BURT FRANKLIN: BIBLIOGRAPHY & REFERENCE SERIES 255

NORTHEASTERN ASIA
A SELECTED BIBLIOGRAPHY

NORTHEASTERN ASIA

A SELECTED BIBLIOGRAPHY

Contributions to the Bibliography of the Relations of China, Russia, and Japan, with Special Reference to Korea, Manchuria, Mongolia, and Eastern Siberia, in Oriental and European Languages

�csᴐ

By ROBERT J. KERNER

In Two Volumes

VOLUME II

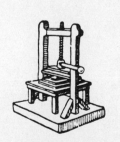

BURT FRANKLIN
NEW YORK

DS
504.5
.Z9
K464
1939a
v.2

Published by BURT FRANKLIN
235 East 44th St., New York, N.Y. 10017
Originally Published: 1939
Reprinted: 1968
Printed in the U.S.A.

Library of Congress Catalog Card No.: 68-58769
Burt Franklin: Bibliography and Reference Series 255

E X P L A N A T O R Y   N O T E

HOW TO FIND MATERIAL

The quickest way to find the items desired is to refer to the Table of Contents. The Subject Index at the end of Volume II gives further assistance. Cross-references may help to find other items.

ARRANGEMENT OF MATERIAL AND ABBREVIATIONS

The material is arranged so that one proceeds from a more general category to the special and from the simple to the more complex. The items are usually listed in chronological order by date of publication or in their historical sequence.

CONTENTS

VOLUME I

PART ONE

ASIA...THE FAR EAST...THE PACIFIC

Numbers

I. BIBLIOGRAPHY................................. 1-42

A. Bibliographies of Bibliography, 1-3. B. General, 4-16. C. Catalogues and Collections, 17-28. D. Bibliographies of Documents, 29-33. E. Newspapers, 34-42.

II. PERIODICAL PUBLICATIONS..................... 43-147

A. General, 43-91. B. Learned, 92-130. C. Missionary, 131-138. D. Special, 139-141. E. Newspapers, 142-143. F. Year-Books, Directories, and Guides, 144-147.

III. GEOGRAPHY AND CARTOGRAPHY...................148-181

A. Bibliography, 148. B. Atlases and maps, 149-164. C. Geographical Accounts, 165-181.

IV. TRAVELS AND SCIENTIFIC EXPEDITIONS..........182-223

V. THE PACIFIC OCEAN: SCIENTIFIC STUDIES AND PILOT DIRECTIONS.............................224-255

A. Periodicals and Publications, 224-226. B. Accounts, 227-255.

VI. ARCHAEOLOGY AND ANTHROPOLOGY................256-272

A. Archaeology, 256-259. B. Anthropology, 260-272.

VII. HISTORY.....................................273-342

A. Chronological Aids, 273-277. B. Historical Atlases and Maps, 278-280. C. Historiography, 281-282. D. General Accounts, 283-342.

Contents

VIII. GENERAL ACCOUNTS........................ 343-449

IX. INTERNATIONAL RELATIONS.................. 450-780

A. Treaty and Documentary Collections, 450-
537: (1) General, 450-451; (2) China, 452-
471; (3) Russia, 472-494; (4) Japan, 495-
513; (5) England, 514-526; (6) United States,
527-530; (7) France, 531-535; (8) Germany,
536-537. B. General Accounts, 538-662:
(1) General, 538-563; (2) Asia, the Far
East, and the Pacific, 564-646; (3) Diplomatic and Peace Machinery, 647-657; (4)
Mandates in the Pacific, 658-662. C.
Problems of War, 663-721: (1) Armed Forces,
663-673; (2) Strategy, 674-681; (3) Strategic Problems, 682-721. D. Washington
Conference (1922) and After, 722-780: (1)
Sources, 722-728; (2) General Accounts,
729-759; (3) Limitation of Arms and Disarmament, 760-780.

X. ECONOMIC FACTORS........................ 781-936

A. Bibliography, 781. B. General Accounts,
782-803. C. Natural Resources and Raw
Materials, 804-823. D. Population Problems,
824-832. E. Agriculture and its Problems,
833-845. F. Industry and its Problems,
846-863. G. Trade and Commerce, 864-898.
H. Fisheries, 899-929: (1) Scientific Studies, 899-905; (2) General Accounts, 906-
929. I. Financial Problems and Currency, 930-936.

XI. CULTURE AND CIVILIZATION................ 937-1046

A. General Accounts, 937-951. B. Philosophy, 952-966. C. Religions and Missions,
967-1012: (1) General, 967-983; (2) Buddhism,
984-996, (a) Bibliography, 984, (b) General
Accounts, 985-996; (3) Christianity, 997-
1010; (4) Mohammedanism, 1011; (5) Shamanism, 1012. D. Education, 1013-1014. E.
Literature, 1015-1016. F. Art, 1017-1044.
G. Theatre, 1045-1046.

XII. COLONIAL REVOLUTIONARY MOVEMENT..........1047-1060

PART TWO

CHINA

I. BIBLIOGRAPHY.........................1061-1087

II. LIBRARIES.............................1088-1093

III. PERIODICAL PUBLICATIONS................1094-1144

A. Guides, 1094-1099. B. Periodicals,
1100-1144.

IV. SINOLOGY..............................1145-1161

V. ENCYCLOPEDIAS.........................1162-1163

VI. BIOGRAPHICAL PUBLICATIONS..............1164-1176

VII. YEARBOOKS.............................1177-1181

VIII. JOURNALISM............................1182-1194

IX. GEOLOGY AND NATURAL RESOURCES...........1195-1234

A. Bibliography, 1195. B. Periodicals,
1196-1200. C. General Accounts, 1201-
1208. D. Mines and Mining Industry, 1209-
1223. E. Iron and Coal, 1224-1232. F.
Other Minerals, 1233-1234.

X. GEOGRAPHY AND CARTOGRAPHY...............1235-1345

A. Bibliography, 1235. B. Periodicals,
1236-1239. C. Atlases and Maps, 1240-
1267. D. Guides, 1268-1276. E. General Accounts, 1277-1317. F. Gazetteers,
1318-1321: (1) Catalogues, 1318-1321; (2)
Gazetteers. G. Historical Geography,
1322-1338. H. Economic Geography, 1339-
1342. I. Climate, 1343-1345.

XI. TRAVELS AND EXPLORATIONS...............1346-1366

XII. ARCHAEOLOGY AND ANTHROPOLOGY...........1367-1395

A. Archaeology, 1367-1378. B. Anthropology, 1379-1395.

Contents

XIII. GENERAL ACCOUNTS......................1396-1525

XIV. HISTORY...............................1526-1921

A. Bibliography, 1526-1527.   B. Periodicals, 1528-1531.   C. Chronology, 1532-1535.
D. General Accounts, 1536-1559: (1) Longer
Accounts, 1536-1547; (2) Shorter Accounts,
1548-1559.   E. History to 1644, 1560-1610:
(1) Longer Accounts, 1580-1582; (2) Shorter
Accounts, 1583-1612;   F. History since
1644, 1613-1921: (1) Sources, 1613-1626; (2)
Longer Accounts, 1627-1638; (3) Shorter Accounts, 1639-1649; (4) Special, 1650-1665;
(5) Nineteenth Century, 1666-1716, (a) Gen-,
eral, 1666-1671, (b) The Taiping Rebellion,
1672-1684, (c) To the End of the Manchu Dynasty (1911), 1685-1716; (6) The Chinese Republic (1911--), 1717-1921, (a) General,
1717-1765, (b) Sun Yat-sen, 1766-1774, (c)
The Rule of the Kuomintang, 1775-1794, (d)
Soviet Movement in China, 1795-1914--(i)
Bibliography, 1795, (ii) Accounts, 1796-
1914,--(e) Since the Sian Coup (1936--),
1915-1921.

XV. GOVERNMENT AND POLITICS...................1922-2003

A. Periodical Publications, 1922-1932.
B. History of Government and Politics,
1933-1937.   C. History of Political
Thought, 1938-1944.   D. General Accounts,
1945-1979.   E. Law and Legislation, 1980-
2003.

XVI. MILITARY AND NAVAL AFFAIRS...............2004-2028

A. Periodicals, 2004.   B. General Accounts,
2005-2019.   C. Strategy, 2020-2028.

XVII. ECONOMIC FACTORS........................2029-2746

A. Periodicals, 2029-2045.   B. Statistics,
2046-2056.   C. Economic History, 2057-2074.
D. General Accounts, 2075-2146.   E. Agriculture, 2147-2297: (1) Bibliography, 2147-
2148; (2) Periodicals, 2149-2153; (3) General Accounts, 2154-2186; (4) Land System
2187-2216; (5) Rice, 2217-2220; (6) Tea

Contents

2221-2227; (7) Silk, 2228-2238; (8) Wheat,
2239-2240; (9) Cotton, 2241-2246; (10)
Wool, 2247; (11) Fruit, 2248; (12) Forestry, 2249-2255; (13) Peasantry, 2256-2260;
(14) Cooperative Movement, 2261-2269; (15)
Rural Reconstruction, 2270-2284; (16) Food-
Supply, 2285-2288; (17) Famines, 2289-2297.
F. Industry, 2298-2361: (1) Periodicals,
2298-2299; (2) General Accounts, 2300-2320;
(3) Special Accounts, 2321-2361. G. Commerce
and Trade, 2362-2477: (1) Periodicals, 2362-
2363; (2) Guides, 2364-2366; (3) History,
2367-2382; (4) General Accounts, 2383-2413;
(5) Inland Trade, 2414-2429, (a) Periodicals,
2414-2417, (b) Accounts, 2418-2429; (6) Oceanic Trade, 2430-2436; (7) Tariff, 2437-2458,
(a) History, 2437-2441, (b) Accounts, 2442-
2458; (8) Commercial Treaties, 2459-2477, (a)
External Tariff, 2462-2472, (b) Internal Tariff (Likin), 2473-2477. H. Communications:
Railroads, Roads, Radio, Aviation, 2478-2539:
(1) Railroads, 2478-2531, (a) Official Publications, 2478-2485, (b) History, 2486-2487,
(c) General Accounts, 2488-2531: (2) Roads,
2532-2536; (3) Radio, 2537; (4) Aviation,
2538-2539. I. Finance, 2540-2661: (1) Official Publications and Periodicals, 2540-
2545; (2) Year-Books (Biographical and Financial), 2546-2548; (3) History, 2549-2551;
(4) General Accounts, 2552-2599; (5) Taxation, 2600-2610; (6) Currency and Exchange,
2611-2648; (7) Stocks, 2649; (8) Foreign
Loans and Investments, 2650-2661. J. Labor
and Labor Problems, 2662-2683: (1) Periodical Publications, 2662-2664; (2) General Accounts, 2665-2683. K. Population Problems,
2684-2715. L. Boycotts, 2716-2729. M.
Colonization and Immigration, 2730-2746:
(1) Bibliography, 2730; (2) Periodical Publications, 2731-2732; (3) General Accounts,
2733-2746.

XVIII. SOCIAL CONDITIONS........................2747-2823

A. Periodicals, 2747. B. General Accounts,
2748-2782. C. Education, 2783-2823: (1)
Official and Learned Society Publications,
2783-2794; (2) Periodicals, 2795-2797; (3)
General Accounts, 2798-2818; (4) Public

Contents

Health, 2819-2823, (a) Official Publications, 2819-2821; (b) General Accounts,
2822-2823.

XIX. CIVILIZATION, RELIGION, AND PHILOSOPHY.....2824-2986

A. History of Civilization, 2824-2828: (1)
Bibliography, 2824; (2) General Accounts,
2825-2828. B. General Accounts, 2829-2854.
C. Art, 2855-2875. D. Literature, 2876-
2885. E. Theatre, 2886. F. Music, 2887-
2889. G. Printing, 2890-2892. H. Science
and Medicine, 2893-2896. I. Religions and
Missions, 2897-2969: (1) Religions, 2897-
2940, (a) History of Religions, 2897-2899,
(b) General Accounts, 2900-2910, (c) Confucianism, 2911-2922, (d) Taoism and Others,
2923-2931, (e) Buddhism, 2932-2938, (f)
Mohammedanism, 2939-2940; (2) Missions,
2941-2969. J. Philosophy, 2970-2986.

XX. FRONTIER PROBLEMS...........................2987-3021

XXI. INTERNATIONAL RELATIONS:...................3022-4705

A. Periodicals, 3022-3028. B. Sources,
3029-3041. C. History, 3042-3095: (1)
General, 3042-3065; (2) Special Periods,
3066-3095. D. General Accounts, 3096-
3109. E. China and Internaional Law,
3110-3112. F. China and the Powers, 3113-
3168. G. Extraterritoriality, 3169-3187.
H. Open Door, 3188-3197. I. Sino-Japanese-
Russian Relations, 3198-4252: (1) Especially
Sino-Japanese, 3198-3695, (a) Bibliography,
3198-3199, (b) Sources, 3200-3202, (c) History, 3203-3214, (d) Sino-Japanese War, 1894-
1895, 3215-3244--(i) Sources, 3215-3219, (ii)
Accounts, 3220-3244,--(e) Relations, 1895-
1931, 3245-3339; (f) Shanghai, 3340-3394--
(i) General Accounts, 3340-3345, (ii) International Settlement, 3346-3352, (iii)
"Incident" of 1932, 3353-3394; (g) North
China, 3395-3488--(i) General Accounts,
3395-3429, (ii) Shantung, 3430-3445, (iii)
Kiao-chow, 3446-3453, (iv) Tsingtao, 3454-
3457, (v) Hopei, 3458-3476, (vi) Peiping
and Tientsin, 3477-3488; (h) Relations,
1931-1936, 3489-3518, (i) The Undeclared

Contents

War, 1937--, 3519-3651, (j) Sino-Japanese
Economic Relations, 3652-3695; (2) Especially Sino-Russian, 3696-3882, (a) Sources,
3696-3735, (b) History to 1917, 3736-3789,
(c) History since 1917, 3790-3882--(i)
Sources, 3790-3801, (ii) General Accounts,
3802-3856,--(d) Economic Relations, 3857-
3882, (3) Especially Russo-Japanese, 3883-
4252, (a) General, 3883-3905, (b) The
Russo-Japanese War, 1904-1905, 3906-4106--
(i) Bibliography, 3906, (ii) Sources, 3907-
3929, (iii) Causes, 3930-3943, (iv) General,
3944-3981, (v) International Law, 3982-3987,
(vi) China and the Russo-Japanese War, 3988-
3989, (vii) Strategy and Tactics, 3990-4001,
(viii) Military Campaigns, 4002-4012, (ix)
Naval Conflicts, 4013-4047, (x) The Trans-
siberian in the War, 4048-4052, (xi) Sakhalin, 4053, (xii) Economic Aspects, 4054-
4061, (xiii) Port Arthur, 4062-4075, (xiv)
Peace of Portsmouth, 4076-4082, (xv) Results and Significance, 4083-4107,--(c)
The Russo-Japanese Alliance. 1907-1917,
4108-4131, (d) Soviet-Japanese Relations,
4132-4252--(i) Periodicals, 4132, (ii) Japanese Intervention in Siberia, 1918-1923,
4133-4167---Documents, 4133-4138, Accounts,
4139-4167,---(iii) Russo-Japanese Agreement of 1925, 4168-4183, (iv) Russo-Japanese Relations since 1925, 4184-4231, (v)
Economic Aspects, 4232-5252. J. British-
Chinese-Japanese Relations, 4253-4361: (1)
Sources, 4253-4267; (2) Early Relations,
4268-4282; (3) Anglo-Japanese Alliance, 1902-
1922, 4283-4309; (4) Since the End of the Alliance, 1922-1937, 4310-4340: (5) Australia,
4341-4350; (6) Singapore, 4351-4358; (7)
Canada, 4359-4361. K. American-Chinese-
Japanese Relations, 4362-4620: (1) Bibliography, 4362: (2) American Diplomatic History, 4363-4371; (3) American Far Eastern
Relations (General), 4372-4380; (4) The
American Navy in the Far East, 4381-4382;
(5) American Far Eastern Relations to 1931,
4383-4503; (6) American Far Eastern Relations since 1931, 4504-4557; (7) The Problem of Orientals in the United States,
4558-4574; (8) The American Monroe Doctrine,
4575-4584; (9) The Hawaiian Islands, 4585-

4589; (10) The Philippines, 4590-4599;
(11) Economic Factors, 4600-4620. L.
French-Chinese-Japanese Relations, 4621-
4657: (1) History of Franco-Chinese Relations, 4621-4637; (2) Franco-Japanese Relations, 4638-4646; (3) General Accounts,
4647-4657. M. Dutch-Chinese-Japanese
Relations, 4658-4678: (1) Sources, 4658-
4663; (2) History, 4664-4669; (3) General
Accounts, 4670-4674; (4) Economic Factors,
4675-4678. N. German-Chinese-Japanese
Relations, 4679-4704. O. Portuguese-
Chinese Relations, 4705.

XXII. MANCHURIA.....................................4706-5804

A. Bibliography, 4706-4720: (1) Works,
4706-4715; (2) Periodical Literature,
4716-4720. B. Periodicals and Newspapers,
4721-4730. C. Atlases and Maps, 4731-
4744. D. Guide-Books, 4745-4746. E.
Year-Books, 4747-4752. F. Travels and
Explorations, 4753-4782. G. Geology,
Natural Resources and Geography, 4783-
4851: (1) Geology and Natural Resources,
4783-4823, (a) Bibliography, 4783, (b)
General Accounts, 4784-4802, (c) Coal,
4803-4811, (d) Iron, 4812-4814, (e) Gold,
4815-4816, (f) Oil, 4817-4823; (2) Geography, 4824-4851. H. Archaeology, 4852-
4855. I. Anthropology, 4856-4869. J.
History, 4870-4920: (1) Sources, 4870-
4876; (2) General Accounts, 4877-4895; (3)
Special Accounts, 4896-4917; (4) Why Study
Manchu? 4918-4920. K. General Accounts,
4921-4991. L. International Relations,
4992-5096: (1) General Accounts, 4992-
5013; (2) Russia and Manchuria, 5014-5026;
(3) Japan and Manchuria, 5027-5096. M.
Government and Administration, 5097-5116;
(1) General Accounts, 5097-5105; (2) Law
and the Judiciary, 5106-5116. N. Economic Factors, 5117-5194: (1) Statistics,
5117-5133; (2) Economic Atlases, 5134-
5135; (3) History and General Accounts,
5136-5166; (4) Japanese Economic Inter-
ests, 5167-5194. O. Agriculture, 5195-
5268: (1) General Accounts, 5195-5216;
(2) By Provinces, 5217-5227; (3) Flora

Contents

5228-5231; (4) Beans, 5232-5242; (5)
Flour, 5243-5245; (6) Millet, 5246; (7)
Rice, 5247-5252; (8) Miscellaneous, 5253-
5261; (9) Furs and Fur-trading, 5262-5264;
(10) Food, Land Utilization Problem, etc.,
5265-5268. P. Forestry--Lumber, 5269-
5288. Q. Industry, 5289-5343. R. Finances, 5344-5379: (1) General Accounts,
5344-5375; (2) Taxation, 5376-5379. S.
Communications: Railroads, Roads, Aviation,
5380-5581: (1) Maps, 5380; (2) Statistics,
5381-5387; (3) General Accounts, 5388-5395;
(4) Special Accounts, 5396-5450; (5) Aviation, 5451; (6) Chinese Eastern Railroad,
5452-5540--(a) Bibliography, 5452, (b)
Sources, 5453-5455, (c) History, 5456-5466,
(d) General Accounts, 5467-5478, (e) International Aspects, 5479-5514--(1) To 1929,
5479-5482, (ii) 1929-1937, 5483-5514, --
(f) Economic Aspects, 5515-5539, (g) Administration and Justice, 5540; (7) South
Manchuria Railroad, 5541-5577, (a) Periodicals, 5541, (b) History, 5542-5550, (c)
General Accounts, 5551-5573, (d) Economic
Conditions, 5574-5577; (8) Water Transportation, 5578-5581. T. Commerce and Trade,
5582-5610: (1) General Accounts, 5582-5599;
(2) Harbors, 5600-5610. U. Labor, 5611-
5617. V. Colonization, 5618-5664: (1)
Statistics, 5618: (2) General Accounts,
5619-5651; (3) The Korean Problem, 5652-
5665. W. Cultural Conditions, 5666.
X. Manchuria by Provinces, 5667-5804: (1)
Kwantung, 5667-5703, (a) Dairen, 5681-5698,
(b) Port Arthur, 5699-5703; (2) Liaoning,
5704-5749; (3) Kirin, 5750-5763, (a) General Accounts, 5750-5758, (b) Mukden, 5759-
5763; (4) Northern Manchuria, 5764-5787,
(a) General Accounts, 5764-5784, (b) Colonization, 5785, (c) Harbin, 5786-5787;
(5) Heilungkiang, 5788-5804.

XXIII.   MANCHUKUO..............................5805-6446

A. The Making of Manchukuo, 5805-6045:
(1) Origins, 5805-5835; (2) The Incident, 5836-5891; (3) The Armed Struggle,
5892-5906; (4) The League of Nations
and Manchuria, 5907-6029; (5) Guerrilla

Contents

Warfare, 6030-6045. B. Manchukuo,
6046-6446: (1) Periodicals, 6046-6050;
(2) Year-Books, 6051-6057; (3) History,
6058-6087; (4) International Relations,
6088-6200, (a) General Accounts, 6088-6127,
(b) Japan and Manchukuo, 6128-6173, (c)
China and Manchukuo, 6174-6182, (d) The
Soviet Union and Manchukuo, 6183-6200; (5)
General Accounts, 6201-6314; (6) Laws, 6315-
6316; (7) Economic Aspects, 6317-6446, (a)
Statistics, 6317-6321, (b) History, 6322,
(c) General Accounts, 6323-6374, (d) Agriculture, 6376-6388, (e) Industry, 6389-6392,
(f) Trade, 6393-6404, (g) Railroads, 6405-
6409, (h) Mining, 6410-6413, (i) Finances,
6414-6429, (j) Colonization, 6430-6446.

XXIV. MONGOLIA...................................6447-6872

A. Eastern Inner Mongolia (Mengkukuo),
6447-6547: (1) Atlases and Maps, 6447-6448;
(2) History, 6449-6453; (3) General Accounts,
6454-6479; (4) Economic Aspects, 6480-6486;
(5) Social and Cultural Aspects, 6487-6488;
(6) Suiyuan, 6489-6503; (7) Chahar, 6504-
6518; (8) Jehol, 6519-6541; (9) Barga, 6542-
6547. B. Outer-Mongolia, 6548-6872: (1)
Geology and Geography, 6548-6560, (a) Maps,
6548, (b) General Accounts, 6549-6560; (2)
Anthropology, 6561-6567; (3) Travels and
Explorations, 6568-6624; (4) History, 6625-
6724, (a) Sources, 6625-6637, (b) General
Accounts, 6638-6678, (c) Special Accounts,
6679-6684, (d) Mongol-Chinese Relations,
6685-6699, (e) Mongol-Russian Relations,
6700-6721, (f) Mongol-Japanese Relations,
6722-6724; (5) General Accounts, 6725-6762;
(6) Republic of Soviet Outer-Mongolia, 6763-
6807; (7) Economic Aspects, 6808-6845, (a)
General Accounts, 6808-6813, (b) Special,
6814-6845; (8) Colonization, 6846-6847; (9)
Social and Cultural Aspects, 6848-6872, (a)
General Accounts, 6848-6859, (b) Religion,
6860-6866, (c) Literature, 6867-6872.

XXV. NORTHWESTERN CHINA........................6873-7144
(Sinkiang, Kokonor [Ch'ing-hai] , Shensi,
Szechwan, Sik'ang)
A. Bibliography, 6873. B. Periodicals,

6874.   C. Atlases and Maps, 6875-6878.
D. Geography, 6879-6896.   E. Gazetteers,
6897.   F. Travels and Explorations, 6898-
6941.   G. Archaeology, 6942-6953.   H.
Anthropology, 6954-6959.   I. History,
6960-6993: (1) Sources, 6960-6978; (2) Accounts, 6979-6993.   J. General Accounts,
6994-7012.   K. Economic and Social Conditions, 7013-7047.   L. Szechwan, 7048-7055.
M. Shensi, 7056-7062.   N. Shansi, 7063-
7064.   O. Kansu, 7065-7068.   P. Sik'ang,
7069-7095.   Q. Sinkiang, 7096-7124.   R.
Kokonor (Ch'ing-hai), 7125-7137.   S. Russia and Northwestern China, 7138-7144.

XXVI.   TIBET...................................7145-7236

A. Travels and Explorations, 7145-7148.
B. Geography, 7149-7156.   C. General Ac-
counts, 7157-7188.   D. Tibetan-Chinese
Relations, 7189-7208.   E. Tibetan-Indian-
British Relations, 7209-7223.   F. Econ-
omic and Social Conditions, 7224-7228.
G. Religious Conditions, 7229-7236.

VOLUME II

PART   THREE

THE JAPANESE EMPIRE

I.   BIBLIOGRAPHY...............................7237-7304

A. General Retrospective Bibliography,
7237-7253.   B. Book-Sellers' Catalogues,
7254-7265.   C. Catalogues of Government
Publications, 7266-7268.   D. Catalogues
of Libraries, 7269-7298.   E. Bibliography
of Periodicals, 7299-7302.   F. Library
Science, 7303-7304.

II.   PERIODICALS...............................7305-7337

A. General, 7305-7326.   B. Government Gazette, 7327-7328.   C. Japan Societies,
7329-7337.

III.   ENCYCLOPEDIAS AND DICTIONARIES............7338-7342

xx

Contents

IV. BIOGRAPHICAL DICTIONARIES...................7343-7357

V. YEAR-BOOKS AND DIRECTORIES.................7358-7365

VI. JOURNALISM AND NEWSPAPERS..................7366-7383

A. History, 7366-7371. B. Newspapers,
7372-7383.

VII. GEOLOGY, GEOGRAPHY, AND NATURAL RESOURCES..7384-7463

A. Periodicals, 7384-7386. B. Maps, 7387-
7406. C. Geology, 7407-7435: (1) General
Accounts, 7407-7415; (2) Natural Resources
and Mining, 7416-7435. D. Geography, 7436-
7463: (1) Periodicals, 7436-7437; (2) General Accounts, 7438-7460; (3) Earthquake of
1923, 7461-7463.

VIII. ARCHAEOLOGY AND ANTHROPOLOGY...............7464-7501

A. Archaeology, 7464-7473: (1) Periodicals,
7464; (2) General Accounts, 7465-7473. B.
Anthropology, 7474-7501: (1) Periodicals,
7474-7476; (2) General Accounts, 7477-7501.

IX. HISTORY....................................7502-7836

A. Bibliography, 7502-7504. B. Historio-
graphy, 7505-7508. C. Periodicals, 7509-
7517. D. Chronologies, 7518-7521. E.
Dictionaries of History, 7522-7523. F.
Collections of Sources, 7524-7541. G.
General History of Japan, 7542-7610: (1)
Longer Accounts, 7542-7571; (2) Shorter
Accounts, 7572-7606; (3) Political History,
7607-7610. H. History by Periods, 7611-
7836: (1) Ancient History, 7611-7624; (2)
Medieval History, 7625-7666; (3) Modern
History, 7667-7836, (a) General Accounts,
7667-7693; (b) Opening of Japan, 7694-7703,
(c) The Imperial Restoration, 7704-7726,
(d) Japan in the World War, 7727-7739; (e)
Recent History, 1918-1937, 7740-7758, (f)
Makers of New Japan, 7759-7836.

X. GENERAL ACCOUNTS OF JAPAN..................7837-7991

XI. JAPANESE NATIONALISM AND PSYCHOLOGY........7992-8043

Contents

XII.   INTERNATIONAL RELATIONS...................8044-8224

A. Periodicals, 8044-8047.   B. Sources,
8048-8052.   C. History, 8053-8224: (1)
General Historical Accounts, 8053-8088;
(2) General Diplomatic Relations, 8089-
8122; (3) History to 1931, 8123-8155; (4)
Recent Japanese Foreign Policy, 1931--,
8156-8224.

XIII. POLITICS AND POLITICAL DEVELOPMENT........8225-8470

A. Periodicals, 8225.   B. General Accounts,
8226-8254.   C. The Feudal Background, 8255-
8277.   D. The Emperor and the Imperial Family, 8278-8288.   E. Constitutional History
and Law, 8289-8326.   F. Administration,
8327-8340.   G. Democratic Elements, 8341-
8344.   H. Parliament, 8345-8354.   I. Political Parties, 8355-8383.   J. Recent Politics, 8384-8429.   K. Communistic and Fas-
cistic Trends, 8430-8470.

XIV.   LAWS AND LEGISLATION......................8471-8532

A. Periodicals, 8471-8472.   B. History
of Law, 8473-8490.   C. Ancient Law, 8491.
D. Medieval Law, 8492-8495.   E. Modern
Law, 8496-8532.

XV.   MILITARY, NAVAL, AND AIR PROBLEMS........8533-8689

A. General Accounts, 8533-8588.   B. The
Army, 8589-8626.   C. The Navy, 8627-8660.
D. Aviation, 8661-8669.   E. Strategy,
8670-8680.   F. War Economics, 8681-8689.

XVI.   PAN-MONGOLIAN AND PAN-ASIATIC MOVEMENTS...8690-8735

A. General Accounts, 8690-8691.   B. The
Japanese Asiatic Monroe Doctrine, 8692-
8697.   C. The Yellow Peril, 8698-8712.
D. The Pan-Mongolian Movement, 8713-8715.
E. The Pan-Asiatic Movement, 8716-8735.

XVII. JAPANESE EXPANSION.......................8736-8885

A. General Accounts, 8736-8804.   B. Japanese Colonial Policies and Island Depend-

Contents

encies, 8805-8841. C. Expansion in the
Pacific, 8842-8854. D. Expansion in
Asia, 8855-8885.

XVIII. ECONOMIC CONDITIONS.....................,...8886-9472

A. Bibliography, 8886-8888. B. Periodicals, 8889-8927. C. Economic Year-Books,
8928-8931. D. Directories and Registers,
8932-8937. E. Statistics, 8938-8989. F.
Economic History, 8990-9009. G. Economic
Geography, 9010-9013. H. General Acccunts,
9014-9093. I. Agriculture, 9094-9168: (1)
History, 9094-9099; (2) General Accounts,
9100-9146; (3) Rice, 9147-9151; (4) Silk,
9152-9167; (5) Tea, 9168. J. Forestry,
9169-9176. K. Industry, 9177-9221: (1)
History, 9177-9182; (2) General Accounts,
9183-9194; (3) Special Accounts, 9195-9221.
L. Commerce and Trade, 9222-9290: (1) History, 9222-9234; (2) General Accounts,
9235-9270; (3) The Commercial Code, 9271-
9279; (4) Tariff, 9280-9290. M. Finances,
9291-9429: (1) History, 9291-9304; (2) General Accounts, 9305-9349; (3) Budget, 9350-
9357; (4) Debts and Loans, 9358-9369; (5)
Currency and Exchange, 9370-9398; (6) Banks
and Banking, 9399-9408, (a) General Accounts,
9399-9405, (b) Central Bank of Japan, 9406-
9408; (7) Taxation, 9409-9420; (8) Index
Numbers and Prices, 9421-9423; (9) Securities and Stock Exchanges, 9424-9426; (10)
War Finance, 9427-9429. N. Communications: Railroad, Marine, and Air Transportation, 9430-9472: (1) History, 9430-9431;
(2) Railroads, 943?-9446; (3) Shipping,
9447-9469; (4) Air Transportation, 9470-
9472.

XIX. SOCIAL CONDITIONS.........................9473-9580

A. Periodicals, 9473-9475. B. History,
9476-9490. C. General Accounts, 9491-
9510. D. Women and Social Life, 9511-
9522. E. Labor Problems, 9523-9544. F.
Population Problems, 9545-9570. G. Immigration, 9571-9580.

XX. CULTURE, RELIGION, PHILOSOPHY.............9581-9842

Contents

A. Periodicals, 9581-9586. B. History,
9587-9616. C. General Accounts, 9617-
9649. D. Education, 9650-9705: (1) Bibliography, 9650; (2) Periodicals, 9651-
9654; (3) History, 9655-9666; (4) General
Accounts, 9667-9702; (5) Institutions of
Higher Learning, 9703-9705. E. Religion,
9706-9767: (1) General Accounts, 9706-
9724; (2) Shintoism, 9725-9730; (3) Buddhism, 9731-9753; (4) Confucianism, 9754-
9755; (5) Christianity, 9756-9764; (6)
Miscellaneous, 9765-9767. F. Philosophy,
9768-9796: (1) Periodicals, 9768; (2) General Accounts, 9769-9796. G. Literature,
9797-9809. H. Art, 9810-9840: (1) General Accounts, 9810-9830; (2) Special Accounts, 9831-9840. I. The Theatre, 9841.
J. Music, 9842.

XXI. KOREA.....................................9843-10290

A. Bibliography, 9843-9848. B. Periodicals, 9849. C. Geology and Natural Resources, 9850-9858. D. Archaeology and
Anthropology, 9859-9864. E. General Accounts, 9865-9911. F. History and International Relations, 9912-10185: (1) Sources,
9912-9965; (2) General Accounts, 9966-9984;
(3) Special Accounts, 9985-10006; (4) Korean-Japanese Relations, 10007-10035; (5)
Annexation of Korea, 10036-10053; (6) Korean National Movement, 10054-10100; (7)
Japanese Rule in Korea, 10101-10184; (a)
Government Reports, 10101-10114; (b) General Accounts, 10115-10147; (c) Japanese
Immigration to Korea, 10148-10155; (d)
Korean-Chinese Relations, 10156-10167;
(e) Laws and Legislation, 10168-10184;
G. Economic Conditions, 10185-10252; (1)
History, 10186-10190; (2) General Accounts,
10191-10205; (3) Agriculture, 10206-10219;
(4) Industry, 10220-10230; (5) Trade and
Finance, 10231-10240; (6) Railroads,
10241-10252; H. Social and Cultural Conditions, 10253-10290: (1) General Accounts,
10253-10257; (2) Religions and Missions,
10258-10290, (a) Buddhism, 10258-10264,
(b) Christianity, 10265-10279; (3) Education, 10280-10290.

Contents

PART FOUR

THE RUSSIAN EMPIRE AND THE SOVIET UNION

IN ASIA AND ON THE PACIFIC

I.   BIBLIOGRAPHY............................10291-10363

A. Bibliographies of Bibliographies,
10291-10294.   B. Bibliographical Periodicals, 10295-10297.   C. General, 10298-
10332.   D. Bibliographies of Articles in
Periodicals, 10333-10340.   E. Bibliography of Russia in Asia and on the Pacific,
10341-10360.   F. Archival Guides, 10361-
10363.

II. PERIODICALS............................10364-10464

A. General, 10364-10385.   B. Government
Publications and Newspapers, 10386-10392.
C. Historical, 10393-10403.   D. Soviet
Union Periodicals, 10404-10409.   E. Econ-
omic, 10410-10423.   F. Local (Siberian),
10424-10464.

III. ENCYCLOPEDIAS............................10465-10467

IV. BIOGRAPHICAL DICTIONARIES................10468-10477

V.   YEAR-BOOKS..............................10478-10484

VI. GUIDES AND HANDBOOKS....................10485-10489

VII. GEOLOGY................................10490-10520

A. Periodical Publications, 10490-10495.
B. General Accounts, 10496-10503.   C.
Special Accounts, 10504-10520.

VIII. GEOGRAPHY AND CARTOGRAPHY..............10521-10583

A. Bibliography, 10521-10522.   B. Periodicals, 10523-10524.   C. Cartography, 10525-
10556: (1) Atlases and Collections, 10525-
10536; (2) Geological, 10537-10538; (3) General Maps, 10539-10546; (4) Special Maps,
10547-10556.   D. History, 10557-10559.   E.
General Accounts, 10560-10572.   F. By Re-

Contents

gions, 10573-10579.   G. Rivers, 10580-
10583.

IX.   TRAVELS AND EXPLORATIONS................10584-10651

X.   RUSSIAN STUDIES ON ASIA AND THE ORIENT..10652-10687

XI.   ARCHAEOLOGY (SIBERIAN)...................10688-10721

A. Periodicals, 10688-10693.   B. History,
10694.   C. General Accounts, 10695-10721.

XII.   ANTHROPOLOGY (SIBERIAN).................10722-10784

XIII.   GENERAL ACCOUNTS.......................10785-11013

A. Especially Russia in Asia, 10785-10850.
B. Russia on the Pacific, 10851-10884.   C.
The Soviet Arctic, 10885-11013: (1) Bibliography, 10885; (2) Maps, 10886; (3) Periodicals, 10887-10888; (4) History and General
Accounts, 10889-10919; (5) Exploration,
10920-10996; (6) Economic Factors, 10997-
11013.

XIV.   HISTORY................................11014-11401

A. General Russian History, 11014-11026.
B. Russian Expansion in Asia, 11027-11044.
C. The Eurasian Interpretation, 11045-
11059.   D. Siberian History, 11060-11401:
(1) Sources, 11060-11096, (a) Archival
Guides, 11060-11070, (b) Collections,
11071-11096; (2) General Siberian History,
11097-11126; (3) Siberian History to the
Eighteenth Century, 11127-11153; (4) From
1689 to 1905, 11154-11178; (5) The Revolutions in Siberia, 11179-11401, (a) Bibliography, 11179-11184, (b) Periodicals,
11185-11188, (c) The Revolutionary Movement to 1905, 11189-11199, (d) The Revolution of 1905, 11200-11241--(i) General
Accounts, 11200-11213; (ii) Special Accounts, 11214-11230, (iii) The Cities in
the Revolution of 1905, 11231-11241,--
(e) The Revolutions of 1917, 11242-11401--
(i) General Accounts, 11242-11273, (ii)
Memoirs, 11274-11281, (iii) Local Self-
Government Movement, 11282-11285, (iv)

Contents

By Regions, 11286-11345---Far East,
11286-11297, Western Siberia and Cen-
tral Asia, 11298-11331, Cities in the
Revolution, 11332-11345,---(v) The Czecho-
Slovaks in Siberia, 11346-11357, (vi)
Intervention in Siberia, 11358-11401.

XV.   INTERNATIONAL RELATIONS TO 1917.........11402-11436

A. Periodicals, 11402. B. Sources,
11403-11414. C. General Accounts,
11415-11436.

XVI. INTERNATIONAL RELATIONS SINCE 1917......11437-11464

A. Periodical Publications, 11437-11439.
B. Soviet International Law, 11440.
C. General Accounts, 11441-11464.

XVII. MILITARY AND NAVAL PROBLEMS.............11465-11494

A. Periodicals, 11465-11471. B. General Accounts, 11472-11494.

XVIII. THE COMMUNIST PARTY AND THE THIRD
INTERNATIONAL.............................11495-11583

A. History of the Communist Party, 11495-
11505. B. The Communist Party in Russia,
11506-11516. C. The Communist Party in
Siberia, 11517-11527. D. The Third International, 11528-11583: (1) Bibliography,
11528; (2) The Seven Congresses, 11529-
11548; (3) Congresses of the Nations of
Asia, 11549-11550; (4) General Accounts,
11551-11583.

XIX. GOVERNMENT AND POLITICS.................11584-11656

A. Before 1917, 11584-11614: (1) Periodicals and Publications, 11584-11598; (2)
General Accounts, 11599-11614. B. Since
1917, 11615-11656: (1) Sources, 11615-
11626; (2) General Accounts, 11627-11648;
(3) Local Government and Regionalism,
11649-11656, (a) Bibliography, 11649, (b)
Periodicals, 11650, (c) Accounts, 11651-
11656.

XX. ECONOMIC CONDITIONS......................11657-12404

A. Statistical Periodicals, 11657-11658.
B. Population Statistics, 11659-11695. C.
Periodicals, 11696-11702. D. Handbooks,
11703. E. Economic History, 11704-11710.
F. Economic Geography, 11711-11717. G.
General Accounts, 11718-11777: (1) Economic Potentialities, 11718-11753; (2) Socialist Construction, 11754-11755; (3)
Water Power, 11756-11762; (4) Western and
Central Siberia, 11763-11765; (5) The Far
Eastern Region, 11766-11777. H. Agriculture, 11778-11882: (1) Bibliography, 11778;
(2) Statistics, 11779-11782; (3) Government Periodicals, 11783-11798; (4) Climate,
11799-11803; (5) Flora and Fauna, 11804-
11810; (6) Soils, 11811-11812; (7) General
Accounts, 11813-11827; (8) Special Accounts,
11828-11838; (9) Agricultural Cooperatives
and Collectives, 11839-11845; (10) Peasantry, 11846-11866; (11) Land Tenure, 11867-
11876; (12) Stock-farming and Meat-Packing,
11877-11882. I. Forestry and Lumber,
11883-11904. J. Furs and Fur-Trade, 11905-
11930. K. Fisheries, 11913-11938. L.
Industry, 11939-11987: (1) Periodicals,
11939; (2) Statistical Publications, 11940-
11943; (3) General Accounts, 11944-11958;
(4) Special Accounts, 11959-11987. M.
Minerals and Mining, 11988-12053: (1) Bibliography, 11988-11989; (2) Periodicals,
11990-11992; (3) Statistics, 11993-11996;
(4) History, 11997-12000; (5) General Accounts, 12001-12016; (6) Gold, 12017-12029,
(a) Bibliography, 12017, (b) General Accounts, 12018-12029; (7) Coal, 12030-12038;
(8) Oil and Gas, 12039-12047; (9) Miscellaneous, 12048-12053. N. Trade and Commerce, 12054-12145: (1) Periodical Publications, 12054-12061; (2) Statistics, 12062-
12070; (3) History, 12071-12078; (4) Laws,
12079; (5) General Accounts of Western Trade,
12080-12089; (6) Domestic Trade, 12090-
12107; (7) Trade in Asia, 12108-12145, (a)
General, 12108-12124, (b) Trade with China,
12125-12139, (c) Trade in Central Asia,
12140-12141, (d) Border Trade, 12142-12145.
O. Railroads and Communications, 12146-

Contents

12216: (1) Periodical Publications, 12146-
12151; (2) History, 12152-12156; (3) General Accounts, 12157-12168; (4) Railroad Rates,
12169-12175; (5) The Transsiberian Railroad,
12176-12197, (a) Guides, 12176-12179, (b)
General Accounts, 12180-12197; (6) The Amur
Railroad, 12198-12202; (7) The Turk-Sib Railroad, 12203-12210; (8) Other Railroads, 12211-
12216. P. Economic Zoning, 12217-12221. Q.
The Five-Year Plans, 12222-12260: (1) Periodicals, 12222-12228; (2) The First Five-Year
Plan, 12229-12247; (3) Between the Two Five-
Year Plans, 12248-12250; (4) The Second Five-
Year Plan, 12251-12260. R. Labor, 12261-
12271. S. Finances, 12272-12300: (1) Government Periodicals and Publications, 12272-
12286; (2) General Accounts, 12287-12300.
T. Colonization, 12301-12394: (1) Bibliography, 12301-12302; (2) History, 12303-
12332; (3) Policy, 12333-12341; (4) Problems, 12342-12364; (5) Colonization and
Agriculture, 12365-12367; (6) Land Settlement, 12368-12385; (7) Colonization by Regions, 12386-12394. U. Siberian Exile
System, 12395-12404: (1) Periodicals, 12395;
(2) Accounts, 12396-12404.

XXI. NON-RUSSIANS IN RUSSIAN ASIA............12405-12437

A. Bibliography, 12405-12407. B. Rus-
sian Policy, 12408-12429. C. The Non-
Russian Peoples, 12430-12435. D. Legal
Rights of the Non-Russians, 12436-12437.

XXII. SOCIAL LIFE.............................12438-12536

A. General, 12438-12440. B. The Russian Orthodox Church and its Problems,
12441-12460: (1) General Accounts,
12441-12444; (2) Church Schools, 12445-
12450; (3) Missions, 12451-12460. C.
The Sectarians, 12461-12464. D. Non-
Christian Religions, 12465-12488. E.
Education and Cultural Conditions,
12489-12536: (1) Bibliography, 12489-
12490; (2) Periodicals, 12491-12492; (3)
Sources, 12493-12496; (4) General Accounts, 12497-12519; (5) Education of
Non-Russians, 12520-12531; (6) Miscel-

Contents

laneous, 12532-12536.

XXIII. RUSSIA IN THE FAR EAST..................12537-12882

A. Bibliography, 12537-12539. B. Maps,
12540-12541. C. Encyclopedias, 12542-
12543. D. Anthropology--Non-Russians,
12544-12579. E. General Accounts, 12580-
12609. F. The Amur Region, 12610-12631:
(1) General Accounts, 12610-12625; (2)
Biro-Bydzhan Territory, 12626-12631. G.
Vladivostok, 12632-12635. H. History,
12636-12654. I. Economic Conditions,
12655-12786: (1) Statistics, 12655-12664;
(2) General Accounts, 12665-12684; (3)
Regionalization, 12685-12690; (4) Geology
and Natural Resources, 12691-12700; (5)
Agriculture and Peasantry, 12701-12742;
(6) Industry, 12743-12745; (7) Railroads,
12746-12747; (8) Finances, 12748-12755;
(9) Labor, 12756-12767; (10) Education,
12768-12776; (11) Communist Party, 12777-
12786. J. Kamchatka, 12787-12823: (1)
Maps, 12787-12789; (2) History, 12790-
12795; (3) General Accounts, 12796-12817;
(4) Economic Conditions, 12818-12823;
K. Sakhalin, 12824-12879; (1) Ethnology,
12824-12827; (2) History, 12828-12838; (3)
General Accounts, 12839-12853; (4) Economic Conditions, 12854-12866; (5) Sakhalin as a Penal Colony, 12867-12869; (6)
Japanese Sakhalin, 12870-12879. L.
Commander Islands, 12880-12882.

XXIV. AUTONOMOUS BURIAT-MONGOLIAN SSR.........12883-12985

A. Bibliography, 12883-12885. B. Buriat
Society Publications, 12886-12888. C.
Maps, 12889. D. Lake Baikal, 12890-12894.
E. Anthropology, 12895-12918. F. History,
12919-12935: (1) Sources, 12919-12927; (2)
Accounts, 12928-12935. G. General Accounts,
12936-12954. H. The Communist Party, 12955-
12958. I. Economic and Social Conditions,
12959-12973. J. Kiakhta, 12974. K. Nerchinsk, 12975-12977. L. Tungusia, 12978-
12985.

XXV. AUTONOMOUS YAKUTSK SSR..................12986-13079

Contents

A. Bibliography, 12983-12988. B.
Maps, 12989-12990. C. Academy Publi-
cations, 12991-12997. D. Anthropology,
12998-13012. E. History, 13013-13021.
F. General Accounts, 13022-13040. G.
The Communist Party, 13041-13043. H.
Economic Conditions, 13044-13071: (1)
Statistics, 13044-13045; (2) Geology and
Geography, 13046-13051; (3) General Ac-
counts, 13052-13071. I. Along the Lena,
13072-13077. J. Dictionaries, 13078-
13079.

XXVI.   THE SIBERIAN REGION (SIBIRSKII KRAI)...13080-13225

A. The Siberian Region, 13080. B.
Along the Yenisei, 13081-13109: (1)
Maps, 13081; (2) General Accounts,
13082-13109. C. Irkutsk, 13110-13139.
D. Omsk, 13140-13148. E. Tomsk, 13149-
13164. F. Turukhansk, 13165-13169.
G. Uriankhai, 13170-13173. H. Khakassk,
13174. I. Oirat Autonomous District,
13175-13225: (1) Geology and Natural Resources, 13175-13190; (2) History, 13191-
13202; (3) General Accounts, 13203-13210;
(4) Economic Conditions, 13211-13220; (5)
Communist Party, 13221-13225.

XXVII.   WESTERN SIBERIA.....................13226-13358
(Chiefly the Ural Autonomous District)
A. Western Siberia (General), 13226-
13261. B. The Ural District, 13262-
13358: (1) Publications, 13262; (2) Geology and Natural Resources, 13263-13271;
(3) History, 13272-13280; (4) General
Accounts, 13281-13288; (5) Economic
Conditions, 13289-13329, (a) Statistical Publications, 13289-13290; (b) General Accounts, 13291-13300; (c) Agriculture, 13301-13309; (d) Industry,
13310-13317; (e) Labor, 13318-13324;
(f) Trade, 13325-13326; (g) Finances,
13327-13329; (h) Cossacks, 13330-13335;
(i) National Question, 13336; (j) Tobolsk,
13337-13342; (k) Cheliabinsk, 13343-13351;
(1) Communist Party, 13352-13358.

XXVIII. RUSSIA IN CENTRAL ASIA.................13359-13866

Contents

A. Bibliography, 13359-13367. B. Periodicals and Newspapers, 13368-13373. C. Guide-Books, 13374-13375. D. Directories, 13376-13377. E. Travels and Explorations, 13378-13426. F. Anthropology and National Zoning, 13427-13446. G. History, 13447-13514: (1) General, 13447-13456; (2) Russia in Central Asia, 13457-13494; (3) The Revolution and Recent History, 13495-13514. H. General Accounts, 13515-13527. I. Anglo-Russian Rivalry, 13528-13548. J. Economic Conditions, 13549-13618: (1) Statistics, 13549-13553; (2) General, 13554-13563; (3) Natural Resources, 13564-13570; (4) Agriculture, 13571-13591; (5) Industry and Labor, 13592-13599; (6) Trade, 13600-13602; (7) Railroads and Highways, 13603-13605; (8) Finances, 13606-13608; (9) Economic Planning and Zoning, 13609-13618. K. Social and Cultural Conditions, 13619-13630. L. Communist Party, 13631-13647. M. By Republics, 13648-13866: (1) Autonomous Tatar SSR, 13648-13675, (a) History, 13648-13654; (b) General Accounts, 13655-13659; (c) Economic Conditions, 13660-13666; (d) Communist Party, 13667-13675; (2) Autonomous Bashkir SSR, 13676-13723, (a) Maps, 13676, (b) Anthropology, 13677-13679, (c) History, 13680-13691--(i) Sources, 13680-13682, (ii) Accounts, 13683-13691,--(d) General Accounts, 13692-13703, (e) Economic Conditions, 13704-13717, (f) Communist Party, 13718-13723; (3) Autonomous Kazak SSR, 13724-13768, (a) Bibliography, 13724-13725, (b) Directories and Dictionaries, 13726-13730, (c) Statistics, 13731, (d) History, 13732-13745, (e) General Accounts, 13746-13749; (f) Economic Conditions, 13750-13768; (4) Turkmen SSR, 13769-13783; (5) Uzbek SSR, 13784-13796; (6) Kirghiz SSR, 13797-13854, (a) Bibliography, 13797, (b) Anthropology, 13798-13805, (c) History, 13806-13819, (d) General Accounts, 13820-13826, (e) Economic Conditions, 13827-13849, (f) Communist Party, 13850-13854; (7) Tadjik SSR, 13855-13866.

XXIX. ANGLO-RUSSIAN RIVALRY IN AFGHANISTAN....13867-13884

PART THREE

I. BIBLIOGRAPHY

See 1-42; 1061-1087.

A. General Retrospective Bibliography

7237. Koseikaku. 大日本書史 Dai Nippon shoshi. (Bibliography of Japan, 1477-1898.) Kyoto, Koseikaku, v. 1, 1929-

7238. Makino, Zenbei. 徳川幕府書籍考 Tokugawa bakufu shoseki-ko. (Books and other general publications of the Tokugawa period, 1600-1867.) (Isseido catalog, 1932.)

7239. Rakuro shoin staff. 日本全書 Nippon zensho. (A complete collection of standard reference books on Japan.) Tokyo, Heiyo tosho kabushiki-kaisha, 1937. 36 v.

7240. Wenckstern, Friedrich von. A bibliography of the Japanese empire. V. I, Leiden, Brill, 1895: reprinted, 1910. 406 p. V. II, Tokyo, 1907. 435 p. (2) Nachod, Oskar. Bibliographie von Japan... (1906-   ). Leipzig, Hiersemann, 1927-   (5 v. in 1937.)

7241. Cordier, Henri. Bibliotheca japonica. Dictionnaire bibliographie des ouvrages relatifs à l'Empire japonais, rangés par ordre chronologique jusqu'à 1870 suivi d'un appendice renfermant la liste alphabétique des principaux ouvrages parus de 1870 à 1912. Publications de l'École des langues orientales vivantes, 5 série, v. 8. Paris, Leroux, 1912. xii p. 762 colonnes.

7242. Ozaki, Tadayoshi. 群書一覧 Gunsho ichiran. (Handbook on classic books of Japan.) Tokyo, Yoshikawa kobunkan, 1931. 1460 p. (2) A guide to Japanese studies. Orientation in the study of Japanese history, Buddhism,

Shintoism, art, classic literature, modern literature.
Kokusai bunka shinkokai. (The society for international
cultural relations.) Tokyo, 1937. 262 p.

7243. Matveev, Z. N. and Popov, A. D. Библиография Японии.
(A bibliography of Japan.) Под редакцией проф. Е. Спальвина.
Vladivostok, Gosudarstvennyi dalnevostochnyi universitet.
Trudy, v. 1, book 2. 1923. 117, 13 p.

7244. Haguenauer, M. Bibliographie des principales publications éditées dans l'empire japonais. Tokyo, 1931. iii,
250 p. (Bulletin de la Maison franco-japonaise. Série
française, v.3: 3-4.)

7245. Satow, Ernest M. The Jesuit mission press in Japan,
1519-1610. Privately printed 1888. (See also, Satow, Translations of the Asiatic society of Japan. Yokohama, 1899,
v. 27, p. 2, and Nippon-yasokai-kanko-shoshi-kaisetsu.
Tokyo, 1926.)

7246. Robertson, James A. "Bibliography of early Spanish-
Japanese relations. Compiled from manuscripts and books in
the Philippine library, Manila." Transactions of the Asiatic society of Japan, 43 (1915):1:1-170.

7247. Slade, William Adams. "A list of books on Japan."
American academy of political and social science. Annals,
v. 122, no.211, Nov. 1925. "The Far East", pp. 227-240.

7248. Gay, Helen Kilduff. Reading list on Japan. 1898.
135 p.

7249. Samura Hachiro. 國書解題 Kokusho kaidai. (A compilation or digest of reviews of the standard literary
works of Japan.) 2 ed. Tokyo, 1926. 2 v.

7250. Wada, Koreshiro. 読書餘錄 日本書籍史 Bosho
yoroku, Nippon shoseki-shi. (History of Japanese books,
memoirs of the books I have read.) Tokyo, Kobu-sho, 1932.
2 v.

7251. 書物展望 Shomotsu tembo. (The survey of books.)
Tokyo, Shomotsu tembosha, (July, 1931-1932, v. 18.)

7252. 享保以後大阪出版書籍目錄 Kyoho igo Osaka shuppan
shoseki mokuroku. (Catalogue of books published in Osaka
since the Kyoho period--1716.) Osaka, Osaka kokusho shuppan
kumiai, 1937. 395 p.

7253. 圖書月報 Tosho geppo. (Monthly bulletin of publications.) Tokyo, Tokyo shoseki-sho kumiai jimusho, 1902-

B. Book-Sellers' Catalogues

7254. 新版月報 Shinpan geppo. (Monthly bulletin of new publications.) Tokyo press association, 1922-

7255. 東京堂月報 Tokyodo geppo. (Monthly bulletin of the Tokyodo publishing company.) Tokyo, Tokyodo, 1914-

7256. Uehara, Nagamori. 出版便覧 Shuppan benran. (A handbook of publications for 1933.) Tokyo, Shuppan shinbun-sha, 1934. 201 p.

7257. 出版年鑑 Shuppan nenkan. (Year-book of publications.) Tokyo, Tokyo shoseki-sho kumiai jimusho, 1928-

7258. 出版年鑑 Shuppan nenkan. (Year-book of publications.) Tokyo, Tokyodo, 1930.

7259. 圖書総目録 Tosho so-mokuroku. (Complete catalogue of books.) Tokyo, Tokyo booksellers' association, 1923. 2318 p.

7260. 圖書分類目録 Tosho bunrui mokuroku. (Classified catalogue of books published in Japan.) Tokyo, Shuppan kyokai, 1930. 279 p.

7261. Mozumi, Takami. 群書索引 Gunsho sakuin. (Index of standard works.) Tokyo, Ganshodo, 1925. 3 v.

7262. 享保十四年合類書籍目録大全 Kyoho 14-nen gorui shoseki mokuroku taizen. (Complete catalogue of books.) Tokyo, Ganshodo, 1729. 13 v.

7263. 新刊書総目録 Shinkan-sho so-mokuroku. (A complete catalogue of newly published books.) Tokyo shigai ikebukuro, Tosho kenkyukai, 1929. 2 v.

7264. Tarumi, Nobuhide. 日本叢書年表 Nippon sosho nempyo. (Chronological table of publications in Japan.) Osaka, Mamiya shoten, 1930. 202 p.

7265. 書物往来 Shomotsu orai. (The journal of books.) Tokyo, Jugoshokosha. (In May, 1924 - Nov. 1925, 19 v.)

C. Catalogues of Government Publications

7266. 官廳刊行圖書目錄 Kancho kanko tosho mokuroku.
(Catalogue of government publications of Japan.) Tokyo,
Naikaku insatsu-kyoku, 1928-

7267. 内務省納本月報 Naimu-sho nohon geppo. (Monthly
bulletin of the books presented to the Department of home
affairs.) Tokyo, Osakayago, 1926-

7268. 外國出版物禁止畫帖 Gaikoku shuppanbutsu
kinshi daicho. (A register of foreign publications censored
in Japan.) Tokyo, Keishicho, 1933.

D. Catalogues of Libraries

7269. Tokyo imperial university. 帝國大學圖書館和漢
書目錄 Teikoku daigaku toshokan Wa-Kan-sho mokuroku.
(A catalogue of Japanese and Chinese books in the Imperial
university library.) Tokyo, Ganshodo.

7270. Imperial library. 帝國圖書館和漢書書名目錄
Teikoku toshokan Wa-Kan-sho shomei mokuroku. (A catalogue
of titles of Japanese and Chinese books in the Japanese
imperial library.) Tokyo, Ganshodo. 2 vols.

7271. Imperial library. 帝國圖書館報
Teikoku toshokanho. (Bulletin of the Imperial library.)
Tokyo, Imperial library, 1908-

7272. Department of imperial household. 帝室和漢圖書目
錄 Teishitsu Wa-Kan tosho mokuroku. (Catalogue of Japanese
and Chinese books in the Japanese imperial household.)
Tokyo, Ganshodo. 2 v.

7273. 奈良帝室圖書館圖書一覽 Nara teishitsu tosho-
kan tosho ichiran. (Catalogue of the books in the Nara
imperial library.) Nara, Nara imperial library, 1929. V.12,
118 p.

7274. Imperial cabinet archives. 内閣文庫圖書陳列目錄
Naikaku bunko tosho chinretsu mokuroku. (A catalogue of
books on exhibition in the Cabinet library.) Tokyo, Ganshodo.

7275. 和漢圖書分類目錄 Wa-Kan tosho bunrui mokuroku.
(Classified catalogue of Japanese and Chinese books in the
Dairen library.) Dairen, South Manchuria railway co., 1927-
1933.

7276. Department of Education. 古今和漢圖書集成分類目録 Kokon Wa-Kan tosho shusei bunrui mokuroku. (A classified catalogue of collection of ancient and modern Japanese and Chinese books.) Tokyo, Ganshodo.

7277. Toyo bunko. 東洋文庫展觀書目 Toyo bunko tenkan shomoku. (Catalogue of books on exhibition in the Oriental library.) Tokyo, Ganshodo. 2 v.

7278. Toyo bunko. モリソン亞細亞文庫目録 Morison Ajia bunko mokuroku. (A catalogue of the Morrison Oriental library.) Tokyo, Ganshodo.

7279. Office of the national shrines. 神宮文庫圖書目録 Jingu bunko tosho mokuroku. (Catalogue of books in the libraries of the National shrines.) Tokyo, Ganshodo.

7280. Buzan university library. 豊山大學圖書館藏書目録 Buzan daigaku toshokan zosho mokuroku. (A catalogue of books in the Buzan university library.) Tokyo, Ganshodo.

7281. Koizumi, Shinzo. 慶應圖書館圖書目録 Keio toshokan tosho mokuroku. (Catalogue of the Keio Gijuku university library.) Tokyo, Keio Gijuku university library, 1929. 1916 p.

7282. Otani university. 大谷大學圖書館和漢書分類目録 Otani daigaku toshokan Wa-Kan-sho bunrui mokuroku. (Classified catalogue of Japanese and Chinese books in the Library of Otani university.) Tokyo, Ganshodo. 2 vols. (2) Otani university. 第二大谷大學和漢圖書分類目録 Dai ni Otani daigaku Wa-kan tosho bunrui mokuroku. (Second classified index of Japanese-Chinese books in the Otani university library.) Kyoto, Otani daigaku, 1935. 1002 p.

7283. Ryukoku university. 龍谷大學和漢書分類目録 Ryukoku daigaku Wa-Kan-sho bunrui mokuroku. (Ryukoku university classified catalogue of Japanese and Chinese books.) Tokyo, Ganshodo.

7284. 圖書目録 Tosho mokuroku. (Catalogue of books in the library in 1930.) Toyama, Asada library, 1930.

7285. Nanki bunko. 南葵文庫藏書目録 Nanki bunko zosho mokuroku. (Catalogue of books in the Nanki library.) Tokyo, Ganshodo. 4 v.

7286. Watanabe, Shin. 青洲文庫古版書目 Seishu bunko kohan shomoku. (Catalogue of old books in the Seishu library.) Tokyo, Ganshodo.

7287. Seikado bunko. 静嘉堂文庫圖書分類目録 Seikado bunko tosho bunrui mokuroku. (Classified catalogue of books in the Seikado library.) Tokyo, Ganshodo.

7288. Hayakawa, Koson. 槇書書堂圖書目録 Shako shoshitsu tosho mokuroku. (Catalogue of books in the Shako library.) Tokyo, Ganshodo. 2 v.

7289. 上高井郡古文書目録 Kamitakai-gun komonjo mokuroku. (Catalogue of old documents published in Kamitakai district.) Nagano, Kamitakai kyoikukai, 1930. 100 p.

7290. Otobe, Senzaburo. 日本圖書分類表及其索引 Nippon tosho bunrui-hyo oyobi sono sakuin. (Classified table of Japanese books with the index.) Nagano, Nagano prefectural library, 1929. 33 p.

7291. Okayama prefectural library. 岡山縣立圖書館和漢圖書目録 Okayama kenritsu toshokan Wa-Kan tosho mokuroku. (A catalogue of Japanese and Chinese books in the Okayama prefectural library.) Tokyo, Ganshodo.

7292. 静岡縣立葵文庫和漢圖書目録 Shizuoka kenritsu Aoi bunko Wa-Kan tosho mokuroku. (Japanese and Chinese books in the Aoi library of Shizuoka prefecture.) Tokyo, Ganshodo, 2 v.

7293. Prefectural library of Yamaguchi. 山口圖書館和漢書分類目録 Yamaguchi toshokan Wa-Kan-sho bunrui mokuroku. (A classified catalogue of Japanese and Chinese books in the Yamaguchi prefectural library.) Tokyo, Ganshodo.

7294. 邦文圖書分類目録 Hobun tosho bunrui mokuroku. (Classified catalogue of the books in Japanese, 1928.) Tokyo, Chamber of commerce and industry, 1929. 439 p.

7295. Office of the Governor General of Formosa. 台湾總督府圖書館和漢圖書分類目録 Taiwan sotokufu toshokan Wa-Kan tosho bunrui mokuroku. (A classified catalogue of Japanese and chinese books in the library of the Office of the Governor General of Formosa.) Tokyo, Ganshodo. 3 v.

7296. Douglas, Robert Kennaway. Catalogue of Japanese printed books and manuscripts in the library of the British museum acquired during the years 1899-1903. 2 v. London, 1904.

7297. Serrurier, L. Bibliothèque japonaise; catalogue
raisonné des livres et des manuscruts japonaise enrégistrés
à la bibliothèque de l'Université de Leyde, 1896. 297 p.

7298. Rosny, L. de. Les documents japonais des bibliothèques
de Londres et d'Oxford. Paris, 1861. 23 p.

E. Bibliography of Periodicals

(1) Periodicals

7299. 分類月刊 Bunrui gekkan (Tokyo), 1, 1931- [Cor-
responding to the German "Dietrich" Internationale bibliographie der zeitschriftenliteratur.]

7300. 雑誌索引 Zasshi sakuin. (Index for the articles
in the magazines published in Japan.) Nagano-machi, Zasshi
hakkosha,   1,   1928-

7301. Association for the investigation of Tokyo municipal
administration. 邦文雑誌記事索引 Hobun zasshi kiji
sakuin. (An index to articles in Japanese language magazines.) Tokyo, Tokyo shisei chosakai, 1929. 326 p.

7302. Eastern Asia society. 満蒙支那関係雑誌重要記事
索引 Man-Mo Shina kankei zasshi juyo kiji sakuin. (Index of
the important articles in magazines on the relation of Japan to China, Manchuria, and Mongolia.) 1928.

F. Library Science

7303. Ota, Tamesaburo. 和漢圖書目錄法 Wa-Kan tosho
mokuroku ho. (Cataloguing method for Japanese and Chinese
books.) Tokyo, Ganshodo.

7304. 圖書館雑誌 Toshokan zasshi. (Journal of the
Japanese library association.) Tokyo, Nippon toshokan kyokai, 1907-

II. PERIODICALS

See 43-147; 1094-1144.

A. General

7305. 中央公論 Chuo koron. (Central review.) Tokyo, Chuo
koronsha, 1886-

7306. Tokutomi, Soho. 國民ノ友 Kokumin no tomo.(The friend

of the nation.) Tokyo, 1887-1912. Discontinued. 17 v.

7307. 日本及日本人 Nippon oyobi Nipponjin. (Japan and
Japanese.) Tokyo, Seikyosha. 1888-

7308. 風俗畫報 Fuzoku gaho. (Illustrated magazine of
manners.) Tokyo, Toyo-do book store, 1889-

7309. 新潮 Shincho. (New tide.) Tokyo, Shinchosha, 1903-

7310. The Japan Magazine. A representative monthly of
things Japanese. Tokyo, Japan magazine company, 1910-

7311. 雄辯 Yuben. (Eloquence.) Dai-Nihon Yuben-kai Kodansha, Tokyo, 1910-   (monthly).

7312. 改造 Kaizo. (Reconstruction.) Tokyo, Kaizosha,
1910-

7313. ダイアモンド Daiamondo. (The diamond.) Tokyo, Diamond
publishing house, 1913-

7314. Голос Японии. Прод. журнала "Вестник Японии".
(1916-1921.) Ред. Уэда. (The Voice of Japan. The continuation of "The Messenger of Japan".)

7315. 日本評論 Nippon hyoron. (The Japan review.)
Tokyo, Nippon hyoronsha, 1926-

7316. 現代 Gendai. (Modern age.) Tokyo, Dai Nippon
yubenkai kodansha, 1921-

7317. 内外公論 Naigai koron. (Domestic and foreign
public opinions.) Tokyo, Naigai koronsha, 1922-

7318. 文藝春秋 Bungei shunju. (Literary digest, including articles on current national problems of Japan.)
Tokyo, Bungei shunjusha, 1923-

7319. 世界ト我等 Sekai to warera. (We and the world.)
Tokyo, Nippon kokusai kyokai, 1927-

7320. 海外之日本 Kaigai no Nippon. (Japan abroad.) Tokyo,
Kaigai no Nipponsha, 1927-

7321. 日本研究 Jih-pên yen-chin. (Research on Japan.) A
monthly. Shanghai, 1931-

7322. 日 ノ 出 Hinode. (Sunrise.) Monthly. Tokyo, Shincho-sha, 1932-

7323. 日本國民 Nippon kokumin. (The Japanese nation.) Monthly. Tokyo, Nippon kokuminsha, 1932-

7324. 新足潮 Shin shicho. (Current opinion.) Tokyo, Shin shichosha, 1932-

7325. Contemporary Japan. A review of Japanese affairs. Quarterly. Tokyo, Foreign affairs association of Japan, 1932- (2) Cultural Nippon. Quarterly. Tokyo, Nippon bunka chuo renmei - Central federation of Nippon culture, 1933-

7326. Tokyo gazette. A monthly report of current policies, official statements and statistics. Tokyo, Foreign affairs association of Japan, 1, July 1937-

B. Government Gazette

7327. 太政官日誌 Dajokan nisshi. (Gazette of the imperial government of Japan.) Tokyo, Dajokan, 1868-

7328. Nisho-do staff. 分類官報 Bunrui kanpo. (Imperial government daily gazette reprinted in classified form.) Monthly. Tokyo, Nisho-do, Jan. 1931-

C. Japan Societies

7329. Japan society. London. Transactions and proceedings... 1, 1892-

7330. Revue française du Japon publié sous le patronage de la Société de langue française. Tokyo, 1, 1892-

7331. Anglo-Japanese gazette. London, 1-16, June 1902 - June 1910.

7332. Société franco-japonaise de Paris. Bulletin. 1, 1902-

7333. Japan society of America. Bureau of international relations. Bulletin. San Francisco. 1, 1914-

7334. Vestnik IAponii. Вестник Японии. (The Messenger of Japan.) Орган русско-японского клуба в Токио. (Publication of the Russo-Japanese club in Tokyo.) Evgeniev (Shneerov), editor. The periodical is in Russian and Japanese. 1915 -

7335. Deutsch-japanische revue. Monatsschrift. Herausgegeben von S. Ikeda. Verlag "Linden", Berlin-Charlottenburg, 1923-

7336. Japanisch-deutsche zeitschrift (Nichi-doku gakugei) zur förderung der wissenschaftlich-technischen, politisch-wirtschaftlichen und kulturellen beziehungen zwischen Japan und Deutschland. Herausgegeben von A. Sata. Osaka (Japan), 1928-

7337. Yamato. Zeitschrift der deutsch-japanischen arbeits-gemeinschaft. Herausgegeben von K. Kanokogi. Verlag Würfel, Berlin-Lankwitz, 1929-

III. ENCYCLOPEDIAS AND DICTIONARIES

See 1162-1163; 10364-10484.

7338. 大百科辭典 Dai hyakka jiten. (Great Japanese encyclopedia.) Tokyo, Heibonsha, 1931-1932. 24 v.

7339. Okuma, Shigenobu. 日本百科大辭典 Nippon hyakka dai-jiten. (Encyclopedia japonica.) Tokyo, Sansei-do, 1908-1919. 10 v.

7340. Yoshida, T. 大日本地名辭書 Dai Nippon chimei jisho. Historical-geographical dictionary of Japan. 1907-1923. 7 v.

7341. Papinot, E. Dictionnaire d'histoire et de géographie du Japon. Tokyo, Sansaisha, Yokohama, Kelly and Walsh, 1906. xviii, 992 p. (Abridged edition, Hongkong, Imprimerie de Nazareth, 1899. vii, 297 p.) English translation of the full edition, Historical and geographical dictionary of Japan. Yokohama, Kelly and Walsh, 1910. xiv, 842 p.

7342. Matsui, K. and Ueda, M. 大日本國語辭典 Dai Nippon kokugo jiten. (Dictionary of the Japanese language.) Tokyo, Fuzanbo co., 1915-1919. 4 v. (1242, 1231, 1258, 1642 p.)

IV. BIOGRAPHICAL DICTIONARIES

See 1164-1175; 10468-10477.

7343. 新撰大人名辭典 Shinsen dai jinmei jiten. (New biographical dictionary.) Tokyo, Heibon-sha, 1937. 8 v.

7344. 大日本人名辭典 Dai Nippon jinmei jisho. (Biographical dictionary of Japan.) Tokyo, Dai Nippon jinmei jisho kan-kokai, 1937. 5 v.

7345. 大日本人名辭書 Dai Nippon jinmei jisho. (A biographical dictionary of Japan.) Tokyo, Keizai zasshisha, 1912. 2754 p.

7346. Haga, Yaichi. 日本人名辭典 Nippon jinmei jiten. (Biographical dictionary of Japan.) Tokyo, Okura book store, 1917. 1174 p. 6th edition.

7347. 日本紳士錄 Nippon shinshi-roku. (Who's who of Japan.) Tokyo, Kojun-sha, 1897-

7348. Omachi, Keigetsu. 日本ノ人傑 Nippon no jinketsu. (Critical biography of the leading statesmen and military men in Japan.) Kobe, Kaibundo, 1928. 216 p.

7349. 現代紳士錄 Gendai shinshi-roku. (Directory of eminent persons in Japan and their personality.) Tokyo, Chuo tanteikyoku (Central detective agency), 1928. 624 p.

7350. Mitani, Kingoro. 大日本実業信用錄 Dai Nippon jitsugyo shinyo-roku. (Who's who among business men in Japan.) Osaka, Dai Nippon jitsugyosha, 1928.

7351. Noride, V. amd Ogita, M. The biography of celebrated statesmen and soldiers of modern Japan. English translation. Tokyo, 1886. 60 p.

7352. 満蒙上海ノ戦野ニ活躍スル陸海将星列傳 Man-Mo Shanghai no senya ni katsuyaku suru rikkai shosei retsuden. (Biographies of generals and admirals active on the battlefields of Manchuria, Mongolia, and Shanghai.) Jitsugyo no sekai. (The industrial world.) Mar. 1932.

7353. Nishino Kiyosaku. 歷代藏相傳 Rekidai zosho den. (Biographies of the successive finance ministers of Japan.) Tokyo, Toyo keizaisha, 1931. 300 p.

7354. Izeki, Kuro.R. 大日本博士錄 Dai Nippon hakushi-roku. (Who's who hakushi: holders of the doctor's degree, 1880-1920.) Text in Japanese and English. Tokyo, 1925.

7355. Kasuga, Shoichiro. 時代ヲ醜ル人々 Jidai wo meguru hitobito. (Men of the times.) Tokyo, Shubunkan, 1931. 604 p.

7356. Washio, Junkei. 日本佛家人名辭書 Nippon bukke jinmei jisho. (Dictionary of prominent buddhists in Japan.) Tokyo, 1917.

7357. Sugihara, Saburo. 大東京紳士錄 Dai Tokyo shinshi-

roku. (Who's who in Tokyo.) Tokyo, Marunouchi shinbunsha.
1928. 932 p.

V. YEAR-BOOKS AND DIRECTORIES

See 1176-1181; 10478-10484.

7358. 日本帝國年鑑 The Japan year-book; complete
cyclopedia of general information and statistics on Japan
and Japanese territories. 1st-27th year, 1905-31. Tokyo,
The Japan year-book office, 1905-31. Superseded by Japan-
Manchoukuo year-book co., 1933-

7359. The Japan year-book. Tokyo, The Foreign affairs association of Japan, 1933-

7360. Japan directory. Annual. Yokohama, Japan gazette,
1867-

7361. Peerage of Japan. Yokohama, Japan gazette, 1912.
951 p.

7362. Japan commercial and industrial directory. 日本商
工營業錄 Nippon shoko yeigyoroku. Tokyo, 1900-

7363. Japan today and tomorrow. Osaka, Osaka mainichi publishing co., 1927-

7364. 日本政治經濟年鑑 Nippon seiji keizai nenkan.
(Japan political and economic year-book.) Tokyo, Iwanami
book store.

7365. Tokyo stock exchange year-book. Tokyo, 1910.

VI. JOURNALISM AND NEWSPAPERS

See 142-143; 1182-1195; 10403-10409.

A. History

7366. Ono, Hideo. 日本新聞發達史 Nippon shinbun
hattatsu shi. (History of the growth of newspapers in
Japan.) Tokyo, Nichi nichi shinbunsha, 1912.

7367. Hanazono, Kanesada. 日本新聞發達史 Nippon shinbun hattatsu-shi. (The development of Japanese journalism.)
Osaka, The Osaka mainichi, 1924. 110 p.

7368. Kawabé, Kisaburo. The press and politics in Japan. A study of the relations between the newspaper and the political development of modern Japan. Chicago, University of Chicago press, 1921. xiii, 190 p.

7369. 新聞總覽 Shinbun soran. (Complete survey of the newspapers published in Japan in 1930.) Tokyo, Nippon denpo tsushinsha, 1930. 774 p.

7370. Martin, Frank Lee. Journalism of Japan. Bulletin of the University of Missouri (Columbia), vol. 19, no. 10. Journalism series 16. 1918.

7371. Young, Morgan A. "The press and Japanese thought." Pacific affairs, 10:4:412-20, December, 1937.

B. Newspapers

7372. 東京、朝日新聞縮刷版 Tokyo asahi shinbun shukusatsu-ban. (Small type edition of the Tokyo sun.) Tokyo, Tokyo asahi shinbunsha, 1919-

7373. 週刊 朝日 Shukan asahi. (Weekly sun.) Osaka, Osaka asahi shinbunsha, 1922-

7374. サンデー 毎日 Sande mainichi. (Sunday weekly published by the Osaka daily.) Osaka, Osaka mainichi shinbunsha, 1922-

7375. Japan mail. Newspaper, review of Japanese literature, commerce, politics and development. Yokohama, in English, 1865-

7376. Japan herald. Newspaper published in Yokohama, in English. 1867-

7377. Japan gazette. Newspaper published in Yokohama, in English. 1867-

7378. Japan chronicle. Newspaper published in Kobe, in English. 1891-

7379. Japan advertiser. A newspaper published in Yokohama, in English. 1895-

7380. Japan times. The only political paper in the English language edited by Japanese. Tokyo, 1897-

7381. Komatsu, Mitsuo. 日本新聞十年史 Nippon shinbun

junen shi. (Ten years of newspaper publication in Japan.)
Tokyo, Nippon shinbunsha,   1936. 78 p.

7382. 日本新聞年鑑 Nippon shinbun nenkan. (Year-book
of newspapers published in Japan.) Tokyo, Shinbun kenkyusho, 1930.

7383. Okamoto, Mitsuzo. 大日本新聞大鑑 Dai Nippon shinbun taikan. (Directory of Japanese newspapers.) Osaka,
Shinbun no sekaisha, 1935. 557 p.

VII. GEOLOGY, GEOGRAPHY, AND NATURAL RESOURCES

See 148-255.

A. Periodicals

7384. 地質学雑誌 Chishitsugaku zasshi. (The Journal
of the Geological society of Tokyo.) Tokyo, Geological
society, 1893-

7385. Seismological journal of Japan, edited by Prof. J.
Milne (forms the continuation of the "Transactions of the
Seismological society of Japan"). Yokohama, 1893-

7386. 日本地理地質報告 Nippon chiri chishitsu hokoku.
(Japanese journal of geology and geography.) Tokyo, National research council of Japan, 1, 1922-

B. Maps

See 149-164; 224-285; 7409.

7387. Collingridge, G. "The early cartography of Japan."
Geographical journal, London, III (1894):403-409.

7388. Dahlgren, E. W. Les débuts de la cartographie du
Japon. Archives d'études orientales, edited by J. A.
Lundell. Vol. 4. Upsala, K. W. Appelberg, 1911. 65 p.

7389. Geological and topographical map of the oil fields of
the Japanese empire. Section-map. Sections 1-21. Tokyo,
Imperial geological survey of Japan, 1902-1923. 1:10,000 -
1:30,000.

7390. Geological map of the Japanese empire. General map.
Tokyo, Imperial geological survey of Japan, 1911. (General
map of the Japanese empire 1:12,000,000; Formosa and Ryukyu
1:4,000,000.)

7391. Mineral map. General map. Mineral distribution of
Japanese empire. Tokyo, Imperial geological survey of Japan,
1911. General map of Japanese empire 1:12,000,000. Manchuria 1:4,000,000. Taiwan 1:400,000.

7392. Topographical map. Sheet-map. (Revised.) Tokyo,
Imperial geological survey of Japan, 5 sheets, 1913-1921.
1:200,000.

7393. Geological and topographical map of the coal fields
and of the mining districts. Johan coal field. Section I.
Tokyo, Imperial geological survey of Japan, 1913. 1:10,000.

7394. Geological and topographical map of the coal fields
and of the mining districts. Karatsu coal field. Tokyo,
Imperial geological survey of Japan, 1917. 1:30,000.

7395. Geological map. Sheet-map. Tokyo, Imperial geological
survey of Japan, 4 sheets, 1921-1923. 1:75,000.

7396. Map of applied geology. Coal of Japan (1921). Iron of
Japan (1922). Copper of Japan (1922). Tokyo, Imperial geological survey of Japan, 1921-1922. 1:3,000,000.

7397. Explanatory text: explanation of the general geological sheet-maps (1:75,000). Abstracts. 1922-1923. Explanation
of the general mineral map 1911. Tokyo, 1911-1923.

7398. See 7389.

7399. Japan. (map.) London, Geographical section general
staff No. 2957, sheet 35, 1923.

7400. Map of Japan and Western Pacific. Equat. Scale
13,100,000. Chicago, A.J. Nystrom and co., 1914.

7401. Mer du Japon. Golfe de Tartarie. Ile de Sakhaline
(Karafuto). Paris, Service hydrographique de la marine,
1928.

7402. 参 謀 本 部 , 地 圖 Sanbo-honbu no chizu.
(Military survey maps of Japan.) Edited and published by
"Rikuchi sokuryobu" (Military land surveying dept.) 3 diff.
editions in scales 1:200,000, 1:50,000 and 1:20,000. The
names are printed in Chinese characters only, folio. Tokyo,
Buyodo publisher 7, Sanchome, Toricho, Nihonbashi.

7403. Ono, Tetsuji. Map showing distribution of population
in the Japanese empire. Tokyo, Fuzambo, 1925. 1:10,000,000.

7404. Coulter, Wesley. "A dot map of the distribution of population in Japan." Geographical review, XVI (1926):283-284.

7405. Sprigade, P. Eisenbahnkarte von Japan, Korea und der Mandschurei. Bearbeitet von P. Sprigade. Berlin, Auswärtiges amt abteilung X (Aussenhandel) No. 290/II. Abschnitt II: Gebietsfragen, sammelmappe: "Deutschland und die weltwirtschaftliche lage". Feb. 1921. 1:7,000,000.

7406. General railway map of Japan. Tokyo, Japanese government, 1912. 1:1,000,000.

C. Geology

(1) General Accounts

7407. Inouye, Kinosuke. The Imperial geological survey of Japan: its history, organization, and work. Tokyo, Imperial geological survey of Japan, 1923. 11 p.

7408. The Imperial geological survey of Japan. 帝國地質調査所報告 Teikoku chishitsu chosasho hokku. Report, No. 1, 1878- [In Japanese. Titles and summaries in English.]

7409. 地質調査所 Chishitsu chosasho. The Imperial geological survey of Japan. Topographical map. General map. 1:1,000,000. 1899. Reconnaisance division-map. 5 divisions 1:400,000. 1884-1894. Division-map. 5 divisions 1:400,000. 1900-1915. Division-map. First division (revised), 1922. Sheet-map. 98 sheets. 1:200,000. 1884-1917. Sheet-map. 5 sheets (revised), 1913-1921. (2) Geological map. General map. 1:1,000,000. 1902. General map. 1:2,000,000. 1911. Reconnaisance division-map. 5 divisions. 1:400,000. 1886-1895. Division-map. 5 divisions 1:400,000. 1902-1916. Sheet-map. 98 sheets 1:200,000. 1885-1919. Sheet-map. 4 sheets 1:75,000. 1921-1923. Special sheet-map. Yoshioka 1:7500. 1921. Special sheet-map. Kune. 1:15,000. 1923. (3) Mineral map. General map. 1:2,000,000. 1911. Division-map. 3d division, 1914. 4th division, 1912. 5th division, 1919. 1:400,000. (4) Geological and topographical map of the Japanese empire. Section-map. Sections 1-21. 1:10,000-1:30,000. 1902-1923. (5) Geological and topographical map of the coal fields and of the mining districts. Joban coal fields. Section 1. 1:10,000. 1913. Karatsu coal field. 1:30,000. 1917. (6) Map of applied geology. Coal of Japan. 1:3,000,000. 1921. Iron of Japan. 1:3,000,000. 1922. Copper of Japan. 1:3,000,000. 1922. (7) Explanatory text. Text of the general geological map. (1:1,000,000) 1902. Explanation of the general geological map. (1:2,000,000.)

1911. 7 texts of the geological sheet-maps (1:75 000).
Abstracts, 1922-1923. 2 texts of the special geological
sheet-maps. Abstracts, 1922-1923. Explanation of the
general mineral map, 1911. 5 texts (sections 17-21) of the
section-map of the oil fields of the Japanese Empire. Abstracts, 1922-1923. Text of Joban coal field section 1.
Abstracts, 1914. (8) Memoirs. Nos. 1-2, 1907-1910.
(9) Bulletin, vols. 11-20, 1898-1907, with English contents.
Vols. 21-25, 1915-1922, with English abstracts. (10) Report. Nos. 83-88, 1921-1923, with English abstracts or contents. (11) Mineral survey report. Nos. 33-34, 1922, with
English contents. (12) Industrial mineral survey report.
Nos. 7-15, 1922-1923. With English abstracts or contents.

7410. St. Petersburg 7th international geological congress
in 1897: Imperial geological survey with a catalogue of
articles and analytical results of the specimens of soil
exhibited. Tokyo, 1897. 47, 28 p. 2 maps.

7411. Imperial geological survey of Japan with a catalogue
of articles exhibited at the Japan-British exhibition held
at London, England, in 1910. Tokyo, Imperial geological
survey of Japan, 1910. 96 p.

7412. Imperial geological survey of Japan. With a catalogue
of articles exhibited at the Panama-Pacific international
exposition held at San Francisco, U. S. A., in 1915. Tokyo,
1915. 65 p.

7413. 日本帝國地質鑛山生產ニ就行 Nippon teikoku
chishitsu kozan seisan ni tsuite. (The geology and mineral
resources of the Japanese empire.) Tokyo, Imperial geological survey of Japan, 1926-

7414. Lyman, Benjamin Smith. Geological survey of Japan.
Reports of progress for 1878 and 1879. Tookei, Public
works department, 1879.

7415. Japan. Imperial geological survey. 鑛業調查報告
Kogyo chosa hokoku. (Industrial mineral survey.) 1-22,
1921-1925.

(2) Natural Resources and Mining

7416. 本邦鑛業一斑 Hompo kogyo ippan. (A survey of the
Japanese mining industry.) Annual, in Japanese and English.
Tokyo, Ministry of agriculture and commerce, 1907-

7417. 地質 鑛 物 調査報告 Chishitsu kobutsu chosa hokoku. (Report on the investigation of geology and minerals
of Japan.) Tokyo, Departments of home affairs and education,
1932. 4 v.   197, 113, 109, 112 p.

7418. Wada, Tsunashiro. 二十五年間 / 鑛業 25-nen kan
no kogyo. (The mining industry in Japan during the last 25
years, 1867-92.) Tokyo, Bureau of commerce and industry of
the imperial Japanese department of agriculture and commerce, 1893. 304 p.

7419. Les mines du Japon, rédigé par le Bureau des mines au
Ministère de l'agriculture et du commerce. Paris, Imperial
commission for the Paris exhibition of 1900, 1900. 530 p.

7420. Wada, Tsunashiro. Minerals of Japan. Tokyo, 1904.
144 p.

7421. Mining in Japan, past and present. Tokyo, Bureau of
mines, Department of agriculture and commerce of Japan,
1909. v, 322 p.

7422. Selwyn-Brown, A. "Mineral resources of the Japanese
empire." Engineer magazine, 40 (1911:347-364, 568-583).

7423. Dyes, W.A. "Gross-Japans bergwirtschaftliche entwicklung." Metall und erz, 14 (1917):289-318.

7424. Adler, W. "Grundlagen und entwicklung der montan-
industrie Japans." Weltwirtschaftliches archiv, chronik und
archivalien, 11 (1917):155-170.

7425. Chenet, Ch. "L'industrie du zinc au Japon. 3e partie.
Les mines de zinc en Corée, en Sibérie, en Mandchourie et
en Chine." Bulletin économique de l'Indo-Chine, 135 (1919):
229-259.

7426. Watanabe, M. On distribution of ore deposits in Japan.
Tokyo, 1925.

7427. Berling, N., Krishtofovich, A., Serk, A., Flerov, A.
"Минеральные ресурсы и горная промышленность Японии." (The
mineral resources and mining industry of Japan.) Novyi Vostok, 16-17 (1927):239-255.

7428. Inouye, K. The coal resources of Japan. Tokyo, 1913.

7429. Schultze, Ernst. "Der kohlenbergbau in Japan." Der
neue Orient, Berlin, 1-12 (1922):314-327.

7430. "The iron ore resources of Japan." Bulletin of the Imperial geological survey of Japan, 25 (1916-1922):27-39.

7431. Wêng, Wên-hao. 日本人如何取得鐵礦砂的供給 Jih-pên jên ju ho chu tê tieh-kung-sha ti kung-chi. (The method of the Japanese in getting the supply of iron.) Tu-li-ping-lun. 1, May, 1932. p. 12-

7432. Kobayashi, G. Geology and oilfields of Japan. Tokyo, 1923.

7433. Fitzner, R. "Die entwicklung der japanischen ölindustrie." Der neue Orient, Berlin, 6 (1919-1920):106-108. Karte.

7434. 我國二於㐀燃料問題 Waga kuni ni okeru nenryo mondai. (The fuel problem in Japan.) To-A keizai chosa kyoku. Materials on economic study of the Far East, v. 11, part 9. See 797.

7435. Hsu,Chung-hao. 日本之資源調查 Jih-pên chih tzu-yüan. tiao-cha. (A survey of the natural resources of Japan.) Kao-shih-yüan kung-pao, no. 11, Nov., 1931, p. 1.

D. Geography

See 148-255; 7386; 7399-7404; 9010-9013.

(1) Periodicals

See 7386.

7436. 地學雜誌 Chigaku zasshi. (A magazine of geography.) Tokyo, Geographical society of Tokyo press, 1899-

7437. 地理學評論 Chirigaku hyoron. (The geographical review of Japan.) Tokyo, Geographical institute, Faculty of science, Imperial university of Tokyo, Association of Japanese geographers, 1925-

(2) General Accounts

7438. Fujita, Motoharu. 日本地理學史 Nippon chirigaku-shi. (History of the geographical study of Japan.) Tokyo, Toko.shoin, 1937. 500 p.

7439. Yamazaki, Naomasa, and Sato, D. 大日本地誌 Dai Nippon chishi. (Geography of Japan.) 1903-1915. 10 v. New printing, Tokyo, 1916-1917.

7440. 日本地理大系,Nippon chiri taikei. (Standard geography of Japan.) Tokyo. Kaizosha, 1929-1930. 14 v.

7441. 日本地理風俗大系, Nippon chirifuzoku taikei. (Great geography of Japan.) Tokyo, Nippon chirifuzoku taikei kankokwai, 1931-1932. 19 v.

7442. Siebold, Ph. von. Geschichte der entdeckungen im seegebiete von Japan, nebst erklärung des atlas von land- und seekarten vom japanischenreiche. Leide, 1852. 204 p.

7443. Pozdneev, Dmitrii. Япония. (Japan.) A geographical statistical sketch. In Izvestiia vostochnogo instituta, vol. 16. Vladivostok, 1906. ii, vi, 154 p.

7444. Haushofer, Karl. Das japanische reich in seiner geographischen entwicklung. Angewandte geographie, bd. 50. Wien, L. W. Seidel'und sohn, 1921. vii, 171 p.

7445. Kiuner, Nikolai V. География Японии. (Физическая и политическая.) (Geography of Japan, physical and political.) Moscow, 1927. 240 p.

7446. Nakamura, Shintaro. 地學論叢 Chigaku ronso. (Collection of essays on geography of Japan.) Kyoto, Kobundo, 1930. 716 p .

7447. Yamamoto, Kumataro. 概観日本地誌 Gaikan Nippon chishi. (A general survey of the geography of Japan.) Tokyo, Kokon shoin, 1930. Vol. 1. 547 p.

7448. Chou, Kuang-cho. 日本地理 Jih-pên ti-li. (A geography of Japan.) Shanghai, Nan-ching shu-tien, 1932.

7449. Trewartha, Glenn Thomas. A reconnaissance geography of Japan. Madison, University of Wisconsin press, 1934. 283 p., 54 diagrams, 49 photographs.

7450. Bishop, Carl Whiting. "The historical geography of early Japan." Geographical review, 13 (1923):40-63. Also in Annual report, Smithsonian institution for 1925. Washington, no. 2859, 1926. 547-568.

7451. Teleki, Graf Paul. "Japans rolle in der geschichte der entdeckung Amerikas. Földrajzi Közlemények. (Geographische mitteilungen der ungarischen geographischen gesellschaft, Budapest.) Abrégé, bd. 34, heft 1, 1906. 10 p.

7452. Yokoyama, Matajiro. 鮮新期後 / 氣候、変化
Senshin kigo no kiko henka. (Climatic changes in Japan
since the Pliocene epoch.) Journal of the College of science, Imperial university of Tokyo, vol. 32, article 5,
1911. 16 p.

7453. Huntington, Ellsworth. "Geographical environment and
Japanese character." Journal of race developement, 2 (1911-
1912):256-281.

7454. Hulbert, H. B. "Japan an isothermal empire." Journal
of race development, 6 (1916):441-453.

7455. Haushofer, Karl. "Die geographischen grundrichtungen
in der entwicklung des japanischen reiches von 1854-1914."
Geographische zeitschrift, 26 (1920):8-25.

7456. Weston, Walter. "The geography of Japan and its influence on the character of the Japanese people." Transactions and proceedings of the Japan society, 20:2-12, 4
plates. (32d session, 1922-1923.)

7457. Weston, Walter. "The influence of nature on Japanese
character." Geographical journal, 63 (1924):106-120.

7458. Haushofer, Karl. "Geopolitische einflüsse bei den
verkörperungsversuchen von nationalem sozialismus und
sozialer aristokratie." Zeitschrift für geopolitik, 1
(1924):127-134.

7459. See 9010-9013.

7460. See 9010-9013.

(3) Earthquake of 1923

7461. Imamura, A. Preliminary note on the great earthquake
of S. E. Japan on September 1, 1923. Imperial earthquake
investigation committee, Seismological notes, no. 6, 1924.
22 p.

7462. Jaggar, T. A. "The Yokohama-Tokyo earthquake of
September 1, 1923." Bulletin of the seismological society
of Americal, 13 (1924):124-146.

7463. Davidson, Charles. "The Japanese earthquake of the 1
September, 1923." Geographical journal, London, 65 (1925):
44-61.

VIII. ARCHAEOLOGY AND ANTHROPOLOGY

See 256-272;1367-1395; 4852-4869; 6561-6567; 6954-6959;
10688-10784.

A. Archaeology

See 7474-7476.

(1) Periodicals

See 7474-7476.

7464. 考古學雜誌 Kokogaku zasshi. (Archaeological
journal) Tokyo, Archaeological society, 1896-

(2) General Accounts

7465. Sato, Torao. 日本考古學 Nippon kokogaku (Japanese
archaeology.) Tokyo, Heibonsha. 1930. 311 p.

7466. Goto, Morikazu. 日本考古學 Nippon kokogaku. (Japanese archaeology.) Tokyo, Shikai shobo, 1927. 332 p.

7467. Munro, Gordon H. Prehistoric Japan. Yokohama, Kelly
& Walsh, 1908. xvii, 705 p. (Second edition, 1911.)

7468. Bénazet, A. Le Japon avant les Japonais: étude d'ethnographie et d'archéologie sur les Aïnou primitifs. Paris,
P. Geuthner, 1911. 33 p.

7469. Maeda, F. "Japanische steinzeit." Mitteilungen der
deutschen gesellschaft für natur- und völkerkunde Ostasiens,
Tokyo, 14(1912):2:157-170. 5 plates.

7470. Matsumoto, H. Notes on the stone age people of Japan."
American anthropologist, 23, 1921.

7471. Munro, N. Gordon. "Primitive culture in Japan."
Transactions of the Asiatic society of Japan, 34 (1906):2:
1-212.

7472. Matsumura, Takeo. 神話學論考 Shinwagaku ronko.
(Treatise on Japanese mythology.) Tokyo, Dobunkan, 1929.
551 p.

7473. Horioka, Bunkichi. 國体起源，神話學的研究
Kokutai kigen no shinwagakuteki kenkyu. (Research in the
origin of Japan with reference to mythology.) Tokyo, Baifu-

kan, 1929. 496 p.

B. Anthropology

(1) Periodicals

7474. 人類學雜誌 Jinruigaku zasshi. (Journal of Anthropology.) Tokyo, Anthropological society, 1886-

7475. 民族ト歴史 Minzoku to rekishi. (Race and history.) Tokyo, Nippon Gakujutsu fukyukai, 1919-

7476. 東京帝國大學理學部紀要:第五類:人類學Tokyo teikoku daigaku rigaku-bu kiyo: dai gorui: jinruigaku. (Journal of the Faculty of science of the Tokyo imperial university.) Section 5. Anthropology. Tokyo, Imperial university of Tokyo. 1925-

(2) General Accounts

7477. Anoutchin [Anuchin], D. N. Matériaux pour l'anthropologie de l'Asie orientale: Tribu des Ainos. (Mémoires de la Société impériale des amis des sciences naturelles, 20 supplement.) Moscou, 1877.

7478. Batchelor, J. The Ainu of Japan. The religion, superstitions, and general history of the hairy aborigines of Japan. London, 1892. 336 p.

7479. Ishida, Shuzo. 北海道アイヌ雑考 "Hokkaido Ainu zakko." (Treatise on the Ainus in Hokkaido.) Jinruigaku zasshi. (Journal of anthropology.) Vol. 26, no. 295. 1910.

7480. Salwey, Charlotte M. "Japanese monographs, no. 14: The Ainu: past and present." Asiatic quarterly review, 31 (1911):315-331.

7481. Torii, R. "Études archéologiques et ethnographiques. Les Ainou des Iles Kouriles." Journal of the College of science, Imperial university of Tokyo, 42:1 (1919). 337 p., 38 plates.

7482. Tsutsumi, Yasujiro. 日支民族論 Nichi-Shi minzoku ron. (A discussion on the Japanese and Chinese races.) Tokyo, Komin domei, 1921. 2 v.

7483. Ramstedt, G. J. "A comparison of the Altaic languages with Japanese." Transactions of the Asiatic society of Japan, 1 (1924):41-54. (Second series.)

7484. Bryan, Ingram J. "The origins of the Japanese race."
Transactions and proceedings of the Japan society, 22:90-
105. (34th session, 1924-1925.)

7485. Matsumura, Akira. On the cephalic index and stature
of the Japanese and their local difference. A contribution
to the physical anthropology of Japan. Journal of the
Faculty of science, Imperial university of Tokyo. Section
5: Anthropology. Vol. 1, part 1, 1925. 312 p.

7486. Hinloopen-Labberton, D. van. "The Oceanic languages
and the Nipponese as branches of the Nippon-Malay-Poly-
nesian family of speech." Transactions of the Asiatic society of Japan, 2 (1925):77-116. (Second series.)

7487. Whytmant, A. Neville J. "The oceanic theory of the
origin of Japanese language and people." Transactions of
the Asiatic society of Japan, 3 (1926): 15-81.

7488. Tanaka, Kanichi. 日本民族ノ將来 Nippon minzoku
no shorai. (The future of the Japanese race.) Tokyo, Baifu-
kan, 1926.

7489. Watanabe, Shujiro. "Ancient Japanese in America and
their descendants." The young East, 2 (1926-1927):17-21.

7490. Batchelor, John. Ainu life and lore. Echoes of a de-
parting race. Tokyo, Kyobunkwan, 1927. 448 p.

7491. Torii, Ryuzo. 人類學上ヨリ見タル我が上代ノ文化
Jinruigaku-jo yori mitaru waga jodai no bunka. (Civilization in the early period of our history from an anthropolog
ical standpoint.) Tokyo, Sobunkaku, 1929. 382 p.

7492. Togami, Komanosuke. 日本民族ノ新研究Nippon minzoku no shin kenkyu. (New research on the Japanese race.)
Tokyo, Toko shoin, 1929. 83 p.

7493. Kanazawa, Shozaburo. 日鮮同祖論Nichi-Sen doso-ron.
(Treatise on the theory that the ancestors of the Japanese
and Koreans are identical.) Tokyo, Toko shoin, 1929. 250 p.

7494. Togami, Komanosuke. 日本ノ民族 Nippon no minzoku.
(The origin and the development of the Japanese race.)
Tokyo, Oka shoin, 1930. 448 p.

7495. 偉大ナル日本民族 Idai naru Nippon minzoku. (The
great Japanese race.) Osaka, Osaka kokugakuin, 1930. 91 p.

7496. Kaneko, Hikoji. 日本國民性ノ實證的研究Nippon

kokuminsei no jisshoteki kenkyu. (Study of the characteristics of the Japanese nation.) Tokyo, Meiji tosho kabushiki-
gaisha, 1930. 358 p.

7497-7498. Watanabe, R. 日本民族特殊性論 Nippon minzoku
tokushusei-ron. (Characteristics of the Japanese race.)
Kyoto, Kokutai kagakusha, 1930. 300 p.

7499. Ning, Mo-kung. 日本種族三所由來 Jih-pên chung-tsu
chih yu-lai. (Origin of the Japanese race.) Hsin-ya-shi-
ya, Vol. 3, no. 3, Dec., 1931, p. 117-

7500. Shimomoru, Hiroshi. 日本民族・將來 Nippon minzoku
no shorai. (The future of the Japanese race.) Tokyo, Tokyo
asahi shinbunsha, 1933. 400 p.

7501. Matsumura, Akira, 日本民族 Nippon minzoku. (The
Japanese race.) Tokyo, Iwanami shoten, 1936. 477 p.

IX. HISTORY

See 273-342; 343-449; 1527-1921.

A. Bibliography

See 1-42; 1061-1087; 1527; 7237-7304; 10291-10363.

7502. Kondo, K. 史籍集覽 Shiseki shuran. (Collection
of books concerning Japanese history.) Tokyo, Kondo press,
1900-1903. 33 v. (2) The same. 續史籍集覽 Zoku: Shiseki shuran.
(Collection of books concerning Japanese history.) Second
series. Tokyo, Kondo press, 1930. 10 v.

7503. 國史研究史集 Kokushi kenkyu shishyu. (A col-
tection of historical research works of Japan.) Kyoto,
Kyoto teikoku daigaku kokushi kenkyushitsu (Kyoto imperial
university), 1933. 70 p.

7504. 國史論文要目 Kokushi rombun yomoku. (Selected
bibliography of essays on national history.) Tokyo, Otsuka
historical association, 1934.

B. Historiography

7505. Kiyohara, Sadao. 日本史學史 Nippon shigaku-shi.
(History of the writing of history in Japan.) Tokyo, Chubunkan, 1928. 333 p.

7506. Nonomura, Kaizo. 史學概論 Shigaku gairon. (Introduction to historiography.) Tokyo, Waseda university, 1929. 393 p.

7507. Nishida, Naojiro. 史 學 論 叢 Shigaku ronso. (A collection of essays on Japanese historiography.) Tokyo, Kobundo, 1930. 741 p.

7508. Kiuner, N. V. Современное состояние японской исторической науки." (Contemporary condition of Japanese historical science.) Istoricheskie izvestiia (Moskva), no 1, 48-78; no 2, 111-139.

C. Periodicals
See 43-147; 7305-7337.

7509. 史 學 雜 誌 Shigaku zasshi. (Journal of history.) Tokyo, Tokyo teikoku daigaku: shiryo hensansho, 1889-

7510. 史 海 Shikai. (The sea of history.) Tokyo, Keizai zasshisha, May, 1891-July, 1896. 4 v.

7511. 歷 史 地 理 Rekishi chiri. (Historical geography.) Tokyo, Nippon chirigakukai, 1899- (2) Hanami, Katsumi. 歷史地理總一卷至第六十卷索引 Rekishi-chiri 1-60 kan sakuin. (The index for vols. 1-60 of the periodical "Historical Geography".) Tokyo, Chijin shokan, 1934. 267 p.

7512. 史 林 Shirin. (Historical quarterly.) Kyoto, Kyoto shigakukai (Historical society of Kyoto imperial university.), 1916-

7513. 歷 史 ト 地 理 Rekishi to chiri. (History and geography.) Tokyo, Shigaku chirigaku dokokai, 1917-

7514. 中 央 史 壇 Chuo shidan. (Historic center.) Tokyo, Kokushi koshukai, 1920-

7515. 新 旧 時 代 Shinkyu jidai. (The times: old and new.) Tokyo, Meiji bunka kenkyukai, 1925-

7516. 史 苑 Shien. (The garden of history.) Tokyo, Keimeisha, 1928-

7517. 史 潮 Shicho. (Tide of history.) Tokyo, Otsuka shigakukai, 1931-

D. Chronologies

See 273-277; 1532-1535.

7518. Takahashi, Shozo. 最新 日本歴史年表 Saishin Nippon rekishi nenpyo. (Latest chronological table of the history of Japan.) Tokyo, Sanseido, 1930.

7519. Satow, E. M. Japanese chronological tables. Yedo, 1874. 50 p. (Privately printed.)

7520. Clement, Ernest W. "Comparative chronological tables of the Christian era, Japanese eras and emperors, Chinese emperors and eras, and Korean kings, with years of the sexagenary cycles, from 660 B. C. to 1910 A. D." Transactions of the Asiatic society of Japan, 37 (1910):133-256. (Supplement.)

7521. Bramsen, William. "Japanese chronological tables, showing the date, according to the Julian or Gregorian calendar, of the first day of each Japanese month from Taikwa 1st year to Meiji 6th year (645 A. D. to 1873 A. D.). With an introductory essay on Japanese chronology and calendars." Transactions of the Asiatic society of Japan, 37 (1910):1-127. (Supplement.)

E. Dictionaries of History

7522. Hayakawa, J., Inobe, S., and Yashiro, K. 國史大辭典 Kokushi daijiten. (The unabridged dictionary of national history.) Tokyo, Yoshikawa kobunkan, 1932. 6 v.   2853 p.

7523. Fujioka, Tsugihei. 日本歴史地理辭典 Nippon rekishi chiri jiten. (Dictionary of historical geography of Japan.) 1907.

F. Collections of Sources

See 496-517; 1536-1547; 1560-1580.

7524. 大日本古文書 Dai Nippon komonjo. (Ancient documents of Japan; 702-772.) Tokyo, Tokyo imperial university, Historiographical institute, 1901-1930. 19 v.

7525. 大日本古文書: 家わけ Dai Nippon komonjo: Iewake. (Documents in archives of the feudal families.) Tokyo, Tokyo imperial university, Historiographical institute. Series: 1. Koyasan monastery. 高野山 1904-1907. 7 v. 2. Asano family. 浅野 1906. 2 v.   3. Date family. 伊達 1911-1914. 10 v.   4. Iwashimizu shrine. 石清水 1909-1915. 6 vols. 5. Sagara family. 相良 1917-1918. 2 v. 6. Kanshinji monastery. 觀心寺 1917. 1 v. 7. Kongoji monastery. 金剛寺 1920. 1 v. 8. Mori family. 毛利 1920-1924.

4 v.   9. Kikkawa family. 吉川 1925-1926. 3 v.
10. Toji temple. 東寺 1925-1933. 3 v.   11. Kobayakawa
family. 小早川 1927. 2 v.   12. Uesugi family. 上杉
1931. 1 v. 13. Aco shrine. 阿蘇 1932. 1 v. (2) 大日本古文
書: 幕末外国関係文書 Dai Nippon komonjo: Bakumatsu
gaikoku kankei monjo. (Official documents of the later Tokugawa era concerning foreign relations; 1853-1858.) 1910-
1932. 21 v.   1913-1926. 4 v.   Supplements.

7526. 大日本史料 Dai Nippon shiryo. (Japanese historical materials.) Tokyo, Tokyo Imperial university, 1902-1932.
119 v.

7527. Toneri, Prince Imperial. 日本書紀 Nihon shoki.
(Chronicle of Japan.) Compiled in 720 A. D. Tokyo, Keizai
zasshisha, Kokushi taikei series, 1904. 574 p.

7528. Ono, Yasumaro. 古事記 Kojiki. (Record of ancient
affairs.) Compiled in 712 A. D. Tokyo, Keizai zasshisha,
Kokushi taikei series, 1904. 170 p. (2) Chamberlain, B. H.
(transl.) Kojiki, or records of ancient matters translated
into English with numerous notes by B. H. Chamberlain.
Yokohama, 1883. lxxv, 369 p.

7529. 文科大学史誌叢書 Bunka daigaku shishi sosho. (History and historical documents.) Kyoto, Kyoto imperial university, College of letters. 6 v.

7530. Arai, Hakuseki. 古史通 Koshi-tsu. (Historical documents of old Japan.) 1871. 4 v.

7531. 史料総覧 Shiryo soran. (Historical materials
of Japan.) Tokyo, Tokyo imperial university, Historiographical institute, 1923-1932. 7 v.

7532. Ota, Ryo. 日韓古代史資料 Nichi-Kan kodaishi shiryo.
(Historical materials for the ancient history of Japan and
Korea.) Tokyo, Isobe koyodo, 1928. 187 p.

7533. 国史大系 Kokushi taikei. (Complete collection of
standard Japanese histories and historical materials.)
Tokyo, Keizai zasshisha, 1897-1904. 17 v.

7534. Kondo, Kameki. 史籍集覧 Shiseki shuran. (Collection
of historical documents and data.) 3d ed Tokyo, Kondo
press, 1918. 32 v.

7535. 維新史料 Ishin shiryo. (History of the Restoration.) Tokyo, Noshidai, 1887-1892. 42 v.

7536. 近 世 實 錄 全 集 Kinsei jitsuroku zensho. (Complete collection of facts and materials on events in recent times.) Tokyo, Waseda university press, 1917-1919. 20 v.

7537. 明 治 維 新 研 究 Meiji ishin kenkyu. (Research on the Meiji reformation, 1868-1912.) Tokyo, Tokyo imperial university, Historical association, 1930. 823 p.

7538. Miyasaka, Kuro. 明治大正昭和歴史資料全集 Meiji, Taisho, Showa rekishi shiryo zenshu. (Complete collection of materials on the history of Meiji, Taisho, and Showa eras.) Tokyo, Jitsugyo no Nihon, 1932.

7539. Hirano, Shin. 明治大正昭和歴史資料大集成：内乱騒擾篇 Meiji, Taisho, Showa rekishi shiryo taishusei: Nairan sojohen. (Collection of source materials on the history of the Meiji, Taisho, Showa eras: on revolts and uprisings.) Tokyo, Shiryo shusei kankokai, 1935. 440 p.

7540. 明治大正昭和歴史資料 Meiji, Taisho, Showa rekishi shiryo. (Historical materials on the Meiji, Taisho, and Showa eras.) Tokyo, Yugosha, 1932-1933. 18 v.

7541. McLaren, W. W. "Japanese government documents." Transactions of the Asiatic society of Japan, 42 (1914):1: 1-681.

G. General History of Japan

See 273-342; 1527-1921; 7837-7901; 8044-8224.

(1) Longer Accounts

7542. Tokutomi, Iichiro. 近世日本國民史 Kinsei Nippon kokumin-shi. (History of the modern Japanese people.) Tokyo, Minyu-sha, 1918-1935. 49 v.

7543. Tokugawa, Mitsukuni. 大日本史 Dai Nihon-shi. (History of Great Japan.) Tokyo, Dai Nippon yubenkai, 1928-1929. 17 vols. (2) 譯文大日本史 Yakubun dai Nihon-shi. (History of Great Japan with Japanese commentary, by Aizan Yamaji.) Tokyo, Koraku shoin, 1912. 243 books in 5 v.

7544. Kobayashi, Shoji. 大日本時代史 Dai Nippon jidaishi. (History of Japan by periods.) Tokyo, Waseda university press, 1926-1927. 14 v.   3d edition.

7545. Yoshida, Togo. 倒 叙 日本史 Tojo Nippon-shi. (History of Japan in reverse order.) Tokyo, Waseda university press, 1917. 10 v.

7546. Aoki, Busuke. 大日本歴史集成 Dai Nippon rekishi shusei. (Complete history of Japan.) 5th ed. Tokyo, Ryubunkan, 1919. 5 v.   1932, Revised edition, 5 v.

7547. Huang, Tsun-hsien. 日本國志 Jih-pên-kuo chih. (A history of Japan.) 1898. 40 v.

7548. Kuroita, Katsumi. 大日本史 Dai Nippon-shi. (Standard history of Japan.) Tokyo, Dai Nippon yubenkai kodansha, 1929. 16 v.

7549. Juken koza kankokai. 國史講座 Kokushi koza. (Lectures on Japanese history.) Tokyo, Juken koza kankokai, 1930-1932. 21 v.

7550. Charlevoix, Pierre François Xavier de. Histoire et description générale du Japon. 1736. 9 v.

7551. Adams, F. O. The history of Japan from the earliest period to the present time. London, 1874-1875. 2 v.

7552. Hayashi, Jo. 本朝通鑑 Honcho tsukan. (Comprehensive history of Japan with commentary.) 1875. 84 v.

7553. Nishimura, Kanebumi. 近世野史 Kinsei yashi. (An unofficial history of modern Japan.) 1875. 15 v.

7554. Inoue, Shukuin. 歴史通覧 Rekishi tsuran. (General survey of the history of Japan.) 1879 3 v.

7555. Takatani, Chu. 日本全史 Nippon zenshi. (Complete history of Japan.) 1880. 10 v.

7556. Iida, Tadahiko. 野史 Yashi. (History of Japan.) Tokyo, Nippon zuihitsu taiseikai, 3d ed. 1929-1930. 5 books in 6 v.

7557. Fujisawa, Nangaku. 日本通史 Nippon tsushi. (History of Japan.) 1885. 16 v.

7558. Ni-Hon Gwai-Si. Histoire indépendente du Japon. Abridged French translation by Oguro Yémon. Paris, 1878-1890. 8 books.

7559. Hagino, Yoshiyuki. 日本歴史評林 Nippon rekishi

hyorin. (Collection of essays on the history of Japan.)
1894. 6 v.

7560. Griffis, William Elliot. The Mikado's empire. Book I:
History of Japan from B. C. 660 to A. D. 1872. Book II:
Personal experiences, observations and studies in Japan,
1870-1874. Tenth edition, with six supplementary chapters,
including history to beginning of 1903. New York, 1904.
2 v. (2) The Japanese nation in evolution. Steps in the
progress of a great people. New York, Crowell, 1907, xii,
408 p.

7561. Ariga, Nagao. 大日本歷史 Dai Nippon rekishi. (History of Great Japan.) Tokyo, Hakubunkan, 1911. 14th edition,
2 v.

7562. La Mazelière, A. T. R. Marquis de. Le Japon, histoire
et civilisation. Paris, 1907-1923. 8 v.

7563. Tsubouchi, Shoyo. 國民ノ日本史 Kokumin no Nipponshi. (People's history of Japan.) Tokyo, Waseda university
press, 1922-1923. 14 v.

7564. Murdoch, James. A history of Japan. With maps by Isoh
Yamagata. Published by the Asiatic society of Japan. Yokohama, Kelly & Walsh; London, K. Paul, Trübner & co., 1903-
1926. 3 v. (2) "A history of Japan. Vol. I. From the
origins to the arrival of the Portuguese in 1542 A. D."
Transactions of the Asiatic society of Japan, Additional
volume, 1910. 667 p and 7 maps. (3) A history of Japan during the century of early foreign intercourse.(1542-1651).
Kobe, 1903.

7565. Kaempfer, Engelbert. The history of Japan: giving an
account of the ancient and present state of government of
the empire; of its minerals, trees, animals and fishes; of
the chronology of the emperors, of the customs and manufactures of the natives, and of their trade, with the Dutch
and Chinese. Together with a description of the Kingdom of
Siam, 1690-1692, written in High Dutch by E. Kaempfer and
tr. from his original manuscript, never before printed by
J. G. Scheuchzer. London, 1728. 2 v. Second ed., Glasgow, James MacLehose and sons, 1906. 3 v.

7566. Kobayashi, Hiroshi. 日本歷史 Nippon rekishi. (History of Japan.) Tokyo, Daido-kan. 1929. 2 v. 856, 945 p.

7567. Miura, Shuko. 日本史ノ研究 Nippon-shi no kenkyu.

(The study of the history of Japan.) Tokyo, Iwanami shoten, 1930. 2 v.

7568. Omori, Kingoro. 大日本全史 Dai Nippon zenshi. (Complete history of Japan.) Tokyo, Fuzanbo, 1932. 3 v .

7569. 岩波講座：日本歴史 Iwanami koza: Nippon reki-shi. (The Iwanami lectures: Japanese history.) Tokyo, Iwa-nami shoten, 1933. 10 v.

7570. 通俗日本全史 Tsuzoku Nippon zenshi. (Complete pop-ular history of Japan.) Tokyo, Waseda university press. 1912-1914. 17 v.

7571. History (official) of the Empire of Japan. Compiled and translated for the Imperial Japanese commission of the World's Columbian exposition in Chicago, U. S. A., in 1893 (translator - Captain Brinkley). Tokyo, Department of edu-cation, 1893. 428 p, 36 plates.

(2) Shorter Accounts

7572. Hagino, Yoshiyuki. 大日本通史 Dai Nippon tsushi. (A comprehensive history of Japan.) Tokyo, Hakubunkan, 1903.

7573. 六國史 Rikkoku-shi. (Six standard national histories compiled by imperial order.) Tokyo, Ikubunsha, 1907. 999 p.

7574. Nadaillac, de. "Le Japon dans l'antiquité et jusqu'à sa dernière évolution." Revue d'Histoire Diplomatique, 22 (1908):24-54.

7575. Omori, Kingoro. 國史概説 Kokushi gaisetsu. (Essen-tials of Japanese history.) Tokyo, Sanseido, 1910. 568 p.

7576. Takakuwa, Komakichi. 日本通史 Nippon tsushi. (Compre-hensive history of Japan.) Tokyo, Kodokan, 1912. 1316 p.

7577. Saito, Hisho. Geschichte Japans. Berlin, F. Dümmler, 1912. x, 262 p. English translation: A history of Japan. Tr. by Elizabeth Lee. London, Kegan Paul, Trench, Trübner & co., 1912. 272 p.

7578. Ito, Gingetsu. 大日本民族史 Dai Nippon minzoku-shi. (History of the Japanese race.) Tokyo, Ryubunkan, 1913. 754 p.

7579. Brinkley, F. and Kikuchi, Baron Dairoku. A history of the Japanese people from the earliest time to the end of

the Meiji era, by Captain F. Brinkley...with the collaboration of Baron Kikuchi. New York, The Encyclopedia britan-
nica co., 1915. xi, 784 p.

7580. Ostwald, P. "Die entwicklungsperioden Japans." Lyze-
um, 2(1915):Nos. 10-11.

7581. Kuroita, Katsumi. 國史'研究:總説'部 Kokushi no
kenkyu: sosetsu no bu. (Introduction to research in national history.) Tokyo, Bunkaido shoten, 1913. 336 p.   (2)The
same.國史'研究:各説部Kokushi no kenkyu:kakusetsu no bu.
(Research in national history.) Tokyo, Bunkaido shoten,
1918. 877 p.

7582. Sakharov, K. V. История Японии. (The history of Japan.) Shanghai, 1920 175 p.

7583. Hara, Katsuro. An introduction to the history of
Japan. Yamato society publication. New York - London, G. B.
Putnam's Sons, 1920. xix, 411 p.   (2) Histoire du Japon des
origines à nos jours. Bibliothèque historique. Paris, Payot,
1926. 307 p.

7584. Hotari, Riichiro. 國民生活'改造Kokumin seikatsu
no kaizo. (On the evolution of the national life of Japan.)
3d ed. 1920. 711 p.

7585. Reznikov, A. I. История Японии. (The history of Japan.) Sbornik trudov professorov i prepodavatelei Irkutskogo gosudarstvennogo universiteta. Irkutsk, 1923.

7586. Hirono, Tokichi.二千六百年史 Nisen roppyakunen-
shi. (History of 2600 years of Japan.) Tokyo, Johoku shobo,
1925. 2230 p.

7587. Yashiro, Kuniharu. 國史叢説 Kokushi sosetsu.
(Collection of essays on national history.) Tokyo, Yoshikawa kobunkan, 1926. 518 p.

7588. Hagino, Yoshiyuki. 日本史講話 Nippon-shi kowa.
(Lectures on Japanese history.) Tokyo, 1926. 1018 p.

7589. Latourette, Kenneth Scott. The development of Japan.
New York, Macmillan, 1918. xi, 237 p. Second edition, 1926.
258 p.

7590. Clement, E. W. A short history of Japan. Chicago,
University of Chicago press, 1915. x, 190 p. Revised edition, Tokyo, Kyobunkwan, 1926. 212 p.

7591. Ch'ên, Kung-lu. 日本全史 Jih-pên ch'uan-shih. (General history of Japan.) Shanghai, Chung-hua book co., 1927.

7592. Mizutani, Jiro. 歴史地理日本三千年史蹟 Rekishi chiri Nippon sanzen-nen shiseki. (Places of interest in the history and geography of three thousand years of Japan.) Tokyo, Nippon shoin, 1929. 1460 p.

7593. Ota, Ryo. 日本史精義 Nippon-shi seigi. (Essentials of Japanese history.) Tokyo, Bunken shoin, 1929. 1110 p.

7594. Oikawa, Giemon. 日本皇室史話 Nippon koshitsu shiwa." (Historical anecdotes of the Japanese imperial household.) Tokyo, Idea shoin, 1929. 218 p.

7595. Yokoi, Haruno. 地理的日本歴史 Chiriteki Nippon rekishi. (Historical geography of Japan.) Tokyo, Monasu, 1929. 560 p.

7596. Miura, Shuko. 日本史研究 Nippon-shi no kenkyu. (Research in the history of Japan.) Tokyo, Iwanami shoten, 1930. 1504 p.

7597. Takahashi, Shunjo. 國民日本歴史 Kokumin Nippon rekishi. (National history of Japan, revised edition.) Tokyo, Fusanbo, 1930. 731 p.

7598. Kihira, Masami. 日本人進路 Nihonjin no shinro. (The course of the Japanese people.) Tokyo, Kaiten jihosha, 1930. 334 p.

7599. Tanaka, Keiji. 史料的日本歴史 Shiryoteki Nippon rekishi. (History of Japan based on historical documents.) Tokyo, Meguro shoten, 1930. 580 p.

7600. Sano, Gaku. 日本歴史研究 Nippon rekishi kenkyu. (Research in the history of Japan.) Tokyo, Kibokaku, 1930. 381 p.

7601. Ch'ên, Pin-ho (tr.). 日本歴史大綱 Jih-pên li-shih ta-kang. (An outline history of Japan.) Shanghai, Commercial press, 1931.

7602. Konrad, N. "Очерк японской истории с древнейших времен до 'революции Мейдзи'." (An outline of Japanese history from ancient times to the 'Meiji revolution'.) IAponia (Moscow, 1934), 229-271.

7603. Nikolaev, A. A. Очерки по истории японского народа. (Outlines of the history of the Japanese people.) Moscow, 1936. 389 p.

7604. 史蹟調査報告 Shiseki chosa hokoku. (Research reports on places of historical interest.) Tokyo, Department of home affairs, Toko shoin, 1932. 2 v. 80, 110 p. (2) 史蹟調査報告 Shiseki chosa hokoku. (Research reports on places of historical interest.) Tokyo, Department of education, Toko shoin, 1932. 2 v.

7605. Asahi, Yutan. 史論ト史實 Shiron to shijitsu. (Historical treatises and facts.) Tokyo, Shokasha, 1932. 350 p.

7606. Kaji, Ijin. 日本國民史 Nippon kokumin-shi. (History of the Japanese people.) Tokyo, Yorozuchosha, 1935. 1057 p.

(3) Political History

See 8225-8470.

7607. Rai, Jo. 日本政記 Nippon seiki (Political history of Japan.) 1876. 16 v.

7608. Kasama, Masuzo. 明治新撰日本政記 Nippon seiki. (Political history of Japan.) 1881. 12 v. (Re-comp. in Meiji era.)

7609. Inada, Shunosuke. 日本政治史要領 Nippon seiji-shi yoryo. (Essentials of Japanese political history.) Tokyo, Yuhikaku, 1912.

7610. Kadota, Fujisaburo. 日本政治史 Nippon seiji-shi. (Political history of Japan.) In Social science lectures, v. 14. Tokyo, Seibundo, 1932.

H. History by Periods

(1) Ancient History

See 1536-1610; 7464-7501.

7611. Mizutani, Kiyoshi. 古事記大講 Kojiki taiko. (Lectures on Kojiki, the ancient records of Japan.) Nagoya, Kojiki taiko kankokai, 1929. 7 v.

7612. Motoori, Norinaga. 古事記傳 Kojiki-den. (Com-

mentary on the records of ancient affairs.) Tokyo, Yoshikawa kobundo, 1935. 2 v.   1176, 1131 p.

7613. Ma-Touan-Lin. Mémoire sur l'histoire ancienne du Japon, d'après le "Ouen Hien Tong Kao de Ma-Touan-Lin" par le
Marquis M. J. L. d'Hervey de Saint-Denys. Paris, 1872. 48 p.

7614. Griffis, Rev. W. E. "Korean origin of Japan." Century, (New York), 25 (1882):224-229.

7615. Wang, Hsien-ch'ien. 日本源流考 Jih-pên yüan-liu
k'ao. (A study of the origin of Japan.) 1902. 22 v.

7616. Nachod, Oskar. Geschichte von Japan. Bd. I: Die ur-
zeit (bis 645 n. Chr.). Allgemeine staatengeschichte, herausgegeben von Karl Lamprecht, Abtlg. 2: Geschichte der
ausseuropäischen staaten, I. Werk. Gotha, Friedrich Andreas
Perthes, 1906. xxxi, 427 p.

7617. Milloué, L. de. "L'histoire primitive du Japon d'après le Kodziki. Valeur de ce livre au point de vue historique." ConférenceMusée Guimet, 26 (1908):59-80.

7618. Ota, Ryo. 日本古代史新研究 Nippon kodai-shi
shinkenkyu. (New research in the ancient history of Japan.)
Tokyo, Isobe koyodo, 1928.

7619. Origuchi, Nobuo. 古代研究 Kodai kenkyu. (Research
in the ancient times in Japan.) Tokyo, Ookayama shoten,
1930. 1266 p.

7620. Tsuda, Sokichi. 日本上代史研究 Nippon jodai-
shi kenkyu. (Research in the ancient history of Japan.)
Tokyo, Iwanami shoten, 1930. 698 p.

7621. Oyabe, Kinichi. 日本及日本國民之起原 Nippon
oyobi Nippon kokumin no kigen.(Origin of Japan and the Japanese people.) Tokyo, Koseikaku, 1931. 393 p.

7622. Hashimoto, Masukichi. 東洋史上ヨリ見タル日本上故研究
Toyo-shi jo yori mitaru Nippon joko-shi kenkyu. (Research
in ancient history from the point of view of Oriental history.) Tokyo, Ookayama shoten, 1932. 612 p.

7623. Reischauer, Robert Carl. Early Japanese history, cir-
ca 40 B. C. - A. D. 1167. Princeton university press; London, Millford, 1937. 2 parts.

7624. Kizaki, Aikichi. 大日本金石史 Dai Nippon kinsekishi. (Japanese epigraphy.) Osaka, Koshokai shuppanbu, 1921. 4 v.

(2) Medieval History

See 7524-7624.

7625. Omori, Kingoro. 日本中世史論考 Nippon chusei-shi ronko. (History of Japanese medieval period.) Tokyo, Shikai shobo, 1929. 537 p.

7626. Hara, Katsuro. 日本中世史之研究 Nippon chusei-shi no kenkyu. (The study of the history of the middle age of Japan.) Tokyo, Dobunkan, 1929. 1088 p.

7627. 吾妻鏡 Azuma kagami. (Historical record of the Kamakura period, 13-14 century.) In Zoku kokushi taikei, vols. 4-5. Tokyo, Keizai zasshisha, 1903. 2 v.

7628. Tschepe, A. "Die grosse niederlage der Mongolen im jahre 1281 bei Tsuschima, dem schauplatze des untergangs der russischen flotte." Ostasiatischer Lloyd, 19 (1905):1: 1165-1168.

7629. Pfizmaier, A. Die geschichte der Mongolen angriffe auf Japan, (from the "Mozokki"). (Sitzungsberichte d. philos.-hist. classe d. kaiserl. akademie, vol. 76, pp. 105 -.) Wien, 1874. 98 p.

7630. Yamada, Nakaba. Ghenkô, the Mongol invasion of Japan. London, Smith, Elder; New York, Dutton, 1916. xx, 276 p.

7631. Tanaka, Yoshinari. 南北朝時代史 Nanbokucho jidai-shi. (History of the period of the northern and southern dynasties.) 3d ed. 1924. 288 p.

7632. Ku, Ying-tai. 明倭寇始末 Ming Wo-kou shih-mo. (An account of the Japanese raids in the Ming dynasty.) 1831. (Hsüeh-hai-lei-pien ed.)

7633. Kokushi kenkyukai. 足利十五代史 Ashikaga jugodai-shi. (History of the fifteen generations of the Ashikaga.) Tokyo, Daidokan, 1912. 404 p.

7634. Tanaka, Yoshinari. 足利時代史 Ashikaga jidai-shi. (History of the Ashikaga period.) 3d ed. 1925. 358 p.

7635. Yanaga, C. "Source materials in Japanese history..." Journal of the American Oriental society, 59:1:38-55.

7636. Tanaka, Yoshinari. 織田時代史 Oda jidai-shi.
(History of the Oda period, 2d half of the 16th century.)
1924. 286 p.

7637. Tanaka, Yoshinari. 豊臣時代史 Toyotomi jidai-
shi. (History of the Toyotomi period, 1597.) 1925. 290 p.

7638. Yamaji, Aizan. 豊太閤 Ho-taiko. (Hideyoshi Toyotomi,
invader of Korea.) 1909. 2 v.

7639. Yamazaki, S. "Hideyoshi." The Japan magazine, 2 (1911-
1912):611-614, 689-691.

7640. Matsumoto, Aiju. 豊太閤征韓秘録 Ho-taiko
seikan hiroku. (Secret memoir of the Korean invasion by Hideyoshi Toyotomi, First series.) 1894.

7641. Sadler, A. L. "The naval campaign in the Korean war of
Hideyoshi (1592-1598)." The transactions of the Asiatic society of Japan, Second series, 14:177-209, June 1937.

7642. Dening, W. A new life of Toyotomi Hideyoshi. Tokyo,
1890. New edition, 1904. 405 p.

7643. Kinoshita, Shinko. 豊太閤征外論 Ho-taiko seigai hen. (History of Hideyoshi's foreign invasion.) Tokyo,
1893.

7644. Sadler, A. L. The maker of modern Japan; the life of
Ieyasu Tokugawa. London, Allen & Unwin, ltd., 1937. 429 p.
(2) Iyeyas[u]. The legacy of Iyeyas (deified as Gongensa-
ma); a posthumous manuscript in one hundred chapters, translated from three collated copies of the original with an introduction by J. F. Lowder. Tokyo, 1902. 7, 37 p.

7645. 徳川實紀 Tokugawa jikki. (Historical record of the
Tokugawa period.) In Zoku kokushi taikei, volumes 9-15. Tokyo, Keizai zasshisha, 1902-1904.

7646. Ihara, Gi. 徳川時代史 Tokugawa jidai-shi.
(History of the Tokugawa period.) Tokyo, Daidokan, 1912.

7647. 江戸時代史論 Edo; jidai shiron. (Histor-
ical survey of the Edo period.) Tokyo, Nippon rekishi chiri
gakkai, 1915. 644 p.

7648. Tochiuchi, Sojiro. 洋人日本探検年表 Yojin Nip-
pon tanken nenpyo. (Chronological table of explorations of
Japan by Westerners.) Tokyo, Iwanami, 1931. 182 p.

7649. Shu Ho.善 隣 國 寳 記 Zenrin kokuho ki. (Documents of diplomatic relations with the continental neighbours.) Tokyo, Bunkyudo, 1932. 200 p.

7650. Inobe, Shigeo. 幕 末 史 / 研 究 Bakumatsu-shi no kenkyu. (Research in history of the later Tokugawa period; the re-opening of Japan.) Tokyo, Yuzankaku, 1927. 700 p. (2)幕 末 史 概 說 Bakumatsu-shi gaisetsu. (Outline of the history of the later Tokugawa period.) Tokyo, Kigensha, 1928. 750 p. (Same author.)

7651. Nagata, Gutoku. 德 川 三 百 年 史 Tokugawa 300-nen shi. (History of 300 years of the Tokugawa period.) Tokyo, Shokabo, 1893.

7652. Shibusawa, Eiichi. 德 川 慶 喜 公 傳 Tokugawa Yoshinobuko. (Life of Yoshinobu (Keiki) Tokugawa, the last shogun.) Tokyo, Ryumonsha, 1918. 8 v.

7653. Bryan, J. Ingram. "The last of the shoguns." Open court. 28 (1914):129-139.

7654. "Count Katsu, the last statesman of the shogunate." The Far East, Tokyo, 2 (1897):508-515, 615-619.

7655. Tokutomi, Soho. 勝 海 舟 傳 Katsu Kaishu den. (Biography of Katsu Kaishu, one of the distinguished men in the last days of the Tokugawa shogunate.) Tokyo, Kaizosha, 1932.

7656. Hokirurien. 井 伊 大 老 Ii tairo. (Ii, regent of the shogunate government.) Tokyo, Taitokaku, 1923.

7657. Mazelière, Marquis de la. "Le Japon des Tokugawa." Bulletin société franco-japonaise, 5 (1906):42-52.

7658. Gubbins, J. H. "Some features of the Tokugawa administration." Transactions of the Asiatic society of Japan, 50 (1922):59-77.

7659. Adams, I. W. Shibusawa; or, the passing of old Japan. London, Putnam, 1906. 284 p.

7660. Dahlgren, E. W. "A contribution to the history of the discovery of Japan." Transactions and proceedings of the Japan society, 11:239-260. (22d session, 1912-1913.)

7661. Hyllander, T. Portugisernas upptäckande af Japan. (The discovery of Japan by the Portuguese.) Ett bidrag till den oraritisk-indagiska geografien. Lund, Hakan Ohlsson, 1911.

7662. **Fukuchi**, Genichiro. 幕 府 衰 亡 論 Bakufu suibo ron. (On the decline and fall of the Tokugawa shogunate.) Tokyo, Manyusha, 1892.

7663. **Asakawa, K.** The documents of the Iriki. Illustrative of the development of the feudal institution of Japan translated and edited with an introduction, bibliography, notes, and the Japanese text of the documents. Yale historical publications and edited texts vol. 10. New Haven, Yale university press; London, Oxford university press, 1929. 576 p.

7664. **Bertin, E.** "Japon avant la féodalité militaire. Anciennes familles et vieilles institutions." Bulletin, société franco-japonaise, 7 (1907):13-40.

7665. **Pletner, O.** "Крестьянские восстания в Японии в эпоху позднего феодализма." (Peasant uprisings in Japan during the epoch of the later feudalism.) Agrarnye problemy, 2 (1928):6:64-71.

7666. **Honjo, Eijiro.** "A short history of social problems in Japan before the restoration." Economic Review (Kyoto), 3 (1928):2:41-85.

(3) Modern History

See 273-342; 1536-1610; 1666-1921; 8044-8224.

(a) General Accounts

7667. **Yamada, Shunzo.** 近 世 事 情 Kinsei jijo. (History of modern Japan.) 1873. 5 v.

7668. 新 日 本 史 Shin Nippon-shi. (Modern history of Japan.) Tokyo, Manchohosha, 1926. 4 v.

7669. **Kokubu, Shigenori.** 大 日 本 現 代 史 Dai Nippon gendai-shi. (History of modern Japan.) 2d edition. Tokyo, Hakubunkan, 1909. 2 v.

7670. **Masuzawa, Chokichi.** 日 本 現 代 史 綱 Nippon gendai shiko. (Modern history of Japan.) Tokyo, 1910, 293 p.

7671. **Kobayashi, Ori.** 明 治 文 明 史 Meiji bunmei-shi. (A history of Japan, 1868-1912.) 2d edition. Tokyo, Bunyodo, 1916.

7672. **McLaren, W. W.** Political history of Japan during the Meiji era, 1867-1912. London, 1916. 379 p.

5565554554

7673. Okuma, Shigenobu. 開國五十年史 Kaikoku 50-nen
shi. (History of 50 years since the re-opening of Japan.)
Tokyo, Jitsugyo no sekaisha, 1917. 2 v.   (2) 日本開
國五十年史 Jih-pên k'ai-kuo wu-shih nien shih. (Fifty
years of Japan's history since the Restoration.) Shanghai,
Commercial press, 1929-1931.

7674. Nakamura, Koya. 日本近世史 Nippon kinsei-shi.
(History of Japan in modern times.) Tokyo, Ikuei shoin,
1917-1919. 3 v.

7675. Takasu, Baikei. 明治大正五十三年史論 Meiji
Taisho 53-nen shiron. (Historical treatise dealing with the
events during the 53 years of the Meiji and Taisho eras.)
Tokyo, Nippon hyoronsha, 1920. 621 p.

7676. Miura, Shuko. 現代史觀 Gendaishikan. (Historical
essays on modern Japan.) Tokyo, Kokon shoin, 1922. 506 p.

7677. 明治大正史 Meiji Taisho shi. (History of the
Meiji and Taisho eras, 1868-1926.) Tokyo, Jitsugyo no sekaisha, n.d. 15 v.

7678. Hayashida, Kametaro. 明治大正政界側面史
Meiji Taisho seikai sokumen-shi. (A side-view of the poli-
tical world of the Meiji and the Taisho eras.) Tokyo, Dai
Nippon yubenkai, 1926. 630 p.

7679. Japans aussen- und innenpolitik seit 1868. Ein über-
blick. Berlin, Eisenschmidt, 1927.

7680. 明治大正國勢總覽 Meiji Taisho kokusei
soran. (General view of the national condition of Japan
during the Meiji and Taisho eras, 1868-1926.) Tokyo, Toyo
keizai shinposha, 1927. 764 p

7681. Kojima, Kenichiro. 現代日本政治史 Gendai Nippon seiji-shi. (Political history of present-day Japan.)
Tokyo, Teikoku kyoiku kenkyu-kai, 1929. 3 v.

7682. 天下史變八十余年近世歷史 Tenka hensen
Hachijuyo-nen kinsei rekishi. (History of modern Japan with
reference to the changes in the political affairs in the
last eighty years.) Tokyo, Tenshodo, 1930. 68 p.

7683. Kiyohara, Sadao. 幕末明治時代史 Bakumatsu
Meiji jidai-shi. (History of the close of the Tokugawa
régime and the Meiji period, 1868-1912.) Tokyo, Juken koza
kankokai. 1930. 302 p.

7684. Ch'ên, To. 日本現代史 Jih-pên hsien-tai shih.
(Modern history of Japan.) Shanghai, Commercial press,
1929-1931. 2 v.

7685. 明治大正史 Meiji Taisho shi. (History of Japan
during the Meiji and Taisho eras, 1868-1926.) Tokyo, Asahi
shinbunsha, 1930-1931. 6 v.

7686. Nitobe, Inazo and others. Western influences in
modern Japan. Chicago, University of Chicago press, 1931.
544 p.

7687. Ku, Tung-tzu (tr.) 日本維新三十年史 Jih-pên
wei-hsin san-shih-nien shih. (A history of Japan thirty
years after restoration.) Shanghai, Hua-tung shu-chü, 1932?

7688. Takeda, Okichi. 國民の日本史：東京 時代
Kokumin no Nippon-shi: Tokyo jidai. (Popular Japanese history: Tokyo period.) Tokyo, Waseda university press, 1932.

7689. 明治史要 Meiji shiyo. (Historical outline of the
Meiji era.) Tokyo teikoku daigaku shiryo hensansho, Hinkodo,
1933. 2 v.

7690. Omori, Kingoro. 現代日本史 Gendai Nippon-shi.
(History of modern Japan.) Tokyo, Fuzanbo, 1935. 608 p.

7691. 明治大正大阪市史(概説篇) Meiji Taisho Osakashi-
shi.(gaisetsu-hen). (History of the city of Osaka during the
Meiji and Taisho eras, introduction.) Tokyo, Nippon hyoronsha, 1935. 998 p.

7692. Misumi, Hiroshi. 明治大正昭和日本勃興秘史
Meiji Taisho Showa Nippon bokko hishi. (A secret history
of the rise of Japan during the Meiji, Taisho, and Showa
eras.) Tokyo, Yashima shobo, 1936. 1153 p.

7693. Omori, Kingoro. 新國史論叢 Shin kokushi
ronso. (A collection of recent dissertations on national
history.) Tokyo, Yoshikawa kobunkan, 1936. 516 p.

(b) Opening of Japan

See 496-517; 4362-4620.

7694. Yamaguchi, Ken. 近世史略 Kinsei shi-
ryaku. (A briefer modern history of Japan.) Tokyo,
1873. 2 v. (2) The same. Translated from the

Japanese into English by E. M. Satow. Yokohama, 1873. 148 p.
2d edition, 1880. 150 p. Revised edition by Shuziro Watanabe. Tokyo, Naigwai shuppan kyokwai, 1906. 178 p. Also
abridged German edition. Mitteilungen des seminars für
orientalische sprachen in Berlin, first division, v. 1, pp.
140-186, and v. 2, pp. 1-54. 1898-1899.

7695. Satow, Sir Ernest Mason. Japan 1853-1864 or Genji
Yume Monogatari. Tokyo, 1905. 242 p.

7696. Shimada, Saburo and Sato, Kenri. 開 國 始 末 Kaikoku
shimatsu. (Circumstances surrounding the opening of the
country.) Tokyo, Dai Nippon tosho kabushiki kaisha, 1908.

7697. Okuma, Shigenobu. 開 國 大 勢 史 Kaikoku taisei-
shi. (General history of the opening of Japan.) Tokyo, Waseda university press, 1923.

7698. Huyssen de Kattendyke, W. J. C. Le Japon en 1857. Ex-
traits du journal, traduits du hollandais par Mme. Thorens
Dollfus. 1924.

7699. Katsu, Kaishu. 開 國 起 原 Kaikoku kigen. (How
Japan was opened up.) Tokyo, Kaizosha,   1929. 2 v.

7700. Otsuka, Takematsu, ed. 川 路 聖 謨 文 書 Kawaji
Toshiakira monjo. (Documents of Kawaji Toshiakira: Docu-
ments concerning commercial treaties with Russia.) Tokyo,
Nippon shiseki kyokai, 1932. V. 1.

7701. Nakayama, Tokugoro. 建 國 ト 其 由 来 Kenkoku to sono
yurai. (Founding of Japan and its history.) Osaka, Bungando,
1932. 527 p.

7702. Osawa, Yonezo. 囘 天 偉 業 幕 末 ノ 全 貌 Kaiten
igyo bakumatsu no zenbo. (Complete view of the great revolutionary undertakings of the later days of the Tokugawa
shogunate.) Tokyo, Toyo bunka kyokai, 1935. 400 p.

7703. Inobe, Shigeo. 維 新 前 史 ノ 研 究 Ishin zenshi no
kenkyu. (A research in the history of the period prior to
the Meiji restoration.) Tokyo, Chubunkan, 1936. 652 p.

(c) The Imperial Restoration

See 7542-7610.

7704. Kitagawa, Shunji. 明 治 新 史 Meiji shinshi. (New
history of the Meiji imperial restoration.) 1876. 2 v.

7705. 明治史要 Meiji shiyo. (Essential historical events of the Meiji period.) Tokyo, Bureau of history, Imperial government, 1876. 4 v.

7706. Sasuhara, Yasuzo. 明治政史 Meiji seishi. (Political history of the early Meiji era.) 1892. 12 v.

7707. Kitahara, Masanaga. 維新七年史 Ishin 7-nen shi. (History of the seven years of the Meiji restoration period.) Tokyo, Keiseisha, 1893.

7708. See 7535.

7709. Hayashi, G. "The fall of the Tokugawa government." Transactions and proceedings, Japan society, London, 4 (1898):2:63-79.

7710. Shigeno, Yasuhira. 大日本維新史 Dai Nippon ishin-shi. (History of the imperial restoration of Japan.) 1899 2 v.

7711. The Japanese revolution of 1867. Quarterly review, London, vol. 200 (No. 399), pp. 268-308. 1904.

7712. Kimura, Takataro. 大日本建國史 Dai Nippon kenkoku-shi. (History of the founding of the Japanese empire.) Tokyo, Hakubunkan, 1909. 398 p.

7713. Mazelière, Marquis de la. "Les idées qui ont inspiré la revolution Japonaise." Bulletin, Société franco-japonaise, 14 (1909):85-107.

7714. Yoshida, Togo. 維新史八講 Ishin-shi hakko. (Eight lectures on the history of the imperial restoration of Japan.) 1910.

7715. Gubbins, J. H. The progress of Japan 1853-1871. London, H. Frowde; Oxford, Clarendon press, 1911. 323 p.

7716. Peace handbook, v. 12, no. 75. Japan: recent history. London, Historical section of the Foreign office of Great Britain, 1920.

7717. Inobe, Shigeo. 明治維新史 Meiji ishin-shi. (History of the Meiji restoration.) Tokyo, Rogosu shoin, 1927.

7718. Shigakukai. 明治維新史研究 Meiji ishin-shi kenkyu. (The study of the history of the imperial restoration of Meiji, 1867-1912.) Fuzanbo, 952 p.

7719. Tsumaki, Chuta. 維 新 後 大 年 表 Ishin-go dai nenpyo. (A chronology since the Meiji restoration.) Tokyo, Yuhodo, 1928. 731 p.

7720. 復 古 記 Fukko-ki. (The imperial restoration in Japan.) Tokyo, Tokyo imperial university, Naigai shoseki kaisha, 1929. 15 v.

7721. Tokutomi, Iichiro. 維 新 回 天 史 , 一 面 Ishin kaiten-shi no ichimen. (A phase of the history of the great restoration in Japan.) Tokyo, Minyusha, 1929. 457 p.

7722. 明 治 維 新 史 , 研 究 Meiji ishin-shi no ken-kyu. (A study of the history of the Meiji restoration.) Tokyo, Tokyo imperial university, Historical association, Fuzanbo, 1932.

7723. Inobe, Shigeo. 維 新 史 考 Ishin-shi ko. (A study of the history of the Meiji restoration.) Tokyo, Chubunkan shoten, 1934. 316 p.

7724. Ooi, Ittetsu. 建 國 由 來 と 皇 道 政 治 Kenko-ku yurai to kodo seiji. (History of the founding of Japan and Japanese imperial rule.) Tokyo, Nippon shakai mondai kenkyusho, 1936. 166 p.

7725. Muto, Teiichi. 日 本 改 新 , 書 Nippon kaishin no sho. (Writings on the renovation of Japan.) Tokyo, Modan Nipponsha, 1937.

7726. Kumada, Ijo. 日 本 建 國 講 話 Nippon kenkoku kowa. (Lectures on the founding of Japan.) Tokyo, Kyobunsha, 1937. 320 p.

(d) Japan in the World War

See 3198-4252.

7727. Yoshimatsu, K. Japans haltung zum europäischen kriege. Der weltkrieg 1914-1915. St. Gallen, W. Beck & co., 1915. 32 p.

7728. Crewdson, W. Japan our ally. Preface by Sir Claude Macdonald. London, Macmillan, 1915. 36 p.

7729. "Japanische stimmen zum kriege Japans mit Deutschland."

Zeitschrift für missionskunde und religionswissenschaft,
Berlin, 30 (1915):84-94. (By Witte.)

7730. Akiyama, A. A Japanese view of the war. London, Unwin,
1917. 15 p.

7731. Kliuchnikov, IU. V. Япония и державы согласия. (Japan
and the Allied powers.) Moscow, D. IA. Makovskii, 1917.
24 p.

7732. Buetz, G. "Die handelsflotte Japans im weltkriege."
Asien, Berlin, 15 (1917-1918):183-193.

7733. Gérard, A. Nos alliés d'Extrême-Orient. Bibliothèque
politique et económique. Paris, Payot et Cie, 1918. xxi,
219 p.   (2) "Nos alliés d'Extrême-Orient. Chine et Japon
(1917-1919)." Revue des deux mondes, 51 (1919):422-443:2.

7734. Dautremer, J. Chez nos alliés Japonais. Esquisse
historique - Passé - Évolution - Présent. Paris, Garnier
Frères, 1918. vi, 296 p.

7735. Diósy, Arthur. "Japan's part in the war, 1914-1917."
Transactions and proceedings of the Japan society, London,
16 (1918):2-14.

7736. Flach, J. La participation militaire du Japon et ses
intérêts vitaux. Séances et travaux de l'Academie des
sciences morales et politiques (Institut de France). Compte
rendu. Mai 1918.

7737. Nakashima, G. "The Japanese navy in the Great War."
Transactions and proceedings of the Japan society, London,
17 (1920):32-39.

7738. Kojima, Shotaro. "The influence of the great war upon
Japanese national economy." Weltwirtschaftliches archiv,
17 (1921-1922):525-548.

7739. Tamura, Kosaku. 日本大戦参加三大事由
Nippon no taisen sanka sandai jiyu. (The three great reasons
why Japan entered the World War.) Gaiko jiho, 77:2:99-132.
January, 1935.

(e) Recent History, 1918-1937

See 283-342; 450-780; 1717-1921; 8053-8224.

7740. Isawa, Hiroaki. 昭和人名辭典 Showa jinmei jiten. (Biographical dictionary of the Showa era.) Osaka,
Kojinsha, 1934. 1500 p.

7741. Tokutomi, Iichiro. 大正ノ青年ト帝國ノ前途
Taisho no seinen to teikoku no zento. (The youth of the
Taisho era, and the future of the empire.) Tokyo, Minyusha,
1923.

7742. Sato, Tetsutaro. 新日本ヘノ道 Shin Nippon e no
michi. (The road to new Japan.) Tokyo, Dai Nippon yubenkai,
1926.

7743. Young, Arthur Morgan. Japan under Taisho Tenno, 1912-
1926. London, 1928.   (2) U. S. edition: Japan in recent
times, 1912-1926. New York, 1929.

7744. Tsuboi, Kumazo. 最近政治外交史 Saikin sei-
ji gaiko-shi. (Recent history of politics and diplomacy.)
Tokyo, Fuzanbo, 1928-1929. 4 v.

7745. 昭和維新ノ要諦 Showa ishin no yotei.
(The essence of the reform of the Showa era, 1926 - .)
Tokyo, Kokka Kyoikusha, 1930.

7746. Kikuchi, Yasaburo. 昭和維新ト國民總動員
Showa ishin to kokumin sodoin. (The reform of the Showa era,
1926 - , and the mobilization of the entire nation.) Tokyo,
Shin Nippon renmei shuppanbu, 1930. 45 p.

7747. Suzuki, Umekichiro. 昭和維新ノ大國是
Showa ishin no dai kokuze. (The great policy of Japan in the
reform of the Showa era, 1926 - .) Tokyo, Teikoku bunka
kyokai, 1930. 50 p.

7748. 昭和三年史 Showa sannen-shi. (History of the
third year of the Showa era [1928] of Japan.) Tokyo, Nenshi
kankokai, 1929. 740 p.   (2) 昭和四年史 Showa yonen-
shi. (History of the fourth year of the Showa era [1929] of
Japan.) Tokyo, 1930. 683 p.   (3) 昭和五年史 Showa
gonen-shi. (History of the fifth year of the Showa era
[1930] of Japan.) Tokyo, 1931. 626 p.   (4) 昭和六年
史   Showa rokunen-shi. (History of the sixth year of
the Showa era [1931] of Japan.) Tokyo, 1933. 688 p.

7749. Li, Tsung-wu. 最近的日本 Tsui-chin ti Jih-
pên. (Japan in recent times.) Shanghai. Kai-ming shu-chü,
1932? (2) Young, A. Morgan. Imperial Japan, 1926-1938.
New York, Morrow, 1938. 328 p.

7750. Sassa, Hiroo. 政局危機、動向 Seikyoku kiki no doko. (The trend of the present political situation leading to its crisis.) Tokyo, Chigura shobo, 1933. 320 p.

7751. Kitamura, Harusaburo. 隠レタル事實：續日本裏面史 Kakuretaru jijitsu: zoku Nippon rimen-shi. (Unknown facts: the inside history of Japan, Series 2.) Tokyo, Yukosha, 1933. 676 p.

7752. Araki, Sadao. 昭和日本、使命 Showa Nippon no shimei. (Japan's mission in the Showa era.) Tokyo, Shakai kyoku kyokai, 1933. 45 p.

7753. Suzuki, Tooru. 日本危シ Nippon ayaushi. (Japan in crisis.) Tokyo, Senshinsha, 1933. 340 p.

7754. Konrad, N. and Zhukov, E. "Новейшая история Японии." (Recent history of Japan.) IAponiia (Moscow, 1934), 295-320.

7755. Kokumin shinbunsha seiji-bu. 非常時日本ニ躍ル人々 Hijoji Nippon ni odoru hitobito. (Men who are active in Japan's crisis.) Tokyo, Gunji kyoikusha, 1934. 207 p.

7756. Kokufukai. 資料近代日本史 Shiryo kindai Nippon-shi. (Data on the recent history of Japan.) Tokyo, Kokufukai, 1934.

7757. Kataoka, Tadanao. 大正昭和政治史、一断面 Taisho, Showa seiji-shi no ichidanmen. (A cross-section of the political history of the Taisho and Showa eras.) Kyoto, Nishikawa hyakushii bunko, 1935. 830 p.

7758. Takeuchi, Tatsuji. War and diplomacy in the Japanese empire. Garden City, Dobleday, Doran and co., 1935. xix, 505 p.

(f) Makers of New Japan

See 7667-7758.

7759. Yoshida, Shoin. 吉田松陰全集 Yoshida Shoin zenshu. (Complete works of Shoin Yoshida.) Tokyo, Iwanami shoten, 1934-1936. 10 v.

7760. Yoshida, Shoin. 幽囚錄 Yushuroku. (Record of my prison life.) 1891.

7761. Noguchi, Katsuichi. 吉田松陰傳 Yoshida Shoin den. (Biography of Shoin Yoshida.) 1891. 5 v.

7762. Tokutomi, Iichiro. 吉田松陰 Yoshida Shoin. (Life of Shoin Yoshida.) 39th edition. Tokyo, Minyusha, 1929. 493 p.

7763. Coleman, Horace E. "The life of Shoin Yoshida, being a translation from the Japanese life of Shoin Yoshida by Mr. Iichiro Tokutomi." Transactions of the Asiatic society of Japan, 45 (1917):1:119-188.

7764. Hirose, Yotaka. 續吉田松陰の研究 Zoku Yoshida Shoin no kenkyu. (On the life of Shoin Yoshida, Series 2.) Tokyo, Musashino shoin, 1933. 357 p.

7765. Miyamoto, Chu. 佐久間象山 Sakuma Shozan. (Life of Shozan Sakuma.) Tokyo, Iwanami shoten, 1932. 705 p.

7766. Katsuda, Sonya. 大久保利通傳 Okubo Toshimichi den. (The life of Okubo Toshimichi.) Tokyo, Dobunkan, 1910. 3 vols.

7767. Kawasaki, Saburo. 大久保甲東 Okubo Koto. (Biography of Koto Okubo, one of the three founders of New Japan.) 1898.

7768. Fukushima, Seiko. 征韓論餘聞：赤坂喰違 / 事變 Seikan-ron yobun: Akasaka kuichigai no jihen. (How and why Okubo Toshimichi was assassinated.) Tokyo, Mayeda Makita, 1929. 232 p.

7769. Courant, M. Tosimitsi Okubo, homme d'état japonais, 1830-1878, Paris, 1904. 203 p.

7770. Kido-ko denki hensan-sho. 松菊木戸公傳 Shokiku Kido-ko den. (Biography of Kido, one of the three founders of New Japan.) Tokyo, Meiji Shoin, 1932. 2300 p.

7771. Ito, Chiyu. 木戸孝允 Kido Koin (Life of Koin Kido.) Tokyo, Heibonsha, 1936. 680 p.

7772. Tsumaki, Chuta. 史實參照：木戸松菊公逸話 Shijitsu sansho Kido Shokiku-ko itsuwa. (An anecdote of Shokiku (Koin) Kido, a national statesman, based on historical facts.) Tokyo, Yuhodo, 1936. 568 p.

7773. Saika, Hakuai. 大西郷全傳 Dai Saigo zenden. (Complete biography of Takamori (Nanshu) Saigo.) Tokyo, Dai Saigo zenden kankokai, 1937. 6 v.

7774. Saigo, Takamori. 大西郷全集 Dai Saigo zenshu.

(Complete works of great Saigo, founder of New Japan.)
Tokyo, Dai Saigo zenshu kankokai, 1926-1927. 3 v.

7775. Iwakura ko kyuseki hozonkai. 岩倉公舊記
Iwakura ko jikki. (Authentic accounts of Prince Tomomi
Iwakura.) Tokyo, Kogogu-shoku, 1927. 3 v. (2) Tokutomi,
Iichiro. 岩倉具視公 Iwakura Tomomi ko. (Life of
Prince Tomomi Iwakura.) Tokyo, Minyusha, 1933. 294 p.

7776. Satoh, Henry. Lord Hotta, the pioneer diplomat of Japan. 2d edition. Tokyo, Hakubunkan, 1908.

7777. Morris, J. The makers of Japan. A series of biographies of H. I. M. the present Emperor and twenty-one statesmen. London, 1906. 350 p. and 24 plates.

7778. Kano, Nobuo. 明治大帝 Meiji taitei. (The great
Emperor Meiji, founder of New Japan.) Tokyo, Kinransha,
1929. 247 p.

7779. Pontus, R. Le Meidji. Le règne de S. M. Mutsu Hito
et le Japon moderne. Bruxelles, Société d'Études belgo-
japonaises, 1913.

7780. Arcambeau, Edme. "Mutsuhito. L'Empereur du Meiji (3
novembre 1852 - 30 juillet 1912)." Bulletin de la Société
franco-japonaise de Paris, 26-27:7-59, June-September, 1912.

7781. Bälz, E. "Der japanische kaiser Mutsuhito oder Meiji-
tenno, seine stellung im staat und volk." Geist des Ostens,
1 (1913-1914):265-268, 329-336, 397-406.

7782. Die wahrheit über Mutsuhito, den kaiser von Japan.
Von einem in Japan lebenden Deutschen. Die Zeitschrift, 2
(1912), Heft 25.

7783. Joly, Henri L. "Meijii Tenno 1852-1912." Transactions
and proceedings of the Japan society, London, 10 (1912-1913):
99-120.

7784. Griffis, W. E. "Mutsuhito the great." North American
review, 196 (1912):328-338.

7785. Mazelière, Marquis de la. "L'empereur Mutsuhito."
Revue des deux mondes, 393-426, September, 1912.

7786. Hiratsuka, Atsushi. 伊藤博文秘錄 Ito Hiro-
bumi hiroku. (Secret memoirs of Hirobumi Ito. Series one.)

Tokyo, Shunjusha, 1931. 524 p.   (2) 續 伊 藤 博 文 祕 錄
Zoku Ito Hirobumi hiroku (Secret memoirs of Hirobumi Ito,
series two.) Tokyo, Shunjusha, 1931. 444 p.

7787. Naito, Morisuke. 伊 藤 公 演 說 全 集 Ito ko enzetsu zenshu. (Complete collection of speeches made by Prince
Hirobumi Ito.) Tokyo, Hakubunkan, 1910. 808 p.

7788. Kokumin shinbunsha editorial staff. 伊 藤 博 文 公
Ito Hirobumi-ko. (Study of the life of Hirobumi Ito.) Tokyo,
Keiseisha, 1931. 125 p.

7789. Akiyama, Goan. 偉 人 研 究 第 七 十 六 篇 : 伊 藤 博 文 言 行 錄
Ijin kenkyu dai 76-hen: Ito Hirobumi genko-roku. (Researches
in great men, no. 76: records of the words and actions of
Hirobumi Ito.) Tokyo, Daikyodo, 1935. 176 p.

7790. Komatsu, Midori. 春 畝 公 卜 含 雪 公 Shunpo ko to
Shasetsu ko. (Prince Shunpo [Hirobumi Ito] and Prince Shasetsu [Aritomo Yamagata].) Tokyo, Gakushi shoin, 1935.
414 p.

7791. Nakamura, Kaju. Prince Ito; the man and statesman; a
brief history of his life. New York, Anraka publishing co.,
1910. xvi, 144 p.

7792. Riess, Ludwig. "Fürst Ito." Meister der politik; 2,
617-657. Stuttgart/Berlin, Deutsche verlagsanstalt, 1922.

7793. Yoshizawa, K. "Prince Ito." Transactions and proceedings of the Japan society, London, 9 (1911):206-228.

7794. Lawton, L. "Prince Ito: his life work and his influence upon the national policy of Japan." Asiatic quarterly
review, 29 (1910):308-337.

7795. Siebold, A. v. "Persönliche erinnerungen an den
Fürsten Ito Hirobumi." Deutsche revue, 35 Jahrgang, May,
1910, 214-231.

7796. Kawakami, K. K. "Prince Ito's confidential papers."
Foreign affairs, 11:3:490-501, April, 1933.

7797. Harada, Toyojiro. 伊 藤 公 卜 韓 國 Ito-ko to Kankoku. (Prince Ito and Korea.) Keijo, 1909. 119 p.

7798. Norman, V. P. Ито; его жизнь, деятельность и влияние
на национальную политику Японии. (Ito: his life, activities

and influence upon the national politics of Japan.) Vestnik
Azii, 5 (1910):131-137.

7799. Bryan, Ingram J. "The passing of a great Japanese
[Count Katsura]." The Japan magazine, 4 (1913-1914):429-423.

7800. Tokutomi, Iichiro. 政治家トシテノ桂公 Seijika
to shite no Katsura-ko. (Prince Taro Katsura as a statesman)
Tokyo, 1927. 265 p.

7801. Tokutomi, Iichiro. 公爵山縣有朋傳 Koshaku
Yamagata Aritomo den. (Life of Prince Aritomo Yamagata.)
Tokyo, Yamagata Aritomo ko kinen jigyokai, 1934. 3 v.

7802. Yamada, Y. "Prince Yamagata." The Japan magazine, 6
(1915-1916):207-211.

7803. Yamazaki, F. "Prince Yamagata." The Japan magazine,
12 (1921-1922):473-483.

7804. Ito, Masanori. 加藤高明 Kato Komei. (Life of
[Premier] Komei Kato.) Tokyo, Hobunkan, 1929. 2 vols. 816,
786 p.

7805. Ito, Jintaro. 元帥東郷平八郎 Gensui Togo
Heihachiro. (Admiral Heihachiro Togo.) Tokyo, Ikubunsha,
1935. 534 p. See also 4042-4044.

7806. Ogasawara, Chosei. 晚年ノ東郷元帥 Bannen no
Togo gensui. (Latter days of Admiral Togo.) Tokyo, Kaizosha,
1935. 313 p.

7807. Sakurai, Shuji. 東郷元帥と乃木將軍 Togo
gensui to Nogi shogun. (Admiral Togo and General Nogi.)
Tokyo, Togo gensui to Nogi shogun hakkosho, 1935. 381 p.

7808. Abe, Shinzo. 東郷元帥直話集 Togo gensui
jikiwa shu. (A collection of the personal conversations of
Admiral Togo.) Tokyo, Chuo koronsha, 1936. 395 p.

7809. Kikuchi, Shiyu. 親トシテノ乃木將軍 Oya to shite no
Nogi shogun. (Life of General Nogi as a parent.) Tokyo, Daiichi shuppansha, 1937. 412 p.

7810. Ono, Sanenobu. 元帥公爵大山巖 Gensui koshaku
Oyama Iwao. (Life of Marshal, Prince Iwao Oyama.) Tokyo,
Oyama gensui den kankokai, 1936. 931 p.

7811. Ono, Sanenobu. 元帥公爵大山巖年譜 Gensui

koshaku Oyama Iwao nenpu. (A chronology of the life of Marshal, Prince Iwao Oyama.) Tokyo, Oyama gensui den kankokai,
1936. 630 p.

7812. Koechlin, Raymond. "T. Hayashi." Bulletin,Société
franco-japonaise, 5 (1906):7-16.

7813. Watanabe, Ikujiro. 文書ヨリ見タル大隈重信侯
Bunsho yori mitaru Okuma Shigenobu ko. (Life of Marquis
Shigenobu Okuma culled from his correspondence and other
documents.) Tokyo, Waseda university, 1933. 288 p.

7814. Watanabe, Ikujiro. 近世之化史上ニ於ケル大隈
重信公 Kinsei bunkashi-jo ni okeru Okuma Shigenobu ko. (The
place of Count Shigenobu Okuma in the history of modern civilization.) Tokyo, Bunmei kyokai, 1929.

7815. Yamamoto, M. "The late Marquis Shigenobu Okuma." The
Japan magazine, 12 (1921-1922):385-399, 453-457.

7816. Ishii, Viscount Kikujiro. 外交餘錄 Gaiko yoroku.
(Memoirs of a diplomat.) Tokyo, Iwanami, 1930. 548 p.

7817. Morris, Roland S. "The memoirs of Viscount Ishii."
Foreign affairs, 10:4:677-688, July, 1932.

7818. Kusakabe, Taro. 新日本ノ先駆者 Shin Nippon no
senkusha. (Leaders of New Japan.) Fukui, Fukui hyoronsha,
1931. 158 p.

7819. See 7748.

7820. Kawai, Tsuguo. 田中義一傳 Tanaka Giichi den.
(Life of [Premier] Giichi Tanaka.) Tokyo, Tanaka Giichi den
hensansho, 1929. 967 p.

7821. Harada, Shigetsu. 田中大將ノ少年時代 Tanaka
taisho no shonen jidai. (Boyhood days of General Tanaka,
Premier.) Tokyo, Kokumin tosho kaisha, 1928. 263 p.

7822. Sakatani, Yoshiro. 世外井上公傳 Seigai Inouye ko
den. (Life of Kaoru Seigai Inouye, a great national statesman.) Tokyo, Naigai shoseki kabushiki-gaisha, 1934. 5 v.

7823. Hirooka, Uichiro. 齋藤實傳 Saito Makoto den.
(Life of [Premier] Makoto Saito.) Tokyo, Jitsuden kankokai,
1934. 998 p.

7824. Harada, Takaichi. 巨星荒木陸相ノ話ル Kyosei

Araki rikusho o kataru. (About the great national leader,
the War minister, General Araki.) Tokyo, Sanyusha, 1934.
122 p.

7825. Kitada, Teiko. 父 懷口 雄 幸 Chichi, Hamaguchi
Yuko. (Life of my father, Yuko Hamaguchi.) Tokyo, Hibiya
shobo, 1932. 311 p.

7826. Kawahara, Yagoro. 犬 養 毅 傳 Inukai Tsuyoshi den.
(Life of [Premier] Tsuyoshi Inukai.) Tokyo, Inukai Tsuyoshi
den kankokai, 1933. 393 p.

7827. Uzaki. Rojo. 犬 養 毅 傳 Inukai Tsuyoshi den.
(A biography of Tsuyoshi Inukai.) Tokyo, Seibundo, 1932.
508 p.

7828. Katayama, Kageo. 木 堂 犬 養 毅 Bokudo Inukai Tsuyoshi. (Life of Bokudo Tsuyoshi Inukai.) San Francisco,
1933. 721 p.

7829. Inukai Bokudo den kankokai. 犬 養 木 堂 傳 Inukai
Bokudo den. (Life of [Premier] Bokudo [Tsuyoshi] Inukai.)
Tokyo, Daikyosha, 1933. 205 p.

7830. Yanagida, Kunio. 平 民 宰 相 犬 養 毅 Heimin sai-
sho Inukai Tsuyoshi. (Commoner Premier Tsuyoshi Inukai.)
Tokyo, Nakamura shoten, 1933. 160 p.

7831. Ozawa, Yonezo. 幕 末 明 治 大 正 回 顧 八 十 年 史 Bakumatsu
Meiji Taisho kaiko hachiju-nen shi. (History from my recollections covering the 80 years period including the latter
days of the Tokugawa shogunate, the Meiji and the Taisho
era.) Tokyo, Toyo bunka kyokai, 1934-1935. 14 v.

7832. Masaki, Naohiko. 回 顧 七 十 年 Kaiko 70-nen. (My
recollection of the last seventy years.) Tokyo, Gakko bijutsu kyokai shuppanbu, 1937. 430 p.

7833. Ishikawa, Mikiaki. 福 澤 諭 吉 Fukuzawa Yukichi.
(Life of Yukichi Fukuzawa.) Tokyo, Iwanami shoten, 1936.

7834. Hayashi, Gonsuke. 我 が 七 十 年 ヲ 語 ル Waga 70-nen
o kataru. (On the 70 years of my life.) Tokyo, Daiichi sho
bo, 1936. 433 p.

7835. Nitta, Munemori. 大 日 本 人 物 史 Dai Nippon
jinbutsu-shi. (Lives of the outstanding men of Japan.) Tokyo, Kokusai rengo tsushinsha, 1933. 867 p.

7836. Baba, Tsunego. 立チイガル 政治家 Tachiagaru
seijika. (Rising statesmen.) Tokyo, Chuo koronsha, 1937.
470 p.

X. GENERAL ACCOUNTS OF JAPAN

See 343-449.

7837. Veniukov, M. Очерки Японии. (Sketches of Japan.)
St. Petersburg, 1869. 441 p.

7838. Giumber, E. Живописная Япония. (Picturesque Japan.)
St. Petersburg, 1870. 414 p.

7839. Rosny, L. de. La civilisation japonaise. Conférences
faites à l'École speciale des langues orientales. Paris,
1883. 400 p.

7840. Fu, Yün-lung. 游歷日本圖經 Yu-li Jih-pên t'u-
ching. (A travel guide of Japan.) Tokyo, 1889.

7841. Chamberlain, Basil Hall. Things Japanese: being notes
on various subjects. London, K. Paul, 1890, 408 p.

7842. Norman, H. The real Japan. Study of contemporary
Japanese manners, morals, administration, and politics.
New York, 1892. 364 p. New edition, London, 1893.

7843. Hearn, Lacfadio. Glimpses of unfamiliar Japan. Boston,
1894. 2 v.   (2) Japan. An attempt at interpretation.
London, 1904. New York, 1904. 541 p.   (3) Glimpses of unfamiliar Japan. Second series. Leipzig, Tauchnitz, 1910.
320 p..   (4) Out of the East. Leipzig, Tauchnitz, 1910.
286 p.

7844. Morris, J. Advance Japan. A nation thoroughly in ear-
nest. London, 1895. xix, 443 p. with about 80 illustrations
by R. Isayama, military artist of Buzen Clan.

7845. Siebold, Philipp Franz von. Nippon. Archiv zur beschreibung von Japan und dessen neben- und schutzländern,
Jezo mit den südlichen Kurilen, Sachalin, Korea und den
Liu-Kiu inselen. Second edition. Würzburg, 1896-1897. ·
2 v.   New completely revised edition. Berlin, Japaninsti-
tut, 1930. 3. v.   (2) Siebold, H. von. Philipp Franz
von Siebold, der erforscher Japans, sein leben und wirken.
Nach der japanischen denkschrift des Dr. S. Kure dargestellt.
Leipzig, L. Woerl, 1909.

7846. Brinkley, Frank. Japan, its history, arts and literature. Boston and Tokyo, J. B. Millet & co., 1901-1902. 8
vols.   (2) Japan; described and illustrated by the Japanese authorities and scholars, ed. by Captain F. Brinkley.
Boston and Tokyo, J. B. Millet & co., 1904. 5 v.

7847. Clement, E. W. A handbook of modern Japan. Chicago,
1903. 395 p.   (2) Golovin, D."Япония прежде и теперь."
(Japan formerly and now.) Russkaia mysl', 7:35-65, July,
1903.

7848. Dumolard, H. Le Japon politique, économique et social
Paris, 1903. 342 p.   Second edition:1904.

7849. 二十世紀初頭，日本 Niju seiki shoto no Nip-
pon. (Japan in the beginning of the 20th century.) Tokyo,
Noshomu-sho (Department of agriculture and commerce), 1904.

7850. Nippold, O. Die entwicklung Japans in den letzten
fünfzig jahren. Berlin, 1904. 42 p.

7851. Sydacoff, B. von. Aus dem reiche des Mikado und die
asiatisce gefahr. Leipzig, 1904. 87 p.

7852. Japan by the Japanese. A survey by its highest authorities, edited by Alfred Stead. First and second edition.
London, 1904, 726 p.

7853. Okakura, Kakuzo. The awakening of Japan. London, Murray, 1905. 240 p.

7854. Bogdanovich, T. Skizzen aus alt- und neu-Japan. St.
Petersburg, 1905. 441 p.

7855. Kawakami, K. K. Japan and the Japanese as seen by foreigners prior to the beginning of the Russo-Japanese war.
Tokyo, 1905. 230 p.

7856. Suyematsu, Baron K. The risen sun. Some papers relating to the problem of the war. London, 1905. 368 p.

7857. Stead, Alfred. Great Japan: a study of national efficiency. With a foreword by Earl of Rosebery. London, J.
Lane, 1906. xiv, 483 p.

7858. Hulbert, H. B. Passing of Japan. London, 1906.
486 p.

7859. Seaman, L. L. The real triumph of Japan. The conquest
of the silent foe. New York, Appleton, 1906. 291 p.

7860. Okuma, Shigenobu. 開 國 五 十 年 史 Kaikoku gojunen-shi. (Fifty years of New Japan.) Tokyo, Waseda university, 1907-1908. 2 v. (English ed.: London, 1910. 2 v.)

7861. Rathgen, K. Staat und kultur der Japaner. Monographien
zur weltgeschichte. V. 27. Bielefeld, Velhangen u. Klasing,
1907. 140 p.

7862. Lorimer, Charlotte. The call of the East. (Japan.)
London, 1907.

7863. Paalzow, H. Das kaiserlich Japan. Berlin, H. Paetel,
1908. 231 p.

7864. Vilenkin, Grigorii. Государственный и экономический
строй современной Японии. St. Petersburg, 1908. 214 p.
English translation. The political and economic organization of modern Japan. 1908. vii, 173 p.

7865. Montgomery, H. B. The empire of the East: a simple
account of Japan as it was, is and will be. London, Methuen
& co., 1908. xii, 308 p. Chicago, McClurg, 1909. 308 p.

7866. Asakawa, Kanichi. 日 本 , 褐 機 Nippon no kaki.
(The crisis of Japan.) Tokyo, Jitsugyo no Nipponsha, 1909.
258 p.

7867. Sales y Ferré, M. La transformación del Japón. Dis-
curso leido ante la Real academia de Ciencias morales y po-
liticas en sesión pública celebrada para conmemorar el L.
Aniversario de su constitución el dia 7 de febr. de 1909.
Madrid, 1909. 151 p.

7868. The Japanese empire. A reprint of the Times,Japanese
edition,July 19, 1910. London, The Times office. O. J.
(1910). 439 p.

7869. Ostrorog, Comte Léon. Conférence de l'Amicale. Conférence sur la renaissance du Japon. Allocutions de M. Sa-
lih Gourdji. Konstantinopel, Ahmed Ihsau, 1911. 91 p.

7870. Cauda, E. Germi della decadenza Nipponica. Turin,
Frayelli Bocca, 1911. xv, 283 p.

7871. Kupchinskii, F. Новая Япония. (New Japan.) St. Petersburg, Posev, 1911. ix, 264 p.

7872. Tunas, M. Anti-Japan: Wahrheitsgetreue aufklärungen
über das land der aufgehenden sonne. Zum nachdenken für

Europäer. Zürich, Kettner, 1911. 132 p.

7873. Nitobe, Inazo. The Japanese nation: its land, its people and its life. With special consideration to its relations with the United States. New York, Putnam, 1912. xiv, 334 p.

7874. Arnoux, J. Le peuple japonais. (Le vieux Japon. Le Japon moderne. Le Japon actuel.) Études internationales. Paris, Marcel Rivière, 1912. 510 p.

7875. Mitford, E. B. Japan's inheritance; the country, its people, and their destiny. London, T. Fisher Unwin, 1913. 398 p.

7876. Griffis, William Elliot. The Mikado's empire. 12th edition. New York, Harper and brothers, 1913. 2 v.   (1st edition, 1876.)   (2) "The empire of the Risen sun." National geographic magazine, 44 (1923):415-463.

7877. Terry, T. Philip. Japanese empire including Korea and Formosa with chapters on Manchuria, the Trans-Siberian Railway, and the chief ocean routes to Japan. A guidebook for travellers. London, Constable & co., 1914. cclxxxiii, 799 p.

7878. Anderson, J. The spell of Japan. Boston, Page, 1914. 414 p.

7879. Giles, Herbert A. Adversaria Sinica. Shanghai, Kelly & Walsh, ltd., 1914-1915. 2 v.

7880. Porter, Robert. Japan, the new world power. Being a detailed account of the progress and rise of the Japanese empire. London, H. Milford, 1915. xxiv, 790 p.

7881. Lotti, Pierre. Japan. New York, 1915.

7882. Kiuner, N. V. Современная Япония. (Contemporary Japan.) Moscow, Granat, 1917.

7883. Kol, H. H. van. Japan. Indrukken van land en volk. Vorwort von M. W. de Visser. Rotterdam, W. L. u. J. Brusse, 1917. xii, 195 p.

7884. Sunderland, Jabez T. Rising Japan: is she a menace, or a comrade to be welcomed to the fraternity of nations? New York - London, Putnam, 1918. xi, 220 p.

7885. Le Roux, Hughes. L'Heure du Japon. Paris, 1918.

7886. Porter, Robert. Japan: the rise of a modern power. London, Milford, 1918. xix, 361 p.

7887. Hershey, Amos and Mrs. Herhsey, Susanne. Modern Japan: Social, industrial, political. Indianapolis, Bobbs-Merrill co., 1919. 382 p.

7888. McGovern, W. Montgomery. Modern Japan, its political, military and industrial development. Preface by Sir E. Denison Ross. London, Fisher Unwin, 1920.

7889. Kol, H. H. van. Oud en nieuw Japan. Grepen uit het leven. Vorrede von M. W. de Visser. Rotterdam, Brusse, 1921. 268 p.

7890. Gleason, G. What shall I think of Japan? New York, Macmillan, 1921. 284 p.

7891. Osborne, Sidney. The new Japanese peril. London, G. Allen & Unwin, 1921. 187 p.

7892. Dautremer, J. Les études japonaises. Société Asiatique. Le livre de centenaire (1822-1922). 2. Cent ans d'Orientalisme en France, 12. Paris, Paul Geuthner, 1922.

7893. Ostwald, Paul. Japans entwicklung zur modernen weltmacht. Seine kultur-, rechts-, wirtschaft- und staatengeschichte von der restauration bis zur gegenwart. Bücherei der kultur und geschichte, Band 28. Bonn-Leipzig, K. Schröder, 1922. 312 p.

7894. Gubbins, John Harington. The making of modern Japan: an account of the progress of Japan from pre-feudal days to constitutional government and the position of a Great power, with chapters on religion, the complex family system, education etc. London, Seeley Service & co., Philadelphia, Lippincott, 1922. 316 p.   (2)   Japan. Handbooks prepared under the direction of the Historical section of the Foreign office no. 73. London, H. M. Stationary office, 1920. 109 p.

7895. Япония. (Japan.) Chita, Politicheskii otdel revoliutsionno-voennogo soveta 5-oi armii, 1923. 320 p.

7896. Pokrovskii, A. M. and Filippov, V. A. Япония накануне землетрясения. Очерки современной Японии. (Japan on the eve of the earthquake. Sketches of contemporary Japan.) Kharkov, Put' prosveshcheniia, 1923. iii, 93 p.

7897. Powers, H. Japan. London - New York, Macmillan, 1923.
x, 278 p.

7898. Konrad, N. I. Япония. Народ и государство. (Japan.
The people and the state.) Petrograd, Nauka i shkola, 1923.
168 p.

7899. Haushofer, K. Japan und die Japaner. Eine landeskunde.
Leipzig, B. G. Teubner, 1923. 166 p.

7900. Vilenskii, Vladimir (Sibiriakov). Япония. (Japan.)
Moscow, Vserossiiskaia nauchnaia assotsiatsiia vostokovedeniia pri Narodnom komissariate po delam natsional'nostei,
1923. 204 p.

7901. Ikeda, S. Welbetrachtungen eines Japaners. Stuttgart,
Verlag Ausland und heimat, 1923. 47 p.

7902. Longford, J. H. Japan. The nations of today series.
1923. ix, 325 p.

7903. Bryan, Ingran J. Japan from within: an inquiry into
the political, industrial, commercial, financial, agricultural, ornamental, and educational conditions of modern Japan. London, Fisher Unwin, 1924. 288 p. New York, 1925.

7904. Kel'in, I. Япония. Культурно-исторический и экономический очерк с приложением карты Японии. (Japan. A cultural-
historical and economic outline with a map of Japan.) Petrograd, Giz, 1924. 168 p.

7905. Pozdneev, Dmitrii M. Япония. Страна, население, история, политика. (Japan. The country, its population and politics.) Moscow, 1925. 351 p.

7906. IUrkevich, T. S. Современная Япония. (Contemporary
Japan.) Экономическо-географический обзор по новейшим источникам. (Economic-geographical survey according to the latest sources.) Vladivostok, Knizhnoe delo, 1925. 191 p.

7907. Popov, A. Япония. (Japan.) Introduction of M. Pavlovich. Moscow, MGSPS Trud i Kniga, 1925. 110 p.

7908. Katayama, Sen. Современная Япония. (Contemporary Japan.) Moscow, Planovoe Khoziaistvo, 1926. 99 p.   (2) Scherer, James A. B. The romance of Japan through the ages.
New York, Doran, 1926. ix, 326 p.

7909. Wakatsuki, Fukujiro. Le Japon traditionnel. Paris, Au sans pareil, 1926. ii, 166 p.

7910. Kharnskii, K. Япония в прошлом и настоящем.(Japan in the past and present.) Vladivostok, Knizhnoe delo, 1926. 411 p.

7911. Ch'ên, Mao-lieh. 最近之日本 Tsui-chin chih Jih-pên. (Modern Japan.) Shanghai, Chung-hua shu-chü, 1926.

7912. Ioffe, A. Япония в наши дни. (Japan in our days.) Moscow, Nauchnaia assotsiatsiia vostokovedeniia, 1926. 76 p. Also in: Krasnaia Nov', 6 (1926):176-187.

7913. Tsurumi, Yusuke. Present-day Japan. New York, Columbia university press; London, H. Milford, 1926. vi, 114 p.

7914. Goldschmidt, Richard. Neu-Japan. Reisebilder aus Formosa, die Ryukyuinseln, Bonininseln, Korea u. d. südmandschurische pachtgebiete. Berlin, Springer, 1927. vii, 303 p.

7915. Brown, Arthur J. Japan in the world of today. New York, 1928.

7916. Allen, G. C. Modern Japan and its problems. London, New York, 1928.

7917. Gastov, G. Япония.(Japan.) Moscow, 1928. 112 p.

7918. Daye, Pierre. Le Japon et don destin. Paris, 1928.

7919. Tai. Chi-t'ao. 日本論 Jih-pên lun. (Japan.) Shanghai, Min-chih shu-chü, 1928.

7920. Paske-Smith, M. Sir Stamford Raffles. Report on Japan to the secret committee of the East India company (1812-1816). With preface and notes. Kobe, London, 1929.

7921. Negishi, Yoshitaro. 堅實性ノ日本 Kenjitsusei no Nippon. (Steadfast Japan.) Tokyo, Toyosha, 1929. 304 p.

7922. 光ハ日本ヨリ Hikari wa Nippon yori. (Japan gleameth.) Tokyo, New Oriental society, Shinchosha, 1929. 370 p.

7923. Kennedy, Captain Malcolm Duncan. The changing fabric of Japan. London, Constable, 1930. vii, 282 p.

7924. 日本研究 Nippon kenkyu. (The study of Japan.)
Tokyo, Waseda daigaku Nippongaku kyokai, 1930. 2 v.

7925. Nuno, Toshiaki. 日本没落 か Nippon botsuraku ka.
(Will Japan ever fall?) Tokyo, Banrikaku, 1930. 446 p.

7926. Japan today and tomorrow. Osaka, 1931.

7927. Sokolov, Boris. Империалистическая Япония. (Imperialistic Japan.) Moscow, Partizdat, 1932. 93 p.   (2) Япония
наших дней. (Contemporary Japan.) Moscow, TSK Mopr SSSR,
1932. 54 p.   (3) Япония. (Japan.) 2nd ed. [Moscow-Leningrad], 1934. 109 p.

7928. Yen, Lu-ching. 日本印象記 Jih-pên yin-hsiang
chi. (Impressions of Japan.) Shanghai, Chün-chung t'u-shu
kung-ssu, 1932?

7929. Takasu, Hojiro. 非常時日本ヲ如何ニスベキか Hijoji
no Nippon o ikani subeki ka? (What measures for Japan in
crisis?) Tokyo, Osakayago, 1932. 360 p.

7930. Ozaki, Yukio. 世界審判，岐路ニ立ツ日本 Sekai
shinpan no kiro ni tatsu Nippon. (Japan at the cross-road
of world judgment.) Tokyo, Chikura shobo, 1932. 98 p.

7931. Ino, Kaju. 日本國策 Nippon kokusaku. (The national
policy of Japan.) Tokyo, Bunrokusha, 1932. 280 p.

7932. Hinode. 非常時讀本 Hijoji tokuhon. (Reading material on the Japanese crisis.) Tokyo, Shinchosha,
1932.

7933. Wang, Shan-Chi. 日本國勢現狀 Jih-pên kuo-shih
hsien-chuang. (The present status of Japan.) Shanghai, Tatung shu-chü, 1932.

7934. Shimomura, Hiroshi. 世界ト日本 Sekai to Nippon.
(Japan and the world.) Tokyo, Asahi shinbunsha, 1932. 500 p.

7935. Hosoi, Hajime. 日本ノ決意 Nippon no ketsui. (Japan's determination.) Tokyo, Dai Nippon yuben kodansha,
1932.   (2) Araki, Sadao. 全日本國民ニ告グ Zen Nippon
kokumin ni tsugu. (A word to all the people of Japan.) Tokyo, Daido shoin, 1932. 300 p.

7936. Toyama, Naotaka. 興國日本ノ苦悶 Kokoku Nippon
no kumon. (The agony of Japan, a rising nation.) Tokyo,
Nitto shoin, 1932.

7937. Honda, Kumataro. 世界ノ不安ト日本ノ立場 Sekai no fuan to Nippon no tachiba. (Insecurity of the world and the position of Japan.) Tokyo, Zenkoku choson kaigi, 1933. 2 vols. 58, 57 p.

7938. Suzuki, Tooru. 日本危シ Nippon ayaushi. (Japan in crisis.) Tokyo, Senshinsha, 1933. 350 p.   See 7753.

7939. Chijiiwa, Fujio. 日本ハ輝ク Nippon wa kagayaku. (Japan shines.) Morioka, Fumeian, 1933. 128 p.

7940. Haushofer, Karl. Japans werdegang als weltmacht und empire. Berlin, 1933.

7941. Shimomura, Hiroshi. 世界ト日本 Sekai to Nippon. (The world and Japan.) Tokyo, Tokyo asahi shinbunsha, 1933. 476 p. See 7934.

7942. See 7935.

7943. Etherton, Percy Thomas and Tiltman, H. H.   Japan: mistress of the Pacific? London, Jarrolds, 1933. 302 p.

7944. O'Conroy, Taid. The menace of Japan. London, Hurst & Blackett, ltd., 1933. 294 p.

7945. Mif, P. and Voitinskii, G. (ed.) Современная Япония. Сборник. (Modern Japan. Symposium.) Moscow, 1934. 229 p.

7946. IUzhnyi, A. Япония. Политико-экономический очерк. (Japan. A political-economic sketch.) 2nd enlarged edition. Moscow, 1934. 395 p.

7947. Grande, Julian. Japan's place in the world. London, H. Jenkins, ltd., [1934]. 254 p.

7948. Scherer, James Augustus Brown. Japan's advance. Tokyo, The Hokuseido press, 1934. xvii, 347 p.

7949. Zhukov, E. and Rozen, A. (ed.) Япония. Сборник статей. (Japan. Collection of articles.) Moscow, 1934. 416 p.

7950. Hattori, Kyoichi. 日本ノ大使命 Nippon no dai shimei. (The great mission of Japan.) Tokyo, Nippon shokumin gakko, 1934. 464 p.

7951. Taga, Munezo. 日本民族ノ根本自覚 Nippon min-zoku no konpon jikaku. (The fundamental self-realization of the Japanese people.) Tokyo, Chokosha, 1934. 122 p.

7952. Kihashi, Toshiro. 帝國ノ危機 Teikoku no kiki. (Crisis of Japan.) Tokyo, Nippon keizai tsushinsha, 1934. 454 p.

7953. Agli, KH. Япония. (Japan.) Kazan', 1935. 138 p.

7954. Yoshida, Katsujiro. 戰爭ノ危機ト皇道日本ノ建設 Senso no kiki to kodo Nippon no kensetsu. (War crisis and the founding of greater Japan.) Sapporo, Katsujiro Yoshida, 1935. 127 p.

7955. Tokyo seiji keizai kenkyu sho. 世界ト日本 Sekai to Nippon. (The world and Japan.) Tokyo, Iwanami shoten, 1935. 605 p.

7956. Tanabe, Saburo. 動ノ日本ノ姿 Ugoku Nippon no sugata. (The condition of Japan in action.) Tokyo, Nitto shoin, 1935. 299 p.

7957. Kennedy, M. D. The problem of Japan. London, Nisbet, 1935. 287 p.

7958. Redman, H. Vere. Japan in crisis; an Englishman's impressions. London, G. Allen & Unwin, ltd., 1935. 223 p.

7959. Pickering, Ernest Harold. Japan's place in the modern world. London, 1936. 326 p.

7960. Smith, Walter. Japan at the crossroads. London, Lawrence & Wishart, 1936. 125 p.

7961. Nagai, Kyo. 新日本論 Shin Nippon ron. (On the new Japan.) Tokyo, Mikasa shobo. 1936. 606 p.

7962. Takayama, Chusuke. 大東京ノ現勢 Dai Tokyo no zensei. (The present condition of great Tokyo.) Tokyo, Tokyo maiyu shinbunsha, 1936. 832 p.

7963. de Garis, Frederic. Their Japan. Yokohama, Yoshikawa, 1936. 204 p., 345 illustrations.

7964. Hayama, U. Япония. (Japan.) Moscow, 1936, 169 p.

7965. Naomi, Zenzo. 日本ハ何ヲ爲スベキカ Nippon wa nani o nasubeki ka. (What is the mission of Japan?) Gaiko jiho, 79:5:48-68, Sept., 1936.

7966. Fujihi, Munehiro. 非常時日本之内患 Hijoji Nippon no naikan. (Internal troubles of Japan in crisis.)

Tokyo, Taishosha, 1936. 218 p.

7967. Sakuma, Teijiro. 変局一断面 Henkyoku ichidanmen. (A cross-section of the national problems.) Tokyo, To-A kenkyukai, 1936. 27 p.

7968. Gota, Akiyoshi. 真日本建設論 Shin Nippon kensetsu ron. (On the founding of an ideal Japan.) Osaka, Akiyoshi Gota, 1936. 543 p.

7969. Ito, Eitaro. 日本ノ運命 Nippon no unmei. (The fate of Japan.) Tokyo, Nippon koronsha, 1936. 302 p.

7970. Yoshizawa, Kiyoshi. 現代日本論 Gendai Nippon ron. (On modern Japan.) Tokyo, Chikura shobo, 1936. 378 p.

7971. Shiota, Morimichi. 皇國大日本ト其ノ使命 Kokoku dai Nippon to sono shimei. (The great Japanese empire and her mission.) Tokyo, Kenkoku koenkai jimusho, 1936. 164 p.

7972. Shimizu, Yoshitaro. 日本経営論 Nippon keiei ron. (On the national governmental undertakings of Japan.) Tokyo, Chikura shobo, 1936. 348 p.

7973. Baba, Yoshio. 萬世一系ノ日本 Bansei ikkei no Nippon. (Japan under the rule of the unbroken imperial lineage.) Tokyo, Kigen kannen fukyukai, 1936. 480 p.

7974. Watanabe, Tetsuzo. 日本ノ力 Nippon no chikara. (The power of Japan.) Tokyo, Shokasha, 1936. 502 p.

7975. See 7984.

7976. Sawada, Otojiro. 日本人ココニアリ Nippon-jin koko ni ari. (The Japanese are here!) Tokyo, Tokyo Ehime kenjinkai, 1936. 353 p.

7977. Kodama, Shoichi. 米國新聞記者ノ見タ日本ト満洲 Beikoku shinbun kisha no mita Nippon to Manshu. (Observations on Japan and Manchuria by American newspaper correspondents.) Tokyo, Nippon shinbun kyokai, 1936. 219 p.

7978. Nitobé, Inazo. Lectures on Japan: an outline of the development of the Japanese people and their culture. Tokyo, Kahkyusha, 1936. 393 p.

7979. Yamakawa, Tadao. "The Yosemite conference and Japan." Pacific Affairs, 9:4:515-524, December, 1936.

7980. Halden, Leon Gilbert and Halden,Sallie Fellman. Japan — colossus of the Far East. Houston, The authors, 1937. 112 p.

7981. Pratt, Helen G. Japan; where ancient loyalties survive. American council. Peoples of the Pacific, 2. Institute of Pacific relations, 1937. 188 p.

7982. Colegrove, Kenneth W. (comp.) Japan as a world power. Selected reading from newspapers, news services, journals, and year books. New York, Institute of Pacific Relations, 1937. 18 p.

7983. Lasker, Bruno. Japan in jeopardy. New York, American council, Institute of Pacific relations, 1937. 18 p.

7984. Hozumi, Shigenori. 日本ノ過去現在反將來 Nippon no kako genzai oyobi shorai. (The past, present and future of Japan.) Tokyo, Iwanami shoten, 1937. 314 p.

7985. Chamberlin, William Henry. Japan over Asia. Boston, Little, Brown and co., 1937. vii, xii, 395 p.

7986. See 7956.

7987. 世界ハ日本ヲドウ見ル Sekai wa Nippon wo do miru. (Japan as observed by the world.) Tokyo, Kokusai josei kenkyukai staff, Taiyokaku, 1937. 560 p.

7988. Okubo,Koichi. 日本ハ強シ. Nippon wa tsuyoshi. (Powerful Japan.) Tokyo, Heiyo tosho kabushiki-kaisha, 1937. 350 p.

7989. Kobayashi, Ichizo. 次ニ來ルモノ Tsugi ni kitaru mono. (Coming events.) Tokyo, Tonan.shoin, 1937. 500 p.

7990. Ozaki, Yukio. 日本ハドウナル力. Nippon wa do naruka. (What will become of Japan.) Tokyo, Hakuyosha, 1937. 445 p.

7991. Scherer, James A. B. Japan defies the world. Indianapolis, Bobbs-Merrill, 1938.

XI. JAPANESE NATIONALISM AND PSYCHOLOGY

See 8690-8735; 9768-9796.

7992. Okakura, Yoshisaburo. The Japanese spirit;with an introduction by George Meredith. New York, J. Pott & co.,

1905. 127 p. German edition: Die japanische volkseele.
Mit einer einleitung von G. Meredith. Autorisierte über-
setzung aus dem englischen von Baronin E. Engerth. Wien-
Leipzig, C. W. Stern. 1906. 142 p.

7993. Leo, J. Die entwicklung des ältesten japanischer
seelenlebens nach seinen literarischen ausdrucksformen (psy-
chologisch-historische untersuchung der quellen). Beitrage
zur kultur- und univeralgeschichte. Heft 2. Leipzig, Voigt-
länder, 1907, vii, 106 p.

7994. Ninakawa, Tatsuo. 日本 武士道史 Nippon bushido-
shi. (History of the bushido, the code of honor of military
men of Japan.) Tokyo, Hakubunkan, 1907. 350 p.

7995. La Vieuville. Essai de psychologie japonaise. La race
des dieux. Paris, A. Challamel, 1908. 183 p.

7996. Takimura, Ryutaro. "Esquisse psychologicue du peuple
japonais." Bulletin, Société franco-japonaise, 12 (1908):
43-53.

7997. Minzinger, Carl. "Zur psychologie des modernen Japans." Beitrage zur kenntnis des Orients, 5 (1908):142-160.

7998. Kennan, G. "Can we understand the Japanese?" Outlook,
101:15 (1912):815-822.

7999. Bryan, Ingram J. "Are the Japanese a warlike people?"
The Japan magazine, 4 (1913-1914):561-564.

8000. Haushofer, Martha. "Die japanische naturgefühl."
Geist des Ostens, 1:147-161, January, 1913 - March, 1914.

8001. Kato, Setsudo. 國民性ト宗教 Kokuminsei to shukyo. (National characteristic of the Japanese and their religion.) Tokyo, Chuo shoin, 1914. 358 p.

8002. Hibino, Yutaka. Pure loyalty: the ideal of the Japanese subject. London, Kegan Paul, Trench, Trübner and co.,
1924. viii, 54 p.

8003. Lincoln, A. E. The psychology of Japanese patriotism.
The new Orient, 1925.

8004. Miyaji, Naoichi. 神祇ト國史 Shingi to kokushi.
(Shinto teaching and the national history of Japan.) Tokyo,
Kokon shoin, 1926. 382 p.

8005. Kanokogi, Kazunobu. "Japanese national spirit as revealed in art." The young East, 2 (1926-k927):179-184.

8006. Watsuji, Tetsuro. 日本精神史研究 Nippon seishin-shi kenkyu. (A research in the history of the developement of nationalism in Japan.) Tokyo, Iwanami shoten, 1927. 430 p. See 8022.

8007. Kiyohara, Sadao. 武士道十講 Bushido jikko. (Ten lectures on Bushido, the way of the samurai.) Tokyo, Meguro shoten, 1927. 274 p.

8008. Nitobé, Inazo. Bushido, the soul of Japan. Tokyo, The student co., 1905. x, 177 p.   French translation: Le Bushidô. L'âme du Japon. Traduction française de Charles Jacob. Préface d'André Bellessort. Paris, Payot, 1927. 267p.

8009. Hibino, Yutaka. Nippon Shindo Ron: or the national ideals of the Japanese people. Translated with an introduction by A. P. MacKenzie. London, Cambridge university press, 1928. xxxviii, 176 p.

8010. Bondegger, Harry W. Die geheimwissenschaft Japans "Buschido". 5 Auflage. Talisman-Bücherei. Dresden, Rudolph, 1929. 2 v.

8011. 日ノ丸由来記 Hinomaru yurai-ki. (An account of the origin of hinomaru, the sun national flag of Japan.) Tokyo, Nichi nichi shinbun, 1929. 62 p.

8012. Hsiao, H. H. "Mentality of the Chinese and Japanese." Journal of applied psychology (Athens, Ohio). 13:9-31, February, 1929.

8013. Sakai, Kohei. 日本國民性,史的研究 Nippon kokuminsei no shiteki kenkyu. (The historical study of the character of the Japanese nation.) Tokyo, Bunshodo, 1930. 475 p.

8014. Kihira, Masami. 日本精神 Nippon seishin. (The soul of Japan.) Tokyo, Iwanami, 1931. 434 p.

8015. Kato, Jinpei. 國民精神發達史 Kokumin seishin hattatsu-shi. (History of the development of Japanese national spirit.) Tokyo, Kyoiku kenkyukai, 1932. 294 p.

8016. Fukumoto, Giryo. 吉田松陰,殉國敎育 Yoshida Shoin no junkoku kyoiku. (Yoshida Shoin's teaching on sacrificing of life for the country.) Tokyo, Seibundo, 1932. 1000 p. See 7759-7764.

8017. Okawa, Shumei. 日本精神研究 Nippon seishin kenkyu. (A study of the soul of Japan.) Tokyo, Bunrokusha, 1932.

8018. Funaguchi, Manju. 國体思想變遷史 Kokutai shiso hensen-shi. (History of the development of the nationalism of Japan.)

8019. Min, Chü-chu. 日本之國民性 Jih-pên' chih kuo-min-hsing. (The national characteristics of Japan.) Nung-lin. hsin-pao. 9:16, June,1932.

8020. Kono, Shozo. 日本精神發達史 Nippon seishin hattatsu shi. (History of the development of the "Japanese spirit".) Tokyo, Ookayama shoten, 1932. 360 p.

8021. 日本精神史論集 Nippon seishin-shi ronsan. (A collection of historical essays on the "Japanese spirit".) Tokyo, Nippon seishin-shi gakkai, Iwanami, 1932.

8022. Watsuji, Tetsuro. 日本精神史研究 Nippon seishin-shi kenkyu. (Research in the history of development of nationalism in Japan.) Tokyo, Iwanami, 1932. 442 p. See 8006.

8023. Nitobé, Inazo Ota and others. Western influences in modern Japan. Chicago, The University of Chicago Press, 1931. 544 p.

8024. Matsunaga, Sai. 日本主義ノ論理 Nippon-shugi no ronri. (Logic of the Japanese doctrine.) Tokyo, Daiyukaku, 1932. 180 p.

8025. Ashida, Masaki. 日本精神ノ哲學 Nippon seishin no tetsugaku. (Philosophy of the Japanese spirit.) Osaka, Shinshindo shoten, 1932.

8026. Nomura, Hachiryo. 上代文學ニ現ハレタル日本精神 Jodai bungaku ni arawareta Nippon seishin. (The "Japanese spirit" as manifested in the ancient literature of Japan.) Tokyo, Ookayama shoten, 1932. 250 p.

8027. Yamamichi, Joichi. 日本再建論 Nippon saiken ron. (Rebuilding of Japan.) Tokyo, Chikura shobo, 1933. 179 p.

8028. Hiraizumi, Cho. 闇齋先生ト日本精神 Ansai sensei to Nippon seishin. (The "Soul of Japan" as expounded by Ansai, the great Japanese teacher.) Tokyo, Shibundo, 1932.

8029. Yanaginuma, Hichiro. 愛國ノ心理 Aikoku no shin-ri. (The psychology of patriotism.) Tokyo, Senshinsha, 1933. 300 p.

8030. Nishimura, Shinji. 日本民族理想 Nippon minzoku riso. (Ideals of the Japanese race.) Tokyo, Tokyodo, 1934. 253 p.   (2) Kiyohara, Sadao. 國史ト日本精神ノ顕現 Kokushi to Nippon seishin no kengen. (National history and the manifestation of the Japanese spirit.) Tokyo, Fujii shoten, 1935. 613 p.

8031. Sakase, Kawaharu. 皇國精神ヲ代表シル西郷南州ト大久保甲東 Kokoku seishin o daihyo shitaru Saigo Nanshu to Okubo Koto. (Nanshu [Takamori] Saigo and Koto [Toshimichi] Okubo: exponents of the Japanese spirit.) Tokyo, Okubo Koto sensei dozo kensetsu kai, 1936. 339 p.

8032. Motoori, Norinaga. 本居宣長全集 Motoori Norinaga zenshu. (Complete works of Norinaga Motoori.) Tokyo, Yoshi-kawa kobunkan, 1937. 13 v.

8033. Yoshimura, Tamotsu. 非常時局ト日本精神 Hijo jikyoku to Nippon seishin. (Critical period and the Japanese spirit.) Kyoto, Kyoto-fu kyoikukai, 1936. 101 p.

8034. Miyanishi, Kazutsumi. 國史ヲ貫ク日本精神 Kokushi o tsuranuku Nippon seishin. (The Japanese spirit which per-meates its national history.) Tokyo, Shinseikaku shoten, 1936. 231 p.

8035. Togo, Minoru. 精神日本ノ建設 Seishin Nippon no kensetsu. (Founding of spiritual Japan.) Tokyo, Tamagawa gakuen, 1936. 248 p.

8036. Sato, Taihei. 櫻ト日本民族 Sakura to Nippon min-zoku. (Cherry blossoms and the Japanese race.) Tokyo, Taito shuppansha, 1937.

8037. Wildes, Harry Emerson. Aliens in the East. Philadel-phia, University of Pennsylvania press, 1937. 360 p.

8038. Kinoshita, Kazuo. 日本道徳學 Nippon dotokugaku. (A study of the moral principles of Japan.) Tokyo, Baifu-kan, 1937. 250 p.

8039. Tozaka, Jun. 日本イデオロギー論 Nippon ideorogi ron. (On the ideologies of Japan.) Tokyo, Hakuyosha, 1937. 450 p.

8040. Nishimura, Shinji. 日本民族理想 Nippon min-

zoku riso. (The ideals of the Japanese race.) 3d edition.
Tokyo, Tokyodo, 1937. See 8030.

8041. Okubo, Koichi. 日本精神信解 Nippon seishin
shinkai. (Explanation of the Japanese spirit.) Tokyo, Heiyo
tosho kabushiki-kaisha, 1937. 150 p.

8042. Kato, Setsudo. 日本偉人信仰實傳 Nippon ijin
shinko jitsuden. (True accounts of the hero worship of Japan.) Tokyo, Taito shuppansha, 1937. 2 vols. 2100 p.

8043. Takamatsu, Toshio. 真日本主義 國民改造ト道
義大亞建設 Shin Nippon-shugi kokumin kaizo to dogi
tai-A kensetsu. (Reforming the nationals according to the
true Japanese doctrine and founding of greater Asia along
our moral principles.) Tokyo, Toko shoten, 1937. 250 p.

XII. INTERNATIONAL RELATIONS

See 450-780; 3022-4705; 4992-5096; 5805-6446; 6772-6724;
8690-8885; 11402-11464.

A. Periodicals

See 43-147; 1088-1093; 7305-7337; 7509-7517.

8044. 外交時報 Gaiko jiho. (Diplomatic review.) Bi-
monthly. Tokyo, Gaiko jihosha, 1, 1898 -

8045. 國際法外交雜誌 Kokusaiho gaiko zasshi.
(The journal of international law and diplomacy.) Bureau
of the Association of international law. 1, 1902·

8046. 國際知識 Kokusai chishiki. (International digest.) Tokyo, Nippon kokusai kyokai. 1, 1921-

8047. 國際時報 Kokusai jiho. (The International review.) Published by the News department of the Ministry of
Foreign affairs, Tokyo,   1, 1926-   (2) 國際評論
Kokusai hyoron. (The international review.) Tokyo, Nippon
gaiji kyokai.(The foreign affairs association of Japan.)
1, 1932-

B. Sources

See 450-538; 3029-3041.

8048. 大日本古文書：幕末外國關係文書 Dai Nippon ko-
monjo: Bakumatsu gaikoku kankei bunsho. (Old historical doc-

uments of Japan: Documents concerning foreign relations during the later part of the Tokugawa shogunate.) Tokyo, Tokyo imperial university, College of literature, Division of
historical material, 1910-1916. 22 v.

8049. 外交志稿 Gaiko Shiko. (Diplomatic history and
official documents.) Tokyo, Department of foreign affairs,
Bureau of records, 1884. 2 v.   822, 311 p.   (2) Oda,
Junichiro. 日清韓交渉録. Nichi-Shin-Kan koshoroku.
(International transactions between Japan, China, and Korea,
and the documents regarding them.) 1894.

8050. 大日本外交文書 Dai Nippon gaiko bunsho. (Japanese diplomatic documents.) Tokyo, Nippon kokusai kyokai,
1936- . [Thus far published 2 vols; v. I:1 (1019 p.), I:2
(1016 p.); II:1 (940 p.), II:2 (894 p.), II:3 (703 p.)
(October, 1867 - December, 1869).]

8051. Japan. Laws statutes, etc. Secretariat of the cabinet,
Section of the archives. 外事 Gaiji. (Laws and ordinances
regarding all treaties and agreements with foreign nations.)
In "Genko Horei Shuran". v. 12, Tokyo, Teikoku chiho gyosei
gakukai, 1931. 1885 p.

8052. Ito, Hirobumi (Hakubun). 秘書類纂外交篇 Hisho
ruisan gaiko hen. (Unpublished documents classified and compiled: on diplomacy.) Tokyo, Hisho ruisan kankokai, 1935.
684 p.

C. History

See 539-662; 3042-3095.

(1) General Historical Accounts

8053. Hayashi, Fukusai. 通航一覧 Tsuko ichiran. (Com-
prehansive history of the national contacts of Japan with
foreign nations.) Tokyo, Kokusho kankokai, 1912-1913.
8 v.

8054. Akagi, Roy Hidemichi. Japan's foreign relations.
1543-1936. A short history. Tokyo, Hokuseido, 1936. 560 p.

8055. Yoshida, Norikata. 外蕃通略 Gaiban tsuryaku.
(Brief history of Japan's international intercourse with
foreign countries.) 1892.

8056. Watanabe, Shujiro. "The Japanese and the outer world."

The Japan magazine, Tokyo, 17 (1926-1927) 474-482; 18 (1927-1928):5-12, 124-132, 136-145 218-226, 253-257; 19 (1928-1929):56-59, 160-163, 238-242, 272-278, 346-350, 437-443, 488-489; 20 (1929-1930):24-29, 61-65.

8057. Nagaoka, H. Histoire des relations du Japon avec l'Europe au XVIe et XVIIe siècle. Paris, 1905. 326 p.

8058. Nagaoka, H. "Les premières relations de l'Europe avec le Japon." Bulletin, Société franco-japonaise, 4 (1906): 35-48.

8059. Dahlmann, J. Japans älteste beziehungen zum Westen 1542-1614 in zeitgenössischen denkmälern seiner kunst. Ein beitrag zur historischen, künstlerischen, religiösen würdigung eines altjapanischen bilderschmuckes. Ergänzungshefte zu den "Stimmen der zeit". Freiburg i/Br., Herder u. co., 1923. viii, 72 p.

8060. Montanus, Arnoldus. Ambassades vers les empereurs du Japon. Amsterdam, 1680. Japanese transl. 日本訳 Nippon-shi.

8061. Boxer, C. R. A Portuguese embassy to Japan (1644-47). Translated from an unpublished Portuguese MS., and other contemporary sources, with commentary and appendices. London, 1928.

8062. Núñez Ortega, Angel. Noticia histórica sobre las relaciones políticas y comerciales habidas entre México y el Japón durante el siglo XVII. Archivo historico diplomático mexicano. No. 2. 1923.

8063. Lera, C. A. "Primeras relaciones oficiales entre el Japón y España tocantes á México." Boletin de la sociedad geográfica (Madrid), 48 (1906):64-80.

8064. Relations officielles entre le Japon et l'Espagne au sujet du Mexique au XVIe siècle. Mélanges (a quarterly review), Tokyo, 2 (1905):6-7:234-241, 294-302.

8065. Nuttall, Zelia. The earliest historical relations between Mexico and Japan (from original documents preserved in Spain and Japan). University of California publications, American archaeology and ethnology 4, No. 1, Berkeley, Calif., University press, 1906. 47 p.

8066. Rammung, Martin. "Über den anteil der Russen an der eröffnung Japans für den verkehr mit den westlichen mächten." Mitteilungen der deutschen gesellschaft für natur- und völkerkunde Ost-Asiens, Band 16, Teil B. Tokyo, 1926.

8067. Urkundige darstellung der bestrebungen von Niederland und Russland zur eroeffnung Japans für aller nationen, von F. Siebold. Bonn, 1854.

8068. Ogawa, Heikichi. 明治外交要錄 Meiji gaiko yoroku. (A record of Japanese diplomacy of recent times.) 1903.

8069. Osadake, Takeki. 國際法ヨリ觀タル幕末外交物語 Kokusai-ho yori mitaru bakumatsu gaiko monogatari. (Diplomatic events of the later Tokugawa period: The re-opening of Japan, viewed from international law.) Tokyo, Bunka seikatsu research association, 1926. 530 p.

8070. Takabe, Taichi. 幕末外交談 Bakumatsu gaiko dan. (An account of the diplomatic transaction in the latter days of the Tokugawa shogunate.) Tokyo, Fuzanbo, 1908.

8071. Yoshino, Sakuzo (compiler). 明治文化全集：外交篇 Meiji bunka zenshu: Gaiko hen. (Japanese diplomacy of the Meiji era, 1868-1912.) In: Complete collection on the culture and civilization of the Meiji era. Tokyo, Nippon hyoronsha, 1928. 572 p.

8072. Yoshino, Sakuzo. 明治外交史ノ一節 Meiji gaikoshi no issetsu. (A section of the history of Japanese diplomacy during the Meiji era, 1868-1912.) In: Series of Social economics and politics, Tokyo, Nippon hyoronsha.

8073. 明治大正史 Meiji Taisho-shi. (History of the Meiji and Taisho eras.) Tokyo, Asahi news, 1930. 6 v. (Vol. 2, 426 p.)

8074. Ariga, Nagao. 最近三十年外交史 Saikin 30-nen gaiko-shi. (Diplomatic history of the past 30 years.) Tokyo, Waseda university press, 1923.

8075. Shinobu, J. 大正外交十五年史 Taisho gaiko jugonen-shi. (A diplomatic history of the fifteen years of Taisho, 1912-1926.) Tokyo, 1927.

8076. Tokutomi, Iichiro. 大戰後ノ世界ト日本 Taisen go no sekai to Nippon. (Relation of the world and Japan after the great war.) 12th ed. 1921. 775 p.

8077. Inahara, Katsuji. 大正外交ノ總決算 Taisho gaiko no so kessan. (Summary of Taisho diplomacy.) Gaiko jiho,

45:2:30-60, January 15, 1927.

8078. Matsubara, Kazuo. 外交及外交史研究 Gaiko oyo-
bi gaiko-shi kenkyu. (Research on diplomacy and our diplomatic history.) Tokyo, Maruzen, 1927. 790 p.

8079. Tsuboi, Kumazo. 最近政治外交史 Saikin sei-
ji gaiko-shi. (History of recent politics and diplomacy.)
Tokyo, Fuzanbo, 1926-1930. 3 v.

8080. The re-orientation of Japan's foreign policy. Foreign
policy reports, v. 6, no. 16 (New York), 1930.

8081. Tsuji, Zennosuke. 海外交通史話 Kaigai kotsu
shiwa. (Diplomatic history of Japan, and the official documents.) Tokyo, Naigai book store ltd., 1930. 816 p.

8082. Tahobashi, Kiyoshi. 近代日本外國關係史
Kindai Nippon gaikoku kankei-shi. (Recent history of the
relations of Japan with the foreign countries.) Tokyo, Toko
book store, 1930. 3 v.

8083. Nagano, Isamu. 日本外交六十年史 Nippon gaiko
60-nen-shi. (Sixty years of Japanese diplomacy.) Tokyo,
Kensetsusha, 1934. 3 vols. 379, 329, 341 p.

8084. Kanagawa, Hikomatsu. 立敎授還曆祝賀外交史論
Tachi kyoju kanreki shukuga gaiko shiron. (Historical dissertations on diplomacy on the celebration of Professor
Tachi's sixtieth anniversary, by his friends.) Tokyo, Yuhikaku, 1935. 507 p.

8085. Tonedate, Masao. 日本外交秘錄 Nippon gaiko hiroku. (Secret memoirs of Japanese diplomacy.) Tokyo, Asahi
shinbun, 1935. 208 p.

8086. Ito, Eitaro. 危機外交秘密史 Kiki gaiko hi-
mitsu-shi. (History of secret diplomacy during critical
periods.) Tokyo, Nippon koronsha, 1935. 376 p.

8087. Funakoshi, Mitsunojo. 日獨國交斷絶秘史
Nichi-Doku koko danzetsu hishi. (Secret history of the sev-
erance of Japanese-German diplomatic relations.) Tokyo,
Nitto shoin, 1935. 326 p.

8088. Kishima, Momotaka. 歷代國務大臣演說集外交篇
Rekidai kokumu-daijin enzetsu shu gaiko-hen. (Collection of
speeches of successive ministers of state--on diplomacy.)
Tokyo, Kokusai keizai shinposha, 1935. 322 p.   (2)T same.

歴代外務大臣演説集 Rekidai gaimu daijin enzetsu-shu.
(A collection of the speeches made by successive foreign
ministers.) Tokyo, Kokusai keizai kenkyusho, 1936. 336 p.

(2) General Diplomatic Relations

8089. Administrative regulations, promulgated by H. I. M.
government. Tokyo, Foreign office (Gwaimusho) in Tokyo,
1884.

8090. Okuma, Count S. "The foreign policy of Japan." Far
East, Tokyo, 1 (1896.):11:6-11.

8091. Clavery, Ed. Les étrangers au Japon et les Japonais a
l'étranger. Étude historique et statistique. Paris, 1904.
31 p. (Reprinted from the "Revue générale d'administration",
v. 79, pp. 5-19, 152-163. Paris, 1904.)

8092. Kaneko, K., Baron. "The 'Yellow peril', the golden
opportunity for Japan." North American review, New York,
179 (1904):641-47.

8093. Hishida, S. G. The international position of Japan as
a great power. Columbia university studies in history, economics and public law, 24, no. 3, New York, Macmillan,
1906. 284 p.

8094. Mutsu, Graf Hirokichi. "The diplomatic and consular
service of Japan." Transactions and proceedings of the Japan society, 7 (1907):434-457.

8095. Laubeuf, A. Naval supremacy, who? England or Germany?
America or Japan? London, S. Hill & Co., 1908.

8096. Revon, M. La politique étrangère du Japon contempo-
rain. Conférence à la Société des anciens élèves de l'École
libre des sciences politiques 10 mars 1909. Paris, Revue de
politique extérieure, 1909. 20 p.   Also in: Questions diplomatiques et coloniales, 27 (1909):446-466.

8097. Dyer, H. Japan in world politics: A study in international dynamics. London, Blackie and son, 1909. xiv, 425 p.

8098. Wilson, G. Grafton. "The family of nations idea and
Japan." Journal of race development, 2 (1911-1912):246-255.

8099. Nakatsuka, Yeiijiro. "The abandonment of consular
jurisdiction in Japan." The Japan magazine, 2 (1911-1912):
63-67, 134-139, 189-194.

8100. Miyaoka, T. Growth of internationalism in Japan. Report of Carnegie endowment for international peace 6. Washington, Carnegie endowment, 1915. 15 p.

8101. Veblen, Thorstein. "The opportunity of Japan." Journal of race development, 1915:23-28.

8102. "Japanische betrachtungen über die zukünftige politik Japans." Korrespondenzblatt der nachrichtenstelle für den Orient, Berlin, 2 (1915-1916):119-120.

8103. Alazard, J. La politique japonaise. Revue des nations latines. Vol. I. April 1, 1917.

8104. Pashkov, B. К характеристике отношений Японии к европейцам в период первого знакомства. (An analysis of the attitude of Japan toward the Europeans during the period of their first acquaintance.) Sbornik statei professorov i studentov Vostochnogo instituta, 1917. 22-25.

8105. Scharschmidt, Clemens. "Eine japanische kommission für auswärtige politik." Der neue Orient, Berlin, 2 (1917-1918):119-121.

8106. Osborne, Sidney. The problem of Japan. A political study of Japan and of her relations with Russia, Great Britain, China, Germany, the United States, the British Colonies, and the Netherlands, and of the world politics of the Far East and the Pacific, by an ex-counsellor of legation in the Far East. Amsterdam, Rotterdam, C. L. van Langenhuysen, 1918. 272 p.

8107. Kawakami, K. K. Japan in world politics. New York, Macmillan, 1917. xxvii, 300 p.   (2)   Japan and world peace. New York, Macmillan, 1919. xv, 196 p.   (3) The real Japanese question. London, Macmillan, 1922. 284 p.   (4) Le problème du pacifique et la politique japonaise. Paris, 1923.

8108. Coleman, F. A. Japan or Germany. New York, 1918. 232 p.

8109. Tsurumi, Y. "The difficulties and hopes of Japan." Foreign affairs, 3:2:253-265, December, 1924.

8110. Rittner, Erich. "Die japanische aussenpolitik." Zeitschrift für politik, 14 (1925):6:501-14.

8111. Matsushita, Masatoshi. Japan in the League of nations. Studies in history, economics and public law, No. 309.

New York, Columbia university press, 1929. 175 p.

8112. Terao, Sachio. 露支人ニ伍シテ Ro-Shi jin ni go-shite. (The Russians and the Chinese as our friends.) Tokyo, Hobunkan, 1926.

8113. See 8163.

8114. Osadake, Takeki. 近世日本國際觀念ノ發達 Kinsei Nippon no kokusai kannen no hattatsu. (The development of the international idea in Modern Japan.) Tokyo, Kyoritsusha, 1932.

8115. Ashida, Hitoshi. 近代世界外交問題解説 Kindai sekai gaiko mondai kaisetsu. (An explanation of diplomatic problems in the modern world.) Tokyo, Taimususha, 1932. 370 p.

8116. Shiga, Tetsuro. 列國ハ日本ヲドウ見ル Rekkoku wa Nippon o do miru. (As the Powers see Japan.) Tokyo, Meiji tosho shuppan kyokai, 1933. 350 p.

8117. Saito, Hiroshi. Japan's policies and purposes; selections from recent addresses and writings. Boston, Marshall Jones co., 1935. x, 231 p.

8118. Hindmarsh, Albert E. The basis of Japanese foreign policy. Cambridge, Harvard university press, 1936. viii, 265 p.

8119. Korovin, E. A. Япония и международное право. (Japan and international law.) Moscow, 1936. 246 p.

8120. Tsuboi, Kumazo. 最近政治外交史 Saikin seiji gaiko-shi. (History of politics and diplomacy of the present day.) Tokyo, Fuzanbo, 1932. 4 v.

8121. Ohira, Shinichi. 日本外交論 Nippor gaiko ron. (On the diplomacy of Japan.) Gaiko jino, 81:5:210-221, March, 1937.

8122. Causton, Eric Edward Nicholson. Militarism and foreign policy in Japan. London, G. Allen & Unwin, ltd., 1936. 207 p.

(3) History to 1931

8123. Hattori, Tooru. 日韓交通史 Nichi-kan kotsu-shi. (History of relations between Japan and Korea.) 1895.

8124. Schurhammer, G. "Die erste japanische gesandtschafts-reise nach Europa (1582-1590)." Katholische missionen, 49 (1920-1921):217-224.

8125. Tsuda, Noritake. "The foreign policy of Iyeyasu." The Japan magazine, 3 (1912-1913):561-567.

8126. Kuiper, Feenstra J. "Some notes on the foreign relations of Japan in the early Napoleonic period (1798-1805)." Transactions of the Asiatic society of Japan, 1 (1924):55-82. (Second series.)

8127. Oyamada, S. "Un précurseur de l'ouverture du Japon aux étrangers:Kwazan Watanabe." Bulletin de la Société franco-japonaise, 55-57:19-25, January - September, 1923.

8128. Satow, E. M. Diary of (Ichikawa Wataru) a member of the Japanese embassy to Europe in 1862-1863. (Chinese and Japanese repository, vol. 3, pp. 305-312, 361-363, 425-437, 465-472, 521-528, and 569-576.) London, 1865. (Unfinished, as the publication of the "Repository" stopped in December, 1865.)

8129. Kurino, S. "Le Japon dans ses rapports avec les puissences occidentales." Revue d'histoire diplomatique, Paris, 13:3:335-344. 1899.

8130. Ito, Marquis H. Marquis H. Ito's experiences. English translation by T. Kuramata. New edition. Nagasaki, 1904. 149 p.

8131. Kijima, Kozo. "Pages de l'histoire diplomatique du Japon. Revue de droit international et de législation comparee. 2 serie. 9(1907):550-569; 11(1909):578-587, 661-678; 12 (1910):160-168.

8132. Mohr, F. W. "Japan und die geschichte der grossmachts konstellationen." Gegenwart, 72 (1907):32.

8133. G., Vicomte E. de. "La politique extérieure du Japon depuis 1895." Questions diplomatiques et coloniales, 25 (1908):141-158.

8134. "Exposé du baron Komura sur la politique extérieure du Japon. Budget: Situation économique du Japon en 1908." Archives diplomatiques, 109 (1909):1:352-359.

8135. Guichen, Vicomte de. "La politique extérieure du Japon depuis quinze ans." Revue d'histoire diplomatique, Jan.1909

8136. Dillon, E. J. "Dual alliance for the Far East." Contemporary review, 107-119, July, 1910.

8137. Challaye, Félicien. "La politique extérieure du Japon moderne." Revue du mois, Nov. 10, 1910. 597-620.

8138. McLaren, W. W. Japan's foreign relations prior to 1911. Washington, 1922.

8139. Ular, A. "Von Ito zu Katsura. (Neueste japanische politik)." Die zeitschrift, 2 (1911-1912):673-678.

8140. Rivetta, Pietro Silvio. "Jutaro Komura (1855-1911)." Nuova antologia, February 1, 1912.

8141. Krüger, K. "Japanische bündnispolitik." Asien, 14 (1916-1917):214-221.

8142. Mackay, F. von. "Japans grosse täuschung." Der neue Orient, 2 (1917-1918):554-556.

8143. Jacob, Gustav. "Japanische ausnutzung der kriegskonjunktur in Lateinamerika." Mitteilungen der ibero-amerikanischen gesellschaft, 1 (1918):14:471-480.

8144. Satow, Sir Ernest Mason. A diplomat in Japan. London, Seeley, Service and co., 1921. 427 p.

8145. Mueller, Herbert. "Japan auf der friedenskonferenz. Territoriale amsprüche und 'race discrimination'." Der neue Orient, Berlin, 5 (1919):149-152.

8146. Sauter, J. A. Die isolierung Japans. Charlottenburg, 1919.

8147. Mackay, F. v. "Japanische weltkriegspolitik." Asien, Berlin, 14 (1916-1917):41-44, 64-67.

8148. Osborne, Sidney. The isolation of Japan, an exposé of Japan's political position after the war. Amsterdam-Rotterterdam, C. L. van Langenhuysen, 1919. 150 p. Translated into German, Die isolierung Japans. Eine darstellung der politischen lage Japans nach dem kriege. Berlin - Charlottenburg, Deutsche verlagsgesellschaft für politik und geschichte, 1919. xi, 158 p.

8149. Pooley, A. M. Japan's foreign policy. London, G. Allen & Unwin, ltd., 1920. 202 p. (2) The same. Japan at the crossroads. London, Allen & Unwin, 1920. 102 p.

8150. Hartwig, A. "Die isolierung Japans." Deutsche rundschau, October, 1921.

8151. Mohr, F. W. "Die räumung Ostsibiriens und Shantungs
durch Japan." Deutsche nation, 5 (1923):1:16-21.

8152. Tchang, Tchiao. "La situation politique du Japon dans
le monde avant et après l'abolition de l'alliance anglo-
japonaise." La Chine et le Monde, Paris, 1 (1925):1.

8153. Ostwald, Paul. "Die japanische politik seit dem weltkriege." Zeitschrift für geopolitik. 3 (1926):916-924.

8154. 長春事情 Chosun jijo. (State of affairs in
Changchun.) Department of foreign affairs, Bureau of commercial affairs, 1929.

8155. Mutsuoku, Munemitsu. 蹇々録外交秘史 Kenken-
roku gaiko hishi. (My humble records of the secret diplomatic history of Japan.) Osaka, Ichiya Koyabu, 1933. 219 p.

(4) Recent Japanese Foreign Policy, 1931 -

See 3198-3695; 5805-6200.

8156. Yueh-fu. 第二次世界大戰與日帝國主義戰爭
準備 Ti-êrh-tzu shih-chieh ta-chan yü Jih ti-kuo-chu-i
chan-chêng chun-pei. (The second world war and the Japanese
imperialistic war preparations.) Japan study monthly, 2:1:
September, 1931.

8157. Fujimoto, Naonori. 我が國三國回答 Waga kuni
san-koku kaito. (The response of Japan to the three countries.) Tokyo, Asahi news, December 29, 1931.

8158. Miura, Etsuro. 極東新時局 Kyokuto shin-jikyoku.
(The new crisis of the Far East.) Tokyo, Nitto book store,
1932.

8159. Ching-tzu. 對抗世界之日本外交 Tui-k'ang
shih-chieh chih Jih-pên wai-chiao. (The anti-world Japanese
diplomacy.) Kuo-wên chou-pao, 9: 15, April 1932.

8160. Moriguchi, Shigeharu. 國際聯盟ト日支問題 Ko-
kusai renmei to Nichi-Shi mondai. (The League of nations and
the Sino-Japanese controversy.) Osaka, Osaka asahi, April,
13, 1932.   See 5907-6029.

8161. Kamikawa, Hikomatsu. 十字路ニ立ツ日本外交

Jujiro ni tatsu Nippon gaiko. (Japanese diplomacy at the
crossroads.) Bungei shunju, 10:4: April, 1932.

8162. Machida, Shiro. 孤立日本ノ解剖 Koritsu Nippon
no kaibo. (Detailed discussion on the isolated position of
Japan.) Chuo koron, 47:4:197-204, April, 1932.

8163. Ashida, Hitoshi. 日本外交ノ功罪 Nippon gaiko
no kozai. (The success and the failure of Japanese diplomacy.) Chuo koron, 47:5:236-243, May, 1932.

8164. Matsumoto, Tadao. 民政党ノ外交方針ノ教術シテ
Minseito no gaiko hoshin wo shiki-en shite. (Expounding the
foreign policy of the Minseito party.) Gaiko jiho, 63:3:
189-199, August 1, 1932.

8165. Saito, Prime minister of Japan. 難局ノ打開セン
Nankyoku wo dakai sen. (We shall surmount the difficult situation.) Osaka, Osaka asahi (daily), August 26, 1932.

8166. Fujita, Shinichiro. 新満洲国ト巴奈馬 Shin
Manshukoku to Panama. (New Manchukuo and Panama.) Gaiko
jiho, 63:5:147-156, September 1, 1932.

8167. Komai, Tokuzo. 東洋平和ノ為ニ日本国民ニ訴フ
Toyo heiwa no tame ni Nippon kokumin ni utto. (An appeal to
the Japanese people for the sake of the peace of the Far
East.) Jitsugyo no Nippon, September 1, 1932.

8168. Izumi, Tetsu. 日支紛争ト類似ノ二事件
Nichi-shi funso to ruiji no ni -jiken. (Two cases similar to
the Sino-Japanese dispute.) Gaiko jiho, 63:6:92-104, September 15, 1932.

8169. Honjo, Shigeru. (Commanding general of the Kwantung
army.) 東洋平和ノ礎石成ル Toyo heiwa no kiseki
naru. (The completion of the foundation of Far Eastern
peace.) Osaka, Osaka asahi, September 18, 1932.

8170. Suehiro, Dr. 満蒙承認ト国際孤立
Man-Mo shonin to kokusai koritsu. (Recognition of Manchuria
and Mongolia and the international isolation of Japan.)
Gaiko jiho, Special number, October 3, 1932.

8171. Hanzawa, Gyokujo. 満洲承認後ノ日本外交史
Manshu shonin go no Nippon gaiko-shi. (History of the diplomacy of Japan since the recognition of Manchukuo.) Gaiko
jiho, Special number on Manchurian recognition, October 3,
1932.

8172. Yoshizawa, Kenkichi. 現下内外危局ニ對スル 感想 Genka naigai kikyoku ni taisuru kanso. (My impressions of the present crisis at home and abroad.) Chuo koron, 23:10, October, 1932.

8173. Ashida, Hitoshi. 極東ノロカルノノ提唱 Kyokuto no Locarno no teisho. (A proposal for a Far Eastern Locarno pact.) Gaiko jiho, 64:4:27-33, November 15, 1932.

8174. 日本若シ孤立セバ Nippon moshi koritsu seba. (If Japan should be isolated diplomatically.) Yuben, 23:12, December, 1932.

8175. Inehara, Katsuji. 清算期ニアル日本ノ外交 Seisan-ki ni aru Nippon no gaiko. (Japanese diplomacy in its liquidation period.) Tokyo, Daijosha, 1932. 250 p.

8176. Maida, Minoru. 外交ハドウナル Gaiko wa do naru. (What will become of the diplomacy of Japan?) Tokyo, Gendai, 1932.

8177. The re-orientation of Japan's foreign policy. Since the Washington conference. Foreign policy assosiation (New York), 6 (1932):16.

8178. 荒木陸相時局談 Araki rikusho jikyoku dan. (Talks on the present situation by the War minister Araki.) Tokyo, Shinbun no shinbunsha staff, Seika shobo, 1932. 47 p.

8179. Mori, Kiyoto. 人間松岡ノ全貌 Ningen Matsuoka no zenbo. (Yosuke Matsuoka, the man.) Tokyo, Jitsugyo no Nipponsha, 1932. 300 p.

8180. Ishii, Kikujiro. "The permanent bases of Japanese foreign policy." Foreign affairs, 11:2:220-230, January, 1933.

8181. Azuma, Toichi. 経済封鎖ト日本前途及列強細部事情 Keizai fusa to Nippon no zento oyobi rekkyo no saibu jijo. (Economic blockade and Japan's future, with detail information on the powers.) Tokyo, Taguchi shoten, 1933.

8182. Kokushi, Gohichi. 日露戦争ヲ顧ミテ國民ノ反省ヲ促ス Nichi-Ro senso o kaerimite kokumin no hansei o unagasu. (Recalling the Russo-Japanese war and urging the reconsideration of the people.) Tokyo, Shina jihen shoi gunjin koenkai, 1933. 124 p.

8183. Inehara, Katsuji. 清算期ニアル日本ノ外交 Seisan-ki ni aru Nippon no gaiko. (The liquidation stage of Japanese diplomacy.) Tokyo, Akira Ozama, 1933.   See: 8175.

8184. Zhukov, E. "Японские теории империалистических захватов. Обзор японской литературы." (Japanese theories of imperialist seizure. A survey of Japanese literature.) Bolshevik, 13-14:129-138, July 1934.

8185. Matsuoka, Yosuke. 聯盟ニ使シテ Renmei ni tsukaishite. (As a delegate to the League of nations.) Tokyo, Shakai kyoiku kyokai, 1934. 40 p.

8186. Hayashi, Masayoshi. 我が非常時外交 Waga hijoji gaiko. (Our diplomacy during the critical period.) Tokyo, Sozosha, 1934. 122 p.

8187. Wada, Toshihiko. 聯盟脱退後ノ日本 Renmei dattai go no Nippon. (Japan after her withdrawal from the League of nations.) Tokyo, Nippon hoso shuppan kyokai, 1934. 133 p.

8188. Sugimura, Yotaro. 國際外交錄 Kokusai gaiko roku. (Memoirs of international diplomacy.) Tokyo, Chuokoronsha, 1934. 508 p.

8189. Aoki, Setsuichi. 日本脱退ノ前後 Nippon dattai no zengo. (The before and aftermath of Japan's withdrawal from the League.) Osaka, Asahi shinbun, 1935. 258 p.

8190. Kishima, Momotaka. 廣田外交ノ対外反響 Hirota gaiko no taigai hankyo. (Foreign reverberation of Hirota diplomacy.) Tokyo, Toryukaku, 1935. 64 p.

8191. Ezaki, Toshio. 北洋日本ノ危機 Hokuyo Nippon no kiki. (Japan's crisis in the northern waters.) Tokyo, Kokusai keizai shinposha, 1935. 207 p.

8192. Ishii, Kikujiro. "Japan and the Franco-Russian rapprochement." Contemporary Japan, 624-635, March 1935.

8193. Yoshitomi, Masanori. 轉換期ノ日本ノ外交 Tenkanki no Nippon no gaiko. (The turning point in the diplomacy of Japan.) Gaiko jiho, 76:4: 76:6: 1-11; 70-89, November, December, 1935.

8194. Inehara, Katsuji. 現代外交ノ動キ Gendai gaiko no ugoki. (The trend of recent diplomacy.) Tokyo, Fukuda shobo, 1936. 503 p.

taykui, 1936. 27 p.

8196. Kishima, Momotaka. 外交智識 Gaiko chishiki. (Diplomatic knowledge.) Tokyo, Kokusai keizai kenkyusho, 1936. 184 p.

8197. Chang, Hsiu-che. 國民政府外交及外交行政 Kokumin-seifu no gaiko oyobi gaiko gyosei. (Foreign diplomacy of the Nationalist government and its administration.) Tokyo, Nichi-Shi mondai kenkyukai, 1936. 438 p. See 3109.

8198. 圖録日本外交大觀 Zuroku Nippon gaiko taikan. (A comprehensive review of Japanese diplomacy with photo-illustrations of clippings and other documents.) Tokyo, Asahi shinbunsha, 1936. 260 p.

8199. Itani, Zenichi. 外交革新,経済的基礎 Gaiko kakushin no keizai teki kiso. (Economic fundamentals of diplomatic reform.) Gaiko jiho, 78:2:23-46, April 1936.

8200. Suehiro, Shigeo. 日獨提攜可能ナリヤ Nichi-Doku teikei kano nariya. (The possibility of a Japan-German alliance.) Gaiko jiho, 78:4:44-56, May 1936.

8201. Okamoto, Tsuramatsu. 同盟ノ進化ト日英米ノ親善 Domei no shinka to Nichi-Ei-Bei no shinzen. (The development of alliance: amity between Japan, England and the United States.) Gaiko jiho, 79:5:81-89, September 1936.

8202. Matsumoto, Tadao. 大日本外交文書,續刊 Dai Nippon gaiko bunsho no zokkan. (Continuous edition of the diplomatic documents of Japan.) Gaiko jiho, 80:4:215-216, November 1936.

8203. "Берлинский сговор главных зачинщиков войны." (Berlin agreement of the chief instigators of war.) [Agreement between Germany and Japan.] Kommunisticheskii internatsional, 18:3-11, December 1936.

8204. Yamaji, Akira. 日獨新協定ノ意義ト効用 Nichi-Doku shin-kyotei no igi to koyo. (The significance and effectiveness of the new Japan-German anti-communist pact.) Gaiko jiho, 80:6:197-205, December 1936.

8205. Naomi, Zenzo. 日獨日伊新協定ノ意義ト効用 Nichi-Doku Nichi-I shin-kyotei no igi to koyo. (Significance and effectiveness of the Japan-German and Japan-Italy

anti-communist pact.) Gaiko jiho, 80:6:147-165, December
1936.

8206. Lemin, I. "Японо-германское соглашение." (Japanese-
German agreement.) 1:11-26, January 1937.

8207. Nakamura, Tsunezo. 日獨伊ノ接近ト日支交渉ノ決裂
Nichi-Doku-I no sekkin to Nichi-Shi kosho no ketsuretsu.
(Closer relationship betwee Japan, Germany and Italy and
the rupture of the Sino-Japanese negotiations.) Gaiko jiho,
81:1:106-117, January 1937.

8208. Kamikawa, Hikomatsu. 日獨協定ノ本質ト其ノ特異性
Nichi-Doku kyotei no honshitsu to sono tokuisei. (Essentials of the German-Japanese anti-communist pact and its
singularity.) Gaiko jiho, 81:1:4051, January 1937.

8209. Nakayasu, Yosaku. 亜細亜ノ嵐ト日獨協定
Ajia no arashi to Nichi-Doku kyotei. (The storm in Asia and
the Japan-Germany anti-communist pact.) Gaiko jiho,' 81:1:
300-317, January 1937.

8210. Suehiro, Shigeo. 秘密外交失敗ノ教訓 Himitsu
gaiko shippai no kyokun. (Teachings from the failures of
secret diplomacy.) Gaiko jiho, 81:2:44-54, January 1937.

8211. Matsunami, Jinichiro. 日獨防共協定ト日本皇道
Nichi-Doku bokyo kyotei to Nippon kodo. (The Japan-Germany
anti-communist pact and the national doctrines of Japan.)
Gaiko jiho, 81:2:110-133, January 1937.

8212. Hayashi, Masayoshi. 日獨協定ニ対スル厳正批判
Nichi-Doku kyotei ni taisuru gensei hihan. (Unsparing criticism of the Japan-Germany anti-communist pact.) Gaiko jiho,
82:2:363-392, January 1937.

8213. Kusuyama, Gitaro. 日獨防共協定ト英國ノ去就
Nichi-Doku bokyo kyotei to Eikoku no kyoshu. (Japan-Germany
anti-communist pact and the course of Great Britain's actions.) Gaiko jiho, 81:1:52-63, January 1937.

8214. Borisov, A. "Японо-германское соглашение. Обзор."
(Japanese-German agreement. A review.) Tikhii Okean, 1:11:
102-113, January-March 1937.

8215. Kishida, Eiji. 満洲國ト日獨日伊兩協定
Manshukoku to Nichi-Doku Nichi-I ryo-kyotei. (Manchukuo and
its relation to the Japan-Germanyand the Japan-Italy anti-
communist pacts.) Gaiko jiho, 81:5:26-49, March 1937.

8216. Muto, Teiichi. 林内閣ニ望ム外交國策
Hayashi naikaku ni nozomu gaiko kokusaku. (The national
diplomatic policy desired by the Hayashi cabinet.) Gaiko
jiho, 81:5:70-88, March 1937.

8217. Kaneu, Kizo. 林内閣ノ外交綱領 Hayashi
naikaku no gaiko koryo. (Diplomatic principles of the
Hayashi cabinet.) Gaiko jiho, 81:5: 88-97, March, 1937.

8218. Ida, Baron Iwakusu. "The meaning of the Japan-German
pact." Contemporary Japan, 5:4:519-527, March 1937.

3219. Tashiro, Shigenori. 帝國外交ノ動向 Teikoku
gaiko no doko. (The trend of Japanese diplomacy.) Gaiko
jiho, 82:1:11-16, April 1937.

8220 Tachi, Sakutaro. 國際法外交史ト日獨防共
協定　Kokusaiho gaiko-shi to Nichi-Doku bokyo
kyotei. (The Japan-Germany anti-communist pact from the
point of view of diplomatic history and international law.)
Gaiko jiho, 83:3: 1-27, August 1937.

8221. Fujisawa, Michio. 日獨防共協定ト思想國策
Nichi-Doku bokyo kyotei to shiso kokusaku. (The German-
Japanese anti-communist pact and the national policy regu-
lated therein.) Gaiko jiho, 83:6:60'68, September 1937.
(2) The same. "Imperial message." Tokyo gazette, 3: 1,
September, 1937. (3) The same. "Documents concerning
the Brussels conference." Tокyo gazette, 5:9-18, November 1937. (4) The same. "The pact against the Comintern." Tokyo gazette, 6: 14-19, December 1937.

8222. Два очага войны. Германия и Япония. Сборник статей.
(Two hotbeds of war. Germany and Japan. Collection of
articles.) Leningrad, 1937. 180 p.

8223. Chamberlin, William Henry. Japan over Asia. Boston,
Little, Brown & co., 1937. 395 p.

8224. Borisov, A. Японо-германское соглашение. Очаг войны
на Востоке. (The German-Japanese agreement. The hotbed of
war in the East.) Moscow, Sotsekgiz, 1937. 103 p.   (2)
Korovin, Evgenii Aleksandrovich. Япония и международное
право. (Japan and international law.) Moscow, Gosudarstvennoe sotsialno-ekonomicheskoe izdatelstvo, 1936. 246 p. See
8119.

XIII. POLITICS AND POLITICAL DEVELOPMENT

See 7502-7836; 7992-8043; 9706-9796.

A. Periodicals

See 7509-7517.

8225. 國家學會雜誌. Kokka gakkai zasshi. (Political science magazine.) Tokyo, Kokka gakkai kyokai (Society for the investigation of political science), 1, 1887-

B. General Accounts

See 7522-7836.

8226. Konakamura, Kiyonori. 官制沿革略史 Kansei enka-ku ryaku-shi. (A brief history of the origin and development of governmental organization in Japan.) 1900. 3 v.

8227. Ariga, N. L'idée de souveraineté dans l'histoire du Japon. Compte rendu du I-er Congrès International des études d'Extrême-Orient à Hanoi, 1902. 1 (1903):52-55.

8228. Kawakami, K. K. The political ideas of modern Japan. Iowa City, 1903. 208 p. (Forms volume of the "Studies in Sociology, economics, politics and history." Bulletin of the State university of Iowa.)

8229. Gollier, T. Essai sur les institutions politiques du Japon. Bruxelles, 1903. 208 p.

8230. Spal'vin, E. G. Обзор политического устройства Японии в прошлом и настоящем. (A survey of the political organization of Japan in the past and present.) Part 1. Vladivostok, 1910. ix, 200 p. Part 2, Vladivostok, 1911. viii, 130 p.

8231. Uyehara, G. Etsujiro. The political development of Japan 1867-1909. Studies in economics and political science, edited by the Director of the London school of economics and political science, No. 19. London, Constable & co., 1910. xxiv, 296 p.

8232. Petrov, Arkadii. Политическая жизнь Японии. (Political life of Japan.) St. Petersburg, Obshchestvo revnitelei znanii, 1910. 92 p.

8233. McLaren, W. W. "The political development of Japan." Transactions of the Asiatic society of Japan, 52 (1914):

2:782-806.

8234. Vinkhuyzen van Maarssen, W. Le Japon. Son ancien régime féodal, son développement en état constitutionnel et l'ouverture de ses ports au commerce universel. Amsterdam, 1918.

8235. Haas, H. Japan. Handbuch der staatengeschichte, Ausland, abteilung 2: Asien- Afrika. Berlin, 1922.

8236. Fujisawa, Rikiharo. Recent aims and political development of Japan. London, Milford, 1923. 222 p. New Haven, Yale university press, 233 p.

8237. Überschaar, J. Die eigenart der japanischen staatskultur. Eine einführung in das denken der Japaner. Leipzig, Th. Weicher, 1925. viii, 108 p.

8238. Pletner, O. Япония. Политические очерки. (Japan. Political sketches.) Moscow, Razvedochnoe upravlenie shtaba R. K. K. A., 1924. viii, 111 p.

8239. Kuroita, Katsumi. 國 体 新 論 Kokutai shinron. (New treatise on the fundamentals of national organization.) Tokyo, Hakubundo, 1925. 272 p.

8240. Satomi, Kishio. 日 本 國 体 概 論 Nippon kokutai gairon. (An introduction to the national organization of Japan.) Hyogo, Satomi Kenkyusho, 1929. 380 p.

8241. Nagai, Kyo. 日 本 國 体 論 Nippon kokutai ron. (A treatise on the national organization of Japan.) Tokyo, Nippon hyoronsha, 1929. 286 p.

8242. Suzuki, Tomokichi. 我 が 國 体 ト 國 民 精 神 Waga kokutai to kokumin seishin. (The unique national structure of Japan and its effect on the national spirit.) Tokyo, Kobundo, 1929. 438 p.

8243. Kitazawa, Naokichi. The government of Japan. Edited with an introduction by William Starr Myers. Princeton, Princeton university press, 1929. 130 p.

8244. Quigley, Harold Scott. Japanese government and politics. New York, Century, 1932. 454 p.

8245. Chun-i. 日 本 的 对 内 宣 傳 Jih-pên ti tui-nei hsuan-chuan. (Japan's internal propaganda.) Shêng-huo chou-Kan. 7:5, February 1932.

8246. Wu, Hsiao-hou (translator). 日本之農村都市
Jih-pên chih nung-tsun tu-shih. (Japanese rural municipal-
ities.) Shanghai, Ta-tung-shu-chü, 1932?

8247. Yamada, Takao. 國体ノ本義 Kokutai no hongi. (Essence of the national organization of Japan.) Tokyo, Hobunkan, 1932. 304 p.

8248. Sato, Kiyokatsu. 大日本政治思想史 Dai Nippon
seiji shiso-shi. (History of Japanese political thought.)
Tokyo, To-A jikyoku kenkyukai, 1935. 835 p.

8249. Kojima, Tokuya. 明治以前大事件ノ真相ト判例
Meiji izen daijiken no shinso to hanrei. (True facts and
judicial precedents on the great incidents [assasinations]
which occurred before the Meiji era.) Tokyo, Kyobunsha,
1935. 857 p.

8250. Ito, Chimazo. 日本國体論 Nippon kokutai ron.
(On the fundamentals of the national organization of Japan.)
Tokyo, Toyo shoin, 1936. 312 p.

8251. Moriyoshi, Yoshiakira. 我國体ト人種民族國民性
Waga kokutai to jinshu minzoku kokumin-sei. (Fundamentals
of the national organization of Japan -- racial and national characteristics.) Gaiko jiho, 81:4:65-92, February 1937.

8252. Watanabe, Hachiro. 國体ト教育 Kokutai to kyoiku.
(Fundamental organization of Japan and education.) Tokyo,
Shunyodo shoten, 1937.

8253. Kakehi, Katsuhiko. 國家ノ研究 Kokka no kenkyu.
(Research in the Japanese state.) Tokyo, Shunyodo shoten,
1937.

8254. Watanabe, Hachiro. 皇國体ノ大義 Kokokutai no
taigi. (Essence of the fundamental organization of imperial
Japan.) Tokyo, Shunyodo shoten 1937.

C. The Feudal Background

See 7542-7666.

8255. Rai, Sanyo. 日本外史 Nippon gaishi. (History of
Japan.) Latest edition. Tokyo, Dai Nippon bunko kankokai,
1938. 2 v. Russian translation by V. M. Mendrin. История
сиогуната в Японии. (The history of the shogunate in Japan.)
With notes and commentary. Vladivostok, 1910-1916. 6 books.

8256. Nikolai (Ordained monk). "Сеогуны и микадо. Истори́че-ский очерк по японским источникам." (The Shoguns and the Em-peror. Historical sketch from Japanese sources.) Russkii vestnik, 84 (1869): 11 and 12, 207-227 and 415-460.

8257. Hall, J. C. (Translator.) "Japanese feudal laws." Asiatic society of Japan. Transactions, 34 (1906)1:1-44; 36 (1908):2:1-23;   38 (1910):4:269-321;   41 (1913):683-804.

8258. 戰 國 時 代 史 論 Sengoku jidai-shi ron. (Histor-ical treatises on the feudal period.) Tokyo, Rekishi chiri gakkai, 1910. 382 p.

8259. Asakawa, Kanichi. "Some of the contributions of feud-al Japan to the new Japan." Journal of race development, 3 (1912-1913):1-32.   (2) The same. "Some aspects of Japanese feudal institutions." Transactions of the Asiatic society of Japan, 46 (1918):1:77-102.

8260. Mendrin, V. M. "К истории сиогуната в Японии."   (On the history of the shogunate in Japan.) Vestnik Azii, 4 (1910):163-178.(2)The same. Сиогун и сейи тай-сиогун. Бакуфу. (Shogun and sei-i tai shogun. Bakufu.) Linguistical historical sketches. Izvestiia Vostochnogo instituta, Vla-divostok, 11 (1916):1. 198 p.

8261. Lange, R. "Die zahl der japanischen lehnfürsten im jahre 1869." Mitteilungen des seminars für orientalische sprachen zu Berlin. 14 (1911):1:354-368.   (2) The same. "Die lehnfürsten nach der schlacht von Sekigahara." Mit-teilungen des seminars für orientalische sprachen zu Ber-lin, 15 (1912):1:184-196.

8262. Hara, Katsuro. 日 本 中 世 史 / 研 究 Nippon chusei shi no kenkyu. (A study of the middle ages of Japan.) Tokyo, Dobunkan, 1929. 1088 p.

8263. 安 土 桃 山 時 代 史 論 Azuchi Momoyama jidai-shi ron. (Historical treatise: the Azuchi and Momoyama period.) To-kyo, Rekishi chiri gakkai, 1916. 440 p.

8264. Nakamura, Koya. 封 建 制 度 論 Hoken seido ron. (On the feudal system.) Kokka oyobi kokkagaku, 4 (1916):12; 5 (1917):1.

8265. Wainwright, S. H. "Japan's transition from the rule of persons to the rule of law." Transactions of the Asiatic society of Japan, 47 (1919):155-171.

8266. Tokimoto, Seiichi. 德川 時代, 封建制度
Tokugawa jidai no hoken seido. (Feudalistic system of the
Tokugawa period.) Seijigaku keizaigaku ronso, 1:1, 2 (1919).

8267. Tsuji, Zennosuke. 武家政治論, 一節 Buke seiji
ron no issetsu. (A chapter on the military rule.) Chuo shidan, 1 (1920):1.

8268. Konrad, N. I. "Вопросы японского феодализма." (Questions concerning Japanese feudalism.) Novyi vostok, 4 (1923):
348-364.

8269. Arai, Hakuseki. 藩翰譜 Hankenfu. (History of feudal families in the Tokugawa period.) Tokyo, Yoshikawa kobunkan, 1925. 12 books in 2 vols. 595, 1216 p.

8270. Akiyama, Kenzo. 日本中世史 Nippon chusei shi. (A
history of the middle ages of Japan.)

8271. Tsuchiya, Takao. 封建社會崩壊過程, 研究
Hoken shakai hokai katei no kenkyu. (A study of the process
of the breakdown of feudalistic society in Japan.) Kyoto,
Kobundo, 1927. 729 p.

8272. Omori, Kingoro. 日本中世史論考 Nippon chusei
shi ronko. (A treatise on the middle ages of Japan.) Tokyo,
1928. (2) The same. 武家時代, 研究 Buke jidai no
kenkyu. (The age of the military.) Tokyo, 1927-1929. 2 vols.

8273. Pletner, O. "К изучению японского феодализма."(The
study of Japanese feudalism.) Agrarnye problemy (Moscow),
1929, 2, 176-188.

8274. Asakawa, Kanichi. The documents of Iriki, illustrative
of the development of the feudal institutions of Japan. New
Haven, Yale university press, 1929. xvi, 442, 134 p.

8275. Slósarczyk, Antoni. "Podstawy sztuki wojennej w dawnej
Japonij." (The bases of military art in old Japan.) Bellona,
44 (1934):64-89.

8276. Zimmermann, Herbert. Politische erziehung der militär-
klasse (Samurai) in Japan zur feudalzeit. Würzburg, Triltsch
1935. 81 p.

8277. Maki, Kenji. 日本封建制度成立史 Nippon ho-
ken seido seiritsu- shi. (History of the formation of the
feudal system in Japan.) Tokyo, Kobundo, 1935. 537 p.

D. The Emperor and the Imperial Family

8278. Fukuzawa, Yukichi. 日本皇室論 Nippon koshitsu-ron. (A treatise on the imperial family of Japan.) Tokyo, Jiji shimposha, 1936. 136 p.

8279. Griffis, W. E. The Mikado: institution and person; a study of the internal political forces of Japan. Princeton, Princeton university press, 1915. 8, 346 p.

8280. Oikawa, Giemon. 皇室ト文化 Koshitsu to bunka. (The imperial family and culture.) Tokyo, Chubunkan, 1930.

8281. Endo, Ryukichi. 勅語ト國家及社會 Chokugo to kokka oyobi shakai. (The imperial rescripts and their effect upon the nation and society.) Tokyo, Taizambo, 1930. 258 p.

8282. Nakano, Tomio. The ordinance power of the Japanese emperor. Johns Hopkins university studies in historical and political sciences, extra volumes, new series, no. 2. Baltimore, 1923. xviii, 269 p.

8283. Überschaar, J. Die stellung des kaisers in Japan. Eine staatsrechtlich-historische skizze. Inaugural-dissertation, Leipzig. Borna-Leipzig, R. Noske, 1912. viii, 89 p.

8284. Onzan. "The surviving genro." (Matsukata, Yamagata, Oyama, Inouye, Itagaki.) The Japan magazine, 3 (1912-1913): 473-476.

8285. Yamaguchi, M. "Japan and her constitutional emperor." The Far East, Tokyo, 11 (1897):589-596.

8286. Balfour, F. H. "Court and society in Tokyo." Transactions and proceedings, Japan society, 3 (1896):1-2:54-74 (London).

8287. Fujikashi, Junji. 皇室大観 Koshitsu taikan. (Directory of matters concerning the imperial family.) Osaka, Osaka mainichi shinbun, 1937. 500 p.

8288. Takasu, Yoshijiro. 水戸學派ノ尊皇及經倫 Mito gakuha no sonno oyobi keirin. (Reverence to the emperor and the administration of state affairs advocated by the scholars of the Mito faction.) Tokyo, Yuzankaku, 1937. 756 p.

E. Constitutional History and Law

8289. Kimura, Seiji. 憲法史料 Kenpo shiryo. (Materials

for the history of the Japanese constitution.) 1878. 37 v.

8290. Ito, Marquis Hirobumi. Commentaries on the constitution of the empire of Japan. English translation by Baron
M. Ito. 2nd edition. Tokyo, Chuo daigaku, 1906. 310 p.   (2)
Komatsu, Midori. 伊藤公全集 Ito ko zenshu. (A complete collection of works of Hirobumi Ito, the framer of the
Japanese constitution.) Tokyo, Showa shuppansha, 1929. 3
vols.   (3) Sato, Hanji. 偉人伊藤公ノ理想
Ijin Ito ko no riso. (The ideals of the great Ito, the framer of the Japanese constitution.) Tokyo, Nanosha, 1929.
118 p.   (4) Ito, Hirobumi (Hakubun). 憲法資料 Kenpo
shiryo. (Source materials on the constitution of Japan.)
Tokyo, Kenpo shiryo kankokai, 1935. 3 v.

8291. Arimori, Sinkiti. Das staatsrecht von Japan. (Inauguraldissertation der staats- und rechtwissenschaftlichen
facultät). Strassburg im Elsass, 1892.

8292. Nosawa, T. Étude sur la constitution du Japon. (Dissertation inaugurale). Genève, 1895. 188 p. (Reissued in
Paris in 1896.)

8293. Clement, E. W. "Constitutional government of Japan."
Annals of the American academy of political science, Philadelphia, 21:209-221, March 1903.

8294. Iyenaga, T. Constitutional development of Japan. Baltimore, The Johns Hopkins press, 1891. 56 p.

8295. Kobayashi, T. Die japanische verfassung, vergleichen
mit ihren europäischen vorbildern. (Inaugural dissertation).
Rostock, 1902. 121 p.

8296. Inada, Shunosuke. 日本憲法論 Nippon kenpo ron. (A
treatise on the constitution of Japan.) Tokyo, Yuhikaku,
1912.

8297. Überschaar, J. "Preussisches und japanisches verfassungsrecht. Ein kulturgeschichtlicher beitrag zu dem thema
'Rezeptionen und renaissancen'." Mitteilungen der deutschen
gesellschaft für natur- und völkerkunde Ostasiens, Tokyo,
14 (1912):171-195.

8298. Okuma, Count. "The future of constitutional government in Japan." The Japan magazine, 3 (1912-1913):527-529.

8299. Kudo, Takeshige. 明治憲政史 Meiji kensei-shi.
(History of constitutionalism in the Meiji era, 1867-1912.)

Tokyo, Yuhikaku, 1914. 2 v.

8300. Uyesugi, S. Japanisches verfassungsrecht 1912-1922.
Jahrbuch des öffentlichen rechts. Bd. 12, 1925. 311 p.

8301. Miyaoka, T. "Treaty-making power under the constitution of Japan." International conciliation, Carnegie endowment, 221 (1926):297-309.

8302. Osadake, Takeki. 日本憲政史 Nippon kensei shi.
(Constitutional history of Japan.) Tokyo, Nippon hyoronsha,
1926.

8303. Takamatsu, T. Japan als konstitutionelle monarchie.
Kurze erläuterungen über die japanische kaiserreichs-verfas-
sung. Berlin, 1928.

8304. Otsu, Junichiro. 大日本憲政史 Dai Nippon kensei-
shi. (History of the constitutionalism of Japan.) Tokyo,
Hobunkan, 1927-1928. 10 v.

8305. Minobe, Tatsukichi. 逐條憲法精義 Chikujo
kenpo seigi. (Detailed commentary on the Japanese constitution.) Tokyo, Yuhikaku, 1929. 738 p.

8306. Kaneko, Kentaro. 明治大帝ト憲法制定 Meiji tai-
tei to kenpo seitei. (Emperor Meiji and the framing of the
constitution of Japan.) Tokyo, Seiji kyoikukai. 1929.

8307. Sasaki, Soichi. 日本憲法要論 Nippon kenpo
yoron. (Essentials of the Japanese constitution.) Tokyo,
Kinratsu shoten, 1930. See 8314.

8308. Kurata, Hanji. 聖徳太子憲法ト法王帝説
研究 Shotoku taishi kenpo to hoo teisetsu no kenkyu.
(A research in the contitution framed by the Imperial regent
Prince Shotoku and in the theory of the authority and the
throne of Japanese emperors.) Tokyo, Sankibo, 1930. 203 p.

8309. Kudo, Takeshige. 大正憲政史 Taisho kensei-shi.
(History of the constitutional government in Japan during
the Taisho era, 1912-1926.) Tokyo, Okano shogakukai, 1931.
436 p.

8310. Sasaki, Soichi. 日本憲法論 Nippon kenpo ron. (A
treatise on the constitution of Japan.) Tokyo, Kinratsu horyudo, 1931. 701 p.

8311. Fujii, Jintaro. 日本憲法制定史 Nippon kenpo

seitei-shi. (History of the framing of the Japanese constitution.) Tokyo, Yuzankaku, 1931.

8312. Kato, Genchi. 日本人ノ國体信念 Nipponjin no kokutai shinnen. (Belief of the Japanese people in the national constitution.) Tokyo, Bunrokusha, 1932. 100 p.

8313. Asai, Kiyoshi. 日本憲法講話 Nippon kenpo kowa. (Lectures on the imperial constitution.) Tokyo, Shunjusha, 1934. 245 p.

8314. Sasaki, Soichi. 日本憲法要論 Nippon kenpo yoron. (On the principles of the imperial constitution.) Tokyo, Kanasashi horyudo, 1934. 708 p. See 8307.

8315. Takeuchi, Osamu. 憲法原論 Kenpo genron. (Principles of the constitution.) Tokyo, Meiji daigaku, 1935. 550p.

8316. Suzuki, Yasuzo. 憲法ノ歴史的研究 Kenpo no rekishi teki kenkyu. (Historical studies on the constitution.) Tokyo, Sobunkaku, 1935. 487 p.

8317. Suzuki, Yasuzo. 日本憲法学ノ生誕ト發展 Nippon kenpo-gaku no seitan to hatten. (Origin of the study of Japanese constitutional law and its development.) Tokyo, Sobunkaku, 1935. 234 p.

8318. Fujii, Shinichi. 日本比較憲法論 Nippon hikaku kenpo ron. (A treatise on the comparative constitutional law of Japan.) Tokyo, Yuseido, 1935. 395 p.

8319. Kanamori, Tokujiro. 帝國憲法要綱 Teikoku kenpo yoko. (Principles of the imperial constitution.) Tokyo, Ganshodo, 1935. 343 p.

8320. Tabata, Shinobu. 帝國憲法逐條要義 Teikoku kenpo chikujo yogi. (Article by article commentary of the imperial constitution.) Kyoto, Seikyo shoin, 1935. 2 v.

8321. Watanabe, Ikujiro. 明治天皇ト立憲政治 Meiji tenno to rikken seiji. (Emperor Meiji and the constitutional government.) Tokyo, Gakushi shoin, 1936. 262 p.

8322. Nomura, Junji. 憲法提要 Kenpo teiyo. (A summary of the imperial constituion.) Tokyo, Yuhikaku, 1935. 456 p.

8323. Kudo, Takeshige. 改訂明治憲政史 Kaitei Meiji kensei-shi. (History of the constitutional government during the Meiji era. Revised edition.) Tokyo, Yuhikaku, 1935.

8324. Minobe, Tatsukichi. 憲法ト政黨. Kenpo to seito. (The constitution and the political parties.) Tokyo, Nippon hyoronsha, 1935. 235 p.

8325. Kuroda, Kaku. 日本憲法論 Nippon kenpo ron. (On the national constitution of Japan.) Tokyo, Kobundo, 1937. 260 p.

8326. Sato, Ushijiro. 帝國憲法講義 Teikoku kenpo kogi. (Lectures on the imperial constitution.) Tokyo, Yuhikaku, 1937. 387 p.

F. Administration

8327. Hagino, Yoshiyuki. 日本制度通 Nippon seido-tsu. (Outline of the administrative system of the government of old Japan.) 1889-1890. 3 v.

8328. Yokose, Yau. 太政官時代 Dajokan jidai. (Period of the administrative councils in Japan, 1608-1890.) Tokyo, Azusa shobo, 1929. 793 p.

8329. Sato, Kiyokatsu. 世界ニ比類ナキ天皇政治 Sekai ni hirui naki tenno seiji. (The imperial administration unparalleled in the world.) Tokyo, Chuseido, 1930. 321 p.

8330. Miyaoka, T. "Japanese law courts: their organization and jurisdiction." The Japan magazine, 5 (1914-1915):404-416.

8331. Shen, Chin-ting. 日本官制官規之研究 Jih-pên kuan-chih kuan-kuei chih yên-chiu. (A study of the Japanese official system and regulations.) Kao-shih-yüan kung-pao, 9, September 1931.

8332. Hsu, Chung-hao. 日本行政制度特質 Jih-pên hsing-chêng chih-tu tê-chih. (The special characteristics of the Japanese administrative system.) Min-ming, 4:1, October 1931.

8333. Hsu, Chung-hao. 日本地方自治制度 Jih-pên tifang tzu-chih chih-tu. (The system of local self-government in Japan.) Kao-shih yüan kung-pao, 10, October 1931.

8334. Hsu, Chung-hao. 日本三行政制度概要 Jih-pên chih hsing-chêng chih-tu kai-yao. (A sketch of the administrative system of Japan.) Chien-kuo yüeh-kan, 6:1, November 1931.

8335. 地方行政 Chiho gyosei. (Local administration.)
Monthly. Tokyo, Teikoku chiho gyosei gakukai.(Society for
the local administration of the Japanese empire.)

8336. Igarashi, Kozaburo. 市制 町村制 丞條 示解
Shisei chosonsei chikujo shikai. (Japanese local govern-
ments and their functioning with a full commentary.) Tokyo,
Jichikan, 1930. 59th edition. 1050 p.

8337. 都市問題 Toshi mondai. (Municipal problems.)
Monthly. Tokyo, Tokyo shisei chosakai(Association for the
investigation of municipal administration).

8338. Li, Mu. 東京市之市政 Tung-ching shih chih shih-
chêng. (The municipal administration in Tokyo.) Shanghai,
Min-chih shu-chü, 1932.

8339. 德川時代警察沿革說 Tokugawa jidai keisatsu
enkaku-shi. (An account of the development of the police
system during the Tokugawa period.) Tokyo, Keisatsu kyokai.
(Police association.) 1930?

8340. Chêng, Tsung-kai. 日本警察組織之系統 Jih-
pên ching-cha tzu-chih chih hsi-tung. (The organic system
of the Japanese police.) Shih-shih-yüeh-pao, 6:2, February
1932.

G. Democratic Elements

8341. Nagano, Akira. 日本自治史觀 Nippon jichi-shi-
kan. (Historical review of self-government in Japan.) Tokyo,
Kensetsusha, 1933. 167 p.

8342. Ozaki, Yukio. The voice of Japanese democracy. Being
an essay on constitutional loyalty. Translated by J. E. de
Becker. Yokohama-Shanghai, Kelly & Walsh, 1918. 108 p.

8343. Sato, Hiroshi. Democracy and the Japanese government.
Present day political problems in Japan. New York, Columbia
university press, 1920. vi, 97 p.

8344. Democracy in Japan. Rise of democratic institutions.
Foreign policy association, 6 (1930):8.

H. Parliament

8345. Ito, Hirobumi (Hakubun). 秘書類纂帝國議會資料
Hisho ruisan teikoku gikai shiryo. (Unpublished documents
classified and compiled: source materials on the imperial

diet.) Tokyo, Hisho ruisan kankokai, 1935. 600 p.

8346. Kudo, Takeshige. 帝國議會史 Teikoku gikai-shi.
(History of the imperial diet of Japan.) Tokyo, Yuhikaku,
1901. 3 v.

8347. 大日本帝國議會説第四五-五十四回議會 Dai Nippon teikoku gikai-
shi: Dai shijugo-gojushi gikai. (History of the Japanese
diet from the forty-fifth to the fifty-fourth session.)
Shizuoka, Gikai shi kankokai, 1931. 4 v.

8348. Colegrove, K. "Parliamentary government in Japan."
American political science review (Menasha, Wis.), 21:835-
852, November 1927.

8349. Clement, Ernest W. and Uyehara, Etsujiro. "Fifty sessions of the Japanese Imperial diet." Transactions of the
Asiatic society of Japan, 2 (1925):5-35. (Second series).

8350. Vostokov, L. "Японский парламент." (The Japanese parliament.) Vostok, 2-6 (1908).

8351. 第六十五回帝國議會：衆議院議事摘要
Dai 65-kai teikoku gikai shugiin kiji tekiyo. (The 65th Imperial diet: a summary of the procedures of the House of
representatives.) Tokyo, Shugiin jimukyoku, 1935. 3 v.

8352. 第六十七回帝國議會：衆議院議事摘要
Dai 67-kai teikoku gikai: shugiin giji tekiyo. (The 67th
session of the Imperial diet: the proceedings of the House
of representatives.) Tokyo, Shugiin jimusho, 1936. 3 v.

8353. Fukao, Hayao. 帝國議會五十年史：自第一議會至
第六十六議會 Teikoku gikai 50-nen shi:dai-1 gikai
yori dai-66 gikai. (50 years of the Imperial diet: from the
1st to 66th sessions.) Tokyo, Shinbunjin kyokai, 1936.
1020 p.

8354. 帝國議會解散史 Teikoku gikai kaisan-shi.
(History of the dissolutions of the Imperial diet.) Tokyo,
Naigaisha staff, 1933. 437 p.

I. Political Parties

8355. Sakamoto, Tatsunosuke. 日本帝國政治年表 Nippon
teikoku seiji nenpyo. (Chronological table of Japanese politics.) Tokyo, Shobundo, 1931. 282 p.

8356. Iwasaki, Uichi. The working forces in Japanese poli-

tics. A brief account of political conflicts, 1867-1920.
New York, Longmans, London, P. S. King, 1921. 141 p.

8357. See 8396.

8358. Ando, Tokki. 歴代内閣論 Rekidai naikaku ron.
(On the successive cabinets.) Tokyo, Genkai shobo, 1936.
144 p.

8359. Hayashida, Kametaro. 日本政党史 Nippon seito-shi.
(History of political parties in Japan.) Tokyo, Nippon yubenkai kodansha, 1927. 2 vols. 506, 452 p.

8360. Nagai, Kyo. 日本政党史 Nippon seito-shi. (History
of political parties in Japan.) Tokyo, Nippon hyoronsha,
1929. 281 p.

8361. Azbelev, N. Политические партии и общественное мнение
в Японии. (Political parties and public opinion in Japan.)
Mir bozhii. 1-2, 1905.

8362. Uda, Tomoi and Wada, Saburo. 自由党史 Jiyuto-shi.
(History of the liberal party of Japan.) Tokyo, Gosharyo,
1910.

8363. Kobayashi, Yugo. 立憲政友会史 Rikken Sei-
yukai-shi. (History of the Seiyukai party.) Tokyo, Seiyukai
press, 1929.

8364. Inoue, Heitaro. 政友会三十五年史 Seiyukai 35-
nen-shi. (35 years of the Seiyukai party.) Tokyo, Seiyukai
35-nen shi hensanbu, 1936. 465 p.

8365. Yoshioka, Usaburo. 立憲民政党史 Rikken Minseito
shi. (History of the constitutional Minseito party.) Tokyo,
Rikken Minseito-shi hensanbu, 1935. 535 p.

8366. Hudson, G. F. "Political parties in Japan." Nineteenth
century, 107:640:792-796, June 1930.

8367. Lay, A. H. "A brief sketch of the history of the rise
of political parties in Japan." Transactions, The Asiatic
society of Japan, 30 (1902):3:363-462.

8368. Tseitlin, I. "Кабинет Хирота и партия сэйюкай."
(The Hirota cabinet and the Seiyukai party.) Tikhii Okean,
1:11:114-127, January-March 1937.

8369. Colegrove, K. "Labor parties in Japan." American political science review (Menasha, Wis.), 23:329-363, May 1929.

8370. Tani, G. "Программа японской пролетарской партии." (The program of the Japanese proletarian party.) Mezhdunarodnoe rabochee dvizhenie, 33 (1925):1-3.

8371. Matsumoto, Junzo. 日本無産政黨 / 現勢 Nippon musan seito no genjo. (Present condition of proletarian parties in Japan.) In Social science lectures, v. 11. Tokyo, Seibundo, 1931.

8372. Asanuma, Inajiro. 無産政黨議會闘争五ヶ年史 Musan seito gikai tóso gokanen-shi. (History of five years' struggle of the proletarian party in the Japanese diet.) In Social science lectures, v. 10. Tokyo, Seibundo, 1931.

8373. Kono, Mitsu. 日本無産政黨史 Nippon musan seito-shi. (History of the proletariat party of Japan.) Tokyo, Hakuyosha, 1931. 764 p.

8374. Asahara, Kenzo. 日本無産政黨發達史 Nippon musan seito hattatsu-shi. (History of the growth of proletarian parties in Japan.) In Social science lectures, v. 7. Tokyo, Seibundo, 1931.

8375. Oi, Ittetsu. 憲政ヲ破壞スル政黨政治 Kensei o hakai suru seito seiji. (Party government which destroys the constitutional government.) Tokyo, Nippon shakai mondai kenkyusho, 1932. 247 p.

8376. The Japanese elections. Foreign policy association. Vol. 3, extra number, 1928.

8377. Nagano, Akira. 自治日本 / 建設 Jichi Nippon no kensetsu. (Founding of self-government in Japan.) Tokyo, Shina mondai kenkyusho, 1933. 287 p.

8378. Katayama, Sen. "Всеобщее избирательное право в Японии." (The general electoral right in Japan.) Kommunisticheskii internatsional, 11 (1925):125-135.

8379. Zumoto, M. "Japan and manhood suffrage." The young East, 1 (1925-1926):7-8.

8380. Kimura, Yosaku. 秘錄五・一五事件 Hiroku go-ichigo jiken. (Secret memoir of the May 15th incident: the assassination of Premier Inukai.) Tokyo, Meiji tosho shuppan kyokai. 1932.

8381. Sato, Kiyokatsu. 政黨政治亡國論 Seito seiji bokoku ron. (On the national ruin under party politics.) Tokyo, Hojosha, 1933. 260 p.

8382. Kodo kakusei domei staff. 既成政黨ヲアバク Kisei seito o abaku. (Exposing the existing political parties.) Tokyo, Zen Nippon kokoku doshikai, 1933. 233 p.

8383. Aono, Gonuemon. 日本政黨變遷史 Nippon seito hensen-shi. (History of the transformation of the political parties in Japan.) Tokyo, Ankyusha, 1936. 346 p.

J. Recent Politics

8384. Arcambeau, E. "La troisième crise ministérielle de l'ére Taisho. Cabinet du Comte Okuma." Bulletin, Société franco-japonaise, 34-35 (1915):77-91.

8385. Griffis, William Elliot. "Okuma and the new era in Japan." North American review, 204 (1916):681-690.

8386. Amurskii, N. V."Кураизава. У Маркиза Окума." (Kurai-zava. At Marquis Okuma's.) Velikii Okean, 3 (1918):6-9.

8387. Brackmann, C. I. "I. Das Ministerium Okuma. II. Das Ministerium Terauchi." Asien, 1:15 (1917-1918):208-218; 2:16 (1918-1919):21-26, 46-48, 58-63, 82-88.

8388. Anesaki, Masaharu. "Social unrest and spiritual agitation in present-day Japan." Harvard theological review, 1922, 305-322.

8389. Okamoto, T. "The record of the Kato administration." The Asiatic review, New series, 19 (1923):209-219.

8390. "La politique japonaise. Le gouvernment de coalition du Vicomte Kato." L'Asie française, 25(1925):228:15-22.

8391. "Фашистское движение в Японии." (The fascist movement in Japan.) Mezhdunarodnoe rabochee dvizhenie, 36 (1925):5-6.

8392. Reilly, H. J. "Revolt of youth in Japan." World today, 1926. 58-66.

8393. Balet, J. C. "Au Japon: le ministère Tanaka." L'Europe nouvelle (Paris), 10 (1927):482:613-616.

8394. Wang, Mao-yüan. 日本最近政潮中之分子與問題 Jih-pên tsui-chin chêng-chao chung chih fên-tzu yu wên-ti. (Elements and problems in the recent political situation of Japan.) Eastern miscellany, 26:2:29-42, January 1929.

8395. Yü-kan. 田中内閣崩潰後的日本新政局 Tien-chung nei-ko p'êng-k'uei hou ti Jih-pên hsin chêng-chü. (The new Japanese political situation after the fall of the Tanaka cabinet.) Eastern miscellany, 26:13:4-7, July 1929.

8396. Hirota, Naomori. 内閣更迭五十年史 Naikaku kotetsu 50-nen-shi. (50 years' history of successive cabinets.) Tokyo, Shunyodo, 1930. 742 p.

8397. Baba, Tsunego. 田中内閣倒壊ノ主役者 Tanaka naikaku tokai no shuyakusha. (Principal factors causing the downfall of the Tanaka cabinet: Saionji, militarism; assassination of Chang Tso Lin.) Chuo koron, 44:8:121-129, August 1930.

8398. Askhi and Matsumoto, Kh. "Надвигающийся фашизм в Японии." (Approaching fascism in Japan.) Krasnyi internatsional professorov, 7 (30), 1930.

8399. Takenaka, Shigeru. 日本各婦人團体關於縣府会議員競選巻對策 Jih-pên ko fu-jên tuan-t'i kuan yü hsien fu hui i-yüan tsung hsuan-chü tui-tsê. (The proposition of Japanese women's organizations in regard to the election of members for the district and prefectural congresses.) Fu-nu-tsa-chih, 17:11, November 1931.

8400. Takenaka, Shigeru. 日本民法改正案全部脱稿後的女権 Jih-pên min-fa kai-chêng-an chuan-pu to kao hou ti nu-chuan. (Women's rights in Japan's civil law after the amendment.) Fu-nu-tsa-chih, 17:11, November 1931.

8401. Sung-hua. 日本犬養毅内閣的成立 Jih-pên Ch'üan-yang-i nei-ko ti ch'êng-li. (The formation of the Inukai cabinet in Japan.) Eastern miscellany, 29:2, January 1932.

8402. Miyake, Setsurei. ファッショ政治ハ日本ニ出来ルヵ Fassho seiji wa Nippon ni dekiru ka? (Is fascist rule possible in Japan?) Jitsugyo no sekai, March 1932.

8403. Shinmei, Masamichi. ファッショニ成ッタラ Fassho ni nattara. (What will become of Japan if she turns fascist?) Bungei shunju. 10:4, April 1932.

8404. Ting, Wên-chiang. 犬養毅被刺與日本政局的前途

Chuan-yang-i pei-tzu yü Jih-pên chêng-chü ti chien-t'u. (The assassination of Inukai and the future of Japanese politics.) Tu-li ping-lun, 1, May 1932.

8405. Ting, Wên-chiang. 日本的新内閣 Jih-pên ti hsin nei-ko. (The new cabinet of Japan.) Tu-li ping-lun, 2, May 1932.

8406. Ming. 犬養被刺與日本政局之前途 Chüan-yang-i pei tzu yü Jih-pên chêng-chü chih chien-t'u. (The assassination of Inukai and the future of   Japanese politics.) Hsin-tung-fang, bi-annual anniversary number, June 1932.

8407. Jui-fu. 日本法西斯蒂運動的蓦進及其前途 Jih-pên fa-hsi-ssu-ti yün-tung ti mu-chin chi ch'i chien-t'u. (The sudden advance of the fascist movement in Japan and its future.) Hsin-tung-fang, bi-annual anniversary number, June 1932.

8408. Tzu-yün. 日本政治演進與中日外交之前途 Jih-pên chêng-chih yên-chin yü Chung Jih wai-chiao chih chien-t'u. (Changes in Japanese politics and the future of Sino-Japanese diplomatic relations.) Hsin-tung-fang, 3:7, July 1932.

8409. Tsai, Shih-hao. 日本議會政治崩潰的原因 Jih-pên i-hui chêng-chih pêng-kuei ti yüan-yin. (The cause of the downfall of the parliamentary system in Japan.) Shên-pao yüeh-kan, 1:1, July 1932.

8410. Chang, Shui-ch'i. 日本武力政治團体概况 Jih-pên wu-li chêng-chih tuan-ti kai-kuang. (The general status of the militaristic political organs in Japan.) Shên-pao yüeh-kan, 1:1, July 1932.

8411. Tu, Kuang-yün. 日本政治制度中内閣的地位 Jih-pên chêng-chih chih-tu chung nei-ko ti ti-wei. (The position of the cabinet in the political system of Japan.) Wu-ta shê-hui-ko-hsüeh chi-k'an, 2 (1932):3.

8412. Political realignments in Japan. Foreign policy association, 8:17, October 1932.

8413. Gorai, Kinzo. 政治ハドウナル Seiji wa do naru. (What will happen to politics in Japan?) Tokyo, Gendai,1932.

8414. Saito, Hitoshi. 父齋藤實ヲ語ル Chichi Saito Makoto wo kataru. (On my father, Makoto Saito, Premier of

Japan.) Hinode, 1:1, October 1932.

8415. Hirano, Kaoru. 本邦ノ政治ノ根本問題 Honpo no seiji no konpon mondai. (Fundamental problems of the politics of Japan.) Tokyo, Hirano shoten, 1933. 203 p.

8416. Sassa, Yoshio. 政局危機ノ動向 Seikyoku kiki no doko. (Trends of the political crisis.) Tokyo, Chikura shobo, 1933. 293 p.

8417. Royama, Masamichi. 日本政治動向論 Nippon seiji doko ron. (On the political trends of Japan.) Tokyo, Koyo shoin, 1934. 554 p.

8418. Kato, Yasuhiro. 明治大正昭和政界秘史 Meiji, Taisho, Showa seikai hishi. (Secret history of Meiji, Taisho, Showa politics.) Tokyo, Ryushokaku, 1935. 310 p.

8419. Kojima, Seiichi. 岡田内閣ト一九三五年 Okada naikaku to 1935 nen. (The Okada cabinet and 1935.) Tokyo, Chikura shobo, 1935. 348 p.

8420. Fujisawa, Chikao. "Japan versus marxism." Contemporary Japan, Tokyo, 1932/33:3:441-452. (2) The same. "A new interpretation of Japanese monarchy." Cultural Nippon, Tokyo, 3:340-356, June 1935.

8421. Takeuchi, Tai. 日本政治ノ動向 Nippon seiji no doko. (The trend of the Japanese government.) Gaiko jiho, 79:4:50-66, August 1936.

8422. Kato, Shuichi. 躍進日本ノ政治動向 Yakushin Nippon no seiji doko. (Political trends of rising Japan.) Tokyo, Nakanishi shobo, 1936. 297 p.

8423. Uemura, Koyu. 國政一新論叢 Kokusei isshin ronso. (Dissertations on the complete reformation of national policies.) Tokyo, Genkai shobo, 1936. 173 p.

8424. Taiheiyo kenkyukai (Institute of Pacific relations). 日本ノ政治 Nippon no seiji. (Political affairs of Japan.) Tokyo, Sobunkaku, 1936. 247 p.

8425. Ozaki, Gakudo. 政戦六十年 Seisen 60-nen. (60 years of political struggle.) Tokyo, Nippon hyoronsha, 1936. 331 p.

8426. Fujisawa, Chikao. 近代政治思想ト皇道 Kindai seiji shiso to kodo. (Modern political thoughts and Japanese imperial doctrine.) Tokyo, Seinen kyoiku fukyukai, 1936.

8427. Yomiuri shinbunsha. 日本ヲドウスル速ニ國策ヲ樹立セヨ Nippon o dosuru, sumiyakani kokusako o juritsu seyo. (Japan; set up your national policy immediately.) Tokyo, Nippon hyoronsha, 1936. 214 p.

8428. Takata, Haruzo. 岡田内閣 Okada naikaku. (The cabinet under Premier Okada.) Tokyo, Okada naikaku hensankai, 1936. 356 p.

8429. Murakami, Teiichi. 巨人齋藤實 Kyojin Saito Makoto. (The great man [Premier] Makoto Saito.) Tokyo, Shinchosha, 1937.

K. Communistic and Fascistic Trends

See 1047-1060; 7992-8043; 8690-8735; 11495-11583.

8430. Vilenskii, V. (Sibiriakov). Революционное движение в Японии (из писем японских рабочих). (Revolutionary movement in Japan: from letters of Japanese workers.) Moscow, Gosizdat, 1919. 24 p.

8431. The socialist and labour movement in Japan. By an American sociologist. Chronicle reprints No. 2. Kobe, Japan chronicle, 1921. 145 p.

8432. Katayama, Sen. Капиталистическое наступление и пролетарская защита в Японии.(The capitalist offensive and proletarian defensive in Japan.) Moscow, Krasnaia Nov', 1923. 40 p.

8433. Voitinskii, G. "Буржуазия и остатки феодализма в Японии." (The bourgeoisie and the remains of feudalism in Japan.) Novyi vostok, 4 (1923):122-128.

8434. Matsokin, N. "Социалистическое движение современной Японии." (Socialist movement of modern Japan.) Vestnik Manchurii, 1-2 (1925):40-45.

8435. Asao, Katsuya. 政界ノ尖端ヲ行ク人々 Seikai no sentan wo yuku hitobito. (Men with radical views in Japan.) Tokyo, Daiichi shuppansha, 1931. 323 p.

8436. 京阪神ニ跨ル共産業大檢擧 Keihanshin ni matagaru kyosanto daikenkyo. (A wholesale roundup of communists arrested in Kyoto, Osaka, and the Kobe region.) Extra, Osaka, Mainichi shinbun, August 25, 1932.

8437. Topekha, P. P. Японский пролетариат в борьбе против

империалискической войны. (The Japanese proletariat in the struggle against imperialistic war.) Moscow, Partizdat, 1932. 60 p.

8438. The rise of fascism in Japan. Foreign policy reports, 8 (1932):17.

8439. Kuusinen, O. "Японский империализм и характер японской революции." (Japanese imperialism and the nature of the Japanese revolution.) Mirovoe khoziaistvo i mirovaia politika, 6:3-14, June 1932.

8440. Fukuoka. "Антивоенное движение в Японии." (Antimilitary movement in Japan.) Krasnyi internatsional profsoiuzov, 13:10-17, July 1932.

8441. Zhukov, E. "К характеристике японского социал-фашизма." (The character of Japanese social-fascism.) Zapiski Instituta vostokovedeniia akademii SSSR, 1 (1932):63-123.

8442. Tadokoro, Teruaki. 無産党十字街 Musanto jujigai. (The proletariat party at the crossroads.) Tokyo, Senshinsha, 1932. 458 p.

8443. Volk, IA. "Революционный подъем в Японии." (Rise of revolutionary spirit in Japan.) Bol'shevik, 21:61-80, November 1932.

8444. Wang, Fu-chuan. 日本法西斯韋主義的展望 Jih-pên fa-hsi-shi-ti chu-i ti chien-wang. (Prospect of fascism in Japan.) Eastern miscellany, 30:3, 23-30, February 1, 1933.

8445. 再生日本共産党/全貌 Saisei Nippon kyosanto no zenbo. (A general view of the revived movement of the communist party in Japan.) Extra. Osaka asahi daily, January 18, 1933.

8446. Ternovskaia, E. "Фашизм в японском рабочем движении." (Fascism in the Japanese labor movement.) Materialy po natsionalho-kolonialnym problemam, 7 (1933):13:3-21.

8447. Radek, K. "Японский и европейский фашизм." (Japanese and European fascism.) Bol'shevik, 21:86-96, November 1933.

8448. Janin, O. "Военно-фашистское движение в Японии."(Military-fascist movement in Japan.) Moscow, 1933. xvi, 270 p.

8449. Kuusinen, O. "Японский империализм и характер япон-

ской революции." (Japanese imperialism and the nature of the
Japanese revolution.) Sovremennaia IAponiia (Moscow), 1
(1934):26-38.

8450. Zhukov, E. "О японском фашизме и социал-фашизме."
(About Japanese fascism and social fascism.) Sovremennaia
IAponiia, 1 (1934):161-209.

8451. Volk, IA. "Рост сил революции и мобилизация сил
контреволюции в Японии." (The rise of revolutionary forces
and mobilization of counter-revolutionary forces in Japan.)
Sovremennaia IAponiia, 1 (1934):210-280.

8452. Atlee, F. "Мелкая буржуазия в структуре японского империализма." (Petty bourgeoisie in the structure of Japanese imperialism.) Sovremennaia IAponiia, 2 (1934):147-177.

8453. Okano. "Опасность войны и задачи коммунистической партии Японии." (The danger of war and the problems of the communist party of Japan.) Bol'shevik, 5:72-87, March 1934.

8454. Lemin, I. "Антисоветская пропаганда в Японии." (Anti-soviet propaganda in Japan.) Tikhii Okean, 1:50-62, July-September 1934.

8455. Itikawa. "Из истории коммунистической партии Японии."
(From the history of the communist party of Japan.) Testimony of Itikawa before the court concerning the history of the
communist party in Japan.) Tikhii Okean, 1:113-168, July-
September 1934.

8456. Tanin, O. and Yohan, E. Militarism and fascism in Japan. New York, International publishers, 1934. 320 p.

8457. Barandov, G. E. Революционное движение в Японии и борьба японской компартии. (Revolutionary movement in Japan and
the struggle of the Japanese communist party.) Moscow, 1934.
58 p. See 8463.

8458. Япония. Сборник статей и метериалов. (Japan. Collection of articles and materials.) [Moscow-Leningrad], 1934.
400 p.

8459. Feldman, N. (ed.) Японская революционная литература.
Сборник статей. (Japanese revolutionary literature. Collection of articles.) Moscow, 1934. 238 p.

8460. Коминтерн и профинтерн по японскому вопросу. Сборник
важнейших документов. (The communist international and the

trade union international on the problem of Japan. Collection of most important documents.) Moscow, 1934. 205 p.

8461. Izabelov. Милитаризация японской школы. (The militarization of the Japanese school.) Moscow, 1934. 39 p.

8462. The trend toward dictatorship in Japan. Foreign policy reports (New York), 10 (1935):25.

8463. Barandov, G. E. Революционное движение в Японии и борьба японской компартии. (Revolutionary movement in Japan and the struggle of the Japanese communist party.) Tashkent, 1935. 83 p. See 8457.

8464. Japan's conflict with the evil of bolshevism in the Far East. Association for the study of international socialistic ideas and movements. Tokyo. 124 p.

8465. Tanaka, Takuji. 日本改造ノ具体案 Nippon kaizo no gutaian. (Concrete ideas on the reorganization of Japan.) Tokyo, Yosei jihyosha, 1936. 197 p.

8466. Nakanishi, Inosuke. 軍閥 Gunbatsu. (Military olique.) Tokyo, Jissensha, 1936. 422 p.

8467. Hamadan, A. Япония на путях к "Большой войне". Заговор 26-29 фев.1936 г.(Japan on the road to a "Big war". The military-fascist plot in Tokyo of February 26-29, 1936.) Moscow, 1936. 46 p.

8468. Kono, Mitsu. "Japan's proletarian movement." Contemporary Japan, 5:4:577-586, March 1937.

8469. Baba, Tsunego. "The anti-comintern pact in domestic politics." Contemporary Japan, 5:4:536-545, March 1937.

8470. Stein, Guenther. "'Totalitarian' Japan." Foreign affairs, 16:2:294-309, January 1938.

XIV. LAWS AND LEGISLATION

See 8225-8470.

A. Periodicals

8471. 法學協會雜誌 Hogaku kyokai zasshi. (The journal of the Jurisprudence society.) Tokyo, Jurisprudence society of the Tokyo imperial university, 1, 1888-

8472. 京都法學會雜誌 Kyoto hogakukai zasshi. (The journal of the Jurisprudence society of Kyoto.) Kyoto, Jurisprudence society of the Kyoto imperial university, 1918-1925. 13 v. (No more published.)

B. History of Law

See 8327-8340; 8345-8354; 8492-8495.

8473. Ikebe, Gisho. 日本法制史解題 Nippon hosei-shi kaidai. (Outline and explanation of all the standard histories of Japanese legislation.) Tokyo, Isseido, 1932. 2 v.

8474. Ikebe, Gisho. 日本法制史 Nippon hosei-shi. (History of legislation in Japan.) Tokyo, Ganshodo, 1912.

8475. Miura, Shuko. 法制史ノ研究 Hosei-shi no kenkyu. (A study of the history of legislation in Japan.) Tokyo, Iwanami, 1919. 1174 p. (2) The same. 續法制史ノ研究 (A study of the History of legislation in Japan, Second series.) Tokyo, Iwanami, 1925. 1563 p.

8476. Takikawa, Seijiro. 日本法制史 Nippon hosei-shi. (History of legislation in Japan.) Tokyo, Yuhikaku, 1929.

8477. Hosokawa, Kameichi. 日本法制史大綱 Nippon hosei-shi taiko. (A general outline of the history of legislation of Japan.) Tokyo, Jichisha, 1935. 246 p.

8478. Kiyoura, Keigo. 明治法制史 Meiji hosei-shi. (History of Meiji legislation.) Tokyo, Meihodo. 1899.

8479. Lönholm, L. The condition of the foreigners and the new treaties. A digest written for the international committee of Yokohama. Tokyo, 1898. 54 p.

8480. Hozumi, Nobushige. Ancestor-worship and Japanese law. Second and revised edition. Tokyo, Osaka and Kyoto, Maruzen kabushiki kaisha, 1912. xxx, 198 p.

8481. Uchida. "The teaching of jurisprudence in Japan." American law school review, 3 (1912):19-25.

8482. Kohler, J. Die orientalischen rechte. 10. Japanisches recht. Kultur der gegenwart II, Abteilung VII, No. 1, 1914: 145-150.

8483. Becker, J. E. de. "Elements of Japanese law." Trans-

actions of the Asiatic society of Japan, Tokyo, 44 (1916):
2:i-xi, 1-473.

8484. Hozumi, Nobushige. Lectures on the new Japanese civil
code as material for the study of comparative jurisprudence.
Second and revised edition. Tokyo, Osaka and Kyoto, Maruzen
kabushiki-kaisha, 1912. xvi, 166 p.

3485. Uyesugi, Shinkichi. "Die öffentlich-rechtliche gesetzgebung in Japan." Jahrbuch des öffentlichen rechts der gegenwart, 4 (1910):530-536.

8486. Katsumoto, M. "Übersicht über die gesetzgebung Japans
in den letzen 15 jahren (1905-1920)." Blätter für verglei-
chende rechtswissenschaft, 17 (1923):73-111.

8487. Otto, Günther v. Geschichte des japanischen straf-
rechts. Inaugural-dissertation. Borna-Leipzig, R. Noske,
1913. ix, 152 p.

8488. Sumida, Shoichi. 日本海法史 Nippon kaiho-shi.
(History of Japanese maritime law.) Tokyo, Ganshodo, 1927.
471 p.

8489. Miyaoka, T. "Japanese law of nationality and the
rights of foreigners in land under the laws of Japan." International conciliation, Carnegie endowment, 206 (1925):
1-20.

8490. See 8347.

C. Ancient Law

See 7611-7624.

8491. Hagino, Yoshiyuki. 日本古代法典 Nippon kodai
hoten. (Codes and laws of ancient Japan.) 1893.

D. Medieval Law

See 7625-7666.

8492. Hall, J. Carey. "Japanese feudal laws." Transactions
of the Asiatic society of Japan, Tokyo, 34 (1906)1:44; 36
(1908):2:1-23; 38 (1911):4:269-331; 41 (1913):683-804.   (2)
The same. "Early feudal law in Japan." Transactions and
proceedings of the Japan society, London, 7 (1907):410-417.

8493. 徳川禁令考 Tokugawa kinrei-ko. (Laws and ord-

inances of the Tokugawa period, 1600-1867.) Tokyo, Department of justice, Yoshikawa kobunkan, 1894-1932. 12 v.

8494. Yoshida, Togo. 德 川 政 敎 考 Tokugawa seikyoko.
(Laws and administration of the Tokugawa period.) 1894.
2 v.

8495. Wigmore, J. H. Materials for the study of private law
in Old Japan. Yokohama, 1892.

E. Modern Law

See 7667-7693; 8225-8470.

8496. 宸 翰 集 Shinkanshu. (Collection of edicts and letters by various emperors of Japan.) Department of the Imperial household. Tokyo, Isseido, 1932. 3 books in 4 v.

8497. Japan. Laws, statutes, etc. The imperial house law.
(Translation.) Tokyo, 1899.

8498. Japan. Laws, statutes, etc. The imperial ordinance relating to the ascension to the throne. (Translation.) 2nd
edition. 1928. 101 p.

8499. Japan. Laws, statutes, etc. Imperial ordinance concerning the House of peers. (Translation.) Tokyo, 1889.

8500. Japan. Laws, statutes, etc. Law of the Houses. (Translation.) Tokyo, 1889. 23 p.

8501. Japan. Laws, statutes, etc. Law of election for the
members of the House of representatives. (Translation.) Tokyo, 1889. 28, 27 p.

8502. Japan. Imperial diet. (Including House of peers, House
of representatives.) 帝 國 議 會: 貴 族 院 衆 議 院 報 告
Teikoku gikai: Kizoku-in, Shugi-in hokoku. The Japanese
chronicle publishes a weekly digest of the proceedings of
the Diet. (Serial publications of foreign governments.) (2)
The same. Records of the Lower house. 1896-1915? 36 v.

8503. Suehiro, Gentaro. 現 代 法 令 全 集 Gendai horei zenshu. (A complete collection of present laws and regulations.)
Tokyo, Nippon hyoronsha, 1936. 18 v.

8504. Japan. Laws, statutes, etc. 法 令 全 書 Horei zensho. (Statutes.) 1867- Index: 1867-1884.

8505. Japan. Laws, statutes, etc. 法令全書 Horei zensho. (A complete collection of laws and ordinances.) Tokyo,
Naikaku insatsukyoku, 1935. 11 v.

8506. Japan. Laws, statutes, etc. Secretariat of the Cabinet, Section of the archives. 現行法令輯覧 Genko
horei shuran. (Complete collection of laws and ordinances
now in force, 1868-1930.) Tokyo, Teikoku chiho gyosei gakukai, 1931. 12 v.

8507. Japan. Laws, statutes, etc. Secretariat of the Cabinet, Section of the archives. 目録索引 Mokuroku sakuin.
(Table of contents and index.) Tokyo, Teikoku chiho gyosei
gakukai, 1931. 512 p. See 8506.

8508. Japan. Laws, statutes, etc. Secretariat of the Cabinet, Section of the archives. 憲法皇室帝国議会官規
Kenpo, koshitsu, teikoku gikai, kanki. (Constitution, imperial house law, laws and ordinances regarding the Imperial diet, and governmental regulations.) In Genko horei shuran, v. 1. Tokyo, Teikoku chiho gyosei gakukai, 1931. 1395
p. (2) The same. 服制微章褒賞恩給文書統計社
寺宗教 Fukusei, kisho, hosho, onkyu, bunsho, tokei,
shaji, shukyo. (Laws and ordinances regarding the uniform
system, badges, rewards, pensions, documents, statistics,
churches and temples, and religions.) In Genko horei shuran,
v. 2. 1593 p. (3) The same. 地方制度警察衛生
Chiho seido, keisatsu, eisei. (Laws and ordinances regarding
the local system, the police, and sanitation.) Genko horei
shuran, v.3. 1487 p. (4) The same. 社會土地 Shakai,
tochi. (Laws and ordinances regarding the social welfare
and land.) Genko horei shuran, v. 4. 1252 p. (5) 財務
Zaimu. (Laws and ordinances regarding national accounting,
taxation, license system, currency, national debt, bond,
post savings, and other financial subjects.) Genko horei shuran, v. 5. 1753 p. (6) 軍事法務 Gunji, homu. (Laws
and ordinances regarding military affairs and legal affairs,
part I.) Genko horei shuran, v. 6. 1737 p. (7) The same.
法務學事 Homu, gakuji. (Laws and ordinances regarding legal affairs, part 2, and education.) Genko horei shuran, v. 7. 2591 p. (8) The same. 産業 Sangyo. (Laws
and ordinances regarding industry.) Genko horei shuran,
vols. 8 & 9. 1286, 2346 p. (9) The same. 交通電氣
Kotsu denki. (Laws and ordinances regarding roads, bridges,
railroads, shipping,harbor and bay, aviation, and electri-
city and gas.) Genko horei shuran, vols. 10 & 11.

8509. Boissonnade, G. Projet de code civil pour l'empire du Japon, accompagné d'un commentaire. Tokyo, 1882-1891. 5 v.

8510. The Civil code of Japan. English translation by J.H. Gubbins, with the Japanese text on the margin. Tokyo, 1897-1899. 2 v.

8511. Hozumi, Nobuzumi. The new Japanese civil code, as material for the study of comparative jurisprudence. A paper read at the International congress of arts and science at the Universal exposition. St. Louis, 1904. 73 p.

8512. Japan. Laws, statutes, etc. The civil code of Japan. Tr. by L. H. Loenholm & R. H. Loenholm. 4th edition, Tokyo, 1906.

8513. Becker, J. E. de. The annotated Civil code of Japan, translated and annotated, with introduction by Count Tadasu Hayashi. Yokohama, Kelly & Walsh; London, Butterworth & co., 1909-1910. 4 v.

8514. Japan. Laws, statutes, etc. Japanese code of civil procedure. Translated by J. E. DeBecker. Yokohama, 1918. 106 p.

8515. Japan. Laws, statutes, etc. The code of civil procedure of Japan. Translated by J. E. DeBecker. London, 1928, 165 p.

8516. (First) Draft of the (revised) Japanese criminal code, translated from the original Japanese text by J. E. DeBecker (Kobayashi beika). Yokohama, 1899. 88 p. (2) (Second) Draft of the (revised) Japanese criminal code, translated from the original Japanese text by J. E. DeBecker. Yokohama, 1903.

8517. Japan. Laws, statutes, etc. The criminal code of Japan. Tr. by J. E. DeBecker. Yokohama, 1918. 100 p.

8518. Makino, Eiichi. 日本刑法 Nippon keiho. (Criminal law of Japan.) Tokyo, Yuhikaku, 1937. 500 p.

8519. Japanisches strafgesetze vom 13 april 1907. Sammlung ausserdeutscher strafgesetzbücher no. 23; zeitschrift für die gesammte strafrechtswissenschaft 28. Berlin und Leipzig, W. de Gruyter & co., 1908.

8520. Japan. Laws, statutes, etc. 日本商法 Nippon shoho. (Commercial code of Japan, annotated.)

8521. Hang, Yang Yin. Commercial code of Japan. University of Pennsylvania Law school series no. 1. Boston, Boston book co., 1911. xxiii, 319 p.

8522. Japan. Laws, statutes, etc. New Japanese laws supplementary to the codes. Tr. by Dr. Ludwig Loenholm, Bremen, 1898. 133, 24 p.

8523. Laws of Japan, translated by H. B. M. Legation in Tokyo and published by the Japan mail. Yokohama, 1899. 3 v.

8524. Okuma, Yokichi. "Japanese marriage law, past and present. Part 1: Japanese marriage law in the past. Part 2: The present marriage law in Japan." Transactions and proceedings of the Japan society, London, 21 (1924):68-82; 22 (1925): 4-36.

8525. The new Japanese and Korean laws concerning patents, trade marks, designs and utility models. With all ordinances and regulations relating thereto. Tokyo, Maruya and co.; Yokohama, Kelly & Walsh, 1909. 200 p.   By L.H. Loenholm.

8526. 判決要録 Hanketsu yoroku. (Important records of the court decisions.) Tokyo, Horitsu shinbunsha, 1934. 33 v.

8527. Oda, Yorozu. 日本行政法原理 Nippon gyoseiho genri. (Principles of the administrative law of Japan.) Tokyo, Yuhikaku, 1934. 422 p.

8528. Watanabe, Sotaro. 改訂：日本行政法 Kaitei: Nippon gyoseiho. (Revised: administrative law of Japan.) Tokyo, Kobundo, 1937. 610 p.

8529. Kanemitsu, Yoshizumi. 大審院民事判例要旨類集 Daishin-in minji hanrei yoshi ruisan. (Classified compendium of judicial precedents of civil cases by the supreme court.) Tokyo, Hosokai, 1935.

8530. 大審院刑事判例要旨類集 Daishin-in keiji hanrei yoshi ruisan. (Classified compendium of judicial precedents of criminal cases by the supreme court.) Tokyo, Hosokai, 1935. 1358 p.

8531. Miyake, Shotaro. 日本判例大成 Nippon hanrei taisei. (A compilation of judicial precedents of Japan.) Tokyo, Hibonkaku, 1935. 24 v.

8532. Ito, Hirobumi. 秘書類纂 官制関係資料

Hisho hensan kansei kankei shiryo. (Unpublished compiled doc-
ument: the source materials relating to the governmental regulations.) Tokyo, Hisho ruisan kankokai, 1936. 618 p.

XV. MILITARY, NAVAL, AND AIR PROBLEMS

See 663-721; 2004-2028; 2987-3021; 3022-4705; 11465-11494.

A. General Accounts

8533. 陸軍省沿革史 Rikugun-sho enkaku-shi. (History
of the development of the department of war of Japan.) Tokyo, Department of war, 1930. 2 v.

8534. Sakurai, Tadaomi. 國防大事典 Kokubo daijiten.
(Encyclopedia of national defense.) Tokyo, Chugai sangyo
chosakai, 1932. 900 p.

8535. Krylov, V. N. Библия японского солдата и матроса.
(The bible of the Japanese soldier and sailor.) K poznaniiu
iaponskoi armii. Chita, 1919. 32 p.

8536. Caltrop. E. F. The book of war, the military classic
of the Far East. London, J. Murray, 1908.

8537. 日本兵器沿革説 Nippon heiki enkaku-shi. (History of the development of the Japanese weapons of war.)
Tokyo, Military library of the Department of war, 1881.
5 v.

8538. Watanabe, Seiyu. 戦國時代史論 Sengoku jidai-
shi ron. (Treatise on the history of the period of wars of
Japan.) Tokyo, Sanseido, 1910. 360 p.

8539. Ishikawa, Daiji. "Die einführung der feuerwaffen in
Japan." Ost-Asien, 9 (1906):103-104.

8540. Hasegawa, Seiki. 倭寇 Wako. (Wako: Japan, the nation
of pirates.) Tokyo, Tokyodo, 1914. 126 p.

8541. Mury, F. "L'organisation militaire du Japon." Bulletin du Comité de l'Asie française, 1907. 306-314.

8542. Misawa, Sukesaburo. "Das japanische feuerwehr- und
feuerlöschwesen der feudalzeit in Tokyo." Mitteilungen der
deutschen gesellschaft für natur- und völkerkunde Ostasiens,
Tokyo, 2 (1908):247-258.

8543. Balet, J. C. Le Japon militaire. Yokohama, Paris,1910.

8544. See 8583.

8545. Richter. "Japans kaisermanöver 1911."Jahrbücher für die deutsche armee und marine, 1 (1912):63-78.

8546.Balet, J. C. Le Japon militaire. L'armée et la marine japonaise en 1910. Yokohama, Kelly and Walsh, 1910. vi, 230 p.   English translations by C. A. Parry: Military Japan. The Japanese army and navy in 1910, with a new map of Japan. London, Gale & Polden; Yokohama, Kelly & Walsh, 1911. 232 p.

8547. Yamato, R. "La politique militaire et navale du Japon." Questions diplomatiques et coloniales, 33 (1912):156-173.

8548. Pozdneev, Dmitrii. Япония. Военно-экономическое описание. (Japan. A military-economic description.) Moscow, Izdanie razvedochnogo upravleniia shtaba R.K.K.A., 1924. 268p.

8549. Chün-i. 日本的國防宣傳 Jih-pên-ti kuo-fang hsüan-ch'uan. (The defense propaganda in Japan.[Correspondence from Japan.]) Shêng-huo, 6:41, October 1931.

8550. Liu, Li-chung. 日本軍事考察記 Jih-pên chün-shih k'ao-ch'a chi. (The account of an observation on the Japanese military affairs.) Huang-pu yüeh-k'an,   2:2, November 1931.

8551. Shên, Chin-ting. 日本國家制度上軍國主義之解析 Jih-pên kuo-chia chih-tu-shang chün-kuo-chu-i chih chieh-hsi. (An analysis of militarism in the national system of Japan.) Shih-shih yüeh-pao, 5:5, November 1931.

8552. Ning, Mo-kung. 歐戰後日本軍事進展之概況 Ou-chan hou Jih-pên chün-shih chin-chan chih kai-k'uang. (The military developments in Japan since the World war.) Shih-shih yüeh-pao, 5:5 & 6, November, December 1931.

8553. Chi-ming. 日本軍備之急進觀 Jih-pên chün-pei chih chi-chin-kuan. (The rapid advance of Japanese armament.) Nanking, Pa-ti shu-tien, 1932.

8554. Nakayama, Shiro. 日米開戰ト赤露ノ襲來 Nichi-Bei kaisen to seki-Ro no shurai. (The outbreak of war between Japan and the United States and the invasion of Red Russia.) Tokyo, Sekirokaku, 1932.

8555. Wan-li. Jih-pên hai-chün ping-hsüeh-hsiao kai-k'uang. 日本海軍兵學校概況 (The conditions of the naval schools in Japan.) Hai-chün ch'i-kan, 4:5, January 1932

8556. Hirata, Shinsaku. ワレ等ノ陸海軍 Warera no
riku-kaigun. (Our army and navy.) 53d edition. Tokyo, Dai-
Nippon yubenkai kodansha, 1932. 300 p.

8557. Barsukov, E. Z. Как вооружается японский империализм.
(How Japanese imperialism is arming.) Khabarovsk, 1933. 22p.

8558. 國防ノ第一線=躍ル Kokubo no dai issen ni odo-
ru. (Activities at the first line of the national defense.)
Tokyo, Kokubo shiso fukyukai, 1933. 568 p.

8559. Goto, Toshio. 眼前=迫ル世界大戰ト英米赤露
ノ襲来 Ganzen ni semaru sekai taisen to Ei-Bei seki-
Ro no shurai. (Imminent world war and the invasion of Japan
by Great Britain, America, and Soviet Russia.) Tokyo, Daikyosha, 1932. 570 p.

8560. Mizushima, Shosuke. 日本ノ國防ハドウスル Nippon
no kokubo wa do suru. (What about the national defense of
Japan?) Tokyo, Kokubo kyokai, 1933. 263 p.

8561. Hata, Shinji. 帝國ノ國防 Teikoku no kokubo. (The
national defense of Japan.) Tokyo, Senshinsha, 1933. 187 p.

8562. Ternovskaia, E. "Как японский империализм готовится к
войне." (How Japanese imperialism is preparing for war.)
Materialy po natsional'no-kolonial'nym problemam, 6 (1933):
12:15-30.

8563. Noyori, Hideichi. 軍部ヲ衝ノ Gunbu o tsuku.
(A criticism of the military faction.) Tokyo, Shubunkaku,
1933. 447 p.

8564. Date, Ryuzo. 國防危シ我=勝算アリヤ Kokubo
ayaushi ware ni shosan ariya. (Insecurity of the national
defense and prospects of a victory.) Tokyo, Meiji tosho
shuppan kyokai, 1933. 788 p.

8565. Etherton, P. T. and Tiltman, H. H. Japan:mistress of
the Pacific? London, Jarrolds, 1934. 302 p.

8566. Hall, J. V. Challenge: behind the face of Japan. New
York, Farrar & Rinehart, 1934. 409 p.

8567. Lemin, I. M. Пропаганда войны в Японии и Германии.
(War propaganda in Japan and Germany.) Moscow, 1934. 169 p.

8568. O'Conroy, T. The menace of Japan. New York, Kinsey,
1934. 294 p.

8569. Asik, M. Вооруженные силы Японии. Справочник. (Armed forces of Japan. Guide.) 2nd revised and enlarged edition. Moscow, 1935. xix, 304 p. See 8599.

8570. Дальневосточный очаг военной опасности. Сборник. (The Far Eastern hot-bed of military danger.) Collection of articles. Saratov, 1936. 132 p.

8571. Colegrove, Kenneth W. Militarism in Japan. World peace foundation. Boston, 1936. 77 p.

8572. Sakamoto, Tatsunosuke. 日本外戰史 Nippon gaisen-shi. (History of foreign wars of Japan.) Tokyo, Mancho-hosha, 1936. 956 p.

8573. Ishihara, Kaizo. 現代ノ國防ト産業 Gendai no ko-kubo to sangyo. (National defense and the productions of to-day.) Tokyo, Gakuji shoin, 1936. 232 p.

8574. Tanin, O. and Johan, E. When Japan goes to war. New York, Vanguard press, 1936. 271 p. Russian translation from the English: Когда Япония будет воевать. Moscow, 1936. 237 p. Also in German: Japan rüstet zum grossen krieg. Moscow, 1936. 315 p.

8575. Causton, E. E. N. Militarism and foreign policy in Japan. London, Allen & Unwin, 1936.

8576. Imura, Kunyu. 東亞安定ノ保障 To-A antei no hosho. (The stability of Eastern Asia and its security.) Gaiko jiho, 78:5:107-119, June 1936.

8577. Otomo, Kisaku. 對蘇國防ノ澁艘 Tai-Ro kokubo no rancho. (The advent of the national defense against Russia.) Tokyo, Naukasha, 1936. 299 p.

8578. Muto, Teiichi. 戰爭 Senso. (War.) Tokyo, Usami publishing office, 1936. 288 p.

8579. Saito, Naomiki. 財政中心國防論 Zaisei chu-shin kokubo ron. (On the national defense based on the national finances.) Tokyo, Gendai shobo, 1936. 350 p.

8580. Ishihara, Kanji. 非常時ト日本ノ國防 Hijoji to Nippon no kokubo. (The critical period and the national defense of Japan.) Yamagata, Asahi insatsu-bu, 1936. 36 p.

8581. Takahashi, Kamekichi. 戰爭ト日本経済力 Senso to Nippon keizai-ryoku. (War and the economic power of Japan.) Tokyo, Chikura shobo, 1937. 318 p.

8582. Ishimaru, Tota. The next world war. London, Hurst,
1937. 352 p.

8583. Kokusai josei kenkyukai staff. 世界ノ見タ日本ノ
陸海軍-Sekai no mita Nippon no riku-kaigun. (The Japanese
army and navy as observed by the world.) Tokyo, Taiyokaku,
1937. 300 p.

8584. Watanabe, Ikujiro. 人物近代日本軍事史 Jinbu-
tsu kindai Nippon gunji-shi. (The characters involved in
the history of military affairs of modern Japan.) Tokyo,
Chikura shobo, 1937. 428 p.

8585. Noda, Yutaka. 軍部ト財界 Gunbu to zaikai. (The military faction and the financial world.) Tokyo, Konnichi no mondaisha, 1937. 240 p.

8586. Oki, Yodo. 人生ト兵法 Jinsei to heiho. (Human life
and military tactics.) Tokyo, Kyozaisha, 1937. 368 p.

8587. Rikimaru, Tota. 次ノ世界戦争 Tsugi no sekai senso. (The next world war.) Tokyo, Shunjusha, 1937. 470 p.

8588. 第二次世界大戦 Dai niji sekai taisen. (The second world war./ Tokyo, Kokusai seiji kenkyukai, 1937. 270 p.

B. The Army

8589. Japan. War department. 陸軍組織年報 Rikugun
soshiki nenpo. (Annual report of the military organization
of Japan.) Tokyo.

8590. Japan. War department. 測量局年報 Sokuryo-kyoku
nenpo. (Land survey. Annual report.) 1922-1928.

8591. Japan. War department. 統計年報 Tokei nenpo. (Annual statistical report.) Tokyo, 1, 1887-

8592. Japan. War department. 日本陸軍衛生統計
Nippon rikugun eisei tokei. Statistique sanitaire de l'armée japonaise.

8593. Katsu, Kaishu. 陸軍歴史 Rikugun rekishi. (History
of the Japanese army.) Vol. 6, in Katsu Kaishu collection.
Tokyo, Kaizosha, 1929.

8594. 日本陸軍史 Nippon rikugunshi. (History of the

Japanese army.) Tokyo, Yuzankaku, 1936. 379 p.

8595. 日本兵制沿革説 Nippon heisei enkaku-shi. (History of the growth of the military system in Japan.) Tokyo, Military library, Department of war, 1880.

8596. 皇朝兵史 Kocho hei-shi.(History of the military system of Japan.) Tokyo, Department of war, 1881.

8597. Inada, Shunosuke. 軍政及軍事 Gunsei oyobi gunji. (Military administration and military affairs of Japan.) Tokyo, Yuhikaku, 1912.

8598. Hirata, Shinsaku. 陸軍讀本 Rikugun tokuhon. (Our army.) 230th edition. Tokyo, Nippon hyoronsha, 1932. 400 p.

8599. Asik, M. Вооруженные силы Японии. Справочник. (Armed forces of Japan. A guide.) Moscow, 1934. 222 p. See 8569.

8600. Masuda, N. Military industries of Japan. New York, Oxford university press, 1922.

8601. Kobayashi, Ushisaburo. Military industries of Japan. Japanese monographs edited by Baron Y. Sakatani. Publications of the Carnegie endowment for international peace, Division of economics and history. New York, Oxford university press, 1922. xv, 269 p.

8602. Arizawa, Hiromi. 軍需工業論 Gunju kogyo ron. (Discussion on the munitions industry.) Chuo koron, 23:9:September 1932.

8603. Matsui, Iwane. The Japanese army and the dispute in the Far East. Geneva, Kundig, 1932. 30 p.

8604. Krivenko, Vasilii. Тактика японской армии. (Tactics of the Japanese army.) St. Petersburg, 1911. 450 p.

8605. Полевой устав японской армии. (Field regulations of the Japanese army.) Translated from the Japanese. Moscow, 1933. 120 p.

8606. Новне методы боя японской пехоты. С японск. (New methods in battle of the Japanese infantry.) Translated from the Japanese by M. Niziaeva and E. Zykova. Second edition. Moscow, 1936. 258 p.

8607. Ivanov, S. Японская артиллерия. (Japanese artillery) Moscow, 1934. 82 p.

8608. Fedorenko. L. (ed.) Японский кавалерийский устав.
(Japanese cavalry regulations.) Tr. from the Japanese. Moscow, 1934. 139 p.

8609. Müller, Herman. Моральное воспитание войск в Германии,
России и Японии. (The moral training of troops in Germany,
Russia and Japan.) A comparative study based on the experi-
ence of the Russo-Japanese war. Translated from the German
by P. Kh. P-v. Moscow, 1907.

8610. Romanovskii, IU. Японская армия. (The Japanese army.)
St. Petersburg, Rittikh, 1910. iii, 208, 8 p. French translation (by G. Wehrlin and A. Le Merre): L'armée japonaise:
son recrutement, son organisation, ses règlements. Paris,
1912.

8611. Washburn, S. Nogi: a man against the background of a
great war. n.p., 1913. 136.

8612. Lisynov, K. P. Материалы по военной администрации Японии. (Sources pertaining to military administration of Japan.) Khabarovsk, Izdanie Shtaba Priamurskogo voennogo okruga, 1913. 143 p.

8613. Krylov, V. N. Краткие сведения о вооруженных силах
Японии. (Brief information regarding the military forces of
Japan.) With statistical data of a general nature. Kharbin,
1915. 72 p.

8614. Krylov, V. N. Очерки японской армии. (Sketches of the
Japanese army.) Chita, 1919. viii, 84 p.

8615. Ogawa, Gotaro. Conscription system in Japan. Publications of the Carnegie endowment for international peace,
Division of economics and history. New York, Oxford university press, 1921. xii, 245 p.

8616. Dolivo-Dobrovol'skii. Боевые силы Японии и Соединенных
Штатов. (The military power of Japan and the United States.)
Voennaia nauka i revoliutsiia, 1922.

8617. Kennedy, M. D. The military side of Japanese life.
London, Constable, 1924. xix, 367 p.

8618. Pogorelov. "Япония и ее армия." (Japan and her army.)
Voennyi vestnik, 1, 1925.

8619. Kennedy, Captain M. D. Some aspects of Japan and her
defense forces. London, K. Paul, 1928. 243 p.

8620. Sychev, Ivan I. Япония и ее вооруженнье силы. (Japan and her armed forces.) Moscow, 1930. 64 p.

8621. Hirata, Shinsaku. 日露ノ陸軍 Nichi-Ro no rikugun (The armies of Japan and Russia.) Chuo koron, 23:9, September 1932.

8622. Tonegava, S. Пособие для изучения военной японской терминологии. (A guide for the study of Japanese military terminology.) Vladivostok, 1935. 48 p.

8623. Endo, Yushiro. 皇國軍人ニ愬フ Kokoku gunjin ni uttau. (An appeal to the imperial soldiers of Japan.) Tokyo, Kinkikai, 1933. 300 p.

8624. Mizuno, Hironori. 日本名將論 Nippon meisho ron. (On the outstanding generals of Japan.) Tokyo, Chuo koronsha, 1937. 460 p.

8625. Aoki, Tamotsu. 兵器讀本 Heiki tokuhon. (Text on arms and ammunition.) Tokyo, Nippon hyoronsha, 1937. 490 p.

8626. 帝國及列國ノ陸軍 Teikoku oyobi rekkoku no rikugun. (The army of Japan and those of other powers.) Tokyo, Rikugun-sho, 1936. 168 p.

C. The Navy

See 663-673.

8627. Japan. Navy department. 海軍省年報 Kaigun-sho nenpo. (Annual report.) 1-36, 1886-1921?

8628. Hirose, Hikota. 海軍要覽 Kaigun yoran. (A handbook of the Japanese navy.) Tokyo, Kaigun yushukai, 1936. 580 p.

8629. 海軍歷史 Kaigun rekishi. (History of the Japanese navy.) Vol. 7, in Katsu Kaishu collection. Tokyo, Kaizosha, 1929.

8630. Katsu, Kaishu. 勝海舟全集 Katsu Kaishu zenshu. (Complete works of Kaishu Katsu, the founder of the navy.) Tokyo, Kaizosha, 1929. 10 v.

8631. Kawashima, Kiyojiro. 海上ヨリ日本 Kaijo no Nippon. (Japan on the seas.) Tokyo, Niyusha, 1914. 686 p.

8632. Sakurai, Kurokawa and Tatsumi. "Les étapes successives

de la marine japonaise de guerre et de commerce." Bulletin,
Société franco-japonaise, 42-43 (1919):87-115; 44-45 (1920):
19-140; 46 (1920):21-28.

8633. Jane, Fred T. The imperial Japanese navy ... assisted
by officers of the Japanese navy. London, 1904. 410 p. with
over 80 illustrations, plates, maps and plans.

8634. Hirata, Shinsaku. 海軍讀本 Kaigun tokuhon. (Our
navy.) 150th edition. Tokyo, Nippon hyoronsha, 1932. 400 p.

8635. 海軍ノ今昔 Kaigun no konseki. (The imperial navy of
Japan, yesterday and today.) Tokyo, Department of navy,
Naval popular education section, 1933.

8636. 時局ト海軍 Jikyoku to kaigun. (Japan's present
national situation: her navy.) Tokyo, Department of navy,
Naval popular education section, 1933.

8637. 十四版海軍諸例則 14 pan Kaigun sho-reiso-
ku. (14th edition: Japanese navy regulations.) Tokyo, Kai-
gun-daijin kanbo, 1936. 4 v.

8638. Hurd, A. S. "Growing power of the Japanese navy."
North American review, New York, 177 (1903):570-678.

8639. Firle. "Die geschichtliche entwicklung der japanischen
marine." Marine-rundschau, 17 (1906):1227-1240, 1368-1377.

8640. Fauvel, A. "La marine de guerre japonaise." Bulletin
du Comité de l'Asie française, 426-449, October 1909.

8641. Nantès. "Les ports de guerre du Japon." La Ligue maritime, November 1910.

8642. Maltzahn, F. v. "Weshalb haben die Japaner Port Arthur als kriegshafen aufgegeben?" Marine-rundschau, 21
(1910):1209-1216.

8643. "Über die organisation des admiralstabes und die im
zusammenhang mit ihm stehenden einrichtungen der japanischen marine." Marine-rundschau, 21 (1910):470-480.

8644. Lion, Captain. Наставление для перевозки войск и де-
сантной операции в японской армии.(Instruction concerning
transport of troops and landing operations in the Japanese
army.) Izdanie Shtaba priamurskogo voennogo okruga. Khabarovsk, 1911. 34 p.

8645. "Admiral Togo." Japan magazine, 2 (1911):315-319.

8646. Grumme. "Flottenpolitik und staatshaushalt in Japan." Marine-rundschau, 22 (1911):174-189, 476-492.

8647. Chechin, P. Настоящее и будущее японского флота. (The present and future of the Japanese navy.) Morskoi sbornik, 1911.

8648. Ogasawara, Chosei. "Histoire de la marine japonaise." Revue maritime, 198 (1913):381-392.

8649. (A Rear-Admiral). "Naval supremacy of the Orient." Japan magazine, 4 (1913-1914):703-709.

8650. Nakashima, G. The Japanese navy in the Great war. Proceedings of the Japan society (London), 17 (1920).

8651. Gorskii, I. Япония на море. (Japan on the sea.) Novyi Vostok, 4 (1924):382-389.

8652. Shvede, E. E. Военные флоты 1925 г. (Military navies in 1925.) Izdanie otdela morsil SSSR, Leningrad, 1925.

8653. Bywater, H. C. "Japanese naval policy." Nineteenth century and after, 98 (1925):689-700.

8654. Kennedy, M. D. "Japanese fighting forces and disarmament." Nineteenth century, 99 (1926):323-337.

8655. 帝國潛水艦／發達 Teikoku sensui-tei no hattatsu. (The development of Japan's submarine fleet.) Tokyo, Department of navy, Naval popular education section, 1933.

8656. Hashimoto, Masao. 我が海軍 Waga kaigun (Our navy.) Tokyo, Kaigun kenkyusha, 1933. 268 p. Another edition in 1936, 256 p.

8657. Knox, U.S. Navy, Captain Dudley W. The Japanese situation. U.S. naval institute proceedings, 61, September 1935.

8658. Saito, Naomiki. 建艦宣言案／檢討 Kenkan sengenan no kento. (Investigation of the proposal for the building of warships.) Gaiko jiho, 76:4:108-121, November 1935.

8659. Arima, Narisuke. 海軍々縮會議ト日本／將來 Kaigun gunshuku kaigi to Nippon no shorai. (Naval armament conference and the future of Japan.) Tokyo, Taiyokai, 1936.

8660. Abe, Nobuo. 海軍讀本 Kaigun tokuhon. (Textbook on the navy.) Tokyo, Nippon hyoronsha, 1937. 420.

D. Aviation

8661. 海ト空 Umi to sora. (Sea and air.) Tokyo, Umi to sorasha, 1932- (Monthly)

8662. Ust'iantsev, L. G. Воздушный флот Японии. (The air fleet of Japan.) Vestnik Vozdushnogo flota, 1, 1924.

8663. Popov-Tativa, N. "Воздушная оборона Японии." (The air defense of Japan.) Voennaia mysl', 140-154, September-October 1924.

8664. Higuchi, Kiichi. 東京ノ防空 Tokyo no boku. (Air defense of Tokyo.) Tokyo, Teikoku kokubo kyokai, 1932. 100 p.

8665. Alekseev. "Японская зенитная артиллерия." (Japanese anti-aircraft artillery.) Vestnik protivovozdushnoi oborony, 3-50, March 1934.

8666. Vladimirov, M. A. Воздушный флот Японии. (The air fleet of Japan.) Moscow, 1934. 59 p.

8667. Byas, Hugh. "Most of all Japan fears an air attack." N. Y. Times magazine section, 6, August 4, 1935.

8668. "Обзор воздушного флота Японии." (A survey of the air fleet of Japan.) Vestnik Vozdushnogo flota, 10:38-46, October 1935.

8669. Taoka, Ryoichi. 空軍ニ依ル海上通商ノ破壊 Kugun ni yoru kaijo tsusho no hakai. (Destruction of maritime commerce by the air force.) Gaiko jiho, 80:1:141-163, October 1936.

E. Strategy

See 663-721.

8670. Yao, Wên-tung. 日本地理兵要 Jih-pên ti-li ping-yao. (A strategical geography of Japan.) Peking, 1884. 8 v.

8671. K. K. "Стратегическое положение Японии относительно С.-Американских Соединенных Штатов." (The strategic position of Japan in regard to the United States.) Morskoi sbornik, 12 (1911):99-111.

8672. "Die geographischen grundlagen der japanischen wehr-kraft." Mitteilungen der geographischen gesellschaft, Mün-chen, 6 (1911):166-188.

8673. "Strategische aufgaben der flotte Japans und ihre wirtschaftlichen rückhalte." Überall, 16 (1914):445-455.

8674. Rivetta, Pietro Silvio. Un grande stratega giapponese: Oyama. Nuova antologia, 1919.

8675. Ballard, Vice Admiral George A. The influence of the sea on the political history of Japan. London, Murray, 1921. 330 p.

8676. Nishinoiri, Alichi. "A Japanese view of the Pacific pact." Asiatic review, 18 (1922).

8677. Futakoishi, Kantaro. 滿 蒙 ト 帝 國 , 國 防 Man-Mo to teikoku no kokubo. (Manchuria and Mongolia, and the defense of the imperial Japanese state.) Yuben, November 1931.

8678. "Стратегические проблемы японского империализма." (Strategic problems of Japanese imperialism.) A survey of articles ... Voennyi zarubezhnik, 6 (1932):141-158.

8679. 米 露 ト 戦 ッ テ 日 本 ハ 勝 ッ カ Bei, Ro to tatakatte Nippon wa katsu ka? (Will Japan be victorious in a war with Russia and the United States?) Conference attended by the army, navy and the air service officers, Hinode, 1:1, October 1932.

8680. Suzuki, Kazuma. 極 東 防 衛 論 Kyokuto boei ron. (A discussion on the defense of the Far East.) Tokyo, Taiyo-sha, 1932.

F. War Economics

See 781-936; 8886-9472.

8681. Pozdneev, Dmitrii M. Япония. Военно-экономическое опи-сание. (Japan. A military-economic description.) Moscow, 1924. 268 p.

8682. 日 本 戦 時 経 済 , 全 貌 Nippon senji keizai no zenbo. (General outlook on the war time economy of Japan.) Tokyo, Toyo keizai shinposha, 1932. 210 p. 46th edition.

8683. Yuzawa, Hiromi. 戦争ト経済 Senso to keizai. (War and economics.) Tokyo, Nippon hyoronsha, 1937. 356 p.

8684. Hatano, Kanae. 我國戦時経済 Waga kuni senji keizai. (War economics of our country.) Tokyo, Nippon hyoronsha, 1937, 214 p.

8685. Saito, Naomiki. 戦争経済讀本 Senso keizai tokuhon. (Text on the war economy of Japan.) Tokyo, Konnichi no mondaisha, 1937. 220 p.

8686. Noda, Yutaka. 戦争ト財産 Senso to zaisan. (War and property.) Tokyo, Konnichi no mondaisha, 1937. 288 p.

8687. Saito, Naomiki. 戦争ト戦費 Senso to senpi. (War and war expense.) Tokyo, Daiamondosha, 1937.

8688. Iwai, Ryotaro. 戦事経済ノ基礎智識 Senji keizai no kiso chishiki. (Fundamental knowledge of war time economics.) Tokyo, Chikura shobo, 1937. 330 p.

8689. See 682-721.

XVI. PAN-MONGOLIAN AND PAN-ASIATIC MOVEMENTS

See 2987-3021; 7992-8043.

A. General Accounts

8690. Takebayashi, Fuyo. 大日本帝國ノ使命ト其ノ將來 Dai Nippon teikoku no shimei to sono shorai. (The mission of Japan and her future.) Kyoto, Seishunsha, 1929. 364 p.

8691. Stepanov, A. К вопросу о панмонголизме. (On the question of Pan-mongolism.) Kazan,1905. 35 p.

B. The Japanese Asiatic Monroe Doctrine

See 4575-4584.

8692. Kaneko, Viscount Kentaro. 日本モンロー主義ト満洲 故ルーズヴェルト氏ノ遠大ナル卓見ヲ憶フ Nippon Monro shugi to Manshu: Ko-Ruzuberuto-shi no endai naru takuken wo omou. (Japanese Monroe doctrine and Manchuria: My recollection of the far-sighted view of Roosevelt.) Osaka, Asahi shinbun, September 1, 2, 3, 1932.

8693. Takeuchi, Tai. 日本モンロー主義ノ必然性 Nippon Monro shugi no hitsuzen-sei. (The necessity for a Japanese Monroe doctrine.) Gaiko jiho, 64:4:46-60, November 15, 1932.

8694. Imura, Isao. 東洋モンロー主義，經濟的基礎Toyo Monro shugi no keizai teki kiso. (The economic basis of the Oriental Monroe doctrine.) Gaiko jiho, 64:5:44-58, Dec. 1, 1932.

8695. Maeda, Yoshinori. 東亞モンロー主義 To-A Monro-shugi. (Eastern Asian Monroe doctrine.) Asahigawa, Asahigawa shinbunsha, 1933. 232 p.

8696. Kiyosawa, Hiroshi. 亞細亞モンロー主義 Ajia Monro shugi. (Monroe doctrine of Asia.) Tokyo, Chikura shoten, 1934. 280 p.

8697. Tsui, Shu-tsin. 亞洲門羅主義與中國門戶開放 Ya-chou mên-lo-chu-i yü Chung-kuo mên-hu-k'ai-fang. (The 'Asiatic Monroe doctrine' and the open door policy in China.) Wai-chiao yüeh-pao, 5:1, July 1934.

C. The Yellow Peril

8698. Vambéry, H. Die gelbe gefahr. Eine kulturstudie. Budapest, 1904. 36 p.

8699. Politikus. "Der kampf gegen die gelbe gefahr." Deutsche kultur, 1 (1905-1906):2.

8700.(Gilbert-Gidel.)"Conférence faite par M. Gilbert-Gidel sur le Péril jaune. - Chine et Japon." Bulletin de la Société de géographie de l'Aisne (Laon). 1907. 181-194.

8701. Goltz, Fritz Frhr. von der. Die gelbe gefahr im lichte der geschichte. Leipzig, Engelmann, 1907. vii, 120 p. Also see:Deutsche rundschau, 34,(1908):6, 339-356.

8702. Peez, A. v. and Wiser, F. v. Die gelbe gefahr in der geschichte Europas. Wien, Lumen, 1908. 38 p.

8703. Stone, Melville E. "Race prejudice in the Far East." National geographic magazine (Washington), 21 (1910):973-985.

8704. Rupert, G. G. The Yellow peril; or the Orient versus the Occident as viewed by modern statesmen and ancient prophets. Choctaw (Oklahoma), Union publisher, 1911. 526 p.

8705. Bland, J. O. P. "The yellow peril." Nineteenth century, 1017-1028, May 1912.

8706. Tavokin, S. N. К вопросу о "желтой опасности". (The problem of the "yellow peril".) Kiev, Vostochnaia biblioteka No. 1, 1913. 32 p.

8707. Spielmann, C. Arier und Mongolien. Weckruf an die europäischen kontinentalen unter historischer und politischer beleuchtung der gelben gefahr. 2. bis auf die gegenwart fortgeführte ausgabe. Halle a/S., Gesenius, 1914. xiv, 334p.

8708. Очерк характеристики японца и "желтая опасность".(An outline of the characteristics of the Japanese and the "yellow peril".) Translated from the French by A. Makalinskii. Morskoi sbornik, 1914.

8709. Du Bois, Fr. "Le péril jaune." Revue de Hongrie, 20 (1918):60:15-25.

8710. Lévy-Bruhl, L. "L'ébranlement du monde jaune." La revue de Paris, 871-894, October 1920.

8771. Fechner, E. Die vernichtung der Westmächte durch den erwachten Orient. Naumburg, Tachré-Verlag, 1921.

8712. Nohara, W. K. Die "gelbe gefahr": Japan und die erhebung der farbigen völker. Stuttgart, Berlin and Leipzig: Union deutsche verlagsgesellschaft, 1936. 214 p.

D. The Pan-Mongolian Movement

See 6722-6724.

8713. Ular, A. v. "Le panmongolisme japonais." La revue, Paris, 48 (1904):413-443.

8714. S-kii, A. F. "Материалы к истории интервенции. Роль Японии в пан-монгольском движении."(Sources pertaining to the history of the intervention. The rôle of Japan in the Pan-Mongolian movement.) Novyi Vostok, 2 (1922):591-603.

8715. Dashidondobe. "Об одной вреднейшей антимарксисткой теории. (О панмонголизме)." (About one, most harmful anti-marxian theory. [About Pan-Mongolism].) Vestnik instituta kul'tury Buriato-Mongol'skoi ASSR, 1 (1931):18-29.

E. The Pan-Asiatic Movement

8716. 大亜細亜主義 Dai Ajia shugi. (The Great Asia doctrine.) Tokyo, Dai Ajia kyokai, 1933-

8717. See 8690.

8718. Reinsch, P. S. "Japan and Asiatic leadership." North American review, New York, 180 (1905):48-57.

8719. "Un nouvel aspect du Panislamisme. Ambitions musulmans relatives au Japon." Questions diplomatiques et coloniales, 22 (1906):559-563.

8720. Singh, Saint Nihal. "Asia for the Japanese." Contemporary review, 9 (1910):341-352.

8721. Sawayanagi, Masataro. "Asianism." The Japan magazine, 10 (1919):141-144.

8722. * * * "Le Japon et l'avenir de l'Extrême-Orient." Le correspondant, January 10, 1921, 3-40.

8723. Gramatzky, A. "Ostasien ist trumpf." Das junge Japan, 1 (1924):220-226.

8724. Haushofer, Karl. "Der ost-eurasiatische zukunftsblock." Zeitschrift für geopolitik, 2 (1925):81-87. (2) The same. Ostasien in rahmen der Panasiatischen frage. Der Bücherwurm (Dachau bei München), 2 (1926). Heft 6. (3) The same. "Asiens erwachen in Japan und China." Das erwachende Asien V. (pp. 97-138). Süddeutsche monatshefte, 24 (1926):2:105-109.

8725. Mitsukawa, Kametaro. 世界變動ト亜細亜復興 Sekai hendo to Ajia fukko. (Political changes of the world, and the revival of Asia.) Taiyo, 32:4:140-148, April 1926.

8726. Zumoto, Motosada. "Japan and Pan-Asiatic movement." The young East, 2 (1926-1927):219-227. See also the News bulletin of the Institute of Pacific relations (Honolulu), February 1927.

8727. "Pan-Asiatic conference at Nagasaki." The young East, 2 (1926-1927):105-106.

8728. Das, Taraknath. "Pan-Asianism, Asian independence and world peace." Modern review, 45:1:44-52, January 1929.

8729. Ming-chao. 亜洲聯邦問題 Ya-chou lien-pang wên-t'i. (The problem of an Asiatic confederation.) Eastern miscellany, 28:15:42-47, August 1931.

8730. Hanaoka, Shiro. 亜細亜ノ覺醒ト支那 Ajia no kakusei

to Shina. (Asia's awakening and China.) Gaiko jiho, July 1931.

8731. Matsuoka, Yusuke. 東亜全局／動揺 To-A zenkyoku no doyo. (The political unrest of Eastern Asia.) Tokyo, Senshinsha, 1931. 149 p.

8732. Uchida, Ryohei. 日本／亜細日亜 Nippon no Ajia. (Japan's Asia.) Tokyo, Kokuryukai, 1932. 350 p.

8733. Shulunov, F. "Из истории пан-азиатской политики японского империализма." (From the history of the Pan-Asiatic policy of Japanese imperialism.) Revoliutsionnyi Vostok, 6 (1934):28:181-195.

8734. Asahi, Norihiko. 日本／大陸建國 Nippon no tairiku kenkoku. (Founding of the continental nations by Japan) Tokyo, Heibonsha, 1933. 115 p. (2) Nakatani, Takeari. 大亜細亜主義ト日支関係. Dai-Ajia shugi to Nichi-Shi kankei. (The Asia doctrine and Sino-Japanese relationships.) Tokyo, Dai Ajia kyokai, 1934. 28 p.

8735. Shishiya, Zenichi. 汎日本ブロツ／結成 Pan Nippon burokku no kessei. (Consolidation of the Pan-Japan blocs.) Gaiko jiho, 82:1:84-101, April 1937.

XVII. JAPANESE EXPANSION

See 496-517; 2987-3021; 3198-4252; 5027-5096; 5805-6446; 6722-6724; 8690-8735; 9843-10290; 11402-11464.

A. General Accounts

8736. Morris, J. "Japan, a forecast of the future expansion." Imperial and Asiatic quarterly review, Third series, Woking, 5 (1898):309-320.

8737. "Our future empire in the Far East, by the author of '1920'." Contemporary review, London, 74 (1898):153-166.

8738. Ransome, S. "Imperial policy of Japan; its bearing on international relations." Fortnightly review, London, 77

8739. Séménoff, E. "Le rôle mondiale du Japon, prédit par un grand écrivain russe." Grand revue, Paris, 29 (1904): 519-528.

8740. Byram, L. Petit Jap deviendra grand! L'expansion japonaise en Extrême-Orient. Préface de J. Claretie. Paris, Berger-Levrault & cie., 1908. xviii, 398 p.

8741. Labroue, H. "L'expansion japonaise en Europe." La revue, 803-820, March 1911.

8742. Labroue, H. L'impérialisme japonais. Paris, Delagrave, 1911. 336 p. (2) (Lebon and Lebroue). L'impérialisme japonaise. Discours de M. le général Lebon et conférence de M. Henri Labroue à la Société de géographie. Archives diplomatiques, 114 (1910):294-302.

8743, Lorin, H. "L'imperialisme japonais." Revue économique internationale, 1912:5:359-377.

8744. Kergant, A. "L'impérialisme japonais." Revue de Paris, June 1, 1912. 547-575.

8745. Okuma, Shigenobu Count. "Что необходимо для заокеанского развития Японии?" (What is necessary for the development of Japan beyond the ocean?) Vestnik Azii, 13 (1913): 73-76.

8746. Jacob, Johanna. "L'idée des Japonais d'autrefois sur le droit internationale public." Revue de droit international et de législation comparée, 2 série, 16 (1914):183-188.

8747. "Die entwicklung der japanischen kolonien. (Nach einem berichte des handelssachverständigen bei dem kaiserlichen general-konsulat in Yokohama)." Berichte über handel und industrie, 19 (1913):195-200.

8748. Polynov, K. "Колониальная политика Японии." (Colonial policy of Japan.) Vestnik finansov, promyshlennosti i torgovli, 11 (1913).

8749. Rivetta, P. S. "L'espansione coloniale giapponese." Rivista coloniale, Rome, 10 (1915):241-259.

8750. Ostwald, Paul. Japans expansionspolitik 1900-1914. Gegenwartsfragen 1913-1915, No. 8. Berlin, Politik, 1916. 44 p.

8751. "Japans expansionsbestreubungen in fernen Osten und in der Südsee." Jahrbuch, Norddeutscher Lloyd, Bremen, 1915-1916. 109-128.

8752. Klocke, Eduard. "Japans weltpläne." Konservative monatsschrift, 73 (1916):8:587-591.

8753. Clement, E. W. Constitutional imperialism in Japan. New York, Academy of political science, 1916. 104 p.

8754. 日本人ノ海外發展 Nipponjin no kaigai hatten.
(Overseas expansion of the Japanese.) Tokyo, Bunmei kyokai,
1916.

8755. Hirai, Banson. "Mitsuru Toyama, ein heros des japanischen imperialismus." (Nach Far Eastern review, September
1916). Korrespondenzblatt der nachrichtenstelle für den
Orient, Berlin, 3 (1916-1917):123-124.

8756. Moslé, A. "Japan und seine stellung in der weltpolitik." Meereskunde, Heft 9, No. 129. Berlin, Mittler und
sohn, 1917. 40 p.

8757. Rivetta, P. S. "L'espansione coloniale giapponese e
la guerra." Memorie e monografie coloniale, Serie:politica,
1918.

8758. Vilenskii, Vl. (Sibiriakov). Империализм современной
Японии и социальная революция. (Imperialism of modern Japan
and the social revolution.) Moscow, Gosizdat, 1919. 79 p.
(2) The same. "Останется ли Япония- великой державой?"
(Will Japan remain a great power?) Khar'kov, Molodoi Rabochii, 1924. 61 p.   (3)The same. Японский империализм.(Japanese imperialism.) Leningrad, Priboi, 1925, 134 p.

8759. Nitobe, Inazo. "Japanese colonization." Transactions
and proceedings of the Japan society, 17:42-51. (28th-29th
sessions, 1918-1920).

8760. Bates, C. J. L. "Japan and the world." The Japan magazine, 10 (1919-1920):187-194.

8761. Chidell, Fleetwood. "The menace of Japan." Contemporary review, 653 (1920):655-662.

8762. Challaye, Félicien. "Les ambitions coloniales de l'imperialisme japonais." Revue de Paris, 27 (1920):18:434-448.

8763. Haushofer, Karl. I. Japans ausdehnungsbestrebungen.
II. Japan im weltkrieg. III. Japans vormacht-stellung im
Osten. Handbuch der politik, II. Berlin-Leipzig, Walther
Rothschild, 1920.

8764. Kuno, Yoshi S. What Japan wants. New York, 1921.154p.

8765. Millard, Thomas. Japan and the "irrepressible expansion" doctrine. Shanghai, The weekly review of the Far East,
1921.

8766. Pitkin, W. B. Political and economic expansion of Japan. New York, Institute of international education, 1921.

8767. К. К. Нужны ли Японии новые земли? (Does Japan need new territory?) Vladivostok, 1921. 12 p.

8768. Kaufman, L. В тисках японского империализма. (In the clutches of Japanese imperialism.) Narody Dal'nego Vostoka, 2 (1922).

8769. Pavlovich, M. (Vel'tman). "Японский империализм на Дальнем Востоке." (Japanese imperialism in the Far East.) Novyi Vostok, 2 (1922):1-58. (2) The same. "Японский империализм." (Japanese imperialism.) Krasnaia nov', 5 (1922): 238-245.

8770. Rine, Victor (pseud.) (Reinstein, Victor). Machiavelli of Nippon. Japan's plan of world conquest willed by Emperor Meiji developed by Premier Tanaka. ("Tanaka Memorial" proven genuine.) New York, The wandering eye (writers-publishers), Incorporated, 1932. 111 p. (2) Tanaka, Giichi. Secret memorial concerning Manchuria, Mongolia, China, U. S. A. and the world; submitted by general Tanaka to the Japanese Emperor in 1927. Published by the China critic. Shanghai, 1931. ii, 42 p. (Cover, Japan and the next war.) (3) "Меморандум о позитивной политике в Манчжурии представленный 25 июля 1927 года премьером Танака императору Японии." (A memorandum concerning the positive policy in Manchuria, presented on July 25, 1927 by Premier Tanaka to the Emperor of Japan.) Kommunisticheskii Internatsional, 33-34 (303-304): 47-62, December 1931. (4) A plan of Japan's proposed military and naval conquest as revealed in the strategic map. Published by the Chinese national salvation publicity bureau, 844 Stockton Street, San Francisco, California. Map and text, 4 p. (5) "Японский империализм в своей отвратительной наготе." (Japanese imperialism in its repellent reality-) Kommunisticheskii internatsional, 33-34 (303-304): 11-14, December 1931. (6) Memorials presented by Premier Tanaka to his majesty the Emperor of Japan outlining the "Positive policy" in Manchuria, privately printed. Peiping, 1929.

8771. Goto, Shinpei. 日本膨脹論 Nippon bocho-ron. (On the expansion of Japan.) Tokyo, Dai Nippon yubenkai, 1926.

8772. Schmitthenner, Heinrich. "Die japanische expansion und kolonisation in Ostasien." Geographische seitschrift, 34 (1928):1-22.

8773. Katayama, Sen. "Die japanische auswanderung und die imperialistischen gegensätze." Der rote aufbau. 2 (1929):4: 161-166.

8774. Watanabe, Kaoru. 延び行ク日本 Nobiyuku Nippon.(Japan that expands.) Tokyo, Nanyo kyokai, 1930. 55 p.

8775. Gastov, Georgii A. Японский империализм. (Japanese imperialism.) A political-economic sketch. Moscow, 1930. 141 p.

8776. Hamabe, Hisaji. 何ガ日本ノ躍進ガセルカ Nani ga Nippon o yakushin saseruka. (What is the motivating power of Japan?) Tokyo, Hakubunsha, 1930. 50 p.

8777. Yüeh-fu. 第二次世界大戦与日本帝国主義戦争準備 Ti-êrh-tzu shih-chieh ta-chan yü Jih-pên ti-kuo-chu-i chan-chêng chun-pei. (The second great world war and the war preparation of the Japanese imperialism.) Jih-pên yên-chiu, 2:1, September 1931.

8778. Ch'ên, Hsin-mu (tr.) 世界王者誰 Shih-chieh wang-chê shui. (Who will be the ruler of the world.) Shanghai, Shên-chou kuo-kuang-shê, 1931.

8779. Lezhnev, I. "Три агентуры японского империализма." (Three agencies of Japanese imperialism.) Voennyi vestnik, 8:4-10, April 1932.

8780. "Отражение японской интервенции в Китае, на Филиппинах и в Индонезии." (The reaction to the Japanese intervention in China upon the Philippines and Indonesia.) Materialy po natsional'no-kolonial'nym problemam, Sbornik, 3 (1932):130-144.

8781. Davydov, K. "Персия и японская интервенция в Китае." (Persia and the Japanese intervention in China.) Materialy po natsional'no-kolonial'nym problemam, Sbornik, 3 (1932): 145-147.

8782. Varga, E. "Японский империализм в центре. мировой политики." (Japanese imperialism in the centre of world politics.) Mirovoe khoziaistvo i mirovaia politika, 5:3-39, May 1932.

8783. Ishimaru, Tota. 日本對世界戦争 Nippon tai sekai senso. (The war between Japan and the world.) Tokyo, Nichigetsusha, 1932.

8784. Takahashi, Masao. 日本帝國主義論 Nippon teiko-ku-shugi ron. (On Japanese imperialism.) Chou koron, 47:6: 57-67, June 1932.

8785. 世界征服ノ夢: 英字新聞ニ誤解サレタル陸相 Sekai seifuku no yume: Eiji shinbun ni gokai saretaru ri-kusho. (Dream of world conquest: War Minister Araki misinterpreted by English papers in China.) Editorial, Osaka, Asahi daily, August 25, 1932.

8786. Kikuchi, Kan and others. 荒木陸相ニ物ヲ訊ノ 座談會 Araki rikusho ni mono wo kiku zadankai. (A round table discussion with War Minister Araki.) Bungei shunju, 10:9, September 1932.

8787. Bogaevskii, B. L. "Археология на службе у японского империализма." (Archeology in service of Japanese imperialism.) Gosudarstvennaia akademiia istorii material'noi kul'tury, 5-6 (1932):7-20.

8788. Liu, Jung-hsia. 日本帝國主義的前途 Jih-pên ti-kuo-chu-i ti ch'ien-tu. (The future of Japanese imperialism.) Shê-hui tsa-chih, 2:5-6, December 1932.

8789. Yamakawa, Hitoshi. 日本及び世界,政局 Nippon oyo-bi sekai no seikyoku. (The political situation of Japan and the world.) Keizai orai, 7:12, December 1932.

8790. Davis, Colonel. 日本怖ルベシ Nippon osorubeshi. (Japan should be feared.) 130th edition. Tokyo, Shinkosha, December 1932.

8791. Iolk, E. "Японский империализм перед новыми авантюрами." (Japanese imperialism on the eve of new adventures.) Bol'shevik, 19:38-55, October, 1933.

8792. Sinani, G. "Япония как новый фактор в империалистической борьбе за южную и Караибскую Америку."(Japan as a new factor in the imperialist struggle for South and Carribean America.) Kommunisticheskii internatsional, 32†374:61-66, November 1933.

8793. Braude, V. D. Японский империализм. (Japanese imperialism.) Moscow, 1933. 56 p.

8794. Varga, E. "Борьба Японии за гегемонию в Азии." (The struggle of Japan for hegemony in Asia.) Sovremennaia IAponiia, Moscow, 2 (1934):3-25.

8795. Zeiskii, M. "Империалистическая Япония как фактор нарушения мира на Дальнем Востоке."(Imperialist Japan as a factor of violation of peace in the Far East.) Voina i krestianstvo, Moscow, (1934):77-90.

8796. Iota. "Пути экспансии японского империализма."(The paths of expansion of Japanese imperialism.) Tikhii Okean, 2:4:11-39, April-June 1935.

8797. Zischka, Antoine. Le Japon dans le monde; l'expansion nippone 1854-1934. Avec 25 photographies et 8 cartes. Paris, Payot, 1935. 325 p.

8798. Scherer, J. A. B. Japan's advance. Tokyo, Hokuseido press, 1935. 347 p.

8799. Eastern menace: The story of Japanese imperialism. Published by the Union of democratic control. London, 1936.

8800. Nagao, Sakuro. 世界ニ於ケル日本ノ植民的發展 Sekai ni okeru Nippon no shokuminteki hatten. (Colonial expansion of Japan in the world.) Gaiko jiho, 78:6:52-63, June 1936.

8801. Orlov, N. "Политика агрессии и нищеты японского империализма." (The policy of aggression and poverty of Japanese imperialism.) Propaganda i agitatsiia, 11 (1936):61-65.

8802. Zischka, Anton. Japan in der welt. Die japanische expansion seit 1854. Leipzig, Goldmann, 1937. 425 p. See 8797.

8803. Tsurumi, Yusuke. 張膨ノ日本 Chobo no Nippon. (Expanding Japan.) Tokyo, Dai Nippon yubenkai kodansha, 1936. 326 p.

8804. Aoki, Tokuzo. 日本民族大陸發展ノ回顧 Nippon minzoku tairiku hatten no kaiko. (Review of continental expansion of the Japanese race.) Gaiko jiho, 83:4: 108-120, August 1937.

B. Japanese Colonial Policies and Island Dependencies

8805. 殖民地便覧 Shokuminchi benran. (Handbook of the Japanese colonies.) Tokyo, Department of Overseas affairs, 1927

8806. Matsuoka, Kinpei. 日本ノ殖民的發展 Nippon no shokumin-teki hatten. (Colonial expansion of Japan.) Tokyo,

Tsuzoku daigakukai, 1912.

8807. 日本 殖民 地ニ 於ル 土民 政策 Nippon shoku-
minchi ni okeru domin seisaku. (Japan's policy on the treatment of natives in the colonies.)In Materials on economic
study of the Far East. Dairen, To-A keizai chosa kyoku,
1915-1931.

8808. Japan's failure as a colonizer. Saturday review, London, 82:358-364, October 1896.

8809. Wertheimer, F. Die japanische kolonialpolitik. Hamburg, L. Friederichsen und co., 1910. 100 p.

8810. Semple, Ellen Churchill. "Japanese colonial methods."
Bulletin of the American geographical society (New York),
45 (1913):255-275.

8811. Riess, L. "Japan als kolonialmacht." Asiatisches jahrbuch, 2 (1913):41-51.

8812. Bigelow, Poultney. Japan and her colonies: being extracts from a diary made whilst visiting Formosa, Manchuria,
Shantung, Korea and Saghalin in the year 1921.London, Arnold,
1923. xii, 276 p.

8813. Hasebe, Genjin. 過去, 我ガ 南洋 Kako no waga Nanyo. (Work undertaken in our South Seas.) Tokyo, Oka shoin,
1933. 231 p.

8814. Yanaihara, Tadao. 南洋群島ノ研究 Nanyo gunto no
kenkyu. (A research in the South Sea islands.) Tokyo, Iwanami shoten, 1936. 552 p.

8815. Kishida, Eiji. 日本ト福建 Nippon to Fukken. (Japan
and Fukien.) Gaiko jiho, 78:4:149-158, May 1936.

8816. Etsuda, Hajime. 南洋ノ重要性ト對南國策
Nanyo no juyo-sei to tai-Nan kokusaku. (Importance of the
South Seas and the national policy regarding them.) Gaiko
jiho, 80:4:35-57, November 1936.

8817. Salwey, Charlotte M. The island dependencies of Japan.
An account of the islands that have passed under Japanese
control since the Restoration, 1867-1912. A series of monographs, reprinted from the Imperial and Asiatic quarterly
review, with additions from native sources, translations,
and new information. London, E. L. Morice, 1913. ix, 147 p.

8818. Okamoto, Ryunosuke. 日魯交渉北海道史稿 Nichi-Ro kosho Hokkaido shiko. (History of Hokkaido with reference to the negotiations between Japan and Russia.) 1898.

8819. Matsuura, Hiroshi. 蝦夷年代記 Ezo nendaiki. (Chronological history of Ezo, Hokkaido.) 1870.

8820. Kobayashi, Shojiro. 蝦夷征服ニ関スル傳說ニ就テ Ezo seifuku ni kansuru densetsu ni tsuite. (Legends concerning the Japanese subjugation of Ezo, Hokkaido.) In the Journal of historical geography, 9 (1907):3-4.

8821. Müller, Max. "Die landwirtschaft, tierzucht und kolonisation Hokkaidos, deren stand und zukunft." Natur- und völkerkunde Ostasiens, Tokyo, 15 (1913):A:1-17.

8822. Davis, Darrell H. "Present status of settlement in Hokkaido." The Geographical review, 24:386-399, July 1934.

8823. Hokkaido-cho Takushoku-bu. 北海道移民史 Hokkaido imin-shi. (Immigration history of Hokkaido.) Hokkaido, Takushoku-bu, 1935. 185 p.

8824. Nippon godo tsushinsha staff. 臺灣大觀 Taiwan taikan. (Directory of Formosa.) Tokyo, Nippon godo tsushinsha, 1933. 690 p.

8825. Takekoshi, Yosaburo. Japanese rule in Formosa. Preface by Baron Shinpei Goto. Translated by G. Braithwaite. London, Longmans, Green & co., 1907. xv, 342 p.

8826. Hishida, Seiji. "Formosa: Japan's first colony." Political science quarterly, 2 (1907):267-282.

8827. Mackay, G. W. "Japanese administration in Formosa." Journal of race development, 2:2:172-187, October 1911.

8828. Ishii, Shinji. "The silent war in Formosa." Asiatic review, 2 (1913) N.S.

8829. Yogi, Seiichi. 臺灣ノ寶庫ト沖繩縣 Taiwan no hoko to Okinawa-ken. (The treasure-house of Formosa and the Okinawa prefecture.) Okinawa, Kyuyo shuppanbu, 1933. 209 p.

8830. Ikeda, Kameyoshi. 臺灣ノ全貌 Taiwan no zenbo. (A general survey of Formosa.) Tokyo, Gunji kaikan, 1936. 181 p.

8831. Rozen, A. "Кровавое сорокалетие. Формоза 1895-1935 гг. К сорокалетию захвата Японией." (A bloody fortieth anniversary. Formosa during 1895-1935. The fortieth anniversary of the annexation of Formosa by Japan.) Tikhii Okean, 3:5:105-122, July-September 1935.

8832. Kobayashi, Kyokei. 琉 球 藩 史 Ryukyu han-shi. (History of the LiuChiu kingdom.) 1874. 3 v.

8833. Leavensworth, Ch. S. "The history of the Loochoo islands." Journal, China branch of the Royal Asiatic society, 36 (1905):103-119.

8834. Schultze, G. Die besitznahme der Riukiu-inseln durch Japan in 1879." Asien, Berlin, 4 (1905):181-183.

8835. Salwey, Charlotte M. "Japanese monographs No. 18: The Kuril islands, called by the Japanese, Chishima." Asiatic quarterly review, 3 series, 34(1912):363-383.

8836. Pogranichnik. Курильские острова. (The Kurile isles.) Novyi Mir, 10 (1929):136-144.

8837. Cholmondeley, Lionel Berners. The history of the Bonin islands from the year 1827 to the year 1876 and of Nathaniel Savory, one of the original settlers, to which is added a short supplement dealing with the islands ... after their occupation by the Japanese. London, Constable, 1915. vii, 178 p.

8838. 我 統治 南 洋 群 島 案 内 Waga toji Nanyo gunto annai. (A guide to the Japanese mandated islands in the Pacific.) Tokyo, Nantosha, 1931. 119 p.

8839. Bell, H. T. Montague. "Japan as the Allies' mandatory." The Royal colonial institute journal, New series, 9 (1918):4:154-158.

8840. 聯盟脱退ト南洋委任統治 Renmei dattai to Nanyo inin toji. (Japan's withdrawal from the League of nations; her mandate rights in the South Sea islands.) Tokyo, Department of navy, 1933.

8841. Akamatsu, Sukekore. 南洋委任統治問題 Nanyo inin toji mondai. (Problems of the South Sea mandates.) Tokyo, Kokusai renmei kyokai, 1934. 100 p.

C. Expansion in the Pacific

8842. Inagaki, Manjiro. Japan and the Pacific, and a Japanese view of the eastern question. London, Unwin, 1890. 265 p.

8843. "Hawaii, die nächste beute Japans." Korrespondenzblatt der nachrichtenstelle für den Orient, 2 (1915-1916):89-90.

8844. Engelhardt, E. "Japans weltpolitik um den Stillen Ozean." Bibliothek für volks- und weltwirtschaft, herausgegeben von F. v. Mammen, Nos. 11-13, Dresden, Globus, 1916. 38 p.

8845. Kawakami, K. K. Japan's Pacific policy; especially in relation to China, the Far East, and the Washington conference. New York, Dutton, 1922. xiv, 380 p.

8846. "Watch-Dog". Main features of the Japanese and other Pacific problems. By "Watch-Dog". London, Sifton-Praed, 1925. 38 p.

8847. Bell, Edward Price. Japan views the Pacific; conversations on vital international issues with Viscount Kato, Premier, and Baron Shidehara. Chicago, Chicago daily news, 1925. 18 p.

8848. Sawayanagi, Masataro. "Japan and the Pacific questions." The young East, 1 (1925-1926):99-105.

8849. Abe, Ginjiro. 比島ト日本 Hito to Nippon. (Philippines Islands and Japan.) Moji, Ginjiro Abe, 1933. 129 p.

8850. Galperin, A. "Японская экспансия в Индонезию, Малайские штаты и Филиппины." (Japanese expansion to Indo-Asia, Malay States and the Philippines.) Tikhii Okean, 1:92-112, July-September, 1934.

8851. Oyoshimi, Chotoku. 我が統治地南洋群島案内 Waga tojichi Nanyo-gunto annai. (A guide to the Japanese mandate in the South Sea islands.) Tokyo, Naigai kenkyusha, 1935. 200 p

8852. Kojima, Ken. 南方政策ノ新意義ト帝國ノ使命 Nanpo seisaku no shin-igi to teikoku no shimei. (New significance of the policy towards the South and the mission of Japan.) Gaiko jiho, 82:1:150-170, April 1937.

8853. Shinmei, Masamichi. 南方政策ノ基調 Nanpo seisaku no kicho. (The keynote of the national policy toward the south.) Gaiko jiho, 83:5:1-14, September 1937.

8854. 世界ノ見タ日本ノ南進政策 Sekai no mita Nippon no nanshin seisaku. (Southern expansion policy of Japan as observed by the world.) Tokyo, Taiyokaku, 1937.

D. Expansion in Asia

8855. Lyman, Benjamin Smith. The future of Japan in its relations with China and Russia. Philadelphia, Sherman & co., 1897. 8 p.

8856. Okuma, Count Shigenoku. "Japan as a continental power." Independent, New York, 51:1215-1219, May 4, 1899.

8857. Wernicke, J. Japan und die ostasiatische frage. Jahrbücher für nationalökonomie und statistik. 3 folge, 31 (1906): heft 4.

8858. Rai, Lajpat. "Asiens misstrauen gegen Japan."Der neue Orient, 1 (1917):133-135.

8859. Immanuel. "Das vorgehen Japans in Ostasien 1918." Militär-wochenblatt, 102 (1918):123:2961-2969.

8860. H. L. "Die japanische gefahr in Ostasien." (Übersetung eines aufsatzes von K. Lee in "Foreign affairs" über Korea). Der neue Orient, Berlin, 6 (1919-1920):129-131.

8861. McKenzie, F. A. "The imperial aspects of the FarEastern problem." The Asiatic review, New series, 17 (1921): 419-424.

8862. See 8769.

8863. Willoughby, W. W. "Japan and natural resources in Asia." North American review, 218 (1923):170-178.

8864. Kaufman, L. "Японский империализм и Корея." (Japanese imperialism and Korea.) Novyi Vostok, 5 (1924):86-100.

8865. Zhigur, IA. "Политика Японии на Дальнем Востоке." (Japan's policy in the Far East.) Voina i Revoliutsiia, Moscow, 5:138-150, May 1926.

8866. Katakura, Tojiro. 對支殖民策 Tai-Shi shokuminsaku. (Japanese colonial policy in China.) Japan and the

Japanese, 97:7-12, April 15, 1926.

8867. Zamiatin, N. "Корея как плацдарм японской экспанции на азиатском побережьи." (Korea as a base for the Japanese expansion on the Asiatic coast.) Voina i revoliutsiia, 4 (1926):131-143.

8868. Hua-lu. 日本的東方政策 Jih-pên ti Tung-fang chêng-ts'ê. (Japan's eastern policy.) Eastern miscellany, 24:13:1-2, July 1927.

8869. Platonov, A. "Основные черты японской политики на азиатском континенте." (The basic features of Japanese policy on the Asiatic continent.) Severnaia Aziia, Moscow, 4 [16] (1927):12-43.

8870. Wang, Chao-yu. 亞洲之日本 Ya-chou chih Jih-pên. (Japan in Asia.) Peiping, 1928.

8871. Murayama, Masataka and Wang, Chao-yu. 支那カラ見タ亞細亞ニ於ケル日本ノ立場 Shina kara mita Ajia ni okeru Nippon no tachiba. (Position of Japan in Asia as viewed by the Chinese.) Tokyo, Masataka Murayama, 1929. 82 p.

8872. Inoue, Masaji. 大亞細亞ヲ興サントスル希望 Dai-Ajia wo okosan to suru kibo. (The desire to found a Greater Asia.) Jitsugyo no Nippon, 33:3:34-39, February 1, 1930.

8873. Hirano, Shunko. 日本ト支那ノ將來 Nippon to Shina no shorai. (The future of Japan and China.) Tokyo, Reigan jusanjo shuppanbu, 1930. 296 p.

8874. Gyohei, Nachitaro. 日本ニ於ケル東方問題ノ重大性 Nippon ni okeru tobo mondai no judai-sei. (The importance of the Eastern Asiatic problems to Japan.) Kaizo, 13:9:28-39, September 1931.

8875. Hsieh, Chêng-fu. 對於日本大陸政策之觀察 Tui yü Jih-pên ta-lu-chêng-ts'ê chih kuan-cha. (An outlook on the Japanese continental policy.) Nan-ching-chêng-fu kung-pao, 93, October 1931.

8876. Kuo, Ying-han. 日本北進政策下之朝鮮 Jih-pên pei-chin-chêng-ts'ê hsia chih Chao-hsien. (Korea under the northward advance policy of Japan.) Hsin-ya-hsi-ya, 3:3, December 1931.

8877. Hashimoto, Masukichi. 我國ト大陸政策 Wagakuni to tairiku seisaku. (Japan and her continental policy.)

Gaiko jiho, 61:1:43-55, January 1, 1932.

8878. Kiyosawa, Retsu. 民主黨内閣，對東洋政策
Minshuto naikaku no tai toyo seisaku. (The Far Eastern policy of the democratic party cabinet.) Gaiko jiho, 64:4:129-
141, November 15, 1932.

8879. Oyama, Ujiro. 極東問題ノ回顧 Kyokuto mondai no
kaiko. (Recollections on the Far Eastern problem.) Keizai
orai, 7:12, December 1932.

8880. Murata, Toshizo北支那獨立，機運 Kita-Shina
dokuritsu no kiun. (The opportunity for the independence
of North China.) Sekai chishiki, December 1932.

8881. Primiakov, V. "Японский империализм на Дальнем Востоке." (Japanese imperialism in the Far East.) Ural'skii
kommunist, 2:38-47, February 1932.

8882. Voitinskii, G. "Японский империализм и война на Дальнем Востоке." (Japanese imperialism and the war in the Far
East.) Tikhii Okean, 1:7-16, July-September 1934.

8883. Mariev, M.A. Империалисты готовят войну и интервен-
цию против СССР. (Imperialists are preparing war and intervention against the USSR.) Leningrad, 1934. 134 p.

8884. Imanaka, Tsugimaro.我ガ大陸政策，基調 Waga
tairiku seisaku no kicho. (The keynotes of our continental
policy.) Gaiko jiho, 80:1:330-346, October 1936.

8885. Kuno, Yoshi S. Japanese expansion on the Asiatic continent. A study in the history of Japan with special reference to her international relations with China, Korea, and
Russia. Publications of the Northeastern Asia seminar, edited by Robert J. Kerner. Berkeley, University of California
press, 1937. v. I, 373 p.; v. II (in press, 1939).

XVIII. ECONOMIC CONDITIONS

See 781-936; 5117-5194; 6317-6448; 7416-7435.

A. Bibliography

See 781; 7237-7304; 9035.

8886. Takimoto, Dr. S. 日本経済叢書 Nippon kei-
zai sosho. (Bibliotheca japonica oeconomiae politicae .)
Tokyo, Nippon keizai sosho kankokai, 1914-1917. 36 v.

8887. Honjo, Eijiro. 日本 經濟史文献 Nippon keizai-shi bunken. (Bibliography on the economic history of Japan.) Tokyo, Nippon hyoronsha, 1933. 908 p.

8888. 經濟文庫圖書目錄 Keizai bunko tosho moku-roku. (Book catalogue of the Economic library.) Tokyo, Tokyo ginko shukaisho, 1930. 495 p.

B. Periodicals

See 7305-7337.

8889. Japan. Department of agriculture and commerce. 統計報告 Tokei hokoku. (Statistical report.) 1-35, 1879-1918. Continued as Agricultural and commercialstatistics, later as Statistics of agriculture, industries and commerce.

8890. Japan. Department of agriculture and commerce.繭年報 Mayu nenpo. (Annual report of cocoons.) 1912-1920. (In Japanese and English. Early volumes as Annual report of raw silk, floss silk and silkworm eggs.)

8891. 東京帝國大學農科紀要 Tokyo teikoku daigaku noka kiyo. (Bulletin of the Tokyo imperial university, College of agriculture.) Continued as Journal of the College of agriculture. (2) 東京帝國大學農科紀要 Tokyo teikoku daigaku noka kiyo. (Journal of the Tokyo imperial university, College of agriculture.)

8892. 東京農業大學紀要 Tokyo nogyo daigaku kiyo. (Journal of the Tokyo agricultural college.)

8893. Bulletin of the Imperial central agricultural experimental station in Nishigahara near Tokyo. 1, 1907-

8894. Japan. Department of agriculture and commerce.茶年報 Cha nenpo. (Annual report on tea.) 1912-1920. Title varies.

8895. Japan. Department of finance.日本財政經濟年鑑 Nippon zaisei keizai nenkan. (Financial and economic annual of Japan.) 1, 1901-

8896.實業之日本 Jitsugyo no Nippon. (Business of Japan.) Tokyo, Jitsugyo no Nipponsha. 1, 1897- (Bi-monthly).

8897. 經濟之日本 Keizai no Nippon. (Economics of Japan.) Tokyo, Keizai no Nipponsha. 1, 1919- (Monthly).

8898. Finanzielles und wirtschaftliches Jahrbuch für Japan.

Herausgegeben vom Kaiserlichen finanzministerium. Tokyo, Quart., Deutsche ausgabe begründet 1904. (English edition, no. 45. French edition, no. 4.)

8899. The Oriental economist. Tokyo, Toyo keizai shinposha, 1, 1934- (Monthly). In English. See 68.

8900. 經済史研究 Keizaishi kenkyu. (Studies in economic history.) Tokyo, Keizaishi kenkyukai, 1, 1929- (Monthly.)

8901. 經済時代 Keizai jidai. (Economic age.) Tokyo, Keizai jidaisha, 1, 1929- (Monthly).

8902. 社會經済學史 Shakai keizai gakushi (Studies in social and economic history.) Tokyo, Shakai keizai gakkai, 1, 1931- (Monthly).

8903. 實業之世界 Jitsugyo no sekai. (The business and industrial world.) Tokyo, Jitsugyo no sekaisha, 1, 1908-

8904. 經済タイムス Keizai taimusu. (Economic times.) Tokyo, Keizai taimususha, 1, 1917- (Monthly).

8905. 人口問題 Jinko mondai. (The population problem.) Tokyo, Jinko mondai kenkyujo, 1, 1936-

8906. 國民經済雜誌 Kokumin keizai zasshi. (Journal of national economy.) Published by the Institute of commercial science of the Kobe university of commerce, Osaka, Hobunkan, 1, 1905- (Monthly).

8907. 經済聯盟 Keizai renmei. (The Japanese economic federation periodical.) Tokyo, Nippon keizai renmei, 1, 1931-

8908. 海外經済事情 Kaigai keizai jijyo. (Overseas economic information.) Tokyo, Trade bureau, Foreign office, 1, 1926-

8909. エコノミスト Ekonomisuto. (The economist.) Osaka, Osaka mainichi shinbunsha, 1, 1923-

8910. 三田學會雜誌 Mita-gakkai zasshi. (Journal published by the department of economics of Keio university.) Tokyo, Rizai gakkai, 1, 1909- (Monthly).

8911. 日英商業時報 Nichi-Ei shogyo jiho. (The Japanese-British commercial news.) A commercial journal edited in English and Japanese.) 1, April 15, 1912- (Bi-monthly).

8912. 財政経済時報 Zaisei keizai jiho. (Review of
finance and economics.) Tokyo, Zaisei keizai jihosha, 1914-

8913. 経済論叢 Keizai ronso. (Economic review.) Kyoto, Kyoto teikoku daigaku: keizai-gakkai, 1, 1915-

8914. 事業之日本 Jigyo no Nippon. (Industry of Japan.)
Tokyo, Jigyo no Nipponsha, 1, 1922-

8915. 経済学論集 Keizaigaku ronshu. (Economics.) Tokyo, Tokyo teikoku daigaku keizaigakubu, 1, 1922- (Monthly).

8916. 資源 Shigen. (National resources.) Tokyo, Kogyo chosakai, 1, 1931- (Monthly).

8917. 銀行論叢 Ginko ronso. (Banking monthly.) Tokyo,
Ginko mondai kenkyukai, 1, 1923-

8918. Japan. Institute for commercial research. 財政経済
統計年報 Zaisei keizai tokei nenpo. (Annual bulletin of the financial and economic statistics of Japan.) Tokyo, 1, 1924-

8919. 農業経済研究 Nogyo keizai kenkyu. (Research
in agricultural economy.) Tokyo, Iwanami shoten, 1, 1925-
(Quarterly).

8920. 企業ト社会 Kigyo to shakai. (Enterprise and society.) Tokyo, Dobunkan, 1926-1928. 24 vols.

8921. 国際経済新報 Kokusai keizai shinpo. (Jour-
nal on international economics.) Tokyo, Kokusai keizai shinposha, 1, 1917- (Monthly).   See 61.

8922. 経済往来 Keizai orai. (Economic intercourse.)
Tokyo, Nippon hyoronsha, 1, 1927-

8923. 財政 Zaisei. (Finance.) Tokyo, Okura zaimu kyokai,
1, 1936- (Monthly).

8924. 税 Zei (Taxation.) Tokyo, Teikoku chiho gyosei gakkai, 1923- (Monthly).

8925. Kanbara, Shuhei.(ed.) 日本経済年報 Nippon keizai nenpo. (An economic annual of Japan.) Tokyo, Toyo keizai shinposha, 1, 1932-

8926. 日本ノ貿易 Nippon no boeki. (Japan trade.) Osaka, Jitsugyosha, 1, 1932- (Monthly).

8927. 日本経済 Nippon keizai. (Economics of Japan.) Tokyo, Nippon keizaisha, 1, 1935-

C. Economic Year-Books

See 144-147; 7338-7365.

8928. 政治経済年鑑 Seiji keizai nenkan. (Political and economic year-book.) Tokyo, Nippon hyoronsha, 1932. 710 p.

8929. Sato, Teijiro. 昭和九年版: 日本経済年誌. Showa 9-nen ban: Nippon keizai nenshi. (Economic year-book of Japan: 1934 edition.) Tokyo, Zenkoku keizai chosa kikan rengokai, 1935. 407 p.

8930. Hirayama, Keizo. 昭和十年版: 日本経済年誌. Showa 10-nen ban: Nippon keizai nenshi. (Economic year-book of Japan: 1935 edition.) Tokyo, Zenkoku keizai chosa kikan rengokai, 1936. 461 p.

8931. 昭和十二年度: 日本経済年報 Showa juni-nen do: Nippon keizai nenpo. (1937, Economic year-book of Japan.) Tokyo, Toyo keizai shinposha, 1937.

D. Directories and Registers

See 144-147; 7358-7365.

8932. 大日本商工録 Dai Nippon shoko roku. (Commercial and industrial directory of Japan.) Tokyo, Dai Nippon shokokai, 1931.

8933. 帝国商工録: 満鮮版 Teikoku shokoroku Man-Sen han. (Imperial commercial and industrial directory:Manchuria and Korea edition.) Fukuoka, Teikoku shokokai, 1931. 239 p.

8934. 日本船舶レヂスター Nippon senpaku rejisuta. (Japanese shipping register.) Kobe, Kobe kaiun shukaisho, 1931. 736 p.

8935. Japan. Bureau of commerce. 日本輸出商人名録 Nippon yushutsu shonin meiroku. (Exporters' directory of Japan.) 1, 1906-

8936. The Japan mercantile and manufacturers' directory 1925-1926 and foreign residents' list. Kobe, The Far Eastern advertising agency, 1926. 1004 p.

8937. The Japan commercial directory. Tokyo, Japan trade promoters' publishers, 1922.

E. Statistics

8938. 日本経済統計總觀 Nippon keizai tokei sokan. (Manual of economic statistics of Japan.) Osaka, Asahi daily news, 1931. 1280 p.

8939. Yanagisawa, Comte Y. de "Histoire critique des travaux statistiques au Japon depuis l'antiquité jusqu'à la restauration impériale." Bulletin de l'Institut international de statistique (Haag), 19 (1912):245-307.

8940. Wäntig, Heinrich. "Die japanische statistik als wissenschaftliches quellenmaterial." Jahrbücher für nationalökonomie und statistik, 3 folge, 48 [103] (1914):244-260.

8941. Saint-Maurice, Graf. Statistiques générales et comparées japonaises. 1911. 55 p.

8942. Japan. Bureau of general statistics. 統計年報 Tokei nenpo. (Statistical annual of the Japanese empire.)1, 1881- (In Japanese. 1917 never issued).

8943. Japan. Bureau of general statistics. 帝國統計年報目録 Teikoku tokei nenpo mokuroku. (Table of contents to the Statistical annual of the Japanese empire.) 1-9, 1880-1888.

8944. Japan. Bureau de la statistique générale. 帝國統計一覧 Teikoku tokei ichiran. (Résumé statistique de l'empire du Japon.) 1, 1887- (In Japanese and French).

8945. Japan. Bureau of general statistics. 日本帝國事情統計 Nippon teikoku jijo tokei. Statistical account of the conditions of the Empire. Tokyo, 31 (1912) (Only edition issued in English).

8946. Japan. Department of home affairs. 日本帝國人口調査年報 Nippon teikoku jinko chosa nenpo. (Annual report of census of Japanese empire.) 1, 1882-

8947. Japan. Bureau de la statistique générale. 人口 増加 / 大勢 Jinko zoka no taisei. (Mouvement de la population.)) (Dispositions sur la manière de recueillir des renseignements.) (Proportions.) 1899-1908, 1910-1915. (2) The same. (Tableaux.) 1899-1918. In Japanese and French. Continued as Résumé statistique du mouvement de la population.

8948. Japan. Bureau de la statistique générale. 帝国 情勢 統計 Teikoku josei tokei. (Statistiques des causes du décès de l'empire du Japon.) 1906-1918. (To 1905 included in Statistique du mouvement de la population de l'empire.) In Japanese and French.

8949. Mouvement de la population de l'empire du Japon depuis l'an 32 jusqu'à l'an 41 de Meiji 1899-1908. (Dispositions sur la manière de recueillir des renseignements.) Tokyo, Cabinet impérial, Bureau de la statistique générale, 1912. iv, 40, 315 p.

8950. Mouvement de la population de l'empire du Japon pendant l'an 43 de Meiji, 1910 (Nombre absolu et proportion). Tokyo, Cabinet impérial, Bureau de la statistique générale, 1913. xii, 276, 90 p.

8951. 昭和七年日本帝国人口動態統計摘要 Showa 7-nen Nippon teikoku jinko dotai tokei tekiyo. (A summary of the statistics on the movement of the Japanese population -- 1932.) Tokyo, Naikaku tokei-kyoku, 1935. 127 p.

8952. Jefferson, M. "The distribution of people in Japan in 1913." Geographical review, 1916: 2: 368-372.

8953. Hanabusa, Naosaburo. Graphiques statistiques sur l' état de la population de l'empire du Japon. Tokyo, Bureau de la statistique générale, Cabinet impérial, 1916. 25 p.

8954. Japan. Bureau de la statistique générale. 人口 増加 統計大勢一覧 Jinko zoka tokei taisei ichiran. (Résumé statistique du mouvement de la population de l'empire du Japon.) 1, 1919- (Continues Mouvement de la population.) In Japanese and French.

8955. État de la population de l'empire du Japon au 31 déc. 1903. Tokyo, Cabinet impérial, Bureau de la statistique générale, 1906. 320 p.

8956. Yanagisawa, Comte Y de. "Sur le recensement des villes de Tôkyô et de Kobé." Bulletin Société franco-japonaise, 17 (1909):13-25.

8957. Takano, J. "The recent movement of population in Japan." Journal of the Royal statistic society, 73 (1910): 738-768.

8958. État de la population de l'empire du Japon au 31 déc. 1908. Tokyo, Cabinet impérial, Bureau de la statistique générale, 1911.45, 285; 59, iv, 132 p.

8959. Hanabusa, Naosaburo. État de la population de l'empire du Japon au 31 décembre 1913. Tokyo, Bureau de la statistique générale, Cabinet impérial, 1916. ix, 335, xxxviii.

8960. Statistiques des causes de décès de l'empire du Japon. Tokyo, Cabinet impérial, Bureau de la statistique générale, 1909- (Annual.)

8961. 日本帝國國勢一班（第四十七囘）Nippon teikoku kokusei ippan. (A general survey of the 47th national census of the empire of Japan.) Tokyo, Section of archives, Secretariat of the Minister of home affairs, Isseisha, 1930. 884 p.

8962. 日本國勢大觀 Nippon kokusei taikan. (A general survey of the National census of Japan.) Tokyo, Yamato shinbunsha, 1930. 2 v.

8963. Naimu-daijin kanbo bunshoka. 日本帝國國勢一班 第五十一囘 Nippon teikoku kokusei ippan dai 51 kai. (51st national census of Japan.) Tokyo, Isseisha, 1935. 966 p.

8964. Naikaku tokei-kyoku. 昭和五年國勢調査報告 Showa 5-nen kokusei-chosa hokoku. (Report on the 1930 national census.) Tokyo, Tokyo tokei-in kyokai, 1936. 161 p.

8965. 昭和八年東京市人口統計 Showa 8-nen Tokyo shi jinko tokei. (The statistics of the 1933 census for the city of Tokyo.) Tokyo, Tokyo shiyakusho, 1936. 502 p.

8966. Japan. Bureau of customs. 外國貿易年報 Gaikoku boeki nenpo. (Returns of the foreign trade.) Comparative statistics for each year from 1868. Title varies. See also Department of finance. Annual return of the foreign trade. 1882-

8967. Japan. Bureau of customs. 對外商業貿易報告

Taigai shogyo boeki hokoku. (Return of the foreign commerce and trade. -1881. In Japanese and English. Three reports issued each year: half year ending June 30, half year ending December 31 and for the year ending June 30. Continued by the Department of finance. Annual return of the foreign trade.

8968. Japan. Department of finance. 外國貿易月報 Gaikoku boeki geppo. (Monthly return of the foreign trade.) In Japanese and English. [To 1882 as Monthly return of His imperial majesty's customs of Japan. Early years issued by the Bureau of customs.] Tokyo, Ministry of finance, 1, 1883-

8969. Monthly trade return of Japan proper and Karafuto (Sakhalin) with Chosen (Korea). Tokyo, 1910-

8970. Japan. Department of finance. 外國貿易年報 Gaikoku boeki nenpo. (Annual return of the foreign trade. 1882. In Japanese and English. [1882-1883, 1885-1890 published by the Bureau of customs; 1884 by the first division of the Board of revenue; 1891 by the Bureau of revenue. Continues Bureau of customs. Return of the foreign commerce and trade]

8971. Japan. Department of finance. 大正十三年大日本外國貿易年表 Taisho 13-nen Dai Nippon gaikoku boeki nenpyo. (Table of Japan's foreign trade for 1924.) Tokyo, Sanshodo, 1926. 420 p.

8972. Statistical report of the Department of agriculture and commerce. Tokyo, Ministry of Agriculture and commerce, 1884- (Annual.)

8973. Japan. Department of agriculture and commerce. 農商務統計表 Noshomu tokeihyo. (Statistical tables of the Ministry of agriculture and commerce.) Tokyo, Ministry of agriculture and commerce, 1886- (Annual.)

8974. Japan. Department of agriculture and commerce. 統計略表 Tokei ryakuhyo. (Abstracts of the statistics.) 1, 1900- (Continued as Statistics of agriculture, industries and commerce.)

8975. Japan. Department of agriculture and commerce. 農工商業統計 No-ko-shogyo tokei. (Statistics of agriculture, industires and commerce.) Tokyo, 1919-1923. Each volume has one leaf in Japanese at end. Continues its Abstracts of the statistics. Continued by the Department of commerce and industry.

8976. Japan. Department of commerce and industry. 農商務省
統計 No-shomu-sho tokei. (Statistics of the Department
of commerce and industry.) 1, 1924-

8977. The statistical abstract of the department of agriculture and forestry 1924. Tokyo, Section of statistics,
Department of agriculture and forestry, 1926. 154 p.

8978. Japan. Department of home affairs. 内地統計年報
Naichi tokei nenpo. (Annual report of the statistics of the
interior.) 1-29, 1887-1915.

8979. Japan. Chamber of commerce and industry. 統計年報
Tokei nenpo. (Annual statistical report.) 1, 1924-

8980. The principal monthly tables in the financial circles.
Tokyo, Shoken jihosha, 1909. (Annual)

8981. Five years' statistics of Japanese banks and companies
for 1904-1908. Tokyo, Koshinjo, 1910. 1049 p.

8982. Economic statistics of Japan,1925. Tokyo, Bank of Japan, 1926. 160 p.

8983. The annual statistical report of the Tokyo chamber of
commerce and industry. 統計年報 Tokei nenpo. Tokyo,
1923-

8984. 統計・顕・ヮル日本ノ進歩 Tokei ni araware-
taru Nippon no shinpo. (Japan's progress as seen in her
statistics.) [In Materials on economic study of the Far
East. Dairen, To-A keizai chosa kyoku, 1915-1931.]

8985. Hsu, Chung-hao. 日本内閣統計局之調査
Jih-pên nei-ko tung-chi-chü chih tiao-cha. (A survey of the
cabinet statistics bureau of Japan.) Kao-shih-yüan kung-pao,
11, November 1931.

8986. 日本及各國國勢圖解 Nippon oyobi kakkoku
kokusei zukai. (Graphical explanations of the national powers of Japan and other nations.) Tokyo, Dai Nippon kokumin
kyoikukai, 1933. 24 p.

8987. Shoko-sho. 昭和八年商工省統計表 Showa
8-nen Shoko-sho tokei hyo. (1933 statistical table published by the department of commerce and industry.) Tokyo, Tokyo tokei kyokai, 1935. 228 p.

8988. Kanbara, Shuhei. 日本経済年報十八 Nippon

keizai nenpo 18. (18th annual economic report of Japan.)
Tokyo, Toyo keizai shinposha, 1935. 365 p.

8989. 大日本帝國内務者第四十六囘統計報告
Dai Nippon teikoku Naimu-sho dai 46 kei tokei hokoku. (46th
statistical report by the Department of home affairs of Japan.) Tokyo, Naimu-daijin kanbo bunshoka, 1935. 586 p.

F. Economic History

See 9010-9013; 9014-9093.

8990. Takekoshi, Yosaburo. 日本経清史 Nippon keizai-
shi. (Economic history of Japan.) Tokyo, Heibonsha, 1935-
1936. 12 v.   (2) The same. The economic aspect of the
history of the civilization of Japan. London, Allen & Unwin,
1930. 3 v.

8991. Honjo, Eijiro. 日本経済史文獻 Nippon keizai-
shi bunken. (Materials on the economic history of Japan.)
Tokyo, Naigai shuppansha, 1914.

8992. Ouchi, Hyoe. 明治前期財政経清史料集成
Meiji zenki zaisei keizai shiryo shusei. (Collection of
historical sources on finance and economics during the early part of the Meiji era.) Tokyo, Kaizosha, 1934. 498 p.

8993. Itani, Zenichi. 明治維新経清史 Meiji ishin
keizai-shi. (Economic history of the Meiji restoration.)
1920.

8994. Uchida, Ginzo. 日本経清史ノ研究 Nippon keizai
shi no kenkyu. (Research in the economic history of Japan.)
Tokyo, Dobunkan, 1921. 794 p.

8995. Yamamoto, Katsutaro. 元禄時代ノ経清学的
研究 Genroku jidai no keizaigakuteki kenkyu. (Research
in the history of the 17th century in Japan from the economic point of view.) Tokyo, Hobunkan, 1925. 762 p.

8996. Honjo, Eijiro and Kuromasa, Iwao. 日本経清史
Nippon keizai-shi. (Economic history of Japan.) Tokyo, Nippon Hyoronsha, 1928. Vol. 6 in Gendai keizaigaku zenshu.
(36 v.)

8997. Takahashi, Kamekichi and others. 日本経清史 Nippon keizai-shi. (Economic history of Japan.) Tokyo, Kaizosha, 1930. Vol. 31 in Keizaigaku zenshu. (1928-1932, 62 v.)

8998. Noro, Eitaro. 日本資本主義發達史 Nippon
shihon-shugi hattatsu-shi. (History of the development of
capitalism in Japan.) In Lectures on Social problems, v. 3.
Tokyo, Shinchosha, 1931. 339 p.

8999. Svetlov, Vladimir P. Происхождение капиталистической
Японии. (The origin of capitalistic Japan.) Moscow, 1931.
124 p.

9000. Takimoto, Seichi. 日本経済史 Nippon keizai-shi.
(Economic history of Japan.) Tokyo, Jiji shinposha, 1931.
577 p. (2) The same. 日本封建経済史 Nippon hoken
keizai-shi. (Economic history of the Feudal age in Japan.)
Tokyo, Maruzen kabushiki kaisha, 1930. 586 p.

9001. Ono, Takeo. 近世地方経済史料 Kinsei chiho
keizai shiryo. (Materials on the recent history of economic sectionalism in Japan.) Tokyo, Ryuginsha, 1932. 10 v.

9002. Koda, Naritomo. 日本経済史研究 Nippon keizai-
shi kenkyu. (Research on Japanese economic history.) Tokyo,
Ookayama shoten, 1932. 930 p.

9003. Tokyo nichi nichi and Osaka mainichi economic bureaus.
経済風土記 Keizai fudo-ki. (History of local economics with reference to geography and customs in Japan.) Tokyo, Tokyo shoin, 1932. 6 v.

9004. Chou, Hsien-wên. 日本社會経済發達史 Jih-pên
shê-hui chin-chi fa-ta-shih. (A history of the social and
economic development of Japan.) Shanghai, Min-chih shu-chü,
1932.

9005. Mitsui. The house of Mitsui, its history, organization and working. (English and Japanese text.) Tokyo, 1903.

9006. 社誌 Sha-shi. (History of the Mitsubishi company.)
Tokyo, Mitsubishi co., Research bureau, General affairs department, 1917. 20 v.

9007. Fukuda, Tokugo. "La cylicité de la vie économique et
de la politique économique éclairée par l'exemple de l'évolution japonaise de 1868 à 1925 dans ses rapports avec l'
éntranger." Journal de économistes, Paris, 84 (1926):3-45.

9008. Sumiya, Etsuji. 日本経済學史，一齣 Nippon
keizaigaku-shi no ikku. (One phase of the economic history
of Japan.) Tokyo, Ohata shoten, 1935. 415 p.

9009. Takahashi, Kamekichi. 最近 / 日本経済史 Sai-
kin no Nippon keizai-shi. (Economic history of present-day
Japan.) Tokyo, Heibonsha, 1935. 581 p.

G. Economic Geography

See 7407-7463.

9010. Japan als economisch-geographisch gebied in't verle-
den en heden. Haag, Muton & co. Tijdschrift voor economisch
geschiedenis, 13 (1922):1. 46 p.

9011. IUrkevich, T. S. Современная Япония. (Contemporary
Japan.) An economic-geographic survey of the most recent
Japanese sources. Vladivostok, 1925. 192 p.

9012. Oseki, K. "The economic geography of Japan." Scottish
geographical magazine, 31 (1915):449-465, 519-531.

9013. Nishida, Uhachi. 日本経済地理講話 Nippon
keizai chiri kowa. (Lectures on the economic geography of
Japan.) Tokyo, Hobunkan, 1929. 721 p.

H. General Accounts

See 7837-7991.

9014. Popov, Konstantin. Япония. (Japan.) Sketches of its
geography and economy. Moscow, 1931. 158 p.

9015. Geerts, Antonius. Les produits de la nature japonaise
et chinoise, comprenant la dénomination,l'histoire et les
applications aux arts, à l'industrie, à l'économie, à la
médicine, etc. Yokohama, 1878-1883.

9016. General view of commerce and industry in the empire
of Japan, edited by the Bureau of the commerce and industry
of the Department of agriculture and commerce of Japan. Tokyo, 1893. 493 p.

9017. Utsunomiya, K. Die warenpreisbewegung in Japan seit
dem jahre 1895, ihre ursachen und ihre einwirkung auf die
volkswirtschaft. (Inaugural-dissertation). Leipzig, 1897.
96 p.

9018. Fukuda, Dr. T. Die gesellschaftliche und wirtschaftliche entwicklung in Japan. (Inaugural dissertation). München, 1900. 75 p.

9019. Japan in the beginning of the 20th century. Edited by
H. Yamawaki by order of the Ministry for agriculture and
commerce. Tokyo, 1903. 804 p.

9020. Viallate, A. "L'avenir économique du Japon." Annales
des sciences politiques, 20 (1905):340-363, 490-508. (Paris)

9021. Igarashi, Eikichi and Takahashi, Hideomi. The national wealth of Japan, revised by H. E. Count Shigenobu Shibusawa. Tokyo, 1906. vi, v, 12, 355 p.

9022. Goossens, F. Le Japon économique. Bruxelles. 1906.
53 p.

9023. Viallate, A. L'avenir économique du Japon. Paris, Marcel Rivière, 1907. 112 p. See 9020.

9024. Saint-Maurice, Graf de. La civilisation économique
du Japon (1908); son expansion en Extrême-Orient. Bibliothèque des Études économiques et financières, 4. Paris,
Roustan, 1908. 116 p.

9025. Saint-Maurice, Graf de. La puissance économique du
Japon (1909). 1909. 90, xxix p.

9026. Mochizuki, Kotaro. "La situation économique et financière du Japon après la guerre." Revue économique internationale, 468-494, June 1910.

9027. Porter, Robert. The full recognition of Japan, being a
detailed account of the economic progress of the Japanese
empire to 1911. London, Henry Frowde, 1911. xii, 789 p.

9028. Rathgen, Karl. Die Japaner in der weltwirschaft. 2
auflage. Aus natur und geisteswelt no. 72. Leipzig, B. G.
Teubner, 1911. viii, 145 p.

9029. A complete account of the monopoly system in Japan.
Tokyo, Direction general of State monopolies, 1912. 68 p.

9030. Petrov, A. Финансово-экономическое положение современной Японии. (The financial and economic situation of contemporary Japan.) A statistical sketch. St. Petersburg,
1912. 94 p.

9031. Kambe, Masao. Die entwicklung der japanischen volkswirtschaft in der gegenwart. Wirtschafts- und verwaltungs-
studien no. 49. Leipzig, Deichert, 1914. 49 p.

9032. Kambe, Masao. "Grundlagen und entwicklungstendenzen der japanischen volkwirtschaft." Weltwirtschaftliches archiv, 5 (1915):63-75.

9033. 我國商工業之現在及將來 Wagakuni shoko-gyo no genzai to shorai. (The present and future of the commerce and industry in Japan.) Tokyo, Department of agriculture and industry, Hokubunkan, 1914. 552 p.

9034. Dautremer, J. L'empire japonais et sa vie économique. Paris, E. Guilmoto, 1910. 308 p.   English translation: The Japanese empire and its economic conditions. Tr. from the French. London, T. Fisher Unwin, 1910. 319 p. New edition, 1915.

9035. Takimoto, Seiichi. 日本経済典籍考 Nippon keizai tenseki ko. (A study of the economic bibliography of Japan.) Tokyo, Nippon hyoronsha, 1928. 482 p. See 8886-8888.

9036. Takimoto, Seiichi (compiler). 日本経済叢書 Nippon keizai sosho. (Series on Japanese economics.) Tokyo, Nippon keizai sosho kankokai, 1914-1917. 36 v.   (2) The same. 續日本経済叢書 Zoku Nippon keizai sosho. (Second series on Japanese economics.) Tokyo, Nippon keizai sosho kankokai, 1923. 3 v.

9037. Hara, Takeshi. "Les problèmes du Japon et les solutions qui en sont proposées." Bulletin de la Société franco-japonaise de Paris, 47:7-9, January-March 1921.

9038. Takahashi, Vicomte Korekiyo. "Exposé d'un plan pour l'avenir économique du Japon. Banquiers, marchands et manufacturiers doivent s'unir en vue d'avantages durables." Bulletin, Société franco-japonaise, 47 (1921:11-15.

9039. Okorokov, A. Япония. Торговля, промышленность, земледелие и экономическое положение. (Japan. Trade, industry, agriculture and economic conditions.) Tokyo, 1923. 280 p.

9040. Voitinskii, G. "Буржуазия и остатки феодализма в Японии." (The bourgeoisie and the remnants of feudalism in Japan.) Novyi Vostok, 4 (1923):122-128.

9041. Ogata, Kiyoshi. The cooperative movement in Japan. Preface by Sidney Webb. London, P.S. King & son, 1923. xv, 362 p.

9042. Katayama, S. Капиталистическое наступление в Японии. (Capitalist encroachment in Japan.) Moscow, 1923. 40 p.

160   The Japanese Empire

9043. Kel'in, I. Япония. Культурно-исторический и экономический очерк. (Japan. A cultural-historical and economic sketch of Japan.) Leningrad, 1924. 168 p.

9044. Uyehara, S. The industry and trade of Japan. London, P.S. King & son, 1926. xv, 326 p.

9045. Tani, G. Капитал и труд в Японии. (Capital and labor in Japan.) Moscow, Profintern, 1926. 106 p.

9046. Tsyrlin, L. M. "Экономическое состояние Японии." (The economic condition of Japan.) (1913-1925). Statistika mirovogo khoziaistva. Izd. Biullet. tsentr. statist. upravleniia, 119 (1926):149-166.

9047. Pogrebetskii, A. I. Экономические очерки современной Японии. (Economic sketches of modern Japan.) Izdanie Obshchestva izucheniia man'chzhurskogo kraia. Harbin, 1927. 166 p.

9048. Micard, Étienne. Le Japon. Monographies économiques. Paris, 1928.

9049. Fujisawa, Chikao. Capitalism, marxism, and Japanese national thoughts. Annals of the Faculty of law and letters of the Kyushu imperial university, 1 (1928):3, Tokyo.

9050. Fan, Tsung-yu. 日本資本主義與帝國主義 Jih-pên tzu-pên-chu-i yu ti-kuo-chu-i. (Japanese capitalism and imperialism.) Eastern miscellany, 26:4:37-46, February 1929.

9051. IUrievskaia, M. "Экономическая экспансия Японии." (Economic expansion of Japan.) Revoliutsionnyi Vostok, 6 (1929):120-145.

9052. Yamasaki, Kakujiro and Ogawa, Gotaro. The effect of the world war upon the commerce and industry of Japan. Economic and social history of the world war, Japanese series. New Haven, Yale university press, 1929. 345 p.

9053. Takimoto, Seiichi. 日本経済大典 Nippon keizai taiten. (Standard work on Japanese economics.) Tokyo, Keimeisha, 1928-1930. 54 v.

9054. Takahashi, Kamekichi and others. 現代日本経済研究 Gendai Nippon keizai no kenkyu (Economic study of present-day Japan.) Part I. Tokyo, Kaizosha, 1929. Vols. 41 and 42 in Keizaigaku zenshu [62 vols., 1928-1932].

9055. Penrose, E. F. Agricultural and mineral production in Japan. Tokyo, The Institute of Pacific relations. Japanese council, 1929. 75 p.

9056. Honjo, Eijiro. "The new economic policy in the closing days of the Tokugawa shogunate." Keizai ronso (Kyoto), 4 (1929):2:52-75.

9057. Penrose, E. F. Food supply and raw materials in Japan. n.p. 1930. 75 p.

9058. Yamamoto, Kumetaro. 經濟國家／提唱 Keizai kokka no teisho. (Improvement of national economy.) Tokyo, Nippon hyoronsha, 1930.

9059. Orchard, John E. Japan's economic position. New York, Whittlesey house, 1930.

9060. Moulton, H. G. with the collaboration of Junichi Ko. Japan. An economic and financial appraisal. Published by the Institute of economics of the Brookings institution. N. p., 1931. xix, 645 p.

9061. Lu, I-ming. 日本資本主義的國內及國市場 Jih-pên tzu-pên-chu-i ti kuo-nei ch'i kuo-wai shih-ch'ang. (The home and foreign markets of Japanese capitalism.) Jih-pên yên-chin, 2:2, October 1931.

9062. Chang, Shao-wu. 世界經濟恐慌中的日本危機 Shih-chieh ching-chi kun-huang chung ti Jih-pên wei-chi. (The crisis of Japan in this world of depression.) Chien-kuo yüeh-kan, 6:1, November 1931.

9063. Inouye, Junnosuke. 戰後ニ於ケル我國　經濟及金融 Sengo ni okeru wagakuni no keizai oyobi kinyu. (Japan's economic conditions and finances after the world war.) Tokyo, Iwanami, 1931. 250 p.

9064. Takahashi, Kamekichi. 日本資本主義／合理化 Nippon shihon-shugi no gorika. (How can the capitalism of Japan be rationalized?) Tokyo, Shunyodo, 1931. 526 p. (2) The same. 日本財閥／解剖 Nippon zaibatsu no kaibo. (Analysis of the plutocrats of Japan.) Tokyo, Chuo koronsha, 1931. 362 p. (3) The same. 日本經濟／現勢 Nippon keizai no gensei. (Present economic condition of Japan.) In Social science lectures, v. 2. Tokyo, Seibundo, 1931.

9065. Huang, Tsung-hai. 日本資本主義的危機及其前途 Jih-pên tzu-pên-chü-i ti wei-chi chi ch'i chien-t'u. (The crisis and the future of Japanese capitalism.) Hsin-ya-hsi-ya yüeh-kan, 3:4, January 1932.

9066. Chung-lien. 日本財閥在政治上經濟上之地位 Jih-pên tsai-fa tsai chêng-chih shang ching-chi shang chih ti-wei. (Japanese capitalists and their positions in politics and economics.) Yin-hang chou-pao, 6:19, May 1932.

9067. 一九三一年日本經濟概況 I-chiu-san-i-nien Jih-pên ching-chi kai-kuang. (The general economic condition of Japan in 1931.) Kung-shang pan-yüeh-kan, 4:10, May 1932.

9068. Nakano, Seigo. 新日本發展，大策 Shin Nippon hatten no taisaku. (A plan for the development of a new Japan.) Yuben, 23:9, September 1932.

9069. Yamazaki, Benji. 日本消費組合運動史 Nippon shohi kumiai undo-shi. (History of the consumers' cooperative movement in Japan.) Tokyo, Nippon hyoronsha, 1932.

9070. Shimizu. Yoshitaro. 日本經濟革命論 Nippon keizai kakumei ron. (Discussion of the Japanese economic revolution.) Tokyo, Chigura shobo, 1932.

9071. 日本戰時經濟，全貌 Nippon senji keizai no zenbo. (A complete view of war time economics of Japan.) Tokyo, Toyo keizai shinposha, 1932. 210 p.

9072. Takahashi, Kamekichi. 非常時經濟 Hijoji keizai. (Economic Japan in the crisis.) Tokyo, Chigura shobo, 1933. 428 p.

9073. Supply of raw materials in Japan. By the Staff of the Tokyo institute of political and economic research. n.p., 1933. 23 p.

9074. Popov, K. A. Технико-экономическая база Японии. (The technical-economic base of Japan.) Moscow, 1934. 230 p.

9075. Tsumura, Hidematsu. 非常時日本財政及經濟 Hijoji Nippon no zaisei oyobi keizai. (Finance and economics of Japan in the crisis.) Tokyo, Hobunkan, 1934. 244 p.

9076. Svetlov, V. P. Происхождение капиталистической Японии. (The origin of capitalistic Japan.) 2nd revised edition, Moscow-Leningrad, 1934. 111 p. See 8999.

9077. Keizai josei kenkyukai. 日本 ／ 経済的發展
Nippon no keizai teki hatten. (Economic development of Japan.) Tokyo, Sobunkaku, 1935. 350 p.

9078. Ishihashi, Jinsai. 我國最近 ／ 経済ト財政
Wagakuni saikin no keizai to zaisei. (Recent economic and financial aspects of our nation.) Tokyo, Heibonsha, 1935. 564 p.

9079. Takeuchi, Kenji. 日本経済 ／ 不安性 Nippon keizai no fuansei. (Economic insecurity of Japan.) Tokyo, Chikura shobo, 1935. 378 p.

9080. Vaintsvaig, N. K. Японские концерны. (Japanese concerns.) Moscow, 1935. 120 p.

9081. Grajdanzev, A. J. Effects of the occupation of Manchuria on Japanese economy. (In English) Nankai social and economic quarterly, 9:3:709-735, October 1936.

9082. Yamaue, Hisashi. 日支経済提携 ／ 動因ト
其將來 Nichi-Shi keizai teikei no doin to sono shorai. (Motives of Sino-Japanese economic cooperation and its future.) Tokyo, Toyo kyokai, 1936. 55 p.

9083. Yano, Kota and Shirosaki, Jinichi. 昭和十年度
日本國勢圖會 Showa 10-nen do: Nippon kokusei zue. (Chart of the national power of Japan based on the 1935 census.) Tokyo, Kokuseisha, 1936. 370 p.

9084. Itani, Zenichi. 日満支経済論 Nichi-Man-Shi keizai ron. (On the economics of Japan, Manchukuo, and China.) Tokyo, Genkai shobo, 1936. 358 p.

9085. Popov, K. A. Экономика Японии. (The economics of Japan.) Moscow, 1936. 551 p.

9086. Shimada, Gyuchi. 資本主義経済ト日本／経済 Shihon shugi keizai to Nippon no keizai. (Capitalistic economics and economics of Japan.) Osaka, Osaka-fu shiso mondai kenkyukai, 1936. 361 p.

9087. Nippon keizai kenkyukai. 日本経済研究 Nippon keizai kenkyu. (A research in the economics of Japan.) Tokyo, Sobunkaku, 1936. 363 p.

164 The Japanese Empire

9088. Mitsubishi economic research bureau. Japanese trade and industry, present and future. Tokyo, London, New York, Macmillan co., 1936. 663 p.

9089. Smith, N. Skene. "Materials on Japanese social and economic history." The Transactions of the Asiatic society of Japan, Second series, 14:1-177, June 1937.

9090. Lévy, R. Les conséquences du développement économique du Japon pour l'empire français. Paris, Hartmann, 1937. 183 p.

9091. Utley, Freda. Japan's feet of clay. New York, Norton, 1937. 393 p.

9092. Lederer, Emil. Japan in world economics. New York, New school for social research, February 1937. 32 p.

9093. 日本経済四季報 Nippon keizai shikiho. (Four seasonal reports of the economics of Japan.) Tokyo, Nippon keizai kenkyusha, 1937.

I. Agriculture

See 804-845.

(1) History

9094. 大日本農史 Dai Nippon no-shi. (Agricultural history of Japan.) Tokyo, Isseido, 1930. [Published by the Department of agriculture and commerce.]

9095. Norin-sho. 大日本農政史 Dai Nippon nosei-shi. (History of the agricultural policy of Japan.) Tokyo, Bungei shunjusha, 1932. 919 p.

9096. Takahashi, Kamekichi. 我が農業経済行詰り史的検討 Waga nogyo keizai yukizumari no shiteki kento. (Historical investigation on the dilemma of our agricultural economy.) Tokyo, Chuo koron, 40:10.

9097. Koda, Naritomo. 日本田制史 Nippon densei-shi. (History of land legislation in Japan.) Tokyo, Ookayama shoten, 1932. 370 p.

9098. Hirano, Gaku. 日本農民運動史 Nippon nomin undo-shi. (History of the peasant movement in Japan.) In Social science lectures, v. 15. Tokyo, Seibundo, 1932.

9099. Yanagida, Kunio. 日本農民史 Nippon nomin-shi.
(History of the Japanese peasantry.) Tokyo, Toko shoten,
1935. 192 p.

(2) General accounts

9100. Keigokee, Quanno. Agriculture and husbandry of the
Japanese islands. Translated into English by William H.
Doyle. Tokyo, 1879.

9101. Louisiana purchase exhibition, 1904. A sketch of the
history and work of the Imperial geological survey of Japan with a catalogue of articles and analytical results of
the specimens of soil exhibited. Tokyo, 1904. 60, 15 p. 2
plates and 4 maps.

9102. Liebscher, G. Japans landwirtschaftliche und allge-
mein landwirtschaftliche verhältnisse, nach eignen beobachtungen dargestellt mit terraindarstellungen und 5 sta-
tistischen karten. Jena, 1882. viii, 183 p.

9103. Fesca, Dr. M. Beiträge zur kenntniss der japanischen
landwirtschaft, herausgegeben von kaiserlich geologischen
reichsanstalt. Berlin, 1890-1893. 2 v.

9104. Ota-Nitobe. "Bauernbefreiung in Japan." Handwörter-
buch der staatswissenschaften. Second edition. Jena, 2
(1899):424-431.

9105. Gonnard, R. La production agricole au Japon. Bruxelles, Revue économique internationale, 1907. 30 p.

9106. Ehrlich. Die landwirtschaftlichen verhältnisse Japans.
Berlin-Gross-Lichterfelde, Wallmann, 1908. 32p.

9107. Ito, C. Activities of the agricultural association of
the Ito family, commemorating the Japan-British exhibition,
1910. Lecture delivered by Choziro Ito. Edited by Heishiro
Okui. London, Kegan Paul, Trübner & co., 1910. 170 p.

9108. Outlines of agriculture in Japan. Published by Agricultural bureau, Department of agriculture and commerce,
Tokyo, 1910. x, 132 p.

9109. The rural life of Japan. Translated and published by
the Bureau for local affairs, Home department. Tokyo, 1910.
51 p.

9110. Exploitation of leased farms owned by the Homma clan of Sakata. Tokyo, 1910. iii, 46 p.

9111. Semple, Ellen Churchill. "Influence of geographical conditions upon Japanese agriculture." Geographical journal, 40 (1912):589-607.

9112. Struthers, J. "Studies in Japanese agriculture." Transactions of the Asiatic society of Japan, 41 (1913):2: 351-377.

9113. Asakawa, K. "The origin of the feudal land tenure in Japan." American historical review, 20 (1914):1:1-23.

9114. Hogesteger, J. F. De agrarische kwestie in Japan. Tijdschrift van economisch geographie, 6, 1, January 1915.

9115. Katayama, S. "Аграрный вопрос в Японии."   (The agrarian question in Japan.) Novyi Vostok, 2 (1922):367-395. (2) The same. "Крестьянское движение в Японии."   (Peasant movement in Japan.) Krestianskii internatsional, 1 (1924): 85-94.   (3) The same.   "К крестьянскому вопросу в Японии." (The peasant question in Japan.) Krestianskii internatsional, 1-2 (1926):41-56.

9116. Scott, J. W. Robertson. The foundations of Japan. Notes made during journeys of 6000 miles in the rural districts as a basis for a sounder knowledge of the Japanese people. London, J. Muray, 1922. xxv, 446 p.

9117. Kol, H. H. van. "De irrigatie in Japan." Indische gids, 35 (1923):429-444.

9118. Hanada. "Аграрная проблема в Японии."   (The agrarian problem in Japan.) Krestianskii internatsional, 7-9 (1924): 89-99.

9119. Kuwada, Shiro. "Pächterbewegung in Japan." Archiv für sozialwissenschaft und sozialpolitik, 54 (1925):424-445.

9120. Volin, V. "Сельское хозяйство и крестьянское движение в Японии." (Rural economy and peasant movement in Japan.) Na agrarnom fronte, 7-8 (1925).

9121. Pletner, O. V. "Развитие капитализма в японском земледелии." (The development of capitalism in Japanese agriculture.) Na agrarnom fronte, 10, 11-12 (1925).

9122. Sako, G. Конгресс японских крестьянских союзов.(The congress of Japanese peasant unions.) Krestianskii internatsional, 2 (1925).

9123. Tselishchev, M. "Сельское хозяйство Японии." (Rural economy of Japan.) Ekonomicheskaia zhizn' Dal'nego Vostoka (Khabarovsk), 1:108-116, January 1926.

9124. Kawada, Shiro. "Agricultural problems and their solution in Japan." Keizai ronso (Kyoto), 1:2:155-191, December 1926. (2) The same. "Tenant systems in Japan and Korea." Keizai ronso (Kyoto), 1 (1926):38-73. (3) The same. Landbauprobleme und ihre lösung in Japan. Keizai ronso (Kyoto), 1 (1926):2.

9125. Honjo, Eijiro. "The agrarian problem in the Tokugawa régime." Keizai ronso, 1:2:75-93, December 1926.

9126. Pletner, O. V. "Крестьянские восстания в Японии в эпоху позднего феодализма." (Peasant uprisings during the later epoch of feudalism.) Agrarnye problemy, 2 (6):64-71, April 1928.

9127. Tani, Gompei. Крестьянство и аграрный вопрос в Японии. (Peasantry and the agrarian problem in Japan.) Moscow, Gosizdat, 1928. 110 p.

9128. Honjo, Eijiro. 日本土地制度論 Nippon tochi seido ron. (Treatise on the land system of Japan.) Tokyo, Seiji kyoiku kyokai, 1927.

9129. Pletner, O. V. Аграрный вопрос в Японии. (The agrarian problem in Japan.) Leningrad, 1928. 246 p.

9130. Nasu, Shiroshi. Land utilization in Japan. Tokyo, The Institute of Pacific relations, Japanese council, 1929. 262 p.

9131. Wen Yuh Swen, with the assistance of Carl L. Alsberg. Japan as a producer and importer of wheat. Wheat studies of the Food research institute, Stanford, 6 (1930):8. 28 p.

9132. Honso, Michio. 日本農民運動ノ現勢 Nippon nomin undo no gensei. (The peasant movement in Japan.) In Social science lectures, v. 10. Tokyo, Seibundo, 1931.

9133. Chang, Chia-chiu. 日本農村経済考察録 Jihpên nung-ts'un ching-chi kao-cha-lu. (An investigation of rural economy in Japan.) Ts'un-chih, 2:6, October 1931.

9134. Hou, Chê-mong. 最近日本之農村合作事業 Tsui-chin Jih-pên chih nung-tsun ho-tso shih-yeh. (The recent rural cooperatives in Japan.) Ho-tso yüeh-k'an, 4:1, 1932.

9135. Chou, Hsien-wên. 日本農村經濟恐慌與其政局 Jih-pên nung-tsun ching-chi kung-huang yü ch'i chêng-chü. (The crisis in rural economy in Japan and its relation with her political condition.) Shên-pao yüeh-k'an, 1:2, August 1932.

9136. Ai, Hsiu-fêng. 日本的農業恐慌 Jih-pên ti nung-yeh kung-huang. (The agricultural crisis in Japan.) (The original in Japanese by Ryuichi Imamura), Tientsin, Ta-kung daily, 1932.

9137. 植物調查報告 Shokubutsu chosa hokoku. (Report on the investigation of plant life in Japan.) Tokyo, Departments of home affairs and education, Toko shoin, 1932. 13 v.

9138. Ono, Takeo. 維新農村社會史論 Ishin noson shakai-shi ron. (Discussion on the agricultural community of the Meiji restoration.) Tokyo, Toko shoin, 1932. 485 p.

9139. Ishikawa, Hakukei. 日本農村問題ト大陸建國 Nippon noson mondai to tairiku kengoku. (Agricultural problems of rural Japan and the founding of a nation on the continent.) Nagano, Shinano mainichi shinbunsha, 1932. 160 p.

9140. 動物調查報告 Dobutsu chosa hokoku. (Report on the investigation of animal life of Japan.) Tokyo, Departments of home affairs and education, Toko shoin, 1932. 2 v.

9141. Katayama, Sen. "Крестьянская борьба в Японии. Исторический обзор."(Peasant struggle in Japan. Historical survey.) Sovremennaia IAponiia (Moscow), 1 (1934):39-72.

9142. Nasu, S. 本邦土地利用ノ研究(桑園ノ部) Honpo tochi riyo no kenkyu (soen no bu). (Land utilization: mulberry farming.) n.p., 1933. vi, 291 p. With map, tables, charts.

9143. IAchmenev, A. I. Японская деревня. (The Japanese village.) Moscow, 1934. 54 p.

9144. Holland, William L. "The plight of Japanese agriculture." Far Eastern survey, 5:1:1-14, January 1, 1936.

9145. Farley, Miriam S. "Japan's unsolved tenancy problem."
Far Eastern survey, 6:14:153-159, July 7, 1937.

9146. Fisher, Galen M. "The landlord - peasant struggle in
Japan." Far Eastern survey, 6:18:201-206, September 1,
1937.

(3) Rice

9147. Japan. Department of agriculture and commerce. 米穀
年報 Beikoku nenpo. (Annual report on rice.) 1912-1920.

9148. Rice inspection and its results, by the Rice inspection office in the Prefecture of Toyama (Japan). 1910. 37 p.

9149. Bachmann, C. Der reis. Geschichte, kultur und geographische verbreitung, seine bedeutung für die wirtschaft und
den handel." Beihefte zum tropenpflanzer, 4 (1912):209-386.

9150. Материалы по рисосеянию в Приморье. (Sources pertaining to rice-sowing in the Maritime province.) Book 1, Results of experimental institutions on rice cultivation in
Japan. Vladivostok, izd. Zemel'nogo upravleniia, 1925. 90 p.

9151. Nakazawa, Benjiro. 日本米價變動史 Nippon bei-
ka hendo-shi. (History of the price fluctuations of rice in
Japan.) Tokyo, Menbundo, 1933. 600 p.

(4) Silk

9152. Gan, O. Развитие шелководства в Японии. (Development of the silk industry in Japan.) Published in the
periodical Promyshlennost' i torgovlia, 1910, number 20.

9153. Bavier, E. de. Japans seidenzucht, seidenhandel und
seidenindustrie, translated from the French. Zürich, 1874.
103 p.

9154. Bolle, J. Der seidenbau in Japan nebst einem anhang
über die gelboder fettsucht der seidenraupe, eine parasitä-
re krankheit. Budapest, 1895. 141 p. (Re-issued, Wien. 1898)

9155. Paton, G. P. Reports on the raw silk industry of Japan, and on habutae (Japanese manufactured silk). British
diplomatic and consular reports, no 672. London, 1909. 55 p.

9156. Martell, Paul. "Die seidenindustrie in Japan." Asien,, Berlin, 10 (1910-1911):2-4, 23-24.

9157. The sericultural industry in Japan. Compiled for the Japan-British exhibition by the Japan sericultural association. Tokyo, 1910. ii, 158 p.

9158. Sericultural investigations. A general report by the sericultural institute. Tokyo, 1910. 203 p.

9159. Bolle, J. La sériculture au Japon. Traduit de l'italien par F. Lambert. Montpellier, Coulet et fils, 1913. 90 p.

9160. Wakatsuki, F. Le pays des cerisiers et de la soie. Paris, Desforges, 1924.

9161. Estrade, C. Etoffes de soie du Japon. Paris, 1925.

9162. One thousand facts about the raw silk industry of Japan. Tokyo (?), The Raw silk association, 1927.

9163. Chang, Hung-tu. 日本人造絲業最近概况 Jih-pên jên-tso-szu-yeh tsui-chin kai-kuang. (The most recent status of the Japanese artificial silk industry.) Chien-yeh yüeh-pao, 11:9, September 1931.

9164. 蠶絲要鑑 Sanshi yokan. (Essentials of sericulture.) Tokyo, Japan silk association, 1931. 468 p.

9165. Yang, Hsien-hsü. 日本三人造絲業 Jih-pên chih jên-tso-szu yeh. (The artificial silk industry of Japan.) Chien-yeh yüeh-pao, 12:2, February 1932.

9166. Tung, Yü-min. 日本蠶絲業與合作制度 Jih-pên chan-szu-yeh yü ho-tso chih-tu. (The Japanese silk industry and the cooperative system.) Ho-tso yüeh-kan, 4:5, May 1932.

9167. Astaurov, B. L. Племенное шелководство в Японии и задачи шелководства СССР. (Silk-worm breeding in Japan and problems of sericulture in the USSR.) Moscow, 1933. 192 p.

(5) Tea

9168. Japonicus. "Japans teekultur in geschichte und neuerer entwicklung." Das junge Japan, 1 (1925):310-328, 389-391.

J. Forestry

9169. Matsunami, Hidemi.明 治 林 業 史要 Meiji ringyo shiyo. (Essence of the History of forestry in the Meiji era, 1867-1912.) Tokyo, Dai Nippon sanrinkai, 1929. 2 v.

9170.日 本 林 制 史 資 料 Nippon rinsei-shi shiryo. (Materials on the history of forestry administration in Japan.) Tokyo, Department of agriculture and forestry, Choyokai, 1931. 3 v.

9171.帝 國 林 業. 鯨. 覧 Teikoku ringyo soran. (Outline of forestry in the empire of Japan.) Tokyo, Imperial forest society, Dai Nippon sanrinkai, 1929. 800 p.

9172. Watanabe, Zen. 日 本, 森 業 Nippon no shingyo. (Forestry in Japan.) Tokyo, Dai Nippon sanrinkai, 1929. 440 p.

9173. Watanabe, Zen and Hayao, Ushimaro. 日 本, 林 業 Nippon no ringyo. (Forestry in Japan.) Tokyo, Teikoku shinrinkai, 1931. 440 p.

9174. Hirata, Tokutaro. Contribution to the problem of the relation between   forest and water in Japan. Forestry experimental station, Meguro, Tokyo, 1929.

9175. "Японский лесной рынок." (Japanese timber market.) lesopromyshlennoe delo, 10-11 (1925):16-21.

9176. Eckbo, N. B. "Forests of Japan." American forestry, 21 (1915):693-711.

K. Industry

See 846-863.

(1) History

9177. Takimoto, Dr. Seiichi.日 本 産 業 資 料 大系 Nippon sangyoshiryo taikei. (Materials for the history of Japanese industry.) Tokyo, Nippon sangyoshiryo kankokai, 1926. 12 v.

9178. Yokoi, Tokifuyu.日 本 工 業 史 Nippon kogyo-shi.(The history of Japanese industry.) Tokyo, Hakuyosha, 1926.

9179. Akramovskaia, V. "Из истории рабочего движения в Японии." (History of the labor movement in Japan.) Vestnik truda, 4, 1925.

9180. Takahashi, Kamekichi. 明治大正産業發達史
Meiji Taisho sangyo hattatsu-shi. (The development of industries during the Meiji and Taisho eras, 1868-1926.) Tokyo, Kaizosha, 1929. 763 p.

9181. Ubara, Yoshitoyo. 日本産業、革命論 Nippon sangyo
kakumeiron. (Treatise on the Industrial revolution in Japan.) Tokyo, Chigura shobo, 1933.

9182. 特許局五十年史 Tokkyo-kyoku 50-nen shi. (History of 50 years of the patent office.) Tokyo, Tokkyo-kyoku, Tokkyo-ho shiko 50-nen kinenkai, 1935. 203 p.

(2) General Accounts

9183. Rein, J. J. Industries of Japan together with an account of its agriculture, forestry, arts and commerce,
translated from the German. London, 1889. 570 p.

9184. Heber, Ernst Arthur. Japanische industriearbeit. Eine
wirtschaftswissenschaftliche und kulturhistorische studie.
Probleme der weltwirtschaft 7. Jena, G. Fischer, 1912. viii,
282 p. (2) The same. Japans industriearbeit, ein faktor
in der politischen entwicklung des Fernen Ostens." Deutsche
politik, (1916):1388-1395.

9185. Kol, H. H. van. De ontwikkeling der groot-industrie
in Japan. Rapport samengestellt ingevolge opdracht van den
Minister van kolonien. Haag, J. Bootsma, 1916. 2 v.

9186. Dyes, W. A. Gross-Japans wirtschaftliche entwicklung
mit berücksichtigung der chemischen und verwandten indust-
rien. Göthen, O. v. Halem, 1917. 48 p.

9187. Bertrand, A. Die entwicklung der chemischen industrie
in Japan. Dokumente zu Englands handelskrieg, no. 331. Die
Chemische industrie, 40 (1917):24.

9188. Berliner, S. und Meissner, K. Die entwicklung der japanischen eisenindustrie während des krieges. Weltwirtschaftliche abhandlungen no. 3. Hannover, Hahn, 1920. 60 p.

9189. Gins, G. "Индустрианизованная Япония." Vestnik IAponii, 5-7 (1925):80-91. A reprint in English -- Japan in-
dustrialized: facts and impressions. Harbin, 1925. 70 p.

9190. Holland, Maurice. Industrial transition in Japan. Tokyo, National research council; New York, Japan society,
1927.

9191. Liu, H. C. 日本工業化問題 Jih-pên kung-yeh-hua wên-t'i. (The problem of industrialization of Japan.) Quarterly review of social sciences, 1:1:29-49, March 1930.

9192. Maurette, Fernand. Social aspects of industrial development in Japan. Studies and reports. Series B (Economic conditions), no. 21. Geneva, International labor office, 1934. 69 p.

9193. Yoshino, Shinji. 日本工業政策 Nippon kogyo seisaku. (Industrial policy of Japan.) Tokyo, Nippon hyoronsha, 1935. 349 p.

9194. Takahashi, Kamekichi. Factors in Japan's recent industrial development. Prepared for the Sixth conference of the Institute of Pacific relations. Japanese council papers. no. 11. Tokyo, 1936. 35 p.

(3) Special Accounts

9195. Ehlers, J. H. Raw materials enering into the Japanese iron and steel industry. Trade information bulletin no 573. Washington, U. S. department of commerce, Bureau of foreign and domestic commerce, Government printing office, 1928.

9196. Takeuchi, Kenji. 世界ノ鉄鉱問題ト日本 Sekai no tekko mondai to Nippon. (Iron ore problem of the world and Japan.) Gaiko jiho, 81:5:60-70, March 1937.

9197. Buetz, G. "Die entwicklung der japanischen kupferindustrie." Der neue Orient, Berlin, 10 (1921-1922):21-23.

9198. Barker, J. Ellis. "The rural industries of Japan." Asiatic quarterly review, Third series, 22 (1906):97-117.

9199. 日本紡織年鑑 Nippon boshoku nenkan. (Japan year-book of spinning and weaving industries.) Tokyo, Nippon boshoku tsushinsha, 1931. 972 p.

9200. Crewdson, Wilson. "The textiles of old Japan." Transactions and proceedings of the Japan society, 11 (1914): 4-25.

9201. Schultze, Ernst."Der sturmschritt der asiatischen textilindustrie." Der neue Orient, Berlin, 1-12 (1922):281-290.

9202. Pfitzner, Johannes. "Die japanische baumwollindustrie." Der neue Orient, Berlin, 5 (1919):187-189.

9203. Fukuhara, H. H. The past, present and future of the cotton industry in Japan. (A paper read before the New England cotton manufacturers' association, Pan-American meeting, held in Buffalo, N. Y. on September 25-26, 1901.) Reprinted Tokyo, no date, 1902(?).

9204. Nishi, Hikotaro. Die baumwollspinnerei in Japan. Tübingen, Laupp, 1911. vii, 264 p. Zeitschrift für die gesammte staatwissenschaft, Ergänzungsheft 40.

9205. Uyeda, Tejíro and others. Small-scale industries of Japan: The cotton industry. Sixth conference of the Institute of Pacific relations, 1936. 101 p.

9206. 米國人ノ觀タル日本綿工業ト其貿易 Beikokujin no mitaru Nippon menkogyo to sono boeki. (Japan cotton industry and cotton trade as viewed by Americans.) In Materials of economic study of the Far East, v. 15, part 9, and v. 16, part 2.

9207. Ho-fa. 日本紡織工業之不景氣 Jih-pên fang-chih kung-yeh chih pu-ching-ch'i. (The depression of the textile industry in Japan.) Kuo-chi-mao-i tao-pao, 2:12, December 1931.

9208. Uyeda, Teijiro. The rayon textile industry. Sixth conference of the Institute of Pacific relations, 1936. 26 p.

9209. Uyeda, Teijiro. The woolen industry. Sixth conference of the Institute of Pacific relations, 1936. 45 pp.

9210. 震災ト本邦纖維工業 Shinsai to honpo seni kogyo. (The Earthquake and the fiber industry of Japan proper.) Materials on economic study of the Far East, v. 10, part 2.

9211. Uyeda Teijiro. The rubber goods industry. Sixth conference of the Institute of Pacific relations, 1936. 55 p.

9212. Uyeda, Teijiro. The electric lamp industry. Sixth conference of the Institute of Pacific relations, 1936. 25p.

9213. Uyeda, Teijiro. The enameled ironware industry. Sixth conference of the Institute of Pacific relations, 1936. 16 p.

9214. Uyeda, Teijiro. The bicycle industry. Sixth conference of the Institute of Pacific relations, 1936. 25 p.

9215. Oku, K. The salt industry of Japan. Tokyo, 1901.

9216. Nishikawa, T. Soda industry of Japan. Manchuria daily news. Monthly supplement. Dairen, 1926.

9217. Saito, S. Japanese culture pearls. Tokyo, 1904.

9218. Bonshtedt, E. M. "Японский жемчуг." (Japanese pearls.) Priroda, 5-6 (1926).

9219. Crewdson, Wilson. "Japanese leather." Transactions and proceedings of the Japan society, London, 14 (1916): 62-70.

9220. Taki, Seiichi. "Causes of development of Japanese artistic industries." Kokka, 18 (1907-1908):173-181.

9221. "Das altjapanische kampfermonopol." Berichte über handel un industrie, 11 (1908):725-745; 12 (1908):221 (Berichtigung).

L. Commerce and Trade

See 864-898; 8938-8989.

(1) History

9222. Endo, Yoshiki. 日本商業史 Nippon shogyo-shi. (Commercial history of Japan.) Tokyo, Hobunkan, 1891.

9223. Yokoi, Tokifuyu. 日本商業史 Nippon shogyo-shi. (The history of Japanese commerce.) Tokyo, Hakuyosha, 1926.

9224. See 894.

9225. Abe, Hidesuke. 近世商業史 Kinsei shogyo-shi. (Recent commercial history of Japan.) Tokyo, Jiji shinposha, 1931. 391 p.

9226. Takimoto, Seichi and Mukai, Shikamatsu. 日本商業史 Nippon shogyo-shi. (Commercial history of Japan.) Tokyo, Chugai shogyo shinposha, 1932. Vol. 8, in Nippon Sangyo shiryo taikei (1926-1932, 13 v.)

9227. Shimada, Sosuke. 日本古代商業史 Nippon kodai shogyo-shi. (History of commerce in ancient Japan.) 1887.

176   The Japanese Empire

9228. Meylan, G. F. Geschichte des handels der Europäer in Japan; translated from the Dutch into German by F. W. Dieterich. Leipzig, 1861.

9229. Münsterberg, O. Japan's auswärtiger handel von 1542 bis 1854 bearbeitet nach quellenberichten. Stuttgart, 1896. 38, 312 p. (Forms v. 10 of the "Münchener volkswirthschaftliche studien".)

9230. Paske-Smith, M. T. "The Japanese trade and residence in the Philippines before and during the Spanish occupation." Transaction of the Asiatic society of Japan, 42 (1914):2:683-710.

9231. 德川 時代 商業 叢書 Tokugawa jidai shogyo sosho. (Commerce in the Tokugawa period, 1600-1867.) Tokyo, Kokusho kankokai, 1931-1932. 3 vols.

9232. 商工省要覧 Shoko-sho yoran. (Department of commerce and industry and its functions.) Tokyo, Naigai shoko jiho, 1931. 590 p.

9233. Tsêng, Yin. 日本貿易局之組織及其改善計劃 Jih-pên mao-i-chü chih tsu-chih chi ch'i kai-shan chi-hua. (The organization of the Japanese trade bureau and the project for its improvement.) Kung-shang pan-yüeh-k'an, 4:1, January 1932.

9234. Kawashima, Shintaro. 過去四十年本邦對外貿易回顧 Kako 40-nen honpo taigai boeki kaiko. (Review of Japan's foreign trade during the last 40 years.) Gaiko jiho, 82:1:280-298, April 1937.

(2) General Accounts

9235. Tateish, S. Japans internationale handelsbeziehungen mit besonderer berücksichtigung der gegenwart. (Inauguraldissertation. Halle, 1902. 98 p.

9236. Hattori, Y. "Foreign commerce of Japan since the restoration, 1869-1900." Johns Hopkins university studies in historical and political science, Baltimore, 22 (1904):9-10:491-570.

9237. Kinoshita, Y. The past and present of Japanese commerce. Columbia university studies in history, economics and law, New York, 16 (1902):1.

9238. Masuda, Takashi. Japan. Its commercial development

and prospects. London, Sisley, 1908. 127 p.

9239. Returns of the foreign trade of the empire of Japan
for the 41 years from 1868 to 1908 inclusive. Tokyo, Bureau
of revenue, Department of finance, 1909. 348 p.

9240. Pringle, J. C. "The significance of the Japanese raw
silk export." Keizai ronso, 21 (1911):289-308.

9241. Clark, W. A. Graham. Cotton goods in Japan and their
competition on the Manchurian market. Department of commerce, Bureau of foreign and domestic commerce, Special
agents series no. 86. Washington, Government printing office, 1914. 282 p.

9242. Yamasaki, Keiichi. "Resources of Japan in their relation to British commerce after the war." Transactions
and proceedings of the Japan society, 15 (1916-1917):78-84.

9243. Schuchart, T. Japans rüstung für den handelskrieg.
Berlin, Deutscher überseedienst, 1918.

9244. United States tariff commission: Japan. Trade during
the war. A study of the trade of Japan, particularly during
the years 1913 to 1917 and with special reference to the
trade with the United States. Washington, Government printing office, 1919. 147 p.

9245. Mossdorf, O. Die förderung des japanischen aussenhan-
dels im weltkriege. Schriften des verbandes für den Fernen
Osten, 5. Berlin, Curtius, 1920. 32 p.

9246. Berliner, S. Organisation und betrieb des japanischen
importhandels. Weltwirtschaftliche abhandlungen. Hannover,
Hahn, 1920. iv, 114 p.

9247. The foreign trade of Japan. A study of the trade of
Japan with special reference to that with the United States.
United States tariff commission. Washington, Government
printing office, 1922. vii, 229 p.

9248. Shlezinger, B. Экспортные возможности Японии. (Export
possibilities of Japan.) Ekonomicheskoe obozrenie (Moscow),
15 (1924).

9249. Takagi, Rokuro. 支那關稅會議ト我貿易ニ及ホス
影響 Shina kanzei kaigi to waga boeki ni oyobosu.
eikyo. (The Chinese tariff convention, and the effect upon
our Chinese trade.) Jitsugyo no Nippon, 28:18, Sept., 1925.

9250. 大正十三年大日本外國貿易年表 Taisho
13-nen Dai Nippon gaikoku boeki nenpyo. (Table of Japan's
foreign trade for 1924.) Tokyo, Department of finance, Sanshodo, 1926. 420 p.

9251. Sumida, Shoichi. 日本海法史 Nippon kaiho-shi.
(History of Japanese marine law.) Tokyo, Ganshodo, 1927.
462 p.

9252. The foreign trade of Japan. Tokyo, Ministry of trade
and industry, Maruzen, 1928.

9253. Koepsel, Kurt. Die entwicklung des japanischen aus-
senhandels, insbesondere der deutsch-japanischen handelsbeziehungen vor dem weltkriege. (Inaugural-dissertation.)
Kassel, Selbstverlag, 1929.

9254. Chêng, Wên-ai. 日本商業與勞工 Jih-pên shang-
yeh yü lao-kung. (Commerce and laborers in Japan.) Ch'ien-
yeh vüeh-pao, 11:9, September 1931.

9255. Japan. Department of finance. 昭和八年日本外國
貿易年報 Showa 8-nen Nippon gaikoku boeki nenpo.
(1933 annual reports of Japanese foreign trade.) Tokyo,
Naikaku insatsu-kyoku, 1935. 2 vols. (2) The same. 昭和
九年：日本外國貿易年報 Showa 9-nen Nippon gaikoku
boeki nenpo. (1934 annual reports of Japanese foreign
trade.) Tokyo, Naikaku insatsu-kyoku, 1936.

9256. Japan's trade expansion. Foreign policy reports (New
York), 10 (1934):16.

9257. Ichikawa, Taijiro. 轉換期日本貿易政策，課題
Tenkanki Nippon boeki seisaku no kadai. (Japan's trade pol-
icy at the turning point and problems involved thereby.)
Gaiko jiho, 79:4:132-143, August 1936.

9258. Japan's trade boom: does it menace the United States?
Foreign policy reports (New York), 12 (1936):1.

9259. Voitinskii, G. (ed.) Торговая экспансия Японии.
(Commercial expansion of Japan.) Collection of articles.
Moscow, 1936. 220 p.

9260. Kamisaka, Seitaro. 日蘭會商ノ經過 Nichi-Ran kai-
sho no keika. (Proceedings of the Dutch-Japanese commercial
parley.) Tokyo, Seitaro, Kamisaka 1936. 144 p.

9261. Recent developments of the foreign trade of Japan, particularly in relation to the trade of the United States. U. S. tariff commission. Washington, D. C., 1936. 207 p.

9262. Tokyo association for the liberty of trading. A brief analysis of Japan's foreign trade. Tokyo, 1936. 58 p.

9263. Miyata, Yasuro. 日本貿易鳥瞰圖 Nippon boeki chokanzu. (A bird's-eye view of Japanese trade.·) Tokyo, Hakuyosha, 1936. 384 p.

9264. Uyeda, Teijiro. The recent development of Japanese foreign trade. With special reference to restrictive policies of other countries and attempts at trade agreements. Prepared for the Sixth conference of the Institute of Pacific relations. Tokyo, 1936. 127 p.

9265. Trademarks. Complete list of trade marks registered at the Japanese patent office since its reformation in 1884 up to December 31, 1904. About 3000 pages in photo-lithography. Tokyo, 1905. 2 v.

9266. 日本登錄商標大全 Nippon toroku shohyo taizen. (A complete work on Japanese registered trade marks.) Tokyo, Tokyo shoin, 1931.

9267. 日本商標彙刊 Jih-pên shang-piao hui-k'an. (A collection of Japanese trade marks.) Shanghai, 1931.

9268. Mahlmann, J. J. The Inland Sea and Coast Pilot. 2nd revised and enlarged edition. Yokohama, 1898. 241 p.

9269. Grosse, V. "Торговые порты запада Японии." (Trade ports of western Japan.) Sbornik konsul'skikh donesenii, 4 (1907):243-262.   (2) Maksimov, A. "Порт Цуруга." (Port Tsuruga.) Sbornik konsul'skikh donesenii, 2 (1907):115-119.

6270. "Japanese shipping." Tokyo gazette, 1:1-11, July 1937.

(3) The Commercial Code

See 8473-8532.

9271. Commercial code of Japan, promulgated on April 26, 1890, came in force on July 1, 1893. Official English translation. Tokyo, 1893. 142 p.

9272. Japanese commercial law, containing the law of bankrupcy of partnerships and companies, and of bills of ex-

change, notes and cheques, in a systematic form. Translated
into English by Dr. L. Loenholm. Tokyo, 1895. 128, 10 p.

9273. Commercial code of 1898 (which came in force on June
16, 1899). English translation by L. Loenholm, fourth edition. Tokyo, 1905. 218 p.

9274. Schroeder, F. Notes on the commercial code of Japan
and the law concerning its operation. (A commentary to the
Commercial code of Japan, based on the German commercial
code and English commercial law). Yokohama, 1900.

9275. The commercial code of Japan, by Yang Yin Hang. Boston, 1911. 319 p.

9276. Commercial code of Japan. Translated by K. Vogt, assisted by G. O. Heath. Second edition. Yokohama, Geiser &
Gilbert, Kelly & Walsh, 1912. (Appendix, index to the Commercial code of Japan.) 71 p.

9277. The commercial code of Japan, laws and ordinances relating thereto. Translated by L. H. & R. N. Loenholm. 6th
edition. Tokyo, 1920. 196 p.

9278. Ripert, G. et Komachiya, Sozo. Code de commerce de l'
empire du Japon. Traduction française avec une introduction
et des notes. Paris, 1924. 292 p.

9279. The commercial code of Japan. Translated by J. E. de
Becker. London, 1927. 280 p.

(4) Tariff

9280. Ota, Seiko. 日本関税発達史論 Nippon kanzei
hattatsu-shi ron. (A discussion on the history of the development of the customs system of Japan.) In Series on social ecnomics. Nippon hyoronsha, Tokyo.

9281. The revised customs import tariff of Japan. Tokyo,
1903. 79, 25 p.

9282. Customs tariff of Japan. (Revised to June, 1912). Introduction by F. R. Rutter. Department of commerce and labor. United States bureau of manufactures, Tariff series 28.
Washington printing office, 1912. 88 p.

9283. Customs tariff of Japan. Washington, 1912. 88 p. Supplement, 1913. Supplement, 1914.

9284. "Japan. Änderungen im japanischen zolltarifgesetz und zolltarif." Deutsches handelsarchiv, 1 (1921):331-336.

9285. Magami, Umeo. Import tariff of Japan, 1926. Tokyo, Japan times, 1926. 320 p.

9286. Takimoto, Seiichi and Mukai Shikamatsu. 我國ノ関税 Waga kuni no kanzei. (Customs duties in Japan.) Tokyo, Chugai shogyo shinposha, 1932. In Nippon sangyo shiryo taikei, v. 10.

9287. Sato, Teijiro. 日満関税政策ノ研究 Nichi-Man kanzei seisaku no kenkyu. (Research in the Japanese-Manchurian tariff policy.) Tokyo, To-A keizai chosa-kyoku, 1934. 283 p.

9288. Kawashima, Shintaro. 對外貿易發展ト関税改正 Taigai boeki hatten to kanzei kaisei. (Foreign trade expansion and the revision of the tariff.) Gaiko jiho, 80:4:1-20, November 1936.

9289. Kawashima, Shintaro 本邦関税改正批判 Honpo kanzei kaisei hihan. (Criticism of the tariff revision of Japan.) Gaiko jiho, 81:3:1-18, February 1937.

9290. Hirano, Tsuneji. 我ガ関税改正ト輸出振興策 Waga kanzei kaisei to yushutsu shinko-saku. (Revision of our tariff and the plan for promoting exportation.) Gaiko jiho, 83:1:138-151, July 1937.

M. Finances

See 930-936.

(1) History

9291. 日本財政經濟史料 Nippon zaisei keizai shiryo. (Materials for financial and economic history of Japan.) Tokyo, Department of finance, Zaisei keizai gakkai, 1922-1925. 11 v.

9292. Andréadès, A. "Japanese finance since the war." Foreign affairs (New York), 10:485-501, April 1932.

9293. Otsuka, Kinnosuke and others. 日本資本主義經達史講座 Nippon shihon-shugi hattatsu-shi koza. (Lectures on the history of the development of capitalism in Japan.) Tokyo, Iwanami shoten, 1932. 7 v.

9294. Takizawa, Matsuyo. The penetration of money economy in Japan and its effects upon social and political institutions. New York, Columbia university press, 1927.

9295. Kuroita, Katsuyoshi. "The financial policy of the Tokugawa shogunate." Japan magazine, 4 (1913-1914):13-19.

9296. 明 治 財 政 史 Meiji zaisei-shi. (Financial history of the Meiji era.) Tokyo, Meiji zaisei-shi kankokai, 1926-1931. 15 v.

9297. 明 治 前 期 財 政 経 済 資 料 集 成 Meiji zenki zaisei keizai shiryo shusei. (Collection of historical materials on the finance and economics of the first part of the Meiji era.) Tokyo, Department of finance, 1931-1933. 18 v.

9298. Ouchi, Hyoe. 明 治 前 期 財 政 経 済 史 料 集 成 Meiji zenki zaisei keizai shiryo shusei. (Collection of materials on the financial and economic history of the early part of the Meiji era.) Tokyo, Kaizosha, 1932.

9299. Kobayashi, Ushisaburo. 明 治 大 正 財 政 史 Meiji Taisho zaisei-shi. (The financial history of the Meiji and the Taisho eras, 1867-1912, 1912-1926.) Tokyo, Ganshodo.

9300. Hijikata, Seibi.明治財政史 Meiji zaisei-shi. (Japanese financial history during the Meiji era, 1868-1912.) In Series on social economics (Finance). Tokyo, Nippon hyoron-sha.

9301. 明 治 大 正 財 政 評 覧 Meiji Taisho zaisei shoran. (Comprehensive study of the finances of Japan during the Meiji and Taisho eras.) Tokyo, Toyo keizai shinposha, 1926. 760 p.

9302. 金 融 六 十 年 史 Kinyu rokujunen-shi. (Sixty years of the history of the finance of Japan.) Tokyo, Toyo keizai shinposha, 1927. 630 p.

9303. Takahashi, Kamekichi. 財 政 経 済 二 十 五 年 誌 (第八巻年誌年表索引) Zaisei keizai nijugonen-shi. (Financial and economic record of twenty-five years. V. 8, Annual records, annual tables, and index.) Tokyo, Jitsugyo no sekai, 1932.

9304. See 867.

(2) General Accounts

9305. The law of finance. (Translation.) Tokyo, 1889. 12 p.

9306. Kuroita, K. "The financial policy of the Tokugawa sho-gunate." The Japan magazine, 4 (1913-1914):13-19.

9307. Nakahashi, T. 日 本 財 政 現 状 Nippon zaisei gen-jo. (Financial standing of Japan.) Osaka, 1900.

9308. Rathgen, K. Zwischen zwei kriegen. Die japanische fi-nanzpolitik von 1895 bis 1904. Leipzig, 1905.

9309. Franconie, J. "Les conséquences financières de la guerre russo-japonaise." Questions diplomatiques et coloni-ales, 20 (1905):8-21. (Paris)

9310. 日 本 財 政 法 一 班 Nippon zaiseiho ippan. (A brief outline of the financial system of Japan.) Tokyo, Department of finance, 1906.

9311. Théry, Edmond. Études économiques et financières. La situation économique et financière du Japon après la guerre de 1904-1905. 2nd edition. Paris, Économiste Européen, 1907. 276 p.

9312. Hoshino, Benzo. Die finanzen und die finanzpolitik Japans während und nach dem russisch-japanischen kriege. (Inaugural-dissertation). Halle a S., Kämmerer, 1908. 79 p.

9313. Büchel, H. Die finanzen Japans. Essen, Bädeker, 1908. vi, 222 p.

9314. Odate, Gyogu. Japan's financial relations with the United States. Columbia university, Studies in history, eco-nomics and public law, 98:2. New York, Longmans Green, 1922. 136 p.

9315. Shiomi, Saburo. "Die entwicklung des volkesinkommens in Japan in den jahren 1903-1919." Archiv für sozialwissen-schaft und sozialpolitik, 53 (1924):141-185.

9316. Shiomi, Saburo. "Seasonal fluctuations of our national finance." Keizai ronso, 1:2:94-127, December 1926.

9317. Shiomi, Saburo. 日 本 財 政 ノ 特 殊 問 題 Nippon zaisei no tokushu mondai. (Special problems in the finance of Japan.) Tokyo, 1928.

9318. Makino, Terutomo. 大正時代経済界,發達
Taisho jidai keizai-kai no hattatsu. (The growth in Japanese finances during the Taisho era, 1912-1926.) In Series of social economics.(Special lecture). Tokyo, Nippon hyoronsha.

9319. Yamamuro, Sobun. 我國,金融 Waga kuni no kinyu. (Japan's finances.) In Series on social economics. (Economic problems). Tokyo, Nippon hyoronsha.

9320. Inouye, Junnosuke. 我國際金融,現状及改善策
Waga kokusai kinyu no genjo oyobi kaizensaku. (Japan's international finances and a plan for improvement.) Tokyo, Iwanami, 1931. 260 p.

9321. 日本國財政概論 Nippon koku-zaisei gairon.
(An outline of national finances of Japan.) In Materials on economic study of the Far East. Dairen, To-A keizai chosakyoku, 1915-1931. See 797.

9322. The Chinese consulate in Yokohama. 日本財政之現状
Jih-pên ts'ai-chêng chih hsien-chuang. (The present financial status of Japan.) Wai-shaio-pu-kung-pao, 4:6, October 1931.

9323. Jung-nung. 日本財界之窮途興內部之一大危機
Jih-pên ts'ai-chieh chih chiung-t'u yü nei-pu chih i-ta-wei-chi. (The end of the road for the Japanese financial circles and the internal danger.) Shêng-huo, 6:50, December 1931.

9324. Chang, Shu-min. 日本在世界経済上之地位 Jih-pên tsai shih-chieh ching-chi shang chih ti-wei. (The financial position of Japan in the world.) Hsin-shê-hui, 1:11, December 1931.

9325. Andreades, A. "Japanese finance since the war." Foreign affairs, 10:3:485-502, April 1932.

9326. Ting, Wên-chiang. 日本的財政 Jih-pên ti ts'ai-chêng. (The finances of Japan.) Tu-li p'ing-lun, 2, May 1932.

9327. Ai, Hsiu-fêng (tr.). 日本改造法案 Jih-pên kai-tsao fa-an. (The reconstruction bill of Japan.) Tientsin, Ta-kung-pao, 1932. (From the Japanese.)

9328. Ouchi, Hyoe. 日本財政論 Nippon zaisei-ron.
(Discussions on Japanese finance.) Tokyo, Kaizosha, 1932.

(V. 23 of Keizaigaku zenshu, 62 v., 1928-1932.)

9329. Araki, Mitsutaro. Financial system of Japan. Tokyo, Imperial university, n.d., 60 p.

9330. Miwashi, Sonjin. 財閥政商政黨 Zaibatsu, seisho, seito. (The financial clique, political merchants, and political parties.) Tokyo, Kojin shobo, 1935. 240 p.

9331. Kishima, Momotaka. 歴代國務大臣演説集, 財政篇 Rekidai kokumu daijin enzetsu-shu, zaisei-hen. (Collection of speeches of successive ministers of state -- on finance.) Tokyo, Kokusai keizai kenkyusho, 1935. 450 p.

9332. See 9337.

9333. Naimu-sho chiho-kyoku. 昭和九年度: 地方財政篇 Showa 9-nen do: Chiho zaisei gaiyo. (An outline of local financial conditions in 1934.) Tokyo, Zenkoku toshi mondai kaigi jimu-kyoku, 1936. 105 p.

9334. Stein Guenther. "Japanese state finance." Pacific affairs, 10:4:393-407, December 1937.

9335. Takahashi, Kamekichi. 日本財閥論 Nippon zaibatsu ron. (On the financial clique of Japan.) Tokyo, Shunjusha, 1937. 350 p.

9336. Makino, Terutoshi. 日本ノ財政論 Nippon zaisei ron.(On the finances of Japan.) Tokyo, Nippon hyoronsha, 1937. 360 p.

9337. Suzuki, Mosaburo. 財界人物讀本 Zaikai jinbutsu tokuhon. (Textbook on the leaders of the financial world.) Tokyo, Shunjusha, 1937. 350 p.

9338. Tsukikata, Narumi. 財政讀本 Zaisei tokuhon. (Textbook on the finance of Japan.) Tokyo, Nippon hyoronsha, 1937. 380 p.

9339. Suzuki, Mosaburo. 日本財閥論 Nippon zaibatsu ron. (On the financial clique of Japan.) Tokyo, Kaizosha, 1937. 453 p.

9340. Iwai, Ryotaro. 三菱コンツェルン讀本 Mitsubishi kontsuerun tokuhon. (Text-book on the Mitsubishi concerns.) Tokyo, Shunjusha, 1937. 350 p.

9341. Wada, Hidekichi. 三井・コンツエルン讀本 Mitsui kontsuerun tokuhon. (Text-book on the Mitsui concerns.) Tokyo, Shunjusha, 1937. 380 p.

9342. Nishino, Kiyosaku. 住友 コンツエルン 讀本 Sumitomo kontsuerun tokuhon. (Text-book on the Sumitomo concerns.) Tokyo, Shunjusha, 1937. 350 p.

9343. Konami, Ritoku. 安田 コンツエルン 讀本 Yasuda kontsuerun tokuhon. (Text-book on the Yasuda concerns.) Tokyo, Shunjusha, 1937. 350 p.

9344. Wada, Hidekichi. 日産 コンツエルン 讀本 Nichi-san kontsuerun tokuhon. (Text-book on the Nichi-san concerns.) Tokyo, Shunjusha, 1937.

9345. Miyake, Kiyoteru. 新興 コンツエルン 讀本 Shinko kontsuerun (Noguchi, Mori, Nichi-so, Riken) tokuhon. (Text-book on the outstanding new concerns: Noguchi, Mori, Nippon soda, Rikagaku kenkyusho.) Tokyo, Shunjusha, 1937. 350 p.

9346. Katsuda, Teiji. 大倉 鴻池 川崎 根津 讀本 Okura, Konoike, Kawasaki, Nezu tokuhon. (Text-book on the Okura, Konoike, Kawasaki, and Nezu concerns.) Tokyo, Shunjusha, 1937. 350 p.

9347. Nishinoiri, Aiichi. 澁澤 大川 淺野 古河 讀本 Shibushawa, Okawa, Asano, Furukawa tokuhon. (Text-book on the Shibusawa, Okawa, Asano, and Furukawa concerns.) Tokyo, Shunjusha, 1937. 350 p.

9348. Kuribayashi, Seishu. 證券財閥（野村小池山一）讀本 Shoken zaibatsu (Nomura, Koike, Yamaichi) tokuhon. (Text-book on the leading stock and bond companies: Nomura, Koike, Yamaichi.) Tokyo, Shunjusha, 1937. 350 p.

9349. Tokyo, Shokokaigisho. (Tokyo chamber of commerce and industry.) 日本財界ノ現勢 Nippon zaikai no gensei. (Present condition of the financial world in Japan.) Tokyo, Kaizosha, 1937.

(3) Budget

9350. Japan. Imperial mint. 造幣局ノ長報告 Zoheikyoku kyokucho hokoku. (Report of the director.) 1, 1871/72-

9351. Japan. Department of finance. 日本財政経済年鑑 Nippon zaisei kizai nenkan. (Annuaire financier et économique du Japon.) 1, 1901-   (Published also in English.)

9352. 帝 國 歲 計 豫 算 史 Teikoku saikei yosan-shi. (History of the annual budget of Japan.) Tokyo, Department of finance, 1894-1909.

9353. Suzuki, Keigi. 帝 國 歲 計 沿 革 史 Teikoku sai-kei enkaku-shi. (Historical record of the annual budget of the empire of Japan.) Tokyo, Kirinkaku, 1915. 1760 p.

9354. "Развитие государственного бюджета Японии." (The development of Japan's state budget.) Ekonomicheskaia Zhizn' Dal'nego Vostoka, 2 (1926):98-110.

9355. Okura-sho shukei-kyoku. 昭 和 九 年 度 帝 國 歲入 歲 出, 豫 算 Showa 9-nen do teikoku sainyu saishutsu yosan. (An estimate of the 1934 national income and expend-iture.) Tokyo, Naikaku insatsu-kyoku, 1935. 232 p.

9356. Okura-sho shukei-kyoku. 昭 和 九 年 度 帝 國 豫 算 提 要 Showa 9-nen do teikoku yosan teiyo. (Summary of the 1934 national budget.) Tokyo, Naikaku insatsu-kyoku, 1935. 276 p.

9357. Okura-sho. 昭 和 十 年 度: 豫 算 / 解 說 Showa 10-nen do: Yosan no kaisetsu. (An explanation of the 1935 national budget.) Tokyo, Nippon hyoronsha, 1936. 84 p.

(4) Debts and Loans

9358. Matsukata, Count M. 日 本 國 債 史 Nippon kokusai-shi. (The history of the national debts in Japan.) Tokyo, 1890. 158 p.

9359. Matsukata, Count M. 戰 後 財 政 行 政 報 告 Sengo zaisei gyosei hokoku. (Report on the post-bellum fi-nancial administration in Japan, 1896-1900.) Tokyo, Imperi-al department of finance, 1901, xviii, 256 p.

9360. Fischer, C. Japanische staats-, städte- und hafenan-leihen nebst angaben über einige eisenbahn-, schiffsbau-und reedereiobligationen. London, 1906. 86 p.

9361. The national debts of Japan. Tokyo, Ministry of fi-nance, 1906. 29 p.

9362. Report on the war finance, issued by the Department of finance. Tokyo, 1906. 57 p.

9363. Manual of Japanese securities: government and munici-pal loans, railway and shippingdebentures, compiled by Dunn,

Fischer and company, London, 1906. 87 p.

9364. Aoki, Tokuzo. 日本國債 Nippon kokusai.(Japan's national debt.) In Series on social economics.(Finance). Tokyo, Nippon hyoronsha.

9365. Askov, A. "Первоначальные накопления капитала в Японии." (Early accumulations of capital in Japan.) Sbornik "Krasnyi vostochnik", Moscow,(1925):46-64.

9366. Japan. Department of finance. 昭和八年度國債統計年報 Showa 8-nen do kokusai tokei nenpo. (1933 annual statistical report of the national debt.) To-kyo, Okura-sho rizai-kyoku, 1935. 159 p.

9367. Okura-sho rizai-kyoku. 國債統計年報・昭和九年度 Kokusai tokei nenpo: Showa 9-nen do. (Annual report of statistics of the national debt -- 1934.) Tokyo, Department of finance, Naikaku insatsu-kyoku, 1936. 159 p.

9368. Takahashi, Kamekichi. 現代公債政策 Gendai kosai seisaku. (Modern policy on public debts.) Tokyo, Chikura shobo, 1937. 512 p.

9369. Ouchi, Hyoe. 日本財政論公債篇 Nippon zaisei ron: Kosai hen. (On the finance of Japan: Public debts.) Tokyo, Kaizosha, 1937.

(5) Currency and Exchange

9370. Japan. Department of finance. 大日本貨幣史参考 Dai Nippon kahei-shi sanko. (Materials on the history of Japanese currency.) Tokyo, 1877. 5 v. (2) The same. 大日本貨幣史 Dai Nippon kahei-shi. (History of the currency in Japan.) Tokyo, 1925-1926. 8 v.

9371. The currency of Japan. A reprint of articles, letters and official reports published in Japan and abroad relating to the currency, paper and metallic, of the empire of Japan, edited by W. H. T. Yokohama, 1882. 331 p.

9372. Japan. Department of finance. 明治貨政考要 Meiji kasei koyo. (Outline of currency legislation in the Meiji era.) Tokyo, 1887. 2 v.

9373. Kusσáka, J. Tsiôsiro (Kusaka, J. Choshiro). Das japanische geldwesen. Geschichtlich und kritisch dargestellt. (Inaugural-dissertation.) Berlin, 1890. 100 p.

9374. Münsterberg, O. Japan's edelmetallhandel von 1542-1854. (Inaugural-dissertation). Freiburg, 1895. 38 p.

9375. Droppers, G. "Monetary changes in Japan, 1877-1897." U. S. foreign affairs, Collected documents, 112 (1898): 1313-1330. (Washington).

9376. Kotégawa, T. "The currency system in Japan: past and present." Far East (Tokyo), 3 (1898):355-363.

9377. Sugi, U. Die reform des japanischen geldwesens im jahre 1897. (Inaugural-dissertation). Göttingen, 1901. 56 p.

9378. Takaki, M. The history of Japanese paper currency from 1868 to 1890. Baltimore, 1903. 59 p.

9379. The currency system of Japan. Tokyo, Department of finance, 1906. 23 p.

9380. Ashida, T. Das geldwesen Japans. Entwicklung und ver-gleichung mit demjenigen in europäischen ländern. 1912. 148 p.

9381. Tsukamoto, T. Old and new coins of Japan. Tokyo, Toyo kahei kyokai, 1925.

9382. Allen, G. C. "Recent currency and exchange policy of Japan." Economic journal (London), 35 (1925):66-83.

9383. Sakuda, S. "The gold-paper standard in the monetary system of Japan." Keizai ronso (Kyoto), 1:1:144-172, July 1926.

9384. Yoshida, Kensuke. 大日本貨幣史 Dai Nippon ka-hei-shi. (History of Japanese currency.) Tokyo, Department of finance, 1872. 16 v.   (2) The same. 大日本貨幣史 Dai Nippon kahei-shi. (History of Japanese currency). Tokyo, Choyokai, 1925-1926. 8 v.

9385. Japan. Department of finance. 貨幣論叢 Kahei ronso. (Collection of treatises on currency.) Tokyo, 1921-1928. 9 v.

9386. Tsukamoto, Toyojiro. 日本貨幣史 Nippon kahei-shi. (History of Japanese currency.) Tokyo, Zaisei keizai gakkai, 1928. 2 v.   (2)   The same. 本邦通貨／専歴 Honpo tsuka no jireki. (History of Japanese currency.) Osa-ka, Senyukai, 1929. 308 p.

9387. Furuya, Seiko Yoshisada. Japan's foreign exchange and her balance of international payments. With special reference to recent theories of foreign exchange. Columbia university studies in history, economics, and public law, 299. London, King & son. New York, Columbia university press, 1928. 208 p.

9388. Obata, Jun. 日本貨幣流通史 Nippon kahei ryutsu-shi. (History of currency circulation in Japan.) Tokyo, Toko shoin, 1931. 458 p.

9389. Takimoto, Seiichi and Mukai, Shikamatsu. 市場金融 Shijo kinyu. (Market and monetary circulation in Japan.) Tokyo, Chugai shogyo shinposha, 1932. Vol. 9 in Nippon sangyo shiryo taikei.

9390. Aono, Takeo. Japan after the gold ban removal. London, Kegan Paul, 1932. 114 p.

9391. See 9297.

9392. Dorfman, Ben D. Japan's reimposition of the gold embargo. North China union language school cooperating with California college in China, Peiping, 1932. 19 p.

9393. Wang, Nien-kuan. 論日本金再禁之前因後果 Lun Jih-pên chin tsai-chin chih ch'ien-yin hou-kuo. (Causes and effects of the second gold embargo in Japan.) Shang-yeh yüeh-pao, 12:1, January 1932.

9394. Wang, Yü-t'ung. 日本重施金禁 Jih-pên ch'ung-shih chin-chin. (A second gold embargo in Japan.) Shang-yeh yüeh-pao, 12:1, January 1932.

9395. Wu, Yü-kan. 日本重申金禁的由來與其影響 Jih-pên ch'ung-shên chin-chin ti yu-lai yü ch'i ying-hsiang. (The cause of the re-embargo of gold in Japan and its effects.) Hsin-shê-hui, 2:1, January 1932.

9396. Feng. 最近日本的政治危機與財政危機 Tsui-chin Jih-pên ti chêng-chih wei-chi yü ts'ai-chêng wei-chi. (Japan's recent political and financial crises.) Hsin-ch'uang-tsao pan-yüeh-k'an, 1:1, April 1932.

9397. Mei, I-pin. 日本金再禁對於日本物價之影響 Jih-pên chin tsai-chin tui-yü Jih-pên wu-chia chih ying-hsiang. (The re-embargo of gold in Japan and the effect on the prices of her goods.) Chung-tung-ching-chi yüeh-k'an, 8:3-4, April 1932.

9398. Ch'ü, Ching-chou. 日本 金 輸 先 再 禁 止 與、日 本
經 濟 Jih-pên chin shu-ch'u tsai-chin-chih yü Jih-pên
ching-chi. (The second gold embargo in Japan and her economic conditions.) Hsin-ya-hsi-ya-yüeh-k'an, 4:1, May 1932.

(6) Banks and Banking

(a) General Accounts

9399. Soyeda, J. History of banking in Japan. (In History
of banking in all the leading nations, edited by W. Dods-
worth. Vol. 4, 409-544). New York, 1896.

9400. Kiga, K. Das bankwesen Japans. (Inaugural-dissertation). Leipzig, 1903. 197 p.

9401. Adler, W. "Das bankwesen Japans." Weltwirtschaftliches
archiv, Chronik und archivalien, 10 (1917):158-170.

9402. Ishizawa, Hisagoro. 本 邦 銀 行 發 達 史 Honpo
ginko hattatsu-shi. (History of the development of banking
in Japan.) Tokyo, Dobunkan, 1920. 644 p.

9403. Allen, G. C. Japan's banking system. Kobe, Japan
chronicle press, 1923.

9404. Chu, Ting. 十 年 來 日 本 銀 行 業 之 變 遷
Shih-nien lai Jih-pên yin-hang-yeh chih pien-ch'ien. (Japanese banks in the past ten years.) Yin-hang chou-pao, 15:
44, November 1931.

9405. Kishitani, Goro. 今 後 二 於 ル 我 國 、 普 通
銀 行 Kongo ni okeru wagakuni no futsu ginko. (Common
banks in Japan from now on.) Tokyo, Daido shoin, 1932.

(b) Central Bank of Japan

9406. 日 本 銀 行 年 報 Nippon ginko nenpo. (Annual report of the Bank of Japan.) Tokyo, Japan times. [For the
year 1912 (condensed) 1913. For 1913 (condensed) 1914.]

9407. 日 本 銀 行 沿 革 史 Nippon ginko enkaku-shi. (History of the development of the Bank of Japan.) Tokyo, Bank
of Japan, 1913. 11 v. (Including index).

9408. Hamaoka, I. A study of the Central bank of Japan.
With an introductory note by H. C. Adams. Tokyo, 1902. 118 p.

(7) Taxation

See 930-936;   8938-8969.

9409. Japan. Tax bureau. 租 税 統 計 年 報 Sozei tokei nenpo. (Annual statistics on taxation.) 1-45, 1874-1918.

9410. Japan. Department of finance. 大 日 本 租 税 志 Dai Nippon sozei-shi. (History of taxation in Japan.) Tokyo, 1926. 3 v.

9411. Kambe, Masao. "Die entwicklung des japanischen steuerwesens vom altertum bis zur gegenwart." Finanz-archiv, 23 (1906).:2:1-45.

9412. Miura, Chiharu. 租 調 考 Socho-ko. (Taxation and requisition system of ancient Japan.) 1868.·

9413. Kambe, Masao. "Höhe und verteilung der steuern Japans, sowie vorschläge zu ihren reformen." Finanz-archiv, 31 (1914):2:625-631.

9414. Nonaka, Jun. 大 日 本 租 税 史 Dai Nippon sozei-shi. (History of taxation in Japan.) Tokyo, Choyokai, 1926. 3 v.

9415. Kambe, Masao. Grundzüge des japanischen steuersystems der gegenwart. Übersetzt und bearbeitet von Kushimoto. 1927.

9416. Kanbe, Masao. 租 税 研 究 Sozei kenkyu. (Study on taxation.) Tokyo, Kobundo, 1919-1932. 10 v.

9417. S. M. R. R. economic research committee. 帝 國 ノ 各 殖 民 地 ニ 於 ケル 課 税 狀 況 Teikoku no kaku shokuminchi ni okeru kazei jokyo. (Conditions of method of taxation in the various colonies of Japan.) Dairen, 1929.

9418. Okura-sho zaisei kenkyukai staff. 新 税 法 要 覽 Shin-zeiho yoran. (A glossary of the new tax regulation.) Tokyo, Sanseido, 1937. 250 p.

9419. Abe, Isamu. 日 本 財 政 論: 租 税 Nippon zaisei ron: sozei. (On the finances of Japan: taxation.) Tokyo, Kaizosha, 1937.

9420. "Growth of Japan's finances." Tokyo gazette, 1:25-30, July 1937.

(8) Index Numbers of Prices

9421. Shiomi, Saburo. "Indexzifferberechnung in Japan. Eine kritische studie über die indexziffern der Bank von Japan." Weltwirschaftliches archiv, Chronik und archivalien, 22 (1925):250-264.

9422. Shiomi, Saburo. "A study in the index numbers of prices of the bank of Japan." Keizai ronso (Kyoto), 1 (1926):111-143.

9423. See 9333.

(a) Securities and Stock Exchanges

9424. See 9363.

9425. Hiraga, Yoshinori. 東京株式取引所五十年史 Tokyo kabushiki torihikisho gojunen-shi. (History of fifty years of the Tokyo stock exchange.) Tokyo, Tokyo stock exchange, 1928. 536 +323 p.

9426. Ch'ên, Hsüeh-t'ao. 東京市之市財政 Tung-ching-shih chih shih ts'ai-chêng. (The municipal finances of Tokyo.) Hsüeh-i, 11:5, September 1931.

(10) War Finance

9427. Ono, Giichi. War and armament expenditures of Japan. Japanese monographs, 7. Publications of the Carnegie endowment for international peace, Division of economics and history. New York, Oxford university press, 1922. xv, 314 p.

9428. Kobayashi, Ushisaburo. War and armament taxes of Japan. New York, Carnegie endowment for international peace, Division of economics and history, 1923. xv, 255 p.

9429. Расходы Японии по ведению русско-японской войны.(The expenses of Japan for the conduct of the Russo-Japanese war.) Vestnik finansov, 12 (1909).

N. Communications: Railroad, Marine and Air Transportation

See 864-898.

(1) History

See 9435-9438.

9430. 日本交通史論 Nippon kotsu-shi ron. (A treatise on the history of communications in Japan.) Tokyo, Nippon rekishi chiri gakukai, 1925. 688 p.

9431. Aoe, Shu. 大日本交通史 Dai Nippon kotsu-shi. (History of communications of Japan.) Tokyo, Choyokai, 1928. 766 p.

(2) Railroads

9432. Japan. Department of railroads. 日本全國鉄道線 路圖附滿鉄線路圖 Nippon zenkoku tetsudo senro-zu: Fu Mantetsu senro zu. (Map of railway lines of Japan: Appendix map of the South Manchuria railway line.) Tokyo, 1930.

9433. Japan. Department of railways. 鉄道局年報 Tetsudo-kyoku nenpo (Annual report.) 1894/1895- At head of title 1907/1908-1916/1917: Imperial government railways of Japan. 1916/1917 as Imperial government railways of Japan. Railway nationalization in Japan. Ten years' progress under state management, 1907/08-1916/17. Most reports include statistics on the South Manchurian railway, also private and light railways in Japan.

9434. Japan. Department of railways. 日本帝國鉄道統 計一覧 Nippon teikoku tetsudo tokei ichiran. (Summary statistics of the government railways of Japan.) 1915/1916 ? -

9435. Noguchi, Masao. 日本運送史 Nippon unso-shi. (History of transportation of Japan.) Tokyo, Kotsu jironsha, 1934. 251 p.

9436. Honjo, Eijiro. 日本交通史ノ研究 Nippon kotsu-shi no kenkyu. (A study on the history of transportation in Japan.) Tokyo, Kaizosha.

9437. Hibata, Sekko. 江戸時代ノ交通文化 Edo jidai no kotsu bunka. (Traffic and transportation development of Japan during the Yedo period, 1603-1867.) Tokyo, Toko shoin, 1932. 550 p.

9438. Trevithick, Francis H. "The history and development of the railway system in Japan." Transactions Asiatic society of Japan, 22 (1894):111-257.

9439. Trevithick, Francis H. "Japan's railway system." Transactions and proceedings of the Japan society (London),

9 (1911):158-180.

9440. Lévy, M. "Le rachat des chemins de fer au Japon." Annales des sciences politiques, 717-739, November 1911.

9441. Baltzer, F. Die eisenbahnverstaatlichung in Japan 1906 und die ergebnisse des staatsbetriebes in den ersten 10 jahren. Zentralblatt der bauverwaltung, 1919. 149 p. Vol. 39, 1921. 549 p.

9442. Watarai, Toshiharu. Nationalization of railways in Japan. New York, Longmans, Green & co., 1915. Columbia university studies in history, economics and public law, 63 (1915):2. 156 p.

9443. Japan. Imperial government railways. 本邦鉄道 ノ社會及ビ經濟ニ反ボセル影響 Honpo tetsudo no shakai oyobi keizai ni oyboseru eikyo. (The Japanese railroads.) Tokyo, 1916. 3 v.

9444. Japan. Department of railways. 日本鉄道史 Nippon tetsudo-shi. (The history of railways in Japan.) Tokyo, 1921. 3 v.

9445. 大日本交通史 Dai Nippon kotsu-shi. (The history of transportation in Japan.) Tokyo, Hyogensha, 1928.

9446. Artemov, I. I. Железные дороги Японии. (Japanese railways.) Moscow, Transpechat', 1929. 115 p.

(3) Shipping

9447. Japanese shipping, ancient and modern. Tokyo, Mercantile marine bureau, Department of communications, 1909. Album of 73 photographs and descriptions.

9448. Sumida, Shoichi. 海事史料叢書 Kaiji shiryo sosho. (A library of materials on maritime affairs.) Tokyo, Ganshodo, 1929-1932. 20 v.

9449. 日本海運資料史 Nippon kaiun shiryo-shi. (Materials on the history of Japanese marine transportation.) Tokyo, Shipping control bureau, Department of communication. 1904.

9450. Kimiya, Y. 日支交通史 Nichi-Shi kotsu-shi. (History of communication between Japan and China.) Tokyo, Kinshi horyudo, 1928. 2 v.

9451. Sumida, Shoichi. 海上運送史論 Kaijo unso shiron. (Historical treatise on marine transportation of Japan.) Tokyo, Ganshodo, 1925. 238 p.

9452. Japanese shipping, ancient and modern. Tokyo, Mercantile marine bureau, Department of communications, 1909.

9453. Takimoto, Seiichi and Mukai, Shikamatsu. 運 輸 業 、日 本 海 運 五 十 年 史 ; 南 満 洲 鉄 道 株 式 會 社 事 業 概 況 Unyugyo. Nippon kaiun gojunen-shi. Nan-Manshu tetsudo kabushiki kaisha jigyo gaikyo. (Transportation industry. Fifty years of Japanese marine transportation. General condition of the enterprise of the South Manchuria R. R. Co.) Tokyo, Chugai shogyo shinposha, 1932. Vol. 11 in Nippon sangyo shiryo taikei.

9454. Goto, R. Die japanische seeschiffahrt. (Inaugural-dissertation.) Berlin, 1901. 30 p.

9455. 日 本 海 上 史 論 Nippon kaijo-shi ron. (Treatise on the maritime history of Japan.) Society of historical geography of Japan, 1911.   See 9465.

9456. Ulrich, Leo. "Handelsschiffahrt und schiffbau Japans während des krieges." Weltwirtschaftliches archiv, chronik und archivalien, 11 (1917):101-123.

9457. Imaoka, Junichiro. 世 界 大 戦 と 日 本 海 運 Sekai taisen to Nippon kaiun. (The world war and Japanese shipping.) Tokyo, Fuzanbo, 1918.

9458. Blair, James. "The Japanese mercantile marine." Transactions and proceedings of the Japan society (London), 16 (1918):38-55.

9459. Simmersbach, Bruno. "Die entwicklung des japanischen schiffsbaues." Asien (Berlin), 16 (1918-1919):100-106.

9460. Purvis, F. P. "Ship construction in Japan. Ancient and modern." Transaction of the Asiatic society (Tokyo), 47 (1919):1-22.

9461. Sakourai, M., Kurokawa et Tatsumi. "Les étapes successives de la marine japonaise de guerre et de commerce." Bulletin de la Société franco-japonaise de Paris, 44-45: 19-140, 36 Abb., Jan.-Sept. 1920; 46:21-28, Oct.-Dec. 1920.

9462. Purvis, F. P. "Japanese ships of the past and present." Transactions and proceedings of the Japan society (London), 23 (1926:51-87.

9463. See 9270.

9464. Kovan'ko, L. "Торговый флот Японии." (The commercial fleet of Japan.) Ekonomicheskaia zhizn' Dal'nego Vostoka, 1 (1928):124-133.

9465. 日 本 海 上 史 論 Nippon kaijo-shi ron. (Treatise on the maritime history of Japan.) Tokyo, Nippon rekishi chiri gakkai, 1930. See 9455.

9466. Masui, Yukio. 交 通 政 策 Kotsu seisaku. (Japan's transportation policy.) Tokyo, Jiji shinposha, 1931. 451 p.

9467. Terashima, Narinobu. 日 本 海 運 政 策 Nippon kaiun seisaku. (Shipping policy of Japan.) In Series on social economics. (Economic problems). Tokyo, Nippon hyoronsha.

9468. Macking, Ludwig. Japans häfen, ihre beziehungen zur landesnatur und wirtschaft. Hamburg, Friederichsen, de Gruyter, 1931.

9469. Teishin-sho. 昭 和 九 年 日 本 船 名 録 Showa 9-nen Nippon senmei roku. (1934 register of Japanese ships.) Tokyo, Teikoku kaiji kyokai, 1935. 682 p.

(4) Air Transportation

9470. 航 空 時 代 Koku jidai. (Aviation age.) Tokyo, Koku jidaisha, 1, 1930-

9471. 航 空 之 日 本 Koku no Nippon. (Aviation of Japan.) Tokyo, Koku no Nipponsha, 1, 1934-

9472. Ogawa, Taichiro. 航 空 讀 本 Koku tokuhon. (Textbook of aviation.) Tokyo, Nippon hyoronsha, 1932. 400 p.

XIX. SOCIAL CONDITIONS

See 937-951; 2748-2782.

A. Periodicals

See 7305-7337.

9473. Kyochokai. 社 會 政 策 事 報 Shakai seisaku jiho. (Journal of social policy.) Tokyo, 1, 1920-

9474. 大 原 社 會 問 題 研 究 所 雑 誌 Ohara shakai mondai kenkyusho zasshi. (Monthly, published by the Ohara research institute of social problems, 1, 1924-

9475. 社會學評論 Shakaigaku hyoron. (Sociological review.) Tokyo, Kyobundo, 1, 1933- (Bi-monthly.)

B. History

See 7502-7836; 8886-9472.

9476. 日本社會事彙 Nippon shakai jii. (Encyclopedia of Japanese sociology.) Tokyo, Keizai zasshisha, 1890,1908. 2 v.

9477. Hasegawa, Yoshinobu. 社會政策大系 Shakai seisaku taikei. (Collection of standard works on social policy.) Tokyo, Daito shuppansha, 1926-1927. 10 v.

9478. Honjo, Eijiro. 日本社會史 Nippon shakai-shi (History of Japanese sociology.) Tokyo, Kaizosha, 1928. Vol. 30 in Keizaigaku zenshu (1928-1932, 62 vols.) (2) The same. Социальная история Японии. (A social history of Japan.) Trudy Moskovskogo instituta vostokovedeniia imeni N. N. Narimanova. Moscow, 1927. 140 p. (3) The same. "Changes of social classes during the Tokugawa period. A cause of the collapse of the feudal system of the Tokugawa régime." Keizai ronso (Kyoto), 3 (1928):1:56-74.

9479. Fujioka, Sakutaro and Hirade, Kenjiro. 日本風俗史 Nippon fuzoku-shi. (History of Japanese manners and customs Tokyo, Toyodo, 1895-1917. 3 v.

9480. Yada, Soun. 江戸から東京へ Yedo kara Tokyo e. (Changes in social life from the Yedo period to the Tokyo period.) Tokyo, Tokokaku, 1921-1925. 9 v.

9481. Uchida, Shigetaka. 日本政治社會思想史 Nippon seiji shakai shiso-shi. (History of social and political ideas of Japan.) Tokyo, Ganshodo, 1931. 452 p.

9482. Japanese people. The manners and customs of the Japanese people from the earliest times. Madras, Sankaran & co., 1906. 116 p.

9483. Saito, Ryuzo. 近世日本世相史 Kinsei Nippon seso-shi. (Development of the life and social organization of modern Japan, 1603-1925.) Third edition. 1926. 1228 p.

9484. Shimode, Junkichi. 明治社會思想研究 Meiji shakai shiso kenkyu. (Research in the social thoughts of the Meiji era.) Tokyo, Asano shoten, 1932. 410 p.

9485. Abe, Kozo. 日本奴隷史 Nippon dorei-shi. (History of slavery in Japan.) Tokyo, Shuhokaku, 1926. 447 p.

9486. Takikawa, Seijiro. 日本奴隷経済史 Nippon dorei keizai-shi. (History of slave economics of Japan.) Tokyo, Toko shoin, 1932. 553 p.

9487. Kikukawa, Tadao. 日本学生社會運動史 Nippon gakusei shakai undo-shi. (History of social movement among students in Japan.) In Social science lectures, vol. 3. Tokyo, Seibundo, 1931.

9488. 社會経済体系 Shakai keizai taikei. (Series on social economics.) Tokyo, Nippon hyoronsha, 1926-1928. 9 v.

9489. Sunada, Kanyei. 日本家族制度史研究 Nippon kazoku seido-shi kenkyu. (Research in the history of the family system in Japan.) Tokyo, Chubunkan, 1926. 285 p.

9490. Tamaki, Hajime. 日本家族制度批判 Nippon kazoku seido hihan. (Criticism of the Japanese family system.) Tokyo, Fukuda shobo, 1936. 340 p.

C. General Accounts

See 7542-7610; 9014-9093.

9491. Matsubara, I. In darkest Tokyo. Sketches of humble life in the capital of Japan. English translation edited by F. Schroeder. Yokohama, 1897. 78 p.

9492. Suyematsu, Baron K. "The ethics of Japan." Annual report, Smithsonian institute for 1905. 1907: 293-307. (Reprinted from the Journal of the Society of arts, London, 53 (1905).)

9493. Vasiliev. Рабочие в Японии.   (Laborers in Japan.) Moscow, 1906. 31 p.

9494. Takakusu, Junjiro. "The social and ethical value of the family system in Japan." International journal of ethics, 17 (1907):100-106.

9495. Préville, A. de. "Le Japon et son évolution sociale, précédé de deux études sur le Japon, viz: E. Demolins, La formule sociale du Japon et G. d'Azambuja, Le péril jaune." Paris, 1904. 96 p.

9496. Krauss, Friedrich S. Das geschlechtsleben in glauben, sitte und brauch der Japaner. Beiwerke zum studium der anthropophyteia bd. 2. Leipzig, Deutsche verlags-aktiengesellschaft, 1907. 161 p.

9497. Petrov, Arkadii. Очерки социального быта современной Японии. (Outlines of social customs of modern Japan.) Izvestiia Vostochnogo instituta (Vladivostok), 15 (1907):6. iii, 40 p.

9498. Heber, E. A. "L'origine des classes sociales japonaises et leur évolution jusqu'à la restauration de Meiji." Revue économique internationale, October 1911. (The same. "Soziale klassenbildung in Japan." Zeitschrift für sozialwissenschaft. Neue folge. 2 (1911):468-480, 576-585.

9499. Kobayashi, Teruaki. La société japonaise. Étude sociologique. Traduit du Japonais par Junkichi Yoshida avec le concours de Madame Laudenbach. Préface de Tongo Takébe. Bibliothèque d'histoire contemporaine. Paris, Felix Alcan, 1914. xx, 223 p.

9500. Tsuda, Sokichi. 我ガ國民思想ノ研究 Waga kokumin shiso no kenkyu. (Japanese social life and customs.) Tokyo, Rakuyodo, 1919-1920. 3 v.

9501. Witte, J. "Die soziale frage in Japan." Zeitschrift für missionskunde und religionswissenschaft (Berlin), 35 (1920):161-173.

9502. Present condition of the child welfare work in Japan. Tokyo, Ministry of the interior, Department of social welfare, 1921.

9503. Mitsukuri, Kakichi. La vie sociale au Japon. Paris, Société franco-japonaise, 1922. 150 p.

9504. Erskine, William Hugh. Japanese customs. Their origin and value. Introduction by E. W. Clement. Tokyo, Kyobunkwan, 1925. xii 236 p.

9505. Bellessort, A. La société japonaise. 9th edition. Paris, 1926.

9506. Petrov, Arkadii N. Японский пролетариат. История.(The Japanese proletariat.) Leningrad, 1927. 182 p.

9507. Wildes, Harry Emerson. Social currents in Japan. With special reference to the press. Chicago university press,

1927. x, 392 p. Reprinted, See 9508.

9508. Wildes, Harry Emerson. Press and social currents in Japan. Philadelphia, University, 1927. ix, 390 p.

9509. Hsü, Chung-hao. 日本之社會事業. Jih-pên chih shê-hui shih-yeh. (Social work in Japan.) K'ao-shih-yüan kung-pao, 10, October 1931.

9510. Hirano,Shin. 明治大正昭和歷史資料大集成: 犯罪篇 Meiji Taisho.Showa rekishi shiryo tai-shusei:hanzai-hen. (Collections of the source materials on the history of the Meiji, Taisho, Showa eras: on crime.) Tokyo, Shiryo shusei kankokai, 1935. 440 p.

D. Women and the Social Life

9511. Japanese women. A report by the Japanese women's commission for the World's Columbian exposition in Chicago. Chicago, 1893. 159 p.

9512. Murphy, U. G. Social evil in Japan and allied subjects with statistics and the social evil test cases and progress of the anti-brothel movement. Second edition. Tokyo, 1904, 113 p. (First edition:1899).

9513. Matignon, "La prostitution au Japon." Archives d'anthropologie criminelle, de criminologie et de psychologie normale et pathologique. Lyon, 21 (1906):697-715.

9514. Miyakawa, S. Frauenleben in Japan. Dokumente des fortschritts. 1909.

9515. Kubota, B. 現代日本ト社會問題 Gendai Nippon to shakai mondai. (Modern Japan and the social question.) 1920. 570 p.

9516. Kaufman, L. "Экономическое положение японской женщины." (Economic status of the Japanese woman.) Narody Dal'nego Vostoka, 4 (1922):465-477.

9517. Katagiri, Tatsuko. 日本婦人ノ使命ト其修養 Nippon fujin no shimei to sono shuyo. (The mission of Japanese women and self-cultivation.) Gifu, Chusei futokukai, 1929. 487 p.

9518. Borisov, A. Работница Японии. (The woman-worker in Japan.) Moscow, 1930. 64 p.

9519. Chu, Chung-fan. 日本首都的職業婦人的調查
Jih-pên shou-tu ti chih-yeh fu-jên ti tiao-ch'a. (An investigation on professional women in Tokyo, Japan.) Fu-nü tsa-
chih, 17:12, December 1931.

9520. Chu, Chung-fan. 日本農村婦人的副業. Jih-pên
nung-ts'un fu-jên ti fu-yeh. (The subordinate profession of
the rural Japanese women.) Fu-nü tsa-chih, 17:11, November
1931.

9521. Chang, Shui-ch'i. 日本陰慝的社會相 Jih-pên
hsien-o ti shê-hui hsiang. (The dangerous social phenomenon
in Japan.) Shên-pao yüeh-k'an, 1:2, August 1932.

9522. Ishimoto, Baroness Shidzue. Facing two ways. New York,
Farrar & Reinhardt, 1935. 373 p.

E. Labor Problems

See 846-863; 9177-9221.

9523. Takano, Iwasaburo. 日本勞働年鑑 Nippon rodo nenkan. (Japan labor year-book.) Tokyo, Doninsha, 1932.

9524. Suzuki, Bunji. 日本勞働運動史 Nippon rodo undo-shi. (History of the Japanese labor movement.) In Series
on social economics. (Social problems). Tokyo, Nippon hyoronsha.

9525. Akamatsu, Katsumaro. 日本勞働組合運動發達史
Nippon rodo kumiai undo hattatsu-shi. (History of the growth
of the labor union movement in Japan.) In Social science
lectures, vol. 8. Tokyo, Seibundo, 1931.

9526. Murayama, Shigeo. 日本勞働爭議史槪觀
Nippon rodo sogi-shi kenkan. (History of labor disputes in
Japan.) Tokyo, Bunmei kyokai, 1929.

9527. Petrov, Arkadii. Рабочий вопрос в Японии. (The labor
question in Japan.) St. Petersburg, 1912. vii, 264 p.

9528. Kuwata, K. "Die gegenwärtige lage der arbeiter in Japan und das neue fabrikgesetz." Archiv für sozialwissen-
schaft und sozialpolitik, 35 (1912):775-790.

9529. Katayama, Sen. The labor movement in Japan. Chicago,
Kerr, 1918. 147 p.

9530. Winther, I. Kagawa, de forkuedes ven: et rids af 'hans liv, viske og tanker. Kopenhagen, Lohse, 1925. 93 p.

9531. Akramovskaia, V. "Из истории рабочего движения в Японии." (History of the labor movement in Japan.) From materials published in "Annuaire du travail Japonois" and "The labor monthly". Vestnik truda, 4 (1925).

9532. Ayusawa, Iwao F. Industrial conditions and labor legislation in Japan. Genf, 1926.

9533. Katayama, Sen. Моя жизнь. (My life.) Moscow, Moskovskii rabochii, 1926. 79 p.

9534. Ayusawa, Iwao F. Législation et conditions du travail dans l'industries au Japon. Genf, Bureau international du travail, Études et documents, 16 (1926). vi, 119 p. (See 9532.)

9535. Harada, Shuichi. Labor conditions in Japan. Studies in history, economics and public law, 301. New York, Columbia university press, 1928. 295 p.

9536. Watanabe, Michitaro. 我國勞働組合/研究 Wagakuni rodo kumiai no kenkyu. (Study of labor unions of Japan.) Tokyo, Rodo jijo chosasho, 1931. 338 p.

9537. Hirano, Gaku. 日本勞働組合運動/現勢 Nippon rodo kumiai undo no gensei. (Present conditions of the labor union movement in Japan.) In Social science lectures, vol. 7. Tokyo, Seibundo, 1931.

9538. Nagai, Kyo. 日本・勞働問題 Nippon no rodo mondai. (Labor problems in Japan.) In Series on social economics. (Social problems). Tokyo, Nippon hyoronsha.

9539. Yamanaka, Tokutaro. 日本勞働組合法案研究 Nippon rodo kumiai hoan kenkyu. (A study of Japan's labor union bill.) Tokyo, Iwanami, 1932. 354 p.

9540. See 9518.

9541. Lukianova, M. I. Как борются японские рабочие. (How the Japanese workers struggle.) Moscow, 1935. 100 p.

9542. Lukianova. "Борьба за профединство в Японии." (The struggle for unity in the labor unions in Japan.) Materialy po natsional'no-kolonial'nym problemam, 11:26-31, June 1936.

9543. Uyeda, Teijiro. The growth of the population and oc-
cupational changes in Japan, 1920-1935. Sixth conference of
the Institute of Pacific relations, 1936. 19 p.

9544. Uyeda, Teijiro and Inokuchi, Tosuke. Cost of living
and real wages in Japan 1914-1936. Sixth conference of the
Institute of Pacific relations, 1936. 30 p.

F. Population Problems

See 824-832.

9545. Inada, Shunosuke. 人 口 問 題 Jinko mondai. (Population problem of Japan.) Tokyo, Yuhikaku, 1912.

9546. Shibusawa, Eiichi. 財 政 経 清 ト 生 活 問 題
Zaisei keizai to seikatsu mondai. (Finance, economy and
the problems of livelihood.) Tokyo, Jitsugyo no sekaisha,
1914. 497 p.

9547. Morimoto, Kokichi. The standard of living in Japan.
Baltimore, Johns Hopkins press, 1918. vi, 147 p.

9548. Chevalier, H. "Le coût de la vie au Japon." Bulletin,
Société franco-japonaise, 40-41 (1918):79-84.

9549. Honjo, Eijiro. 徳 川 時 代 ニ 於ケル日本ノ人口 Tokugawa jidai ni okeru Nippon no jinko. (The population of Japan
in the Tokugawa era.) Kyoto, 1923.

9550. Allen, G. C. "The population problem in Japan." Economica, 17 (1926):170-186.

9551. "The population problem of Japan." The young East, 2
(1926-1927):171-174.

9552. Yamamoto, Kyohei. "The question of population in Japan." Kyoto university economic review, 2 (1927):1:52-62.

9553. Yamamoto, Miono. "The principles of emigration policy." Kyoto university economic review, 2 (1927):2:103-112.

9554. Gowen, H. H. Over-population in Japan. Proceedings of
the Institute of international relations (Riverside, Calif.)
First session. Vol. 1, 1927.

9555. Kudo, Takeo. 我 國 人 口 問 題ト 満 蒙 Wagakuni
jinko mondai to Man-Mo. (The population problem of Japan,
and Manchuria and Mongolia.) Dairen, S.M.R.R., 1928.

9556. Orchard, John E. "The pressure of population in Japan." Geographical review, 18 (1928):374-401.

9557. Taigin, I."Страдает ли Япония от перенаселения?" (Does Japan suffer from overpopulation?) Mirovoe khoziaistvo i mirovaia politika, 12 (1928):24-33.

9558. Huang, Hsia-ch'ien. 日本之人口問題 Jih-pên chih jên-k'ou wên-t'i. (The population problem of Japan.) Eastern miscellany, 26:9:29-47, May 1929.

9559. Honjo, Eijiro. 人口及人口論 Jinko oyobi jinko ron. (The population and population problems of Japan.) Tokyo, Nippon hyoronsha, 1930. 258 p.

9560. Crocker, Walter Russell. The Japanese population problem: the coming crisis. London, Allen & Unwin, 1931. 240 p. [Population control in the Tokugawa period.]

9561. P'ei, Hsi-hêng. 談談日本的人口與糧食問題 T'an-t'an Jih-pên ti jên-k'ou yü liang-shih wên-t'i. (Some remarks on the question of population and food in Japan.) Shê-hui tsa-chih, 2:3, September 1931.

9562. Hsieh, Shih-tsun. 日本果真人口過剩食糧不足嗎 Jih-pên kuo-chên jên-k'ou-kuo-shêng shih-liang-pu-tsu ma? (Is it true that Japan is over-populated and lacks food?) Nung-yeh-chou-pao, 1:24, October 1931.

9563. Pao, Huai-pai. 日本殖民與人口問題 Jih-pên ch'ih min yü jên-k'ou wên-t'i. (The problem of emigration and population in Japan.) Shanghai, Li-ming-shu-chü, 1932.

9564. Oikawa, Jinnojo. 日本人口地理 Nippon jinko chiri. (Population-geography of Japan.) Tokyo, Koseisha, 1933. 348 p.

9565. Uyeda, T. Future of the Japanese population. Tokyo, Tokyo commercial university, 1933. 25 p.

9566. Penrose, E. F. Population theories and their application, with special reference to Japan. Stanford university press, 1934. 347 p.

9567. Alsberg, Carl L. Japanese self-sufficiency in wheat. Wheat studies of the food research institute, 12 (1935):3. 43 p. (Stanford.) (2) Droppers, Garrett. "The population of Japan in the Tokugawa period." Transactions of the Asiatic society of Japan, v. 22, part 2.

9568. Kondo, Tsuneji.日 本 ノ 人 口 問 題 Nippon no jinko mondai. (The population problems of Japan.) Tokyo, Nankosha, 1936, 275 p.

9569. Pelzer, Karl J. "Japanese migration and colonization."
Limits of land settlement, prepared under the sponsorship
of the American coordinating committee for international
studies and published by the Council on foreign relations.
New York, 1937.

9570. Ishii, Ryoichi. Population pressure and economic life
in Japan. London, King, 1937. xix, 259 p.

G. Immigration

See 833-845; 5265-5268; 10191-10205.

9571. Takaoka, K. Die innere kolonisation Japans. Leipzig,
1904.

9572. Straus, V. "La colonisation du Hokkaido." Bulletin
de la Société franco-japonaise de Paris, 28:99-103, December 1912.

9573. Grünfeld, Ernst. "Die japanische auswanderung." Mitteilungen der deutschen gesellschaft für natur- und völkerkunde Ostasiens (Tokyo), 14:(1913):Suppl. 8:1-157.

9574. Müller, Max. "Die landwirtschaft, tierzucht und kolonisation Hokkaidos, deren stand und zukunft." Mitteilung-
en der deutschen gesellschaft für natur- und völkerkunde
Ostasiens, Tokyo, 15 (1913):A:1-17.

9575. Wertheimer, Fritz. "Das eingeborenen-problem in Formosa und die japanische kolonisierungs-arbeit." Geist des
Ostens, 1:208-218, January 1913 - March 1914.

9576. Schultze, Ernst. "Die japanische auswanderung." Petermanns geographische mitteilungen, 61 (1915):1:129-133.

9577. Nopitsch, T. "Die tatsachen der japanischen auswanderung und ihre völkerpsychologische wirkung." Zeitschrift
für geopolitik, 1 (1924):416-424.

9578. Derber, P. "Японская эмиграция в Соединенные Штаты."
(Japanese emigration to the United States.) Novyi Vostok,
6 (1924):19-30.

9579. 東洋拓殖株式會社二十年誌 Toyo takushoku kabushiki kaisha nijunen-shi. (Twenty-year history of Toyo takushoku kabushiki kaisha.) Toyo takushoku kabushiki kaisha, 1928.

9580. Kashiwagi, Minetaro. ブラジル移民ノ割當緩和 Buraziru imin no wariate kanwa. (Adjustment of the allocation of Japanese immigrants to Brazil.) Gaiko jiho, 78:5: 120-132, June 1936.

XX. CULTURE, RELIGION, PHILOSOPHY

See 937-1046.

A. Periodicals

See 7305-7337; 7509-7517.

9581. 東京帝國大學紀要：文科 Tokyo teikoku daigaku kiyo: bunka. (Tokyo imperial university, College of literature, memoirs.) 1, 1887-

9582. 學藝志林 Gakugei shirin. (Journal of arts and science.) Tokyo, Tokyo daigaku, 1887-1899. 18 v.

9583. 藝文 Geibun. (Journal of Japanese literature and history.) Literature society of the Kyoto imperial university. 1910-1931. 22 v. No more published.

9584. 風俗研究 Fuzoku kenkyu. (Journal of study of ancient customs and manners.) Society of the history of customs. 1, March 1916-

9585. 佛教美術 Bukkyo bijutsu. (Quarterly journal of Buddhistic art.) Kyoto, Bukkyo-bijutsusha, 1924-

9586. Japan. Imperial household museums department. 帝室博物館報告 Teikoku hakubutsukan hokoku. (Annual report of the imperial household museums.) Tokyo and Nara, 1, 1925-

B. History

See 7502-7836.

9587. Yoshino, Sakuzo. 明治文化全集 Meiji bunka zenshu. (Complete collection of works on culture during the Meiji era, 1868-1912.) Tokyo, Nippon hyoronsha, 1927-1930. 24 v.

9588. 風俗研究 Fuzoku kenkyu. (Research on manners and customs.) Tokyo, Fuzoku kenkyukai. (115 v. in 1933.)

9589. Ukita, Kazutami (editor). 大日本文明協會刊行書 Dai Nippon bunmei kyokai kankosho (Complete works of the Japan culture association.) Tokyo, Dai Nippon bunmei kyokai, 1, 1908- (302 v. in 1930).

9590. Kiyohara, Sadao. 改撰日本文化史年表 Kaisen Nippon bunka-shi nenpyo. (Revised edition of the chronological table of the cultural history of Japan.) Tokyo, Chubunkan shoten, 1931. 434 p.

9591-92.日本文化史 Nippon bunka-shi. (History of Japanese civilizaion.) Tokyo, Taishokaku, 1922. 12 v.

9593. Kitagaki, Yasujiro. 日本文化史談 Nippon bunka shidan. (Historical accounts of Japanese civilization.) Tokyo, Jitsugyo no sekaisha, 1934. 3 v.

9594. Yoshida, Togo. 日本文明史話 Nippon bunmei shiwa. (Historical account of Japanese civilization.) Tokyo, Kobundo, 1915. 454 p.

9595. Nishimura, Fuminori. 日本文化生活史 Nippon bunka seikatsu-shi. (History of culture and life in Japan.) Tokyo, Yuzankaku, 1924. 752 p.

9596. See 9602.

9597. Kurita, Motoji. 解説日本文化史 Kaisetsu Nippon bunka-shi. (Cultural history of Japan. A commentary.) Tokyo, Meiji tosho kabushiki gaisha, 1930. 591 p.

9598. Naito, Torajiro. 日本文化史研究 Nippon bunka-shi kenkyu. (Research in the cultural history of Japan.) Kyoto, Kobundo, 1930. 397 p.

9599. Kiyohara, Sadao. 日本道徳史 Nippon dotoku-shi. (History of the morals of Japan.) Tokyo, Chubunkan, 1930. 756 p.

9600. Sasagawa, Tanero. 日本文化史 Nippon bunka-shi. (History of Japanese civilization.) Tokyo, Yufukan, 1931.

9601. Nishida, Naojiro. 日本文化史序説 Nippon bunka-shi josetsu. (Introduction to the cultural history of Japan.) Tokyo, Kaizosha, 1933. 645 p.

9602. Nishimura, Shinji. 日本文化史點描 Nippon bunka-shi tenbyo.(An outline of the cultural history of Japan.) Tokyo, Tokyodo, 1937. 346 p. 13th edition.

9603. Sato, E. 日本古代印刷史 Nippon kodai insa-tsu-shi. (Notes on the early history of printing in Japan.) Transactions of the Asiatic society of Japan, 10 (1881):1: 48-83.

9604. 鎌倉文明史論 Kamakura bunmei-shi ron. (Trea-tise on the history of the development of culture and civi-lization in the Kamakura period, 1192-1333.) Tokyo, 1909.

9605. Kiyohara, Sadao. 明治初期文化史 Meiji sho-ki bunka-shi. (Cultural history during the early part of the Meiji era.) Tokyo, Kenbunkan, 1935. 398 p.

9606. Shimaya, Seiichi. 印刷文明史 Insatsu bunmei-shi. (History of civilization, stressing the art of print-ing.) Osaka, Insatsu bunmei-shi kankokai, 1932. 5 v.

9607. Omachi, Yoshiye. 日本文明史 Nippon bunmei-shi. (History of Japanese civilization.) Tokyo, Hakubunkan, 1909. 302 p.

9608. Kato, Setsudo. 日本風俗史 Nippon fuzoku-shi. (History of Japanese manners and customs.) Second edition. 1919. 3 v.

9609. Kamijioto, Choshu. 日本風俗史 Nippon fuzoku-shi. (History of Japanese customs and manners.) Tokyo, 1924. 283 p.

9610: Sakamoto, Kenichi. 日本風俗史要 Nippon fuzoku shiyo. (A brief history of Japanese manners and customs.) Tokyo, Musashino shoin, 1926. 331 p.

9611. Ema, Tsutomu. 日本風俗史 Nippon fuzoku-shi. (History of Japanese manners.) Tokyo, Juken koza kankokai, 1930. 333 p.

9612. Nakayama, Taro. 日本民族学 Nippon minzoku-gaku. (Japanese manners and usages.) Tokyo, Ookayama shoten, 1932. 4 v

9613. Yoshino, Sakuzo (compiler). 明治文化全集：文明開化篇 Meiji bunka zenshu: bunmei kaika hen. (Civilization and culture of the Meiji era.) In Complete collection on the culture of the Meiji era. Tokyo, Nippon hyoronsha, 1929.

9614. Fujisawa, Ehiko. 明治風俗史 Meiji fuzoku-shi.
(History of Japanese manners and customs of the Meiji era,
1868-1912.) Tokyo, Shunyodo, 1929. 503 p.

9615. Matsuoka, Shizuo. 日本古俗誌 Nippon kozoku-shi.
(Record of old customs of Japan.) Tokyo, Toko shoin, 1932.
371 p.

9616. Osadake, Takeki. 明治文化研究論叢 Meiji
bunka kenkyu ronso. (A collection of dissertations on
research in the culture of the Meiji era.) Tokyo, Ichigen-
sha, 1935. 348 p.

C. General Accounts

9617. Ichikawa, Daiji. Die kultur Japans. Berlin, Curtius,
1907. 149 p.

9618. Brandt, M. v. Die grundlagen der japanischen kultur-
entwicklung. Internationale wochenschrift für wissenschaft,
kunst und technik. 2: December 26, 1908. 22 p.

9619. Giles, H. A. "Japan's debt to China." Adversaria Sinica (Shanghai), 7 (1909):189-203.

9620. Takakusu, Junjiro. What Japan owes to India. Journal
of the Indo-Japanese association. January 1910.

9621. Yamasaki, N. L'action de la civilisation européenne sur
la vie japonaise avant l'arrivée du commodore Perry. (Inaugural-dissertation.) Paris, 1910. 127 p.

9622. Lowell, Percival. The soul of the Far East: Japan.
New edition. London - New York, Macmillan, 1911. x, 226 p.

9623. Matsusaki. "Ähnlichkeiten in der politischen, kulturellen und wirtschaftlichen entwicklung Deutschlands und Japans." Japan und China, 2 (1911-1912):221-223.

9624. Arima, Sukemasa. 國民道德叢書 Kokumin dotoku sosho. (Collection of works on the national morals of Japan.)
Tokyo, Hakubunkan, 1911. 3 v.

9625. Okakura, Yoshisaburo. The life and thought of Japan.
London, Dent & sons, 1913. viii, 150 p.

9626. Wainright, S. H., Anezaki, M., Schwartz, H. B. and
Naruse, J. Aspects of Japan, being 4 series of lectures delivered at the Summer school for missionaries, Karuizawa,

1913. Tokyo, Kyobunkan, 1914. 191 p.

9627. Brou, A. Les Japonais peints par eux-mêmes. Études. 20 (1914):3:737-759.

9628. Gérard, A. "Le Japon. Sa mission et son rôle dans les rapports entre l'Orient et l'Occident." Bulletin, Société franco-japonaise, 36-37 (1916):83-92.

9629. Inoue, Tetsujiro. 國民道德概論 Kokumin doto-ku gairon. (Essentials of the national morals of Japan.) Tokyo, Sanseido, 1918. 518 p.

9630. Tagore, Rabindranath. Der geist Japans. Übersetzt von Helene Meyer-Francke. Der neue geist (Leipzig), 1 (1918).

9631. Tanimoto, Tomi. 日本文化ト佛教 Nippon bunka to bukkyo. (Japanese culture and Buddhism.) Tokyo, Chojiya shoten, 1922. 396 p.

9632. Satomi. Kishio. Japanese civilization. Its signifi-cance and realization, Nichirenism and the Japanese natio-nal principles. Trubner's Oriental series. London, 1923. xiv, 238 p.

9633. Yoshitomi, Maçaomi. Le Japon et sa civilisation. Gre-noble, Drevet, 1924.

9634. Takagi, Toshio. 日本神話傳説ノ研究 Nippon shinwa densetsu no kenkyu. (Research in Japanese mythology and traditions.) Tokyo, 1925. 570 p.

9635. Kiyohara, Sadao. 神道ト日本文化 Shindo to Nippon bunka. (Shintoism and Japanese culture and civilization.) Tokyo, Taishokaku, 1926. 175 p.

9636. Ku, H.-M. "Civilization and monarchy, or the moral problem of the Far Eastern question." Ex Oriente (Tokyo), 2-3 (1926):125-137.

9637. Griffis, W. E. Some of Japan's contributions to civi-lization. New York, Japan society, 1927.

9638. Nitobe, Inazo. Japanese traits and foreign influences London, 1927.

9639. Bryan, John Thomas Ingram. The civilization of Japan. Home universal library of modern knowledge. London, Williams & Norgate; New York, Holt & co., 1928. vii, 256 p.

9640. Witte, J. Japan zwischen zwei kulturen. Leipzig, 1928. 505 p.

9641. Young, Walter C. Japan as tutor to the West. N.p., 1929. 28 p.

9642. Inage, Sofu. 日本文化ノ創造ト教育 Nippon bunka no sozo to kyoiku. (Cultural development of Japan and its effect upon education.) Tokyo, Toyo tosho kaisha, 1929. 494 p.

9643. Ueno, Shunei. 日本文化ノ権威 Nippon bunka no keni. (On Japanese civilization.) Tokyo, Taishokaku, 1930. 73 p.

9644. 光ハ日本ヨリ Hikari wa Nippon yori. (Japan sends out her light.) Tokyo, Shinchosha, 1930. 370 p.

9645. Sansom, George B. Japan -- a short cultural history. New York, Appleton-Century co., 1931. 537 p.

9646. Nitobe, Inazo and others. Western influences in modern Japan. N.P., 1931. xii, 532 p.

9647. Kido, Bantaro. 古代日本人ノ世界観 Kodai Nipponjin no sekaikan. (Ancient Japanese view of the world.) Tokyo, Iwanami, 1932. 272 p.

9648. Sawada, Ushimaro. 日本文化ノ再建 Nippon bunka no saiken. (The reformation of Japanese culture.) Tokyo, Nitto shoin, 1932.

9649. See 9587.

D. Education

See 937-951; 7992-8043.

(1) Bibliography

See 7237-7304.

9650. 圖書目録 Tosho mokuroku. (Catalogue of books in the [Educational] library.) Toyama, Kyoiku toshokan, 1930. 249 p.

(2) Periodicals

See 7305-7337.

9651. Japan. Department of education. 文部大臣年報
Monbu daijin nenpo. (Annual report of the Minister of state
for education.) Tokyo, 1, 1873- (47, 1919-1920 never issued.)

9652. 日本帝國文部省年報 Nippon teikoku monbu-
sho nenpo. (Annual report of the Minister of state for education.) Tokyo, Section of archives, Department of education. (Continued). 1925-

9653. 日本教育 Nippon kyoiku. (Japanese education.)
(Monthly). Tokyo, Nankosha.

9654. 教育修身研究 Kyoiku shushin kenkyu. (Research
in moral education.) (Monthly). Hongo, Tokyo, Nippon kyoiku
gakkai.

(3) History

9655. 日本教育史資料 Nippon kyoiku-shi shiryo. (Materials for the educational history of Japan.) Tokyo, Department of education, 1890-1892. 2 v.

9656. Ose, Jintaro. 日本現代教育學大系. Nippon gen-
dai kyoiku-gaku taikei. (A complete collection of modern
Japanese pedagogy.) Tokyo, Monasu, 1929. 427 p.

9657. Ototake, Iwazo. 日本庶民教育史 Nippon sho-
min kyoiku-shi. (History of the education of the masses in
Japan.) Tokyo, Meguro shoin, 1930. 3 v.

9658. 日本教育史 Nippon kyoiku-shi. (History of education in Japan.) Tokyo, Department of education, Kodokan,
1925. 284 p.

9659. Takahashi, Shunjo. 日本教育史 Nippon kyoiku-shi.
(History of education in Japan.) Tokyo, Kyoiku kenkyukai,
1930. 485 p.

9660. Ishikawa, Ken. 日本庶民教育史 Nippon shomin kyoiku-shi. (History of the education of the masses in Japan.)
Tokyo, Toko shoin, 1932. 458 p. See 9676.

9661. Keenleyside, Hugh L. and Thomas, A. F. History of Japanese education and present educational system. Tokyo, The
hokuseido press, 1937. 365 p.

9662. "Histoire de l'éducation au Japon (660 A. C. - 1602
A.D.)." Ex Oriente, 2-3:138-154, July 1926.

9663. Haruyama, Sakuju. 王朝教育史資料 Ocho kyoiku-shi shiryo. (Materials on the history of education in the Ocho period in Japan, 8th-11th century.) Tokyo, Nagasaki shobo, 1930. 91 p.

9664. Lombard, Frank Alanson. Pre-Meiji education in Japan. A study of Japanese education previous to the restoration of 1868. Tokyo, Kyobunkan, 1914. 275 p.

9665. Machida, Noribumi. 明治国民教育史 Meiji kokumin kyoiku-shi. (History of the education of the people in Japan during the Meiji era, 1868-1912.) Tokyo, Showa shuppansha, 1929. 538 p.

9666. Miura, Tosaku 大正年間日本教育史 Taisho nenkan Nippon kyoiku-shi. (A history of education in Japan during the Taisho era, 1912-1926.) Tokyo, Shuzando bunko, 1929. 293 p.

(4) General

See 1013-1014; 7992-8043.

9667. Pieters, A. The educational system of Japan. Prepared from official sources. Nagasaki, 1906. 79 p.

9668. Koroniev, N. "Эволюция воспитания в Японии." (The evolution of education in Japan.) Russkaia Shkola, 12 (1908):139-161.

9669. Kikuchi, Dairoku. Japanese education. Lectures delivered in the University of London. London, J. Murray, 1909. xvi, 398 p.

9670. Lamprecht, K. Rede bei übernahme des rektorats der Universität Leipzig am 31 Okt. 1910. Zwei hochschulreform. Berlin, Weidmann, 1910. 45 p.

9671. Mackay, F. v. "Zur reform und psychologie des japanischen schulwesens." Asien, Berlin, 10 (1910-1911):65-68.

9672. Nikolaenko, P. M. Материалы по коммерческому образованию в Японии. (Sources pertaining to commercial education in Japan.) Izvestiia Vostochnogo instituta (Vladivostok), 37 (1911):2. viii, 92 p.

9673. Clavery, Édouard. "L'institut historique de Tokyo shiryo hensan kakari." Bulletin de la Société franco-japonaise de Paris, 25 (1912):127-138.

9674. Sorokoletov, G. Материалы по начальному образованию в Японии. (Sources pertaining to primary education in Japan.) Izvestiia Vostochnogo instituta (Vladivostok), 57 (1915):1. iv, vii, 24 p.

9675. Mizuno, Tsunekichi. The kindergarten in Japan. Its effects upon the physical, mental and moral traits of Japanese school children. Boston, Stradford co., 1917.

9676. Ishikawa, Ken. 日本庶民教育史 Nippon shomin kyo-iku-shi. (History of common education in Japan.) Tokyo, Toko shoten, 1929. 472 p. See 9660.

9677. Kato, Naoshi. "The educational system of Japan." Transactions and proceedings of the Japan society (London), 16 (1918):132-145.

9678. Katayama, H. 日本語問題及教育ニ及ボセル問題 (The language question as it affects education in Japan.) Nippongo mondai oyobi kyoiku ni oyoboseru mondai. Transactions and proceedings of the Japan society, 19:54-74. (31 session, 1921-1922).

9679. Mas'ūd, Syed Ross. Japan and its educational system. Being a report compiled for the government of H. H. the Nizam. Hyderabad-Deccan, Government central press, 1923. v, 369 p.

9680. Seryshev, Innokentii. "Основы японской системы образования." (The foundations of the Japanese system of education.) Vestnik Asii, Harbin, 1923:51:115-178; 52:167-233.

9681. Il'in, N. "Японская система народного образования." (Japanese system of public education.) Narodnoe prosveshchenie, 3 (1926):136-143.

9682. A general survey of education in Japan. Tokyo, Department of education, 1926. 88 p.

9683. Imamiya, Sensho. 純粋日本教育原理 Junsui Nippon kyoiku genri. (Fundamental principles of Japanese education.) Tokyo, Meguro shoten, 1929. 322 p.

9684. 昭和新教育ニ即スベキ教育名論卓説集 Showa shinkyoiku ni sokusubeki kyoiku meiron taku-setsu-shu. (Collection of well-accepted views applicable to education of the present day.) Tokyo, Research institute of materials for teaching, Toyo tosho kaisha, 1929. 292 p.

9685. Watari, Shozaburo. 教育勅語ト學校教育
Kyoiku chokugo to gakko kyoiku. (The imperial rescript on
education and formal schooling.) Tokyo, Chubunkan, 1930.
757 p.

9686. Nogami, Sokichi. 日本教育界暴露記 Nippon kyoikukai bakuroki. (The secret of educational circles in Japan.) Tokyo, Jiyusha, 1930. 156 p.

9687. Sasaki, Fujinosuke. 昭和教育革新論 Showa
kyoiku kakushin ron. (The discussion for reform of the present educational system.) Tokyo, Daidokan, 1930. 220 p.

9688. Ito, Chimazo. 教育勅語述義 Kyoiku chokugo ju-
tsugi. (Commentary on the imperial rescript on Japanese
education.) Tokyo, Bunkosha, 1930. 409 p.

9689. Chin, Jung-hsüan. 最近日本勞働者教育運動概觀
Tsui-chin Jih-pên lao-tung-chê chiao-yü yün-tung kai-kuan.
(An outlook on the educational movement for laborers in Ja-
pan.) Chiao-yü-tsa-chih, 23:8, August 1931.

9690. Yang, Hsi-ming. 現代日本教育的解剖 Hsien-tai
Jih-pên chiao-yü ti chieh-p'ou. (An analysis of the education of modern Japan.) Chiao-yü tsa-chih, 23:9, September
1931.

9691. Wu, Tzu-ch'iang. 日本教育制度的缺陷與勞動
者的教育 Jih-pên chiao-yü-chih-tu ti chüeh-hsien yü
lao-tung-chê ti chiao-yü. (The defects of the Japanese education and the education for the labor class.) Chiao-yü
tsa-chih, 23:9, September 1931.

9692. Wu, Tzu-ch'iang. 日本的專門大學教育 Jih-pên ti
chuan-mên ta-hsüeh chiao-yü. (Higher technical education in
Japan.) Hsüeh-i, 11:5, September 1931.

9693. Hsü, Chung-hao. 日本考試制度 Jih-pên k'ao-shih
chih-tu. (The examination system in Japan.) Kao-shih-yüan
kung-pao, 10, October 1931.

9694. Wu, Tzu-ch'iang. 日本的高等普通教育 Jih-pên
ti kao-têng p'u-t'ung chiao-yü. (The higher general education in Japan.) Hsüeh-i, 11:7, November 1931.

9695. Lin, Li-ju. 日本師範教育的特点 Jih-pên shih-
fan chiao-yü ti t'ê-tien. (The special characteristic of
normal school education in Japan.) Chiao-yü yen-chiu, 32,
December, 1931.

9696. Chuang, Tsê-hsüan. 日本學制概要 Jih-pên hsüeh-chih kai-yao. (The Japanese educational system.) Chiao-yü yen-chiu, 32, December 1931.

9697. Hsü, Hsi-ling. 日本教育制度的哲學背境 Jih-pên chiao-yü chih-tu ti chê-hsüeh pei-ching. (The philo-sophical background of the Japanese educational system.) Chiao-yü yen-chiu, 32, December 1931.

9698. Lei, T'ung-ch'ün. 日本教育思潮的綜合批評 Jih-pên chiao-yü ssu-ch'ao ti tsung-ho p'i-p'ing. (A com-prehensive criticism on the educational thoughts of Japan.) Chiao-yü yen-chiu, 32, December 1931.

9699. Chiang, Ch'i. 日本現代教育哲學的發生與派別及其總勢 Jih-pên hsien-tai chiao-yü chê-hsüeh ti fa-shêng yü p'ai-pieh chi ch'i ch'ü-shih. (The birth of the modern Japanese educational philosophy, its different schools and tendencies.) Chiao-yü yen-chiu, 32, December 1931.

9700. Chung, Tao-chan. 日本三職業教育 Jih-pên chih chih-yeh-chiao-yü. (Vocational education in Japan.) Chiao-yü yü chih-yeh, 133-135, May 1932.

9701. Li, Chih-lin. 考察日本教育筆記 K'ao-ch'a Jih-pên chiao-yü pi-chi. (Notes on the investigation of educa-tion in Japan.) Peiping, Tung-hua shu-chü, 1932.

9702. Tanaka, Kotaro. 教養と文化基礎 Kyoyo to bunka no kiso. (Fundamentals of education and culture.) Tokyo, Iwanami shoten, 1937. 658 p.

(5) Institutions of Higher Learning

9703. 日本科學界 Nippon no kagakukai. (The scienti-fic world of Japan.) Tokyo, Bummei kyokai, 1916.

9704. Konrad, N. I. "Японские университеты." (Japanese uni-versities.) Nauchnyi rabotnik, 7-8 (1926):113-124.

9705. Scientific Japan: past and present. (Prepared in con-nection with the Third Pan-Pacific science congress.) Tokyo, 1926. 359 p.

E. Religion

See 967-1012; 2897-2938; 7992-8043.

(1) General Accounts

9706. Naganuma, Kenkai. 日本京. 教史/研究 Nippon shukyo-shi no kenkyu. (A study of the religious history of Japan.) Tokyo, Kyoiku kenkyukai, 1929. 1019 p.

9707. Ito, Kobi. 日本京. 教制度史料類聚考 Nippon shukyo seido shiryo ruishuko. (Collection of materials for the history of religious systems in Japan.) Tokyo, Ganshodo, 1930. 758 p.

9708. Kawaomote, Bonji. 祖神垂示. 天照. 大神宮 Soshin suiji Tensho daijingu. (Divine revelation and instructions of the Sun-Goddess, the Imperial ancestress of Japan.) Tokyo, Ryoikai, 1929. 1642 p.

9709. Hiyane, Yasusada. 日本京. 教史 Nippon shukyo-shi. (History of Japanese religions.) 1925. 1142 p.

9710. Griffis, W. E. The religions of Japan from the dawn of history to the era of Meiji. 4th edition. New York, 1901. (1st edition, 1895).

9711. Tsuchiya, Senkyo. 日本京. 教史 Nippon shukyo-shi. (History of religions in Japan.) 1907.

9712. Knox, G. W. The development of religion in Japan. American lectures on the history of religions, 6. London - New York, Putnam & sons, 1907. xxi, 204 p.

9713. Haas, Hans. Japans zukunftsreligion. Berlin, Curtius, 1907. 164 p.

9714. Reinhardt, L. Jung-Japan und seine bedeutung für das reich Gottes und die entwicklungsgeschichte der menschheit. Warte des tempels. München, Reinhardt, 1908. 58 p.

9715. Kirby, R. J. "Ancestral worship in Japan." Transactions of the Asiatic society of Japan (Tokyo), 38 (1911):4:233-267.

9716. Anesaki, Masaharu. "Le sentiment religieux chez les Japonais." Revue du mois, 5 (1908):655-674. (Appears in 1st report of the Association concordia of Japan, Tokyo, 1913. 94-114.)

9717. Harada, Tasuku. The faith of Japan. London, New York, Macmillan, 1914. ix, 190 p.

9718. Japanese temples and their treasures. Edited by H. I. Japanese Majesty's commission to the Panama-Pacific international exposition. Special edition. Tokyo, Shinbi shoin, 1915. 3 maps and 529 plates.

9719. Dahlmann, P. J. La religion du Japon. Manuel d'histoire des religions, 5. Paris, Beauchesne, 1916.

9720. Holtom, D. C. "A new interpretation of Japanese mythology and its bearing on the ancestral theory of Shinto." Journal of religion, 58-77, January 1926.

9721. A general view of the present religious situation in Japan. Tokyo, Bureau of religions, Department of education, 1920.

9722. Kato, Genchi. "A study of the development of religious ideas among the Japanese people as illustrated by Japanese phallicism." Transactions of the Asiatic society of Japan, 1 (1924):5-70. (Supplement to vol.1, 2nd series.)

9723. Florenz, K. "Die Japaner." Lehrbuch der religionsgeschichte von A. Bertholet und E. Lehmann, begründet von Chantepie de la Saussaye. 4 Auflage, Bd. 1, 262-422. Tübingen, J. C. B. Mohr, 1925.

9724. Shikado, Yasuhei. 神國大日本，眞髓 Shinkoku dai Nippon no shinzui. (The spirit of Japan, the sacred land.) Tokyo, Seishinkan, 1929. 212 p.

(2) Shintoism

9725. Azukizawa, Hideo and Takano, Yoshitaro. 神職便覧 Shinsoku binran. (Handbook for Shinto priests.) Tokyo, Kyoiku kenkyūkai, 1932. 600 p.

9726. Ono, Seishu. 神道十三敎，敎理ト歷史 Shinto jusan-kyo no kyori to rekishi. (The tenets and history of the thirteen sects of Shinto.) Kyoto, Bunseido, 1929. 278 p.

9727. Aston, W. G. Shinto, the ancient religion of Japan. London, Constable, 1907. New edition, 1921. 83 p.

9728. Holtom, D. C. "The political philosophy of modern Shinto. A study of the state religion of Japan." Transactions of the Asiatic society of Japan (Tokyo), 49 (1922):2:1-iv, 1-325.

9729. Shinto, der weg der Götter in Japan. Der Shintoismus, nach den gedruckten und ungedruckten berichten der japanischen Jesuitenmissionäre des 16 und 17 jahrhunderts. Bonn-Leipzig, K. Schroeder, 1923. 210 p.

9730. Martin, J.-M. Le Shintoïsme. Religion nationale. I. Les origines; essai d'histoire ancienne du Japon. Hongkong, Imprimerie de nazareth, 1924, vi, 223 p.

(3) Buddhism

9731. Oda, T. Bukkyo daijiten. 佛教大辞典 (Dictionary of Buddhism.) Published by the Okura book store, 1929. 1874 p.

9732. Hashikawa, Tadashi. 綜合日本佛教史 Sogo Nippon bukkyo-shi. (Comprehensive history of Japanese Buddhism.) Tokyo, Meguro shoten, 1932. 598 p.

9733. Oya, Tokujo. 日本佛教史ノ研究 Nippon bukkyo-shi no kenkyu. (A study of the history of Buddhism in Japan) Kyoto, Toho bunken kankokai, 1929. 590 p.

9734. Matsumoto, Bunzaburo. 國譯大藏経 Kokuyaku daizokyo. (Japanese translation of Buddhist tripitaka.) Tokyo, Nippon daizokyo hensankai, 1914-1921. 50 v. and index.

9735. Nanjo, Fumio; Takakusu, Junjiro; and Mochizuki, Shinryo. 大日本佛教全書 Dai Nippon bukkyo zensho. (Complete work on Japanese Buddhism.) Tokyo, Dai Nippon bukkyo zensho kankokai, Yuseido, 1932. 150 v.

9736. 真宗全書 Shinshu zensho. (Complete series of books concerning the Shin Shuh, one school of Japanese Buddhistic religion.) Tokyo, Zokyo shoin, 1913-1915. 74 v.

9737. Toyoda, Yasoyo. 國文學ニ現ハレタル佛教思想ノ研究 Kokubungaku ni arawaretaru bukkyo shiso no kenkyu. (A study of Buddhist thought found in Japanese national literature.) Tokyo, Ookayama shoten, 1932. 230 p.

9738. Eliot, Sir Charles Norton Edgecumbe. Japanese Buddhism. London, Arnold & co., 1935. xxxv, 449 p.

9739. Steinilber-Oberlin, E. The Buddhist sects of Japan. London, Allen & Unwin, 1937.

9740. Anesaki, Masaharu. "Buddhist influence upon the Japanese. (Abstract.)" Transactions of the Third international congress for the history of religions (Oxford 1908), 1 (1908):154-157.

9741. Lloyd, Arthur. "Formative elements of Japanese Buddhism." Transactions of the Asiatic society of Japan (Tokyo), 35 (1908):191-244.

9742. Takakusu, J. "Buddhism as we find it in Japan." Transactions and proceedings of the Japan society (London), 7 (1907):264-279.

9743. Anesaki, Masaharu. "Honen, the pietist saint of Japanese Buddhism." Transactions of the Third international congress for the history of religions (Oxford 1908):122-128.

9744. Holtom, D. C. "Shintoism and its significance." Annual report Smithsonian institution for 1913, 2304 (1914):607-615.

9745. "What Buddhism has done for Japan." The Japan magazine, 3 (1912-1913):196-200, 224-227.

9746. Osumi, S. "Le bouddhisme et son influence civilisatrice au Japon." Bulletin de la Société franco-japonaise de Paris, 50:25-31, Oct.-Dec. 1921.

9747. Nanjo, Bunyu. A history of the twelve Japanese Buddhist sects. Translated from the original Japanese. Tokyo, 1886. 31, 172 p.

9748. Suzuki, Daisetz Teitaro. "The development of the pure land doctrine in Buddhism." The eastern Buddhist, 3:4:285-326, January-March 1925.

9749. Imai, Kinachi and Matsutani, Motosaburo. The ideals of the Shinran-followers. A short exposition of the religion that is professed by most of the educated Japanese people. Tokyo, 1918. 7, 42, 45 p.

9750. Kita, Reikichi. "Über die japanische mystik." Ex Oriente, 2-3:114-124, July 1926.

9751. Washio, Junkei. 皇室ト佛敎 Koshitsu to bukkyo. (The imperial family and Buddhism.) Tokyo, Taitc shuppansha, 1937. 550 p.

9752. Fukushima, Masao. 忠孝・本義・佛教 Chuko no hongi no bukkyo. (Buddhism based on the true essence of loyalty and filial piety.) Tokyo, Meguro shoten, 1937. 200 p.

9753. Hosokawa, Kameichi. 日本佛教經濟史論考 Nippon bukkyo keizai-shiron ko. (Study of historical treatises on Buddhist economy in Japan.) Tokyo, Hakutosha, 1932. 596 p.

(4) Confucianism

See 2911-2922.

9754. Kato, Totsudo. 國民思想叢書・儒教篇 Kokumin shiso sosho: jukyo-hen. (National thought library: Confucianism.) Tokyo, Seishinsha, 1929. 546 p.

9755. Spal'vin, E. G. Конфуцианские идеи в этичном учении японского народа. (Confucian ideas in the ethical teachings of the Japanese people.) Izvestiia Vostochnogo instituta, Vladivostok, 31 (1913):3:1-22.

(5) Christianity

See 997-1010.

9756. The Christian movement in its relation to the new life in Japan. Year-book 4. Yokohama, D. C. Greene, 1906. 245, 40 p.

9757. Allier, R. Le protestantisme au Japon (1859-1907). Bibliothèque d'histoire contemporaine. Paris, Alcan, 1908. ii, 262 p.

9758. Cary, Otis. A history of Christianity in Japan. Protestant missions. Roman Catholic and Greek Orthodox missions. New York - London, Revell co., 1909. 2 v.

9759. Vogt, A. Der katholizismus in Japan. Wissenschaft und religion 24. Strassburg i. E., Le Roux, 1909. 64 p.

9760. "Из донесений начальных российских духовных миссионеров о состоянии православной церкви в Японии за 1911 г." (Reports of the first Russian religious missionaries regarding the conditions of the Orthodox church in Japan during the year 1911.) TSerkovnye vedomosti, 12-13 (1912):500-511.

9761. Vogt, A. Le Catholicisme au Japon. Paris, 1915. See 9759..

9762. Turkevich, L. and Tucker, H. "St. G. Archbishop Nikolai (von Turkevich). The orthodox apostle of Japan (von Tucker)." Constructive quarterly, 553-565, December 1919.

9763. Tucker, H. St. G. Missionary problems and policies in
Japan. Being the Reinecke lectures delivered at the Virgi-
nia theological seminary 1921. New York, Department of missions, Protestant Episcopal church, 1922. 47 p.

9764. Davis, J. Merle. "Feudalism and Christianity in Japan." International review of missions, 12 (1923):527-542.

(6) Miscellaneous

9765. Takakusu, J. "What Japan owes to India." The young
East, 1 (1925-1926):70-75, 106-109, 144-149, 183-186, 214-
217, 349-352, 385-391.

9766. Vambéry. "Japan and the Mohammedan world." Nineteenth
century and after (London), 57 (1906):573-576.

9767. Farjenel, F. "Le Japon et l'Islam." Revue du monde
musulman, 1 (1907):101-114.

F. Philosophy

See 952-966; 2970-2986; 7992-8043.

(1) Periodicals

See 7305-7337.

9768. 哲 学 雑 誌 Tetsugaku zasshi. (Journal of philosophy.) Tokyo, Iwanami shoten. (Monthly).

(2) General Accounts

See 7992-8043.

9769. 大 思 想 エンサイクロペデア Dai shiso ensaikurope-
jia. (Encyclopedia of great thought.) Tokyo, Shunjusha,
35 v.

9770. 大 日 本 思 想 全 集 Dai Nippon shiso zenshu. (Complete collection of works on Japanese thought.) Tokyo, Dai
Nippon shiso zenshu kankokai, 1932. 18 v.

9771. Washio, Junkei. 日 本 思 想 闘 諍 史 料 Nippon shiso toso shiryo. (Historical material regarding the develop-

ment and the dispute of thought and idea in Japan.) Tokyo, Tobo shoin, 1930-1931. 10 v.

9772. 福澤全集 Fukuzawa zenshu. (Complete works of Fukuzawa, one of the great thinkers of the early Meiji era.) Tokyo, Kokumin tosho kaisha, 1925-1926. 10 v.

9773. Kato, Setsudo. 國民思想叢書：民衆篇 Kokumin shiso sosho: Minshu hen. (A collection on Japanese national thought. Section on the people.) Tokyo, Seishinsha, 1930. 572 p.

9774. Tsuda, Sokichi. 文學＝現ハレタル我國民思想ノ研究 Bungaku ni arawaretaru waga kokumin shiso no kenkyu. (Research in the development of life and thought.) Tokyo, Rakuyodo, 1919. 4 v.

9775. Kato, Jinpei. 國民精神發達史 Kokumin seishin hattatsu-shi. (History of the development of the mind of the Japanese people.) Tokyo, Kyoiku kenkyukai, 1930.

9776. Honaga, Mosuke. 日本思想史 Nippon shiso-shi. (History of Japanese thought.) Tokyo, Kyoiku kenkyukai, 1932. 500 p.

9777. Takasu, Yoshijiro. 日本思潮十六講 Nippon shicho juroku-ko. (Sixteen lectures on Japanese thought.) Tokyo, Shinchosha, 1929. 476 p.

9778. Holtom, D. C. The national faith of Japan: a study in modern Shinto. London, Kegan Paul, ltd., 1938 585 p.

9779. Muraoka, Tsunetsugu. 日本思想史研究 Nippon shiso-shi kenkyu. (Research in the history of Japanese thoughts.) Tokyo, Oka shoin, 1935. 607 p.

9780. Inouye, T. Kurze übersicht über die entwicklung der philosophischen ideen in Japan. Translated from the French into German by A. Gramatzky. Berlin, 1897. 25 p.

9781. Nagai, Kyo. 日本思想論 Nippon shiso-ron. (Treatise on Japanese thought.) Tokyo, Waseda university, Publication department, 1929. 417 p.

9782. Honaga, Mosuke. 日本思想ノ研究 Nippon shiso no kenkyu. (Research in Japanese thought.) Tokyo, Kyoiku kenkyukai, 1929. 476 p.

9783. Kishinami, T. The development of philosophy in Japan. London, Milford, 1916.

9784. Kiyohara, Sadao. 日本道德論 Nippon dotoku ron. (On the moral virtues of Japan.) Tokyo, Kaizosha, 1926. 556 p.

9785. Iwazumi, Junsei. 日本倫理思想發達史 Nippon rinri shiso hattatsu-shi. (History of the development of ethical ideas in Japan.) Tokyo, 1915. 2 v.

9786. Inoue, Tetsujiro and Kanie, Yoshimaru. 日本倫理 彙論 Nippon rinri iron. (Treatise on Japanese ethics.) Tokyo, 1930. 10 v.

9787. Satomi, Kishio. The discovery of Japanese idealism. Trubner's Oriental series. London, Kegan Paul, 1924. vi, 178 p.

9788. Kiyohara, Sadao. 明治時代思想史 Meiji jidai shiso-shi. (Life and thought in the Meiji era, 1868-1912.) Tokyo, Taishokaku, 1921. 383 p.

9789. Tsuchida, Kyoson. Contemporary thought of Japan and China. Library of contemporary thought. London, Williams & Norgate; New York, Knopf, 1927. 240 p.

9790. Oyama, Kotaro. Der geist des Absoluten schicksals. Das ideal des lebens, der politik, der erziehung. Konstanz, A. G. Neuenschwander, 1922. 253 p.

9791. Lloyd, Arthur. "Historical development of the Shushi philosophy in Japan." Transactions of the Asiatic society of Japan, 34 (1907):4:1-80.

9792. Fujisawa, Chikao. Die gegenwärtigen abendländischen geistesströmungen und der echtjapanische geist. Annalen für die Juristisch-literarische fakultät der Kyushu kaiserlichen universität (in Fukuoka). Vol. 1:1. Fukuoka, Tokyo, 1928.

9793. Kato, Naoshi. "Eastern ideas and the Japanese spirit." Transactions and proceeding of the Japan society (London), 13 (1915):116:148.

9794. Spencer, J. Kennard. Thinking in Japanese. London, Kegan Paul, 1925. 120 p.

9795. Takayama, Shun. "Developpement de la philosophie occidentale au Japon." Ex Oriente, 1:81-87, April 1925.

9796. Matsunaga, Zai. 日本主義' 哲 学 Nippon shugi no tetsugaku. (Philosophy based on Japanese nationalism.) In Tetsugaku taikei. Tokyo, Shobundo, 1929. 551 p.

G. Literature

See 1015-1018.

9797. Lange, Rudolf. Thesaurus japonicus. Berlin, Reimer, 1913-1920. 3 v.

9798. Florenz, Karl. Geschichte der japanischen litteratur. Die litteraturen des Ostens in einzeldarstellungen, 10. Leipzig, Amelang, 1906. x, 642 p.

9799. Adler-Revon (P. Adler). Japanische litteratur. Geschichte und auswahl von den anfängen bis zur neuesten zeit. Taschenbücher der litteratur, 1. Frankfurt a. M., Frankfurter verlag-Anstalt, 1925. 430 p.

9800. Wilson, E. Japanese literature: including selections from Genji Monogatari and classical poetry and drama of Japan. With critical and biographical sketches. New York, Lamb, 1908. 2 v.

9801. Revon, Michel. Anthologie de la littérature Japonaise des origines au 20ᵉ siècle. Collection "Pallas". Paris, Delagrave, 1910. 476 p. Another edition, 1919.

9802. Yoshitomi, M. Anthologie de la littérature japonaise contemporaine. Grenoble, Drevet, 1924.

9803. Marquis de la Mazelière. "La littérature japonaise dans l'ère de Meiji." Bulletin de la Société franco-japonaise de Paris, 29:85-95, April 1913.

9804. Tanakadate, A. "Japanese writing and the Romazi movement." Introduction by Hiroshi Saito (74-76). Transactions and proceedings of the Japan society, 17 (1920):74-98.

9805. Asataro, Miyamori. Masterpieces of Japanese poetry, ancient and modern. Tokyo, Maruzen, 1937. 2 v.

9806. Page, C. H. Japanese poetry. An historical essay with 230 translations. Boston and New York, Houghton, Mifflin ɔo., 1923. 181 p.

9807. Fujisawa, Ehiko. 日本傳説研究 Nippon densetsu kenkyu. (Research in Japanese traditions and folklore.) Tokyo,

Rokubunkan, 1931. 6 v.

9808. Smith, R. G. Ancient tales and folk-lore of Japan.
London, Black, 1908. 378 p.

9809. 日 本 文 學 講 座 Nippon bungaku koza. (Lectures on
Japanese literature.) Tokyo, Shinchosha, 1932. 15 v. (2)
Igarashi, Chikara. 新 國 文 學 史 Shin kokubungaku-shi.(A
new history of Japanese literature.) Tokyo, 1923. 800 p.

H. Art

(1) General Accounts

9810. 東 洋 美 術 大 觀   Toyo bijutsu taikan. (A choice collection of art relics in Japan and other eastern countries.)
Tokyo, 1908-1918, Published by the Shinbi shoin. (1-7 vols.
Japanese paintings and 8-12 vols. Chinese paintings and 13-
15 vols. Japanese and Chinese sculptures.)

9811. Nakamura, Ishisaburo. Catalogue of the national treasures of paintings and sculptures in Japan. Kyoto, Daikoku-
ya; Yokohama, Kelly & Walsh, 1915. vi, 167 p.

9812. Toyei, Shuko. An iluustrated catalogue of the ancient
Imperial treasury called Shosoin. Revised edition. Compiled
by the Imperial household. Tokyo, Shinbi shoin, 1908-1909.
Latest edition, 1926.

9813. Japanese temples and their treasures (Kokuho gajo).
Compiled by the Department of the interior. Tokyo, Shinbi
shoin, 1910. 223 p. and 629 plates.

9814. Kümmel, O. "Neue japanische monumental-publikationen."
Zeitschrift für bildende kunst, 1910. 124-128.

9815. Ikeda, T. 增 補 日 本 書 畫 骨 董 辞 典 Zoho Nippon sho-
ga kotto daijiten. (Dictionary of Japanese caligraphy,
painting and antiques.) Revised edition. 1922.

9816. Kuroda, Hoshin. 大 日 本 美 術 史 Dai Nippon biju-
tsu-shi. (History of Japanese art.) Tokyo, Seibundo, 1922.
1024 p.

9817. Brinkley, F. The art of Japan. Boston, Millet & co.,
1901. 2 v.   (2) Tanabe, Koji. 東 洋 美 術 史 Toyo biju-
tsu-shi. (History of Oriental fine arts.) Tokyo, Heibonsha, 1930-1933. 2 v.

9818. Huish, M. B. Japan and its art. Third edition, revised and enlarged. London, Batsford, 1912.

9819. Joly, H. L. Legend in Japanese art. A description of h historical episodes, legendary characters, folk-lore, myths, religious symbolism, illustrated in the arts of Old Japan. London - New York, John Lane, 1907. xliv, 453 p.

9820. Binyon, L. Japanese art. London, B. Quaritch; T. F. Unwin, 1909. 60 p.

9821. Seidlitz, W. v. History of Japanese color-prints. London, Heinemann, 1910. xvi, 207 p.

9822. Bowie, H. On the laws of Japanese paintings. An introduction to the study of the art of Japan. With prefatory remarks by Iwaya Sazanami and Hirai Kinza. San Francisco, Elder, 1911. 15, 117 p.

9823. Noguchi, Yone. The spirit of Japanese art. London, Murray, 1915.

9824. Gonse, Louis. L'art japonais. Paris, 1926. 340 p.

9825. Martin, Henry. L'art japonais. Paris, Ducher, 1926.

9826. Blacker, J. F. The ABC of Japanese art. London, 1929. 460 p.   (2) Tsuda, Noritake. ABC of Japanese art. Tokyo, Board of tourist industry, Japanese government railways, Toppan printing co., 1937. 87 p.

9827. Warner, Langdon. The craft of the Japanese sculptor. New York, McFarlane, Ward, McFarlane and Japan society. 1936. 85 plates.

9828. Morrison, A. The painters of Japan. London, T. C. & E. C. Jack, 1911. 2 v.

9829. Baltzer, F. Die architektur der kultbauten Japans. Berlin, Ernst u. sohn, 1907. iv, 354 p.

9830. Bayard, Émile. Le style japonais. L'art de reconnaître les styles. Paris, Garnier frères, 1928.

(2) The Arts

9831. Dillon, E. The arts of Japan. Little books on art series. London, Methuen & co., 1906. 2nd edition, Chicago, McClurg, 1909.

9832. Piggott, Sir F. Studies in the decorative art of Japan. London, Batsford; Yokohama, Kelly & Walsh, 1910. 130 p.

9833. Taki, Seiichi. "Causes of development of Japanese artistic industries." Kokka, 18 (1907-1908):173-181.

9834. Koop, J. A. Guide to Japanese textiles. London, Victoria and Albert museum, 1920. 2 v.

9835. Ballot, M.-J. La céramique japonaise. Paris, 1927. 40 p. and 46 plates.

9836. Franks, Sir A. W. Japanese pottery: being a native report (prepared by M. Shioda and translated by T. Asami) with an introduction and a catalogue. 2nd edition. Victoria and Albert museum art handbooks. London, 1906. xxi, 119 p. (1st edition, 1880).

9837. Kurth, Julius. Die geschichte des japanischen holzschnitts. Leipzig, Hiersemann, 1925. viii, 445 p.

9838. Seidlitz, W. v. Geschichte des japanischen farbenholzschnitts. 2 auflage. Dresden, kühtmann, 1910. 228 p.

9839. Anderson, W. Japanese wood engravings. Their history, technique and character. New edition. London, Seeley; New York, Dutton, 1908. 222, 20 p. (1st edition, London, 1895).

9840. Denike, B. P. Японская цветная гравюра. (Japanese colored engraving.) [History of development of colored engraving in Japan.] Moscow, 1935. 198 p.

I. The Theatre

See 1045-1046; 2886.

9841. Maybon, A. Le théâtre japonais. Paris, Laurens, 1925. 132 p.

J. Music

9842. Piggott, Sir Francis. The music and musical instruments of Japan. With notes by T. L. Southgate. Second edition. Yokohama, Kelly and Walsh; London, B. T. Batsford, 1909. xviii, 196 p. First edition, London, 1893. (2) Tanabe, Takao. 東洋音樂史 Toyo ongaku-shi. (History of Oriental music.) Tokyo, Yuzankaku, 1932. 574 p. [In v. 13 of Lectures on Oriental history.]

XXI. KOREA

See 1-1060; 1527-1921; 2987-3021;3022-4705; 4706-6446;
7542-7836; 8044-8224; 8690-8885.

A. Bibliography

See 1-42; 1061-1087; 4706-4720; 7237-7304.

9843. Courant, Maurice. Bibliographie coréenne; tableau lit-
téraire de la Corée, contenant la nomenclature des ouvrages
publiés dans ce pays jusqu'en 1890 ainsi que la description
et l'analyse détaillées des principaux d'entre ces ouvrages.
Paris, E. Leroux, 1894-1896. 3 vols. Supplément a la Bibliographie coréenne. Paris, Leroux, 1901. x, 122 p.

9844. 朝鮮古書目錄 Chosen kosho mokuroku. (A catalog
of ancient Korean books.) Tokyo, Chosen kosho kankokai.

9845. 朝鮮總督府圖書目錄 Chosen Sotokufu
tosho mokuroku. (Catalogue of books in the office of the
Governor general of Korea.) Tokyo, Chosen Sotokufu. 2 v.

9846. 朝鮮帝室圖書目錄 Chosen teishitsu tosho
mokuroku. (A catalogue of books in the Korean royal household.) Tokyo, Department of the Korean royal household.

9847. Underwood, Horace H. Partial bibliography of Occidental works on Korea with a paper on Occidental literature on
Korea. English publication of Chosen Christian college,
Seoul, 1931. Reprint from the Transactions of the Korea
branch of the Royal Asiatic society, 20 (1931): 1-185.

9848. "A Korean cyclopedia." Korea review, 6 (1906):217-223,
244-248.

B. Periodicals

See 45-247; 1088-1093; 4721-4730; 7305-7337.

9849. Royal Asiatic society of Great Britain and Ireland.
Korea branch. Transactions. Seoul, 1, 1900-

9850. 개벽 Kaebyŏk. (The dawn.) Seoul, 1916-1936.
(Monthly). Discontinued. (2) 우라기 Urak'i (The Roc-
ky.) Seoul, 1, 1920-   (Quarterly). (3) 동광 Tong-
gwan. (Eastern light.) Seoul, 1922-1927. (Monthly). Discontinued.

9885. Griffis, William E. Corea the hermit nation. New York, 1911. 9th edition.

9886. Lushington, M. A. and Hamilton, A. Korea; its history, its people, and its commerce. Oriental series. Boston, J.B. Millet, 1911. 16, 326 p.

9887. Immanuel, F. "Korea im besitze Japans. Eine militärge-ographische beurteilung." Petermanns geographische mitteil-ungen, 57 (1911):1:220-223. (2) The same. "La Corée japon-aise, essai de géographie militaire." Internationale revue über die gesamten armeen und flotten, 1911. 368-376.

9888. "Corea: a Confucian polity." Economic review, 22 (1912):392-414.

9889. Kiuner, N. V. Стат.-географический и экономический очерк Кореи, ныне японская губерния Циосен. (A statistical-geographic and economic outline of Korea, now the Japanese province, Chosen.) Izvestiia Vostochnogo instituta (Vladi-vostok), 41-43 (1912). vi, xxx, 656, 32 p.

9890. Kirillov, N. V. Корея. (Korea.) A medico-anthropologi-cal sketch. Zapiski Priamurskogo otdela Imperatorskogo rus-skogo geograficheskogo obshchestva, 1913. Vol. 9:1.

9891. Haegeholz, W. Korea und die Koreaner. Nach englischen quellen dargestellt. Stuttgart, Steinkopf, 1913. 296 p.

9892. Gale, J. S. Korean folk-tales: imps, ghosts and fai-ries; translated from the Korean of Im Bang and Yi Ryuk by J. S. Gale. London, Dent & sons, 1913. 246 p.

9893. Keir, R. Malcolm. "Modern Korea." Bulletin of the American geographical society, 46 (1914):756-769, 817-830.

9894. Grünfeld, Ernst. "Eine kurze geschichte der fremden in Korea." China-Archiv. Archiv für den Fernen Osten, 2 (1916): 651-656.

9895. Coleman, Frederick. "The Chosen of today and the Korea of yesterday." Fortnightly review, 102 (1918):612:905-916.

9896. Muzio, C. Manciuria e Corea. Mailand, Sonzogno, 1920. 31 p.

9897. La Corée contemporaine. Paris, J. Dumoulin, 1921. 96 p.

9851. 青丘學叢 Seikyu gakuso. (Quarterly review of the Korean historical society.) Keijo, 1929-1938. Discon-tinued. (2) 震檀學報 Chindan hakpo. (Quarterly journal of Korean studies.) Seoul, 1934-

9852. 태평양주보 T'aep'yŏngyang chubo. (Korean Pa-cific weekly.) Honolulu, 1, 1914- (irregular in early years.) (2) Minjok hyŏngmyŏng. 민족혁명 (National revolution.) Nanking, 1936- (Monthly). (3) 신한민보 Sinhan minbo. (The New Korea.) San Francisco, 1906-1937; Los Angeles, 1938- . [The first few volumes under: 공립신보 Kongnip sinbo. (United Korea.).] (4) 국민보 Kungminbo. (Korean national herald.) Honolulu, 1, Octo-ber 1907- (Weekly).

C. Geology, Natural Resources, and Geography

See 1235-1345.

9853. Karte der russisch-asiatischen grenzendistrikte. Sek-tion 16: Korea. Neue ausgabe, July 1913. 1:1,680,000.

9854. Inouye, K. (comp.). General geological map of Korea. Tokyo, Imperial survey, 1911. 1:1 500 000. (2) Kawasaki, S. Geology and mineral resources of Korea. Tokyo, 1916.

9855. O, Taehwan. 大韓地理 대한지리 Taehan Chiri. (Geography of Korea.) Seoul, Pangmunsa, 1904. 2 v.

9856. Fukuchi, N. 朝鮮鑛產物 Chosen kosanbutsu. (The minerals of Chosen.) Beiträge zur mineralogie von Japan, Tokyo, 1915, 207-305. (2) Shihara, Genzo. 新朝鮮風土記 Shin-Chosen fudo-ki. (The natural features of new Korea.) Tokyo, Banrikaku, 1930.

9857. Robbins, H. R. "The mineral resources of Korea." Transaction of the American institute for mining and engi-neering, 1908, 587-800. (2) Fermor, L. Leigh. "On the geo-logy and coal resources of the Korean state, Central provin-ces." Memoirs, Geological survey of India, 41 (1914):2:I-III, 148-245. (3) Mills, E. W. "Gold mining in Korea." Transactions of the Korea branch of the Royal Asiatic soci-ety, 7 (1916):1:3-39.

9858. Niu-shan. 朝鮮鑛業的現狀 Ch'ao-hsien k'uang-yeh ti hsien-chuang. (Korean mining at present.) New Orient month-ly, 1:10:87, October 1930.

9859. Chong, Unmo. 대한십삼도유람하 Taehan sipsamdo yuramha (Geography of the 13 provinces of Korea.) Seoul, 1909. 2 v.

D. Archaeology and Anthropology

See 256-272.

9860. 朝鮮總督府古蹟調査報告 Chosen Sotokufu ko-
seki chosa hokoku (Annual report of the Archaeological survey in Korea.) Published by the Goverment-general of Chosen,
1916-1922. 7 v.

9861. Tsuboi, Heigoro. 朝鮮人種 Chosen no jinshu.
(Korean racial origins.) Chiri to rekishi, 141-146, November 1, 1910. (Special edition: Annexation of Korea.)

9862. Hulbert, Homer B. "Korean and Ainu." Korea review, 6
(1906):223-228.

9863. Kubo, T. Beitrage zur physischen anthropologie der
Koreaner. Mitteilungen der Medizinischen fakultät der Kaiserlichen universität, 12. Tokyo, 1913. 676 p.

9864. Korf, Baron N. A. "О численности населения в Корее."
(On the number of inhabitants in Korea.) Izvestiia Imperatorskogo russkogo geograficheskogo obshchestva, 40:330-354.

9865. Shinoda, Jisaku. 朝鮮民族, 北進 Chosen minzoku
no hokushin. (Northward advance of the Korean race.) Gaiko
jiho, 81:5:98-113, March 1937.

E. General Accounts

See 343-449.

9866 . Oppert, Ernst. A forbidden land. London, 1880. 349 p.
(2) Lowell, Percival. Chosön, the land of the morning calm.
Boston, 1888. 412 p. (3) Carles, W. R. Life in Korea. London-New York, 1888. 317 p.

9867. Podzhio, M. Очерки Кореи. (Sketches of Korea.) St. Petersburg, 1892. 391 p. (2)Chaillé-Long, Colonel Charles. La
Corée ou Tchösen (La terre du calme matinal. Paris, 1894.
(3) Landor, Arnold H. S. Corea; or, Cho-sen, the land of
morning calm. London, 1895.

9868. Bishop, Isabella L. (Bird). Korea and her neighbours.
London, 1898. 2 v. (2) Gale, James S. Korean sketches. New
York, 1898. 256 p. (3) The same. The vanguard. New York,
1904. 320 p.

9869. Genthe, Siegfried. Korea: reiseschilderungen...
Berlin, 1905. 343 p.

9870. Hamilton, Angus. Korea. London, Heine
xlii, 315 p.   2nd rev. ed. Boston-Tokyo, 1

9871. Allen, Horace N. Korea, fact and fanc

9872. Sieroszewski, W. Korea land und volk nac
schauung gemeinverständlich geschildert. Übers
Stefania Goldenring. Berlin, Gutmann, n.d. (190
The same. Korea: klucz Dalekiego Wschodu. Warsaw

9873. Vaskevich, P. К вопросу о современном сост
(On the present condition of Korea.) Vladivostok,

9874. "Kennan and Korea." Korea review, 6 (1906):

9875. Speshnev, Captain. Корея. (Korea.) A geograph
sketch, edited by N. V. Kiuner. Vladivostok, 1907.

9876. McKenzie, F. A. The tragedy of Korea. London,
& Stoughton, 1908. xii, 312 p.

9877. Underwood, Frau Lilias H. Fifteen years among th
knots; or life in Korea, with an introduction by F. F.
linwood. 2nd edition revised and enlarged. New York, Am
can tract society, 1908. xvii, 354 p.

9878. Underwood, H. G. The call of Korea. Political, so
religious. London, Edinburgh, New York, Fleming, H. Revel
& co., 1908. 204 p.

9879. Allen, H. N. Things Korean. A collection of sketches
and anecdotes, missionary and diplomatic. New York, Fleming
Revell & co., 1908. 256 p.

9880. Gollier, T. Une nation qui meurt: la Japonisation de
la Corée. 1909.

9881. Kröbel, Emma. Wie ich an den koreanischen kaiserhof
kam. Reiseeindrücke und erinnerungen, Berlin, Jacobstahl,
1909. 188 p.

9882. Kolokol'nikova, V. Корея. (Korea.) 2nd edition. Moscow, Panafidina, 1909. 24 p.

9883. Rossov, P. "Корейская армия."   (The Korean army.)
Voennyi sbornik, 10 (1909):227-236.

9884. Longford, J. H. The story of Korea. London, Unwin,
1911. vii, 400 p.

9898. Shirman, G. V. Корея. (Korea.) Historical and political economic sketch. Moscow, Institut vostokovedeniia, 1923. 52 p.

9899. I, Kwangsu. 朝鮮 의 現在 와 將未 조선 의 현재 와 장래 Chosonui hyonjae wa changnae. (The present and the future of Korea.) Seoul, 1923. 198 p.

9900. Chêng, Tz'u-ch'uan. 高麗一瞥 Kao-li i-pieh. (A glimpse of Korea.) Shanghai, Commercial press, 1924.

9901. Curzon of Kedleston, Marquess. "In the diamond mountains of Korea." National geographic magazine, 46 (1924): 353-374.

9902. Kim.. Под гнетом японского империализма. (Under the oppression of Japanese imperialism.) A sketch of modern Korea. Edited by K. Kharnskii. Vladivostok, Knizhnoe Delo, 1926. 151 p.

9903. Ireland, Alleyne. The new Korea. New York, Dutton & co., 1926. xii, 354 p.

9904. Takeuchi, Bunpin. 二ッノ朝鮮問題 Futatsu no Chosen mondai." (The two Korean problems.) Gaiko jiho, 52:2: 146-153, October 15, 1929.

9905. Huang, Yen-p'ei. 朝鮮 Ch'ao-hsien. (Chosen.) Shanghai, Commercial press, 1930.

9906. Yên, Ping-hao. Ch'ao-hsien. 朝鮮 (Korea.) Current events, 2:5:170, May 1930.

9907. Tokutomi, Iichiro. 文祿慶長以後日本ニ於ヶル 朝鮮ノ感化 Bunroku Keicho igo Nippon ni okeru Chosen no kanka.) (The influence of Korea in Japan after the Bunroku and Keicho eras.) Tokyo, Chuo Chosen kyokai, 1931. 56p.

9908. Yamamoto, Sanehiko. 満鮮 Man-Sen. (Manchuria and Korea.) Tokyo, Kaizosha, 1932.

9909. Ono, Kyutaro. 朝鮮ト満洲國 Chosen to Manshukoku. (Korea and Manchukuo.) Seoul, Chosen keizai nipposha, 1933. 200 p.

9910. Kamada, Sawaichiro. 朝鮮ハ起ヶ上ル Chosen wa tachiagaru. (Risen Korea.) Tokyo, Chikura shobo, 1934. 358 p.

9911. Ugaki, Kazunari. 朝 鮮 , 語 ∿ Chosen wo kataru.
(About Korea.) Tokyo, Jitsugyo no Nipponsha, 1936. 166 p.

F. History and International Relations

See 273-342; 450-780; 3022-4705; 8044-8224; 8690-8885; 11402-11464.

(1) Sources

9912. Kim, Pusik. 三 國 史 記 Samguk sagi. (History of
the Three kingdoms.) 50 books in 10 v. (Compiled in compliance with the royal request of King Injong, 1123-1147, seventeenth ruler of the Koryo dynasty.)

9913. Yi, P'a, Kim, Kyech'ang, and others. 三 國 史 節 要
Samguksa Choryo. (Outline history of the Three kingdoms of
Korea.) 14 books in 7 v. (Compiled in compliance with the
royal request of King Songjong, 1470-1494, 9th ruler of the
Yi dynasty.)

9914. Ch'oe, Inji. 高 麗 史 Koryo-sa. (History of Korea.)
139 books in 100 v. (Compiled in compliance with the royal
request of King Sejo, 1419-1450, 4th ruler of the Yi dynasty.) (2) The same. 高 麗 史 節 要 Koryo-sa choryo. (Outline of the History of Korea.) 35 books in 25 v. (3) Yu,
Kye. 麗 史 提 綱 Yosa chegang. (Outline history of Korea.)
23 books in 23 v.

9915. Sŏ, Kŏjŏng. 東 國 通 鑑 Tongguk t'onggam. (History
of Korea.) 56 books in 28 v. (Compiled in compliance with
the royal request of King Songjong, 1470-1495, 9th ruler of
the Yi dynasty.) (2) Hong, Yŏha. 東 國 通 鑑 提 綱
Tongguk tonggam chegang. (Outline of the Complete history
of the Eastern country, Korea.) 13 books in 7 v. (3) Im,
Sangdŏk. 東 史 會 綱 Tongsa hoegang. (History of the East,
Korea.) 1719. 27 books in 9 v. (4) An, Chŏngbok. 東 史 綱 目
Tongsa kangmok. (Classified history of the East, Korea.) 20
books in 20 v.

9916. Kwŏn, Nam. 國 朝 寶 鑑 Kukcho Pogam. (National history of Korea.) 7 books in 3 v. (Compiled in compliance with
the royal request of King Sejo, 1456-1468, 7th ruler of the
Yi dynasty.) Revised and continued by Cho Kyong at the request of King Chŏngjo, 1777-1800. 56 books in 19 v.; and by
Ch'oe Wonyong at the request of King Honjong, 1835-1849. 82
books in 24 v., with a supplement by Kim Ch'iin. 10 books in
3 v. Final edition by a board of editors appointed by the
last king of the dynasty, King Sunjong, 1907-1910. 90 books
in 28 v.

9917. 東國文獻備考 Tongguk munhŏn pigo. (Official
Korean encyclopedia.) 100 books in 40 v. (Compiled in compliance with the request of King Yongjo, 1725-1777.) Revised
and enlarged edition published at the request of King Ko-
jong, 1864-1907. 250 books in 50 v.

9918. Chŏng, Ch'angsun. 同文彙考 Tongmun hwigo. (Documents of foreign relations.) 129 books in 60 v. (Compiled
at the request of King Chongjo, 1777-1800.) Two volumes of
a projected edition of 12 volumes, published by Keijo imperial university, were released in 1938.

9919. Kim, Kyŏngmun. 通文館志 T'ongmun'gwanji. (Records
of the Office of interpreters, or Foreign office.) Seoul,
1881. 12 books in 6 v.   Abridged edition by the Council on
Korean history of the Government general of Chosen, 1913. 1 v.

9920. 李朝實錄 리 조 실 록 Yi-jo sillok. (The Yi dynasty annals.) 1392-1864. Seoul, Government general of Chosen and Keijo imperial university, 1930-1934. 864 v.   (2)
McCune, G. M. "The Yi dynasty annals of Korea." Transactions, Korea Branch, Royal Asiatic society, Seoul, 1938.

9921. 太祖實錄 T'aejo sillok. (Chronicle of the reign
of King T'aejo, 139.-1399, first ruler of the Yi dynasty.)
Tokyo. See 9920.

9922. 定宗實錄 Chŏngjong sillok. (Chronicle of the reign
of King Chongjong, 1399-1400, 2nd ruler of the Yi dynasty.)
6 books in 4 v. See 9920.

9923. 太宗實錄 T'aejong sillok. (Chronicle of the reign
of King T'aejong, 1401-1418, 3rd ruler of the Yi dynasty.)
36 books in 35 v. See 9920.

9924. 世宗實錄 Sejong sillok. (Chronicle of the reign
of King Sejong, 1419-1450, 4th ruler of the Yi dynasty.)
163 books in 154 v. See 9920.

9925. 文宗實錄 Munjong sillok. (Chronicle of the reign
of King Munjong, 1451-1452, 5th ruler of the Yi dynasty.)
13 books in 12 v. See 9920.

9926. 端宗實錄 Tanjong sillok. (Chronicle of the reign
of King Tanjong, 1453-1455, 6th ruler of the Yi dynasty.)
14 books in 15 v. Also: 端宗實錄附錄 Tanjong sillok purok. (Supplement...) See 9920.

9927. 世 祖 實 錄 Sejo sillok. (Chronicle of the reign of King Sejo, 1456-1468, 7th ruler of the Yi dynasty.) 49 books in 42 volumes. See 9920.

9928. 脊 京 實 錄 Yejong sillok. (Chronicle of the reign of King Yejong, 8th ruler of the Yi dynasty. 1469.) 8 books in 5 v. See 9920.

9929. 成 京 實 錄 Songjong sillok. (Chronicle of the reign of King Songjong, 1470-1494, 9th ruler of the Yi dynasty.) 297 books in 150 v. See 9920.

9930. 燕 山 君 日記 Yŏnsan-gun ilgi. (Chronicle of the reign Prince Yŏnsan, 1495-1505, 10th ruler of the Yi dynasty.) 63 books in 46 v. See 9920.

9931. 中 京 實 錄 Chungjong sillok. (Chronicle of the reign of Chungjong, 1506-1544, 11th ruler of the Yi dynasty.) 105 books in 102 v. See 9920.

9932. 仁 京 實 錄 Injong sillok. (Chronicle of the reign of King Injong, 1545, 12th ruler of the Yi dynasty.) 2 books in 2 v. See 9920.

9933. 明 京 實 錄 Myŏngjong sillok. (Chronicle of the reign of King Myŏngjong, 1546-1567, 13th ruler of the Yi dynasty.) 34 books in 34 v. See 9920.

9934. 宣 祖 實 錄 Sŏnjo sillok. (Chronicle of the reign of King Sŏnjo, 1568-1608, 14th ruler of the Yi dynasty.) 221 books in 125 v. (2) Revised edition, 42 books in 8 v. (3) Yi, Tanha. 宣 廟 寶 鑑 Sŏnmyo pogam. (Biography of King Sŏnjong.) 10 books in 5 v. (Compiled in compliance with the royal request of King Sukehong, 1675-1720, 19 ruler of the Yi dynasty.) See 9920.

9935. 光 海 君 日記 Kwanghae-gun ilgi. (Chronicle of the reign of Prince Kwanghae, 1609-1622, 15th ruler of the Yi dynastry.) 187 books in 40 v. See 9920.

9936. 仁 祖 實 錄 Injo sillok. (Chronicle of the reign of King Injo, 1623-1649, 16th ruler of the Yi dynasty.) 50 books in 50 v. See 9920.

9937. 孝 京 實 錄 Hyojong sillok. (Chronicle of the reign of King Hyojong, 1650-1659, 17th ruler of the Yi dynasty.) 21 books in 22 v. See 9920.

9938. 顯宗實錄 Hyŏnjong sillok. (Chronicle of the reign of King Hyŏnjong, 1660-1674, 18th ruler of the Yi dynasty.) 22 books in 23 v.   Also a revised edition, 28 books in 29 v.

9939. 肅宗實錄 Sukchong sillok. (Chronicle of the reign of King Sukchong, 1675-1720, 19th ruler of the Yi dynasty.) 65 books in 73 v. (2) Yi, Tŏksu. 肅廟寶鑑 Sungmyo Pogam Sukchong. (Biography of King Sukchong.)   15 books in 8 v. (Compiled in compliance with the royal request of King Yŏngjo, 1725-1776, 21st ruler of the Yi dynasty.)

9940. 景宗實錄 Kyŏngjong sillok. (Chronicle of the reign of King Kyŏngjong, 1721-1724, 20th ruler of the Yi dynasty.) 15 books in 7 v. Also a revised edition, 5 books in 3 v.   See 9920.

9941. 英祖實錄 Yŏngjo sillok. (Chronicle of the reign of King Yŏngjo, 1725-1776, 21st ruler of the Yi dynasty. 127 books in 83 v.   See 9920.

9942. 正祖實錄 Chŏngjo sillok. (Chronicle of the reign of King Chŏngjo, 22nd ruler of the Yi dynasty, 1777-1800.) 54 books in 56 v.   See 9920.

9943. 純祖實錄 Sunjo sillok. (Chronicle of the reign of King Sunjo, 1801-1834, 23rd ruler of the Yi dynasty.) 34 books in 36 v.   See 9920.

9944. 憲宗實錄 Hŏnjong sillok. (Chronicle of the reign of King Hŏnjong, 1835-1849, 24th ruler of the Yi dynasty.) 16 books in 9 v.   See 9920.

9945. 哲宗實錄 Chŏlchong sillok. (Chronicle of the reign of King Chŏlchong, 1850-1863, 25th ruler of the Yi dynasty.) 15 books in 9 v.

9946. Breher, Theodor. Das Toung Tien des Tu über Ko-kourye. Materialen zur geschichte Koreas. Berlin, 1920.

9947. 東國歷代史略 Tongguk yŏktae saryak. (Brief history of the Eastern country, Korea, according to the rule of the successive kings.) Seoul, Department of education of the Korean government, 1899. 6 books in 3 v.

9948. 朝鮮史 Chosen-shi. (History of Korea.) Seoul, Government general of Korea, Association of the publication of Korean historical materials, 1933-1938. 35 v.

9949. Cheng, Lin-chih (Korean). 高麗史 Kao-li shih. (History of Korea.) 1452. 2 v.(Presented to the Chinese emperor.)

9950. Sekino, Tadashi. 朝鮮古蹟圖譜 Chosen koseki zufu. (An illustrated catalogue of ancient monuments and historical remains in Korea.) Published by the Government-general of Chosen, 1915-1932. 12 v. (2) Hamada, Seiryo. 慶州金冠塚ト其遺寶 Keishu Kinkanzuka to sono iho. (A royal tomb "Kinkan-tsuka" or the Gold town at Keishu in Korea, and its treasures.) Published by the Government-general of Chosen, 1924-1927. 3 v.

9951. Chung, Henry. Korean treaties. New York, 1919. 226 p.

9952. Sands, William Franklin. Undiplomatic memories. New York, Whitlesey house, McGraw Hill, 1930. 238 p.

(2) General Accounts

9953. Klaproth, J. (transl.). 三國通覽圖說 San kokf tsou ran To sets ou Aperçu général des Trois royaumes. Paris, 1832.

9954. Zhdan-Pushkin, P. I. Корея. (Korea.) Sbornik istoriko-statisticheskikh svedenii o Sibiri i sopredel'nykh ei stran, 1 (1875):1-16.

9955. Ross, John. History of Korea, ancient and modern. Paisley (Scotland), Parlane, [1879]. 404 p.

9956. Dadeshkaliani, Prince. "Краткий очерк современного состояния Кореи."   (A brief sketch of the present condition of Korea.) Izdanie Voenno-uchenogo komiteta Glavnogo shtaba, St. Petersburg, 22 (1884):61-118.

9957. Taka, Gonzo. 朝鮮政治史綱 Chosen seiji shiko. (Outline of the political history of Korea.) Tokyo, Nagata shoten, 1934. 304 p.

9958. Nakayama, Kyushiro. 朝鮮通信隣好史一面 Chosen tsushin rinko-shi no ichimen. (One phase of the history of international relations of Korea.) Gaiko jiho, 82: 1:130-149, April 1937.

9959. 高麗史 Korai-shi. (History of Korea.) Tokyo, Kokusho kankokai, 1932. 3 v.

9960. Fukuda, Yoshinosuke. 新 羅 史 Shiragi-shi. (History of Shiragi.) Tokyo, Osakayago, 1923.

9961. Hsüeh, P'ei-jung. 東 藩 紀 要 Tung-fan chi-yao. (An outline history of Korea.) Shanghai, 1882.

9962. Chŏng, Inho. 大 韓 歷 史 Taehan yŏksa. (History of Korea.) Seoul, Imun'gwan, 1904. 170 p.

9963. See 3044.

9964. Hulbert, Homer B. The history of Korea (from the earliest times up to the beginning of the Japan-Russian war of 1904-1905). Seoul, 1905 2 v.   (2) The same. 大 東 紀 年 Dai-To kinen. (Chronological history of the East, Korea.) Shanghai, 1905. 5 books in 5 v.

9965. Tokunaga, Kunbi. 韓 國 總 覽 Kankoku soran. (Summary of events of Korea.) Tokyo, Hakubunkan, 1907. 1489 p.

9966. 歷 史 地 理 臨 時 増 刊 朝 鮮 號 Rekishi chiri rinji zokan: Chosen go. (History and geography: special Korean number.) Tokyo, Nippon rekishi chiri gakkai, Sanseido, 1910. 311 p.

9967. Baelz, E. Korea von seinen anfängen bis zu seinem ende. Frankfurt a. M., 1910. 24 p.

9968. Longford, Joseph Henry. Story of Korea. New York, 1911.

9969. Tai-pai-k'uang-nu. 韓 國 痛 史 Han-kuo t'ung-shih. (The tragic history of Korea.) Ta-t'ung-pien-i-chü, 1915.

9970. Hayashi, Taisuke. 朝 鮮 通 史 Chosen tsushi. (A comprehensive history of Korea.) Tokyo, Fuzanbo, 1917. 608 p. 4 maps.

9971. Aoyagi, Nanmei. 朝 鮮 四 千 年 史 Chosen 4000-nen-shi. (Four thousand years' history of Korea.) Tokyo, Osaka-yago, 1923.

9972. Aoyagi, Nanmei. 朝 鮮 五 百 年 史 Chosen 500-nen-shi. (Five hundred years' history of Korea.) Tokyo, Osaka-yago, 1923 .

9973. Aoyagi, Nanmei. 李 朝 史 大 全 Richo-shi taizen. (History of the Yi dynasty.) Tokyo, Isseido, 1922. 966 p.

9974. Shidehara, Hiroshi. 朝 鮮 史 話 Chosen shiwa. (Tales of Korean history.) Tokyo, Fuzanbo, 1925. 531 p.

9975. Taka, Gonzo. 近 代 朝 鮮 政 治 史 Kindai Chosen seiji-shi. (Political history of Korea in recent times.) Tokyo, Tetto shoten, 1930.

9976. Huang, Hung-hsien. 朝 鮮 國 紀 Ch'ao-hsien-kuo chi. (An account of the kingdom of Korea.) 1931.

9977. Kang, Younghill. The grass roof. NewYork-London, Scribner's, 1931. viii, 367 p.

9978. Treat, P. J. "China and Korea, 1885-1895." Political science quarterly, 49 (1935):34:506-543.

9979. Banasiński, Eugenjusz. "Korea." 1860-1919. Przegląd politiczny, Warsaw, 46 (1932):21-31.

(3) Special Accounts

9980. Hsü, Ching. 宣 和 奉 使 高 麗 圖 經 Hsüan-ho fêng-shih Kao-li t'u-ching. (An account of a mission to Korea in the Hsuan-ho period, 1119-1125.) Shanghai, 1921. 40 v.

9981. Parker, E. H. "The Manchu relations with Korea." Transactions of the Asiatic society of Japan, 15 (1887): 96-102.

9982. Trollope, Mark Napier. "An account of the shipwreck of a Dutch vessel on the coast of the isle of Quelpaert, together with a description of the kingdom of Korea." Transactions of the Korea branch of the Royal Asiatic society, 9 (1918):91-148. (Tr. from the French.)

9983. Koei-Ling. Journal d'une mission en Corée (traduit du Chinois par F. Scherzer). Paris, 1877.

9984. Ratzel, F. "Korea und die Liu-Kiu inseln und die zwei asiatischen grossmächte, viz. China und Japan." Oesterreichische monatschrift f. d. Orient, Wien, 5 (1879):189-196.

9985. Paullin, Charles Oscar. "The opening of Korea by Commodore Shufeldt." Political science quarterly, 25 (1910): 470-499.

9986. Pollard, R. T. "American relations with Korea 1882-1895." The Chinese social and political science review, 16: 3: 425-471, October 1932.

9987. Petrov-Baturich, S. V. Исторический очерк возникновения и развития корейского вопроса. (An historical outline of the origin and development of the Korean problem.) Russkii vestnik, 1894:10.

9988. Okudaira, Takehiko. 朝鮮開國交涉始末 Chosen kaikoku kosho shimatsu. (Diplomatic accounts of the opening of Korea.) Tokyo, To-A shoten, 1936. 209 p.

9989. 清光緒八年處理朝鮮大院君倡亂事件案檔之一斑 Ch'ing Kuang-hsü pa-nien ch'u-li Ch'ao-hsien Ta-yüan-chün ch'ang-luan shih-chien mi-tang chih i-pan. (Secret archives on the managing of the rebellion of the Korean emperor's father in the 8th year of Kuang-hsü, 1872.) Jên-wên, 1:7, September 1930.

9990. Noble, Harold J. "The Korean special mission to the United States in 1883." Transactions, Korea branch, Royal Asiatic society, Seoul, 18 (1929):1-27.

9991. Duncan, Chesnay. Corea and the powers. Shanghai, 1889. Pamphlet.

9992. Pokotilov, D. Корея и японо-китайское столкновение. (Korea and the Sino-Japanese war.) St. Petersburg, 1895.

9993. Wilkinson, W. H. The Corean government: Constitutional changes, July 1894 to October 1895, with an appendix on subsequent enactments to 30th June, 1896. Shanghai, 1897.

9994. Villetard de Laguérie, R. La Corée indépendente, russe ou japonaise. Paris, 1898. 304 p. (Forms a volume of the Collection de voyages illustrés.)

9995. Villetard de Laguérie, R. La Corée et la guerre russo-japonaise. Paris, 1904. 176 p.

9996. Hulbert, Homer B. The passing of Korea. London, William Heinemann, 1906. xii, 473 p.

9997. Li-ch'i. 亡國後的朝鮮 Wang-kuo hou ti Ch'ao-hsien. (Korea after the annexation.) Current events, 2:3: 131- , March 1930.

9998. Der geplante japanische kriegshafen Chinhai bei Masampo auf Korea. Petermanns geographische mitteilungen, 58:2 (1912). 244 p.

9999. Chung, Henry. The case of Korea. A collection of evidence on the Japanese domination of Korea, and on the development of the Korean independence movement. Preface by Selden P. Spencer. London, Allen & Unwin, 1922. 367 p. See 363.

10000. Yin, Wei-lien. 朝鮮史地反其現在 Ch'ao-hsien shih ti chi ch'i hsien-tsai. (Korea. Its history, geography and the present.) Hsin-ya-hsi-ya, 3:5, February 1932.

(4) Korean-Japanese Relations

See 8044-8224; 8690-8885.

10001. Schlegel, G. Het geschil tusschen China en Japan in Korea. Verslagen en mededeelingen der kon. akademie von wetenschappen, Afdeeling letterkunde. 3rd series, 11, 159-174. Amsterdam, 1894.

10002. Higasa, Mamoru. 日鮮関係ノ史的考察ト其研究 Nichi-Sen kankei no shiteki kosatsu to sono kenkyu. (The historical consideration and study of Japanese-Korean relations.) Tokyo, Shikai shobo, 1931. 250 p.

10003. "Японо-германское соглашение и Корея." (Japanese-German agreement and Korea.) Tikhii Okean, 1:11:216, January-March, 1937.

10004. Ota, Ryo. 日本古代史新研究 Nippon kodai-shi shin-kenkyu. (New study on Japan's ancient history: Japan's relation with Korea.) Tokyo, Isobe koyodo, 1928. 622 p

10005. Jones, G. H. "The Japanese invasion of Korea under Taiko Hideyoshi at the end of the 16 century." Korean repository, Seoul, 1 (1892):1-7, 10-16, 46-50, 116-121, 147-152, 182-188, 217-222, 308-311.

10006. Yamagata, I. "Japanese-Korean relations after the Japanese invasion of Korea in the 16 century." Transactions of the Korea branch of the Royal Asiatic society, 4 (1913):2: 1-11.

10007. Hulbert, H. B. Korean relations with Japan, translated from "The Cheung-jung Kyo-rin ji". Korean review, Seoul, 3 (1903-1904):294-300, 347-349, 394-398, 438-443, 492-497, 537-544; 4 (1904-1905):9-13.

10008. Jones, G. H. "The Japanese invasion under Taiko Hideyoshi at the end of the 16 century." Korean repository, 1 (1892):1-7.

10009. Jones, G. H. "The Japanese invasion of Korea in 1592, taken from Korean sources." China review, Hongkong, 23 (1898-1899):4-5:215-219, 239-254.

10010. Aston, W. G. "Hideyoshi's invasion of Korea." Transactions of the Asiatic society of Japan, 6 (1878):227-248; 9 (1881):87-93; 9 (1881):213-222; 11 (1883):117-125.

10011. Tsuji, Zennosuke. 德川時代初期ニ於ケル日韓ノ關係 Tokugawa jidai shoki ni okeru Nichi-Kan no kankei. (The relation between Japan and Korea during the early Tokugawa period.) History and geography (Annexation of Korea, special edition), 230:253, November 1, 1910.

10012. Yoshida, Togo. 日韓古史断 Nichi-Kan koshi dan. (Historical shifting of events and the pre-historic relations between Japan and Korea.) Tokyo, Fuzanbo, 1911. 586 p

10013. Yamagata, Isoh. "Japanese-Korean relations after the Japanese invasion of Korea in the 16 century." Transactions of the Korea branch of the Royal Asiatic society, Seoul, 4 (1913):2:1-11.

10014. Hagino, Yoshiyuki. 國史上ヨリ見タル朝鮮 Kokushi jo yori mitaru Chosen. (Korea as viewed from the national history of Japan.) History and geography (Annexation of Korea, special edition), 95-105, November 1, 1910.

10015. Omori, Otokichi. 明治維新以後ニ於ケル日韓ノ交渉 Meiji Ishin igo ni okeru Nichi-Kan no kosho." (Negotiations between Japan and Korea after the Meiji restoration period.) History and geography (Annexation of Korea, Special edition), 280-290, November 1, 1910.

10016. Hoshino, Ko. 歴史上ヨリ見タル日韓同域ノ復古ト確定 Rekishi jo yori mitaru Nichi-Kan doiki no fukko to kakutei. (Historical aspects of the restoration of the former relations between Japan and Korea.) History and geography (Annexation of Korea, special edition), 24:41, November 1, 1910.

10017. Vaskevich, P. "Очерк сношений Японии с Кореей." (An outline of the relations between Japan and Korea.) Vestnik Azii, 2 (1909):20-25.

10018. Takeda, Katsuzo. 明治十五年朝鮮事変ト花房公使 Meiji jugonen Chosen jihen to Hanafusa koshi. (Minister Hanafusa and the Korean incident of 1882.) Tokyo, Takeda Katsuzo, 1931. 103 p.

10019. Saizau, M. "Le Japon moderne et la question coréenne." Revue politique et parlementaire, Paris. 5, Nov. 1894.

10020. Bushby, H. N. G. "Korea from the Japanese standpoint." Nineteenth century (London), 49 (1901):834-839.

10021. Longford, J. H. "Japan's relations with Korea in the 19 century." Eclectic magazine, New series, New York, 11: 142 (1904):540-550. Nineteenth century, 55 (1904):618-629.

10022. Krahmer, J. Die beziehungen Russlands zu Japan mit besonderer berücksichtigung Koreas. Leipzig, 1904. 221 p. (Russland in Asien).

10023. O, Sung-Keun. "The Korean prefecture." The Korea review, 6 (1906):378-382.

10024. McKenzie, F. A. The colonial policy of Japan in Korea. Proceedings of the Central Asian society, December 1906. 27 p.

10025. R., C. "Corée. Comment fut conclu le traité japonais." Revue française de l'étranger et des colonies et exploration, 30 (1906):303-311.

10026. Поглощение Кореи. (The absorption of Korea.) Politicheskoe obozrenie. Niva, 30 (1907).

10027. Ladd, George Trumbull. In Korea with Marquis Ito. New York, Scribners, 1908. xiii, 477 p.

10028. Lee, S. S. and Song, J. H. Japan's action in Korea. Being the story from within of Japan's relations with Korea, from the conclusion of the Russo-Japanese war to the present date. 1908. 15 p.

10029. McKenzie, F. A. "The Japanese in Korea." Contemporary review, 1 (1908):55-64.

10030. Vay de Vaya. "La fin d'un empire. La japonisation de
la Corée." Revue des deux mondes, 43 (1908):178-210.

10031. Kate, H. ten. "De Japanners in Korea." Vragen des
tijds, 271-315, March 1909.

10032. "Staryi sotrudnik." "Письма с Дальнего Востока."
(Letters from the Far East.) About the annexation of Korea.
Sovremennyi mir, 11 (1910):29-48.

10033. Kennedy, J. R. "The regeneration of Korea." Japan
magazine, 1 (1910):15-20.

10034. Rossi-Toesca, V. I diritti del Giappone sulla Corea.
Rom, Istituto coloniale italiano, 1910. 27 p. Biblioteca di
studi coloniali, dir da R. Paoli, no. 2.

10035. Riess, L. "Korea und Japan." Marine-rundschau, 21
(1910):1237-2155.

(5) Annexation of Korea

10036. 韓國, 合併ニ就テ Kankoku no gappei ni tsuite. (On
the annexation of Korea.) In Materials on economic study of
the Far East. Dairen, To-A keizai chosa kyoku, 1915-1931.
See 797.

10037. Kida, Sadakichi. 韓國, 併合ト國史 Kankoku no heigo to kokushi. (The annexation of Korea and its history.)
Tokyo, Sanshodo, 1910. 182 p.

10038. Kassei, Yoshihisa. 日韓合邦秘史 Nichi-Kan gap-
po hishi. (The secret history of the annexation of Korea.)
Tokyo, Kokuryukai, 1931. 2 v.

10039. Yoshioka, Shigezane. 斉明天智両天皇, 御鴻業
Saimei, Tenchi ryo Tenno no gokogyo. (Achievements of Empe-
ror Saimei, and Emperor Tenchi: regaining suzerainity in
Korea.) Tokyo, Seikyosha, 1931.

10040. Daugny, J. "L'annexation de la Corée." La nouvelle
revue, 508-514, October 1910.

10041. Аннексия Кореи. (The annexation of Korea.) A political review. Niva, 21 and 35, 1910.

10042. Terriou, R. Le statut international de la Corée an-
térieurement au 29 août 1910. 1911. 247 p.

10043. "L'annexion de la Corée." T'oung Pao, 11 (1910):542-546. (Documents in French).

10044. "Verträge und verordnungen betreffend das verhältnis zwischen Japan und Korea." Zeitschrift für völkerrecht und bundesstaatsrecht, 4 (1910):261-270.

10045. Kataphronète. "L'annexion et le régime international de la Corée." Bulletin du comité de l'Asie française, 419-428, Oct. 1910.

10046. Iyenaga, Toyokichi. "Japan's annexation of Korea." Journal of race development, 3 (1912-1913):201-223.

10047. Ivanovskii, A. P. "Аннексия Кореи и отношение ее к христианству в этой стране." (The annexation of Korea and its relation to Christianity in that country.) Vestnik Azii, 7 (1911):13-19.

10048. Pesotskii, V. D. "Корея накануне аннексии." (Korea on the eve of annexation.) Zapiski Priamurskogo otdela Imperatorskogo obshchestva vostokovedeniia, 1:93-114.

10049. Ladd, George Trumbull. "The annexation of Korea. An essay in 'benevolent assimilation'." Yale review, new series, 1:639-656, July 1912.

10050. "La fin de la vieille Corée." Asie française, 73-90, February 1913.

10051. See 10032.

10052. Yoshida, Togo. 韓半島，併合せル大局面 Kan-hanto wo heigo seru daikyokumen. (The general state of affairs regarding the annexation of the Korean peninsula.) History and geography (Annexation of Korea, special edition), 83-97, November 1, 1910.

10053. Shidehara, Hiroshi. 日韓交通概要 Nichi-Kan kotsu no gaiyo. (Summary of diplomatic relations between Japan and Korea.) History and geography (Annexation of Korea, special edition), 9-21, November 1, 1910.

(6) Korean National Movement

10054. Rossov, P. Национальное самосознание корейцев. (National self-consciousness of the Koreans.) St. Petersburg, P.A.Artemiev, 1906. 40 p.

10055. Baird, Annie L. Daybreak in Korea: a tale of transformation in the Far East. New York, Revell co., 1909. 124p.

10056. Rhee, Sungman. 獨立精神 독 립 정 신
Tongnip chŏngsin. (The spirit of independence.) San Francisco, 1910. 296 p.

10057. Li, Chih-fu. 朝鮮亡國史 Ch'ao-hsien wang-kuo
shih. (A history of the extermination of Korea as a nation.)
Chihli, Educational book co., 1911.

10058. Changha No Pangsil (Pak Unsik). 安重根傳 안중근전
(The life of An Chunggun.) Shanghai, Taedong pyongupkuk,
1914. 24 p.

10059. The Korean situation. No. 1: Authentic accounts of
recent events by the eye-witnesses. No. 2: - New York, Issued by the Commission on relations with the Orient of the
Federal council of the Churches of Christ in America. No.
1919. No. 2, 1920. 27 p.

10060. L'Independance de la Corée et la paix. La question
coréenne et la politique mondiale japonaise. Paris, Bureau
d'information coréenne, 1919. 36 p.

10061. Kendall, Carlton Waldo. The truth about Korea. 2nd
edition. San Francisco, Korean national association, 1919.
104 p.

10062. Yi, Yŏngyŏl. 韓國眞相 한국진상 Han'guk chinsang. (The true Korean situation.) Shanghai, Samil insŏgwan, 1920. 50 p.   (2) The same. 韓國獨立運動의眞相
Han'guk tongnip undongŭi chinsang. (The true state of the
Korean independence movement.) Shanghai, 1920. 52 p.

10063. Draves, J. W. The renaissance of Korea. Philadelphia,
1920.

10064. McKenzie, F. A. Korea's fight for freedom. New York,
Revell, 1920. 330 p.

10065. Cynn, Hugh Hueng-Wo. The rebirth of Korea: the reawakening of the people: its causes and the outlook. London, Society for promoting Christian knowledge, 1920.
272 p. (2) 독립운동사려 Tongnip undong saryŏ. (Source material of the independence movement.) Sinhan chŏngnyŏn,
Shanghai, 1:6-102, Dec., 1919. (3) Yi, Changbaek. 한족의장매
Hanjŏgŭi changmae. (The future of the Korean nation.) Sinhan ch'ŏngnyŏn, 1:116-122, December 1919.

10066. Kim Pyŏngjo. 韓國獨立運動史 한국독립운동사 Han'guk tongnip undong-sa. (History of the Korean independence movement.) Shanghai, Samil insogwan, 1921. 2 v.

10067. Pak Unsik. 韓國獨立運動之血史 한국동립운동지혈사 Han'guk tongnip undong chihyŏl-sa. (History of the bloody independence movement of Korea.) Shanghai, Yusinsa, 1920. 272 p.

10068. The Korean provisional government. 大韓民國臨時憲法 대한민국림시헌법 Taehan min'guk imsi hŏn-pŏp. (Constitution of the Korean provisional government.) Shanghai, 1920. (2) The same. 大韓民國臨時官制 대한민국림시판제 Taehan min'guk imsi kwanje. (Administrative regulations of the Korean provisional government.) Shanghai, 1920. (3) The same. 改正臨時議政院法 개정림시의정원법 Kaejŏng imsi ŭijŏng wŏn-pŏp. (Revised regulations concerning ths administration.) Shanghai, 1920.

10069. McKenzie, F. A. "The problem of Korea." The Asiatic review, new series, 17 (1921):23-29.

10070. Pak, Unsik. 韓國獨立運動史 한국동립운동사 Han'guk tongnip undong-sa. (History of the Korean independence movement.) Shanghai, Sonusa, 1922. 236 p.

10071. Norman, Irand. Этапы освободительного движения в Корее. (Landmarks in the emancipation movement of Korea.) Narody Dal'nego Vostoka, 5 (1922).

10072. Speranskii, A. F. "Национальное движение в Корее." (The national movement in Korea.) Novyi Vostok, 3 (1923): 122-138.

10073. Dalin, S. Молодежь в революционном движении в Корее. (Youth in the revolutionary movement in Korea.) Moscow, 1924. 126 p.

10074. See 9999.

10075. Pak, Diktun'. "К 7-ой годовщине революции в Корее." (The seventh anniversary of the revolution in Korea.) Krestianskii internatsional, 3-5 (1926):78-86.

10076. The Korean conspiracy. Full report of the second trial. Kobe, Japan chronicle press, 1927 (?).

10077. Baty, Thomas. "Korea, Japan, and freedom." Asiatic review, new series, 24 (1928):78:213-224.

10078. Li, Hsien-ming 朝鮮民族運動概觀 Ch'ao-
hsien min-tsu yün-tung kai-kuan. (A general view of the
Korean national movement.) Eastern miscellany, 26:20:125-
146, October 1929.

10079. Ho-ling. 朝鮮獨立運動的今昔觀 Ch'ao-hsien
tu-li yün-tung ti chin-hsi-kuan. (Past and present aspects
of the Korean independence movement.) Min-kuo jih-pao, 30:
40, February 3, 1930.

10080. Fang, Shu-hua. 朝鮮民族革命之過去與現在
Ch'ao-hsien min-tsu ko-ming chih kuo-ch'ü yü hsien-tsai. (The
past and present of the Korean nationalistic revolution.)
Chung-yang jih-pao, 239-240, February 9-11, 1930.

10081. Yen, Ping-hao. 朝鮮 Ch'ao-hsien. (Korea. The complete story of the Kuang-chou affair) Current events, 2:3,
March 1930.

10082. Yü-yen. 一九三〇年朝鮮運動概況 I-chiu-san-
ling-nien Ch'ao-hsien yün-tung kai-kuang. (The general status
of the Korean movement in 1930. New Orient monthly, special
anniversary number, June 1931.

10083. Shao, Lin-shên. 朝鮮民族的獨立運動 Ch'ao-
hsien min-tzu ti tu-li yün-tung. (The independence movement
of the Koreans.) The progressing youth, 140:54, February
1931.

10084. Yu-chu. 一九三一年朝鮮革命運動概況 I-chiu-
san-i-nien Ch'ao-hsien ko-ming yün-tung kai-k'uang. (An account of the revolutionary movement in Korea in 1931.) Hsin-
tung-fang, bi-annual anniversary number, June 1932.

10085. Gorshenin, I. "Кризис и подъем революционного движения в Корее." (Crisis and rise of the revolutionary movement in Korea.) Sovremennaia IAponiia, Moscow, 2 (1934):
96-146.

10086. Serebriakov. "Кризис и революционное движение в Корее."
(Crisis and revolutionary movement in Korea.) Materialy po
natsional'no-kolonial'nym problemam, 3 (1934):18:53-68.

10087. Korean patriotic society. 윤봉길의사 자서 략 략 급유촉
尹奉吉義士自書略歷及囑 Yun ponggil ŭisa chasŏ
yangyŏk kŭp yuch'ok. (Yun Ponggil, patriot and martyr, his
biography and last will and testament.) Shanghai, Korean
patriotic society, 1934.

10088. 혁명당의런합분제 Hyŏngmyŏng-dangŭi yŏnhap munje.
(The question of the unification of revolutionary parties.)
Chin'gwang, Shanghai, 1, January 1934. (2) 민종분제연구
Mingjok munje yŏn'gu. (Study of the problem of nationalism.)
Chin'gwang, Shanghai, 2-3, March, April, 1934. (3) 대당조
직분제 Taedang chojik munje. (The problem of organizing
a single party.) Chingwang, Shanghai, 4, May 1934. (4) 일본
의필연부리 Ilbonŭi p'iryŏn punggoe. (The inevitable collapse of Japan.) Chin'gwang, Shanghai, 5, June 1934. (5)
조선혁명당재동부공작 Chosŏn hyŏngmyŏngdang chae tong-
buk kongjak. (Activities of the Korean revolutionary party
in Manchuria.) Chin'gwan, Shanghai, 6, September 1934.

10089. 대한민국림시정부공보 Taehan min'guk imsi
chŏngbu kongbo. (Gazette of the Provisional government of
the Korean republic.) Imsi chŏngbu pisŏguk, Shanghai, 57,
April 15, 1934.

10090. К. "Положение и борьба трудящейся молодежи в Корее."
(The situation and struggle of the working youth in Korea.)
Materialy po natsional'no-kolonial'nym problemam, 3 (1934):
18:68-83.

10091. Serebriakov, V. "К годовщине мартовского восстания в
Корее в 1919 г." (The anniversary of the March uprising in
Korea in 1919.) Bor'ba klassov, 4:71-77, April 1935.

10092. 삼월일일가념 Samwŏl iril kinyŏm. (Remembrance of
March 1 [Korean independence day].) Hanmin, Shanghai, 1,
March 15, 1936.

10093. 윤의사가념의의 Yun ŭisa kinyŏmŭi ŭiŭi. (The significance of the commemoration of the patriot and martyr,
Yun.) Hanmin, Shanghai, April 29, 1936.

10094. 한국군면당삼일절가념선언 Han'guk
kungmindang samilchŏl kimyŏn sŏnŏn. (Declaration of
the Korean nationalist party in commemoration of March
first [the Korean independence day].) Shanghai, March
1, 1937.

10095. 조선혁명당선언 Chosŏn hyŏngmyŏngdang sŏnŏn.
(Declaration of the Korean revolutionary party.) Central
executive committee of the Korean revolutionary party,
Shanghai, May 1937. (2) Rappoport, V. Партизанское движение
в районах северной Кореи. (Guerilla movement in north Korea.)
Tikhii okean, 2 (12):15-40, April-June 1937. (3) Tsou, Shen-
wu. Вопрос о гегемонии пролетариата в корейской революции.
(Question of the hegemony of the proletariat...) Moscow, 1935.

10096. 민 족 동 일 문 제 Minjok tongil munje. (The problem of national unity.) Minjok hyŏngmyŏng, Shanghai, 5, June 20, 1937.

10097. 동 포 들 이 여 맹 성 하 자 Tongp'odŭriyŏ maengsŏng-haja. (Bretheren, let us awake and act!) Apkil, Shanghai, 24, August 9, 1937.

10098. 중 일 전 쟁 에 대 하 야 Chungil chŏnjaenge taehaya. (On the Sino-Japanese war.) Apkil, Shanghai, 25, August 16, 1937.

10099. 한 국 광 복 운 동 단 제 연 합 선 언 Han'guk kwangbok undong tanch'e yŏnhap sŏnŏn. (Joint declaration of the Korean independence movement parties.) Shanghai, August 1, 1937. (2) The claim of the Korean people...for liberation from Japan. Korean delegation, Peace conference, Paris, 1919. 8, 23 p.

10100. 독 립 운 동 발 흥 에 대 하 야 Tongnip undong parhŭnge taehaya. (Concerning the progress of the independence movement.) Tongnip, Nanking, 192, September 3, 1927.

(7) Japanese rule in Korea

(a) Government Reports

10101. The material progress of Korea for the last five years (1905-1910) compiled by H. I. M. Residency General. Seoul, 1910. iv, iii, 52 p.

10102. Annual report for 1907 on reforms and progress in Korea. Compiled by H. I. M. Residency General. Seoul, 1908. viii, 140 p.

10103. The second annual report on reforms and progress in Korea, 1908-1909. Compiled by H. I. M. Residency General. Seoul, 1909. viii, 215 p.

10104. The third annual report on reforms and progress in Korea 1909-1910. Seoul, Residency General, 1911. viii, 194 p.

10105. Annual report on reforms and progress in Chosen (Korea) 1910-1911. Keijo (Seoul), Government General, 1911. 268 p.

10106. Results of three years' administration of Chosen since annexation. Keijo (Seoul), Government General of Chosen, 1914. 66, 95 p.

10107. Annual report on reforms and progress in Chosen (Korea). Keijo (Seoul), Government General of Chosen, 1911-1912:1913. xi, 272 p.   1912-1913:1914. xii, 271 p.   1913-1914:1915. ix, 167 p.   1914-1915:1916. x, 183 p.   1917-1918:1920. xiii, 171 p.

10108. Annual report on reforms and progress in Chosen 1918-1921. Keijo (Seoul), 1921.

10109. La nouvelle administration de la Corée d'après la brochure publiée en Juillet 1921 par le Gouvernement Général de la Corée. Paris, Pierre Roger et cie., 1922. 117 p.

10110. The new administration in Chosen. Compiled by the Government General of Chosen, 1921. iv, 76, xxx p.

10111. Statistics for 1922. Compiled by the Government General of Chosen. Chosen print, 1922.

10112. Annual report on reforms and progress in Chosen, 1922. Keijo (Seoul), Government General of Chosen, 1922. 280 p.

10113. Annual report on administration of Chosen, 1922-1923. Seoul, 1923. 240 p.

10114. Annual report on administration of Chosen, 1923-1924. Compiled by the Government General of Chosen. Keijo (Seoul), 1925. vii, 189 p.

(b) General Accounts

10115. 朝鮮ニ於ケル日本ノ施政ニ就テ Chosen ni okeru Nippon no shisei ni tsuite. (On the Japanese administration of Korea.) In materials on economic study of the Far East. Dairen, To-A keizai chosa kyoku, 1915-1931.

10116. Backhausen, A. Die japanische verwaltung in Korea und ihre tätigkeit. Berlin, Reimer, 1910. ii, 79 p.

10117. Bürgers, R. "Die reform Japans in Korea." Zeitschrift für kolonialpolitik, kolonialrecht und kolonialwirtschaft, 12 (1910):569-578.

10118. Kennedy, J. R. "The regeneration of Korea." Japan magazine, 1 (1910-1911):15-20.

10119. Saito, Hisho. "Das verhältnis Koreas zu Japan." Japan und China, 2 (1911-1912):5-6, 105-107, 153-155.

10120. Komatsu, Midori. "The old people and the new government." Transactions of the Korea branch of the Royal Asiatic society (Seoul), 4 (1912):1:1-12.

10121. Kazan, F. "The reformation of Korea." Japan magazine, 3 (1912-1913):481-488.

10122. See 10059.

10123. Chevalier, H. "Des réformes et des progrès réalisés en Corée par le Gouvernement Général japonais." Bulletin de la Société franco-japonaise de Paris, 30:85-96, July 1913; 31-32 (1914):137-151.

10124. See 10107.

10125. Surugue, R. "L'oeuvre japonaise en Corée." Revue Indo-chinoise, Jan.-Febr., 1915, 117-140.

10126. Brown, Arthur Judson. "Japanese nationalism and mission schools in Chosen." International review of missions, 6 (1917):74-98.

10127. "The Japanese administration of Korea." By a Korean. Der Neue Orient (Berlin), 4 (1918-1919):437-440.

10128. Administrative reforms in Korea. Articles reprinted from the "Seoul press". Seoul, "Seoul press", 1919. 76 p.

10129. Osuga, J. "Reform in Korea." Japan magazine, 10 (1919-1920):219-222.

10130 Ponsonby, Richard Fane. "Japanese administration in Korea today."Japan magazine, 12 (1921-1922):248-252.

10131. Pieters, Albertus. "Japanese rule in Korea past and present. A reply to General Crozier and Mr. R. Ponsonby Fane." The Japan magazine, 12 (1921-1922):259-262.

10132. Powell, E. Alexander. "Japan's policy in Korea." Atlantic monthly, 1922. 395-412.

10133. Hayden, Ralston. "Japan's new policy in Korea and Formosa." Foreign affairs, 2:3:474-488, March 1924.

10134. Yamagata, Isoh. "Korea under the administration of viscount Saito." Young East, 1 (1925-1926):15-20.

10135. Sherrill, Charles H. Korea and Shantung versus the White peril. Seoul, Seoul press, 1920. 36 p.

10136. Smith, Frank Herron. The other side of the Korean question. Fresh light on some important factors. Reprinted by the "Seoul press" from the "Japan advertiser". Seoul, 1920. 33 p.

10137. Li, Kolu. Unabhängigkeitsbewegung Koreas und japanische eroberungspolitik. Berlin, J. Sittenfeld, 1924. 32 p.

10138. Carpenter, Frank George. Japan and Korea, 1925. 324 p.

10139. Soejima, Dosei. 朝鮮統治ノ現在及將來 Chosen tochi no genzai oyobi shorai. (The present and the future of our Korean administration.) Gaiko jiho, 47:8:69-80, April 15, 1928.

10140. Kim, Nik. "Эволюция японской политики в Корее." (Evolution of the Japanese policy in Korea.) Novyi Vostok, 25 (1929):103-126.

10141. Ch'ên-ti. 日本帝國主義支配下滿廿年的朝鮮 Jih-pên ti-kuo-chu-i chih-p'ei-hsia man nien-nien ti Ch'ao-hsien. (Korea, twenty years under control of Japanese imperialism.) New Orient, 1:11; November 1930.

10142. Wang, Chih-pin. 日人治下的高麗 Jih-jên chih-hsia ti Kao-li. (Korea under Japanese rule.) Progressing youth, 139, January 1931.

10143. Chang, Ch'ên-fu (tr.) 日本治下的朝鮮 Jih-pên ch'ih-hsia ti Ch'ao-hsien. (Korea under Japanese control.) Chung-yang jih-pao fu-kan, Ta-tao, 151, April 1931.

10144. Mizuno, Rentaro. 對支關係ト朝鮮統治ノ問題 Tai-Shi kankei to Chosen tochi no mondai. (Our Chinese relations and the problem of the Korean administration.) Gaiko jiho, 59:3:1-8, August 1, 1931.

10145. Ost, K. "Японская армия в Корее." (The Japanese army in Korea.) Na rubezhe, 4:80-84, July-August 1936.

10146. Matsuoka, Masao. 朝鮮臺灣總督ノ更迭 Chosen Taiwan sotoku no kotetsu. (Changes of the governors-general of Korea and Formosa.) Gaiko jiho, 79:6:208-215, September 1936.

10147. Kamada, Sawaichiro. 宇 垣 一 成 Ugaki Kazunari.
(Life of [Governor General of Korea] Kazunari Ugaki.) Tokyo, Chuo koronsha, 1937. 470 p.

(c) Japanese Immigration to Korea

10148. "Japanese immigration." Korea review, 6 (1906):341-
346.

10149. Labroue, H. "La colonisation japonaise en Corée."
Revue politique et parlamentaire, 1908. 346-370.

10150. Millard, T. F. "Japanese immigration into Korea."
Annals of the American academy of political and social science, 34 (1909):403-409.

10151. Gollier, T. "Le Japon colonisateur. Les Japonais en
Corée." Revue économique internationale, 4 (1909):244-282.

10152. Halot, Alexandre. "La colonisation japonaise en Corée." Bulletin de la Société franco-japonaise de Paris,
26-27:61-74, June-September 1912.

10153. See 10030.

10154. Preyer, W. D. von. "Die japanische kolonisation in
Korea und ihre weltwirtschaftlichen wirkungen." Weltverkehr
und weltwirtschaft, 7-8 (1913).

10155. Kanbe, Masao. 朝 鮮 農 業 移 民 論 Chosen nogyo
imin ron. (A discussion on Japanese immigrant farmers to
Korea.) Tokyo, Yuhikaku, 1929.

(d) Korean-Chinese Relations

10156. Rockhill, William W. "Korea and its relations with
China." Journal of the America Oriental society, 13 (1889).

10157. Rockhill, William W. China's intercourse with Korea
from the XV century to 1895. London, 1905.

10158. Wên-yü. 光 緒 十,十一 両 年 間 清 廷 處 理 朝 鮮 亂 事
關 係 文 件 Kuang-hsü shih shih-i liang-nien-chien
Ch'ing-ch'ên ch'u-li Ch'ao-hsien luan-shih kuan-hsi wên-
chien. (Documents in relation to Ch'ing officials managing
the rebel movement in Korea in the 10 and 11 years of Kuang-
hsü (1874-1875).) Jên-wên, 2:8, October 1931. (2) Sŏn, Su-
jŏng (ed.). 事 大 文 軌 Sadae Mun'gwe. (Documents concern-
the serving of China.) Seoul, 1937. 23 v.

10159. Li-Kang. Манчжурские события и Корея. (Manchurian events and Korea.) Translated from the Korean. Materialy po natsional'no-kolonial'nym problemam, sbornik, 3 (1932): 95-110.

10160. Tsai, Yüan-pei and others. 萬鮮慘案專輯 Wan Hsien ts'an-an chuan-chi. (Special issue on the Wan-pao-shan case.) Hsin-ya-hsi-ya, 3:1, October 1931.

10161. Wang, Jung-pao (former Chinese Minister to Japan.) 朝鮮排華慘案調查報告 Ch'ao-hsien p'ai Hua ts'an-an t'iao-ch'a pao-kao. (A report on the investigation of the anti-Chinese incident in Korea.) Eastern miscellany, 28:21: 116-119, November 1931.

10162. 朝鮮慶尚南道華僑現狀 Ch'ao-hsien Ch'ing-shang-nan-tao Hua-ch'iao hsien-ch'uang. (The present status of Chinese in Ching-shang-nan-tao, Korea.) Central oversea Chinese affairs monthly, 9:19, April 1931.

10163. Chang, Wei-ch'êng. 朝鮮華僑概況 Ch'ao-hsien Hua-ch'iao kai-k'uang. (The general status of Chinese in Korea.) Current events, 2:6, June 1930.

10164. 瀋案與旅韓華僑之影響 Shên-an yü lü-Han Hua-ch'iao chih ying-hsiang. (The Mukden incident and its effect on the Chinese in Korea.) Wai-chiao-pu kung-pao, 4:7, 1931.

10165. Nanking, Ministry of Foreign affairs. 新義州華僑之工商業及經濟狀況人數之增減 Hsin-i-chou Hua-ch'iao chih kung-shang-yeh chi ching-chi chuang-kuang jên-shu chih tsêng-chien. (Industrial and commercial enterprises of the Chinese in Hsin-i-chou and their economic condition and numbers.) Foreign affairs gazette, 2:8:70, December 1929.

10166. Chang-ch'ün provisional bureau. 萬寶山事件調查報告 Wan-pao-shan shih-chien tiao-ch'a pao-kao. (A report on the investigation of the Wan-pao-shan incident.) Eastern miscellany, 28:21:113-116, November 1931.

10167. Ch'ao-hsien Hua-kung chih tai-yü. 朝鮮華工之待遇 (The treatment of Chinese laborers in Korea.) Wai-chiao-pu-kung-pao, 4:7, November 1931.

(e) Laws and Legislation

10168. Asami, Rintaro. 朝鮮法制史稿 Chosen hosei-

shi-ko. (A manuscript on the history of Korean legislation.)
Tokyo, Ganshodo, 1930. 469 p.

10169. 朝鮮法規輯覧 Chosen hoki shuran. (A collection of laws and regulations of Korea.) Tokyo, Teikoku
chiho-gyosei gakkai, 1935. 6 v.

10170. Crémazy, Laurent. Texte complémentaire du Code pénal
de la Corée. Paris, Marchal et Billard, 1906. 28 p.

10171. "The Korean mining laws." Korea review, 6 (1906):
241-244.

10172. "The Korean emigrant protection law." Korea review,
6 (1906):256-258.

10173. Office of the Korean Governor General. 朝鮮法令
輯覧 Chosen horei shuran. (Laws and ordinances of Korea.)
Tokyo, Society of Imperial regional administration, 1923.

10174. Japan. Laws, statutes, etc. 朝鮮總督府官規
Chosen sotokufu kanki. (Korean government and its organization.) Regarding the official ranks, degrees, salaries, and
their appointment. In Genko horei shuran, 1:3:699-704,
1060-1071.

10175. Japan. Laws, statutes, etc. 朝鮮總督府
Chosen sotokufu. (Korean government and its organization.)
Regarding the mineral industry, silk industry, fishing industry, industrial and savings banks, weights and measures,
inspection of cereals and soya beans, encouragement of immigration into new lands, foreigners in the fishing industry, etc. In Genko horei shuran,8-9:16:168-2187.

10176. Japan. Laws, statutes, etc. 朝鮮總督府
Chosen sotokufu. (Korean government and its organization.)
Regarding research on the mineral industry, on ports and
bays, on private railways, on factories, and on the census
of 1930, etc. In Genko horei shuran, 2:6:242-474.

10177. Japan. Laws, statutes, etc. 朝鮮總督府
Chosen sotokufu. (Korean government and its organization.)
Regarding the regional system. In Genko horei shuran, 3:8,
259-316.

10178. Japan. Laws, statutes, etc. 朝鮮總督府
Chosen sotokufu. (Korean government and its organization.)
Regarding general rules and regulations, land laws, regional annual expenditures, election, etc. In Genko horei shuran, 3:8: 259-461.

10179. See 8525.

10180. Japan. Laws, statutes, etc. 朝 鮮 總· 督 府
Chosen sotokufu. (Korean government and its organization.)
Regarding its relation with Kanto consular jurisdiction, re-
gistration of ships, factory ordinance, registration of the
Korean fishing industry association, etc. In Genko horei
shuran, 6-7:14:101-1041.

10181. See 8508.

10182. Japan. Laws, Statutes, etc. 朝 鮮 總· 督 府
Chosen sotokufu. (Korean government and its organization.)
Regarding exportation and importation at border lands,
steamship clearance tax, tonnage duties, exportation of
leaf tobacco, tariff charges, commission charges at customs
office, etc. In Genko horei shuran, 5:12:655-1370.

10183. Japan. Laws, statutes, etc. 朝 鮮 總· 督 府
Chosen sotokufu. (Korean government and its organization.)
Regarding its educational affairs. In Genko horei shuran,
7:15:424-537.

10184. Tamagawa, Kengo. 朝 鮮 警 察 法 大 意 Chosen
keisatsu-ho taii. (Outline of the Korean police laws.) Tokyo, Osakayago, 1923.

G. Economic Conditions

(1) History

10185. Paik, Earl K. 한 국 경 제 사 Han kuk kyong che-sa.
(Economic history of Korea.) San Francisco, Korean national
association, 1919. 129 p.

10186. Frescura, B. Giappone e Corea, studio di geografia
economica. Società ligustica di science naturali e geogra-
fiche (Genua), 1 (1910).

10187. Hoshino, T. Economic history of Chosen. Compiled in
commemoration of the decennial of the Bank of Chosen. Seoul, 1920. x, 266 p.

10188. Itani, Zenichi. 朝 鮮 経 済 史 Chosen keizai-shi.
(Economic history of Korea.) Tokyo, Taishokaku, 1929. 323 p.

10189. Keijo imperial university. 朝 鮮 経 済 / 研 究 Chosen keizai no kenkyu. (Study of Korean economy.) Tokyo, Toko shoin, 1932. 773 p.

10190. Ladd, George Trumbull. "The development of Korea in
most recent times." Journal of race development, 431-438,
April 1918.

(2) General Accounts

10191. 鮮 滿 經 濟 十 年 史 Sen-Man keizai junen-shi.
(Ten-year economic history of Korea and Manchuria.) Published by the Korean bank, 1919.

10192. Numanami, Tamane. 鮮 滿 風 物 記 Sen-Man fubutsu-
ki. (An account of the land and produce of Korea and Manchuria.) Tokyo, Osakayago, 1923.

10193. Economic development of Korea and Manchuria. Tokyo,
Japan times publishing co., 1923. 319 p.

10194. "Экономическое положение Кореи и Маньчжурии в оцен-
ке Чосен-банка."(The economic position of Korea and Manchuria as seen by the Chosen bank.) Ekonomicheskii biulleten', Harbin, 17-18 (1925):8-10.

10195. Yü-kan. 日本統治下之朝鮮産業發展現況
Jih-pên t'ung-chih-hsia chih Ch'ao-hsien ch'an-yeh fa-chan
hsien-k'uang. (The present status of the development of the
products of Korea under Japanese rule.) Eastern miscellany,
24:7:48-50, April 1927.

10196. Yü-kan. 日本統治下之臺灣産業發展現況
Jih-pên t'ung-chih-hsia chih Tai-wan ch'an-yeh fa-chan hsien
k'uang. (The present status of the development of the products of Formosa under Japanese rule.) Eastern miscellany,
24:7:46-48, April 1927.

10197. Aoyama, Tendo. 朝鮮滿蒙大觀 Chosen Man-Mo
taikan. (General outlook of Korea, Manchuria, and Mongolia.)
1928.

10198. 朝鮮經濟研究 Chosen keizai no kenkyu. (Research on the economic development of Korea.) Tokyo, Keijo
imperial university law association, Toko shoin, 1929.
772 p.

10199. Nanking, Ministry of Industry and commerce. 駐朝鮮
總領事館商情報告概要 Chu Ch'ao-hsien tsung-
ling-shih-kuan shang-ch'ing pao-kao kai-yao. (Report on
business conditions issued from the Chinese general consulate in Korea.) Industry & commerce gazette, 17, Oct.,1929.

10200. Nishinoiri, Aiichi. 露 国 ' 鮮 銀 壓 迫 真 相
Rokoku no sengin appaku shinso. (The truth about Russian
pressure upon the Bank of Korea.) Gaiko jiho, 56:2:122-130,
October 15, 1930.

10201. English parliamentary papers. Correspondence respect-
ing the ownership of land and mines by British subjects in
Corea. 1911. [Cd. 5717.]

10202. 朝 鮮 華 僑 人 口 職 業 統 計 表 Ch'ao-hsien Hua-ch'iao jên-
k'ou chih-yeh t'ung-chi-piao. (A statistical table showing
the number and occupation of the Chinese in Korea.) Central
oversea Chinese affairs monthly, 2, October 1929.

10203. Ch'ao-hsien li-nien Hua-ch'iao jên-kou tiao-ch'a
tung-chi. 朝 . 鮮 歷 年 華 僑 人 口 調 查 統 計 (A statistical investigation on the Chinese population in Korea.)
Wai-chiao-kung-pao, 4:8, December 1931.

10204. 鮮 南 華 僑 之 生 活 狀 況 Hsien-nan Hua-ch'iao
chih shêng-huo, chuang k'uang. (Living conditions of the
Chinese people in southern Korea.) Central oversea Chinese
affairs monthly, 9:19, April 1931.

10205. Takahashi, Kamekichi. 現 代 朝 鮮 経 済 論 Gendai Chosen keizai ron. (On the economics of present Korea.) Tokyo,
Chikura shobo, 1936. 593 p.

(3) Agriculture

10206. Van Buskirk, J. D. "The climate of Korea and its
probable effect on human efficiency." Transactions of the
Korea branch of the Royal Asiatic society, 10 (1919):1-58.

10207. Hofmann, A. "Die forstlichen produktionsverhältnisse
von Korea. (Eine reise im lande der morgenfrische.)" Mitteilungen der deutschen gesellschaft für natur- und völkerkunde Ostasiens, Tokyo, 11 (1906):1:47-107.

10208. Nakai, T. Flora Koreana. Tokyo, Journal of the College of science, Imperial university of Tokyo, 1909 and
1911. 2 parts.

10209. Koto, B. Journeys through Korea. Tokyo, Journal of
the College of science, Imperial university of Tokyo, 1909
and 1910. 2 parts.

10210. Wilson, Ernest H. "The vegetation of Korea." Transactions of the Korea branch of the Royal Asiatic Society, IX (1918):1-16.

10211. Lee, Hoon K. Land utilization and rural economy in Korea. Tr. from the Korean. Shanghai, Kelly & Walsh, 1936. 289 p.

10212. Nam-Manchun. "Положение крестьянства и его движение в Корее." (Peasant conditions and the peasant movement in Korea.) Krestianskii internatsional, 8-9 (1925):72-90.

10213. Pletner, O. "К аграрному вопросу в Корее." (The agrarian problem in Korea.) Na agrarnom fronte, 11 (1926): 124-138.

10214. Chinese consulate in Korea. 商農參之產題及其栽培製造 Kao-li-sen chih ch'an-o chi ch'i tsai-p'ei chih-tsao. (The ginseng raising, its extent and its manufacure in Korea.) Agriculture gazette, 23, April 1930.

10215. Chuang, Hsin-tsai. 朝鮮革命與農業問題 Ch'ao-hsien ko-ming yü nung-yeh wên-t'i. (The Korean revolution and the problem of agriculture.) National construction monthly, 4:3, January 1931.

10216. Chiba, Toyoharu. 朝鮮ニ於ケル獨逸人經營機械農場 Chosen ni okeru Doitsujin keiei kikai nojo. (The mechanical farming managed by Germans in Korea.) Dairen, S. M. R. R., 1925.

10217. Moose, J. R. Village life in Korea. Nashville, Tenn., Publishing house of the M. E. Church, 1911. 242 p.

10218. Gillett, P. L. "The village guilds of old Korea." Transactions of the Korea branch of the Royal Asiatic society, 4 (1913):2:13-44.

10219. Koons, E. W. "Afforestation in Korea." Transactions of the Korea branch of the Royal Asiatic society, 6 (1915): 1:35-42.

(4) Industry

10220. Yakeda, H. "Some Korean industries." Japan magazine, 3 (1912-1913):489-493.

10221. Emerson, Gertrude. "Industrial Korea. The Hermit kingdom under Japanese administration." Asia, 208-213, May

1917.

10222. Fujimoto, Jitsuya. 鮮 滿 反 北 支 那 之 產 業、
Sen-Man oyobi kita Shina no sangyo. (Industry in Korea,
Manchuria and North China.) 1926.

10223. Harizuka, Chotaro. 鮮 滿 ' 繅 絲 業. Sen-Man no san-
shigyo. (Silk-reeling industry in Manchuria and Korea.)
Ueda, Ueda sanshi dosokai, 1929. 183 p.

10224. Shanghai. Bureau of industrial and commercial information: 韓 稅 海 重 徵 我 國 絲 織 品 Han shui-kuan
chung-sheng wo-kuo szu-chih-p'in. (Korea's high tariff on
our silk textile goods.) Industry and commerce bi-weekly,
2:23:4, December 1930.

10225. Nanking. Ministry of Foreign affairs. 朝 鮮 工 業
之 現 狀 反 其 將 來 Ch'ao-hsien kung-yeh chih hsien-
chuang chi ch'i chiang-lai. (The present status of Korea's
industry and its future.) Foreign affairs gazette, 3:4;120,
August 1930.

10226. 朝 鮮 仁 川 中 日 鮮 勞 工 工 資 比 較 表 Ch'ao-hsien
Jên-ch'uan Chung Jih Hsien lao-kung kung-tzu pi-chiao-piao.
(A comparative table showing the wages of Chinese, Japanese,
and Korean laborers in Jen-chuan, Korea.) Central oversea
Chinese affairs monthly, 2, October 1929.

10227. Lee-Kang. "Рабочее движение в Корее." (Labor movement in Korea.) Materialy po natsional'no-kolonial'nym problemam, 7 (1933):13:35-70.

10228. 朝 鮮 元 山 華 僑 之 工 商 業 反 人 數 之 調 Ch'ao-
hsien Yüan-shan Hua-ch'iao chih kung-shang-yeh chi jên-shu
chih tiao-ch'a. (A survey of Chinese industry, commerce,
and number of people in Yuan-shan, Korea.) Central oversea
Chinese affairs monthly, 1:43, September 1929.

10229. 華 綢 絕 跡 朝 鮮 市 場 Hua ch'ou chüeh-chi
Ch'ao-hsien shih-ch'ang. (Chinese silk goods disappear in
Korean markets.) Shanghai, Industry and commerce bi-weekly,
2:24:5, December 1930.

10230. Chinese consulate at Fu-shan. 鮮 境 夏 布 之 消 費 與
其 供 給 Hsien ching hsia-pu chih hsiao-fei yü kung-chi.
(The consumption and the supply of Chinese linen in Korea.)
Wai-chiao-pu kung-pao, 4:3, October 1931.

(5) Trade and Finance

10231. Korea. Trade of Korea for the year 1906. London,
Foreign office, Diplomatic and consular reports annual series no. 3880, 1907. 27 p.

10232. Korea. Report for the year 1907 on the trade of Korea. Diplomatic and consular reports annual series no. 4120,
1908. 16 p.

10233. Korea. Imperial maritime customs returns of trade
and trade reports. Seoul, 1906, 1907, 1908.

10234. Korea. Tables of the foreign trade and shipping.
Published by oreder of the chief commissioner of customs
for the year 1908. Tokyo, 1908.

10235. Japan. Bureau of customs. 朝鮮貿易年報 Chosen
boeki nenpo. (Annual return of Korean trade of the empire
of Japan.) In Japanese and English.

10236. Ettingen, V. von. Чемульпо.(Port Chemulpo.) Sbornik
konsul'skikh donesenii, 2 (1908):331-341.

10237. 朝鮮各道ニ於ケル國庫補助金下附ニ就テ
Chosen kakudo ni okeru kokko hojokin kafu ni tsuite. (On
the grants of national subsidies in the provinces of Korea.)
In Materials on economic study of the Far East, Dairen,
To-A keizai chosa kyoku, 1915-1931.

10238. Ichihara, M. "Coinage of old Korea." Transactions of
the Korea branch of the Royal Asiatic society (Seoul), 4
(1913):2:45-74.

10239. Ramsdeh, H. A. "Modern coins of Korea. New coin issue of 1909 for Korea." Numismatist (Philadelphia), 22
(1909):101-103, 339.

10240. Shibuya, Reiji. 朝鮮銀行二十五年史 Chosen
ginko 25-nen shi. (Twenty-five years of the Bank of Korea.)
Chosen, Chosen ginko, 1936. 276 p.

(6) Railroads

10241. Bureau of management, S. M. R. R. 朝鮮鐵道旅
行案内 Chosen tetsudo ryoko annai. (Guide-book to the
Korean railways.) Tokyo, Osakayago, 1923.

10242. Chosen sotoku-fu. 朝 鮮 鐵 道 史 Chosen tetsudo-shi. (History of the railways in Korea.) Seoul, Office of the Governor General, 1915.

10243. Taylor, W. W. "Korean roads past and present." Transactions of the Korea branch of the Royal Asiatic society, 15 (1924):35-56.

10244. Haushofer, K. "Der ausbau des eisenbahnnetzes in Korea." Petermanns geographische mitteilungen, 60 (1914):2: 1-56.

10245. Railways of Chosen. I. Report on the Korean railways for 1912. II. Report for 1914-1915. Far Eastern review, 109-116, August 1915; 189-192, October 1916.

10246. Preyer, W. D. von. "Die eisenbahnen in Korea." Archiv für eisenbahnwesen, 1914. 402-418, 728-743.

10247. "Report on investigations, no. 2. January 1924. Development and trend of the automotive transportation in Chosen." Transactions of the Korea branch of the Asiatic society (Seoul), 15 (1924):57-82.

10248. 朝 鮮 ニ 於 テル 鐵 道 Chosen ni okeru tetsudo. (Railways in Korea.) In Materials on the economic study of the Far East, 5:6, To-A keizai chosa kyoku.

10249. See 9433.

10250. Takeuchi, Toraji and Suzuki, Kiyoshi. 朝 鮮 ノ 私 設 鐵 道 Chosen no shisetsu tetsudo. (Private railways in Korea.) Dairen, S. M. R. R., 1925.

10251. B-n, A. "Новое железнодорожное строительство в Корее и его экономическое значение." (The new railway construction in Korea and its economic importance.) Ekonomicheskoe obozrenie, 8-9 (30-31) (1929):14-19.

10252. 朝 鮮 ニ 於 テ 外 國 企 業 家 ニ 對 スル 鐵 道 建 設 ノ 許 可 ノ 可 否 ニ 就 テ Chosen ni oite gaikoku kigyo-ka ni taisuru tetsudo kensetsu no kyoka no kahi ni tsuite. (On the advisability of granting permission to foreign capitalists for the construction of railways in Korea.) In Materials on economic study of the Far East. Dairen, To-A keizai chosa kyoku, 1915-1931.

H. Social and Cultural Conditions

(1) General Accounts

10253. Inaba, Kunzan. 朝鮮文化史研究 Chosen bunka-shi kenkyu. (Research on the cultural history of Korea.) Tokyo, Yuzankanku, 1925. 378 p. See 937-1046.

10254. Maeno, Fukuzo. 朝鮮ノ文化ト迷信 Chosen no bunka. to meishin. (Civilization and culture of Korea and super-stition.) Yamaguchi, Ryuseido, 1931. 260 p.

10255. Shio, Genzo. 新朝鮮風土記 Shin Chosen fudo-ki. (New account of Korean manners and customs.) Tokyo, Banrikaku, 1931. 519 p.

10256.. Keijo imperial university. 朝鮮支那文化ノ研究 Chosen Shina bunka no kenkyu. (Study of the development of Chinese culture and civilization in Korea.) Tokyo, Toko shoin, 1932. 603 p.

10257. 朝鮮國書解題 Chosen kokusho kaidai. (Out-line and explanation for the standard literary works of Ko-rea.) Seoul, Government General of Korea, 1932. 578 p.

(2) Religions and Missions

(a) Buddhism

10258. Hodges, Cecil H. N. "A plea for the investigation of Korean myths and folklore." Transactions of the Korea branch of the Royal Asiatic society, 5 (1914):1:41-53. See 937-1046.

10259. Courant, Maurice. "Sommaire et historique des cultes Coréens." T'oung pao, 1 (1900) 2nd series.

10260. Takahashi, Tooru. 朝鮮思想史大系：李朝佛教 Chosen shiso-shi taikei: Ri-cho bukkyo. (Standard history of the development of Korean thought: Buddhism in Yi dy-nasty.) Tokyo, Hakubunkan, 1929. 1062 p.

10261. Starr, Frederick. Korean Buddhism. History, condition and art. Boston, M. Jones & co., 1918. xix, 104 p.

10262. Trollope Bishop Mark Napier. "Introduction to the study of Buddhism in Korea." Transactions of the Korea branch of the Royal Asiatic society (Seoul), 8 (1917):1-41.

10263. Eckardt, Andreas. "Verehrung Buddhas in Korea."
Geist des Ostens, 2:34-47, 146-158, April 1914 - April 1915.

10264. Witte, J. "Die Japaner und die christliche mission
in Korea." Der Neue Orient, Berlin, 5 (1919):321-322.

(b) Christianity

10265. Delpech, J. Le Christianisme en Corée. Paris, Société générale d'impression, 1913. 110 p.

10266. Dallet, Ch. Histoire de l'église de Corée. Paris,
1874. 2 v.

10267. Trollope, Bishop Mark Napier. The church in Korea.
London, Mowbray, 1915. 132 p.

10268. Dalmen. Le Catholicisme en Corée. Son origine et son
progrès. Hongkong. Imprimerie de la Société des Missions
étrangères de Paris, 1924. 122 p.

10269. The Catholic church in Korea. Hongkong, 1924.

10270. Les débuts du catholicisme en Corée. Bethléem,
1929.

10271. Cadaras. Chez les vieux chrétiens de Corée. Les
mission Catholiques, 1923.

10272. Documents relatifs aux martyrs de Corée de 1839 à
1846. Hongkong, Imprimerie de Nazareth, 1924. vii, 146 p.

10273. Documents relatifs aux martyrs de Corée de 1866.
Hongkong, Imprimerie de Nazareth, 1926. 168 p.

10274. Nedachin, S. V. Православная церковь в Корее. (The
orthodox church in Korea.) A historical sketch. St. Petersburg, 1911. 59 p.

10275. Corfe, C. J. The Anglican church in Korea. London,
Rivingtons, 1906. 37, 139 p.

10276. Paik, L. George. The history of Protestant missions
in Korea, 1832-1910. Pyeng Yang, Korea, 1929.

10277. Nedachin, S. V. К вопросу о принятии корейцев в
христианство. (On admission of Koreans to Christianity.) A
report to the general meeting of the Society of Russian
Orientalists [Obshchestvo russkikh orientalistov], held

January 17, 1912. St. Petersburg, Izdanie V. M. Skvortsova, 1913. 15 p.

˜0278. Миссионерное дело в Корее и в уссурийском краю.
(Missionary affairs in Korea and in the Ussuriisk province.)
A private letter from Seoul. Published in the Tserkovnye
vedomosti, 6 (1912):203-206.

10279. Gordon, E. A. "Some recent discoveries in Korean temples..."Transactions, Korea branch of the Royal Asiatic society, 5 (1914):1:1-39. (2) Yi, Manch'ae.閔 衛. 綸 Pyŏwi p'yŏu. (Catholic persecution.) 1777-1850. Seoul, 1931. 2 v.

(3) Education

10280. Underwood, Horace Horton. Modern education in Korea.
New York, 1926. 351 p.

10281. Manual of education of Koreans. Seoul, The Government General of Chosen. Department of Internal affairs.
Bureau of Education, 1913.

10282. Aston, W. G. "Writing, printing, and the alphabet
in Korea." Royal Asiatic Society of Great Britain and Ireland, 1895. v. I, 505-

10283. Gale, J. S. "The Korean alphabet." Transactions of
the Korea branch of the Royal Asiatic society, Seoul, 4
(1912):1:12-62.

10284. Chevalier, H. "La réforme de l'instruction publique
en Chosen (Corée) d'après les rapports officiels du Gouverneur Général." Bulletin, Société franco-japonaise, 36-37
(1916):37-51.

10285. Bowman, N. H. "The history of Korean medicine."
Transactions of the Korea Branch of the Royal Asiatic society, 6 (1915):1:1-34.

10286. Sekino, Tadashi. "Korean architecture." Japan magazine, 5 (1914-1915):613-621. (2) Eckardt, Andreas. Geschichte der koreanischer kunst. Leipzig, Hiersemann, 1929. xxiii, 225 p. 506 ill.

10287. Courant, M. "Essai historique sur la musique class-
ique des Chinois, avec un appendice relatif à la musique
coréenne." Encyclopédie de la misique et dictionnaire du
conservatoire, 77-241. Dissertation univ. Lyon. Paris, Delagrave, 1912. 165 p.

10288. I-yü. 朝 鮮 的 婦 人 運 動 Ch'ao-hsien ti fu-jên
yün-tung. (The Korean womens movement.) Women's journal,
17:4:65, April 1931.

10289. Gale, James Scarth. The unabridged Korean-English
dictionary. Third edition. Seoul, 1931. xviii, 1781 p.

10290. Koto, B. and Kanazawa, S. A catalogue of the Roman-
ized geographical names of Korea. Tokyo, 1903. 90, 88 p.
(2) McCune, G. M. and Reischauer, E. O. "Romanization of
the Korean language." Transactions of the Korea branch of
the Royal Asiatic society, Seoul, 1938.

P A R T   F O U R

THE RUSSIAN EMPIRE AND THE SOVIET UNION

IN ASIA AND ON THE PACIFIC

See 1-1060.

I. BIBLIOGRAPHY

See 1-42.

A. Bibliographies of Bibliography

See 1-3.

10291. Fomin, A. G. Путеводитель по библиографии, био-библиографии, историографии, хронологии и энциклопедии литературы. (Guide to Russian works and periodicals printed in the years 1736-1932.) Leningrad, 1934. 335 p. (2) Библиография, обзор трудов библиографического содержания. (Bibliography, a survey of bibliographies.) St. Petersburg, 1900. 50 p.

10292. Vykotich, N.A. Материал для списка указателей русской периодической печати. (Sources for lists of guides of Russian periodical press.) Leningrad, 1928. (Published by the Academy of sciences. 631 numbers).

10293. Lisovskii, Nikolai M. Список указателей к русским периодическим изданиям 18-19 ст. (A list of guides to Russian periodical publications of the 18-19 cent.) St. Petersburg, 1903. 64 p.

10294. Mezier, Avgusta Vladimirovna. Словарный указатель по книговедению. (A dictionary-guide to library science.) Leningrad, 1924. 926 p.

B. Bibliographical Periodicals

10295. Книжный вестник. (Book messenger.) St. Petersburg, 1-31 (1889-1914).

10296. Книжная летопись. (Book annals.) Moscow, 1907-1919, weekly; 1920, 48 issues; 1921-1925, semi-monthly; 1926-1929, weekly; 1930- , every 5 days. (2) Алфавитный перечень запрещенных изданий. (Alphabetic index of banned publications.) Separately paged and bearing in some years same numbers as the periodical. 1907 - 1917.   (3) Специальный выпуск. (Special issue.) Quart. 1928- (Lists books in languages of the national minorities.)   (4) Сводный список непериодических изданий выходящих в пределах союзных республик (кроме РСФСР). (Cumulative list of non-periodical publications issued within the Soviet republics, except RSFSR) Quarterly, 1928-

10297. Ежегодник книги СССР. Систематический указатель. (Annual guide to book publications in the USSR.) Ed. by I. T. Morozov and V. I. Soloviev. Moscow, All-Union book chamber, 1, 1936-

C. General

10298. Pulner, I. M. "Ближайшие задачи советской национальной библиографии." (Immediate problems of Soviet national bibliography.) Sovetskaia bibliografiia, 3 (1937):17:33-46.

10299. Ikonnikov, V. S. Опыт русской историографии. (A study in Russian historiography.) Kiev, 1891-1908. 2 v.

10300. Sopikov, V. Опыт российской библиографии. (A study in Russian bibliography.) St. Petersburg, 1813-1821. 5 v. New edition, 1904-1906. 5 parts in 1 volume.

10301. Материалы для библиографии по истории народов СССР XVI-XVII вв. (Materials for the bibliography of the history of the peoples of the USSR.) Leningrad, 1933. 360 p.

10302. Adelung, F. von. Kritisch-literatur. Übersicht der reisenden in Russland bis 1700. St. Petersburg, 1846. 2 v.

10303. Guberti, N. V. Материалы для русской библиографии. Хронологическое обозрение редких и замечательных книг XVIII ст. 1725-1800 гг. (Materials for Russian bibliography. A chronological survey of rare and remarkable Russian books of the XVIII century.) Moscow, 1878-1891. 3 v.

10304. Mezhov, Vladimir Izmailovich. Систематический каталог с 1825 до 1869 и дополнения. (Systematic catalogue and supplements.) St. Petersburg, 1859-   (2) Efremov, P. Систематическая роспись книгам, 1855-1866. (A systematic catalogue of books, 1855-1866.) St. Petersburg, 1867; sup-

plements 1867-1873. St. Petersburg, 1869, 1874. (3) Mezhov,
V. Систематическая роспись книгам, 1873-1881. (A systematic catalogue of books, 1873-1881.) St. Petersburg, 1880;
with supplements, 1881-1892; 1883-1887, St. Petersburg,
1884, 1889. (4) Mezhov, V. Русская историческая библиография, 1800-1854. (Russian historical bibliography.) St.
Petersburg, 1892-1893. 3 v.   (5) Lambin, P. and B.
ibid., 1854-1864 (10 vols). St. Petersburg, 1861-1864.   (6)
Mezhov, V. Ibid., 1865-1876. St. Petersburg, 1882-1890.
8 v.

10305. Главное управление по делам печати. Список книг вышедших в России. (List of books published in Russia.) St.
Petersburg, 1885-1907.

10306. Список повременных изданий за ... год. (List of ser-
ials for the year ...) Moscow, Gosudarstvennaia tsentral'-
naia knizhnaia palata, 1917-1918 (?)   2 v.

10307. Каталог изданий Государственного издательства и его
отделений, 1919-1925. (A catalogue of the publications of
the [Russian] National publication house and its divisions,
1919-1925.) Moscow, 1927.

10308. Библиографический обзор изданий за 10 лет, 1918-
1928. (Bibliographical survey of publications for 10 years,
1918-1928.) Moscow, TSentral'noe statisticheskoe upravlenie,
1928.

10309. Kerner, Robert J. Slavic Europe. A selected bibliography in the Western European languages. Cambridge, Harvard university press, 1918. 402 p.

10310. Viktorov-Toporov, V. Rossica et Sovietica. Bibliographie des ouvrages parus en français de 1917 à 1930 in-
clus relatifs à la Russie et à l'U.R.S.S. Saint Cloud, Éditions documentaires et bibliographiques, 1931-1932. 2 v.

10311. Mehnert, Klaus. Die Soviet-Union, 1917-1932. Bibliographie. Berlin, Ost-Europa verlag, Königsberg-Berlin,
1932. 200 p.

10312. Burtsév, A. Описание редких российских книг. (A description of rare Russian books.) St. Petersburg, 1897. 5
vols.

10313. N. B. (Berezin, Nikolai Il'ich). Русские книжные
редкости. (Russian book rarities.) Moscow, 1902-1903. 2 v.

10314. Sreznevskii, I. I. Сведения и заметки о малоизвест-
ных и неизвестных памятниках. (Information and memoranda
concerning obscure and unknown historical sources.) St.
Petersburg, 1867-1876. 2 v.

10315. Каталог изданий Императорской академии наук. (A catalogue of the publications of the [Russian] Imperial academy of sciences.) St. Petersburg,1912-1915. 2 parts.

10316. Каталог русских книг библиотеки Императорского Ст.-
Петербургского университета. (A catalogue of Russian books
in the library of the Imperial St. Petersburg university.)
St. Petersburg, 1897-1902. 2 v.

10317. Систематический указатель изданий Академии наук
С. С. С. Р., вышедших в свет с 1 января 1917 г. по 1 сентября 1925 г. (Catalogue systématique des publications de
l'Académie des sciences de l'Union des Républiques Soviétiques Socialistes.) Leningrad, 1925.

10318. Научная литература СССР. Систематический указатель
книг и журнальных статей. (Scientific literature of the
USSR. Systematic guide to books and magazine articles.)   1.
Medicine; 2-3. Social sciences; 4. Natural sciences; 5.
Technology; 6-7. Agriculture. Moscow, 1928-

10319. Catalogue systématique des publications de l'Académie des sciences d'Ukraine, 1918-1929. Kiev, 1931. 284 p.
(A list with a carefully compiled index, of the publications of the Ukrainian Academy of sciences in Kiev. Bearing also a Ukrainian title.)

10320. Материалы для библиографии русских научных трудов за
рубежом, 1920-1930. (Sources for bibliography of Russian
scientific works abroad, 1920-1930.) Belgrad, Izdanie Russkogo nauchnogo instituta v Belgrade, 1, 1931. 394 p. (Russian émigré literature.)

10321. Artsimovich, E. V., Ishmenetskoi, M. V., Kapitsa,
B. G., Knats, M. I., Strakhovoi, M. I. Указатель книг по
истории и общественным вопросам. (A guide to books on history and social problems.) St. Petersburg, 1909. 556, 56,
7, v p.

10322. Общественные науки СССР, 1917-1927. (Social sciences
in the USSR.) A symposium, edited by B. P. Volgin, G. O.
Gordon, I. K. Luppol. Moscow, 1928.

10323. Каталог изданий. (Catalogue of publications.)
TSentrarkhiv RSFSR, Gosizdat, 1928. 87 p.

10324. Müller, Frederik. Essai d'une bibliographie néer-
lande-russe. Amsterdam, 1859. 174 p.

10325. Бюллетень торгового сектора Государственного издательства. (Bulletin of the trade department of the State
publishing house.) Moscow, 1924-

10326. Каталог изданий. (Catalogue of publications [of
the State publishing office].) Moscow, Gosudarstvennoe izdatel'stvo, 1919/1925; 1928- Supplement, 1926-1927, nos.
1-3.

10327. Ежегодник. (Year-book [of the State central book
chamber].) Moscow, Gosudarstvennaia tsenral'naia knizhnaia
palata, 1925- (?)

10328. Библиография. (Bibliography.) Moscow, Gosudarstvennaia tsentral'naia knizhnaia palata, 1929- (Quarterly).

10329. Бюллетень. (Bulletin.) Moscow, Gosudarstvennoe izdatel'stvo, 1921-

10330. Moskva. Publichnaia biblioteka SSSR imeni Lenina.
Сборник. (Annals of the Moscow branch of the Lenin public
library of the USSR.) Moscow, 1928-

10331. Leningrad. Publichnaia biblioteka. Сборник Российской публичной библиотеки. (Annals of the Russian public
library.) Leningrad, 1:1, 1920; 2:1, 1924.

10332. Печать СССР в 1936 году. (The press of USSR in 1936.)
Statistical material. Compiled and prefaced by K. I. Pro-
pin. Ed. by V. I. Soloviev. Published by the Knizhnaia palata,
Moscow, 1937. 116, 2 p.

D. Bibliographies of Articles in Periodicals

10333. Lisovskii, Nikolai M. Русская периодическая печать,
1703-1900. (The Russian periodical press, 1703-1900.) Petrograd, 1915. 1067 p.

10334. Miliutin, A. N. Указатель к сибирским изданиям в работе Лисовск.(A guide to the Siberian publications in N. M.
Lisovskii's work.) Reprint from the Sibirskie trudy Tomskogo kraevogo muzeia. Tomsk, 1927.

10335. Sreznevskii, Vsevolod I. Список русских повременных изданий с 1703 по 1899 год. (A list of Russian periodical publications from 1703 to 1899.) St. Petersburg, 1901.

10336. Neustroev, Aleksandr N. Указатель к русским повременным изданиям и сборникам за 1703-1802. (A guide to periodical publications and miscellanies for the period 1703-1802.) St. Petersburg, 1898. 805 p.

10337. Ulianov, N. A. Указатель журнальной литературы. (A guide to periodical literature.) Moscow, 1911-1913. 2 v.

10338. Журнальная летопись. (Annals of periodicals.) Moscow, 1926-1928, quarterly; 1929, bi-monthly; 1930, monthly; 1931- semi-monthly. (Subject index of all articles published in the periodicals.)

10339. Газетная летопись. Орган государственной библиографии. (Newspaper annals. Publication of the Knizhnaia palata Bibliographical division.) Semi-monthly, 1936-1937. Continued as: Летопись газетных статей. (Annals of newspaper articles.) Issued three times a month, 1, 1938-

10340. Azadovskii, M. K. Рукописные журналы в Восточной Сибири в первой половине XIX века. (Handwritten magazines in Eastern Siberia in the first half of the 19 century.) In Sbornik statei k sorokaletiiu uchenoi deiatel'nosti akademika A. S. Orlova. Leningrad, 1934. 594 p.

E. Bibliography of Russia in Asia and on the Pacific

10341. Mezhov, Vladimir Izmailovich. Библиография Азии. (Bibliographia asiatica.) St. Petersburg, 1891-1894. 6 vols First series: Bibliographia Sibirica. 1891-1892. 4 vols in 3. Second series: Bibliographica Asiatica. 1891-1894. 2 vols in 1.

10342. IAkushev, I. A. Материалы для сибирской библиографии. (Sources for a Siberian bibliography.) Praha, 1930.

10343. Материалы для истории русских заселений по берегам Восточного океана. (Materials on the history of Russian settlements on the shores of the Pacific ocean.) Supplement to Morskoi Sbornik, 1-4, 1861.

10344. Mameev, S. N. Материалы для библиографии Сибири. (Materials for a Siberian bibliography.) Tobolsk, 1892.

10345. Ternovskii, A. A. Материалы для библиографии Сибири. (Materials for a bibliography of Siberia.) Tobol'sk, 1893.

10346. Azadovskii, Mark. Обзор библиографий Сибири. (A survey of Siberian bibliographies.) Tomsk, 1920. (2) The same. Задачи сибирской библиографии. (Problems of Siberian bibliography.) Sibirskie zapiski, 6 (1919).

10347. Egorov, Dmitrii Nikolaevich (editor). Библиография Востока. (Bibliography of the Orient.) Moscow, Nauchnaia assotsiatsiia vostokovedeniia pri TsIK, SSSR. 1, 1928. (2) Библиография Востока. (Bibliography of the Orient.) Leningrad, Institut vostokovedeniia Akademii nauk SSSR, 1, 1932- [Vol. 10, 1936].

10348. Belov, A. M. Материалы к указателю литературы о Сибири на европейских языках. С 1917-1930 г. (Sources for a guide to the literature of Siberia in European languages.) 1917-1930. In Trudy Soveta po izucheniiu proizvoditel'nykh sil. Akademiia nauk SSSR, 1931. 35 p.

10349. Grachev, V. A. Обзор источников по истории Приамурья и Охотско-Камчатского края. (Aperçu des sources pour l'histoire des provinces d'Amour, d'Ochotsk et de Kamchatka.) Part 1: From the earliest times to the middle of the 19 century. Vladivostok, 1927. 49 p. In Trudy Gosudarstvennogo Dal'ne-vostochnogo universiteta. Series 3, no. 5.

10350. Zdobnov, N. V. Указатель библиографических пособий по Уралу. (A bibliographical guide for the Ural region.) Includes Bashkiriia and the Siberian regions of the Ural Oblast'. 1, Moscow, 1927.

10351. KHoroshikh, P. P. Указатель литературы по археологии Иркутского края. (Guide to literature on the archaeology of the Irkutsk region.) Izvestiia Biol.-geograficheskogo instituta pri Gosudarstvennom irkutskom universitete, 1:1 (1924). 8 p.

10352. Matveev, Z. N. Что читать о Дальне-восточной области. (What to read on the Far-Eastern province.) Vladivostok, 1925. 248 p.

10353. Bartol'd, Vasilii Vladimirovich. История изучения Востока в Европе и России. (History of the study of the Orient in Europe and in Russia.) 1st ed. 1911; 2nd ed. Leningrad, 1925. German translation: Die geographische und historische erforschung des Orients. Mit besonderer berücksichtigung der russischen arbeiten. Leipzig, Figulla, 1913.

10354. Zdobnov, N. "Современное состояние и задачи урало-
сибирской библиографии." (Modern conditions and problems
of Uralo-Siberian bibliography.) Severnaia Aziia, 1-2
(1925):114-122.

10355. Matveev, Z. N. Состояние библиографической литературы
Дальне-восточного края. (Condition of bibliographical literature of the Far Eastern region.) Vladivostok, Gosudarstvennyi universitet. Trudy, 3rd series,no. 2.   12 p.

10356. Bakai, N. N. Замечательное книгохранилище в восточной Сибири. (Библиотека Г. В. Юдина.) (A remarkable library
in eastern Siberia.) [The Yudin library was acquired by the
Library of Congress in 1907]. Moscow, 1896. 15 p.

10357. Badmaev, I. M. Десять лет большевистской печати в
Калмыкии. (Ten years of bolshevist press in Kalmykia.)
Elista, 1931. 32 p.

10358. Алфавитный указатель литературы по вопросам Азии и
Дальнего Востока за 1911 г. (An alphabetical guide to literature pertaining to questions of Asia and the Far East during the year 1911.) Books and pamphlets published in Russian, French, German and English.   Supplement to the magazine "Dal'nevostochnoe obozrenie". St. Petersburg, 1911.

10359. Tiumin, M. S. Указатель периодических и повременных
изданий, выходивших в г. Харбине на русском и других европейских языках по 1-е января 1927. (A guide to the periodical literature published in Harbin in Russian and other
European languages up to January 1, 1927.) Harbin, 1927.

10360. Slonim, M. "Современная сибирская литература." (Contemporary Siberian literature.) Vol'naia Sibir', 5 (1929):
24-47.

F. Archival Guides

10361. Drezden, A. K. (editor). Архивы СССР.   (Archives of
the USSR.) Leningradskoe otdelenie TSentral'nogo istoriche-
skogo arkhiva. Leningrad, Lenoblizdat, 1933. 280 p.

10362. Putsillo, M. P. Указатель делам и рукописям   относящимся   до Сибири. (A guide to manuscripts pertaining to
Siberia.) Moscow, 1879. 123 p. See 11070.

10363. Kaidanov, N. I. (compiler). Систематический каталог
делам Сибирского приказа, Московского коммисарства и других
бывших учреждений по чьсти промышленности и торговли, хра-

нящихся в архиве Департамента таможенных сборов. (A systematic catalogue of the Siberian documents of the Moscow commissariat and other institutions for trade and industry, kept in the archives of the Department for customs duties.) St. Petersburg, 1888. 202 p. See 11068.

II. PERIODICALS

See 43-147.

A. General

10364. Журнал Министерства народного просвещения. (Journal of the Ministry of public education.) St. Petersburg, 1802-1917. Index, 1803-1864; 1867-1900. (Title varies.)

10365. Annuaire diplomatique de l'Empire de Russie. St. Petersburg, Ministry of foreign affairs, 1861-1917. 54 v.

10366. Правительственный вестник. (The government messenger.) St. Petersburg, 1879-1902.

10367. Вестник Европы. (The messenger of Europe.) Moscow, 1866-1917. (Monthly).

10368. Мир божий. (God's world.) St. Petersburg, 1892-1906. Succeeded by (2) Современный мир. (Contemporary world.) St. Petersburg, 1906-1918. (Monthly).

10369. Отечественные записки. (Fatherland annals.) St. Petersburg, 1820-1830. Started anew: 1839-1884.

10370. Русская мысль. (Russian thought.) Moscow, Sofia, Berlin, 1880-1924. (Monthly).

10371. Русский вестник. (The Russian messenger.) Ed. by M. Katkov. Moscow-St. Petersburg, 1856-1906. 306 v.

10372. Русское богатство. (Russian wealth.) St. Petersburg, 1894-1914. (Monthly).

10373. Судебный вестник. (Juridical messenger.) St. Petersburg, 1866-1877. Succeeded by: (2) Северный вестник. (The northern messenger.) 1877-1878. (Daily).

10374. Северный вестник. (The northern messenger.) St. Petersburg, 1885-1891; 1891-1898.

10375. Сын отечества. (Son of the fatherland.) Ed. by N. I.
Grech. St. Petersburg, 1812-1828.   (2) Северный архив.
(The northern archives.) Ed. by F. V. Bulgarin. 1822-1828.
(3) Сын отечества и северный архив.   (Son of the fatherland
and the northern archives.) 1829-1852.

10376. Вестник Азии. (The messenger of Asia.) Harbin, Society of Russian orientalists, 1909-

10377. Восток. (The East.) Moscow-Leningrad, 1922-1925.

10378. Жизнь национальностей. (Life of the nationalities.)
Moscow, 1923-1924.

10379. Новый Восток. (The new East.) Moscow, Nauchnaia assotsiatsiia vostokovedeniia SSSR, 1922-1930. 29 v.

10380. Obshchestvo izucheniia Urala i Dal'nego Vostoka.
Северная Азия. (North Asia.) Moscow, 1925- (2) The same.
Труды. (Transactions.) 1, 1928-

10381. Сибирские вопросы. (Siberian problems.) St. Petersburg, 1905-1913.

10382. Сибирский вестник. (The Siberian messenger.) Ed. by
G. I. Spasskii. St. Petersburg, 1818-1824. (2) Азиатский
вестник. (The Asiatic messenger.) Continues the above.
St. Petersburg, 1825-1827.

10383. Восток. (The East.) Ed. by N. N. Durnovo. Moscow,
1879-1886. (Weekly; after 1881, bi-weekly).

10384. Окраины России. (The borderlands of Russia.) St. Petersburg, 1906-1912. (Weekly). (2) Сибирь. (Siberia.) St.
Petersburg, 1897-1898.

11385. Новое время. (New times.) St. Petersburg, 1868-1917.
(Daily). (2) Русские ведомости. (The Russian gazette.)
Moscow, 1863-1917. (Daily).

B. Recent Government Publications and Newspapers

10386. Russia. Provisional government. Вестник Временного
правительства. (Bulletin of the Provisional government.)
March 5/18 - October 27/November 9, 1917.

10387. Известия Центрального исполнительного комитета Союза
советских социалистических республик и Всероссийского центрального исполнительного комитета советов рабочих, крестьянских и красноармейских депутатов. (News of the Central ex-

эcutivе committee of the Union of soviet socialist republics, and of the All-Russian central executivе committee of
the councils of workers', peasants', and red soldiers' deputies.) Petrograd, 1917-   (Daily).

10388. Правда. (Truth.) Moscow, All-Union communist party,
1917-   (2) Бюллетень Правды. (Bulletin of the Truth.)
Moscow, 1927-   (Reprints of important articles from the
newspaper Pravda).

10389. Правда Востока. (Truth of the East.) Tashkent, 1,
1924- (Daily).

10390. Советская Сибирь. (Soviet Siberia.) Novosibirsk,
West Siberian division of the Communist party, 1, 1924-
(Daily).

10391. Тихоокеанская звезда.(Pacific star.) Khabarovsk, Far
Eastern division of the Communist party, 1, 1924- (Daily).

10392. Красная звезда. (Red star.) Moscow, 1928- (Daily).

C. Historical

10393. Императорский московский университет. Общество исто-
рии и древностей российских. (Imperial Moscow university.
Society for the study of history and antiquities of Russia.)
Publications: Труды и летопись. (Transactions and annals.)
1815-1837. 8 v. (2) The same. Русские достопамятности.
(Russian monuments [of antiquity].) 1815-1844. 3 v. (3)
The same. Русский исторический сборник.   (Russian historic-
al miscellany.) 1837-1844. 8 v. Succeeded by (4) Чтения.
(Lectures.) 1845-1848. Succeeded by (5) Временник.
(Annals.) 1849-1857. Succeeded by (6) Чтения. (Lectures.)
1858- ? (7) Исторический вестник.(Historical bulletin.)
Moscow, Historical society of Moscow university, 1916-1917.

10394. Istoricheskoe obshchestvo Nestora letopistsa. Чтения.
(Lectures.) Kiev, 1873-1900. 14 v. (2) Novorossiiskii universitet. Записки.(Journal.) Odessa, 1865-1913. 113 v. (4)
St. Petersburg university. Historico-philological faculty.
Записки. (Journal.) 1876-1918. 143 v. (5) Kharkov university. Historico-philological society. Сборник.(Miscellany.)
1886-1907. 18 v.   (6) Warsaw university. Society of history... Записки. (Journal.) Warsaw, 1902-1914. 7 v.

10395. Вестник археологии и истории. (Bulletin of archeology and history.) St. Petersburg, Archeological institute,
1886-1918. 23 v.

10396. Исторический вестник. (The historical messenger.)
St. Petersburg, 1880-1917. 148 v. (Monthly).

10397. Историческое обозрение. (The historical review.) St.
Petersburg university, Historical society, 1890-

10398. Русский архив. (Russian archives.) Ed. by P. Bar-
tenev. Moscow, 1863-1916.

10399. Русский исторический журнал. (Russian historical
journal.) Petrograd, Academy of sciences, 1917-1922. 8 v.

10400. Русская старина. (Russian antiquities.) St. Petersburg, 1870-1918. 173 v.

10401. Историк и современник. (Historian and contemporary.)
Berlin, 1922-1923.

10402. Eurasia septentionalis antiqua. Helsinki, 1926-

10403. Красный архив.(Red archives.) Moscow, 1922-   (2)
Борьба классов. (Class struggle.) Moscow, TSentrarkhiv,
1924.(3) Историк-марксист. (Marxist historian.) Institut istorii Kommunisticheskoi akademii, 1, 1922-

D. Soviet Union Periodicals

10404. Большевик. (Bolshevik.) Moscow, 1924-   (2) Молодая
гвардия. (The young guard.) Moscow, 1929-   (3)   Октябрь.
(October.) Moscow, 1924-   (4) Под знаменем марксизма. (Under the marxist banner.) Moscow, 1922-

10405. Звезда. (The star.) Leningrad-Moscow, 1924-   (2)
Красная новь. (Red virgin soil.) Moscow, 1921-   (3) Новый
мир. (The new world.) Moscow, 1925-

10406. Война и революция. (War and revolution.) Moscow,
Osoviakhim, 1924-

10407. Революционный Восток. (Revolutionary East.) 1927-1937.
(Discontinued).

10408. Революция и национальности. (Revolution and the nationalities.) 1, 1930-   (Monthly).

10409. Soviet union review. Washington, Soviet union information bureau, 1923-1934.

E. Economic

10410. Вестник финансов, промышленности и торговли.(Bulletin of finance, industry, and commerce.) St. Petersburg, Ministry of finance, 1865-1917. (Weekly).

10411. Амурский земледелец. (The Amur agriculturist.) Blago veshchensk, 1912-

10412. Вестник золотопромышленности и горного дела вообще. (Bulletin of gold mining and mining in general.) Tomsk, 1892-1903. (2) Горные и золотопромышленные известия. (Mining and gold mining news.) Tomsk, 1904- ?

10413. Забайкальский хозяин. (The Transbaikal economist.) Chita, 1912- (2) Приморский хозяин. (The Maritime economist.) Vladivostok, 1913-1922. (3) Труды Тобольского общества сельского хозяйства. (Transactions of the Tobolsk society of rural economy.) Tobolsk, 1897- ?

10414. Moskovskoe obshchestvo sel'sk. khoz. Krasnoiarsk department. Труды. (Transactions.) 1, 1894- ? (2) Протоколы. (Protocols.) 1, 1894- ?

10415. Сибирская торговая газета. (Siberian commercial newspaper.) Tiumen, July 1897- ? (Daily).

10416. Экономист России.(The economist of Russia.) St. Petersburg, 1910-1913.

10417. All-Union chamber of commerce. Quarterly review. Moscow, 1931- (2) Торговля СССР с Востоком. (Russian trade with the East.) Moscow, All-Union Eastern chamber of commerce, 1923- (3) Ежегодник внешней торговли.(Yearbook of foreign trade.) Moscow, Gosizdat, 1932-

10418. Труды финансовой секции. (Transactions of the financial section.) Moscow, National commissariat of finance, Institute of economic research, 1928-

10419. Плановое хозяйство.(Planned economy.) Moscow, 1925-

10420. Русское экономическое обозрение. (The Russian economic review.) St. Petersburg, 1897- (Monthly).

10421. Сибиреведение. (Study of Siberia.) Novosibirsk, Society for the study of Siberia and her productive power, 1, 1929-

284   Russia

10422. Sowjetwirtschaft und aussenhandel. Berlin, 1, 1922-

10423. Экономическая жизнь Дальнего Востока.(Economic life
of the Far East.) Chita-Khabarovsk, 1922-   (2) Экономическая жизнь Приморья. (Economic life of the Maritime province.) Vladivostok, 1923- (Monthly).

F. Local (Siberian)

10424. Тобольские губернские ведомости. (Tobolsk gubernia
gazette.) Tobolsk, 1857-? (2) Иркутские губернские ведомости. (Irkutsk gubernia gazette.) 1857-? (3) Енисейские
губернские ведомости. (Yeniseisk gubernia gazette.) 1857-?
(4) Томские губернские ведомости. (Tomsk gubernia gazette.)
1857-? (5) Забайкальские областные ведомости. (Transbaikal
region gazette.) Chita, 1865- ? (6) Акмолинские областные
ведомости. (Akmolinsk region gazette.) 1871-? (7) Семи-
палатинские областные ведомости. (Semipalatinsk region
gazette.) 1871- ? (8) Якутские областные ведомости.(Yakutsk
region gazette.) 1892- ? (9) Приморские ведомости. (Maritime region gazette.) Khabarovsk, 1894- ?

10425. Иркутские епархиальные ведомости. (Irkutsk diocese
gazette.) Irkutsk, 1862-1921 (2) Томские епархиальные
ведомости. (Tomsk diocese gazette.) 1880-1918. (3) Тобольские епархиальные ведомости. (Tobolsk diocese gazette.)
1882-1918. (4) Енисейские епархиальные ведомости. (Yeniseisk diocese gazette.) Krasnoiarsk, 1884- ? (5) Якутские
епархиальные ведомости. (Yakutsk diocese gazette.) 1887-
? (6) Камчатские епархиальные ведомости. (Kamchatka diocese gazette.) Blagoveshchensk, 1894- ? (7) Омские епархиальные ведомости. (Omsk diocese gazette.) 1898-1918 ?
(8) Благовещенские епархиальные ведомости. (Blagoveshchensk
diocese gazette.) 1899- (9) Забайкальские епархиальные
ведомости. (Transbaikal diocese gazette.) Chita, 1900- ?
(10) Владивостокские епархиальные ведомости.(Vladivostok
diocese gazette.) 1900-

10426. Государственный дальневосточный университет. (State
Far Eastern university.) Ученые записки. (Learned journal.)
Vladivostok, Historico-philological faculty, 1, 1919- (2)
The same. Бюллетень. (Bulleten.) 1, 1921- (3) The same.
Труды. (Transactions.) 1923- (4) Иркутский государственный
университет. (Irkutsk state university.) Труды. (Trans-
actions.) Irkutsk, 1921- (5) Tomsk university. Известия.
(Bulletin.) 1, 1889-

10427. Иртыш, превращающийся в Ипокорену. (Irtysh becoming
the Ipokorena.) Tobolsk, 1789-1794.

10428. Ленская волна. (The Lena wave.) Yakutsk, 1913-1915.

10429. Сибирская неделя. (Siberian week.) Irkutsk, 1913-1914.

10430. Сибирские записки. (Siberian notes.) Krasnoiarsk, 1916-1919.

10431. Сибирский архив. (Siberian archives.) Minusinsk-Irkutsk, 1911-1916.

10432. Ежегодник Тобольского губернского музея. (Year-book of the Tobolsk gubernia museum.) Tobolsk, 1893-1918.

10433. Russkoe tekhnicheskoe obshchestvo. East Siberian department. Записки. (Journal.) Irkutsk, 1869- ?

10434. Obshchestvo vostokovedeniia.   Amur department. Записки. (Journal.) Khabarovsk, 1912-1913.

10435. Tomskoe obshchestvo estestvopytatelei i vrachei. Труды. (Transactions.) Tomsk, 1889-1913.

10436. Tomskoe obshchestvo izucheniia Sibiri. Труды. (Transactions.) Tomsk, 1913-

10437. Амур. (The Amur.) Irkutsk, 1860. (Weekly). Succeeded by (2) Амур. Газета Восточной Сибири. (Amur. A newspaper of Eastern Siberia.) Irkutsk, 1861-1862. (Bi-weekly).

10438. Амурская газета. (The Amur newspaper.) Blagoveshchensk, 1895- ? (Weekly).

10439. Амурский край. (The Amur region.) Blagoveshchensk, 1899- ? (3 times a week).

10440. Байкал. (The Baikal.) Kiakhta, 1897-1899.

10441. Владивосток. (Vladivostok.) 1883-1894 ? (Weekly).

10442. Восточный вестник.   (The Eastern bulletin.) Vladivostok, 1898- ?

10443. Восточное обозрение. (Eastern review.) St. Petersburg-Irkutsk, 1882-1906. [Ed. by N. M. IAdrintsev]. (2) Сибирский сборник. (Siberian miscellany.) Irkutsk, 1886-1906. Supplement to the Eastern Review.

10444. Дальний Восток. (The Far East.) Vladivostok, 1892-1918. (Daily).

10445. Листок Приморского областного статистического комитета. (Leaflet of the Maritime provincial statistical committee.) Vladivostok, 1900- ? (Semi-monthly).

10446. Россия и Азия. (Russia and Asia.) Kiev, 1897-1901. (Weekly).

10447. Сибирская газета. (The Siberian newspaper.) Tomsk, 1881-1888. (Weekly).

10448. Сибирский вестник. (The Siberian messenger.) Irkutsk, 1864-1868.

10449. Сибирский вестник политики, литературы и общественной жизни. (The Siberian messenger of politics, literature, and social life.) Tomsk, 1885- ? (Weekly).

10450. Сибирский листок. (Siberian pamphlet.) Tobolsk, 1891- ? (Semi-weekly).

10451. Сибирь. (Siberia.) Irkutsk, 1873-1887. (2) Сборник газеты "Сибирь". (A supplement to the newspaper "Siberia.")

10452. Справочный листок Енисейской губернии. (Information leaflet of the Yeniseisk gubernia.) Krasnoiarsk, 1889-1891. Continued as (2) Енисейский справочный листок. (Yenisei information leaflet.) 1891-1892. (3) Енисейский листок. (Yenisei leaflet.) 1892-1894. (4) Енисей. (The Yenisei.) 1894-

10453. Томский справочный листок. (The Tomsk information leaflet) Tomsk, 1894-1900. Continued as (2) Сибирская жизнь. (Siberian life.) Tomsk, 1900- ? (Daily).

10454. Екатеринбургская неделя. (The Ekaterinburg week.) Ekaterinburg, 1879-1897. Continued as (2) Урал. (The Urals) 1897- ? (Weekly).

10455. Уралец. (The Uralian.) Uralsk, 1897-

10456. Деловой корреспондент. (The business correspondent.) Ekaterinburg, 1886-1898. Continued as (2) Уральская жизнь. (Ural life.) 1899- ? (Daily).

10457. Уральский листок (объявлений). (The Ural leaflet [of advertisements].) Uralsk, 1893- ?

10458. Уральское горное обозрение. (The Ural mining review.) Ekaterinburg, 1898- ? (Weekly).

10459. Улан-Залат. Ulan-Zalat. Prague, 1927- In Russian
and Kalmuk.

10460. Жизнь Сибири.(Life of Siberia.) Novonikolaevsk,
1922- (Monthly).

10461. Новый Дальний Восток. (The new Far East.) Vladivostok, 1923-

10462. Сибирская живая старина. (Siberian living antiquities.) Irkutsk, 1923-

10463. Сибирские огни. (Siberian fires.) Novosibirsk, 1922-

10464. Труды Томского краевого музея. (Transactions of the
Tomsk regional museum.) Tomsk, 1, 1927-

III. ENCYCLOPEDIAS

10465. Энциклопедический словарь (Encyclopedia.) St. Petersburg, Brokgauz and Efron, 1890-1907. 82 v., 4 v. of
supplement. Later edition, 1911-1916. 58 v. (Discontinued
on the word Отто.)   (2) Энциклопедический словарь. (Encyclopedia.) Moscow, A. and I. Granat, 1910-   (1934, v. 50
[up to Эволюция внешнего быта] was published.)

10466. Большая советская энциклопедия. (The great soviet
encyclopedia.) Moscow, 1926- (Publication continues.) (2)
Малая советская энциклопедия. (The small soviet encyclopedia.) Moscow, 1930-1931. 10 v. (Completed). (3) Литератур-
ная энциклопедия. (The literary encyclopedia.) Pub. by the
Communist academy, 1929-1935. 9 v.(Discontinued on the word
Романтизм.)

10467. Сибирская советская энциклопедия.(The Siberian soviet encyclopedia.) Ed. by B. Z. Shumiatskii. Moscow, Sibirskoe kraevoe izdatel'stvo, 3 v. (Discontinued after the
letter "N".)

IV. BIOGRAPHICAL DICTIONARIES

10468. Русский биографический словарь. (Russian biographical dictionary.) St. Petersburg, 1896-1918. 25 v.

10469. IAzykov, D. D. Обзор жизни и трудов покойных русских
писателей. (A survey of the lives and works of deceased
Russian writers.) St. Petersburg and Moscow, 1885-1916.
13 v.

10470. Vengerov, Semen Afanasievich. Критико-биографический
словарь русских писателей и ученых. (Critical biographical
dictionary of Russian writers and scholars.) St. Petersburg,
1897-1906. 6 v.

10471. Vengerov, S. A. Источники словаря русских писателей.
(Sources for a dictionary of Russian writers.) St. Petersburg, 1900-1917. (To: Nekrasov).

10472. Gennadi, Grigorii N. Справочный словарь о русских
писателях и ученых, умерших в 18 и 19 столетиях, и список
русских книг с 1725 по 1825 г. (A dictionary-guide of Russian writers and scientists who died during the 18 and 19
centuries, and a list of Russian books from 1725 to 1825.)
Berlin-Moscow, 1876-1908. 3 v.

10473. Strahl, Philipp. Das gelehrte Russland. Leipzig, F.
Fleischer, 1828 (to the end of the 18 century). 514 p.

10474. Kozmin, P. (editor). Писатели современной эпохи.
(Writers of the contemporary epoch.) Moscow, 1928. (Biobibl)

10475. Vladislavlev, Ignatii Vladislavovich (Gul'binskii).
Русские писатели. (Russian writers.) 4th edition. Moscow,
1924. (A biobliography).

10476. Nevskii, Vladimir Ivanovich. Материалы для биографи-
ческого словаря социал-демократов, вступивших в российское
рабочее движения за период от 1880 до 1905 г. (Sources for
a biographical dictionary of the social-democrats who joined
the Russian labor movement during the period 1880-1905.)
Mosc ow,1923.

10477. Zdobnov, Nikolai V. Материалы для сибирского словаря
писателей.   (Sources for a Siberian dictionary of writers.)*
Moscow, 1927. 61 p.

V. YEAR-BOOKS

See 144-147.

10478. Soviet Union year-book. London, Allen & Unwin, 1925-
(6 vols. in 1930).

10479. Malevskii-Malevich, P. (editor). Russia - USSR. A
complete handbook. New York, Payson, 1933. 712 p.

10480. Весь СССР. (The entire USSR.) Information and address
book for the year. Moscow, 1, 1924-

10481. Политико-экономический ежегодник СССР. (Political-economic year-book of the USSR.) Moscow, 1925-26-   (?)

10482. Весь СССР. Экономический, финансовый, политический и административный справочник. (The entire USSR. Guide on economics, finance, politics and administration.) Moscow, 1, 1926-

10483. Сельское хозяйство СССР, ежегодник 1935.(Agriculture of the USSR, 1935 year-book.) Moscow, Sel'khozgiz, 1935.

10484. Социалистическое строительство СССР. Статистический ежегодник. (Socialist construction of the USSR. Statistical year-book.) Soiuzorguchet, Moscow, 1936.

VI. GUIDES AND HANDBOOKS

10485. Dolgorukov, V. Путеводитель по всей Сибири и средне-азиатским владениям России. (Guide through all of Siberia and the Central-Asiatic possessions of Russia.) Tomsk, 1900. 540 p.

10486. От Урала до Великого океана. (From the Urals to the Pacific.) A guide-book. Moscow, 1928.

10487. Great Britain. Admiralty. A handbook of Siberia and Arctic Russia. Compiled by the Geographical section of the Naval intelligence division. London, 1920.

10488. Radó, Alexander (comp.) Guide-book to the Soviet Union. Issued by the Society for cultural relations of the Soviet Union with foreign countries. New York, International-al publishers co., 1928. 855 p.

10489. Lipovetskii, Grigorii Aleksandrovich. От Урала до Тихого океана по Великому сибирскому пути. (From the Urals to the Pacific along the Great Siberian railway.) Guide-book. Moscow, Sovetskaia Azia, 1931. 151 p. (Later edition, 1933. 168 p.)

VII. GEOLOGY

See 804-823; 1196-1234.

A. Periodical Publications

10490. Krishtafovich, N. I. (editor). Ежегодник по геологии и минералогии России.   (Year-book on geology and mine-ralogy of Russia.) Novo-Alexandria, 1896-1908. V.1, Warsaw.

10491. Русская геологическая библиотека. (Russian geological library.) St. Petersburg, Geologicheskii komitet, 1885-1901. 17 v.

10492. Каталог изданий геологического комитета. (Catalogue of the Geological committee's publications.) Moscow, Geologicheskii komitet, 1926-

10493. Труды Геологического комитета. (Transactions of the Geological committee.) St. Petersburg, 1903-1930. 189 v.

10494. Материалы по геологии и полезным ископаемым Дальнего Востока. (Materials on the geology of the Far East.) Glavnoe geologo-razvedochnoe upravlenie, Dal'nevostochnoe otdelenie, 1920-

10495. Известия.(Bulletin de Filiale de la Siberie d'Ouest du Comité géologique.) Glavnoe geologo-razvedochnoe upravlenie, Zapadno-sibirskoe otdelenie, 1919- (Bi-monthly).

B. General Accounts

10496. Obruchev, V. A. История геологического исследования Сибири. (A history of the geological survey of Siberia.) Period one: XVII and XVIII centuries (Gmelin, Pallas, Georgi). Izd. Akademii nauk, 1931. 153, 18 p.

10497. Borisiak, Aleksei A. Очерк геологии Сибири. (Sketch of the geology of Siberia.) St. Petersburg, 1923. 140 p.

10498. Obrutschew, V. (Obruchev). Geologie von Sibirien. (Fortschrifte der geologie und palaeontologie, Heft 15). Berlin, Gebrüder Borntraeger, 1926. 572 p. See 10,500.

10499. Сборник по геологии Сибири, посвященный двадцатипятилетнему юбилею научно-педагогической деятельности проф. М. А. Усова. (Collection of essays concerning the geology of Siberia, dedicated to Prof. M. A. Usov on the occasion of his twenty-fifth jubilee of scientific-pedagogical activity.) Tomsk, 1933. x, 348 p.

10500. Obruchev, V. A. Геология Сибири. (Geology of Siberia.) Moscow, Academy of sciences, 1935-1936. 2 v.   See 10,498.

10501. Геологические исследования и разведочные работы вдоль сибирской железной дороги. (Geological explorations and prospecting works along the Siberian railroad.) St. Petersburg, Geologicheskii komitet, 1896-1912. 32 v.

10502. Геология СССР. (Geology of the USSR.) Moscow, Geologicheskii komitet, 1917-1929.

10503. See 165-181.

C. Special Accounts

10504. Материалы по геологии и полезным ископаемым Дальнего Востока. Полезные ископаемые Дальнего Востока.(Geology and mineralogy of the Far East.) Vladivostok, 1923. 5, 285, 338 p.

10505. Arseniev, A. К вопросу о байкальской нефти. (On the question of oil in the Baikal region.) In Materialy po geologii i poleznym iskopaemym Dal'nego Vostoka, no. 30. Vladivostok, 1924. 29 p.

10506. Bogdanovich, K. (Bohdanowicz, Karol). Геологический очерк западного побережья Охотского моря от Николаевска на Амуре до Охотска. (Sketch of the geology of the western coast of the Sea of Okhotsk from Nikolaevsk on the Amur to Okhotsk.) In Izvestiia Imperatorskogo russkogo geograficheskogo obshchestva, St. Petersburg, 42 (1904).

10507. Obruchev, V. A. Геологический очерк Прибайкалья и Ленского района. (A geological study of the Baikal and Lena districts.). Izd. Akademii nauk SSSR, 1932. 128 p. 2 maps.

10508. Bogdanovich, K. (Bohdanowicz). Материалы по геологии и полезным ископаемым Иркутской губернии. (Sources pertaining to the geology and minerals of the Irkutsk guberniia.) In Geologicheskie issledovaniia po linii Sibirskoi zheleznoi dorogi, 2, 1896.

10509. IAchevskii, L. A. Северный енисейский горный округ. (Northern Yenisei mountain region.) In Gornyi zhurnal, St. Petersburg, January 1894.

10510. Keidel, Hans. Geologische untersuchungen in südlichen Tian-Schan nebst beschreibung einer obercarbonischen brachiopodenfauna aus dem Kukurtuk-Tal. Neues jahrbuch für miner., geolog. und paläont. Beilage, band 22,1906.

10511. Friederichsen, M. Zur morphologie des Tien-schan. Zeitschr. d. Gesellschaft für erdkunde (Berlin), 34, 1899.

10512. Friederichsen, M. Geologische ergebnisse der Mezbacherschen expedition in den zentralen Tien-schan in den jahren 1902-1903. Petermanns mitt. 1907.

10513. Ziablov, M. F. Ангаро-Илим. (Angara-Ilim.) A geological economic sketch. Moscow-Irkutsk, 1934. 56 p.

10514. Churakov, A. N. История геологического развития южной части Средней Сибири. (History of the geological development of the southern part of Central Siberia.) Moscow, Academy of sciences, 1935. 29 p.

10515. Vasiliev, A. A. and Kataev, V. A. (ed.) Геофизические методы разведки в Западной Сибири. (Geophysical methods of exploration in Western Siberia.) Collected articles. Tomsk, 1935. 259 p.

10516. Frederiks, G. N. Геологический очерк района Вашкурского водохранилища на реке Чусовой. (Geological sketch of the regional Vashkur water preservation on the river Chusovaia.) Leningrad, 1933. 56 p.

10517. Nekhoroshev, V. P. Геологический очерк Алтая. (A geological study of Altai.) Izd. Akademii Nauk, 1932. 46 p.

10518. Бюллетень. (Bulletin.) Glavnoe geologo-razvedochnoe upravlenie, Sredne-aziatskoe raionnoe upravlenie, 1930-

10519. Luchitskii, O. V. Гидрогеологические исследования в среднем и нижнем течении реки Сурхан-Дарьи. (Hydro-geological explorations in the central and lower currents of the river Surkhan-Daria.) Samarkand, 1935. 63 p.

1520. Burachek, A. (ed.) К геологии Восточного Памира. (Contributions to the geology of Western Pamir.) Collected articles. Tadjik-Pamir expedition of 1933. Leningrad, 1935. 140 p.

VIII. GEOGRAPHY AND CARTOGRAPHY

See 148-161.

A. Bibliography

See 148.

10521. Belkin and Trirogov. Систематический указатель всех изданий Восточно-сибирского отдела Русского географического Общества, помещенных в них статей и заметок за десятилетие 1891-1901 гг. (A systematic guide to all the publications of the East-Siberian Russian geographical society, articles and notes issued during the decade 1891-1901. Irkutsk, n.d.

10522. Обзор деятельности Забайкальского отдела Русского
географического общества и Краевого музея имени А. К. Куз-
нецова за тридцать лет, 1894-1924. (Survey of the activities
of the Transbaikal division of the Russian geographic society, 1894-1924.) Chita, 1924. 91 p.

B. Periodicals

10523. St. Petersburg. Императорское русское географическое общество. (Государственное русское географическое общество, 1917-). (Imperial Russian geographic
society [National Russian geographic society, 1917-].)
Publications: Географические известия. (Geographic bulletin.)
1848-1850. (Irregular). (2) The same. Вестник. (Bulletin.) Continues the above. 1851-1860. (3) The same. Записки. (Journal.) 1846-1859. (4) The same. Записки.
(Journal.) Continues the Bulletin [2]. 1861-1865. (5) The
same. Известия. (Bulletin.) 1865- ? ; 1924- (6) The
same. Записки по общей географии. (Journal of general
geography.) 1867-1916. (7) The same. Отчет. (Reports.)
1850- ? (8) The same. Труды. (Transactions.) 1889- ?
(9) The same. Ежегодник. (Year-book.) 1890-1899. (10)
Живая старина. (Living antiquities.) 1890-1916. (Published
by the Division of ethnography.)

10523a. Императорское Русское географическое общество. Западносибирский отдел. (Imperial Russian geographic society. West-Siberian department.) Omsk. Publications:
Записки. (Journal.) 1878-1916; 1927- (2) The same. Известия. (Bulletin.) 1913-1917. (3) The same. Отчет. (Reports.) 1880-1912(?) (4) Труды. (Transactions.) 1922-
(5) Алтайский сборник. (The Altai miscellany.) Barnaul,
Amateur society for the study of Altai (Общество любителей
исслед. Алтая), 1894-1919. (6) Императорское русское
географическое общество. Западносибирский отдел. Семипалатинский подотдел. (Imperial Russian geographic society.
West-Siberian department. Semipalatinsk subdepartment.)
Записки. (Journal.) Semipalatinsk, 1903- ? ; 1924- as:
Государственное русское географическое общество. Семипалатинский отдел. (National Russian geographic society.
Semipalatinsk department.) (7) Императорское русское географическое общество. Туркестанский отдел. (Imperial
Russian geographic society. Turkestan department.) Записки. (Journal.) Tashkent, 1898- ? (8) Сибирская
живая старина. (Siberian living antiquities.) Irkutsk,
East-Siberian department of the Imperial Russian geographic society, 1, 1923-

10524. Императорское русское географическое общество. Сибирский отдел. (Восточносибирский отдел, 1877-   ). [Госу-
дарственное русское географическое общество,1917-].
(Imperial Russian geographic society. Siberian department.
[East-Siberian department, 1877-   ].[National Russian geographic society, 1917-   ].) Записки. (Journal.) St. Petersburg, 1856-1862; Irkutsk, 1863-1876,   1877-1885; 1886-
1896 in 3 series: general geography, statistics, and ethnography. Continued as: (2) Труды. (Transactions...) Irkutsk, 1897- ? (3) Известия.   (Bulletin.) Irkutsk, 1870-
1876; 1877-   (4) Отчет.   (Reports.) St. Petersburg,
1856-1862; Irkutsk, 1863- ?   (5) Этнографический бюллетень. (Ethnographic bulletin.) Irkutsk, 1922-1923.   Continued as: Бюллетень. (Bulletin.) Irkutsk, 1924-   (6)
И.Р.Г.О. Восточносибирский отдел. Красноярский подотдел. (Г.
Р.Г.О. Среднесибирский отдел.)   (I.R.G.S. East-Siberian
department. Krasnoiarsk subdepartment. [Central-Siberian
department, 1922(?)-   ].) Записки.   (Journal.) Krasnoiarsk,
1903-1914. (7) The same. Известия.   (Bulletin.) Krasnoiarsk, 1901-1915; 1922-   (8) И.Р.Г.О. Восточносибирский
отдел. Якутский подотдел.(Г.Р.Г.О. Якутский отдел.)
(I.R.G.S. East-Siberian department. Yakutsk subdepartment.
[Nat. R. G. S. Yakutsk department.].) Известия. (Bulletin.)
Yakutsk, 1915- ? ; 1928-   (9) И.Р.Г.О. Приамурский отдел.
(Г.Р.Г.О. Дальневосточный отдел.)   (I.R.G.S. Amur department. [Nat.R.G.S. Far Eastern department, 1922-   ].)
Записки. (Journal.) Khabarovsk, 1888- ? ; 1922-   (10) The
same. Труды. (Transactions.) Khabarovsk, 1895-   (11) Общество изучения Амурского края. (И.Р.Г.О. Приамурский отдел.
Владивостокское отделение. Г.Р.Г.О. Владивостокский отдел.
(Society for the study of the Amur region. [I.R.G.S. Amur
department. Vladivostok division.] [Nat.R.G.S. Vladivostok
department.].) Записки. (Journal.) Vladivostok, 1888- ?
(12)   The same. Отчет. (Report.) Vladivostok. (Annually).
(13) И.Р.Г.О. Приам. отд. Троицкосавско-кяхтинское отделение.(I.R.G.S. Amur dept. Troitskosavsk-Kiakhta division.) Протоколы. (Protocols.) 1894- ? (14) The same. Труды. (Transactions.) 1898-   (15) И.Р.Г.О. Приамурский отдел. Читин-
ское отделение. (I.R.G.S. Amur department. Chita division.)
Записки. (Journal.) 1896.   (16) Г.Р.Г.О. Южноуссурийский
отдел. (Nat.R.G.S. South-Ussuri department.) Известия.
(Bulletin.) 1922-   (17) The same. Записки. (Journal) 1924-

C. Cartography

See 149-164; 1240-1267.

(1) Atlases and collections

10525. Большой всемирный настольный атлас Маркса. (The great
world atlas of Marks.) St. Petersburg, 1905.

10526. Большой советский атлас мира. (The great Soviet world atlas.) Ed. by V. E. Motylev. Moscow, TsIK, 1938-

10527. Атлас Союза советских социалистических республик. (Atlas of the USSR.) Moscow, TsIK, 1928. 108 p.

10528. Kordt, V. P. Материалы по истории русской картографии. (Sources pertaining to the history of Russian cartography.) Kiev, 1899; 2nd series, 1906; 3rd series, 1910.

10529. Atlas russicus. (Text in Latin and French). St. Petersburg, Imperial academy of sciences, 1745.

10530. Материалы для историко-географического атласа России. (Sources for a historico-geographical atlas of Russia.) St. Petersburg, Archeographical commission, 1871.

10531. Bagrov, S. L. Карты Азиатской России. (Maps of Asiatic Russia.) Petrograd, 1914.

10532. Cahen, G. Les cartes de la Sibérie au XVIII-e siècle. Nouv. arch. des missions scientifiques et littéraires. Nouv. série. Paris, 1911. 544 p.

10533. Чертежная карта Сибири Семена Ремезова. (Ancient map of Siberia by Semen Remezov.) Ed. by the Archeographical commission. St. Petersburg, 1882.

10534. Grigoriev, A. V. "Подлинная карта Сибири XVIII в." (An authentic map of Siberia of the XVII century.) Zhurnal Ministerstva narodnogo prosveshcheniia, 11(1907):374-381.

10535. Nordenskiöld, N. A. E. Den Första pa verklige jakttagelser grundade karte öfver norra Asien. Stockholm. Ymer, VII: 1887: 133-144. (The Godunov map of Siberia [1667] with reproductions of it from MS. copies made by Cronman and Prutz [1669].)

10536. Kudriashev, K. V. Русский исторический атлас. (Russian historical atlas.) Moscow-Leningrad, Gosizdat, 1928. 18 maps.

(2) Geological

10537. Геологическая карта Азиатской России. (Carte géologique de la Russie d'Asie.) Scale 1:10,500,000. Petrograd, 1922. Also 1924. Also: Carte géologique de la partie asiatique de l'USSR. Scale 1:2,100,000. Leningrad, 1927.

10538. Frederiks, G. N. Геологическая карта Урала. (Geological map of the Urals.) 1:200,000. Moscow-Leningrad, 1931.

(3) General Maps

10539. **Карта** Азиатской России с прилегающими к ней владениями. (A map of Asiatic Russia and its adjacent territories.) Compiled by the military topographical department of the General staff (1884). Scale 100 versts per inch. St. Petersburg, 1910-1911.

10540. Карта путей сообщения Азиатской России. (A map of road communications of Asiatic Russia.) Izd. Otdela statist. i kartograf. Ministerstva putei soobshcheniia, 1911. St. Petersburg. Scale: 100 versts per inch.

10541. Военно-дорожная карта Азиатской России.(A map of military roads of Asiatic Russia.) Compiled in 1895 by the military topographical department of the General staff. Scale: 50 versts per inch. 1912.

10542. Серия географических карт СССР по зонам. (Series of geographic maps of the USSR according to zones.) Explanatory texts. Moscow, 1936.

10543. Союз Советских Социалистических Республик. (The Union of Soviet Socialist Republics.) Leningrad, 1924.

10544. Административная карта СССР. Европейская часть. Экономическое районирование по проэкту Госплана. (A map of adminitrative districts of the USSR. European part. Economic zoning according to the project of the State planning commission.) Leningrad, 1924. Published by the Commissariat of internal affairs.

10545. Административная карта СССР. Азиатская часть. (Administrative map of the USSR. Asiatic part.) Leningrad, Narodnyi komissariat vnutrennikh del, 1925.

10546. Сводная карта народного хозяйства СССР. (Collated map of the national economy of the USSR.) Moscow, Plankhozgiz, 1932.

(4) Special Maps

10547. Konogorov, P. F. Картография Северной Азии. (Cartography of Northern Asia.1917-1927.) Bibliographical guide. Moscow, 1928. 78 p.

10548. Tornau, N. N. Атлас к отечествоведению. (A national atlas.) Part 2. Siberia and Turkestan. St. Petersburg, 1906.

10549. Примерная карта установленных границ новых образований в Средней Азии. (A map of the newly established boundaries in Central Asia.) Tashkent, 1924.

10550. Карта Западной Сибири. (A map of Western Siberia.) Conpiled by V. P. Semenov-Tian-Shanskii. Scale 100 versts per inch. Supplement to "Russia. A complete geographical description of our fatherland." v. 16. St. Petersburg, A.F. Devrien, n.d.

10551. Карта Иркутской губернии. (Map of the Irkutsk guberniia. Scale: 50 versts per inch.

10552. Карта Забайкальской области. (A map of the Transbaikal province.) Sostavlena Mezhevym otdeleniem Voiskovogo khoziaistvennogo pravleniia Zabaikal'skogo kazach'ego voiska, 1909. Scale: 20 versts per incn.

10553. Doi, Shozo. Ro-ryo enkai shu oyobi setsujo chiho zu. 嘉領沿海州及接壌地方圖 (Map of Russian coastal provinces and adjacent territories.) 1:2 000 000. Dairen, S. M. R. R., 1923.

10554. Dal'ne-vostochnoe oblastnoe ekonomicheskoe soveshchanie. Карта Дальне-восточной области (Приморской, Амурской и Забайкальской губерний) и сопределенных территорий Я. А. С.С.Р., Б.М.А.С.С.Р., Монголии и Северной Манчжурии, с приложением карты Камчатки. (A map of the Far Eastern province (Coastal territory, Amur, and Transbaikal guberniia) and adjacent territories of Yakutia, Buriat - Mongolia, Northern Manchuria and Kamchatka.) Khabarovsk, 1925.

10555. Upravlenie vnutrennikh vodnykh putei Sibiri. Сплавная карта р. Олекмы. Порожистая часть от р. Хани до р. Енюка. (A nautical map of the Olekma river. The rapids between the river Khani to Eniuk.) Irkutsk, 1924.

10556. Upravlenie vnutrennikh vodnykh putei Sibiri. Навигационная карта р. Лены от устья р. Витима до р. Якутска. (A nautical map of the Lena river from the mouth of the river Vitim to the river Yakutsk.) Irkutsk, 1924.

D. History

10557. Berg, L. S. Очерк истории русской географической науки. (A sketch of the history of Russian geographical science.) Leningrad, Academy of sciences, 1929.

10558. Semenov, P. P. История полувековой деятельности
Императорского русского географического общества, 1845-1895.
(History of activity of the Imperial Russian geographical
society, 1845-1895.) St. Petersburg, 1896. 3 v.

10559. Kaulbars, Baron Nicolas. Société impériale russe de
géographie. Aperçu des travaux géographiques en Russie.
St. Petersburg, Trenké et Fusnot, 1889. iv, 292 p.

E. General Accounts

10560. Mikhailov, Nicolas. La nouvelle géographie de l'U.S.
S.R. Paris, 1936.

10561. MacKinder, Sir H. S. Soviet geography. The new industrial and economic distributions of the USSR. London,
Methuen & co., 1935. 232 p. 38 maps.

10562. Berg, L. Устройство поверхности Азиатской России.
(Structure of the surface of Asiatic Russia.) St. Petersburg, 1914.

10563. Berg, L. S. Физико-географические зоны С.С.С.Р.
(Physical-geographical zones of the USSR.) Leningrad, 1936.
427 p.

10564. Berg, L. S. Ландшафтно-геогр. зоны СССР. (Structural
-geographical zones of the USSR.) Leningrad, Vsesoiuznaia
akademiia sel'skokhoziaistvennykh nauk imeni Lenina, Institut rastenievodstva, 1930.

10565. Oyama, Takeo. 露領極東地誌 Ro-ryo kyokuto
chishi. (Geography of Russia in the Far East.) Dairen,
S.M.R.R., 1927. 2 v.   (Uchiyama, Peteru co-author ?)

10566. Abramov, N. A.   Очерк Березовского края.
(A description of the Berezovsk region.) St. Petersburg,
1857.

10567. Savitsky, P. N. "Из прошлого русской географии:
периодизация русских географических открытий."   (From the
past of Russian geography: the periodization of Russian geographic discoveries.) Nauchnye trudy Narodnogo univesiteta,
Praha, 4, 1931.

10568. Savitskii, P. N. Географические особенности России.
(Geographical peculiarities of Russia.) Evraziiskoe knigoizdatel'stvo, 1927. 180 p.

10569. Краеведение. (Regional geography.) Moscow, TSentral'-
noe biuro kraevedeniia, 1924-1929.

10570. Вопросы географии и картографии. (Problems pertaining to geography and cartography.) Moscow, 1936. 377 p.

10571. Schultz, A. Sibirien, eine landeskunde. Breslau, F.
Hirt, 1923. 212 p.

10572. Россия. Полное географическое описание нашего отечества. (Russia. A complete geographical description of our
fatherland.) Vol. XVI. Западная Сибирь. (Western Siberia.)
St. Petersburg, 1907. Vol. XVIII. Киргизский край.
(The Kirghiz province.) St. Petersburg, 1903. Vol. XIX.
Туркестанский край. (Turkestan province.) St. Petersburg,
1913.

F. By Regions

10573. Semenov, P. P. La Russie extra-européenne et polaire.
Sibérie, Caucase, Asie centrale, Extrême Nord. Paris, 1900.
242 p.

10574. Stakheev, D. Байкал. (Baikal.) In: Sbornik "Zhivopisnaia Rossiia". (Under the general edit. of P.P.Semenov.)
12:1, St. Petersburg, 1895.

10575. Prasolov, L. Южное Забайкалье. (Southern Transbaikal.)
Izd. Akademii nauk, Leningrad, 1929. 131 p.

10576. Kaulbars, A. Материалы по географии Тянь-шаня.
(Sources pertaining to the geography of Tian-shan.) Zapiski
Imperatorskogo Russkogo geograficheskogo obshchestva po ob-
shchei geografii, 5 (1875).

10577. Kropotkin, P. A. "Общий очерк орографии Восточной
Сибири." (A general sketch of the orography of Eastern
Siberia.) Zapiski Russkogo geograficheskogo obshchestva, 5
(1875): 1-91.

10578. Труды комиссии по изучению озера Байкала. (Publications of the Commission for the study of Lake Baikal.) St.
Petersburg, Akademiia nauk, 1918-1930. 3 v.

10579. Arseniev, V. K. В горах Сихотэ-Алиня. (In the mount-
ains of Sihote-Alin.) A sketch of the expedition of the
Amur   division of the Russian geographical society, from
June 24, 1908 to January 20, 1910.) Moscow, 1937. 273 p.

G. Rivers

10580. Rodevich, V. M. (ed.) Исследование рек СССР.   (A study of rivers of the USSR.) Leningrad, No. 8, 1936. 216 p.

10581. Molodykh, I. F. Водные пути Восточной Сибири. (Water routes of Eastern Siberia.) Irkutsk, 1926.

10582. Malyshev, V. M. and Molodykh, I. F. Исследования рек Восточной Сибири.· (River explorations of Eastern Siberia.) Irkutsk, 1924. 54 p. (2) Koriako, N. IA. Проблема рек Оби и Иртыша. (The problem of the rivers Ob and Irtysh.) Leningrad, Gidroproiz, 1937. 147 p.

10583. Cherntsov, M. Краткое описание исследования реки Ангары. (Sketch of the exploration of the Angara river.) St. Petersburg, 1899.

IX. TRAVELS AND EXPLORATIONS

See 182-223; 1346-1366.

10584. Henning, G. Die reiseberichte über Sibirien von Herberstein bis Ides.   In Verein für erdkunde, Leipzig, 1906.

10585. Alekseev, M. P. Сибирь в известиях западно-европейских путешественников и писателей.   (Siberia as described by western European travelers and writers.) Irkutsk, 1932-1936. 2 v.

10586. "Описание путешествия в Сибирь и далее в различные местности страны.   (Description of travel in Siberia and beyond in different places of the country.) Istoricheskii arkhiv, 1 (1936).

10587. Morgan, E. D. and Coote, C. H. Early voyages and travels to Russia and Persia by Anthony Jenkinson and others. (Hakluyt society). London, 1886. 2 v.

10588. Herberstein, Sigismund von. Gratae posteritati H. actiones suas reliquit. Vienna, 1560.

10589. Berg, L. S. Открытие Камчатки и экспедиции Беринга. (Discovery of Kamchatka and the Bering expeditions.) Leningrad, 1935. 412 p.

10590. Strahlenberg, P. I. von. Das nord- und ostliche theil von Europa und Asia ... Stockholm, 1730. (English translation, London 1738.)

10591. **"Академики Миллер и Фишер и описание Сибири."**
(Academicians Müller and Fischer and the description of
Siberia.) Chteniia v Imperatorskom obshchestve istorii i
drevnostei rossiiskikh pri Moskovskom universitete, 3:15-30
July-September 1866.

10592. Gmelin, J. G. von. Reise durch Sibirien 1733/43.
Göttingen, 1751-1752. 4 v.   French translations, Paris,
1767. 2 v.   (2) The same. Путешествие по России.
(Travels through Russia.) St. Petersburg, 1773-1785. 3 parts,
4 books. (3) The same. Путешествие по Сибири. Источники для
изучения Пермского края. (Travels through Siberia. Sources
pertaining to the study of the Perm region.) Perm, 1876.

10593. Bell, John. Travels from St. Petersburg in Russia to
diverse parts of Asia. Glasgow, R. & A. Foulis, 1763. 2
2 v.   Another edition, London, 1788. 2 v.

10594. Georgi, I. G. Bemerkungen einer reise in den jahren
1772-1774. St. Petersburg, 1775. 2 v.

10595. Pallas, P. S. Reise. St. Petersburg, 1771-1776.
3 v.   French translation. Paris, 1788-1793. 6 v.

10596. Billings, Jos. Reise nach Sibirien. Kamtschatka. Aus
dem englischen übersetzt. Berlin und Hamburg, 1803.

10597. **"Путешествие И. Е. Миллера из Иркутска в Нерчинск,**
в августе 1811 г., им самим описанное."   (Journey of I.E.
Müller from Irkutsk to Nerchinsk in August 1811, described
by himself.) Dukh zhurnalov, 13 (1816):28:67-72; 29:97-102;
30:161-168;31:205-214.

10598. Klaproth, Jul. von. Reise durch Russland und Sibirien
nach der Mongolischen Tartarei. Tübingen, Gotta, 1815.

10599. Martynov, A. Живописное путешествие от Москвы до
китайской границы. (A picturesque journey from Moscow to
the Chinese boundary.) St. Petersburg, 1819. 67 p.

10600. Cochrane, Captain John Dundas. Narrative of a pedes-
trian journey through Russia and Siberian Tartary, from the
frontiers of China to the frozen sea and Kamchatka; per-
formed during the years 1820, 1821, 1822, and 1823. London,
Murray, 1824. 564 p.

10601. Fal'k, I. Полное собрание ученых путешествий по
России. (Full collection of scientific travels in Russia.)
St. Petersburg, 1824. 6 v.

10602. Martos, A. **Письма о восточной Сибири.** (Letters on
eastern Siberia.) Moscow, 1827. 291 p.

10603. Ledebour, Carl F. Reise durch das Altai-gebirge und
die soongorische Kirgisensteppe. Berlin, 1829-1830. 2 v.

10604. Soloviev, M. M. Ученая экспедиция в Бухару в 1841-
1842 гг. (The scientific expedition to Bokhara in 1841-1842)
Moscow, Academy of sciences, 1936. 216 p.

10605. Shchukin, Nikolai S. Поездка в Якутск. (A journey to
Yakutsk.) 2nd edition. St. Petersburg, 1844. 315 p.

10606. Middendorff, A. T. von. Reise in den äussersten
norden u. osten Sibiriens, 1843-1844. St. Petersburg, 1847-
1874. 4 v.   (2) The same. Sibirische reise. St. Petersburg, 1859. 2 v.   (3) The same. Путешествие на север и
восток Сибири. (A journey to the Siberian North and East.)
St. Petersburg, 1860-1878. 2 parts. (4) The same. Бараба.
(Baraba [Siberia].) St. Petersburg, 1871. 122 p.

10607. Erman, Adolph. Travels in Siberia. Including excursions northwards, down the Obi, to the Polar circle, and
southwards to the Chinese frontier by Adolph Erman, translated from the German, by William Desborough. Cooley. London,
Longman, 1848. 2 v.

10608. 10608. Castrén, M. A. Reiseberichte und briefe aus
den jahren 1845-1849. St. Petersburg, 1856.

10609. Bulychev, I. D. Путешествие по Восточной Сибири. (A
journey through Eastern Siberia.) St. Petersburg, 1856.
3 v.

10610. Atkinson, Thomas Witlam. Oriental and western Siberia: a narrative of seven years of explorations and adventures in Siberia, Mongolia, the Kirghis steppes, Chinese
Tartary, and part of Central Asia. London, Hurst and Blackett, 1858. xii, 611 p. (2) The same. Travels in the regions of the upper and lower Amoor and the Russian acquisitions on the confines of India China. With adventures among
the Mountain Kirghis; and the Manjours, Manyars, Toungouz,
Touzemts, Goldi, and Gelyaks: the hunting and pastoral
tribes. London, Hurst & Blacklett, 1860. xiii, 553 p.

10611. Maak, R. Путешествие на Амур в 1855 г. (A journey to
the Amur in 1855.) St. Petersburg, 1859. (2) The same.
Путешествие по долине реки Уссури. (A journey through the
Ussuri river valley.) St. Petersburg, 1861. 2 v.

10612. Collins, MacDonough, Perry. A voyage down the Amour
with a land journey through Siberia and incidental notices
of Manchooria, Kamschatka, and Japan. New York, Appleton &
co., 1860.

10613. Radde, Gustav F. R. Reisen im Süden von Ost-Sibirien
in den jahren 1855-1859. St. Petersburg, 1862. 2 vols.

10614. Etsel and Wagner. Путешественники по Сибири: Мид-
дендорф, Радде и др. (Travelers in Siberia: Middendorff,
Radde, and other.) St. Petersburg, 1865.

10615. Schrenk, Leopold von. Reisen und forschungen im
Amur lande in den jahre 1854-1856. St. Petersburg, 1858-
1860, 1877.

10616. Michi, A. Путешествие по Амуру и Восточной Сибири А.
Мичи. (The journey through the Amur and Eastern Siberia by
A. Michi.) Translated from the German. St. Petersburg,
1868. 351 p.

10617. Stakheev., D. I. За Байкалом и на Амуре. (Beyond the
Baikal and on the Amur.) St. Petersburg, 1869. 347 p.

10618. Przheval'skii, N. M. Путешествие в Уссурийском крае
1866-1869 гг.(A journey through the Ussuriisk region 1866-
1869.) St. Petersburg, 1870. (2) The same. Уссурийский
край. Новая территория России. (The Ussuriisk region. The
new Russian territory.) Vestnik Evropy, 5, May 1870.

10619. Veniukov, M. Путешествия по окраинам Русской Азии и
записки о них. (Travels through the borderlands of Russian
Asia and memoirs on them.) St. Petersburg, 1868. 526 p.

10620. Poliakov, I. Письма и отчеты о путешествии в долину
р. Оби. (Letters and reports of a journey to the Ob valley.)
St. Petersburg, 1877.

10621. Bunge, Al. Naturhistorische beobachtungen. Fahrten in
Lena-delta. Bull. Acad. Sc., St. Petersburg, 29, 1884.
(2) The same. Bericht über fernere fahrten im Lena-delta.
Bull. Acad. Sc., St. Petersburg, 30, 1885-1886. (3) The
same. Berichte über die von der K. Akademie der wissenschaften ausgerüstete expedition nach den Neusibirischen
inseln und dem Jana-lande. Beiträge z. Kennt. des Russ.
reich. 3, 1887.

10622. Sorokin, N. Путешествие по русскому Тянь-шаню в 1884 г. (Journey through the Russian Tian-shan in 1884.) Izvestiia Imperatorskogo russkogo geograficheskogo obshchestva, 21, 1885.

10623. Miu, Yu-sun. 俄 遊 集 編 (Travel notes on Russia.) 1889. 4 v.

10624. Radloff, Wilhelm. Aus Sibirien. Löse blätter aus dem tagebuche eines reisenden linguisten. Leipzig, Weigel, 1893. 2 vols. in 1.

10625. Semenov, V. I. Забытый путь из Европы в Сибирь: Енисейская экспедиция 1893 года. (A forgotten route Europe to Siberia: the Yenisei expedition of 1893.) St. Petersburg, 1894. 185 p.

10626. Katanov, N. F. Отчет о поездке совершенной с 15 мая по 1 сент. 1896 г. в Минусинский округ, Енисейской губернии. (Report on an expedition from May 15 to September 1, 1896, in the Minusinsk district of the Yeniseisk guberniia.) Kazan, 1897.

10627. Diudlov, V. L. Через Сибирь. (Through Siberia.) n.p., 1900.

10628. Stadling, J. Through Siberia. Westminister, A. Constable & co., 1901. 315 p.

10629. Arseniev, V. K. Дерсу Узала. Повесть об экспедиции в Уссурийский край в 1907 г. (Dersu Uzala. The story of the expedition to the Ussuriisk region in 1907.) 3d edition, revised. Moscow, 1936. 284 p.

10630. Murov, G. I. По русскому Дальнему Востоку. (In the Russian Far East.) Moscow, 1909, 1911. 2 vols.

10631. Nansen, Fridtjof. Gjennem Sibirien. (Through Siberia) Kristiania, 1914. 386 p. (2) English translation, London, 1914.

10632. Voitinskii, Vl. and Gornshtein, A. В тайге по Сибири. (In the taiga through Siberia.) Petrograd, "Kniga", 1917. 178 p.

10633. Chiang, Hang-hu. 新 俄 遊 記 Hsin-O yu-chi. (A trip through Russia.) 1923

10634. Ch'ü, Ch'iu-pai. 新 俄 國 遊 記 Hsin O-kuo yu-chi. (Notes of a tour in Soviet Russia.) Shanghai, Commercial press, 1923. 131 p.

10635. Gorodkov, B. N. Западно-Сибирская экспедиция Российской академии наук и Русского географического общества. (The West-Siberian expedition of the Russian academy of science and the Russian geographical society.) Leningrad, 1924.

10636. Sementovskii, V. Экскурсия на Урал. (An excursion to the Ural.) Moscow, 1926. 72 p.

10637. Kao, Têng-yüan. 赤 俄 遊 記 Ch'ih-O yu-chi. (A trip to red Russia.) Shanghai, Min-shih Book store, 1928.

10638. Karger, N. and Koz'minskii, I. Гарино-Амгунская экспедиция 1926 г. (The Garin-Amgunsk expedition of 1926.) Leningrad, Akademiia nauk, 1929. 48 p.

10639. Arseniev, Vladimir K. Сквозь тайгу. (Through the taiga.) A travel diary of the expedition from Sovetskaia gavan' to Khabarovsk. Moscow, 1930. 195 p.

10640. Hu, Yü-chih. 莫 斯 科 印 象 記 Mo-szu-k'o yin-hsiang chi. (Impressions of Moscow.) Shanghai, 1931.

10641. Severin, N. A. По Абакану. С Алтая на Енисей. (Through Abakan. From Altai to the Yenisei.) Moscow, 1931. 88 p.

10642. Vadkovskaia, IU. Путешествие по Алтаю. (Travel in the Altai.) Moscow, 1931. 38 p.

10643. Tsao, Ku-ping. 蘇 俄 視 察 記 Su-O shih-cha chi. (An account of a trip of investigation to Soviet Russia.) Tientsin, Ta-kung daily press, 1931.

10644. Rubin, A. M. "Нижне-Тунгусская экспедиция Академии Наук СССР в 1932 г." (Expedition of the Academy of sciences of the USSR to the Lower Tunguska in 1932.) Doklady Akademii nauk SSSR-A, 15 (1932):369-373.

10645. Ting, Han-min. 新 俄 羅 斯 考 查 記 Hsin O-lo-szu kao-cha chi. (Notes on a visit to new Russia.) Peiping, Lu-chun-ta-hsueh, 1932 ?

10646. Экспедиции Всесоюзной академии наук 1932 г. (Expeditions of the All-Union academy of sciences in 1932.) Leningrad, 1933. 352 p. (Published by the Academy of sciences.)

10647. Экспедиции Академии наук СССР 1934 г. Сборник статей,
(Expeditions of the Academy of sciences of the USSR of 1934.
Collected articles.) Second revised and enlarged edition.
Moscow, 1936. 508 p. [Practically the entire material deals
with Siberia and the Arctic.]

10648. Кулундинская экспедиция Академии наук СССР. (Kulun-
dinsk expedition of the Academy of sciences of the USSR.)
1931-1933. Leningrad, 1934. 225 p.

10649. Polikashin, A. I. Советская Печора.   (Soviet Pechora.) Travel sketches. 2nd edition. Archangel, 1935.
181 p.

10650. Якутская экспедиция Академии наук СССР. (Yakutsk
expedition of the Academy of sciences of the USSR.) Moscow,
Academy of sciences, 1936. 23 p.

10651. Krylenko, N. V. Пять лет по Памиру. Итоги Памирских
экспедиции 1928-1933 гг. (Five years through the Pamir. Summaries of the expeditions of 1928-1933.) Moscow, 1935.
326 p.   (2) Таджикско-Памирская экспедиция 1933 г. (Tadjik-
Pamir expedition of 1933.) Reports and accounts. Leningrad,
1934. 523 p.   (3) Таджикско-Памирская экспедиция 1934 г.
Итоги работ. (Tadjik-Pamir expedition of 1934. Summaries
of the work.) Ed. by A. E. Fersman, N. P. Gorbunov, and
others. Moscow, Academy of Sciences, 1935. 504 p.   (4)
Памир. Северный Памир и ледник Федченко. Сборник статей.
(Pamir. Northern Pamir and the glacier Fedchenko. Collected
articles.) Leningrad, 1936. xxxvii, 485 p.   (5) Arkhangel'skii, A. D. (editor). Научные итоги работ Таджикско-
Памирской экспедиции. Сборник статей. (Scientific summaries of the work completed by the Tadzhik-Pamir expedition.)
Collected articles. Moscow, 1936. 563 p.

X. RUSSIAN STUDIES ON ASIA AND THE ORIENT

See 224-255; 1145-1161.

10652. Bartold, V. V. История изучения Востока в Европе и
в России. (The history of study of the Orient in Europe and
in Russia.) 2nd edition. Leningrad, 1925. viii, 318 p.

10653. "Список статей по востоковедению в 'Изв. Росс. Акад.
наук' за 1895-1917."(A list of articles on Oriental studies,
1895-1917.) Aziatskii sbornik, 1918, 3-15.

10654. Востоковедение в Петрограде,   1918-1922. (Study of
the Orient in Petrograd, 1918-1922.) Petrograd, 1923. 89 p.

10655. Pekarskii, Petr P. История Императорской академии
наук в Петербурге. (History of the Imperial academy of sciences in St. Petersburg.) St. Petersburg, 1870-1873. 2 v.

10656. Struve, V. V., Muratov, KH. I. and Kalianov, V. I.
"Институт востоковедения." (The Institute of Oriental studies.) Vestnik Akademii nauk SSSR, 10-11 (1930):266-279.

10657. Pavlovich, M. (Vel'tman). "Академия наук и востоковедения." (The Academy of sciences and the study of the Orient.) Novyi Vostok, 10-11 (1925):212-215.

10658. Kniazev, G. A. (editor). Архив Академии наук.
(Archives of the Academy of sciences.) A survey of the archival materials. Leningrad, 1933. 259 p.

10659. Вестник Академии наук СССР. (Review of the Academy
of sciences of the USSR.) Edited by N. P. Gorbunov. 1, 1931-
(Monthly).

10660. Kozin, S. A. "Азиатский архив при Институте востоковедения Академии наук СССР. Краткий обзор материалов."
(Asiatic archives at the Institute of Oriental studies of
the Academy of sciences. Brief survey of sources.) Bibliografiia Vostoka (Leningrad), 5-6 (1934):56-66.

10661. Akademiia nauk SSSR. Institut-vostokovedeniia. Leningrad-Moscow. Записки.(Memoirs.) 1, 1932- (2) The same.
Труды.(Transactions.) 1, 1932- (3) Библиография Востока.
(Bibliography of the Orient.) 1, 1932- (4) Отдельные издания. (Separate publications.) 1932- (8 to 1937).

10662. Казанские известия. (Kazan news.) Kazan, 1811-1820.
(2) Казанский вестник.   (The Kazan messenger.) Kazan, Kazan university, 1821-1833. (Monthly). (3) Ученые записки,
издав. Импер. казанским университетом. (Scientific memoirs,
published by the Imperial Kazan university.) 1834-1861.
(Quarterly).. (4) Ученые записки Императорского казанского
университета по отделению историко-филологических и поли-
тико-юридических наук. (Scientific memoirs of the Imperial
Kazan university.) 1862-1864. (Semi-yearly). (5) Известия
и ученые записки Императорского казанского университета.
(Publications and scientific memoirs of the Imperial Kazan
university.) 1865-1883-1884. (Bi-monthly).   (6) Ученые
записки Импер. казанского университета (по факультетам).
(Scientific memoirs of the Imperial Kazan university.)
1884-1889.   (7) Ученые записки Императорского казанского
университета. (Scientific memoirs of the Imperial Kazan
university.) 1890-

10663. Протоколы заседаний конференций Восточного института
(Protocols of the sessions of the Oriental institute's conferences.) Vladivostok, 1907-1913. 6 v.

10664. Восточный институт в г. Владивостоке. (The Oriental
institute in Vladivostok.) Vladivostok, 1909. 58, lxxxii p.

10665. Известия Харбинского отделения Императорского общества востоковедения под ред. А. М. Баранова. (Publications of the Harbin branch of the Imperial society of Oriental studies.) Harbin, 1910. 180 p. (No more published).

10666. Записки Приамурского отдела Императорского Общества
востоковедения. (Memoirs of the Amur branch of the Imperial society of Oriental studies.) Edited by L. G. Ul'-
ianitskii. Khabarovsk.

10667. Доклады группы востоковедов на сессии Академии наук
СССР. (Reports of a group of orientalists at the session of
the Academy of sciences of the USSR.) March 20, 1935. Published in Moscow, 1936. 198 p.

10668. Veselovskii, N. Сведения об оффициальном преподава-
нии восточных языков в России. (Information concerning the
official teaching of Oriental languages in Russia.) St.
Petersburg, 1879. 162 p.

10669. Reby, J. "L'enseignement des langues orientales en
Russie." Revue du monde musulman, 10:357-380, Mar. 1910.

10670. Восточные заметки. (Oriental sketches.) Articles by
Prof. Vasiliev, Marr, Khvol'son, Zhukovskii, Pozdneev and
others. St. Petersburg, 1895.

10671. Ignatiev, S. I. "Наши востоковеды. (По поводу возникновения нового Общества ориенталистов в С. Петербурге.)"
(Our orientalists.) Istoricheskii vestnik, 603-613, August
1910.

10672. Ch'i-shui. 蘇俄的中國研究與東方雜誌
Su-O ti Chung-kuo yen-chiu yü Tung-fang-tsa-chih. (Sino-
logical study in Soviet Russia and the Eastern miscellany.)
Eastern miscellany, 22:7:24-31, April 1925.

10673. Oldenburg, Serge. "Les études orientale dans l'Union
des republiques soviétiques." Journal asiatique, 215 (1929):
117-139.

10674. Grebenshchikov, A. V. Программа преподавания в Восточном институте по предметам маньчжурской словесности, административного устройства Маньчжурии и торгово-промышленной деятельности и быта Маньчжурии. (The program of teaching in the Oriental institute...) Vladivostok, 1912. 12 p.

10675. Kiuner, N. V. Дальний Восток и Приамурский край за минувшие 20 лет в связи с развитием деятельности Восточного института. (The Far East and the Amur province for the last twenty years in their relation to the activities of the Oriental institute.) Vladivostok, 1920. 38 p.

10676. Matveev, Z. N. "История Восточной Азии как предмет изучения и преподавания." (History of Eastern Asia as a subject of study and teaching.) Biulleten' Obshchestva vostokovedeniia, Vladivostok, 1-2 (1929):54-68.

10677. Karakhan, L. "Задачи востоковедения." (The problems of Oriental studies.) Novyi Vostok, 7 (1925):3-4.

10678. Khodorov, A. E. "M. H. Покровский и изучение Дальнего Востока." (M. N. Pokrovskii and the study of the Far East.) Novyi Vostok, Moscow, 25 (1929):1-28. (2) Gurko-Kriajin, V. "M. H. Покровский и изучение истории Востока. (M. N. Pokrovskii and the study of the history of the Orient.) Novyi Vostok, Moscow, 25 (1929):29-46.

10679. Pavlovich, M. (Vel'tman). "Задачи Всероссийской научной ассоциации востоковедения." (Problems of the All-Russian scientific association for the study of the Orient.) Novyi Vostok, 1 (1922):3-15.

10680. "Пятилетие Института востоковедения им. тов. Нариманова." (The fifth anniversary of the Oriental institute established in honor of comrade Narimanov.) Novyi Vostok, 10-11 (1925):367-369.

10681. Borozdin, I. N. "Изучение Востока в современной России." (Study of the Orient in contemporary Russia.) Kolonial'nyi Vostok, 1924:343-353.

10682. Pavlovich, M. (Vel'tman). "История и задачи новых востоковедных вузов." (The history and problems of the new colleges of Oriental studies.) Novyi Vostok, 10-11 (1925): 3-11.

10683. Деятельность Общества изучения советской Азии в 1932 г. (Activity of the Society for the study of Soviet Asia in 1932.) Moscow, Sovetskaia Aziia, 1933. 50 p.

10684. Наука и научные работники СССР. (Science and scientists of the USSR.) Moscow, 1925- (Vols. 2,4,6 of the series had appeared to 1928.)

10685. Geier. Центральный институт востоковедения.   (The Central institute for Oriental studies.) Novyi Vostok, 5 (1924):457-458.

10686. Азиатский сборник. (Mélanges asiatiques.) In Izvestiia Rossiiskoi akademii nauk, Petrograd, 1918. xv, 2310 p.

10687. Азиатский музей Российской академии наук. (The Asiatic museum of the Russian academy of sciences.) 1818-1918. Petrograd, 1920. 115 p.

XI. ARCHAEOLOGY (SIBERIAN)

See 256-259; 1367-1378; 4852-4855; 6568-6684;6942-6953; 7145-7148.

A. Periodicals

10688. Материалы по археологии.   (Materials on archaeology of Russia.) St. Petersburg, Arkheologicheskaia komissiia, 1866-1918. 37 v.

10689. Известия Археологической комиссии.(Publications of the Archaeological comission.) Petrograd, 1915-1917. Supplements to nos. 58, 59, 63, and 64.

10690."Протоколы заседаний Восточного отдела Русского археологического общества за 1916 г." (Protocols of the meetings of the Oriental division of the Russian archaeological society for the year 1916.) In Zapiski Vostochnogo otdeleniia Russkogo arkheologicheskogo obshchestva. 24 (1917):1-29.

10691. Ежегодник Государственного музея имени Н.М. Мартьянова в г. Минусинске. (A year-book of the Minusinsk state museum.) Minusinsk, 2:3 (1924). 107 p.

10692. Труды Восточного отделения Императорского русского археологического общества. (Transactions of the Oriental division of the Imperial Russian archaeological society.) St. Petersburg, 1855- ? (Irregularly.) (2) Rozen, V.A. (editor). Записки Восточного отделения Императорского Русского археологического общества.(Memoirs of the Eastern division of the Imperial Russian archaeological society.) 1866- ?

10693. Советская археология. (Soviet archaeology.) Published by the Academy of sciences of the USSR, Institute of anthropology, archaeology and ethnography. Moscow, 1937-

B. History

10694. Veselovskii, N. I. История Императорского русского археологического общества. (History of the Imperial Russian archaeological society.) St. Petersburg; 1900. 514 p.

C. General Accounts

10695. Древности восточные. (Oriental antiquities.) In Trudy Vostochnoi komissii Moskovskogo arkheologicheskogo obshchestva, Moscow, 1889-1915. 5 v.

10696. Pervukhin, A. Материалы по археологии восточных губерний России. (Materials for the archaeology of the eastern provinces of Russia.) Moscow, 1896.

10697. Tallgren, A. M. "Die russische und asiatische archäologischen sammlungen in Nationalmuseum Finnlands." Eurasia septentrionalis antiqua, 3 (1928).

10698. Uvarov, Count A. Археология России. (Archaeology of Russia.) Moscow, 1881.

10699. Katanov, N. F. Восточная хронология. (An Oriental chronology.) In Izvestiia Severo-vostochnogo arkheologicheskogo i etnograficheskogo instituta v Kazani (Kazan), 1 (1920):133-239.

10700. Minns, Ellis H. Scythians and Greeks. A survey of ancient history and archaeology on the north coast of the Euxine from the Danube to the Caucasus. Cambridge, 1913. 720 p. (2) Zolotarev, A. "The ancient culture of North Asia." American anthropologist, January 1938.

10701. Grakov, B. "Monuments de la culture scythique entre le Volga et les monts Oural." Eurasia septentrionalis antiqua, 3 (1928).

10702. Sulotskii, Alexander (Archpriest). "Исторические сведения об иконописании в Сибири." (Historical data concerning painting of holy images [ikons] in Siberia.) In Chteniia v Imperatorskom obshchestve istorii i drevnostei rossiiskikh pri Moskovskom universitete, 3:29-51, July-September 1864.

10703. Aspelin, R. De la civilisation préhistorique des
peuples permiens. In 3e Congrès internat. des orientalistes.
Leide, 1878.

10704. Tallgren, A. M. "Permian studies 1-3." Eurasia septentrionalis antiqua, 3 (1928).

10705. Merhart, Gero von. Bronzezeit am Jenissei. Ein beitrag urgeschichtes Sibiriens. Wien, 1926. 189 p.

10706. Radlov, V. V. Сибирские древности. (Siberian antiquities.) St. Petersburg, 1888-1892. 4 vols.

10707. Spasskii, G. I. Записки о сибирских древностях.
(Notes on Siberian antiquities.) Sibirskii vestnik, St. Petersburg, 1818. Parts 1,2,3, and 7.

10708. Aurbach and Sosnovskii. "Остатки древнейшей культуры
человека в Сибири." (Remains of ancient culture in Siberia.)
Zhizn' Sibiri, 5-6 (1924):199-219.

10709. Палеолит СССР. (Paleolith of the USSR.) Moscow,
Izvestiia Gosudarstvennoi akademii istorii material'noi
kul'tury, 1935. 118 p.

10710. Zakharov, A. "Materials on the archaeology of Siberia." Eurasia septentrionalis antiqua, 3 (1928).

10711. Montandon, George. "Craniologié paléosibérienne (Néo
lithiques, Mongoloïdes, Tschouktchi, Eskimo, Aléoutes, Kam-
tchadales, Aïnou, Ghiliak, Négroïdes du Nord.)" L'Anthropologie, 1926:209-296.

10712. Brechkevich, M. V. "Северо-восточный археологический
и этнографический институт в Казани." (The North-eastern
archaeological and ethnographical institute at Kazan.) In
Izvestiia Severo-vostochnogo arkheologicheskogo i etnograficheskogo instituta v Kazani, Kazan, 1 (1920):1-24.

10713. Klements, D. Древности Минусинского музея. (Antiquities of the Minusinsk museum.) Tomsk, 1886. 185 p.

10714. Gorodtsov, V. A. "Археологические раскопки и разведки
в Советской России 1919-1923." (Archaeological excavations
and explorations in Soviet Russia 1919-1923.) Drevnii Mir,
1, 20.

10715. Khoroshikh, P. P. Указатель литературы по археологии Иркутского края. (A guide to archaeological literature of the Irkutsk province. Irkutsk, 1924.

10716. Iokhel'son, V. I. (Jochelson, Waldemar). "Археологические исследования на Камчатке." (Archaeological explorations in Kamchatka.) Izvestiia Gosudarstvennogo russkogo geograficheskogo obshchestva, 62 (1930):3:199-242.

10717. Iosifov, G. "Археологические находки в Амурской губернии." (Archaeological discoveries in the Amur gubernia.) Vostochnaia studiia, 13-16 (1925):269-271.

10718. Sosnovskii, G. "К археологии Ангарского края." (The archaeology of Angara province.) Sibirskaia zhivaia stariia, Irkutsk, 1 (1923):121-140.

10719. Granö, I. G. Beiträge zur kenntnis des eiszeit in der nordwestlichen Mongolei und einigen ihrer südsibirischen grenzgebirge. Fennia, Helsingfors, 25 (1910):5.

10720. Oldenburg, S. F. "Русские археологические исследования в Восточном Туркестане." (Russian archaeological explorations in Eastern Turkestan.) Kaz. Muz. Vestn. 1-2 (1921):25-30.

10721. Smolin, V. F. Археологический очерк Татреспублики. (An archaeological sketch of the Tartar republic.) Kazan, 1925. 70 p.

XII. ANTHROPOLOGY (SIBERIAN)

See 260-272; 1379-1395; 4856-4869; 6487-6488; 6954-6959; 7145-7148; 7224-7228; 7474-7501.

A. Bibliography

10722. Azadovskii, Mark. "Литература по этнографии Сибири." (Siberian ethnographic literature.) Sibirskaia zhivaia starina, Irkutsk, 2(1924):191-222.

10723. Azadovskii, Mark. "Этнография в Сибири. Обзор этнографических изучений в Сибири за 1918-1925." (Ethnography in Siberia. A survey of ethnographic studies in Siberia, 1918-1925.) Severnaia Aziia, Moscow, 5-6 (1926):111-132.

B. Maps

10724. Veniukov, M. Этнографическая карта Азиатской России.
(Ethnographic map of Asiatic Russia.) St. Petersburg, 1873.

C. Periodicals

See 10523-10524.

10725. Известия Общества любителей естествознания, антропологии и этнографии. (Publications of the Society.of lovers
of natural sciences, anthropology, and ethnography.) Moscow,
Moscow university, 1866-   Also:Этнографическое обозрение.
(Ethnographic review.) Moscow, 1889-1916.   (2) Известия
Общества археологии, истории и этнографии. (Publications
of the Society of archaeology, history and ethnography.)
Kazan, Kazan university, 1878-   (3) Этнографический
сборник. (Collected articles on ethnography.) St. Petersburg, Imperatorskoe russkoe geograficheskoe obshchestvo,
1853-1864 ?   (4) Записки Отделения этнографии Русского
географического общества. (Publications of the Ethnographic
branch of the Russian geographical society.) St. Petersburg,
1867-1914. (5) Сборник.   (Collected articles.) St. Petersburg, Akademiia nauk, Muzei po antropologii i etnografii,
1900-   (6) Русский антропологический журнал. (Journal
russe anthropologique.) Moscow, 1900-   (7) Протоколы.
(Protocols.) St. Petersburg, Russkoe antropologicheskoe obshchestvo, 1888-1906 ?   (8) Ежегодник. (Year-book). St.
Petersburg, St. Petersburg university, Russkoe antropologicheskoe obshchestvo, 1905-

10726. Сибирская живая старина. (Living Siberian history.)
1923-1926. (Discontinued).   (2) Советская этнография.
(Soviet ethnography.) Published by the Academy of sciences
of the USSR. 1926- (Bi-monthly).

D. General Accounts

10727. Pypin, A. N. История русской этнографии. (History of
Russian ethnography.) Vol. 4. White Russia and Siberia.
St. Petersburg, 1892.

10728. Jochelson, Waldemar. Peoples of Asiatic Russia. New
York, American museum of natural history, 1928. 278 p.

10729. Czaplicka, M. A. Aboriginal Siberia. Clarendon press
Oxford, 1914. 374 p.

10730. Kulisher, M. I. Очерки сравнительной этнографии и
культуры. (Outlines of comparative ethography and culture.)
St. Petersburg, 1887. 287 p.

10731. Georgi, I. Описание всех в Российском государстве
обитающих народов. (A description of all the peoples living
in Russia.) St. Petersburg, 1776-1777. 2nd edtion, 1799.

10732. Rémusat, J. P. Abel. Recherches sur les langues tar-
tares. Paris, 1820.

10733. Radlov, Vasilii Vasilievich. Briefe aus der Altai.
In Ermans archiv, etc., 1841. (2) The same. Aus Sibirien.
Lose blätter aus dem tegebuch eines linguisten. (Sprachfor-
shcers). Leipzig, 1884. 2 v.

10734. Pauli, F. Kh. Народы России. Этнографический обзор
населения России. (The peoples of Russia. An ethnographic
survey of the population of Russia.) St. Petersburg, 1862.

10735. Samokvasov, D. IA. Сборник обычного права сибирских
инородцев. (A collection of customary law among the aboriginies of Siberia.) Warsaw, 1876.

10736. See 10522.

10737. Bezsonov, P. A. "Мнимый 'Туранизм'русских." (The
so-called "Turanism" of the Russians.) In Chteniia v Imperatorskom obshchestve istorii i drevnostei rossiiskikh
pri Moskovskom universitete, 2:1-135, April-June 1885.

10738. Samokvasov, D. IA. "Общества кочевых народов." (Societies of nomadic peoples [in Siberia].) Varshavskie universitetskie zapiski, 9 (1886):1-25.

10739. Potanin, G. N. Несколько вопросов по изучению поверий,
сказаний, суеверных обычаев и обрядов у сибирских инородцев.
(Queries concerning the study of the beliefs, proverbs,
superstitions, customs and ceremonies of the Siberian aboriginies.) St. Petersburg, 1888.

10740. Ivanovskii, A. A. Указатель этнографических статей
и заметок, помещенных в сибирских газетах от начала их издания.(A guide to ethnographical essays and notes published
in the Siberian newspapers from the beginning of their publication.) Moscow, 1890.

10741. IAdrintsev, N. M. Сибирские инородцы, их быт и современное положение. (Siberian aboriginies, their condition

and the present mode of living.) St. Petersburg, 1891.
308 p.

10742. Talko-Gryntsevich. Народности Центральной Азии.
(Peoples of Central Asia.) An anthropological sketch. Moscow, 1892.

10743. Osipov, N. Ритуал сибирской свадьбы. (Rituals of a
Siberian marriage.) St. Petersburg, 1893.

10744. Chugunov, S. Материалы для антропологии Сибири.
(Sources pertaining to Siberian anthropology.) Izvestiia
Imperatorskogo tomskogo universiteta, 7 (1895).

10745. Накануне всеобщей переписи. Алфавитный список народов, обитающих в Российской Империи.   (On the eve of a
general census. An alphabetical list of the peoples living
within the Russian empire.) St. Petersburg, Izd. Kantseliarii Komiteta ministrov, 1895.

10746. Chugunov, S. М. Материалы для антропологии Сибири.
(Sources for Siberian anthropology.) Tomsk, 1899.

10747. Maksimov, A. Из истории семьи у русских инородцев.
(Contribution to the history of the family among the aboriginies of Russia.) Moscow, 1902.

10748. Ivanovskii, A. A. Об антропологическом составе населения России. (Anthropological constituents of the population of Russia.) Moscow, 1904.

10749. Osokin, G. М. На границе Монголии.   (On the Mongolian frontier.) Petrograd, 1906. 304 p.

10750. Patkanov, S. O. О приросте инородческого населения
Сибири. (Concerning the increase of the native population
of Siberia.) Statistical materials. St. Petersburg, Akademiia nauk, 1911. 210 p. Also 1912.

10751. Patkanov, S. K. Статистические данные, показывающие
племенной состав населения Сибири, язык и роды инородцев.
(Statistical data showing the racial composition of the
population of Siberia, language and kind of natives.) In
Zapiski Rus. geogr. obshchestva po Otdel. statistiki, 11:3,
St. Petersburg, 1912.

10752. Shternberg, L. The Turano-Ganowanian system and the
nations of North-east Asia. Proceedings of the 18 international congress of Americanists, London, 1912.

10753. Shternberg, L. IA. "Культ орла у сибирских народов."
(The eagle cult of the Siberian peoples.) In Sbornik Muzeia
antropologii i etnografii pri Rossiiskoi akademii nauk, 5:
2:717-746.

10754. Makarenko, A. Сибирский народный календарь в этнографическом отношении. (Siberian ethnographic calendar.)
In Zapiski Imperatorskogo russkogo geograficheskogo obshchestva, 36 (1913).

10755. Rudenko, S. Антропологическое исследование инородцев
северно-западной Сибири. (An anthropological study of the
natives of north-western Siberia.) Petrograd, 1914.

10756. Arseniev, V. K. "Этнологические проблемы на востоке
Сибири." (Ethnological problems in eastern Siberia.) Vestnik Azii, 38-39 (1916):50-76.

10757. Vishnevskii, B. N. "К антропологии древнего населения Восточного Туркестана."(Anthropology of the ancient population of Eastern Turkestan.) Kaz. Muz. Vestn. 1-2 (1921):
88-102.

10758. Patkanov, S. K. Spisok narodnostei Sibiri. (A list
of Siberian native tribes.) In Izvestiia Rossiiskoi akademii nauk, Petrograd, 1923.

10759. Современное состояние туземных племен Дальнего Вос-
тока. (Present condition of the native tribes of the Far
East.) In.Materialy po tuzemnomu voprosu na Dal'nem Vostoke,
Chita, 1924. 38 p.

10760. Malakhovskii, Vs. Об изучении русских говоров
Сибири. (A study of Russian dialects in Siberia.) Irkutsk,
1925. 48 p.

10761. Известия Обшества археологии...(Publications of the
Archaeological society...) Kazan, Kazanskii gosudarstvennyi
universitet, 1925. (Vol. 33. 158 p.)

10762. Zarubin, I. I. Список народностей СССР. (A list of
peoples of the USSR.) Leningrad, Academy of sciences, 1927.

10763. Popov, A. V. "Чудь, как древнейшее население Сибири."
(Chud' as the most ancient population of Siberia.) Izvestiia Vostochno-sibirskogo otdela Gosudarstvennogo russkogo
geograficheskogo obshchestva, Irkutsk, 1927.

10764. Ostrovskaia, P. E. Народы СССР. Очерк труда, быта и природы. Объяснительный текст к картинам I серии, народы Севера, Алтая и Средней Азии.   Издание Государственного Из дательства, Москва-Ленинград. (Peoples of the USSR. Explanatory text to illustrations of the peoples of the North, the Altai and Central Asia.) Moscow-Leningrad, Gosizdat, 1929. 120 p.

10765. 亞 細 亞 露 西 亞 ／ 住 民 Ajia Roshia no jumin. (The inhabitants of Asiatic Russia.) Research bureau, S.M. R.R.Co., Osaka mainichi, 1929.

10766. 露 領 極 東 ニ 於 ケ ル 黄 色 人 種 問 題 Roryo kyokuto ni okeru koshoku jinshu mondai. (The yellow-race problem in Far Eastern Russia.) In Section 27, Library of economic research on Russia, Tokyo, Nichi nichi shinbun, 1927-1932.

10767. 露 西 亞 諸 民 族 ／ 研 究 Roshia shominzoku no kenkyu. (Study of the various races in Russia.) In Section 4, Library of economic reasearch on Russia, Tokyo, Nichi nichi shinbun, 1927-1932.

10768. Shternberg, L. IA. Семья и род у народов северо-восточной Азии. (Family and clan among the peoples of northeastern Asia.) Leningrad, 1933. xix, 188 p.

10769. Poppe, N. N. Лингвистические проблемы Восточной Сибири. (Linguistic problems of Eastern Siberia.) Moscow-Irkutsk, 1933. 54 p.

10770. Kozmin, N. P. К вопросу о турецко-монгольском феодализме. (Concerning the question of Turco-Mongolian feudalism.) With an introduction by M. Gudoshnikov. Ogiz, 1934. 148 p.

10771. Khudiakov, M. G. "Дореволюционное сибирское областничество и археология." (Prerevolutionary Siberian autonomous movement and archaeology.) Problemy istorii dokapitalisticheskogo obshchestva, 9-10:135-143, September-October 1934.

10772. Alkor, IA. P. (editor). Языки и письменность народов Севера. (The spoken and written languages of the peoples of the North.) Part 3, Languages of the paleo-Asiatic peoples. Moscow, 1934. 238 p.

10773. Potapov, L. P. Разложение родового строя у племен Северного Алтая. (Decay of the clan order among the tribes of Northern Altai.) Moscow, 1935. 120 p.

10774. Из истории родового общества на территории СССР. (From the history of clan society in the territory of the USSR.) Contributions by O.N. Bader, M.V. Voevodskii, P.A. Dmitriev, A.V. Zbruev, P.N.Tretiakov, and A.V.Shmidt. Gosudarstvennaia akademiia istorii material'noi kul'tury, Izvestiia (Moscow), 1935. 346 p.

10775. Kruglov, A. P. and Podgaevskii, G. V. Родовые общества степей восточной Европы.(Clan society in the plains of Eastern Europe.) Moscow, 1935. 119 p.

10776. Kartsov, V. G. Народы Сибири. Очерки . (Peoples of Siberia. Sketches of the past.) Moscow, 1935. 195 p.

10777. Stepanov, N. N. "К вопросу об остяко-вогульском феодализме. (Concerning the question of Ostiak-Vogul feudalism.) Sovetskaia etnografiia, 3 (1936):19-35.

10778. Kennan, G. Кочевая жизнь в Сибири. (Nomadic life in Siberia.) St. Petersburg, 1896.

10779. Rudnev, A. D. "Заслуги И. А. Ровинского перед востоковедением." (Contributions of I. A. Rovinskii to the study of the Orient.) In Izvestiia Russkogo geograficheskogo obshchestva, 3 (1916):7:563-565.

10780. Oldenburg, S. F. "Василий Васильевич Радлов." (Vasilii Vasilievich Radlov [orientalist].) Izvestiia Rossiiskoi akademii nauk, 1918:1233-2136.

10781. Shirokogorov, S. Sh. "В. В. Радлов." (V. V. Radlov.) Uchenye zapiski Istoriko-filologicheskogo fakul'teta v g. Vladivostoke, 1 (1919):2:1:21-24.

10782. Samoilovich, A. "Радлов, как турколог." (Radlov as an authority on the Turkic peoples.) Novyi Vostok, 2 (1922): 707-712.

10783. Ratner-Shternberg, S. A. "Л. Я. Штернберг и Ленинградская этнографическая школа 1904-1927 гг. По личным воспоминаниям и архивным данным." (L. IA. Shternberg and the Leningrad ethnographic school, 1904-1927. Personal reminiscences and archival data.) Sovetskaia etnografiia, 2 (1935):134-154.

10784. Shavrov, K. B. "В. И. Иохельсон. Этнограф. К 80-летию
со дня рождения." (V. I. Jochelson. Ethnographer. On his
eightieth birthday.) Sovetskaia etnografiia, 2 (1935):3-15.

XIII. GENERAL ACCOUNTS

A. Especially Russia in Asia

10785. Азиатская Россия. (Asiatic Russia.) Published by
"Glavnoe upravlenie zemleustroistva i zemledeliia, Pereselencheskoe upravlenie." St. Petersburg, 1914. 3 v. and an
atlas.

10786. Courant, Maurice. La Sibérie colonie russe jusqu'à
la construction du Transsibérien. Paris, 1920. 95 p.

10787. Russia. Glavnyi shtab. Сборник географических, топографических и статистических материалов по Азии.
(A collection of geographic, topographic and statistical
materials pertaining to Asia.) St. Petersburg, Glavnyi
shtab, 1883-1896. 70 v.

10788. Высочайшие отметки с 1881 по 1890 г. по всеподданней-
ших отчетах по Сибири и Степному краю и сведениям о местностях лежащих по маршруту путешествия его императорского
высочества наследника Николая Александровича из г. Владивостока в г. Уральск. (Comments on the memoranda concerning
Siberia and the steppe region presented on the occasion of
the travels of the Tsarevich 1881-1890.) St. Petersburg,
1891. 167 p.

10789. Shperk, Frants. Россия Дальнего Востока. (The Russian Far East.) In v. 14, Zapiski po obshchei geografii, St.
Petersburg, 1885. 503 p.

10790. Baiazitov, M. A. Отношение ислама к науке и иновер-
цам. (The attitude of Islam toward science and religious
dissidents.) St. Petersburg, 1887.

10791. Наши окраины. (Our frontier provinces.) Siberia,
Turkestan, the Caucasus, and the polar region of European
Russia. Edited by P. P. Semenov. St. Petersburg, 1900.

10792. Deutsch, L. 16 лет в Сибири. (Sixteen years in Siberia.) St. Petersburg, 1900. 249 p.

10793. Fraser, Sir John Foster. The real Siberia, together
with an account of a dash through Manchuria. London, Cassell; New York, Appleton, 1902. xvi, 279 p.

10794. Subbotich, D. I. Задачи России на Дальнем Востоке. (Russia's problems in the Far East.) Revel, 1903.

10795. Labbé, Paul. Les Russes en Extrême-Orient. Paris, 1904. 277 p.

10796. Golovachev, P. Россия на Дальнем Востоке. (Russia in the Far East.) St. Petersburg, E. D. Kuskova, 1904. 216 p.

10797. Miliukov, Pavel N. Russia and its crisis. Chicago, Chicago university press, 1905. 589 p.

10798. René, C. Russland und die ostasiatische frage. Berlin, Puttkammer & Mühlbrecht, 1905. 135 p.

10799. Великая Россия. Географические, этнографические и культурно-бытовые очерки современной России. (Great Russia. Geographic, ethnographic and cultural outlines of modern Russia.) Under the general supervision of Professor D. N. Anuchin. V. I. Siberia. (P. I. Golovachev, ed.) 236 p.

10800. Golovachev, P. N. Сибирь. Природа. Люди. Жизнь. (Siberia. Nature. Peoples. Life.) Second, revised edition. Moscow, IU. Bazanova, 1905. 400 p. (First edition, 1902.)

10801. Taburno, I. P. Как наилучшим образом обеспечить свободное развитие России на Дальнем Востоке и неприкосновенность ее границ. (The best means for assuring a free development of Russia in the Far East and the inviolability of her boundaries.) St. Petersburg, 1908. 99 p.

10802. Mel'nik, I. S. (editor). Сибирь, ее современное состояние и ее нужды. (Siberia, its present condition and needs.) Collected articles. St. Petersburg, 1908.

10803. Kozmin, N. N. Очерки прошлого и настоящего Сибири. (Outlines of the past and present of Siberia.) St. Petersburg, 1910.

10804. Voshchinin, V. P. На Сибирском просторе. (In the Siberian plains.) St. Petersburg, 1912. 91 p.

10805. Denisov, Vasilii I. Россия на Дальнем Востоке. (Russia in the Far East.) St. Petersburg, 1913. 142 p.

10806. Seredonin, S. M. Азиатская Россия. (Asiatic Russia.) 1914.

10807. Nansen, Fridtjof. Sibirien ein zukunftsland, Leipzig, Brockhaus, 1914. 383 p.

10808. Palferov, IA. Сибирь и ее возможности. (Siberia and its possibilities.) Voprosy kolonizatsii, St. Petersburg, 15 (1914).

10809. Williams, Albert Rhys. Soviet Russia and Siberia. Chicago, 1919.

10810. Moore, Frederick F. Siberia today. New York - London, D. Appleton, 1919. 333 p.

10811. Kolosov, E. E. Дальний Восток и наше будущее. (The Far East and our future.) Krasnoiarsk, 1919. 47 p.

10812. Pasvolsky, Leo. Russia in the Far East. London, Macmillan & co., 1922. 181 p.

10813. Miliukov, Pavel N. Russia today and tomorrow. New York, Macmillan, 1922. 392 p.

10814. Korostovets, I. IA. Россия на Дальнем Востоке. (Russia in the Far East.) Peking, 1922. 157 p.

10815. Vilenskii, Vl. (Sibiriakov). Советская Россия у берегов Тихого Океана. (Soviet Russia on the Pacific.) Moscow, 1923. 43 p.

10816. Vilenskii, Vl. (Sibiriakov). Россия на Дальнем Востоке. (Russia in the Far East.) Moscow, 1923. 89 p.

10817. Советский Дальний Восток. (The Soviet Far East.) Chita-Vladivostok, 1923. 160 p. 1 map. (S.F.Sukhovii, ed.)

10818. Kiuner, N. V. Сношения России с Дальним Востоком на протяжении царствования дома Романовых. (Russia's relations with the Far East during the reign of the house of Romanovs.) Vladivostok, 1914. 59 p.

10819. Canning, C. G. Fairfax. Siberia's untouched treasure. New York and London. 1923.

10820. Pavlovich, M. (Vel'tman). "СССР и Восток." (The USSR and the Orient.) Novyi Vostok, 6 (1924):3-12.

10821. Arsharuni, A. СССР и народы Востока. (The USSR and the peoples of the Orient.) Moscow, 1925. 41 p.

10822. Lavrov, V. M. (ed.). Сибирь в 1923-1924 г. (Siberia in 1923-1924.) Articles and sources. Novonikolaevsk, 1925. 267 (24) p.

10823. Essén, Rütger. Zwischen der Ostsee und dem Stillen ozean. Frankfurt a. M., 1925.

10824. Lavrov, V. M. (ed.). Будущее Сибири. (The future of Siberia.) Collected articles. Novosibirsk, 1926.

10825. IUrtovskii, N. S. Современная Сибирь. (Contemporary Siberia.) Novosibirsk, 1928 74 p.

10826. Cleinow, George. Neu-Sibirien. Berlin, Hobbing, 1928. 426 p.

10827. Galkowitsch, M. G. Der Osten und die USSR. Moscow, Kommunistische akademie, 1928. 122 p.

10828. Jakuschev, I. A. Die zukunft Sibiriens. Prag, 1928. 212 p.

10829. Heller, Otto. Sibirien ein anderes Amerika. Berlin, Neuer deutscher verlag, 1930. 256 p.

10830. Furusawa, Toshitaro. アヂアı之シア,國土ι產業Ajia Roshia no kokudo to sangyo. (Territory and products of Russian Asia.) Dairen, S.M.R.K., 1930. 2 v.

10831. Hanaoka, Shiro. 露國,将来 Ro-koku no shorai. (The future of Russia.) Gaiko jiho, 56 (1930):1,2,3,4,5:236-251, 113-121, 138-146, 151-165, 126-136.

10832. Fedotov, G. Проблемы будущей России. (Problems of future Russia.) Sovremennye zapiski, Paris, 43 (1930).

10833. Makarov, Nikolai N. По советскому Востоку.(In Soviet Orient.) Moscow, 1930. 168 p.

10834. Arsharuni, Arshaluis Mikhailovich. Очерки панисламизма и пантюркизма в России. (Sketches of panislamism and panturkism in Russia.) Moscow, 1931. 138 p.

10835. Bach, L. Orient soviétique. Paris, Valois, 1931. 296 p.

10836. Nikitin, Mikhail. Второй гигант.(The second giant.) Siberian sketches. Moscow, 1931. 128 p.

10837. Leonov, F. G. Восточная Сибирь на путях социалистической реконструкции.   (Eastern Siberia on the road toward socialist reconstruction.) Irkutsk, 1931. 79 p.

10838. Yakhontoff, Victor A. Russia and the Soviet union in
the Far East. New York, Coward-McCann, 1931. 454 p.

10839. 東 洋 ト ソ ヴエ ッ ト 聯 邦 Toyo to Sovietto renpo.
(The Far East and the Soviet union.) In Section 58, Library
of Economic research on Russia. Tokyo, Research Bureau,
S. M. R. R. co., Nichi nichi shinbun, 1927-1932.

10840. Kondo, Yoshiharu. 東 西 ヨリ ロシヤ-ヲ 觀ル Tozai
yori Roshia wo miru. (Looking at Russia from the east and
the west.) Tokyo, Roshia Tsushinsha, 1932. 250 p.

10841. Baikalov, Anatole. "Siberia since 1894." Slavonic
review, 11 (1933):32: 328-340.

10842. Bezborodov, S. K. Die entdeckung Sibiriens. Moscow -
Leningrad, Verlagsgenossenschaft ausländischer arbeiter in
der USSR, "Internationale, 1933. 148 p.

10843. Kisch, Egon Erwin. Изменившаяся Азия. (Changed Asia.)
Sketches of Soviet Asia. Moscow, 1934. 167 p.

10844. Bezborodov, S. K. Большевики открыли Сибирь.
(Bolsheviks discovered Siberia.) Leningrad, 1934. 186 p.

10845. Chernykh, P. IA. Русский язык в Сибири. (The Russian language in Siberia.) Moscow, 1934. 82 p.

10846. Webb, Sidney and Beatrice. Soviet communism: a new
civilization. London, Longmans, 1935. 2 v. 1200 p.

10847. Strong, Anna Louise. This Soviet world. New York,
Henry Hold & co., 1936. 298 p.

10848. Klimovich, L. I. Ислам в царской России. (Islam in
tsarist Russia.) Moscow, 1936. 406 p.

10849. Hata, Hikosaburo. 隣 邦 ロ シ ア Rinpo Roshia. (Russia, our neighbor nation.) Tokyo, Tonan shoin, 1937. 370 p.

10850. Сибирь в прошлом и настоящем. (Siberia, past and
present.) Sources for propagandists and agitators. Novosibirsk, 1937.

                    B. Russia on the Pacific

See 224-285.

10851. Kerner, Robert J. "Russian expansion to America: its

bibliographical foundations." Papers of the bibliographical society of America, 25 (1931):111-129.

10852. See 227.

10853. Coxe, W. Account of the Russian discoveries between Asia and America. London, 1780. xxii, 344 p.

10854. Markov, Al. Русские на Восточном океане. (Russians on the Pacific.) Moscow, 1849. Second, revised and enlarged edition, St. Petersburg, 1856.

10855. Wagner, Henry R. The cartography of the northwest coast of America to the year 1800. Berkeley, University of California press, 1937. 2 v.

10856. Steller, G. W. Reise von Kamtschatka nach Amerika mit dem Commander-Capitän Bering. St. Petersburg, 1793. 133 p.

10857. Shelekhov, Grigorii. Странствование российского купца Григорья Шелехова. (Travels of the Russian merchant Grigorii Shelekhov.) St. Petersburg, 1791. English translation: The voyage of Gregory Shelekhov, a Russian merchant, from his own journal. London, 1795.

10858. Zagoskin, L. A. Пешеходная опись части русских владений в Америке.(A description of Russian possessions in America.) St. Petersburg, 1847-1848. 2 v.

10859. Материалы для истории русских заселений по берегам Восточного океана. (Documents pertaining to the history of... the Pacific Ocean.) Supplement to Morskoi sbornik, 1-4, 1861.

10860. Berg, L. S.Известия о Беринговом море и его берегах до Беринга и Кука. (Data concerning the Strait of Bering and its coasts before Bering and Cook.) Zapiski po gidrografii, 42 (1920). (2) The same. Открытие Камчатки и экспедиции Беринга, 1725-1742. (The discovery of Kamchatka and the expedition of Bering, 1725-1742.) Leningrad, 1935. 411 p.

10861. Golder, F. A. Bering's voyages. An account of the efforts of the Russians to determine the relation of Asia and America. New York, American Geographical society, 1922-1925. 2 v.

10862. Kireev, I. A. (ed.). Восточно-сибирское и Чукотское
моря, Берингов пролив и Берингово море. (The East-Siberian
and Chukotsk seas, Bering straits and Bering sea.) Collected
articles. Leningrad, 1936. 180 p.

10863. Berkh, V. N. Хронологическая история открытия Алеутских островов. (A chronological history of the discovery of
the Aleutian islands.) St. Petersburg, 1823.

10864. Polonskii, A. Курилы. (The Kuriles.) Zapiski Geograficheskogo obshchestva, Etnograficheskii otdel, 4 (1871).

10865. Berg, L. S. "Из истории открытия Алеутских островов."
(From the history of the discovery of the Aleutian islands.)
Zemlevedenie (Moscow), 26 (1914):1-2:114-132.

10866. Itin, V. A. Выход к морю. (Outlet to the sea.) Novosibirsk, 1935. 249 p.

10867. Sokolov, A. Экспедиция к Алеутским островам капита-
нов Креницына и Левашева 1764-1769 гг. (The expedition of
Captains Krenitsyn and Levashev to the Aleutian islands,
1764-1769.) Zapiski gidrograficheskogo departamenta, 9
(1852).

10868. Markov, Sergei. "Колумбы российские. Колонизаторская
деятельность русских купцов на Аляске, XVIII-XIX в." (Russian Columbuses. Colonization activities of Russian merchants in Alaska, XVIII-XIX centuries.) Sovetskoe kraevedenie, 6:48-58, June 1936.

10869. Vakhtin, V. Русские труженики моря. Первая морская
экспедиция Беринга для решения вопроса, соединяется ли Азия
с Америкой. (Russian sea-explorers. The first sea expedition of Bering for the determination of the question whether
Asia and America are connected.) St. Petersburg, 1890. 124 p.

10870. Tikhmenev, P. Историческое обозрение Российско-
американской компании и действий ее до настоящего времени.
(Historical survey of the Russian-American company and its
activities to the present time.) St. Petersburg, 1861-1863.
2 v.

10871. Pilder, Hans. Die Russisch-amerikanische handels-kom-
panie bis 1825. Berlin - Leipzig, G. Göschen, 1914. 174 p.

10872. Bancroft, Hubert H. History of Alaska, 1730-1885.
San Francisco, A. L. Bancroft, 1886. 775 p.

10873. Bancroft, Hubert H. History of California. San Francisco, The History co., 1884-1890. 7 v.

10874. Basanov, V. "Archives of the Russian church in Alaska in the Library of Congress." Pacific historical review, 2 (1930).

10875. Ross, Frank E. "The retreat of the Hudson's bay company in the Pacific northwest." Canadian historical review, 18:3:262-280, September 1937.

10876. Mahr, August C. The visit of the "Rurik" to San Francisco in 1816. Palo Alto, Stanford university press, 1932. 194 p.

10877. Chevigny, Hector. Lost empire. The life and adventure of Nikolai Petrovich Rezanov. New York, Macmillan, 1937. 356 p.

10878. Maksimov, Aleksandr IA. Наши задачи на Тихом океане. (Our problems of the Pacific.) Political studies. St. Petersburg, Babkin, 1894.

10879. Mazour, Anatole u. "Doctor Yegor Scheffer: dreamer of a Russian empire in the Pacific." Pacific historical review, 6:1:15-20, March 1937.

10880. Mazour, Anatole G. "Dmitry Zavalishin: dreamer of a Russian-American empire." Pacific historical review, 5:1: 26-37, March 1936.

10881. Okun, S. "Политика русского царизма на Тихом океане в XIX веке." (The policy of Russian tsarism in the Pacific in the XIX century.) Bor'ba klassov, 9:34-43, September 1935.

10882. Heller, Otto. Die rote fahne am Pazific. Zehnjahre sowietmacht in Fernen Osten. Moscow, Internationale, 1933. 56 p.

10883. Heller, Otto. Wladiwostok! Der kampf um den Fernen Osten. Berlin, Neuer deutscher verlag, 1933. 308 p.

10884. Hoffman, Karl. "Die russische erdölfrage in der politik." Zeitschrift für politik, 19 (1930):657-675.

C. The Soviet Arctic

See 182-223.

(1) Bibliography

10885. Popov, A. N. Северная библиография. (Northern bibliography.) A systematic guide to books and magazine articles
for 1929. Archangel, 1932. 39 p.

(2) Maps

10886. Belavin, A. F. (comp.). О картах Северного края.
(Concerning maps of the Northern region.) [Archangel], 1934.
78 p.

(3) Periodicals

10887. Труды Института по изучению Севера. (Transactions of
the Institute for scientific exploration of the North.)
Leningrad, 1920-

10888. Советская арктика. (The Soviet arctic.) Edited by
G. A. Ushakov and A. A. Dolgomarov. Published by the chief
administration of the Northern sea route. 1, August 1935-

(4) History and General Accounts

10889. Byhan, A. Die polarvölker. Leipzig, 1909.

10890. Mecking, L. Die polarländer. Allgemeine länderkunde.
Leipzig, 1925.

10891. Vize, Vladimir IU. История исследования Советской
Арктики. (History of the exploration of the Soviet Arctic.)
Archangel, 1934. 209 p.   (2) The same. История исследования
Советской Арктики. Карское и Баренцово моря. (History of
the exploration of the Soviet Arctic. The Kara and Barents
seas.) 3rd corrected and enlarged edition. Archangel, 1935.
232 p.   (3) The same. Моря Советской Арктики. (The seas
of the Soviet Arctic.) Sketches of the history of explorations. Leningrad, 1936. 493 p.   (4) Arctica. (Collected articles under ed. of Vize, and R. L. Samoilovich.) Leningrad,
1933-

10892. Anufriev, I., Banovich, IA. and others. Как исследу-
ют Арктику. (How the Arctic is being explored.) Kharkov,
1934. 202 p.

10893. Diakonov, M. A. Путешествия в полярные страны. (Journeys into the Arctic territories.) A sketch of the history of geographic discoveries.) Edited by V. I. Vize. Leningrad, 1933. 206 p.

10894. Rybin, S. A. and Sholtz, F. A. Северный морской путь из Европы к устьям Оби и Енисея. (The northern sea route from Europe to the mouths of the Ob and Yenisei rivers.) Novonikolaevsk, 1924.

10895. Petrov (IUman), D. P. Завоеватели севера. (Conquerors of the North.) Cheboksary, 1935. 140 p.

10896. Joffe, Semen. The northern sea route as a transport problem. Sixth conference of the Institute of Pacific relations, 1936. 27 p.

10897. Pinegin, N. V. Записки полярника. Воспоминания о походах в Арктику в дореволюционное и советское время. (Memoirs of an Arctic explorer. Reminiscences of explorations in the Arctic prior to the revolution and under the Soviet regime.) Archangel, 1936. 328 p.

10898. Breitfuss, Leonid. Die erforschung des Polargebietes Russisch-Eurasiens. See- und landreisen während der jahre 1912-1924. Gotha, 1925. 113 p.

10899. Smolka, H. P. 40,000 against the Arctic. New York, Morrow & co., 1937. 109 p.

10900. Gaister, A. I. (ed.). Проблемы Севера. (Problems of the North.) Moscow, Sovetskaia Azia, 1933. 421 p.

10901. Shilov, P. N. (comp.) Инструкция для начальников експедиций Всесоюзного арктического института. (Instruction to the heads of the expeditions of the All-Union Arctic institute.) Leningrad, 1936. 51 p.

10902. Sibirtsev, N. Северный морской путь и Карские экспедиции. (Northern sea route and the Kara expeditions.) Novosibirsk, 1936. 229 p.

10903. Itin, V. A. Морские пути Советской Арктики. (Sea routes of the Soviet Arctic.) Moscow, Sovetskaia Aziia, 1933. 106 p.

10904. Groza, I. P. and Dubenskii, P. S. (editors). Славным завоевателям Арктики. (To the renowned conquerors of the Arctic.) Moscow, 1934. 179 p.

10905. Samoilovich, Rudol'f L. Путь к полюсу. (The road to
the pole.) A historical sketch of the polar expeditions.
Leningrad, 1933. 64 p.

10906. Samoilovich, R. L. Во льдах Арктики.   (In the Arctic ice.) Leningrad, 1934. 340 p.

10907. Obruchev, S. V. На самолете в Восточной Арктике.
(In an aeroplane in the Eastern Arctic.) Leningrad, 1934.
184 p.

10908. Kal'nitskii, IA. Огни в Арктике.   (Lights in the Arctic.) Kharkov - Kiev, 1934. 168 p.

10909. Lesshaft, E. Das Karische meer als seeweg nach Sibiri-
en. Annalen der hydrografie, 1914.

10910. Dubravin, A. I. Самолеты в арктических условиях.
(Aeroplanes in the arctic conditions.) Leningrad, 1936.
132 p.

10911. Северный. полюс завоеван большевиками. Экспедиция
СССР на Северный полюс. (The North pole is conquered by the
Bolsheviks. The expedition of the USSR to the North pole.)
Moscow, Partizdat, 1937. 255 p.

10912. За освоение Арктики.   (For the familiarization with
the Arctic.) Leningrad, 1935. 256 p.

10913. Lakhtin, V. L. "Борьба за Арктику." (The struggle
for the Arctic.) Vozdushnye puti severa (Moscow), 1933, 108-
136.

10914. Samoilovich, R. L. "История полетов в Арктику."
(History of the flights to the Arctic.) Vozdushnye puti severa (Moscow), 1933, 10-49.

10915. Zinger, M. E. Основные законы по крайнему северу.
Право на полярные пространства и организация органов управления. (Fundamental laws pertaining to the extreme north.
The right to the Arctic and organization of administrative
organs.) An essay at a systematic description.   Moscow,
1937. Glavsermorput'. 144 p.

10916. Edelman, S. IA. (ed.). Проблемы освоения севера Западной Сибири. (Problems concerning the acquisition of the
northern part of Western Siberia.) Novosibirsk, 1935. 259 p.
(2) Taracouzio, T. A. Soviets in the Arctic. New York, Macmillan, 1938.   563 p.

10917. Сталинская трасса. Москва--Северный полюс--Северная Америка. (The Stalin trail. Moscow -- North pole -- North America.) Moscow, Partizdat, 1937. 112 p.

10918. Сталинский маршрут продолжен. Москва--Северный полюс--Северная Америка.(The Stalin route extended. Moscow -- North pole -- North America.) Moscow, Partizdat, 1937. 108 p.

10919. Smolka, H. P. "Soviet strategy in the Arctic." Foreign affairs, 16:2:272-279, January 1938.

(5) Exploration

10920. Ogloblin, N. N. "Восточно-сибирские полярные мореходы XVII с." (East-Siberian arctic mariners of the XVII c.) Zhurnal Ministerstva narodnogo prosveshcheniia, 5 (1903).

10921. Müller, Gerhard F. Nachrichten von seereisen und zur see gemachten entdeckungen, die von Russland aus längs den küsten des eismeeres und auf dem östlichen weltmeere gegen Japan und Amerika geschehen sind. Sammlung russischer geschichte, 3, St. Petersburg, 1758. (2) The same. Russian translation: Описание морских путешествий по Ледовитому и Восточному морю с российской стороны учиненных. (Description of the sea voyages in the Arctic and Eastern seas undertaken by Russia.) [Ezhemesiachnye] sochineniia i perevody k pol'ze i uveseleniiu sluzhashchie, May - October 1758.

10922. Ostrovskii, B. G. Великая Северная экспедиция, 1733-1743. (The great Northern expedition, 1733-1743.) 2nd enlarged edition. Archangel, 1937. 206 p. (2) Sokolov, A. Северная экспедиция,1733-1743 гг.(The Northern expedition of 1733-1743.) Zapiski Gidrograficheskogo departaments, 9 (1851):190-469. Maps. (3) "Из истории освоения Северного морского пути. Экспедиция Беринга 1732-1743 гг." (From the history of the exploration of the Northern sea route. Bering's expedition, 1732-1743.) Krasnyi arkhiv, 4 (1935):71: 137-169.

10923. Voyages from Asia to America, for completing the discoveries of the northwest coast of America. London, 1761. viii, xliii, 76 p.   Second edition. London, 1764. viii, 120 p.

10924. Sarychev, G. Путешествие флота Сарычева по сев.-вост. части Сибири, Ледовитому морю и Восточному океану. (The voyage of Sarychev's fleet along the north-east coast of Siberia, through the Arctic sea and the Pacific in 1785-1793.) St. Petersburg, 1802.

332 Russia

10925. Wrangel, F. Путешествие по северным берегам Сибири и по Ледовитому морю, совершенное в 1820-1824 г. (Journey to the northern shores of Siberia and to the Arctic.) St. Petersburg, 1841.

10926. Soloviev, M. M. Бэр на Новой Земле. ([K.E. von] Baer on Novaia Zemlia.) Expedition of 1837. Leningrad, 1934. 51 p.

10927. Beliaevskii, A. Поездка к Ледовитому океану. (A journey to the Arctic ocean.) Moscow, 1883.

10928. Shvede, E. "История открытия и завоевания острова Врангеля." (History of the discovery and conquest of Wrangel island.) Krasnyi flot, 10 (1924):111-120.

10929. Гидрология рек Советской Арктики. (Hydrology of the rivers of the Soviet Arctic.) Leningrad, Glavsevmorput', 1938. 242 p. [The Lena, Ebetem, Indigirka, Khatanga, Yenisei and Kolyma].

10930. Kozhevnikov, M. IA. Чукотская экспедиция 1909-1910 г. (The Chukotka expedition of 1909-1910.) Leningrad, Academy of sciences, 1934. 15 p.

10931. Zinger, Maks E. Сквозь льды в Сибирь (Through the ice into Siberia.) The Kara expedition of 1929. Moscow, 1930. 153p.

10932. Bogdanovich, K. Очерки Чукотского полуострова. (Sketches of the Chukotsk peninsula.) St. Petersburg, 1901. 238 p.

10933. Diachkov, G. T. Анадырский край. (The Anadyr region.) Vladivostok, 1893.

10934. Gondatti, N. Поездка из села Маркова на р. Анадыре в бухту Провидения, Берингова пролива. (Trip from the Markovo village on the river Anadyr, to Providence bay on Bering strait.) Khabarovsk, 1898.

10935. Obrutschev, S. Das Tschuktsche gebiet. Petermanns mitteilungen. Gotha, 1934. Heft 10.

10936. Osluev, A. V. Общий очерк Анадырского округа. (A general sketch of the Anadyr district.) St. Petersburg, 1896.

10937. Shklovskii, Isaak. Очерки крайнего Северо-востока. (Sketches of the extreme Northeast.) Irkutsk, 1892.

10938. Sarychev, Gavriil. Путешествие Кап. Биллинга чрез Чукотскую землю от Берингова пролива до Нижне-колымского острога.(Captain Billing's journey through the Chukotsk land, from Bering strait to the Lower Kolyma ostrog.) St. Petersburg, 1811.

10939. Stankevich, V. and Stankevich, K. На великом Севере. (In the great North.) 1922.

10940. Shklovskii, Isaak V. In far Northeast Siberia. London, Macmillan, 1916. 264 p.

10941. Toll, Eduard V. Die russische polarfahrt der "Sarja". Berlin, G. Reimer, 1909. 635 p. (Voyage of 1900-1902).

10942. Toll, Ed. Экспедиция Императорской академии наук 1893 г. на Ново-сибирские острова и побережье Ледовитого океана. (The expedition of the Imperial academy of sciences in 1893 to the New Siberian islands and the coast of the Arctic sea.) In Izvestiia Imperatorskogo russkogo geograficheskogo obshchestva, 30 (1894).

10943. Ogloblin, N. "Семен Дежнев (1638-1671 гг.)." (Semen Dezhnev, 1638-1671.) Zhurnal Ministerstva narodnogo prosveshcheniia, 272 (1890):249-306.

10944. Pinegin, N. V. В ледяных просторах. Экспедиция Г. Я Седова к северному полюсу.   (In the polar regions. G. IA. Sedov's expedition to the North pole.) Leningrad, 1933. 305 p.

10945. Andersen, P. S. Ледокол "Казак Поярков".(The icebreaker "Cossack Poiarkov".) Khabarovsk, 1933. 15 p.

10946. Diakonov, M. A. Четыре тысячи миль на "Сибирякове". (Four thousand miles on the "Sibiriakov".) Leningrad, 1934. 63 p.

10947. Gromov, B. V. Поход "Сибирякова". (The expedition of the "Sibiriakov".) Moscow, 1934. 252 p.

10948. Mironov, A. E. Поход "Челюскина". (The expedition of the "Cheliuskin".) 2d revised edition. Archangel, 1935. 180, 2 p.

10949. Героическая эпопея. Арктический поход и гибель "Челюскина". (Heroic epic. The Arctic expedition and loss of the "Cheliuskin".) Moscow, 1935. 154 p.

10950. Дневники челюскинцев. По дневникам, записям и воспоминаниям участников героической экспедиции. (Diaries of the Cheliuskin crew. According to the diaries, notes and reminiscences of the participants of the heroic expedition.) Leningrad, 1935. 567 p.

10951. Gromov, B. V. Гибель Челюскина. (The loss of the "Cheliuskin".) Moscow, 1936. 377 p.

10952. IUzhin, D. Подвиг "Красина". (Heroic exploit of the "Krasin".) Kharkov, 1934. 166, 9 p.

10953. Lavrov, B. Первая Ленская. Очерки о первом караване советских судов, прошедших через Северный ледовитый океан к устью реки Лены. (The first Lena [journey]. Sketches of the first caravan of Soviet ships that passed through the Arctic ocean to the mouth of the Lena river.) Moscow, 1936. 286 p.

10954. Segal, A. Новый форпост. Из блокнота участника арктического рейса "Малыгин".   (The new outpost. From the notebook of a participant of the "Malygin" Arctic expedition.) [Leningrad], 1933. 50 p.

10955. Vize, V. IU. Владивосток--Мурманск на "Литке". Экспедиция 1934 г. (From Vladivostok to Murmansk on the "Litka." Expedition on 1934.) Leningrad, 1936. 154 p.

10956. Esipov, V. K. Петр Пахтусов. Экспедиции на Новую Землю. (Peter Pakhtusov. Expeditions to Novaia Zemlia.) Archangel, 1936. 73 p.

10957. Замечательная работа Молокова. Героический перелет по всей территории Крайнего Севера и трассе Северного морского пути от Берингова пролива до Белого моря 22 июля - 19 сентября 1936 г. (Molokov's remarkable work. The heroic flight across the entire territory of the Far North and the trail of the Northern sea route from the Bering strait to the White sea, July 22 - September 19, 1936.) Collected articles. Moscow, Partizdat, 1936. 128 p.

10958. Lebedenko, A. G. Осада полюса. Полярные экспедиции и путешествия.   (Siege of the Pole. Polar expeditions and journeys.) Leningrad, 1934. 308 p.

10959. Samoilovich, R. L. Моя восемьнадцатая экспедиция. (My eighteenth expedition.) Leningrad, 1934. 114 p.

10960. Pinegin, N. V. Семьдесят дней борьбы за жизнь. По дневнику участника экспедиции Брусилова штурмана В. Альбанова. (Seventy days of struggle for life. From the diary of a participant of the Brusilov expedition, Pilot V. Albanov.) Archangel, 1934. 134 p.

10961. Steber, Charles. La Sibérie et l'extrême-nord soviétique. Paris, Payot, 1936. 245 p.

10962. Esipov, V. K. Острова Советской Арктики: Новая Земля, Вайгач, Колгуев, Земля Франца-Иосифа. (Islands of the Soviet Arctic: Novaia Zemlia, Vaigach, Kolguev, Franz-Josef Land.) Archangel, 1933. 149 p.

10963. Mineev, A. I. Пять лет на острове Врангеля 1929-1934. (Five years on Wrangel island, 1929-1934.) Leningrad, 1936. 444 p.

10964. Markov, S. "У самого Белого моря. Г. Архангельск." (At the White sea itself. The city of Archangel.) Sovetskoe kraevedenie, 12:45-71, December 1936.

10965. Urvantsev, N. N. Два года на северной земле. (Two years in the northern land.) Leningrad, 1935. 362 p.

10966. Труды Арктического института. (Transactions of the Arctic institute.) Vol 38. Geology. Materials concerning geology and petrography of Novaia Zemlia. Leningrad, Glavsevmorput', 1936. 152, 11 p.

10967. Ostrovskii, B. G. Форпосты советской науки в Арктике. Полярные станции СССР. (Outposts of Soviet science in the Arctic. Polar stations of the USSR.) Archangel, 1933. 48 p.

10968. Научные результаты экспедиции на "Сибирякове" в 1932 г. (Scientific results of the expedition on the "Sibiriakov" in 1932.) Leningrad, Academy of sciences, 1933. 208 p.

10969. Метеорологические и гидрографические наблюдения произведенные в Северном ледовитом океане. (Meteorological and hydrological observations made on the Arctic ocean.) Annual. St. Petersburg, Gidrograficheskoe upravlenie, 1898-1915.

10970. Научные результаты экспедиции на "Малыгине" на Землю Франца-Иосифа в 1932 г. (Scientific results of the expedition on the "Malygin" to the Franz-Josef Land in 1932.) Leningrad, 1935.

10971. Описание маяков, башен и знаков Российской империи
по берегам Белого моря и Северного ледовитого океана.
(Description of lighthouses, towers and signals of the Russian empire along the coast of the White sea and Arctic
ocean.) St. Petersburg, Gidrograficheskoe upravlenie, 1882.

10972. Sergeevskii, B. A. Гидрографическое исследование
юговосточной части Карского моря, Обь-Енисейского района.
(Hydrographic study of the southeastern part of the Kara
sea in the Ob-Yenisei region.) Leningrad, 1936. 416 p.

10973. Лоция Карского моря и Новой Земли. (Pilot to the Kara
sea and Novaia Zemlia.) Supplement. Leningrad, 1930-

10974. Лоция Самоедского берега Северного ледовитого океана.
(Pilot for the Samoed coast of the Arctic ocean.) Supplement.
Leningrad ? n.d. Published by the Gidrograficheskoe uprav-
lenie.

10975. Laktionov, A. F. Северная земля. (The northern land.)
Archangel, 1936. 117 p.

10976. Siglan, P. "Колыма." (Kolyma.) Historical geographic
sketch. Sovetskoe kraevedenie, 2:56-68, February 1936.

10977. Klimov, A. Сердце тундры. (The heart of the Tundra.)
Sketches of the conquest of IA-mal.) Omsk, 1935. 105 p.

10978. Vlasov,-A. "Национальные северные округа Восточной
Сибири."(Northern national regions of Eastern Siberia.) Na
sovetskoi stroike, 1:14:16, January 1932.

10979. Esipov, V. K. Земля Франца-Иосифа. (Franz-Josef
land.) Archangel, 1935. 73 p.

10980. Sokolov-Mikitov, I. S. Белые берега. Новая Земля,
Земля Франца-Иосифа, Северная земля, Шпицберген. Очерки.
(White shores. Novaia Zemlia, Franz-Josef land, Northern
land, Spitzbergen. Sketches.) Archangel, 1936. 228 p.

10981. Dioneo. На крайнем северо-востоке Сибири. (In the
extreme northeast of Siberia.) St. Petersburg, 1895. 287 p.

10982. Kalinnikov, N. Наш крайний Северо-восток. (Our
far Northeast.) St. Petersburg, 1912. 246 p.

10983. Vilenskii, Vl. (Sibiriakov). Северная Азия. (Northern Asia.) Moscow, 1925. 23.

10984. Daurkin. "Известия о Чукотском носе."(Records of Cape Chukotsk.) Mesiatsoslov istoricheskii i geograficheskii na 1780 god, Izd. Akademiei nauk, 1780, 36-46.

10985. Tolmachev, A. I. Северные полярные страны.(Northern polar countries.) The Arctic. Archangel, 1935. 136 p.

10986. Ostrovskii, B. G. Остров Врангеля. (Wrangel island.) Archangel, 1935. 86 p.

10987. Sergeev, M. A. Корякский национальный округ. (Koriak national region.) Nauchno-issled. assotsiatsiia Instituta narodov severa TsIK SSSR. Trudy po ekonomike, v. I.   Izd. Narodov severa TsIK SSSR, 1934. 142 p.

10988. Tekki Odulok. На крайнем севере. Северная Якутия. (In the far north. Northern IAkutiia.) Moscow, 1933. 173 p.

10989. Научно-промысловая экспедиция на Новую Землю, 1931-1934 гг. (The scientific trade expedition to Novaia Zemlia, 1931-1934.) Collected articles. Leningrad, 1937. 91 p.

10990. Ivanov, I. M. Новосибирские острова. (New Siberian islands.) Archangel, 1935. 66 p.

10991. Pinegin, N. V. Новая Земля. (Novaia Zemlia.) Archangel, 1935. 126 p.

10992. Sokolov, M. P. "Полуостров Таймыр и Северный морской путь. (The Taimyr peninsula and Northern sea route.) Severnyi morskoi put', 2 (1935):7-39.

10993. See 10963.

10994. Obruchev, S. Колымская землица.   (Kolyma land.) Two years of vagabonding. Moscow, Sovetskaia Aziia, 1933. 174 p.

10995. Чукотская летная экспедиция 1932-1933 гг. (The Chukotsk flying expedition of 1932-1933.) Collected articles. Leningrad, 1936. 184 p.

10996. Rikhter, Z. V. В снегах Эльбруса. Во льдах Арктики. За Полярным кругом.(In the snows of Elbrus. In the ice of the Arctic. Beyond the Polar region.) The expedition of the icebreaker Litke to Wrangel island. The Kol'sk peninsula. Moscow, 1936. 349 p.

(6) Economic and Cultural Factors

10997. Похозяйственная перепись приполярного севера СССР.
1926-1927 гг.(Census of economic units in the north Arctic
region of the USSR.) Territorial and group totals. Moscow,
1929.

10998. Sinel'nikov, S. M. Северный край. (Northern region.)
An economic geographic sketch. Archangel, 1936. 143 p.

10999. Крайний Север в 1934 году. (The Far North in 1934.)
Collection of materials pertaining to economic and cultural
construction. Moscow, 1934. 176 p.

11000. Dmitriev, S. N.Тундра. (The tundra.) Sketches and
narratives. Moscow, 1935. 70 p.

11001. Perfiliev, I. A. Флора Северного края. (Flora of
the Northern region.) Archangel, 1936. 397 p.

11002. Фауна Тимана и Колымско-Индигирского края. (Fauna of
the Timan and the Kolyma-Indigir region.) Leningrad, 1936.
136 p.

11003. Геологические исследования в восточной части Арктики.
(Geological explorations of the eastern part of the Arctic.)
Collected articles. Leningrad, 1936. 123 p.

11004. Геологические исследования Новой Земли и Вайгача.
(Geological explorations of Novaia Zemlia and Vaigach.)
Collected articles. Leningrad, 1936. 142 p.

11005. Novoselov, N. A. Земледелие на Крайнем севере Восточной Сибири. (Agriculture in the extreme Northeast of Siberia.) Irkutsk, 1934. 92 p.

11006. Gorbatskii, G. V. Тундровая полоса Северного края.
(The tundra zone of the Northern region.) Economic geographical description. Archangel, 1933. 60 p.

11007. Vilenskii, D. G. and Ponagaibo, N. D. (editors).
Почвенно-агрономическое исследование на Крайнем Севере.
(Soil-agronomy exploration in the extreme North.) Moscow,
Academy of agricultural sciences, Transactions, 19 (1937).
179 p.

11008. Tsinzerling, Iu. D. Материалы по растительности
северо-востока Кольского полуострова. (Materials concerning the vegetation of the northeast   part of. the Kolsk

peninsula.) Moscow, Academy of sciences, 1935. 161 p.

11009. Smirnov, N. A. (ed.). Звери Арктики. (Animals of the
Arctic.) Leningrad, 1935. 579 p.

11010. Pavlov, S. G. "Торф на Чукотке." (Turf in Chukotka.)
Sovetskaia Arktika, 1:89-93, January 1937.

11011. Lebedeva, L. A. Грибы арктического побереж. (Mushrooms
on the Arctic coast of Siberia.) Trudy Komissii po izucheniiu IAkutskoi ASSR, 12 (1928). 23 p. Idz. Akademii nauk
SSSR.

11012. Академику Н. Я. Маppy. (Academician N. IA. Marr.)
A jubilean volume, edited by I. I. Meshchaninov. Moscow-
Leningrad, Academy of sciences, 1935. 787 p.

11013. Dudorov, F. (comp.). Песни народов Дальнего Севера.
(Songs of the peoples of the Far North.) Moscow, 1935. 144 p.

XV. HISTORY

See 273-342; 343-449; 450-780;3198-4252: 5014-5026; 6183-
6200; 6700-6721; 7138-7144.

A. General Russian History

11014. Soloviev, S. M. История России с древнейших времен.
(History of Russia from the earliest times.) Moscow, 1851-
1879. 29 v. Last edition, St. Petersburg, 1893-1897. 24 v.
in 6, index. (2) Karamzin, N. M. История государства
российского. (History of the Russian state.) St. Petersburg,
1818-1829. 12 v.

11015. Kostomarov, N. I. Собрание сочинений, исторические
монографии и исследования. (Collected works, historical
monographs and studies.) St. Petersburg, 1903-1906. 21 v.

11016. Kliuchevskii, V. O. Курс русской истории. (A course
in Russian history.) Moscow, 1908-1921. 5 v. English
translation by C. J. Hogarth. London-New York, Dutton & co.,
1911-1931. 5 v.

11017. Platonov, S. F. Лекции по русской истории. (Lectures
in Russian history.) 8th revised and enlarged edition. St.
Petersburg, 1913. 743 p.

11018. Pokrovskii, M. N. Русская история с древнейших
времен. (Russian history from the earliest times.) 2nd edition. Moscow, Mir, 1913-1914. 5 v.

11019. Miliukov, P. N. Очерки по истории русской культуры.
(Studies in the history of Russian culture.) St. Petersburg,
1896-1903. 3 v. in 4 parts. Latest edition, revised and
enlarged. Paris, 1930- (2) Miliukov, P. N., Seignobos,
C. and Eisenmann, L. Histoire de Russie. Paris, Leroux,
1932-1933. 3 v.

11020. Pares, Sir Bernard. A history of Russia. New York,
Knopf, 1926. xxiii, 558 p. 3d revised edition, New York,
Knopf, 1937. xxiii, 570 p. (2) Vernadskii, George V. A
history of Russia. New Haven, Yale university press, 1929.
397 p. Later edition: Political and diplomatic history
of Russia. Boston, Little, Brown, & co., 1936. 499 p.
(3) Rambaud, Alfred N. Histoire de la Russie. Paris, Hachette et cie., 1914. 963 p. See 11045-11059.

11021. Ch'a, Liang-chien. 俄 國 現 代 史 O-kuo hsien-
tai shih. (Modern history of Russia.) Shanghai, Commercial
press, 1929-1931.

11022. Iliukovich, M. История народов СССР. (History of the
peoples of the USSR.) Leningrad, 1933. 207 p.

11023. Dean, Mrs. Vera Micheles. The Soviet Union as a
European power. Foreign policy reports (New York), 9:11:
117-128, August 1933. (2) Soviet Russia: 1917-1936. World
affairs pamphlets (New York), Revised edition, 2, 1936.

11024. Akagami, Yoshitsugu. 近 世 露 西 亜 政 治 史 Kinsei
Roshia seiji-shi. (Modern political history of Soviet Russia.) Tokyo, Shokasha, 1935. 272 p.

11025. Pratt, Helen G. Russia from tsarist empire to socialism. American council. Peoples of the Pacific. (No. 3).
Institute of Pacific relations, 1937. 202 p.

11026. Mazour, Anatole G. "Modern Russian historiography."
The Journal of modern history, 9:2:169-202, June 1937.

B. Russian Expansion in Asia

11027. Seredonin, S. M. Исторический очерк завоевания
Азиатской России. (Historical sketch of the conquest of
Asiatic Russia.) St. Petersburg, 1914.

11028. Semjonow, Juri. Die eroberung Sibiriens. Berlin, Ul-
stein, 1937.

11029. Romanov, B. A. Россия в Манчжурии (1892-1906). (Russia in Manchuria, 1892-1906.) Leningrad, 1928. 605 p. See 5016.

11030. Vladimir (Volpicelli, Z.) Russia on the Pacific and the Siberian railway. London, 1899. 373 p.

11031. Golder, F. A. Russian expansion on the Pacific, 1641-1850. Cleveland, A.H.Clark, 1914. 368 p.

11032. Lobanov-Rostovsky, Prince A. Russia and Asia. New York, Macmillan, 1933. 334 p.

11033. Rambaud, A. "The expansion of Russia, problems of the East and the Far East." International monthly, Burlington, 2:211-251, 341-361, October 1900.

11034. Krahmer, Gustav (ed.). Russland in Asien. Bd. 8. Der Ferne Osten, seine geschichte, seine entwicklung in der neuesten zeit und seine lage nach dem russisch-japanischen kriege. Berlin, 1907. vi, 276 p.

11035. Wartenburg, Maximilian Graf Yorck von. Das vordringen der russischen macht in Asien. Zweite auflage, Berlin, Mittler & sohn, 1900. 67 p.

11036. Friedrichsen, M. Russland in Zentral- und Ostasien. Hamburg, Friedrichsen & co., 1918. (2) Skrine, Francis H.B. The expansion of Russia, 1815-1900. 3rd edition. Cambridge, University press, 1915. 386 p.

11037. Georgievskii, A. P. Русские на Дальнем Востоке. (Russians in the Far East.) Vladivostok, 1926.

11038. Vernadskii, Georgii V. "О движении русского племени на Восток." (On the movement of the Russian people toward the east.) Nauchnyi istoricheskii zhurnal, 1:2 (1914). (2) The same. "Против солнца." (Against the sun.) Russkaia mysl', January 1914.

11039. Vernadsky, George (Vernadskii). "The expansion of Russia." Transactions of the Connecticut academy of arts and sciences, 31:391-425, July 1933.

11040. Veniukov, M. "Поземельные приобретения и уступки России за последние 50 лет, 1830-1880 гг." (Territorial acquisitions and cessions of Russia for the last fifty years, 1830-1880.) Russkaia mysl', 24-141, April 1880.

11041. Kotliarevskii, S. "Правовые достижения России в Азии."
(Legal accomplishments of Russia in Asia.) Novyi Vostok,
1 (1922):34-44.

11042. Beveridge, A. J. The Russian advance, London, 1904.
485 p.

11043. Kleinbort, L. Русский империализм в Азии. (Russian
imperialism in Asia.) St. Petersburg, Izd. "Znanie", no.
309, 1906. 47 p.

11044. Движение России на Дальний Восток. (Russia's advance
in the Far East.) St. Petersburg, 1913. 72 p.

C. The Eurasian Interpretation

11045. Евразийский временник. (Eurasian annals.) Berlin,
1923-1927.. 5 issues.

11046. Евразийская хроника. (Eurasian chronicle.) Berlin,
192?-1927 ? (Up to 1927, 9 issues published).

11047. Vernadskii, G. V. Начертание русской истории. (Outline of Russian history.) Prague, Evraziiskoe knigoizdatel'-
stvo, 1927. 264 p.   (2) The same. Опыт истории Евразии.
(An essay at a history of Eurasia.) Berlin, 1934.

11048. Trubetskoi, Prince N. S. Европа и человечество.
(Europe and mankind.) Sofia, 1920.

11049. Suvchinskii, P.P., Savitskii, P.N., Trubetskoi,
Prince N.S., and Florovskii, G. Исход к востоку. (Exodus
to the east.) Sofia, 1921.

11051. Россия и Латинство. (Russia and Latin civilization.)
Berlin, 1923.

11052. Наследие Чингисхана. (The heritage of Genghis Khan.)
Berlin, 1925.

11053. Trubetskoi, Prince S. N. К проблеме русского самопо-
знания. (Contributions to the problem of Russian self-know-
ledge.) Paris, 1927.

11050. Suvchinskii, P.P., Savitskii, P.N., Trubetskoi,
Prince N.S., G. Florovskii, and others. На путях. (On the
roads.) Berlin, 1922 2 v.

11054. Savitskii, P. N. Россия особый географический мир.
(Russia, a distinct geographical entity.) Prague, 1927.

11055. Savitskii, P. N. Географические особенности России.
(Geographical characteristics of Russia.) Vegetation and
soil. Prague, 1927.

11056. Anonymous. Евразийство. (Eurasianism.) Paris, 1926.

11057. Евразийский сборник. (The Eurasian miscellany: politics, philosophy, and the study of Russia.) Prague, 1929.

11058. Miliukov, Paul. "Eurasianism and Europeanism in Russian history." Festschrift Th. G. Masaryk zum 80 geburts-
tage. (Supplement to Der Russische gedanke), 1:225-236.
Bonn, 1930.

11059. Vernadskii, G. V. Звенья русской культуры. (Links of
Russian culture.) n.p. 1938-

D. Siberian History

(1) Sources

See 450-517;   3696-3736.

(a) Archival Guides

11060. Исторический архив. (Historical archive.) Moscow,
TSentral'nyi arkhiv, 1919.

11061. Архивное дело. (Archival work.) Moscow, TSentral'nyi
arkhiv, 1923- (Quarterly).

11062. Okun', S. "Сибирский комитет. Обзор архивных фондов."
(The Siberian committee. A survey of archival depositories.)
Arkhivnoe delo, 1 (1936):38:92-103.

11063. Andreev, V. "По сибирским архивам." (Through Siberian archives.) Arkhivnoe delo, 4 (1936):41:129-136.

11064. Istniuk, D. "Архивы Сибири." (The archives of Siberia.) Arkhivnoe delo, 5-6 (1926):168-176.

11065. Senkovskii, E. F. Архивное дело на Дальнем Востоке.
(Archival work in the Far East.) Arkhivnoe delo, 8-9 (1926):
104-114.

11066. Westberg, F. К анализу восточных источников о восточной Европе. (On the analysis of Oriental sources on Eastern Europe.) Zhurnal Ministerstva narodnogo prosveshcheniia, New series, 14. St. Petersburg, 1908.

11067. Ogloblin, N. N. Обозрение столбцов и книг Сибирского приказа (1592-1768 гг.). (A survey of rolls and books of the Siberian office, 1592-1768.) Moscow, 1895-1900. 4 v.   (2) The same. Библиотека сибирского митрополита Игнатия. 1700 г. (Library of the Siberian metropolitan Ignatii. 1700.) St. Petersburg, 1893.

11068. Kaidanov, N. I. (editor). Систематический каталог по делам Сибирского приказа.   (A systematic catalogue of the documents.of the Siberian office.) St. Petersburg, 1888.

11069. Golitsyn, N. V. (editor). Портфели Г. Ф. Миллера. (Portfolios of G[erhard] F[riedrich] Müller.) Moscow, 1899. 150 p.

11070. Putsillo, M. P. Указатель делам и рукописям относящимся до Сибири и принадлежащим Главному архиву Министерства иностранных дел. (A guide to records and manuscripts pertaining to Siberia and belonging to the Main archive of the Ministry of foreign affairs.) Moscow, 1879.   See 10363.

(b) Collections

11071. Каталог изданий. (Catalogue of publications.) St. Petersburg, Arkheograficheskaia komissiia, 1836 and 1893.

11072. Полное собрание русских летописей.   (A complete collection of Russian chronicles.) St. Petersburg, Arkheograficheskaia komissia, 1841-1921. 24 v. in 30 books.   (2) Lebedev, V (editor). Древнерусские летописи. (Old Russian chronicles.) Translation and commentary by V. Popov. Leningrad, Academia, 1936. xxiii, 390 p.

11073. Cross, Samuel (tr.). The Russian primary chronicle. (Harvard studies and notes in philology and literature, 12.) Cambridge, 1930. p. 74-320.

11074. The Chronicle of Novgorod, 1016-1471. Tr. by R. Michell and Neville Forbes, with an introduction by C. Raymond Beazley. Royal historical society Camden series, 3rd series, London, 25 (1914).

11075. Акты исторические... 1334-1700. (Historical documents.) St. Petersburg, Arkheograficheskaia komissiia,1841-1843. 5 v. and index.   Also: Дополнения к Актам историческим.

(Supplements to the Akty istoricheskie.) St. Petersburg,
1846-1872. 12 v.

11076. Полное собрание законов Российской империи. (A complete collection of the laws of Russia [1649-1825].) First
series. St. Petersburg, 1830-1839. 49 v.

11077. Сибирские летописи. (Siberian chronicles.) St. Petersburg, Arkheograficheskaia komissiia, 1907. 397, 20 p.

11078. Памятники сибирской истории XVIII века. (Records of
Siberian history in the XVIII century.) St. Petersburg,
Arkheograficheskaia komissiia, 1882-1885. 2 v.

11079. Акты, собранные в библиотеках и архивах Российской
империи Археологическою экспедицею. (Documents collected
by the Archeographic expedition in the libraries and archives of the Russian empire.) St. Petersburg, 1836. 4 v. and
index, 1838.

11080. Русская историческая библиотека. (Russian historical
library.) Collected documents. St. Petersburg, Arkheograficheskaia komissiia, 1872-1927. 39 v.

11081. Müller, Gerhard Friedrich. Sammlung russischer geschichte. St. Petersburg, Buchhandlung der Kaiserl. akademie der wissenschaften, 1732-1818. 10 v.

11082. Veselovskii, N. I. (editor). Материалы для истории
Российской духовной миссии в Пекине. (Documents pertaining
to the history of the Russian ecclesiastical mission in
Peking.) St. Petersburg, 1905. 71 p.

11083. Акты Московского государства, изданные Императорскою
академиею наук.(Documents of the Muscovite state published
by the Imperial academy of sciences.) St. Petersburg, 1890-
1901. 3 v.

11084. Remezov. Краткая сибирская летопись (Кунгурская).
(A brief Siberian chronicle [Kungur].) St. Petersburg, 1880.
39, 47, iii p. 154 illustrations.

11085. Potanin, G. N. Материалы для истории Сибири. (Sources for the study of Siberian history.) Chteniia Obschestva
istorii i drevnostei rossiiskikh, October-December 1866, 1-
128; January-March 1867, 129-230; April-June 1867, 231-324.
(Moscow university).

11086. Kuznetsov-Krasnoiarskii, P. (editor). Исторические
акты (1630-1699). (Historical documents [1630-1699].) Tomsk,
1890-1897. 2 v.

11087. Maikov, L. N. "Для истории сношений России с Китаем
при Петре Великом." (Documents relating to the Russo-Chinese relations during the reign of Peter the great.) Izvestiia Imperatorskogo russkogo arkheologicheskogo obshchestva (St. Petersburg), 8 (1877):545-551. See 3696-3735.

11088. Материалы для истории Сибирского казачьего войска.
(Sources pertaining to the history of the Siberian cossacks)
Omsk, Akmolinskie oblastnye vedomosti, 9-13, 25-18, 1878.
Edited by Zolotov.

11089. Strelov, E. D. Акты архивов Якутской области (с
1650 до 1800). (Documents from the archives of the Yakutsk
province.) Izvestiia Yakutskoi arkh. obl. komissii. Yakutsk,
1916, 1. 308, xxvi p.   (2) Al'kor, IA. P., and Grekov,
B. D. (editors). Колониальная политика московского государства в Якутии XVII в. (Colonial policy of the Muscovite
state in Yakutia in the XVIII c.) Leningrad, Institut narodov severa, 1936. 281 p.   (3) Al'kor, Ia. P. and Dresen,
A. K. (ed.). Колониальная политика царизма на Камчатке и
Чукотке в XVIII в. (The colonial policy of tsarism on the
Kamchatka and Chukotka peninsulas.) Leningrad, Institut narodov severa, 1935. 277 p.

11090. Priklonskii, V. L. Летопись Якутского края. (A chronicle of the Yakutsk region. Compiled from official sources.)
Krasnoiarsk, 1896.

11091. Stroev, P. M. Архив П. М. Строева. (The archive of
P. M. Stroev.) In Russkaia istoricheskaia biblioteka, 32
(1915); 35 (1917). St. Petersburg.

11092. Struve, B. V. Воспоминания о Сибири 1848-1854. (Reminiscences of Siberia, 1848-1854.) St. Petersburg, 1889.

11093. Падение царского режима. (The fall of the tsarist
régime.) Stenographic accounts of the examination and testimony given before the Extraordinary investigation commission of the Provisional government in 1917.   Petrograd,
1926-1927. 7 v.

11094. Ukhtomskii, Prince Esper E. Путешествие на Восток
Его Императорского высочества Государя наследника цесаревича
1890-1891. St. Petersburg, 1893-1895. 2 volumes, 4 parts.
English translation: Travels in the East of H.I.H. the

Tsarevich Nicolas Aleksandrovich in 1890-1891. Tr. by R.
Goodlet. London, 1896-1900. 2 v.   French translation by L.
Leger: Voyage en orient de S. A. I. le Césarevitch (S. M.
Nicholas II). Paris, 1893-1898. 2 v.

11095. Vitte, Sergei IUlievich. The memoirs of Count Witte.
Translated from the Russian manuscript and edited by Abra-
ham Yarmolinsky. Garden City, New York, and Toronto, Doubleday, Page & co., 1921. 445 p.

11096. Krasnyi Arkhiv (v. 52, pp. 54-124). "First steps of
Russian imperialism in the Far East." The Social and political science review, 18:2:236-281, July 1934.

(2) General Siberian History

11097. Golovachev, P. "Ближайшие задачи исторического изучения Сибири." (Current problems of historical investigation of Siberia.) Zhurnal Ministerstva narodnogo prosveshcheniia, 9, 1902 - 10, 1905.

11098. Leibovich, E. S. Хронологические таблицы по истории
народов СССР. (Chronological tables of the history of the
peoples of the USSR.) IX-XVIII c. Moscow, 1936. 17 p.

11099. Shcheglov, I. V. Хронологический перечень важнейших
данных из истории Сибири. (A chronological list of the most
important data in the history of Siberia.) 1032-1882. Irkutsk, 1883. 778 p.

11100. Znamenskaia, R. A. Хрестоматия по истории Сибири.(A
chrestomathy of the history of Siberia.) Novosibirsk, 1930.
263 p.

11101. Gudoshnikov, M. A. Сибирь. (Siberia.) Historical
chrestomathy. Moscow-Irkutsk, 1932. 244 p.

11102. Ogorodnikov, V. I. Очерк истории Сибири до начала
XIX века. (An outline of Siberian history to the XIX c.)
Part I. Введение. История до-русской Сибири. (Introduction.
History of pre-Russian Siberia.) Irkutsk, 1920. Part II:1.
Завоевание русскими Сибири. (Russian conquest of Siberia.)
Vladivostok, 1924.   Part II:3. Русская государственная
власть и сибирские инородцы XVI-XVIII в.в.   (Russian sov-
reignty and the Siberian natives in the XVI-XVIII c.) In
Sbornik trudov professorov i prepodavatelei Gosudarstvenno-
go irkutskogo universiteta, 1:1. Irkutsk, 1921. Also sepa-
rately: Irkutsk, 1920. (2) The same. Из истории покорения
Сибири. (History of the conquest of Siberia.) Conquest of

the IUkagir region. Chita, 1922. 104 p. 1 map.

11103. Platonov, S. F. Великий Новгород до его подчинения
Москве в 1478 году и после подчинения до Ништадского мира
1721 г. (The Great Novgorod before its submission to Moscow
in 1478 and after its submission until the treaty of Nystad,
1721.) Novgorod, 1916. 11 p.

11104. Baddely, John F. Russia, Mongolia, China: being some
record of the relations between them from the beginning of
the seventeenth century to the death of Tsar Alexei Mikhailovich, A. D. 1602-1676, rendered mainly in the form of
narratives dictated or written sent by the Russian tsars...
to the Kalmuck and Mongol khans and princes and to the emperors of China. London, Macmillan & co., 1919. 2 v.

11105. Arseniev, IU. V. Статейный список посольства Н. Спафария в Китай 1675-1678. (A systematic account of Spafari's
embassy to China, 1675-1678.) In Vestnik Arkheologii i istorii izd. Imp. arkh. institutom, 17. St. Petersburg, 1906.
(2) The same. Новые данные о службе Николая Спафария в
России,1671-1708. (New information concerning Nicholas Spa-
fai's service in Russia, 1671-1708.) Izd. Imp. obshchestvo
istorii i drevnostei rossiiskikh pri Moskovskom universitete. Moscow, 1900. See 3703.

11106. Berkh, Vasilii N. Царствование царя Михаила Феодоро-
вича. (The reign of Tsar Michael Feodorovich.) St. Petersburg, 1832. 2 parts. (2) The same. Царствование царя
Феодора Алексеевича и история первого стрелецкого бунта.
(The reign of Tsar Feodor Alekseevich and the history of
the uprising of the streltsy.) St. Petersburg, 1834-1835.
2 v.

11107. Barsukov, Aleksandr P. Списки городовых воевод ...
Московского государства XVII ст. (Lists of municipal military heads ... of the XVII century Muscovy state.) St. Petersburg, 1902.

11108. Butsinskii, Petr N. К истории Сибири. (History of
Siberia.) Surgut, Narym, and Ketsk to 1645. Kharkov, 1893.

11109. Debol'skii, V. N. Сибирские пути XVI и XVII веков.
(Siberian routes of the XVI and XVII centuries.)

11110. Wirth, Albrecht. Geschichte Sibiriens u. der Mandschurei. Bonn, Georgi, 1899. vii, 220 p.

11111. Ogloblin, Nikolai N. Источники чертежной книги
Сибири Семена Ремезова.(Sources for Semeon Remezov's map of
Siberia.) St. Petersburg, 1891. (2) Zamyslovskiĭ, E. E.
"Чертежи сибирских земель XVI-XVII в." (In Zhurnal Minister-
stva narodnogo prosveshcheniia, June 1891.)

11112. Oksenov, A. V. Слухи и вести о Сибири до Ермака.
(Rumors and news of Siberia before Ermak.) In Sibirskii
sbornik (St. Petersburg), 4 (1887).

11113. Petrov, A. L. Материалы для истории Угорской Руси.
(Sources pertaining to the history of Ugrian Russia.) St.
Petersburg, 1912.

11114. Presniakov, Aleksandr E. Образование Великорусского
государства. (Formation of the Great-Russian state.) Outlines in the history of the XIII-XV centuries. Petrograd,
1918.

11115. Remezov, S. Чертежная книга Сибири составлена в
1701. (A book of maps on Siberia collected in 1701.) Izd.
Arkheograficheskoi komissii, St. Petersburg, 1882.

11116. Sadovnikov, D. N. Наши землепроходцы. Рассказы о заселении Сибири   1581-1792 гг. (Our landexplorers. Tales of
the settlement of Siberia, 1581-1792.) Moscow, 1898. 198 p.

11117. Suvorin, Aleksei S. Русские замечательные люди.
Ермак Тимофеевич, покоритель Сибири. (Remarkable Russians.
Ermak Timofeevich, conqueror of Siberia.) 3rd edition. St.
Petersburg, 1887. 191 p.

11118. Titov, Andrei A. Сибирь в XVII веке.   (Siberia in
the XVII century.) A collection of ancient Russian articles
on Siberia and lands bordering upon it. Moscow, IUdin, 1890.
216 p.

11119. Müller, Gerhard F. История Сибири. (History of Siberia.) Moscow-Leningrad, Academy of Sciences of the USSR,
1, 1937-   (2) The same. Описание Сибирского царства и всех
происшедших в нем дел от начала, а особливо от покорения
его российской державе по сии времена. (A description of the
Siberian kingdom and all the important events from beginning, and particularly from its conquest by the Russian
state up to the present time.) St. Petersburg, 1787. 368 p.
First edition: St. Petersburg, 1750.   p.   (3) The same.
Conquest of Siberia, and the History of the transactions,
wars, commerce, & c. & c., carried on between Russia and
China, from the earliest period. Translated from the Rus-

sian... London, Smith, Elder, & co., 1842. v, 153 p. (4)
The same. Voyages from Asia to America, for completing the
discoveries of the northwest coast of America. London, 1761.
viii, xliii, 76 p. (5) Voyages et découvertes faites par
les Russes... Amsterdam, 1766. 2 v.

11120. Fischer, Johann Eberhard. Sibirische geschichte von
der entdeckung Sibiriens bis auf die eroberung dieses lands
durch die russische waffen. St. Petersburg, 1768. 2 v. (2)
The same. Russian translation: Сибирская история с самого
открытия Сибири до завоевания сей земли российским оружием.
St. Petersburg, 1774. 631 p. 2 maps. (3) The same. Recherches historiques sur les principales nations établies
en Siberie et dans les pays adjacens lors de la conquête
des Russes; ouvrage traduit du russe, par M. Stollenwerck.
Paris, 1803. xxiv, 295 p.

11121. Andrievich, V. K. История Сибири. (A history of Siberia.) St. Petersburg, 1889. 2 parts. 220, 487 p. (2) The
same. Пособие к написанию истории Забайкалья. (A guide to
the writing of history of the Transbaikal region.) Irkutsk,
1885. (3) Краткий очерк истории Забайкалья с древнейшего
времени до 1762 г. (A brief outline of the history of the
Transbaikal region from ancient times to 1762.) St. Petersburg, 1887. 237 p. (4) The same. Сибирь в XIX веке.
(Siberia in the XIX century.) St. Petersburg, 1889. 2 parts.
298, 425 p.

11122. Firsov, N. Чтения по истории Сибири. (Readings in
Siberian history.) Moscow, 1921. 2 parts. 67, 71 p.

11123. Slovtsov, P. A. Историческое обозрение Сибири. (Historical survey of Siberia.) 2nd edition. St. Petersburg,
1886. 326, iv, xxvi, 364, v p. (First edition: 1838-1844.)

11124. Kiuner, N. V. Лекции по истории и географии Сибири.
(Lectures on the history and geography of Siberia.) Vladivostok, 1919. 273 p.

11125. Selishchev, A. M. Диалектологический очерк Сибири.
(A dialectological sketch of Siberia.) Irkutsk, 1921. 294 p.

11126. Kartsov, V. G. Очерки истории народов в западной
Сибири. (Sketches in the history of the peoples of western
Siberia.) Moscow, Sotsekgiz, 1937. 132 p.

(3) Siberian History to the XVIII Century

See 3696-3789.

11127. Сказания иностранных писателей о России.   (Narrations of foreign writers about Russia.) Arkheograficheskaia komissiia, St. Petersburg, 1851-1868. 2 v.

11128. Iakinf (Bichurin). Историческое обозрение Ойратов и Калмыков с XV ст. (Historical survey of the Oirats and Kalmyks from the XV century.) St. Petersburg, 1834.

11129. Anuchin, D. N. "К истории ознакомления с Сибирью д о Ермака." (Historical data concerning Siberia before its conquest by Ermak.) In Drevnosti, Moscow, 15 (1890). (2) Pypin, A. N. "Первые известия о Сибири и русское ее заселение." (First news of Siberia and its settlement by the Russians.) Vestnik Evropy, 8 (1891):741-790.   (3) Tyzhnov, I. I. "Обзор иностранных известий о Сибири 2-ой половины XVI в." (Survey of foreign reports concerning Siberia in the second half of the XVI century.) In Sibirskii sbornik (St. Petersburg), 1887; and separately, Irkutsk, 1890.

11130. Platonov, S. F.. Прошлое русского севера. (The past of the Russian north.) Petrograd, Vremia, 1923. 79 p.   (2) Oksenov, A. V. Сношения Новгорода Великого с Югорской землею. (Relations between Great Novgorod and the IUgra region.) In the IAdrintsev Sbornik. St. Petersburg, 1885: 425-446.

11131. Oksenov, A. V. Сибирское царство до эпохи Ермака. (The Siberian kingdom prior to Ermak.) Tomskie gubernskie vedomosti, 14-19 (1888).   (2) The same. "Старые пути из пределов Московского государства в Сибирскую землю. (Old routes from the Muscovy state to Siberia.) Tomskie gubernskie vedomosti, 12 (1888).   (3) Новые данные к истории Сибири XVII века.(New data concerning the history of Siberia of the XVII century.) Irkutsk, 1895.

11132. Martiushev, A. M. "Поход Курбского на Печору и за Урал в 1499 г." (Kurbskii's expedition to the Pechora and beyond the Ural in 1499.) In Zapiski Obshchestva izucheniia Komi kraia, 5 (1930):66-84.

11133. Adrianov, A. V. "К вопросу о покорении Сибири." (On the question of the conquest of Siberia.) Zhurnal Ministerstva narodnogo prosveshcheniia (St. Petersburg), 4 (1893).

11134. Akulinin, I. G. Ермак и Строгановы. (Ermak and the
Stroganovs.) Historical research of Siberian chronicles and
government instruction. Paris, 1933. 62 p. (2) Mironov,
A. M. "Покоритель Сибири Ермак Тимофеевич в сибирских
летописях и старинных намятниках искусства."
(Conqueror of Siberia, Ermak Timofeevich, as pictured in
the Siberian chronicles and literature.) In Izvestiia ob-
shchestva arkheologii, istorii i etnografii pri Kazanskom
universitete, Kazan, 30:4 (1920):443-463.   (3) Stavrovich,
A. M. "Строгановская летопись." (The Stroganov chronicle.)
In Sbornik...posv. S. F. Platonovu (Petrograd), 1922:285-
293.   (4) Vvedenskii, A. A. "Аника Строганов." (Anika Stroganov.) Sbornik... Platonovu (Petrograd), 1922:90-113.   (5)
Dmitriev, A. A. "Строгановы и Ермак." (Stroganovy and Ermak)
Permskaia starina, 4 (1892).   (6) The same. "Покорение
Югорских земель и Сибири." (Conquest of the Iugrian lands
and Siberia.) Permskaia starina, 5 (1894).   (7) The same.
"Первые годы после Ермака и Смутное время." (The first years
after Ermak and the Times of trouble.) Permskaia starina,
6 (1895).   (8) The same. "Верхотурский край в XVII веке."
(The Verkhotursk region in the XVII century.) Permskaia
starina, 7 (1897).   (9) Golovachev, P. "Покорение Сибирского царства и личность Ермака."   (The conquest of Siberia
and the personality of Ermak.) In Sibirskii Sbornik, 1
(1891).   (10) Ilovaiskii, D. I. "Ермак и покорение Сибири."
(Ermak and the conquest of Siberia.) Russkii vestnik, 19
(1889).   (11) Tikhomirov, E. Ермак Тимофеевич, покоритель
Сибири. (Ermak Timofeevich, conqueror of Siberia.) Moscow,
1881. 53 p. (12) Nebol'sin, Pavel. Покорение Сибири. (The
conquest of Siberia.) St. Petersburg, 1849.

11135. Sadovnikov, D. Подвиги Русских в Сибири. (Russian ex-
ploits in Siberia.) Erofei Khabarov and Semen Dezhnev. Moscow, 1906. 61 p.

11136. Kotoshikhin, G. K. О России в царствование Алексея
Михайловича. (Russia during the reign of Aleksei Mikhailovich.) St. Petersburg, 1840. 2nd edition, 1859. 3d edition
1884. See 10589.

11137. Bakhrushin, S. V. "Остяцкие и вогульские княжества в
XVI-XVII веках."   (Ostiak and Vogul principalities in the
XVI-XVII centuries.) Izvestiia. Nauchno-issledovatel'skaia
assotsiatsiia narodov Severa, Leningrad, 3 (1935):1-91.
Also separately, Leningrad, 1935. 86 p.

11138. Butsinskii, P. N. Заселение Сибири и быт первых ее
насельников.   (The peopling of Siberia and the customs of
the first settlers.) Kharkov, 1889. iv, 345 p.

11139. Кунгур. Материалы для истории города XVII и XVIII
столетий. (Kungur. Materials pertaining to the history of
the town in the XVII and XVIII centuries.) Moscow, 1886.
112 p.

11140. Томск в XVII веке. (Tomsk in the XVII century.) Materials pertaining to the history of the city.) St. Petersburg, n. d., 169 p.

11141. Пермский сборник. (The Perm miscellany.) Moscow,
1859-1860.

11142. Tumenets and Petrov. Cossack mission to the Altyn
Khan, 1616. Deposition made in Tomsk. In Fischer, Sib. Ge-
schichte, VI. 366 seq. (For deposition made subsequently in
Moscow see I. A. N. Izvestiia otd. russkogo iazyka etc.
Petrograd, 1914.)

11143. Spafarii, Nikolai. Путешествие через Сибирь от Тобольска до Нерчинска и границ Китая, русского посланника Н.
Спафария в 1675 г. (Travels, through Siberia from Tobolsk to
Nerchinsk and the boundaries of China, of the Russian ambas-
sador Nikolai Spafarii in 1675.) Spafarii's travel diary,
with preface and commentary by IU. V. Arseniev. St. Petersburg, 1882. 214 p.   (2) IAtsimirskii, A. I. Николай Милеску
Спафарий. (Nikolai Milesku Spafarii.) Kazan, 1908. 15 p.
(3) Arseniev, IU. V. "Николай Спафарий и его время."   (Nikolai Spafarii and his time.) Russkii arkhiv, 2 (1895):7:
349-360.   (See 11105.)

11144. Remezov, S. "Туземные легенды в 'Сибирской истории'."
(Native legends in the "Siberian history".) Istoricheskie
izvestiia. Moscow, 3-4 (1916).

11145. Massa, Isaac. Завоевание Сибири. (The conquest of
Siberia.) Translated into Russian by Tyzhnov. In the Sibirskii vestnik, 1887:105-110.

11146. Pal'mov, N. N. Этюды по истории приволжских калмыков
XVII и XVIII века. Ч. I. (Historical studies of the Volga
Kalmyks, XVII-XVIII centuries.) Astrakhan, 1926. 265 p.

11147. Tokarev, S. "Колониальная политика Московского
государства в Сибири в XVII веке." (Colonial policy of the
Muscovite state in Siberia in the XVII century.) Istoriia
v shkole, 4:73-99, July-August 1936.

11148. Alkor, IA. P. and Grekov, B. D. (ed.). Колониальная
политика Московского государства в Якутии XVII в.   (Colonial

policy of the Muscovite state in Iakutia in the XVII century.) Leningrad, 1936. xxxii, 281 p.   See 11089.

11149. Инструкция письмяному голове Пояркову.   (Instructions to Captain Poiarkov.) Chteniia v Imperatorskom obshchestve istorii i drevnostei rossiiskikh pri Moskovskom universitete, 1:1-22, January-March 1861.

11150. Ragoza (Lt.-Colonel). Краткий очерк занятия Амурского края и развития боевых сил Приамурского военного округа. (A brief description of the occupation of the Amur province and the development of the military forces of the Amur region.) Khabarovsk, 1891.

11151. Parshin. История города Албазина.   (History of the city of Albazin.) Moscow, 1844. 208 p.

11152. Ogorodnikov, V. I. "Туземное и русское земледелие на Амуре в XVII в."   (Native and Russian farming in the Amur region in the XVII century.) Trudy Gosudarstvennogo Dal'nevostochnogo universiteta. Vladivostok, 1927. 3:4: 1-91.

11153. Vernadskii, G. V. "Государевы служилые и промышленные люди в Восточной Сибири XVII века." (The military men and traders of Eastern Siberia in the XVII century.) Zhurnal Ministerstva narodnogo prosveshcheniia, April (?) 1915.

(4) From 1689 to 1905

See 3696-3789.

11154. "Албазин и осада его Маньчжурами." (Albazin and its siege by the Manchurians.) Morskoi sbornik, 5 (1861):14-25.

11155. Nikolai (Ordained monk). История Пекинской духовной миссии в первый период ее деятельности (1685-1742). (The history of the Pekin religious mission during the first period of its activities. 1685-1742.) Kazan, 1887.

11156. Bantysh-Kamenskii, D. N. Деяния знаменитых полководцев и министров, служивших в царствование Государя императора Петра Великого. (Deeds of the famous generals and ministers serving in the reign of Peter the Great.) With portraits. 2nd edition. Moscow, 1821.

11157. Lebedev, V."Посольство в Хиву в 1716, 1717 и 1718 гг." (The embassy to Khiva in 1716, 1717, and 1718.) Zhurnal Ministerstva narodnogo prosveshcheniia, 51 (1846).

11158. Unkovskii, I. Посольство к зюнгарскому Хун-Тайджи-Цеван Рабтану капитана от артиллерии Ивана Унковского и путевой журнал его за 1722-1724. (The embassy to the Zungar Khun-Taidji-Tsevan Rabtan headed by Captain of artillery, Ivan Unkovskii, and his diary for 1722-1724.) St. Petersburg, 1887.

11159. Vatin, V. Минусинский край в XVIII веке. (The Minusinsk region in the XVIII century.) Minusinsk, 1913. 212 p.

11160. Terentiev, A. A. Закрепощение ненцев Канинской и Тиманской тундр в XVIII веке. (Enserfment of the Nentsy of the Kanin and Timan tundras in the XVIII century.) Leningrad, 1934. 40 p.

11161. Shashkov, S. S. "Материалы для истории северовосточной Сибири в XVIII веке." (Sources pertaining to the history of northeastern Siberia.) In Chteniia v Imperatorskom obshchestve istorii i drevnostei rossiiskikh pri Moskovskom univеrsitete, 3:63-93, July-September 1864.

11162. Okun', S. "Колониальная политика царизма в Охотско-Камчатском крае в XVIII веке."(Colonial policy of tsarism in the Okhotsk-Kamchatka region in the XVIII century.) Bor'ba klassov, 12:82-89, December 1934.

11163. Golovachev, P. Сибирь в Екатерининской комиссии. (The question of Siberia in Catherine's Committee.) A study in the history of Siberia in the XVIII century. Moscow, 1889. 127 p.

11164. Dmitriev-Mamonov, A. I. Пугачевщина в Сибири. (The Pugachev rebellion in Siberia.) Moscow, 1898. 152 p.

11165. Vagin, V. I. Исторические сведения о деятельности графа М. М. Сперанского в Сибири. (Historical data concerning the activities of Count M. M. Speranskii in Siberia. 1819-1822.) St. Petersburg, 1872. 2 v.

11166. Hedenstrom, M. M. "Записки о Сибири." (Notes on Siberia.) Zhurnal Ministerstva vnutrennikh del, 1 (1829): 1:123-158; 2 (1830):1:111-126; 2:83-103; 3:165-182; 3(1831): 4:149-158.

11167. Обозрение главных оснований местного управления... (Survey of the main principles of local administration of Siberia.) St. Petersburg, 1841.

11168. А. С. Пушкин и Сибирь. (A. S. Pushkin and Siberia.)
Collected articles. Irkutsk, Vostsiboblgiz, 1937.

11169. Dmitriev-Mamonov, A. I.Декабристы в Западной Сибири.
(Decembrists in Western Siberia.) Moscow, 1895. 210 p. Later edition, 1905. 261 p.

11170. Barsukov, Ivan. Граф Н. Н. Муравьев-Амурский. (Count
N. N. Muraviev-Amurskii.) Moscow, 1891. 2 v. (2) Butsinskii,
Petr N. Граф Н. Н. Муравьев-Амурский. (Count N. N. Muraviev-
Amurskii.) St. Petersburg, 1895. 78 p.

11171. Goncharov, Ivan A. Воспоминания Гончарова о восточной Сибири и Муравьеве-Амурском. (Goncharov's memoirs of
Eastern Siberia and Muraviev-Amurskii.) Russkoe obozrenie,
1 (1891).

11172. Whittingham, P. Bernard. Notes on the late expedition
against the Russian settlements in Eastern Siberia; and of
a visit to Japan and to the shores of Tartary, and of the
Sea of Okhotsk. London, 1856. xv, 300 p.

11173. Du Hailly, Ed. "Les escadres de la France et de l'
Angleterre sur les côtes du Japon et de la Tartarie à pour-
suite de l'escadre russe en 1855." Revue des deux mondes,
Septembre 1858.

11174. Bogdanov, R. K. Воспоминания амурского казака о
прошлом с 1849 по1880 год. (Reminiscences of an Amur cossack, 1849-1880.) Zapiski Priamurskogo otdeleniia Imperatorskogo russkogo geograficheskogo obshchestva, 5:3.

11175. Strel'bitskii, I (comp.). Земельные приобретения
России в царствование императора Александра II с 1855 по
1881 год. (Territorial acquisitions of Russia during the
reign of Alexander II from 1855 to 1881.) St. Petersburg,
1881. 56 p.

11176. Veniukov, M. I. "Амур в 1857-1858 г."(The Amur province in 1857-1858.) Russkaia starina, 24 (1879).

11177. Zavalishin, D. I. "Амурское дело и влияние его на
Восточную Сибирь и государство." (The Amur affair and its
influence upon Eastern Siberia and the state.) Russkaia
starina, September-October 1881.

11178. Dmitriev, A. A. К истории Сибирского вопроса. (On the
history of the Siberian question.) Perm, 1895. 17 p.

(5) The Revolutions in Siberia

(a) Bibliography

11179. Mandel'shtam, Roza S. Революционное движение в России XVII-XX с. (The revolutionary movement in Russia in the XVII-XX cent.) A systematic guide to the literature published in 1925. Moscow, 1928. 112 p. (Ed. by B. P. Kozmin).

11180. Turunov, A. N. and Vegman, V. D. (comp.). Революция и гражданская война в Сибири. (The revolution and civil war in Siberia.) An index of books and periodical articles. Novosibirsk, 1928. 136 p.

11181. Matveev, Z. N. "Периодическая печать на Дальнем Востоке в период революции 1917-1922. (Periodical literature in the Far East during the revolutionary period, 1917-1922.) In Izvestiia Priamurskogo Gub. Arkh. Biuro, 3 (1923). And separately, 1923. 22 p.

11182. Печать и революция.(The Press and revolution.) Moscow, 1, 1921-

11183. Porshnev, I. Книжная летопись Иркутска за годы революции. (A bibliography of Irkutsk during the revolutionary years.) Irkutsk, 1920. 75 p.

11184. Matveev, Z. N. "Печать на Дальнем Востоке в период революции. (The press in the Far East during the revolutionary period.) Novyi Dal'nii Vostok, 1923:12-13. Cf. 11181.

(b) Periodicals

11185. Архив гражданской войны. (Archives of the Civil war.) Izd. Russkoe tvorchestvo, Berlin, 1, 1922-

11186. Архив русской революции. (Archive of the Russian revolution.) Izd. Slovo, Berlin, 1, 1921-

11187. Гражданская война. (Civil war.) Sources on the history of the Red army. Moscow, 1, 1923-

11188. Партизанское движение в Сибири. (The partisan [guerrilla] movement in Siberia.) Moscow, TSentral'nyi arkhiv, 1, 1925- (irregular).

(c) The Revolutionary Movement to 1905

11189. К 30-летию большевистких партийных организаций в Сибири. (Thirty years of Bolshevik party organizations in Siberia.) 1903-1933. Moscow, Staryi bol'shevik, 1934. 140 p.

11190. Filippov, A. N."Пугачевское движение в Сибири."
(The Pugachev movement in Siberia.) Severnaia Azia (Moscow), (1926):3:67-78; 4:73-89.

11191. Glumov."К декабрьским дням." (December days.) In
Otkliki sovremennosti, 2. St. Petersburg, 1906. pp 128-152.

11192. Gubaidulin, A. "Участие татар в Пугачевщине." (Tatar participation in the Pugachev rebellion.) Novyi Vostok,
7 (1925):262-268.

11193. Riazanov, A. F. "Отголоски Пугачевского восстания на
Урале в Киргиз-Кайсацкой малой орде и в Поволжье." (Rever-
berations of the Pugachev rebellion among the Kirghiz-Kais-
sak Horde in the Urals and along the Volga region.) In Trudy Obshchestva izucheniia Kazakstana, 6 (1925):195-241.

11194. Savich, A. Очерки истории крестьянских волнений на
Урале в XVIII-XX вв.(Historical sketches of the peasant unrest in the Ural region in the XVIII-XX cent.) Moscow, 1931.
178 p.

11195. Zavalishin, Dmitrii I. Записки декабриста. (Memoirs
of a decembrist.) St. Petersburg, 1906. 464 p.

11196. Bender, I. G."Златоустовская забастовка в 1903 г."
(The Zlatoustovsk strike in 1903.) In Arkhiv istorii truda
v Rossii, 4:2 (1922):50-53.

11197. Shilov, A. A. and Karnaukova, M. G. Деятели революционного движения в России. (Workers of the revolutionary
movement in Russia.) Moscow, 1927-1928.

11198. Участники русского революционного движения эпохи борьбы с царизмом. (Participants of the Russian revolutionary
movement in the period of struggle with tsarism.) Moscow,
1927.

11199. See 11179.

(d) The Revolution of 1905.

(i) General Accounts

11200. 1905 год в документах. (Year 1905 in documents.) Moscow, Komissiia dlia prazdnovaniia 20-tiletiia revoliutsii
1905 goda, 1925-

11201. Stankevich, A. P. Первая революция на Дальнем Востоке. (The first revolution in the Far East.) A chronology of revolutionary events, 1903-1908. Khabarovsk, 1930. xliv, 236 p.

11202. 1905 год в Сибири. (Year 1905 in Siberia.) Collected essays and reminiscences. Novonikolaevsk, 1925. 200 p.

11203. 1905 год в Сибири. (Year 1905 in Siberia.) Collected materials. Novonikolaevsk, 1925. 48 p.

11204. Godes, M. S. (ed.). Пробуждение Азии. 1905 год и революция на Востоке. (The awakening of Asia. Year 1905 and the revolution in the East.) Collected articles. Leningrad, 1935. xi, 228 p.

11205. Rafail, M. "Ленин, 1905 г. и .Восток." (Lenin, the year 1905, and the East.) Novyi Vostok, 10-11 (1925):1-14.

11206. Zaitsev, D. M. "Революция и контр-революция в Сибири." (Revolution and counter-revolution in Siberia.) In Nevskii sbornik, St. Petersburg, 1 (1906):181-262.

11207. Vetoshkin, M. "Большевики и меньшевики в 1905 году на Дальнем Востоке." (The bolsheviks and mensheviks in 1905 in the Far East.) Proletarskaia revoliutsiia, Moscow-Leningrad, 4 (51):158-192, April 1926.

11208. Vetoshkin, M. "Подготовка вооруженного восстания в Сибири в 1905 г." (Preparation for the armed rebellion in Siberia in 1905.) Sibirskii Soiuz RSDRP, Moscow, (1935): 20-45.

11209. Shumiatskii, B. Z. В Сибирском подполье. (In the [political] "underground" of Siberia.) Sketches, 1903-1908. Moscow-Leningrad, 1926. 192 p.

11210. Сибирь. Архив освободительного движения 1905-1906 г, (Siberia. Archives of the liberal movement in 1905-1906.) St. Petersburg, 1907. 160 p.

11211. Maksakov, V. "Железнодорожники Сибири в революционном движении 1905 г." (Siberian railway employees in the revolutionary movement of 1905.) Istoriia proletariata SSSR, Moscow, 6 (1931):210-225.

11212. Ashenbakh, G. "Дело о восстании 402-х." (The case of the rebellion of 402 men.) The Siberian military fleet in the revolutionary movement. In the miscellany: Na vakhte revoliutsii (Leningrad), 2 (1926):5-21.

11213. Baranskii, N. В рядах Сибирского социал-демократического союза, (In the ranks of the Siberian social democratic union.) Memoirs of underground work, 1897-1908. Novonikola-evsk, 1923. 89 p.

(ii) Special Accounts

11214. Dvorianov, S. "Ташкентская социал-демократическая организация в революции 1905 года." (The Tashkent social-democrat organization in the revolution of 1905.) Krasnaia letopis' Turkestana, Tashkent, 1-2 (1923):7-21.

11215. Parenkov, A. "Самарканд в революции 1905 года." (Samarkand in the revolution of 1905.) Krasnaia letopis' Turkestana, Tashkent, 1-2 (1923):24-43.

11216. Berezovskii, F. Таежные застрельщики. (Snipers of the Taiga.) Sketches of the revolutionary struggle of 1905. Leningrad, 1926. 134 p.

11217. Koz'min, N. N. 1905 год и буряты. (Year 1905 and the Buriats.) Irkutsk, 1926. 9 p.

11218. 1905 год в Прибайкалье. (Year 1905 in the Baikal region.) Verkhneudinsk, 1925. 77 p.

11219. Pavlov, E. На Дальнем Востоке в 1905 г. (The Far East in 1905.) Moscow, 1907. 106 p.

11220. "1905-1906 гг. на Дальнем Востоке." (1905-1906 in the Far East.) In Dal'istpart. Sbornik, Vladivostok-Chita, 1 (1923):189-208.

11221. Революционное движение на Дальнем Востоке. (The revolutionary movement in the Far East.) Vladivostok, 1925. 274p

11222. Osokin, S. P. 1905 год в Челябинске. (Year 1905 in Cheliabinsk.) Reminiscences of a participant of the revolutionary events.) Cheliabinsk, 1936. 126 p.

11223. Batashev, P. N. Ленский расстрел. (The Lena executions.) Reminiscences. 2nd edition. Moscow, 1936. 93 p.

11224. Petrov, S. Большевики Урала в революции 1905-1907 гг. (The Ural bolsheviks in the revolution of 1905-1907.) Sverdlovsk, 1931. 120 p.

11225. Beloborodov, A. "Из истории партизанского движения
на Урале. (History of the partisan movement in the Urals.)
(1906-1909).) Krasnaia Letopis', Moscow-Leningrad, 1 (16):
(1926):92-99.

11226. Murashev, P. "Страничка революционного движения на
Урале в 1905 году." (A page from the revolutionary movement
in the Urals in 1905.) Katorga i Ssylka, Moscow, 2 (1927):
16-40.

11227. Революционные события 1905 г. в г. Уфе и уральских
заводах. (The revolution of 1905 in Ufa and the Ural factories.) Ufa, 1925. 257 p.

11228. Baranov, Aleksei V. 1905 год на Урале. (Year 1905 in
the Urals.) Moscow, 1929. 110 p.

11229. Baranov, A. and Mutnykh, V. Металлисты Урала накануне и в период 1905 г. (Ural metal workers on the eve and
during the 1905 period.) Collected materials and documents.
Sverdlovsk, 1926. 219 p.

11230. Maksakov, V. (comp.). Карательные экспедиции в Сибири в 1905-1906 гг. (Punitive expeditions to Siberia in
1905-1906.) Documents and materials. Moscow, RSFSR, TSentral'nyi arkhiv, 1932. 463 p. (2)"К истории карательных
экспедиций в Сибири." (History of the punitive expeditions
in Siberia [in 1905].) Krasnyi arkhiv, 1 (1922):329-343.
(3) Pokrovskii, M. N. 1905. История революционного движения.
(1905. History of the revolutionary movement.) Moscow-Leningrad, Gosizdat, 1925-1927. 3 v. in 4.

(iii) The Cities in the Revolution of 1905

11231. Октябрьские дни в Томске. (The October days in Tomsk)
Description of the bloody events of October 20-23... Tomsk,
1905. 71 p.

11232. Дело о погроме в г. Томске в 1905 г. (The pogrom in
Tomsk in 1905.) Tomsk, 1909. 101 p.

11233. Borziakov, G. "Томск в октябрьские дни 1905 г."
(Tomsk during the October days of 1905.) Iz epokhi bor'by s
tsarizmom. Sbornik, 4. Kiev, 1925:5-24.

11234. Babailov, I. "Революционная Чита с 1905 по 1909 г."
(Revolutionary Chita from 1905 to 1909.) In Dal'istpart,
Sbornik, Vladivostok, 2 (1924):67-74.

11235. Shumiatskii, B. Z. Красноярское восстание 1905 года.
(The Krasnoiarsk uprising of 1905.) Moscow, 1926. 56 p.

11236. Novogreshnov, IA. 1905 год в Красноярске. (1905 in
Krasnoiarsk.) Krasnoiarsk, 1925. 63 p.

11237. Kogan, L. "Страничка из истории Красноярской республики 1905 года." (A page from the history of the Krasnoiarsk republic of 1905.) In: 1905 god v vospominaniakh ego
uchastnikov.Rostov n/D., 1925: 81-89 p.

11238. K-in, A. "Восстание в Красноярске." (The uprising in
Krasnoiarsk.) In: Narodnoe delo, Sbornik (Paris), 4 (1909):
35-84.

11239. Papikas, R. "Читинская организация РСДРП в 1905-1906
гг." (The Chita organization of the Russian social democratic workingmen's party in 1905-1906.) In: Dal'istpart,
Sbornik,(Chita-Vladivostok), 1923:1:153-160.

11240. Dranitsyn, V."Вооруженное восстание во Владивостоке
в 1907 году." (The armed uprising in Vladivostok in 1907.)
Na vakhte revoliutsii (Leningrad), 2 (1926):23-48.

11241. Livshits, S. I. "Военное восстание во Владивостоке
16-17 октября 1907 г." (The military uprising in Vladivostok, October 16-17, 1907.) Katorga i ssylka, Moscow, 2
(1927):102-122.

(e) The Revolutions of 1917

(i) General Accounts

11242. История гражданской войны. (History of the civil
war.) Leningrad-Moscow, 1932-   (Projected history in 16 v.
V. 13 to deal with the Far East; v. 12, Central Asia.)

11243. Miliukov, P. N.   История второй русской революции.
(History of the second Russian revolution.)   Sofia, 1921-
1924. 3 parts.

11244. Chamberlin, W. H. The Russian revolution. New York,
1935. 2 v.

11245. Bunyan, James and Fisher,H.H. The Bolshevik revolution, 1917-1918. Documents and materials. Stanford university press, 1934. 735 p.   (2) Bunyan, James. Intervention,
civil war, and communism in Russia, April-December 1918.
Documents and materials. Baltimore, 1936. xv, 594 p.

11246. Poliak, A. Действия пятой Красной армии от реки То-
боль до озера Байкал. (Operations of the fifth Red army
from the Tobol river to Lake Baikal.) Moscow, 1922.

11247. Sakharov, K. V. Белая Сибирь.(White Siberia.) Internal warfare, 1918-1920. München, 1923.

11248. Steidler, F. Наше выступление в России в 1918 г.
(Our Russian debut of 1918). Prague, Pamiatniki voiny, 1923.

11249. Революция на Дальнем Востоке. (Revolution in the Far
East.) Moscow, Istpart, 1923. 433 p.

11250. Краткий отчет Сибирского революционного комитета.
(A brief report of the Siberian revolutionary committee.)
Novonikolaevsk, 1924. 37 p.

11251. Vladimirova, Vera. Из недавнего прошлого. (From the
recent past.) I. The military organizations of the bolsheviks. II. February and October revolutions in Siberia. Moscow, 1924. 20 p.

11252. Turunov, A. N. and Maksakov, V. V. Партизанское
движение в Сибири. (The partisan movement [guerrilla war-
fare] in Siberia.) Moscow, 1925.

11253. Piontkovskii, S. A. Гражданская война в России.
(1918-1921). (The civil war in Russia, 1918-1921.) Moscow,
1925.

11254. Vel'man, V. "Февральская революция в Сибири." (The
February revolution in Siberia.) Proletarskaia revoliutsiia, 3:38 (1925):167-200.

11255. Гражданская война.(The civil war.)(Operations on the
seas, and river and lake systems.) Moscow, 1925-   (To be
complete in 4 v. V. 1 to be published last.)

11256. Первый съезд революционных организаций Дальнего Востока. (First congress of the revolutionary societies of the
Far East.) Collected articles. Petrograd, Ispolkom Komin-
terna, n.d. 360 p.

11257. Parfenov, Petr S. (Petr Altaiskii). Гражданская
война в Сибири 1918-1920. (The civil war in Siberia, 1918-
1920.) Revised edition. Moscow, 1925. 168 p.

11258. Maksakov, V. Хроника гражданской войны в Сибири.
1917-1918 гг.(Chronicle of the civil war in Siberia, 1917-

1918.) Moscow, 1926. 299 p. (Turunov, A., co-author).

11259. Zenzinov, V. Государственный переворот Адмирала
Колчака в Омске, 18 ноября, 1918 г. (Admiral Kolchak's
coup d'etat in Omsk, November 18, 1918.) Paris, 1919.

11260. Smirnov, M. I. Адмирал Колчак. (Admiral Kolchak.)
Paris, 1930.

11261. Harima, Narakichi. 赤露内訌ノ史的考察.
Seki-Ro naiko no shi-teki kosatsu. (Historical study of the
internal disturbances of Red Russia.) Gaiko jiho, 44:1:118-
130, January 1, 1926.

11262. Samoilov, F. "Большевицкая фракция IV Государственной
думы в Енисейской ссылке перед февральской революцией."
(The Bolshevik faction of the IV Duma in Yenisei exile before the February revolution.) Proletarskaia revoliutsiia,
2-3 (1927):209-239.

11263. Miliukov, P.N. Россия на переломе. (Russia at the crossroads.) Paris, 1927. 2 v. (2) Shumiatskii, B. Сибирь на путях
к Октябрю. (Siberia on the road to October.) Moscow, 1927. 126 p.

11264. Vegman, V. D. Горняки Сибири. (Siberian miners.)
Collected articles and memoirs. 1917-1927. Novosibirsk,
1927. 326 p.

11265. Kirilov, A. A. "Сибирская армия в борьбе за освобож-
дение." (The Siberian army in the struggle for liberation.) Vol'naia Sibir', 4 (1928):36-69.

11266. Ilíukhov, N. Партизанское движение в Приморье,
1918-1920 гг. (The partisan movement in the Maritime region.) Leningrad, 1928. 252 p.

11267. Yang, Yu-chiung. 俄國革命史 O-kuo ko-ming-shih.
(History of the Russian revolution.) Shanghai, 1928.

11268. Shmelev, V. I. Профсоюзы Сибири в борьбе за власть
советов 1917-1919. (Trade unions of Siberia in the struggle
for a Soviet government.) Novosibirsk, 1928. vii, 240 p.

11269. Arsharuni, A. M. Эпос советского Востока. (Poetry
of the Soviet East.) Pre-revolutionary and post-October
motifs. Leningrad, 1930. 131 p.

11270. Vegman, V. Восстания рабочих и солдат в Сибири.
(Uprisings of the workers and soldiers in Siberia.) Novosibirsk, 1932.

11271. Борьба за советы на Дальнем Востоке. (The struggle for the soviets in the Far East.) In Sbornik Dal'ne-Vostochnogo zemliachestva pri muzee RKKA. Moscow, 1932.

11272. "Уфимское совещание и Временное сибирское правительство." (The Ufa convention and the Provisional Siberian government.) Krasnyi arkhiv, 6 (1933):61:58-81.

11273. Rossevin, Stepan. Гражданская война. (The civil war.) Riga, Etikas, 1937. 440 p.

(ii) Memoirs

11274. 1917-1918 гг. в освещении белогвардейцев. (1917-1918 as interpreted by the Whites.). Correspondence of the public prosecutor of the Chita circuit court. Dal'istpart (Vladivostok), 1 (1923):170-189.

11275. IUdin, N. "Воспоминания о революции 1917 г. в Бодайбо." (Recollections of the revolution of 1917 in Bodaibo.) Kommunist, 3 (1923):14-22. (Irkutsk).

11276. Budberg, Aleksei. Дневник барона Алексея Будберга. (The diary of Baron Alexis Budberg.) In: Arkhiv russkoi revoliutsii, 12 (1923):197-291; 13 (1924):197-313; 14 (1924): 225-342; 15 (1924):254-345.

11277. Miliukov, P. N. "Роковые годы." (Fated years.) Russkie zap., 4-

11278. Pepeliaev, V. N. "Развал колчаковщины. Из дневника." (The collapse of the Kolchak movement. From a diary.) Krasnyi arkhiv, 31 (1928):51-80.

11279. Rudnev, S. P. При вечерних огнях. (In evening lights.) Memoirs. Harbin, 192(?). 467 p.

11280. Lipman, N. I. Записки красноармейца-дальневосточника. (Memoirs of a Far Eastern Red army soldier.) Moscow, [1933], 258 p.

11281. Golionko, V. "Красная гвардия на Дальнем Востоке в 1917-1918 гг., по личным воспоминаниям и документам." (The Red guard in the Far East in 1917-1918, according to personal reminiscences and documents.) Bor'ba klassov, 9: 80-89, September 1936.

(iii) Local Self-Government Movement

11282. IAkushev, I. A. "Очерки областного движения в Сибири."

(Outlines of the separatist movement in Siberia.) Vol'naia
Sibir', 2-7 (1927-1929). Prague.

11283. Krol', M. A. "Сибирское правительство и Сибирская областная дума." (The Siberian government and the Siberian
provincial duma.) Vol'naia Sibir', 4 (1928):69-83.

11284. Февральская революция и сибирское областничество.
(The February revolution and Siberian separatism.) Vol'naia
Sibir', 2 (1927):3-12.

11285. IAkushev, I. A. "Февральская революция и сибирские
областные съезды." (The February revolution and the Siberian provincial conferences.) Vol'naia Sibir', 2 (1927):13-40.

(iv) By Regions

(') Far East

11286. Georgievskii, A. P. Архив русской революции. (The
archive of the Russian revolution.)(Sources of the Maritime
government Archival bureau.) Vladivostok, 1923.

11287. Dal'istpart. Сборник материалов по истории революционного движения на Дальнем Востоке. (Collected sources pertaining to the history of the revolutionary movement in the
Far East.) Vladivostok, 1923-1925. 4 parts.

11288. TSypkin, S. Октябрьская революция и гражданская
война на Дальнем Востоке. (The October revolution and civil
war in the Far East.) Chronicle of events, 1917-1922. Moscow-Khabarovsk, 1933. 305 p.

11289. Pokus, IA. Борьба за Приморье.(The struggle for the
Maritime region.) Moscow, 1926. 112 p.

11290. Reznikov (Izgoi). Революционная хроника Забайкалья
1917-1918 гг. (A chronicle of the revolution in the Transbaikal region, 1917-1918.) Revoliutsiia na Dal'nem Vostoke,
Moscow, 1, 1923. 281 p.

11291. О февральской революции в Якутии. (The February revolution in Yakutia.) A letter. Proletarskaia Revoliutsiia,
3:50. (1926).

11292. Революция и бурят-монголы. (The revolution and the
Buriat-Mongols.) Irkutsk, 1921. 26 p.

11293. Potapov, S. Герои гражданской войны в Якутии. (Heroes of the civil war in Yakutia.) Yakutsk, 1931. 108 p.

11294. Purin, A. A. "В дни революции в Охотско-Камчатском и Чукотско-Анадырском крае." (Revolutionary days in the Okhotsk-Kamchatka and Chukotsk-Anadyr regions.) Vol'naia Sibir', 2 (1927):61-62.

11295. Grigoriev, F. S. and Shapirstein-Lers, IA. E.К истории рабочего и революционного движения в Бодайбинском золотопромышленном районе. (History of the labor and revolutionary movement in the Bodaibinsk [Lena] gold mining region.) Bodaibo, 1924. vii, 222 p.

11296. Okuntsov, P. A. Участие Забайкалья в революционном движении рабочего класса. (The participation of the Transbaikal region in the revolutionary movement of the labor class.) Chita, 1927. 75 p.

11297. Karpenko, Z. Гражданская война в Дальне-Восточном крае, 1918-1922 гг. (The civil war in the Far Eastern region in 1918-1922.) Khabarovsk, 1934. 167 p.

('') Western Siberia and Central Asia

11298. Seleznev, K. (comp.). Партизанское движение в Западной Сибири в 1918-1919 гг. Партизанская армия Мамонтова и Громова. (The guerrilla movement in Western Siberia in 1918-1919. The guerrilla army of Mamontov and Gromov.) Collected documents. Novosibirsk, 1936. 374 p.

11299. Gan, B. M. "Февральская революция в Томской губернии." (The February revolution in the Tomsk gubernia.) Severnaia Aziia, 1 (13) (1927):13-23.

11300. Партизанское движение в Сибири. (The guerrilla movement in Siberia.) Moscow, 1925. 295,xv p.

11301. Zhigalin, IA. "Партизанское движение в Западной Сибири." (The guerrilla movement in Western Siberia.) Proletarskaia revoliutsiia, Moscow, 11 (106) (1930):98-114.

11302. Tanaev, A. P. Колчаковщина на Урале (1918-1919). (Kolchak in the Urals, 1918-1919.) Sverdlovsk, 1930. 72 p.

11303. Podshivalov, I. Гражданская борьба на Урале, 1917-1918 г. (The civil war in the Urals, 1917-1918.) Moscow, 1925. 221 p.

11304. Kiikov, A. Из былого Урала.   (From the Ural past.)
Sources pertaining to the history of the revolutionary
movement, 1905-1916. Ufa, 1923. 150 p.

11305. Brazul, D. На освобожденном Урале и в освобождаемой
Сибири. (In the free Urals and the liberated-to-be Siberia.)
Moscow, 1921.

11306. Bykov, P. M. and Niporkin, N. G. Рабочая революция
на Урале. (Proletarian revolution in the Urals.) Ekaterinburg, 1921.

11307. Chernyshev, E. I. "Из истории крестьянских движений
в Казанском крае в 1917 г." (History of the peasant movements in the Kazan region in 1917.) Izvestiia arkheologii,
istorii i etnografii pri Kazanskom universitete imeni B. I.
Ulianova-Lenina. 34:1-2 (1928):4-98.

11308. Glukhov, I. K. Очерки по истории революционного движения в Калмыкии. (Historical sketches of the revolutionary
movement in Kalmukia.) Astrakhan, 1927. 114 p.

11309. Borisov, T. "Революция в Калмыцкой степи." (Revolution in the Kalmuk steppe.) Proletarskaia revoliutsiia,
Moscow-Leningrad, 2 (49):(1926):114-124.

11310. Karmashev, V. Последние дни советской власти в западной Сибири 1918 г. (The last days of Soviet rule in Western Siberia.) Moscow, 1921.

11311. Galuzo, P."Восстание 1916 г. в Средней Азии."
(The 1916 uprising in Central Asia.) Krasnyi arkhiv, Moscow
3:34 (1929):39-45.

11312. Broido, G. I. Восстание киргиз в 1916 г. (The Kirghiz
uprising of 1916.) Moscow, 1925. 28 p.

11313. Broido, G. I. "Материалы к истории восстания киргиз
1916 г." (Sources pertaining to the history of the Kirghiz
uprising of 1916.) Novyi Vostok, 6 (1924):407-434.

11314. Bochagov, A. Краткий исторический очерк о националь-
но-буржуазном движении в Казакстане в 1917-1919 гг. (A
brief historical sketch of the national bourgeois movement
in Kazakstan in 1917-1919.) Kzyl-orda, KSSR, 1927.

11315. Очерки революционного движения в Средней Азии.
(Sketches of the revolutionary movement in Central Asia.)
Collected articles. Moscow, 1926. 152 p.

11316. Революционное прошлое (The revolutionary past.)
Ufa, 1923. 176 p.

11317. Сборник указаний по борьбе с басмачеством. (A collection of instructions for the struggle with the basmach [bandit] movement.) Tashkent, 1924. 73 p.

11318. Saifi, Fatukh. Татары до Февральской революции. (The Tatars prior to the February revolution.) Kazan, 1930. 46p.

11319. Samoilov, F. "Малая Башкирия в 1918-1920 гг."(Little Bashkiria in 1918-1920.) Proletarskaia revoliutsiia, Moscow, 58:196-223, November 1926; 59:185-207, December 1926.

11320. Soloveichik, L. "Революционная Бухара."(Revolutionary Bokhara.) Novyi Vostok, 2:272-288.

11321. Гражданская война. (The civil war.) Sources. Vol.III. Moscow, 1924. 160 p.

11322. Сборник материалов революционного движения в Тагильском округе. (Collected documents pertaining to the revolutionary movement in the Tagilsk region.) Novotagil'sk, 1925. 117 p.

11323. Shoizhelov, S. A. Тувинская народная республика. (The Tuvinsk people's republic.) Moscow, 1930. 100 p.

11324. Brainin, S. and Shafiro, Sh. "Советский переворот в Семиречье в 1918 г." (The Soviet coup d'état in Semirechie in 1918.) Bol'shevik Kazakstana, 3:54:53-63, March 1936.

11325. Brainin, S. Восстание казахов Семиречья в 1916 году. (The uprising of the Kazakhs of Semirechie in 1916.) Alma-Ata, 1936. 103 p.

11326. Gidlevskii, Kensorin. Минусинская коммуна 1917-1918 гг. (The Minusinsk commune, 1917-1918.) From the history of the October revolution in Siberia. Moscow, 1934. 296 p.

11327. Kumach, I. В Акмолинских степях. (In the Akmolinsk steppes.) Alma- Ata, 1936. 84 p.

11328. Aiupov, K. Татары и башкиры в революционных движениях на Средней Волге. (The Tatars and Bashkirs in the revolutionary movements of the Central Volga region.) Moscow, Samara, 1934. 112 p.

11329. Tretiak, I. I. Партизанское движение в горном Алтае,

1919. (Guerrilla movement in the mountainous Altai, 1919.)
Novosibirsk, 1933. 168 p.

11330. Dvoinykh, Z. IA. Таежные партизаны. (Taiga guerrillas.) Reminiscences, 1918-1922. Moscow, 1936. 188 p.

11331. Таежные походы. (Taiga campaigns.) Episodes from
civil war in the Far East.) 2nd ed. Moscow, 1936. 501 p.

('''') Cities in the Revolution

11332. Petrenko, A. "Февральская революция в Томске." (The
February revolution in Tomsk.) Proletarskaia revoliutsiia,
2 (1926):49:91-100.

11333. Shotman, A. "Февральская революция в Томске." (The
February revolution in Tomsk.) Proletarskaia revoliutsiia,
2-3 (1927):240-251.

11334. Smirnov, I. N. "Февральская революция в Томске."
(The February revolution in Tomsk.) Severnaia Aziia, 1
(1927):8-12.

11335. Fefelova, A. K. "История революционного движения г.
Красноярска. (History of the revolutionary movement in
Krasnoiarsk.) In: Trista let goroda Krasnoiarska, 1628-1928.
[Miscellany]. Krasnoiarsk, 1928:19-48.

11336. Gurevich, V. IA. "Февральская революция в Красноярске." (The February revolution in Krasnoiarsk.) Vol'naia
Sibir', 2 (1927):112-132; 3 (1928):28-61.

11337. Gidlevskii, K., Safianov, M., and others. Минусинская коммуна 1917-1918 гг. (The Minusinsk commune of 1917-
1918.) Moscow, Sotsekgiz, 1934. 295 p.

11338. Cherkunov, A. N. Календарь революции гор. Иркутска
1917-1924 гг. (Calendar of the revolution of the city of
Irkutsk, 1917-1924.) Irkutsk, Dvigatel', 1924. 24 p.

11339. Porshnev, G. I. Книжная летопись г. Иркутска за годы
революции,1917-1919. (A chronicle of the city of Irkutsk for
the revolutionary years, 1917-1919.)   Irkutsk, 192 (?). 75p.

11340. Ognetov, "Борьба за советскую власть в Иркутской
губернии в 1917 г." (The struggle for Soviet government in
the Irkutsk guberniia.) Kommunist, Irkutsk, 10 (1922):3-5.

11341. Sokolov, V. N. "Февральский переворот в Чите." (The February revolution in Chita.) Severnaia Aziia, 1 (1927): 36-41.

11342. Teterin, N. I. "Новониколаевск в февральской револю-ции." (Novonikolaevsk in the February revolution.) Severnaia Aziia, 1 (1927):24-28.

11343. Bochkov, A. Три года советской власти в Казани. (Three years of Soviet rule in Kazan.) Kazan, 1921.

11344. ьорьба за Казань. (The struggle for Kazan.) Kazan, 1924. 256 p.

11345. Okuntsev, P. 1917-1918 гг. в Нерчинске и его уезде. (1917-1918 in Nerchinsk and the Nerchinsk uezd.) Dal'ist-part, 1, 1923. 120 p.

(v) The Czechoslovaks in Siberia

11346. Zahraniční politika. Praha, Orbis, 19 - (Monthly). (2) Naše revoluce. Praha, 1923- (Quarterly).

11347. Masaryk, T. G. The making of a state. New York, Mac-millan, 1933. 518 p. (Czech ed. Praha, Orbis,1933. 640 p.) (2) Klecanda, J. Operace čs. vojsku na Rusi v 1. 1917-20. Praha.

11348. Ackerman, Carl W. Trailing the Bolsheviki. New York, Scribner's, 1919. 308 p.

11349. Kudela, I. F. О российском золотом запасе и чехосло-вацких легионах. (Concerning the Russian gold reserve and the Czechoslovak legions.) Praha, 1923. 28 p.

11350. Baerlein, Henry P. B. The march of the seventy thou-sand. London, Parsons, 1926. 287 p.

11351. Vergé, Arsène. Avec les Tchécoslovaques. 2nd edition. Paris, 1926.

11352. Papoušek, J. "Причины чехословацкого выступления." (Causes of the Czechoslovak uprising.) Volia Rossii, 8-9, 1928.

11353. Glos, I. "Чехословаки и Сибирская областная дума." (The Czechoslovaks and the Siberian provincial duma.) Vol'-naia Sibir', 4 (1928):28-36.

11354. Dragomiretskii, V. S. Чехословаки в России 1914-1920.

(The Czechoslovaks in Russia, 1914-1920.) Paris-Prague,
1928. (2) Zmrhal, K. Vlada Sovětu a Čechoslovaci. Praha, 1919.

11355. Shteidler, F. "Выступление чехословакох в России 1918
года." (The Czechoslovak uprising in Russia in 1918.) Vol'-
naia Sibir', 4 (1928):9-28.

11356. Popov, F. Чехословацкий мятеж и Самарская учредилка
(The Czechoslovak rebellion and the Samara Constitutional
assembly.) Moscow, 1932. 232 p.

11357. Klante, Margarete. Von der Volga zum Amur. Die
tschechische legion und der russische bürgerkrieg dargestellt auf grund authentischen materials. Königsberg-Berlin,
Ost-Europa verlag, 1933-

(vi) Intervention in Siberia

11358. Собрание документов, относящихся до интернирования
Атамана Калмыкова и его побега при посещении помещения
консульства. (A collection of documents pertaining to the
interning of Ataman Kalmykov and his escape during his visit to the consulate.) Peking, 1920.

11359. Nikiforov, P. Исторические документы о действиях и
замыслах международных хищников на Дальнем Востоке. (Historical documents concerning the activities and plans of
the international brigands in the Far East.) Moscow, 1923.
64 p.

11360. Vasiliev, E. P.   Алфавитно-предметный указатель-
справочник постановлений Дальне-Восточного революционного
комитета. (An alphabetic and subject index-directory of all
decrees of the Far Eastern revolutionary committee.) Chita,
1923. 35 p.

11361. Действия Японии в Приамурском крае.(Japan's activities in the   Amur province.) Vladivostok, 1926. 142 p.

11362. Varneck, Elena and Fisher, H. H. (editors). The testimony of Kolchak and other Siberian materials . In: Hoover
war library publications, 10. Stanford university press,
1935. 466 p. Russian original: Допрос Колчака. Leningrad, 1925.

11363. "К истории интервенции в Сибири." (History of the
intervention in Siberia.) Krasnyi arkhiv, 39 (1929):126-165.

11364. Nazimovich, N. F. (editor). Документы из истории
японской интервенции на Дальнем Востоке. (Documents per-

taining to the history of Japanese intervention in the Far
East.) Moscow, 1931. 61 p.

11365. Mints, I. (comp.). Японская интервенция 1918-1922
гг. в документах. (Japanese intervention in 1918-1922 in
documents.) Moscow, TSentrarkhiv, 1934. 235 p.

11366. United States. Department of State. Papers relating
to the foreign relations of the United States, 1918-1919.
Russia. Washington, 1931-1937. 4 v. (Publication 222, 330,
390, 987.)

11367. Coleman, Frederick. Japan moves north: the inside
story of the struggle for Siberia. New York, Cassell, 1918.
177 p.

11368. Daya, W. Der aufmarsch im Osten. Russisch-Asien als
deutsches kriegs- und wirtschaftsziel. Dachau bei München,
Einhorn, 1920. iii, 181 p.

11369. Vilenskii-Sibiriakov, Vl. D. Черная година сибирской
реакции. (The dark hour of Siberian reaction.) Intervention
in Siberia. Moscow, 1919. 56 p.

11370. Zenzinov, V. Государственный переворот ... Колчака
в Омске 18 ноября 1918. (The Kolchak coup d'état in Omsk,
November 18, 1918.) Paris, 1919.

11371. Burevoi, K. Колчаковщина. (The Kolchak rule.) Moscow, 1919.

11372. Russian-American relations, March, 1920. (Documents
and papers compiled and edited by C. K. Cumming and others).
New York, 1920.

11373. Spargo, J. Russia as an American problem. New York,
Harper, 1920. 444 p.

11374. Rakitnikov, N. I. Сибирская реакция и Колчак. (The
Siberian reaction and Kolchak.) Moscow, 1920.

11375. Сибирь, союзники и Колчак. (Siberia, the Allies, and
Kolchak.) Peking, 1921. 2 v.

11376. Villeneuve-Trans, R. de. A l'Ambassade de Washington,
octobre 1917-avril 1919: les heurs decisive de l'intervention americaine. Paris, Bossard, 1921. 287 p.

11377. Kurteev, K. K. Угроза русскому Дальнему Востоку.
(The menace to the Russian Far East.) Vladivostok, 1922.
16 p.

11378. Борьба за русский Дальний Восток. (The struggle for
the Russian Far East.) Edited by B. Shumiatskii. Biblioteka
politprosvetrabotnika, 19. Chita, 1922.

11379. Grondijs, Ludovic-H. La guerre en Russie et en Sibérie. Paris, Bossard, 1922.

11380. Norton, Henry K. The Far Eastern republic of Siberia.
London, 1923. 316 p.

11381. Ward, John. With the "Die-Hards" in Siberia. New
York, 1920. Russian translation: Союзная интервенция в
Сибири 1918-1919 г. Moscow, 1923.

11382. Kolosov, E. E. Сибирь при Колчаке.(Siberia during
the Kolchak reign.) Prague, Byloe, 1923.

11383. Raivid, N. and Bykov, P. (editors). Колчаковщина.
(The Kolchak rule.) Ekaterinburg, 1924.

11384. "Омские события при Колчаке."(The Omsk events under
Kolchak.) Krasnyi arkhiv, 7 (1924):201-246; 8 (1925):176-
192.

11385. Союзническая интервенция на Дальнем Востоке и в
Сибири. (Allied intervention in the Far East and in Siberia.)
Moscow, Gosizdat, 1925.

11386. Solodovnikov, G. Сибирские авантюры и генерал Гайда.
(Siberian adventures and General Gayda.) Prague, 192 (?).
292 p.

11387. El'tsin, V. "Крестьянское движение в Сибири в период Колчака." (Peasant movement in Siberia during Kolchak.) Proletarskaia revoliutsiia, Moscow-Leningrad, 49:
5-48, February 1926.

11388. Boldyrev, V. Директория, Колчак, интервенты. (The
Directory, Kolchak, and the intervention.) Novonikolaevsk,
1925. 564 p.

11389. Levidov, M. К истории союзной интервенции в России.
(History of the allied intervention in Russia.) Leningrad,
1925.

11390. Khachaturov, G. Японская интервенция 1918-1922 гг. (Japanese intervention.) Moscow, TSentrarkhiv, 1934. 235 p.

11391. IAkushkin, E. E. Колчаковщина и интервенция в Сибири. (Kolchak and the intervention in Siberia.) Moscow, 1928. 96 p.

11392. Chuchin, F. "Империалистическая интервенция на Дальнем Востоке в Сибири, 1917-1919 гг." (Imperialist intervention in the Far East. Siberia, 1917-1919.) Proletarskaia revoliutsiia, Moscow, 11 (106) (1930):21-51.

11393. Parfenov, Petr S. (Altaiskii, Petr). Борьба за Дальний Восток.1920-1922. (The struggle for the Far East, 1920-1922.) Leningrad, 1928. 386 p. 2nd revised edition: 1931. 358 p.

11394. Graves, General William S. America's Siberian adventure. New York, Cape & Smith, 1931. 363 p. Russian edition, Moscow, 1932. 248 p.

11395. Goriunov, Iv. (ed.). Колчаковщина. (The Kolchak movement.) Moscow-Samara, 1932. 112 p.

11396. Stewart, George. The white armies of Russia: a chronicle of counter-revolution and allied intervention. New York, Macmillan, 1933. 469 p.

11397. Girchenko, V. P. Революционная деятельность иностранных интернационалистов военно-пленных в Восточной Сибири. (Revolutionary activity of foreign internationalists war-prisoners in Eastern Siberia.) Verkhneudinsk, 1933. 32 p.

11398. 4-5 апреля 1920 г. (April 4-5, 1920.) Collected documents concerning the Japanese intervention in the Maritime region. Khabarovsk, Dal'giz, 1937. 87 p.

11399. Reikhberg, G. "События 4-5 апреля 1920 г. и Приморье." (The events of April 4-5, 1920, and the Maritime province.) Istorik marksist, 5-6 (1935):45-46:3-38.

11400. Колчаковщина. (The Kolchak movement.) Collected articles. Novosibirsk, 1935. 160 p.

11401. Strakhovsky, Leonid I. The origins of American intervention in North Russia (1918). Princeton, N. J., Princeton university press, 1938. ix, 140 p. (2) Борьба за советский Дальний Восток. (Struggle for the Soviet Far East.) Collected articles. Khabarovsk, Dal'giz, 1938. 103 p.

XV. INTERNATIONAL RELATIONS TO 1917

See 450-495; 539-721; 3198-4252; 5014-5026; 6183-6200;
6700-6721; 7138-7144.

A. Periodicals

11402. Восточный сборник. (Oriental miscellany.) St. Petersburg, Ministry of foreign affairs, 1877.

B. Sources

See 472-495; 3696-3735; 3736-3801.

11403. Памятники дипломатических сношений древней России с
иностранными державами. (Monuments of the diplomatic relations of ancient Russia with foreign powers.) St. Petersburg, Vtoroe otdelenie cobstvennoi ego imperatorskogo veli-
chestva kantseliarii, 1851-1871. 10 v.

11404. Обзор внешних сношений России (по 1800 год). (Survey of Russian foreign relations to 1800.) St. Petersburg,
Komissiia pechataniia gosudarstvennykh gramot i dogovorov,
1894-1902. 4 parts, index.

11405. Veselovskii, N. I.   Памятники дипломатических и
торговых сношений Московской Руси с Персией.   (Sources
pertaining to the diplomatic and trade relations between
Muscovite Russia and Persia.) In Trudy Vostochnogo otdeleniia Imperatorskogo russkogo arkheologicheskogo obshchestva, St. Petersburg, 1890-1898. V. 20-22.

11406. Сборник дипломатических документов, касающихся событий в Персии.   (Collection of diplomatic documents pertaining to the events in Persia.) St. Petersburg, Ministry
of foreign affairs, 1911-1913. 7 v.

11407. Popov, A. "Дальневосточная политика царизма в 1894-
1901 годах." (The Far Eastern policy of tsarism during 1894-
1901.) Istorik marksist, 11 (1935):51:38-57.

11408. Pokrovskii, M. N. (ed.). Переписка Вильгельма II с
Николаем II. (The correspondence between Wilhelm II and
Nicholas II.) Moscow, 1923.   (2) Bernstein, H. The Willy-
Nicky correspondence, being the secret and intimate tele-
grams between the Kaiser and the Tsar. New York, Knopf,
1918. 11-158 p.

11409. Witte, S. IU. Воспоминания. (Memoirs.) Moscow-Petrograd, Gosizdat, 1923-1924. 3 v.   Berlin, Slovo, 1922.
2 v. (2) The same. The memoirs of Count Witte. Transl. and ed. by A. Yarmolinsky. London, Heinemann, 1921. 445 p. (3) The same. Вынужденные разъяснения по поводу отчета ген-ад. Куропаткина о войне д Японией.   (Some forced explanations concerning General Kuropatkin's report on the war with Japan.) Moscow, Sytin, 1911. 100 p.

11410. Korostovets, I. Страница из истории русской дипломатии. (A page from the history of Russian diplomacy.) Diary of the secretary to Count Witte. 2nd edition. Peking, 1923. (2) Lamsdorff, V. N. Дневник,1886-1890. (Diary, 1886-1890.) Moscow, 1926. 395 p. (3) The same. Дневник, 1891-1892. (Diary, 1891-1892.) Moscow-Leningrad, Academia, 1934. 409 p.

11411 Romanov, B. A. "Лихунчанский фонд." (The Li Hung-chang fund.) Bor'ba klassov, 1-2 (1924):77-126.

11412. "Англо-русское соглашение о разделе Китая (1899)." (The Anglo-Russian agreement concerning the partition of China, 1899.) Krasnyi arkhiv, 15 (1927):111-134.

11413. "Царская дипломатия о задачах России на Востоке в 1900 г."(Tsarist diplomacy regarding the problems of Russia in the Orient in 1900.) Krasnyi arkhiv, 18 (1926):3-29.

11414. Iswolsky, A. Memoirs ... Edited and translated by Charles Louis Seeger. London, Hutchinson & co., 1920. 288 p.
(2) The same. Recollections of a Foreign Minister. Garden City, Doubleday, Page & co., 1921. 303 p.   (3) The same. Mémoirs (1906-1910). Paris, Payot, 1923. 313 p.   (4) The same. Die diplomatische schriftwechsel ... Ed. by Friedrich Stieve. Berlin, Deutsche verladsgesellschaft für politik u. geschichte, 1924. 4 v.   (5) The same. Correspondence diplomatique, 1906-1911. Ed. by Hélène Iswolsky. Paris, Les editions internationales, 1937. 438 p.

C. General Accounts

11415. Kaidanov, I. Краткое изложение дипломатии российского двора со времени восшествия на престол дома Романовых до кончины Государя императора Александра I. (A brief exposition of the diplomacy of the Russian court from the time of the ascent to the throne of the House of Romanovs to the death of Emperor Alexander I.) St. Petersburg, 1833. 189, 240 p.

11416. Veselovskii, N. Татарское влияние на русский посоль-
ский церемониал в московском периоде русской истории.
(Tatar influence upon ambassadorial ceremony during the
Moscow period of Russian history.) St. Petersburg, 1911.

11417. Grigoriev, V. V. Об отношениях России к Востоку.
(About Russia's attitude to the East.) Odessa, 1840.

11418. Korff, Baron S. A. Russia's foreign relations during
the last half century. New York, 1922. (2) The same. Russia
in the Far East. Washington, Carnegie endowment, 1921. 47 p.
(3) The same. "Russia in the Far East." American journal of
international law, 17:252-284, April 1923.

11419. Kiuner, N. V. Сношения России с Дальним Востоком в
период царствования дома Романовых. (Relations between Russia and the Far East during the reign of the House of Romanovs.) Vladivostok, 1914.

11420. Skalkovskii, K. Внешняя политика России и положение
иностранных держав. (Foreign policy of Russia and the condition of foreign powers.) St. Petersburg, 1897. 560 p.

11421. Korostovetz, V. de. "Russia's foreign policy past
and present, with special reference to Asia." Journal of
the Royal Central Asian society, 19:1:121-130, January 1932.

11422. Материалы, относящиеся до пребывания в Китае Н. П.
Игнатьева в 1859-1860 гг. (Sources pertaining to N. P. Ignatiev's stay in China, 1859-1860.) St. Petersburg, 1895.
486 p.

11423. Semennikov, V. P. (ed.). За кулисами царизма. (Back
stage of tsarism.) Archive of the Tibetan physician Badmaev. Leningrad, 1925. 175 p.

11424. Skvirskii, F. B. "Царская авантюра на Дальнем Востоке." (Tsarist adventure in the Far East.) Vestnik Man'-
chzhurii, 1 (1931):92-97.

11425. Roustam Bek. Корень зла. Царские опричники на Дальнем
Востоке. (L'origine du mal. Les satellites du tsar en
extrême-orient.) Nice, 1909. 264 p.

11426. Popov, A. "Кризис дальневосточной политики царизма
накануне революции 1905 года." (Crisis in the Far Eastern
policy of tsarism on the eve of the revolution of 1905.)
Istorik marksist, 12 (1935):52:3-25.

11427. Schön, Hauptmann Joseph. Über die ziele Russlands in Asien. Zweite auflage. Wien, Seidel & sohn, 1900. 96 p.

11428. Toepfer, Hauptmann H. "Russland auf dem wege zur vorherrschaft in Ostasien. Nach dem bericht des Finanzministers Witte über seine reise nach dem Fernen Osten." Asien, 6 (1903):85-90.

11429. Golovachev, P. Россия на Дальнем Востоке. (Russia in the Far East.) St. Petersburg, Koskova, 1905.

11430. Subbotich, D. I. Задачи России на Дальнем Востоке. (Russia's problems in the Far East.) Revel, 1908.

11431. Semenov-Tian-Shanskii, A. Наши ближайшие задачи на Дальнем Востоке. (Our immediate problems in the Far East.) St. Petersburg, 1908.

11432. Rosen, R. R. Forty years of diplomacy. New York, 1922. 2 v. (2) The same. Европейская политика России. (The European policy of Russia.) Petrograd, 1917. 40 p.

11433. Dillon, E. J. The eclipse of Russia. New York, 1918.

11434. Kasianov, N. A. Сибирь и немецкий поход на Восток. (Siberia and the German march to the East.) Lausanne, 1918. (2) The same. La Sibérie et la poussée allemande. Berne, 1918.114

11435. Mackay, F. B. L. von. "Sibirien und das ostasiatische problem." Der Türmer, 20 (1918):22.

11436. Ostwald, Paul. "Die russische ostasienpolitik und ihr zusammenbruch." Asien, Berlin, 16 (1918-1919):1-7. (2) Stanton, John M. Foundations of Russian foreign policy in the Far East, 1847-1875. Unpublished Ph. D. thesis, Berkeley, University of California, 1932. 584 p.

XVI. INTERNATIONAL RELATIONS SINCE 1917

A. Periodical Publications

11437. Годовой отчет ... к ... Съезду советов. (Annual report [of the People's commissariat for foreign affairs to the ... Congress of Soviets.) Moscow, 1918/19-

11438. Международная политика за ... год. (International policy during the year ...) Moscow, Narodnyi komissariat po inostrannym delam, 1921- (Annual).

11439. Ежегодник.   (Year-book.) Moscow, Narodnyi komissariat po inostrannym delam, 1925-

B. Soviet International Law

11440. Korovine, E. Das völkerrecht der übergangszeit. Berlin, 1929.   (2) The same. "La république des Soviets et le
droit international." Revue générale du droit international
public, 32 (1925).

C. General Accounts

11441. Fischer, Louis. Soviets in world affairs. New York,
Cape & Smith, 1930. 2 v.

11442. Dennis, A. L. P. The foreign policies of Soviet Russia. New York, Dutton, 1924. 501 p.

11443. Tanin, M. 10 лет внешней политики СССР (1917-1927).
(Ten years of foreign policy of the USSR, 1917-1927.) Moscow, 1927. 259 p.

11444. Maiskii, M. Внешняя политика РСФСР, 1917-1922. (Foreign policy of the RSFSR.) Moscow, 1923.

11445. Developments in Russia's foreign relations. Since
1917. Foreign policy association, 3 (1927):10.

11446. Hartlieb, Wilhelm Walter. Das politische vertrags-
system der Sowjetunion, 1920-1935. Leipzig, Universitätsver-
lag, 1936.

11447. Pasvolsky, L. Russia in the Far East. New York, Macmillan, 1922. 181 p.

11448. Vilenskii, Vl. (Sibiriakov). Советская Россия у
берегов Тихого океана.   (Soviet Russia on the shores of the
Pacific.) Moscow, Krasnaia Nov', 1923.

11449. Hurwicz, Elias. "Zehn jahre bolschewistischer orient-
politik,1918-1928." Ost-Europa, 4:645-665, July 1929.

11450. Ivangorodskii, P. "Советская политика на Дальнем Востоке.   (Soviet policy in the Far East.) Sibirskie ogni,
Novosibirsk, 1:175-182, January-Ferbuary 1927.

11451. Levin, J. O. "La politique orientale des Soviets."
Monde slave, 6:8:161-175, August 1929; 6:9:321-349, September 1929.

11452. Pavlovich, M. (Vel'tman). "Русский вопрос" в английской внешней политике 1922-1924. (The "Russian question" in English foreign policy 1922-1924.) Moscow, 1924. 54 p.

11453. Pavlovich, M. "Английский ультиматум и основной план великобританского империализма на ближнем и Среднем Востоке. (The English ultimatum and the main plan of British imperialism in the Near and Middle East.) Voennyi vestnik, 13 (1923):42-44.

11454. Pavlovich, M. Советская Россия и капиталистическая Англия. (Soviet Russia and capitalist England.) Moscow, 1922. 201 p. 2nd edition.

11455. Pavlovich, M. "Советская россия и англо-французские интриги на Востоке."(Soviet Russia and the Anglo-French intrigues in the Orient.) Kommunisticheskii internatsional, 14 (1920):2769-2780.

11456. Мировая политика в 1924 году. (World politics in 1924.) Collected articles, edited by F. Rotshtein. Moscow, 1925. 332 p.

11457. Kliuchnikov, IU. V. Мирные договоры империалистической войны в конспективном изложении.(An outline of the peace treaties of the World war.) Moscow, Kommunisticheskaia akademiia, 1925. 166 p.

11458. Zamyslovskaia, E. СССР и мир. (The USSR and peace.) Moscow, TsK. zheleznodorozhnikov "Gudok", 1925.

11459. Bessedovsky, Grigory. Revelations of a Soviet diplomat. Translated by Matthew Norgate. London, Williams & Norgate, 1931. 276 p.

11460. Ching-tzu. 蘇 俄 外 交 之 縱 横 Su-O wai-chiao chih tsung-hêng. (Whither Soviet Russia's foreign policy.) Kuo-wên chou-pao, 9:21, May 1932.

11461. Litvinov, M. M. Внешняя политика СССР. (Foreign policy of the USSR.) 1927-1935. 2nd ed. Moscow 1937. 432 p. (2) Против агрессии.(Against aggression.) Moscow, 1938. 112 p.

11462. Kishida, Eiji. 極 東 ト 蘇 聯 Kyokuto to Soren.(The Far East and Soviet Russia.) Gaiko jiho, 80:5:117-141, December 1936.

11463. The Soviet Union and the path to peace. A collection of statements and documents, 1917-1936. London, 1936. 201 p.

11464. Stalin, J. Беседа с председателем американского
газетного объединения "Скриппс-Говард Ньюспейперс" г-ном
Рой Говардом 1 марта 1936 г. (Conversation with the chairman
of the American news-paper trust, "Scripps-Howard newspapers," Mr. Roy Howard, on March 1, 1936.) Moscow, Partizdat,
1937. 19 p.   (2) Советско-Китайский конфликт 1929 г. (The
Sino-Soviet conflict of 1929.) Collected documents. Moscow,
Litizdat NKID, 1930. 89 p.

XVII. MILITARY AND NAVAL PROBLEMS

See 663-780.

A. Periodicals

11465. Военный сборник. (Military miscellany.) St. Petersburg, 1858-1917. 60 v.   (2) Военно-исторический сборник.
(Military-historical miscellany.) Supplement to the Military miscellany.

11466. Морской сборник. (Naval miscellany.) St. Petersburg, 1848-1917. (2) Библиотека морского сборника. (Library of the Naval miscellany.) Supplement. 1916-1917. (3)
медицинские прибавления. (Medical supplements.) 1861-1914.
(4) Occasional monographs. [Last 3 items, supplements.]

11467. Военная энциклопедия. (Military encyclopedia.) St.
Petersburg-Petrograd, Sytin, 1911-1915. 18 v.

11468. Военно-статистическое обозрение Российской империи.
(Military statistical survey of the Russian empire.) St.
Petersburg, Glavnoe upravlenie General'nogo shtaba, 1849-
1853. 15 v. V. 16, 1858.

11469. Материалы для географии... (Geographical and statistical data on Russia, collected by officers of the General
staff.) St. Petersburg, Glavnoe upravlenie General'nogo
shtaba, 1860-1868. 23 v.

11470. Russia. Provisional government, Army. Армия и флот
в свободной России. (The army and navy in free Russia.)
June 15-November 21, 1917.

11471. Известия Народного комиссариата по военным делам.
(News of the People's commissariat for war.)Moscow, 1918-
1922. 5 v.

B. General Accounts

11472. Niedermayer, O. von, Semyonov Juri. Die Sowjetunion.

Eine geopolitische problemstellung. Berlin-Grunewald, Kurt
Vowinckel verlag, 1934. 151 p.

11473. Andreev, G. А. Железные дороги и оборона СССР. (Railways and the defense of the USSR.) Moscow, 1933. 31 p.

11474. Veniukov, M. I. Опыт военного обозрения русских
границ в Азии. (A military survey of the Russian boundaries
in Asia.) St. Petersburg, 1876.

11475. Zavadskii, E. Военная география. (Military geography.) St. Petersburg, 1909. 184 p.

11476. Veniukov, M. Путешествие по окраинам Русской Азии и
записки о них. (A journey through the border provinces of
Russian Asia and data concerning them.) St. Petersburg,
1868. ii, 526 p.

11477. Druzhinin, K. I. Наша современная политико-стратегия
на Дальнем Востоке. (Our contemporary political strategy
in the Far East.) St. Petersburg, 1910. 78 p. (Secret).

11478. Denikin, A. I. Русско-китайский вопрос. (The Russo-
Chinese question.) Warsaw, 1908. 95 p.

11479. Kostenko, L. F. Туркестанский край. (The Turkestan
region.) St. Petersburg, 1880. 3 v.

11480. Tunoshenskii, G. Наш Дальний Восток и его оборона.
(Our Far East and its defense.) St. Petersburg, 1911.

11481. D. I. Поглощение Дальнего Востока. (The engulfment
of the Far East.) Okrainy Rossii, 19 (1911).

11482. Jane, Fred T. The Imperial Russian army. London,
Thacker, 1899.

11483. Golovin, N. N. Участие России в мировой войне. (Russia's participation in the World war.) Paris, Les éditeurs
réunis, 1938. 450 p.

11484. Takenouchi, Kenzaburo. 蘇 聯 赤 軍 / 編 成 及
極 東 ニ於ケル其兵備 Soren sekigun no hensei oyobi
Kyokuto ni okeru sono heibi. (The organization of Soviet
Russia's red army, and its equipment in the Far East.) Dairen, S. M. R. R., 1929.

11485. Kitazawa, Sukeo. 蘇 聯 邦 / 軍國主義 So-Renpo no
gunkoku shugi. (Militarism of the Soviet Union.) Gaiko jiho,
54:6:92-103, June 15, 1930.

11486. Tu, Jo. 蘇俄之備戰 Su-O chih pei-chan. (War preparation of Soviet Russia.) Shên-pao yüeh-k'an, 1:1, July 1931.

11487. Chang, Kuo-tung. 蘇聯遠東軍之鳥瞰 Su-lien Yüan-tung chün chih niao-kan. (A bird's eye view of the Soviet Union's Far Eastern army.) Shih-shih yüeh-pao, 6:2, February 1932.

11488. Ching-tz'u. 蘇俄紅軍總司令費羅諾夫 Su-O hung-chün tsung-szu-ling Fei-lo-lo-fu. (Voroshilov, commander of Soviet Russia's Red army.) Kuo-wên chou-pao, 9:18, May 1932.

11489. Ching-kuo. 蘇俄軍隊之實力 Su-O chün-tui chih shih-li. (The actual power of Soviet Russia's military force.) Shên-pao yüeh-k'an, 1:1, July 1932.

11490. Kasahara, Yukio. 蘇聯邦ノ軍備ト東方經營 So-Renpo no gunbi to Toho keiei. (The Soviet Union's military preparations and her Far Eastern program.) Gaiko jiho, 63:2:164-171, July 15, 1932.

11491. Hirata, Shinsaku. 赤軍ノ極東作戰 Sekigun no Kyokuto sakusen. (Military plans of the Red army in the Far East.) Bungei shunju, 10:9:September 1932.

11492. Fujitsuka, Shisao. 極東軍ノ配備ト防備施設 Kyokutogun no haibi to bobi shisetsu. (Distribution and defensive plans of the Soviet Far Eastern army.) Sekai chishiki, September 1932.

11493. Hirata, Shinsaku. 赤軍ノ作戰ト勝敗豫想 Sekigun no sakusen to shohai yoso. (Military plans of the Red army and a conjecture on the results of the war in the event of Soviet-Japanese conflict.) Sekai chishiki, September, 1932.

11494. Parry, Albert and Kiralfy, Alexander. "Soviet submarines in the Far East." Pacific affairs, 1:10:31-42, March 1937.

XVIII. THE COMMUNIST PARTY AND THE THIRD INTERNATIONAL

See 1047-1060.

A. History of the Communist Party

11495. IAroslavskii, E. (ed.). История ВКП (б). (History of the All-Union communist party [bolshevik].) Moscow, 1, 1926-

11496. Levin and Tatarov (editors). История ВКП (б) в документах. (History of the All-Union communist party in documents.) Moscow, 1926- (v. I, 1883-1916).

11497. Popov, N. Outline history of the Communist party of the Soviet Union. London, Martin Lawrence, 1935. 2 v.

11498. Rosenberg, Arthur. Geschichte d. Bolschewismus v. Marx bis gegenwart. Berlin, Rewohlt, 1932. 239 p. (2) English translation: A history of Bolshevism, from Marx to the first five years' plan. London, Oxford university press, Milford, 1934. 250 p.

11499. 蘇聯共產黨黨爭之過去及現在
Su-Lien kung-chan-tang tang-chêng chih kuo-chü chi hsien-tsai. (The past and present of inner disputes of the Communist party in Soviet Union.) Wai-chiao-pu kung-pao, 5:1, January 1932.

11500. Памяти В. И. Ленина. Сборник статей к десятилетию со дня смерти. (V. I. Lenin. In memoriam. Collected articles commemorating the tenth anniversary of his death.) 1924-1934. Moscow-Leningrad. 1934. 929 p.

11501. Pavlovich, M., Narimanov, N., Khodorov, A. Ленин и Восток. (Lenin and the Orient.) Moscow, 1924. 65 p. (2) Narimanov, N. "Ленин и Восток." (Lenin and the Orient.) 5 (1924):9-13. (3) Rafail, M. Ленин и Восток. (Lenin and the Orient.) Collected articles. 2nd ed. Moscow, 1925. 80 p.

11502. Stalin, I. Сборник статей. (Collected articles.) Tula, Gosizdat, 1920. 103 p. (2) The same. Национальные моменты в партийном и государственном строительстве. (Moments of national importance in party life and state reconstruction.) Moscow-Leningrad, GIZ, 1923. 43 p. (3) The same. "Революция в Китае и задачи Коминтерна." (The revolution in China and the problems of the Communist international.) Bol'shevik, Moscow, 10:13-27, March 1927.

11503. Tiushevskii, N. "Сталин как теоретик большевизма в национально-колониальном вопросе." (Stalin as a theoretician of bolshevism in the national-colonial question.) Krasnaia letopis, 2 (1933):18-59.

11504. Trotskii, L. Запад и Восток. (West and East.) Moscow, 1924. 152 p. (2) The same. The Third international after Lenin. New York, 1936. 357 p.

11504 b. Report of court proceedings in the case of the
Anti-Soviet Trotskyite center. Moscow, People's commissariat of Justice of the USSR, 1937. 580 p. (2) The case of
Leon Trotsky. Report of hearings on the charges made against
him in the Moscow trials, by the Preliminary commission of
inquiry, John Dewey, Chairman... New York, Harper, 1937.
602 p. (3) Collard, Dudley. Soviet justice and the trial
of Radek and others. London, Gollancz, 1937. 208 p.

11505. IAnson, IA. "Сибирские большевики в борьбе за власть
советов и за построение социализма." (Siberian Bolsheviks
in the struggle for Soviet government and for the construction of socialism.) Sibirskii Soiuz RSDRP (Moscow), 1935:
76-103.

B. The Communist Party in Russia

11506. VIII съезд РКП (б). (The 8th Congress of the Russian communist party.) Moscow, March 18-23, 1919. Moscow,
1919. 415 p. (Stenographic account).

11507. Стенографический отчет X съезда РКП. (A stenographic account of the 10th Congress of the Communist party.)
Petrograd, 1921. 204 p. (March 8-16, 1921).

11508. Двенадцатый съезд РКП (б). (The 12th Congress of the
Russian Communist party.) Stenographic account, April 17-25,
1923. Moscow, 1923. iv, 509, 43 p.

11509. Съезд советов Союза Советских Социалистических Республик. (Congress of the Soviets of the USSR.) Stenographic
account. Moscow, 1922-

11510. Съезд советов Союза Советских Социалистических Республик. Постановления. (Congress of the Soviets of the
USSR. Resolutions.) Moscow, 1922-

11511. Всесоюзная коммунистическая партия. Резолюции съезда.
(Resolutions of the Congress of the Communist party...) Moscow, 1923-

11512. ВКП. Революция и ВКП (б) в материалах и документах.
(The revolution and the All-Union communist party [bolshe-
vik] in the documents and materials.) Moscow, VKP, 1924-
1928. 7 v.

11513. Всесоюзная коммунистическая партия. Конференция.
(The All-Union communist party. Conference.) Stenographic
report. Moscow, 1925-

11514. Всесоюзная коммунистическая партия. Резолюции принятые конференцией ... (All-Union communist party. Resolutions passed by the Conference...) Moscow, 1925-

11515. Совет народных комиссаров. От съезда к съезду. (The Soviet of the People's commissars. From Congress to Congress) Moscow, 1927-

11516. Всесоюзная коммунистическая партия. Партийное строительство. (All-Union communist party. Party building.) Moscow, 1929-

C. The Communist Party in Siberia

11517. "Обзор социалистического строительства Северной Азии на XVI съезде ВКП (б)." (A survey of the socialist development [of Northern Asia] presented to the XVI Congress of the All-Union communist party.) Sovetskaia Aziia, Moscow, 5-6 (35-36) (1930):295-303.

11518. Сибирский союз РСДРП. К 30 летию большевистской партийной организации в Сибири, 1900-1933. (The Siberian union of the Russian social-democratic labor party. Concerning the 30th anniversary of the Bolshevik organization in Siberia.) Moscow, 1935. 141 p.

11519. Baranskii, N. "Краткий очерк истории Сибирского союза РСДРП." (A brief sketch of the history of the Siberian union of the R[ussian] S[ocial]-D[emocratic] L[abor] P[arty].) Sibirskii soiuz RSDRP, Moscow, 1935:9-19.

11520. Резолюции 1-ой Сибирской краевой конференции РКП(б). (8-11 мая 1924 г.). (Resolutions of the 1st Siberian regional conference of the Communist party. May 8-11, 1924.) Novonikolaevsk, 1924. 16 p.

11521. Итоги VII Омской губернской партийной конференции. Резолюции и постановления. (Resolutions and decisions of the VII Omsk guberniia [Communist] party conference.) Omsk, 1924. 87 p.

11522. Резолюции и постановления VIII Томской губернской партийной конференции РКП(б). 25-28 апреля 1924 г. (Resolutions and decisions of the 8th Tomsk guberniia [Communist] party conference.) Tomsk, 1924. 20 p.

11523. Материалы 2-го Окружного съезда советов Тобольского округа Уральской области. (Materials pertaining to the 2nd Regional congress of Soviets of the Robolsk region.) Tobolsk, 1925. 99 p.

11524. Сборник обязательных постановлений и правил к ним
приказов и циркуляров Новониколаевского губернского исполнительного комитета и главнейших постановлений и распоряжений центральной власти. (A collection of obligatory decrees
of the Novonikolaevsk guberniia executive committee and of
the main decrees and orders of the central government.)
Novonikolaevsk, Novonikolaevskii gubernskii ispolnitel'nyi
komitet, 1924. 148 p.

11525. Материалы (7-ой) Новониколаевской губернской партийной конференции (18-21 апреля 1924 г.). (Materials pertaining to the 7th Novonikolaevsk gubernia [Communist] party
conference, April 18-21, 1924.) Novonikolaevsk, Novonikola-
evskaia gubernskaia organizatsiia Rossiiskoi kommunisticheskoi partii, 1924. 110 p.

11526. Gal'perin, A. I. Комсомол в Сибири. (The Komsomol
in Siberia.) Novosibirsk, 1930. 159 p.

11527. Kolesnikov, L. Комсомольский Восток. (The Komsomol
Orient.) A sketch of the Young communist organizations in
Central Asia.) Leningrad, 1925. 123 p.

D. The Third International

(1) Bibliography

11528. Коминтерн 1919-1929. Каталог книг. (Comintern, 1919-
1929. Catalogue of books.) Gosizdat, 1929. 72 p.

(2) The Seven Congresses

11529. Bantke, S. (comp.). Борьба большевиков за создание
Коммунистического интернационала. (The struggle of the Bol-
sheviks for the creation of the Communist international.)
Materials and documents, 1914-1919. Moscow, 1934. xi, 246p.

11530. Коммунистический интернационал. Орган Исполнитель-
ного комитета Коммунистического интернационала. (The Commu-
nist international. Organ of the Executive committee of the
Communist international.) Leningrad-Moscow, Pravda, 1, 1919-
(Appears simultaneously in English, Russian, French, and
German.)

11531. Коммунистический интернационал. Конгресс. Стенографические отчеты. (The Communist international. Congress.
Stenographic accounts.) 1, 1919-

11532. Доклады II конгрессу Коммунистического интернационала. (Reports presented to the II congress of the Communist international.) Petrograd, 1920. 408 p.

11533. Tsitovich, IA. "Второй конгресс Коммунистического интернационала, 19 июля - 20 августа, 1920 г." (Second congress of the Communist international, July 19 - August 20, 1920.) Kommunisticheskii internatsional, 20-21:434-435:165-176, July 1935.

11534. Piatnitskii, O., Manuilskii, D., and Knorina, V. (ed.) Второй конгресс Коминтерна, июль-август 1920 г. (The second congress of the Communist international, July - August 1920.) Leningrad, 1934. xiv, 754 p.

11535. Pjatnizki, O. A. (Piatnitskii). Die vom II weltkongress der Komintern angenommenen aufnahmebedingungen der Kommunistischen parteien. Moskau-Leningrad, 1933. 52 p.

11536. II конгресс Коммунистического интернационала. Стенографический отчет. (A stenographic account of the II congress of the Communist international.) Petrograd, 1921. 682 p.

11537. III всемирный конгресс Коммунистического интернационала. Стенографический отчет. (A stenographic account of the III world congress of the Communist international.) Petrograd, 1922. 500 p.

11538. IV всемирный конгресс Коммунистического интернационала. (The IV world congress of the Communist international.) November 5 - December 3, 1922. Selected reports, speeches, and resolutions. Moscow-Petrograd, 1923. 427 p.

11539. V всемирный конгресс Коммунистического интернационала. (The V world congress of the Communist international.) Theses, resolutions, decrees. Moscow, 1924. 206 p.

11540. V всемирный конгресс Коммунистического интернационала (The V world congress of the Communist international.) June 17-July 8, 1924. Stenographic account. Part I. Moscow - Leningrad, 1925. 1010 p.

11541. "Созревание мирового революционного кризиса--борьба за советскую власть во всем мире." (The ripening of the world revolutionary crisis and the struggle for soviet power in the entire world.) Summaries of the XIII plenum of the Executive committee of the Communist international.) Kommunisticheskii internatsional, 36:378:3-18, Dec. 1933.

11542. Communist international. Executive committee. Plenum, December 1933. Theses and decisions. Thirteenth plenum of the E.C.C. Moscow-Leningrad, Cooperative publishing society of foreign workers in the USSR, 1934. 31 p.

11543. Послевоенный капитализм в освещении Коминтерна. Сборник документов и резолюций конгрессов и Исполкома Коминтерна. (Postwar capitalism in the light of the Komintern. Collection of documents and resolutions of the congresses and the Executive committee of the Comintern.) Moscow, 1933. 209 p.

11544. Коммунистический интернационал пред VII всемирным конгрессом. Материал.(The Communist international before the VII world congress. Materials.) Moscow, Partizdat, 1935. 606 p.   (2) Die Kommunistische internationale, vor dem 7 weltkongress. Materialen. Moskau, 1935. 720 p.

11545. Седьмой всемирный конгресс Коммунистического интернационала. Стенографический отчет. (Stenographic account of the seventh congress of the Communist international [held in Moscow, August 1935].)

11546. Резолюции VII всемирного конгресса Коммунистического интернационала. (Resolutions of the VII world congress of the Communist international.) Moscow, Partizdat, 1935. 101p.
 (2) Resolutions of the Seventh congress of the Communist international. New York, 1936.

11547. VII конгресс Коммунистического интернационала о молодежи. (VII congress of the Communist international concerning the youth.) Excerpts from reports. Moscow, 1935.

11548. James, C. L. World revolution, 1917-1936. The rise and fall of the Communist international. New York, Pioneer publishers, 1937. 429 p.

(3) Congresses of the Nations of Asia

See 1047-1060.

11549. Стенографические отчеты. I съезд народов Востока. (Stenographic accounts. I congress of the peoples of the East.) Baku, 1-8 September, 1920. Petrograd, Komintern, 1920. 232 p.

11550. Der Ferne Osten. Der erste кongress der kommunistischen und revolutionären organisationen im Fernen Osten, Moskau, Januar 1922. Hamburg, 1924.

11551. Troianovskii, K. Восток и революция. (The East and the revolution.) Moscow, 1918. 71 p.

11552. Gorter, G. Империализм, мировая война и социал-демократия. (Imperialism, the world war, and social democracy.) Moscow, 1920. viiv, 152 p.

11553. Pavlovich, M. (Vel'tman). Вопросы национальной и колониальной политики и III Интернационал. (Problems of national and colonial policies and the III International.) Moscow, 1920. 71 p.

11554. Pavlovich, M. (Vel'tman). Восточный вопрос на III конгрессе и перспективы революционного движения в странах Ближнего и Среднего Востока. (The Eastern question at the III congress and the perspective of the revolutionary movements in the Near East and Central Asia.) Krasnaia nov', 1 (1921):276-283.

11555. Коммунистический университет трудящихся Востока. (The Communist university of the proletarian Orient.) In: Otchet Narkomnatsa za 1921 g. :13-18. (2) Коммунистический университет трудящихся Востока имени тов. Сталина (The Comrade Stalin communist university of the proletarian Orient.) In: Shest' let natsional'noi politiki sovetskoi vlasti i narkomantsa, Moscow, 1924:159-200. (3) Stalin, I. О политических задачах Университета народов Востока. (Concerning political problems of the University of Oriental peoples.) Moscow, 1925. 22 p. (4) Советский Восток. (The Soviet East.) 2nd edition. Moscow, Kommunisticheskii universitet trudiashchikhsia Vostoka I.V. Stalina, 1930. 113 p.

11556. Safarov, G. "Национально-колониальный вопрос на IV конгрессе Коминтерна." (The nationality-colonial question at the IV congress of the Communist international.) Novyi Vostok, 2 (1922):58-74.

11557. Palmieri, A. La Politica asiatica dei Bolscevichi. V. I. Cina, Giappone, India, Persia. Bologna, 1924. 291 p.

11558. Ivin, A. Китай и Советский Союз. (China and the Soviet Union.) Moscow, 1924. 144 p.

11559. Manuilskii, D. Z. Национально-колониальный вопрос. (The nationality-colonial problem.) Report at the V world congress of the Communist international, July 30, 1924. 27 p.

11560. Katayama, Sen. "Коминтерн и Дальний Восток."(The Communist international and the Far East.) Kommunisticheskii internatsional, Moscow, 1 (1924):205-212. (2) "Япония и Советская Россия." (Japan and Soviet Russia.) Kommunisticheskii internatsional, 9:1277-1280.

11561. Красный Восточник.(The red Orientalist.) Miscellany. Moscow, 1925. 154 p.

11562. "Мировое положение и задачи Коминтерна." (The world situation and the problems of the Communist international.) Kommunisticheskii internatsional, 8 (1925):5-27.

11563. Coates, Charles H. The red theology in the Far East. London, Thynne and Jarvis, 1926. 202 p.

11564. Vansov, V. "Делегация профессиональных союзов СССР в Китае и Японии." (The trade union delegation of the USSR in China and Japan.) Krasnyi internatsional profsoiuzov, 11 (1925):32-33.

11565. Voitinskii, G. "Колониальный вопрос на расширенном пленуме ИККИ." (The colonial question in the enlarged plenum of the Executive committee of the Communist international.) Kommunisticheskii internatsional, 4 (1925):64-71.

11566. Kasparova, V. Женщина Востока. (The woman of the Orient.) Leningrad, 1925. 90 p. (2) The same. Раскрепощение женщины Востока. (The emancipation of the Oriental woman.) Moscow, 1925. 80 p.

11567. Waksow, Viktor. "Die gewerkschaftsdelegation der USSR in China und Japan." Rote gewerkschafts-internationale, 5 (1926):2:262-267.

11568. Rafes, M. "Китайская революция и задачи коммунистов." (The Chinese revolution and the problem of the communists.) Kommunisticheskaia revoliutsiia, Moscow, January 1927:43-57.

11569. Mitarevsky, N. World wide Soviet plots. Tientsin, 1927. 211 p.

11570. Nikitine, B. "L'union sovetique et l'Orient musulman." Revue des sciences politiques, 51:593-610, Oct.-Dec. 1928.

11571. Lobanov-Rostovsky, A. "Bolshevism and Asia." Edinburgh review, 248:506:349-357, October 1928.

11572. Roy, Manabendra Nat. Китайская революция и Коммунистический интернационал. (The Chinese revolution and the Communist international.) Moscow, 1929. 207 p.

11573. Hayashi, Nobuo. 露 國 赤 化 宣 傳，真 相 Ro-koku sekka senden no shinso. (The truth about Russia's communistic propaganda.) Gaiko jiho, 52:5:145-152, December 1, 1929.

11574. Pan-shu (tr.). 蘇 俄 的 東 方 政 策 Su-O ti Tung-fang chêng-ts'ê. (Soviet Russia's Eastern policy.) Shanghai, Tai-p'ing-yang shu-tien, 1930.

11575. Chiang, Ting-fu. 鮑 羅 廷 時 代 之 蘇 俄 遠 東 政 策 Pao-lo-ting shih-tai chih Su-O Yüan-tung chêng-tsê. (Soviet Russia's Far Eastern policy in the time of Borodin.) Tu-li ping-lun, 6, June 1932.

11576. 年 鑑 サヴエート 現 勢 資 料 Nenkan-Sovieto gensei shiryo. (Materials on contemporary conditions in Soviet Russia.) Roshia tsushinsha, 1932. 1100 p.

11577. Kun, Bela. Die II internationale in auflösung. Moskau-Leningrad, 1933. 85 p.

11578. Мировое профессиональное движение. (Universal trade union movement.) V. VI, Eastern section. Moscow, Krasnyi internatsional professional'nykh soiuzov. 383 p.

11579. Florinsky, Michael. World revolution and the USSR. New York, Macmillan, 1933. 264 p.

11580. Nikonov, A. "Проблема дальневосточных противоречий." (The problem of Far Eastern contradictions.) Kommunisticheskaia revoliutsiia, 11:48-58, November 1934.

11581. Kuchumov, V. "Созревание мирового революционного кризиса и колониальный Восток." (The looming world revolutionary crisis and the colonial Orient.) Revoliutsionnyi Vostok, 1 (1934):23:25-35.

11582. Mif, P. "Современный этап революционной борьбы на колониальном Востоке." (The present stage of revolutionary struggle in the colonial Orient.) Revoliutsionnyi Vostok, 1 (1934):23:36-48.

11583. Mödlhammer, Franz Ludwig. Moskaus hand im Fernen Osten. Berlin, Nibelungen-verlag, 1937. 186 p.

XIX. GOVERNMENT AND POLITICS

A. Before 1917

(1) Government Periodicals and Publications

11584. Полное собрание законов Российской империи с 1649 года. (Complete code of laws of the Russian empire since 1649.) St. Petersburg, 1830-1916. Series I, 46 v.; series II, 58 v.; series III, 33 v.

11585. Правительственный вестник. (Government messenger.) Official gazette, organ of all ministries and government departments. St. Petersburg, 1869-1917.

11586. Положение о земских учреждениях. (Material on local self-government organizations.) St. Petersburg, Khoziaistvennyi departament, 1885-1886. 2 v.

11587. Обозрение главных оснований местного управления Сибири. (A survey of basic laws of local administration of Siberia.) St. Petersburg, 1841. 136, ii p.

11588. Журналы Комитета министерств (1802-1826). (Journals of the Committee of the ministries, 1802-1826.) St. Petersburg, 1889-1891. 2 v.

11589. Государственный совет (1906-1917. Верхняя палата). Стенографический отчет. (State council. 1906-1917 Upper chamber. Stenographic accounts.) St. Petersburg, 1906-1917. 13 v. Приложение- (Appendix.) Sessions, 3-5. 1907-1910. Указатель- (Index.) Session 1-12, 1906-1916.

11590. Государственная Дума. Стенографические отчеты. (The State Duma. Stenographic accounts.) St. Petersburg, 1906-1917. 36 v. Приложения к стенографическим отчетам. (Supplements...) 40 v., 1907-1916. Закрытые заседания. (Closed meetings.)

11591. Государственная Дума. Справочный листок. (Information leaflet of the State Duma.) St. Petersburg, 1908/09-1917.

11592. Государственная Дума. Проекты законов, принятых Государственной Думой. (Bills passed by the State Duma.) St. Petersburg, 1907-1916.

11593. Государственная Дума. Обзор деятельности. (Survey of activities of the State Duma.) St. Petersburg, 1907-1912. 3 v.

11594. Государственная Дума. Обзор деятельности комиссий и отделов. (Survey of the activities of the committees and departments of the State Duma.) St. Petersburg, 1907-1916.

11595. Государственная Дума. Наказ Государственной Думы. (Rules of the State Duma.) St. Petersburg, 1909, 1914, 1915.

11596. Государственная Дума. Материалы к стенографическим отчетам. (Material appended to the stenographic accounts.) St. Petersburg, 1906-1907.

11597. "Временное правительство Автономной Сибири." (The Provisional government of Autonomous Siberia.) Krasnyi Arkhiv, 35 (1929):37-106; 36 (1929):31-60.

11598. Мемуары и дневники царских сановников. (Memoirs and diaries of tsarist dignitaries.) Moscow, TSentral'nyi arkhiv, 1926-

(2) General Accounts

11599. Gradovskii, A. D. Высшая администрация России XVIII века. (The higher administration of Russia in the XVIII century.) St. Petersburg, 1866.

11600. Mrochek-Drozdovskii, P. N. Областное управление России XVIII века. (Russian provincial government in the XVIII century.) Moscow, 1876.

11601. Krusser, G. Сибирские областники. (Siberian separatists.) From 1864 to Kolchak. Novosibirsk, 1931. 97 p.

11602. Shteingel', V. I. Сибирские сатрапы. (Siberian satraps.)

11603. Serebrennikov, I. I. "К истории Сибирского правительства." (Contribution to the history of the Siberian government.) Vol'naia Sibir'. Sibirskii arkhiv. 1, 1929, 5-22.

11604. Shreider, G. Земство и город. (Zemstvo and the city.) Narodnoe khoziaistvo (St. Petersburg), 1900:7,8,10.

11605. Romanovich-Slovatinskii, A. V. Исторический очерк губернского управления. (Historical outline of the provincial administration.) Kiev, 1859.

11606. Ivanovskii, V. V. "Административное устройство окраин." (Administration of the Russian border provinces.) Uchenye zapiski Kzaanskogo universiteta, 63 (1891):6.

11607. Prutchenko, S. Сибирские окраины.   (Siberian provincial governments.) Historical juridical sketches. St. Petersburg, 1899. 2 v.   See 11165.

11608. Vernadskii, G. Государственная уставная грамота. (State charter.) Prague, 1925.

11609. Lantzeff, George V. Russian colonial administration. Ph. D. thesis, University of California, Berkeley, 1938. x. 350 p.

11610. Veselovskii, B. B. Земство в Сибири. (Zemstvo in Siberia.) Obrazovanie, 1908:12.

11611. Polner, T. I. Общеземская организация на Дальнем Востоке. (The Zemstvo organization in the Far East.) St. Petersburg, 1910. 2 v.

11612. Vinogradskii, N. N. Земство в Сибири. (Zemstvo in Siberia.) Petrograd, 1917.

11613. Veisman, P. L. Правовые запросы Сибири.   (Problems of law and justice in Siberia.) St. Petersburg, 1909.

11614. Graf Alfred Keyserling erzählt. Kaunas-Leipzig, Pribaêis, 1937.

B. Since 1917

(1) Sources

11615. Территориальное и административное деление СССР. (Territorial and administrative divisions of the USSR.) Moscow, Narodnyi komissariat vnutrennikh del, Statisticheskii otdel. 1917-

11616. Список губерний, уездов и волостей РСФСР, УССР и ССРБ. (List of provinces, counties, and rural districts of the RSFSR, the UkrSSR, and W-RSSR.) Moscow, Narodnyi komissariat vnutrennikh del, 1921-1922.

11617. Гражданский кодекс. (The civil code.) Moscow, 1923-

11618. Сборник действующих на территории РСФСР административных законов. (Collection of administrative laws in force in the RSFSR.) Comp. by Kurskii. Moscow, 1927.

11619. Собрание узаконений и распоряжений рабочего и крестьянского правительства. (Collection of statutes of the worker and peasant government.) Moscow, 1, 1917-

11620. Гражданский кодекс с постатейно-систематизированным материалом. (Civil code annotated, with systematically arranged subsequent changes.) Ed. by Aleksandrovskii. Дополнение. (Supplement to the 2nd edition.)

11621. Гражданский кодекс. Коментарии. (Civil code annotated.) Ed. by Goikhbarg. Moscow, 1925-

11622. Dimanshtein, S. and Krylenko, N. Материалы к докладам о 2-ой годовщине конституции СССР. (Sources pertaining to the reports on the 2nd anniversary of the USSR constitution.) Moscow, 1925. 23 p.

11623. Vinogradov, B. (comp.). Конституция Союза ССР и союзных республик. (The constitution of the USSR and the allied republics.) Ed. by G. Gurvich. Moscow, 1933. 204 p.

11624. Gurvich, G. Принципы автономизма и федерализма в советской системе. (Principles of autonomy and federalism in the Soviet system.) Moscow, 1924. 75 p.

11625. Совет народных комиссаров. СССР. Год работы правительства. (Annual report of the government of the USSR.) Moscow, 1924/25-

11626. Совет народных комиссаров. Год работы правительства РСФСР. (Annual report of the government of the RSFSR.) Moscow, 1924/25-

(2) General Accounts

11627. Harper, Samuel N. The government of the Soviet Union New York, D. Van Nostrand co., 1938. vii-xviii, 204 p. (2) The same. Civic training in Soviet Russia. Chicago, University of Chicago press, 1929. xvii, 401 p. (3) The same. Making bolsheviks. Chicago, University of Chicago press, 1931. xix, 167 p.

11628. Пять лет власти Советов. (Five years of Soviet rule.) Moscow, 1922. 571 p.

11629. Trainin, I. СССР. Союз Советских Социалистических Республик. (USSR. Union of the Soviet Socialist Republics.) Moscow, 1923. 90 p.

11630. Kantor, E. (Davydov). Что дала советская власть народам России. (What the Soviet government has given to the peoples of Russia.) Moscow, 1923. 39 p.

11631. Ch'ien, Chiang-ch'un. 蘇維埃俄羅斯 Su-wei-yai
O-lo-szu. (Soviet Russia.) Shanghai, Commercial press, 1924.

11632. Kotliarevskii, S. A. СССР и союзные республики.
(The USSR and the allied republics.) Moscow, 1924. 139 p.

11633. День СССР.(The USSR day.) A jubilee edition. Collec-
tec articles ed. by G. I. Broido. Moscow, 1925. 256 p.

11634. Arkhipov, K. Советские автономные области и респу́б-
лики. (The Soviet autonomous provinces and republics.)
Moscow, 1925. 123 p.

11635. Magerovskii, D. A. Союз Советских Социалистических
Республик. (The Union of Soviet Socialist Republics.) A sur·
vey and sources. Moscow, 1925. 185 p.

11636. Shih-chieh-shih chu-jên. 蘇俄評論 Su-O ping-
lun. (Criticisms on Soviet Russia.) Shanghai, Hsin-yüeh shu-
tien, 1927.

11637. Uchiyama, Peteru. シベリヤノ行政経済事情 Shiberia
no gyosei keizai jijo. (The administrative and economic condition of Siberia.) Dairen, S. M. R. R., 1929. 2 v.

11638. Gins, G. and Van-tsyn-shung. Новые законы и правила
регистрации. (The new laws and rules of registration.) Harbin, 1930. 79 p.

11639. Wang, Chi-tang (tr.). 新俄羅斯 Hsin O-lo-szu.
(New Russia.) Shanghai, Commercial press, 1931.

11640. Hsi-hsia. 蘇俄聯邦制度的研究 Su-O Lien-
pung chih-tu ti yen-chiu. (A study of the system of the Soviet Union.) Wu-ta shê-hui-k'o-hsüeh chi-k'an, 1:2, June
1930.

11641. Su-O chih chêng-shih shê-chi. 蘇俄之城市設計
(City projects of Soviet Russia.) Kung-chêng i-pao, 2:4,
October 1931.

11642. Ling, Chi-han. 蘇俄私法的改進 Su-O szu-fa
ti kai-ching. (The improvements on civil law in Soviet Russia.) Hsin-chuang-tso pan-yüeh-k'an, 11:1, April 1932.

11643. Chang, Chün-mai. 我之俄國觀 Wo chih O-kuo kuan.
(My opinion on Russia.) Tsai-shêng, 1, May 1932.

11644. Chang, Yüan-jo. 蘇聯人民的自由權 Su-Lien jên-min ti tzu-yu-chuan. (People's civil rights in Soviet Union.) Hsin-ch'uang-tsao, 1:6, July 1932.

11645. Yamauchi, Hosuke. ソ聯邦ノ權力爭覇戰 So-Renpo no kenryoku soha sen. (The contest for supremacy of power in Soviet Union.) Sekai chishiki, Decmeber 1932.

11646. Yamakawa, Hitoshi. ソヴェート十五周年 Soveto jugo shunen. (Fifteenth anniversary of Soviet Union.) Kaizo, 14:11: November 1932.

11647. 謎ノ赤露解剖號 Nazo no Seki-Ro kaibo go. (The analysis of puzzling Red Russia.) Sekai chishiki, September 1932.

11648. Предложения трудящихся Западной Сибири к проекту Сталинской конституции СССР. (Suggestions of the workers of Western Siberia concerning the projected Stalin constitution of the USSR.) Novosibirsk, 1936. 240 p.

(3) Local Government and Regionalism

(a) Bibliography

11649. Kazarinov, P. "Сибирское краеведение."(Regional study of Siberia.) A short bibliographical survey. Sibirskaia zhivaia starina, Irkutsk, 2 (1924):159-190.

(b) Periodicals

11650. Советское краеведение. (Soviet regional study.) Ed. by A. A. Shirmov. Pub. by TSentral'noe biuro kraevedeniia TSentral'nogo nauchno-issledovatel'skogo instituta metodov kraevednoi raboty. 1, 1925- (Monthly).

(c) Accounts

11651. Vladimirskii, M. Организация советской власти на местах.(The organization of Soviet local-government.) Moscow, 1919. 63 p.

11652. Mikhailov, G. S. Местное советское управление. (Local Soviet administration.) Moscow, 192 .

11653. Mirotvortsev, K. N. К вопросу о районировании Сибири. (The question of zoning Siberia.) Irkutsk, 1924. 35 p.

11654. Marr. N. IA. Краеведение. (Regional geography.) Leningrad, 1925. 20 p.

400   Russia

11655. Alendeev, G., Romanov, N., Kostin, M. Краеведение.
(Regional geography.) Cheboksary, Chuvashiia, 1933. 64 p.

11656. Stepanov, N. L. П.А. Словцов. У истоков сибирского
областничества.   (P. A. Slovtsov. At the source of
Siberian separatism.) Leningrad, Institute for the study of
the peoples of the north of the USSR, 1935. 42 p.

XX. ECONOMIC CONDITIONS

See 781-936.

A. Statistical Periodicals

11657. Статистический ежегодник России. (Statistical year-
book of Russia.) St. Petersburg, TSentral'nyi statisticheskii komitet, 1905-1918. 13 issues.

11658. Вестник статистики. (Statistical messenger.) Moscow,
TSentral'noe statisticheskoe upravlenie, 1919-1930 (?) 34 v.

B. Population Statistics

See 824-832.

11659. Klochkov, M. Население России при Петре Великом.
(The population of Russia during the reign of Peter the
Great.) St. Petersburg, 1911.

11660. Статистическое обозрение Сибири, составленное на
основании сведений, почерпнутых из актов правительства и
других достоверных источников. (Statistical survey of Siberia, compiled on the basis of official decrees and other
reliable sources.) St. Petersburg, 1810. 361 p.

11661. Arseniev, K. Статистические очерки России. (Statistical outlines of Russia.) St. Petersburg, 1848.

11662. Военно-статистическое обозрение Российской империи.
(Military statistical survey of the Russian empire.) 1848-
1853. St. Petersburg, Pervoe otdelenie General'nogo shtaba,
1854.

11663. Hagemeister, IU. A.Статистическое обозрение Сибири.
(A statistical survey of Siberia.) St. Petersburg, 1854.
3 parts.

11664. Материалы для статистики России. (Materials for statistics of Russia.) St. Petersburg, Ministerstvo gosudarstvennykh imushchestv, 1858-1871. 6 v.

11665. **Miliutin, B. A.** (ed.) Сборник историко-статистических сведений о Сибири и странах к ней прилегающих. (A collection of historical statistical data concerning Siberia and its adjacent countries.) St. Petersburg, 1875. 2 v.

11666. Временник Центрального статистического комитета. (Annals of the Central statistical committee.) St. Petersburg, TSentral'nyi statisticheskii komitet, 1888-1903. 52 v.

11667. Общий свод по Империи результатов разработки данных первой всеобщей переписи населения. (General summaries for the Empire of the analysis of data of the first general census of population, 1897.) St. Petersburg, 1905. 2 v.

11668. Dépouillement des données sur la nationalité et classification des peuples de l'Empire de Russie d'après leur langue (1897). St. Petersburg, 1899.

11669. Первая всеобщая перепись населения Российской Империи 1897 года. (First general census of population of the Russia empire in 1897.) St. Petersburg, 1899-1905. 89 v. (128 issues).

11670. Численность и состав рабочих в России на основании данных 1-ой всеобщей переписи населения Российской империи 1897 года. (Industrial statistics of Russia, 1st general census, 1897.) St. Petersburg, 1906. 2 v.

11671. **Patkanov, S.** Главнейшие данные по статистике населения крайнего Востока Сибири. (Chief data for the statistics of the population of Far Eastern Siberia.) St. Petersburg, 1903.

11672. Первая всеобщая перепись населения Российской империи. (The first general census of the population of the Russian empire, 1897.) LXII: The Amur province, 1 and 2, 1899. LXXVI: The Maritime province, 1,2,3, 1899-1904. St. Petersburg, 1907-1908.

11673. **Klements, D.** Население Сибири. (The population of Siberia.) St. Petersburg, 1908.

11674. **Shvetsov, S. P.** Сибирь, кто в ней живет и как живет. (Siberia: who lives in that country and how.) St. Petersburg, 1909.

11675. **Patkanov, S. K.** О приросте инородческого населения Сибири. (The increase of the native population in Siberia. St. Petersburg, 1911.

11676. Предметный указатель материалов в земско-статистических трудах с 1860-х годов по 1917-й год. (Subject index to the material included in the zemstvo statistical publications, 1860-1917.) Moscow, TSentral'noe statisticheskoe upravlenie, 1926-1927. 2 v.

11677. Сборник географических, топографических и статистических материалов по Азии. (A collection of geographic, topographic and statistical data concerning Asia.) St. Petersburg, 1883-1913. 86 v.

11678. Статистика Российской империи. (Statistics of the Russian empire.) St. Petersburg, 1887-1917. 94 v. Published by the TSentral'nyi statisticheskii komitet.

11679. Всеобщая перепись 1920 года. (General census, 1920.) Moscow, 1920.

11680. Всероссийская перепись населения 1920 года. Симбирская губерния. (The All-Russia census of 1920. Simbirsk gubernia.) Simbirsk, Simbirskoe gubernskoe statisticheskoe biuro, 1923. 125 p.

11681. Материалы по статистике Дальнего Востока. Итоги Всероссийской городской переписи 1923 года на Дальнем Востоке. (Statistical materials for the Far East. Returns of the All-Russian urban census of population in the Far East, 1923.) Moscow, 1923-1924.

11682. Предварительные итоги Всероссийской городской переписи 1923 года на Дальнем Востоке. (Preliminary totals of the All-Russian urban census of 1923 in the Far East.) Chita, Upravlenie upolnomochennogo tsentral'nogo statisticheskogo upravleniia na Dal'nem Vostoke, 1923. 11 p.

11683. Материалы по статистике Дальнего Востока. (Statistical materials on the Far East.) Chita, Upravlenie upolnomochennogo tsentral'nogo statisticheskogo upravleniia na Dal'nem Vostoke, 1924. vi, 99 p.

11684. Всесоюзная перепись населения 1926 года. Краткие сводки. (All-Union census of population, 1926. Short summaries.) Moscow, 1928-1929. 10 v.

11685. Всесоюзная перепись населения 1926 года. (All-Union census, 1926.) Moscow, 1926.

11686. Итоги десятилетия советской власти в цифрах. (Tenth anniversary of Soviet rule presented in figures.) Moscow, TSentral'noe statisticheskoe upravlenie, 1927.

11687. Предварительные итоги демографической переписи 1926 года в Сибирском крае. (Preliminary results of the demographic census of 1926 in Siberia.) Novosibirsk, Sibkraistatotdel, 1927. 63 p.

11688. Furusawa, Toshitaro. 亜 細 亜 露 西 亜 ' 住 民 Ajia Roshia no jumin. (The population of Asiatic Russia.) Dairen, S.M.R.R., 1925. Also an edition in 1929.

11689. Ten years of Soviet power in figures. Moscow, 1927. See also 11686.

11690. Shneider, A. P. and Dobrova-IAdrintseva, L. A. Население Сибирского края. (The population of the Siberian region.) Sibkraiizdat, 1928. 110 p.

11691. Boldyrev, V. and Skurskii, F. Сибирский край в цифрах. (The Siberian region in figures.) Novonikolaevsk, 1926. 36 p.

11692. Сибирский край. Статистический справочник. (The Siberian region. A statistical guide-book.) Novosibirsk, Sibirskii krai, Planovaia komissiia, Statisticheskii sektor, 1930. xvi, 804 p.

11693. IAkushev, I. A. "Районированная Сибирь в цифрах." (Regionalized Siberia in figures.) Vol'naia Sibir', Prague, 8 (1930):46-71; 9 (1930):64-84.

11694. Hopper, Bruce. "Population factors in Soviet Siberia." Limits of Land settlement, prepared under the sponsorship of the American coordinating committee for international studies and published by the Council of foreign relations. New York, 1937.

11695. See 824.

C. Periodicals

11696. Бюллетень мирового хозяйства.   (Bulletin of world economy.) Moscow, 1924-

11697. Проблемы экономики.   (Problems of economics.) Ed. by K. Butaev. Pub. by the Institute of economics of the Academy of sciences of the USSR. Published 6 times a year. 1, 1929-

11698. Народный комиссариат путей сообщения. Экономическое бюро. Труды.   (People's commissariat of transportation, Economics bureau, Transactions.) Moscow, 1925-

11699. Производительные силы Дальнего Востока. (Productive forces of the Far East.) "Knizhnoe delo," Khabarovsk-Vladivostok, 1, 192(?)-

11700. The Soviet union monthly. London, Torgovaia delegatsiia v Anglii, 1921-   1921-1924 as Russian information and review.   1925- as Soviet union review.

11701. La vie économique des Soviets. Paris, Torgovoe predstavitel'stvo vo Frantsii, 1925-   ---Supplement: Le pétrole russe. 1927-

11702. Информационный бюллетень(Information bulletin.) Paris, Torgovoe predstavitel'stvo vo Frantsii, 1926-

D. Hand-books

11703. Economic handbook of the Soviet Union. New York, American-Russian chamber of commerce, 1931. 151 p.

E. Economic History

11704. Kulisher, I. M. История русского народного хозяйства. (Economic history of Russia.) Moscow, 1925. 2 v.   German edition: Russische wirtschaftsgeschichte. Jena, G. Fischer, 1925.

11705. Mavor, James. An economic history of Russia. London-New York, Dutton, 1925. 2 v. 2nd ed. rev. and enl.

11706. Lawton, Lancelot. An economic history of Soviet Russia. London, Macmillan, 1932. 2 v.

11707. Bowden, Witt, Karpovich, Michael, and Usher, Abbott Payson. An economic history of Europe since 1750. New York, American book co., 1937. 948 p. (Chapters 14, 29, 34, and 38 deal with Russia.)

11708. Bazilevich, K. "Таможенные книги, как источник экономической истории России."   (Customs records as sources for the economic history of Russia.) In Problemy istochnikovedeniia, Sb. I, Trudy Istoriko arkheograficheskogo instituta Akademii nauk SSSR, 9:110-129.

11709. Ulianov, N. I. "Феодальная колонизация и экономика Мурмана в XVII веке." (Feudal colonization and economic policy of Murman in the XVII century.) Istoricheskii sbornik, 1 (1934):89-139.

11710. Bazilevich, K. V. "Крупное торговое предприятие в Московском государстве в первой половине XVII века." (A large commercial enterprise in the Muscovite state of the first half of the XVII century.) Izvestiia Akademii nauk SSSR, Otdelenie obshchestvennykh nauk, Seriia VII, 9 (1932): 783-811.

F. Economic Geography

11711. Baranskii, N. N. Краткий курс экономической географии. (A brief course in economic geography.) Moscow-Leningrad, 1929. 654 p. (2) The same. Экономическая география СССР. (Economic geography of the USSR.) Moscow, 1935. 408 p.

11712. Grin, M. F. Экономическая география СССР по областям, краям и республикам. (Economic geography of the USSR according to provinces, regions, and republics.) Moscow, 1933. 360 p.

11713. Morozov, N. and IUniev, I. Хрестоматия по экономической географии. (A handbook on economic geography.) Moscow, 192?.

11714. Golovachev, P. Экономическая география Сибири. (An economic geography of Siberia.) Moscow, 1914.

11715. Anson, A. A. (ed.). Экономическая география Сибири. (An economic geography of Siberia.) Novosibirsk, 1928.

11716. Davidenkova, V. S. Сибирь. (Siberia.) Moscow-Leningrad, 192?. 112 p. 1 map.

11717. Konstantinov, O. A. Уральская область (с приложением очерка Башкирской республики.) (The Ural province, with a supplement of a sketch of the Bashkir republic.) Moscow-Leningrad, 192?. 155 p.

G. General Accounts

(1) Economic Potentialities

11718. Krzhizhanovskii, G. M. and Osadchii, P. S. (editors). К проблеме Сибирской сверхмагистрали. (On the problem of the principal trunk line across Siberia.) Moscow, Plankhozgiz, 1929.

11719. Kolosovskii, N. N. Сибирская сверхмагистраль. (The principal trunk line across Siberia.) Moscow, Plankhozgiz, 1930.

11720. Экономическое состояние городских поселений Сибири. (Economic conditions of urban settlements in Siberia.) St. Petersburg, Khoziaistvennyi departament, 1882.

11721. IAdrintsev, Nikolai M. Культурное и промышленное состояние Сибири. (The state of culture and industry in Siberia.) St. Petersburg, 1884. 32 p.

11722. Olan'on, K. Сибирь и ее экономическая будущность. (Siberia and her economic future.) St. Petersburg, 1903. 252 p.

11723. Stroev, S. "Статистико-финансовая картина в Сибири в 1698-1700." (The picture of financial statistics in Siberia in 1698-1700.) Moskovskii telegraf, 1825: 21: 45-57 and 22:139-150.

11724. Grigoriev, V. IU. Перемены в условиях экономической жизни населения Сибири. (Changes in the economic life of the Siberian population.) Krasnoiarsk, 1904. 104 p.

11725. Pistor, E. Durch Sibirien nach der Südsee. Wirtschaftliche und unwirtschaftliche reisestudien aus den jahren 1901 und 1902. 1905. 512 p.

11726. Chuprov, A. I. Речи и статьи. (Speeches and articles.) Moscow, 1909. 2 v.

11727. Chuprov, A. I. Ученые труды. (Scientific works.) Moscow, 1910.

11728. Вопросы советского хозяйства и управления. (Problems of Soviet economy and administration.) Moscow, Narodnyi komissariat raboche-krest'ianskoi inspektsii, 1924. 9 v.

11729. Развитие народного хозяйства СССР за 1913-1927 гг. в диаграмах. (The development of national economy in the USSR during the years 1913-1927, in diagrams.) Moscow, Ekonomicheskii kabinet Kom. universiteta imeni IA. M. Sverdlova, 192?. 2nd revised and enlarged edition.

11730. Сборник грамот Коллегии экономии. (Collection of documents of the Board of economy.) Moscow, Kollegiia ekonomii, 1922-

11731. Miliutin, V. P. Перспективы хозяйственного развития СССР. (Perspectives of the economic development of the USSR) Moscow, Krasnaia pechat', 1926.

11732. Сборник решений и постановлений ВКП(б) и соввласти по экономполитике. (A collection of resolutions and decrees of the Communist party and the Soviet government regarding economic policy.) Moscow, Kom. universitet im. IA. M. Sverdlova, 192?

11733. Danckworth, P. W. Sibirien und seine wirtschafliche zukunft. Leipzig-Berlin, Teubner, 1921. 270 p.

11734. Pohle, Richard. Sibirien als wirtschafsraum. Bonn-Leipzig, 1921.

11735. Canning, C. G. Fairfax. Siberia's untouched treasure. New York, 1923.

11736. Отчет Пятого Сибирского экономического совещания с представителями губерний и уездов 4-7 января 1924 г. (An account of the Fifth Siberian economic conference, January 4-7, 1924.) Novonikolaevsk, 1924. 131 p.

11737. Lavrov, V. M. (ed.). Будущее Сибири. (The future of Siberia.) Novonikolaevsk, 1925. 138 p.

11738. Kolosovskii, N. N. "Хозяйственная проблема Сибири." (The economic problem of Siberia.) Planovoe khoziaistvo, May 1925: 236-247.

11739. Belorusets, L. "Практические моменты построения перспективного плана народного хозяйства Сибирского края." (Planned economy of the Region of Siberia.) Planovoe khoziaistvo, February 1926:301-308.

11740. Rudakov, A. V. "К вопросу о развитии производительных сил Сибири." (The problem of development of the productive forces of Siberia.) Transport i khoziaistvo, Moscow, 2: 54-60, February 1926.

11741. Geischuni, G. Die konzessionspolitik Sowjetrusslands. Berlin, R.L.Prager, 1927.

11742. Shotwell, James T. (ed.). Economic and social history of the world war, Russian series. New Haven, Yale press, 1928-1931. 12 v.

11743. Dobb, Maurice and Stevens, H. C. Russian economic development since the revolution. New York, Dutton, 1928. 2d edition, 1929. 415 p.

11744. Zhdanov, B. N. "O производственных перспективах Сибири."(The prospects of Siberian production.) Severnaia
Aziia, Moscow, 1 (25) (1929):5-28.

11745. Lalevich, I. "Строительство социалистических городов
Сибири." (The building of socialist cities in Siberia.)
Sovetskaia Aziia, Moscow, 1-2 (1931):262-266.

11746. Ch'ên, Ta-chung. 西 伯 利 亜 的 産 業 Hsi-po-li-
ya ti ch'an-yeh. (Natural products of Siberia.) New Asia
monthly, 2:1, April 1931.

11747. Malkin, Georgii V. Природные богатства Сибири. (The
natural wealth of Siberia.) Moscow, 1931. 96 p.

11748. 西 比 利 亜 , 行 政 経 済 事 情 Shiberia no
gyosei keizai jijo. (Administrative and economic conditions
of Siberia.) In section 36, Library of economic research on
Russia. Tokyo, Research bureau, General affairs department,
S.M.R.R., Nichi Nichi shinbun, 1927-1932. 2 v.

11749. 露 亜 経 済 調 査 叢 書 Ro-A keizai chosa so-
sho. (Series of economic research on Russian Asia.) Tokyo,
Research bureau, General affairs dept., S.M.R.R., Nichi
Nichi shinbun, 1927-1932.

11750. Chiang, Kuo-yen (tr.). 蘇 俄 的 経 済 組 織
Su-O ti ching-chi tzu-chih. (The economic system of Soviet
Russia.) Shanghai, Tai-ping-yang shu-tien, 1932.

11751. Социалистическая реконструкция областей, краев и республик СССР в постановлениях партийных и советских органов.
(Socialist reconstruction of the provinces, regions, and
republics of the USSR according to the resolutions of party
and soviet organs.) Ed. by N. N. Baranskii. Moscow-Leningrad, Sotsekgiz, 1932.

11752. Lorwin, L. L. and Abramson, A. The present phase of
economic and social development in the USSR. Paper presented to the Sixth conference of the Institute of Pacific relations, 1936. 38 p.

11753. Darinsky, A. (comp.). Nature and natural resources
of the Soviet Far East. New York, Secretariat of the Institute of Pacific relations, 1936. 62 p.

(2) Socialist Construction

11754. Советское строительство. (Construction of the Soviet
state.) Moscow, ·TS.I.K., SSSR, 1926-   (Monthly).

11755. Sixth conference of the Institute of Pacific relations. Indices of socialist construction in the Union of Soviet Socialist Republics. 1936. 30 p.

(3) Water Power

11756. Kopylov, N. A. (ed.). Справочник по водным ресурсам. (Guide to the water resources.) Leningrad, 1933.

11757. Nekrasov, B. P., Prigorovskii, M. M., and Kryshtofovich, A. N. (ed.). Power resources of the USSR. Leningrad-Moscow, 1933. 40 p.

11758. Krzhizhanovskii, G. M. (ed.). Энергетические ресурсы СССР. (Power resources of the USSR.) Moscow, Academy of sciences, 1937. 635 p.

11759. Vasiliev, B. Энергетика Сибири. (Energy potentialities of Siberia.) Novosibirsk, 1931. 106 p.

11760. Kravtsov, V. A. Энергоресурсы Дальневосточного края. (Energy resources of the Far Eastern region.) Khabarovsk, 1933. 47 p.

11761. Vinter, A. V., Krzhizhanovskii, G. M., and Lomov, G. I. Атлас энергических ресурсов СССР. (An atlas of power resources of the USSR.) V. II. The Far Eastern region. Moscow, 1934. 119 p.

11762. Kolosovskii, N. N. "Перспективы использования энергии р. Ангары в связи с хозяйством Сибири." (Prospects of utilizing the energy of the Angara river in relation to Siberian economy.) Planovoe khoziaistvo, Moscow, 4:253-268, April 1929.

(4) Western and Central Siberia

11763. Nagnibeda, V. IA. Продукция Томской губернии за 1923 год. (Production of the Tomsk guberniia for 1923.) Tomsk, 1924. 9 p.

11764. Народное хозяйство Томской губернии. (National economy of the Tomsk guberniia.) Tomsk, 1924. 232 p.

11765. Podnek, A.Казахстан в системе народного хозяйства СССР. (Kazakstan in the national economic system of the USSR.) Alma-Ata, 1930. 56 p.

(4) The Far Eastern Region

11766. Takahashi, Kokki and Ichikawa, Tagui. 露領極東
及び西比利亞ノ經濟事情 Ro-ryo Kyokuto oyobi
Shiberia no keizai jijo. (Economic conditions of the Russian
Far East and Siberia.) Dairen, S.M.R.R., 1925. 2 v.

11767. Neresov, M. N. Экономические очерки Дальнего Востока. (Economic sketches of the Far East.) Moscow, 1926.
120 p.

11768. Krylov, L. V. Капитальное строительство Дальневосточного края.   (Capital construction of the Far East.) Vladivostok, 1926. 32 p.

11769. Экономика Дальнего Востока.   (Economy of the Far
East.) Collected articles ed. by N.N.Kolosov and others.
Moscow, Planovoe khoziaistvo, 1926. 357 p.

11770. Kolobov, M."К развитию производительных сил Дальнего
Востока." (Development of the productive forces of the Far
East.) Sibirskie ogni, Novosibirsk, 1:160-175, January-Feb-
ruary 1928.

11771. 露領極東，資源ト産業。 Ro-ryo Kyokuto no
shigen to sangyo. (Resources and industries of the Russian
Far East., Osaka, Osaka mainichi, 1929. 316 p.

11772. Chi-shêng (tr.). 蘇聯在太平洋岸底經濟
發展 Su-Lien tsai-t'ai-p'ing-yang-an ti ching-chi fa-
chan. Soviet Russia's economic development on the Pacific
coast.) Ta-kung-pao's Fu-kan on social sciences, 31, September 16, 1930.

11773. Курорты Дальнего Востока.   (Resorts of the Far East.)
Irkutsk, 1930. 199 p.

11774. Sokolov, P. Сибирская тайга и ее культурная пригодность. (The Siberian taiga and its economic possibilities.)
Izvestiia I.R.G.O.,28.

11775. Pavlovskii, E. Тайга и ее богатства. (The taiga and
its wealth.) Siberia and the Yakutsk ASSR. Leningrad, 1931.
88 p.

11776. Raikhman, E. and Vvedenskii, V. The economic development of the Soviet Far East. Prepared for the Sixth conference of the Institute of Pacific relations. USSR council
papers, 2. Moscow, Institute of Pacific relations,1936. 50 p.

11777. Nature and natural resources of the Soviet Far East.
Prepared for the Sixth conference of the Institute of Pacific relations. USSR, Council papers, 4. Moscow, Institute
of Pacific relations, 1936. 62 p.

H. Agriculture

See 833-845

(1) Bibliography

11778. Указатель книг по сельскому хозяйству за ... гг.
(Index of books on agriculture issued in ...) Moscow,
Vsesoiuznaia akademiia sel'sko-khoziaistvennykh nauk imeni
V. I. Lenina, Biuro sel'skokhoziaistvennoi bibliografii,
1918-1922; 1928-1930.

(2) Statistics

11779. Сельско-хозяйственная перепись 1916-го года. Предварительные итоги. (Agricultural census of 1916. Preliminary
returns.) St. Petersburg, 1916-1917. 3 v.

11780. Всероссийская сельско-хозяйственная и поземельная
перепись, 1917 год. (All-Russian agricultural and land census, 1917.) Preliminary returns by provinces... Moscow,
1919.

11781. Сельско-хозяйственная выборочная перепись 1919 года.
(Selective agricultural census [sample survey] of 1919.)
Returns by provinces of the 10 percent sample selective ag-
ricultural census of peasant farms in 1919. Moscow, 1920.

11782. Наемный труд в сельском и лесном хозяйстве СССР в ...
году. (Hired labor in agriculture and forestry of the USSR
in the year ...) Moscow, TSentral'noe statisticheskoe
upravlenie, 1926-

(3) Government Periodicals

11783. Сельскохозяйственное ведомство за 75 лет его деятельности (1937-1912). (Seventy five years of the activities
of the government administration of agriculture, 1837-1912.)
St. Petersburg, Glavnoe upravlenie zemleustroistva i zemledeliia, 1914.

11784. Полная энциклопедия русского сельского хозяйства.
(A complete encyclopedia of Russian agricultural economics.)
St. Petersburg, 1900-1905. 11 v.

11785. Patkanov, S. Материалы для изучения экономического
быта государственных крестьян и инородцев Западной Сибири.
(Materials for the study of the economic conditions of the
state peasants and aborigines of Western Siberia.) St. Petersburg, Ministerstvo gosudarstvennykh imushchestv, 1888-
1894. 21 issues.

11786. Работа землеустроительных комиссий. (Activity of the
agrarian commissions.) St. Petersburg, Glavnoe upravlenie
zemleustroistva i zemledeliia, 1907-1911.

11787. Труды комиссий по подготовке аграрной реформы.
(Transactions of the commissions for the preparation of the
agrarian reform.) Petrograd, Glavnyi zemel'nyi komitet,
1917-1918. 5 v.

11788. Очередные вопросы современного земледелия. (Current
problems of modern agriculture.) St. Petersburg, Departament
zemledeliia, 1913. 9 issues.

11789. Обзор сельско-хозяйственной жизни заселяемых районов
Азиатской России за...год по данным переселенческой текущей
статистики. (Survey of agricultural conditions in the colo-
nized regions of Asiatic Russia for the year ... according
to the current colonization statistics.) St. Petersburg,
Pereselencheskoe upravlenie, 1913.

11790. Народный комиссариат земледелия. Отчет. (People's
commissariat of agriculture. Report.) Moscow, 1917-1920;
1921-

11791. Департамент земледелия. Ежегодник. (Department of
agriculture. Year-book.) St. Petersburg, 1907-1914.

11792. Труды Земплана. (Transactions of the Agrarian planning commission.) Moscow, Narodnyi komissariat zemledeliia,
1924-

11793. Социалистическое землеустройство.(Socialist agrarian organization [land tenure settlement].) Moscow, Narodnyi
komissariat zemledeliia, 1927- (Monthly).

11794. Пути обобществления сельского хозяйства. (The ways
of collectivization of agriculture.) Moscow, Narodnyi komissariat zemledeliia, 1928-

11795. Социалистическое земледелие. (Socialist agriculture.)
Moscow, Narodnyi komissariat zemledeliia, 1929-   (Daily).

11796. Бюллетень узаконений и распоряжений по сельскому и лесному хозяйству. (Bulletin of laws and enactments on agriculture and forestry.) Moscow, Narodnyi komissariat zemledeliia, 1928-1930. 3 v.

11797. Сельское хозяйство и пути сообщения. (Agriculture and ways of communication.) Moscow, Narodnyi komissariat putei soobshcheniia, 1922-1923. 12 issues.

11798. Новая деревня. (The new village.) Moscow, Narodnyi komissariat zemledeliia, 1921-   (Since 1925 semi-monthly).

(4) Climate

11799. Климатологический атлас Российской империи. (Climatological atlas of the Russia empire.) St. Petersburg, Nikolaevskaia glavnaia fizicheskaia observatoriia, 1900.

11800. Breitigam, P. Материалы для климатологии Западной Сибири и Степного края. (Sources pertaining to the climatology of Western Siberia and the Steppe region.) Zapiski Zap.-Sib. Otd. I.R.G.O., Omsk, 1894-1899.

11801. Partanskii, M. Климатические условия Приморья. (Climatic conditions of the Maritime province.) Vladivostok, 1924.

11802. Voznesenskii. Климат Восточной Сибири.   (The climate of Eastern Siberia.) Irkutsk, Eniseiskii peres. raion, 1913.

11803. Partanskii, M. Климат Владивостока.   (Climate of Vladivostok.) Vladivostok, 1923.

(5) Flora and Fauna

11804. Litvinov, D. I. Библиография флоры Сибири. (Bibliography of Siberian flora.) St. Petersburg, 1909.

11805. Serebriakov, K. K. История растительного мира СССР. (History of the flora of the USSR.) Leningrad, 1936. 180 p.

11806. Флора Сибири и Дальнего Востока. (Flora of Siberia and the Far East.) Izd. Botanicheskogo muzeia Akademii nauk SSSR, 1931. 713 p.

11807. Vavilov, N. "О восточных центрах происхождения культурных растений." (The eastern centers of original culture plants.) Novyi Vostok, 6 (1924):291-305.

11808. Флора Сибири и Дальнего Востока издаваемая Ботаническим музеем Российской академии наук. Flora Sibiriae et Orientis extremi a Museo botanico Academiae rossicae scientiarum edita. Petrograd, 1919.

11809. Borodin, I. P. Коллекторы флоры Сибири(Collectors of the flora of Siberia.) St. Petersburg, 1908.

11810. Опыт сибирских мичуринцев. (Works of the Siberian followers of Michurin.) Collected articles. Novosibirsk, 1936. 104, 3 p.

(6) Soils

11811. Prasolov, L. О почвенной карте Азиатской России. (Soil map of Asiatic Russia.) Izvestiia Dokuchaevskogo pochvennogo komiteta, 1-2 (1913).

11812. Материалы по изучению русских почв. (Materials for the study of Russian soils.) St. Petersburg, 1886-1912 ? 21 v. [Ed. by A. V. Sovetov and others.]

(7) General Accounts

11813. Liashchenko, P. I. Русское зерновое хозяйство в системе мирового хозяйства. (Russian grain economy in the system of world economy.) Moscow, 1927.

11814. Сборник материалов к изучению сельского хозяйства Сибири.(A collection of material pertaining to the study of rural economy in Siberia.) Novonikolaevsk, 1924. 2 parts.

11815. Сельское хозяйство Сибирского края. (Rural economy in Siberia.) Novosibirsk, Sibirskoe zemleupravlenie, 1926. 2 parts.

11816. Avchinnikov, I. I. "Сельское хозяйство Сибири и перспективы его развития." (Agriculture in Siberia and the prospects of its development.) Planovoe khoziaistvo, October 1925:261-272.

11817. Bazhaev, V. О системах земледелия в Томской губернии. (Agricultural systems in the Tomsk guberniia.) In: Trudy Tomsk. otdela Imp. mosk. obshch. sel'sk. khoz., Tomsk, 1 (1896).

11818. Miretikov, M. S. Деревенское огородничество в условиях Сибири. (Rural gardening in Siberia.) 3d revised edition. Irkutsk, 1924. 66 p.

11819. Kiziurin, A. D. Плодоводство Сибири. (Horticulture in Siberia.) Omsk, 1934. 39 p.

11820. Lu, Chia. 今年蘇俄的收獲及其對於全世界的影響 Chin-nien Su-o ti shou-hu chi ch'i tui-yü chüan-shih-chieh ti ying-hsiang. (Soviet Russia's harvest this year and its effect on the whole world.) Nung-yeh chou-pao, 1:30, November 1931.

11821. Kaufman, A. A. Влияние переселенческого элемента на развитие сельско-хозяйственной и общинной жизни в Западной Сибири. (The influence of the migratory element on the development of agriculture and communal life in Western Siberia.) Severnyi vestnik, 4 (1891):27-51.

11822. Перспективный план работ Сибсельксоюза по восстановлению сельского хозяйства на период 1924-1928 гг.(Prospective plan of the Siberian agricultural union for the restoration of agriculture for the period 1924-1928.) Novonikolaevsk, Sibirskii oblastnoi soiuz sel'sko-khoziaistvennoi kooperatsii, 1924. 100 p.

11823. IArmosh, A. "Проблема изжития хлебного дефицита в Дальневосточном крае." (The problem of liquidating the grain deficit in the Far-Eastern region.) Planovoe khoziaistvo, November 1926:215-229.

11824. Материалы к сельско-хозяйственному районированию. (Materials for agricultural regional division.) Moscow, TSentral'noe statisticheskoe upravlenie, 1927-

11825. Chinese consulate at Khabarovsk. 蘇聯二期五年計劃鄉村經濟問題 Su-Lien erh-ch'i wu-nien-chi-hua hsiang-tsun ching-chi wên-t'i. (The problem of rural economy in Soviet Union's second Five-year plan.) Wai-chiao-pu kung-pao, 4:6, October 1931.

11826. Резолюции 5-го Сибирского совещания земельных работников. (Resolutions adopted by the 5th Siberian conference of agricultural workers.) Novonikolaevsk, Upravlenie upolnomochennogo narodnogo komissariata zemledeliia, 1925. 62 p.

11827. Roze, A. M. and Osipov, I. I. Агрономическая организация Сибири. Формы и принципы организации. (The forms and principles of the agronomists' organization in Siberia.) Novonikolaevsk, 1925. 54 p.

(8) Special Accounts

11828. Korolev, A. M. Сибирская молочная кооперация: прошлое и настоящее. (Siberian dairy cooperation: past and present.) Moscow, 1926. 59 p.

11829. Stepanenko, I. and Komkov, M. Сибирское маслоделие. (Siberian butter-industry.) Sibkraiizdat, 1928. 201 p.

11830. Kochergin, S. M. Транспорт и холодильное дело молочных и продуктов в Сибири. (Transportation and refrigeration of dairy products in Siberia.) Omsk, 1924. 61 p.

11831. Monin, V. A. Масло и маргарин на мировом рынке и восстановление маслоделия в Сибири. (Butter and margarine on the world market and the restoration of butter production in Siberia.) Berlin, Sotrudnik, 1923. 59 p.

11832. Monin, W. (V.A.) Butterproduktion und genossenschaftswesen in Russland und Sibirien. Berlin, Osnowa,1924.

11833. Хлопковое дело. (The cotton industry.) Moscow, Glavnyi khlopkovyi komitet, 1922-1930.

11834. Milkich, Alexander. Stand und aussichten des baumwollbaus in der Sowjet-Union. Berlin, Parey, 1933.

11835. Korablin, I. I. Овес в Западной Сибири. (Oats in Western Siberia.) Omsk, 1933. 49 p.

11836. Gordienko, I. Der reisbau in Russland. Der Kulturtechniker, 2, April-June 1933.

11837. Voronetskii, B. A. and Savostin, P. V. К проблемам агрохимии Западной Сибири. (Problems of agricultural chemistry of Western Siberia.) Novosibirsk, 1934. 133 p.

11838. IAmzin, I. О новых явлениях в сельском хозяйстве Сибири. (New phenomena in Siberian agriculture.) Kiev, 1910.

(9) Agricultural Cooperatives and Collectives

11839. Сибирская потребительная кооперация в 1923 г. и перспективы ее дальнейшего развития. (Siberian consumers' cooperatives in 1923 and their prospects for further development.) Novonikolaevsk, Sibirskii kraevoi soiuz potrebitel'nykh obshchestv, 1924. 87 p.

11840. Pankratov, I. I. Состояние Сибирской потребительской кооперации. (The state of the Siberian consumers' cooperatives.) Novonikolaevsk, 1925. 22 p.

11841. Makhov, V. Потребительская кооперация Сибири за первую четверть 1924 г. (Consumers' cooperatives of Siberia for the first quarter of 1924.) Novonikolaevsk, 1924. 35 p.

11842. Материалы исследования развития кооперативного крестьянского хозяйства. (Results of an inquiry into the development of peasant cooperative farming.) Moscow, Narodnyi komissariat raboche-krestianskoi inspektsii, 1928-

11843. Odintsov, B. N. "Хлебные фабрики в России и Сибири." (Grain factories in Russia and Siberia.) Vol'naia Sibir', 5 (1929):69-76

11844. Колхозы Дальнего Востока.(The collective farms of the Far East.) Khabarovsk, Soiuz soiuzov sel'sko-khoziaistvennoi kooperatsii Dal'nevostochnogo kraia, 1930. 47 p.

11845. Chinese consulate at Chita. 蘇聯農村集團現状 Su-Lien nung-tsun chi-tuan hsien-chuang. (The present status of the collectivized farms in Soviet Union.) Wai-chiao-pu kung-pao, 4:6, October 1931.

(10) Peasantry

11846. Материалы по истории крестьянских движений в России. (Sources for the study of the revolutionary movement of peasants in Russia.) TSentral'nyi arkhiv, 1923-

11847. Viktorov, V. История крестьянских движений XVII-XVIII вв. (History of the peasant movements of the XVII-XVIII centuries.) Moscow, Kom. Univ. im. IA. M. Sverdlova, 1923.

11848. Shunkov, V. "К истории крестьян в Сибири в XVIII в." (History of the Siberian peasants in the XVIII century.) Severnaia Aziia, Moscow, 5-6 (29-30) (1929):82-103.

11849. Kaufman, A. A. Экономический быт государственных крестьян и оседлых инородцев Туринского округа Тобольской губ. (Economic condition of the state peasants and settled natives of the Turinsk district of the Tobolsk gubernia.) St. Petersburg, 1890.

11850. Bogdanovskii, A. I. Сибирская община и ее роль в политико-экономическом отношении. (The Siberian commune and its political and economic significance.) Tobolsk, 1898.

11851. Kaufman, A. A. Крестьянская община в Сибири по местным исследованиям в 1886-1892. (Peasant communes in Siberia
according to local investigation in 1886-1892.) St. Petersburg, 1897.

11852. Remezov, S. IU. Материалы для изучения быта крестьян
Западной Сибири. (Sources for the study of peasant life
in Western Siberia.) St. Petersburg, 1889-1892.

11853. Pchelin, S. S. Экономический быт государственных крестьян Тюкалинского округа Тобольской губ. (Economic conditions of the state peasants of the Tiukalinskii district of
the Tobolsk gubernia.) Collection of materials. St. Petersburg, 1889.

11854. Patkanov, S. K. Экономический быт государственных
крестьян и инородцев Тобольского округа, Тобольской губернии. (Economic conditions of the state peasants and
natives of the Tobolsk district of the Tobolsk gubernia.)
Collection of materials. St. Petersburg, 1891.

11855. Kafka, S. P. Экономический быт государственных
крестьян и оседлых инородцев юго-западной части Томского
округа Томской губернии. (Economic conditions of the
state peasants and sedentary natives of the southwestern
part of the Tomsk district of the Tomsk gubernia.) Collection of materials. St. Petersburg, 1892.

11856. Osipov, N. O. Экономический быт государственных
крестьян Курганского округа Тобольской губернии.
(Economic life of the state peasants of the Kurganskii district of the Tobolsk gubernia.) Collection of materials.
St. Petersburg, 1894, 1898.

11857. Kaufman, A. A. Очерк крестьянского хозяйства в Сибири
(A sketch of the peasant economy in Siberia.) Tomsk, 1894.

11858. Novombergskii, N. По Сибири. (Through Siberia.) St.
Petersburg, 1903.

11859. Материалы, относящиеся до земельного и экономического положения Амурского и Уссурийского казачьих войск.
(Materials pertaining to the agrarian and economic conditions of the Amur and Ussuri cossack troops.) St. Petersburg, Komitet ministrov, 1902. 4 v.

11860. Novoselov, A. A. "Классовой состав земельно-родовой
общины казаков Семипалатинской области в начале XX века."
(Class structure of the cossack agrarian clan commune at the
beginning of the XX century.) In: Trudy Saratovskogo plano-

vogo instituta, 2 (1934):141-160.

11861. Kornilov, A. A. О нуждах и вопросах крестьянского
дела обнаруженных при ревизии крестьянских учреждений
Иркутской и Енисейской губ. осенью 1899 г.(Peasant needs
and problems revealed during the inspection of the peasant
institutions in the Irkutsk and Eniseisk guberniias in the
fall of 1899.) Irkutsk, 1900.

11862. Shvetsov, S. P. Волостная община и поземельное
устройство в Сибири. (The volost commune and the agrarian
system in Siberia.) Sibirskie voprosy, 1 (1905).

11863. Owen, Launcelot A. The Russian peasant movement,
1906-1917. London, King, 1937. 267 p.

11864. IArovoi, I. V. Экономика Сибирской деревни. (Economics of the Siberian village.) Novonikolaevsk, 1926. 63 p.

11865. TSelishchev, M. "К вопросу об экономическом рассло-
ении крестьянства Дальневосточного края." (On the problem
of economic stratification among the peasants of the Far
East region.) Ekonomicheskaia zhizn' Dal'nego Vostoka,
Khabarovsk, 1:108-116, January 1926.

11866. IArovoi, I. V. Экономическое расслоение деревни и
характеристика основных групп крестьянства Сибири.
(Economic stratification in the villages and the characteristics of the principal peasant groups.) Novonikolaevsk,
1924. 39 p.

(11) Land Tenure

11867. Vasil'chikov, A. Землевладение и земледелие.   (Land-
tenure and agriculture.) St. Petersburg,•1876. 2 v.

11868. Материалы для изучения современного положения землевладения и сельскохозяйственной промышленности в России.
(Materials for the study of the present state of land tenure and agricultural industry in Russia. St. Petersburg,
Ministerstvo gosudarstvennykh imushchestv, 1880.

11869. Ostafiev, V. A. Землевладение и земледелие Сибирского казачьего войска. (Land tenure and agriculture of
the Siberian cossacks.) St. Petersburg, 1897.

11870. Dokuchaev, V. К вопросу о переоценке земель Европейской и Азиатской России с классификацией почв.
(The problem of land revaluation in European and Asiatic

Russia with a classification of the soils.) Moscow, 1898.

11871. Материалы по статистике движения землевладения в России. (Statistical material on changes in land tenure in Russia.) St. Petersburg, Departament okladnykh sborov, 1896-1915. 24 v.

11872. Материалы по землевладению и экономическому быту оседлых инородцев Тобольской губернии. (Sources pertaining to land tenure and economic conditions of the natives of the Tobolsk guberniia.) By. I. A. Andronikov and others, Tobolsk, 1911.

11873. Shkunov, M. Землеустройство инородцев в горном Алтае. (Land settlement of the Altai natives.) In: Voprosy kolonizatsii, St. Petersburg, 1909:5.

11874. Maksimov, V. E. Формы землепользования в Сибири. (Forms of land utilization in Siberia.) Novonikolaevsk, 1925. 62 p.

11875. Земельный кодекс. (Land code.) Moscow, 1927-

11876. Koizumi, Noriumi. 露 國 土 地 法 / 研 究 Ro-koku tochiho no kenkyu. (Research on Russian land laws.) Dairen, S. M. R. R., 1927.

(12) Stock-Farming and Meat-Packing

11877. Ognev, S. I. Звери СССР и прилежащих стран.   (Animals of the USSR and adjacent countries.) Moscow, 1935. viii, 752 p.

11878. Yamashita, Yoshio. 露 領 黑 龍 州 / 畜 產 業. Ro-ryo Kokuryushu no chikusangyo. (Cattle industry in the Russian Amur province.) Dairen, S. M. R. R., 1927. 2 v.

11879. Скотобойное дело в Петропавловске. (Meat-packing industry in Petropavlovsk.) Stepnoi krai, 1896: 77.

11880. Silantiev, A. A. Оленеводство в России. (Reindeer breeding in Russia.) Ezhegodnik Gl. Upr. Z. i Z. po Depart. Zeml. za 1908 g. St. Petersburg, 1909.

11881. Plotnikov, M. Оленеводство. (Reindeer breeding.) Chita, 1924. 12 p.

11882. See 11905.

I. Forestry and Lumber

11883. Лесопромышленное дело. (Lumber industry.) Moscow,
Gosudarstvennoe vsesoiuznoe ob"edinenie lesnoi promyshlennosti i lesnogo khoziaistva, 1922-   Supplement: Лесной
рынок. (Lumber market.) 1925, nos. 1-19.

11884. Лесное хозяйство и лесная промышленность. (Forestry
and lumber industry.) Moscow, Gosudarstvennoe vsesoiuznoe
ob"edinenie lesnoi promyshlennosti i lesnogo khoziaistva,
1922-1930, 1-85.

11885. Лесное хозяйство РСФСР и перспективы его развития.
Forestry of RSFSR and prospects for its development.) Moscow, Narodnyi komissariat zemledeliia, Upravlenie lesami,
1927-

11886. Лес и завод. (Forest and mill.) Moscow, Gosudarstvennoe vsesoiuznoe ob"edinenie lesnoi promyshlennosti i
lesnogo khoziaistva, 1930-

11887. Лесной кодекс РСФСР. (Forestry code of the RSFSR.)
Moscow, series 1, 1926-   ; series 2, 1928-

11888. 露 領 極 東   森 林 利 權 Ro-ryo
Kyokuto no shinrin riken. (Forest rights in the Russian
Far East.) Osaka mainichi news, Research bureau, S. M. R. R.,
1929. 174 p.

11889. Budishchev, A. F. Описание лесов части Приморской области. (Description of the forests of the Maritime province.) Zapiski Sibirskogo otd. I.R.G.O., Irkutsk, 1867:
9,10.

11890. Состояние и нужды казенного лесного хозяйства в
Сибири. (Conditions and needs of the state forestry in Siberia.) St. Petersburg, Ministerstvo zemledeliia i gosudarstvennogo imushchestva, Lesnoi departament, 1899.

11891. Очерк лесов Камчатки. (A description of the Kamchatka forests.) Ezhegodnik lesnogo departamenta, 1910.

11892. Strogii, A. A. О лесах Сибири. (Concerning the forests of Siberia.) St. Petersburg, 1911.

11893. Shostakovich, V. B. Лесные пожары в Сибири в 1915 г.
(Forest fires in Siberia in 1915.) Irkutsk, 1924. 8 p.

11894. Semenov, K. S. Лесное хозяйство Урала. (The Ural
lumber industry.) Sverdlovsk, 1925. 117 p.

11895. Fedoseev, S. K. "Лесное хозяйство Западной Сибири."
(Forestry in Western Siberia.) Planovoe khoziaistvo, October 1925:272-285.

11896. Лесное хозяйство Сибирского края. (Forestry in the
Siberian region.) Novosibirsk, Sibirskoe kraevoe zemel'noe
upravlenie, 1926. 256 p.

11897. Nedrigailov, S. N. Лесные ресурсы Ленско-Алданского
плато и Заалданско-Верхоянского горного района. (Forest resources of the Lena-Aldan plateau and of the Transaldan-
Verkhoiansk mountain region.) In: Materialy komissii po izucheniiu IAkutskoi Avtonomnoi SSR. Vypusk 12. Izd. Akad.
Nauk SSSR, 1928. 468 p.

11898. Vasiliev, IA. IA. Леса и лесовозобновление в районах
Братска, Илимска и Усть-Кута. (Forests and forest conserva-
tion in the regions of Bratsk, Ilimsk and Ust'-Kut.) Leningrad, Academy of sciences, 1933. 111 p.

11899. Abramov, N. Лесохимия Северного края. (Forest
chemistry of the Northern region.) Archangel, 1933. 61 p.

11900. Лесной экспорт СССР. (Lumber export of the USSR.)
Moscow, 1933. 94 p.

11901. Bashkirov, 'I. A. (ed.). Лесной экспорт СССР. Дальний
Восток и Сибирь. (Lumber export of the USSR. The Far East
and Siberia.) Moscow-Leningrad, 1933. 88 p.

11902. Nenarokov, V. Советский лесоэкспорт в Японию. (Soviet timber export to Japan.) Moscow, 1933. 130 p.

11903. Gnedkov, N. E. Лесосырьевые ресурсы Западной Сибири.
(Lumber resources of Western Siberia.) Novosibirsk, 1934.
124 p.

11904. Tsymek, A. The forest wealth of the Soviet Far East
and its exploitation. Prepared for the Sixth conference of
the Institute of Pacific relations held at Yosemite Park,
California, August 15 to 29, 1936. USSR council papers no.
3. Moscow, Institute of Pacific relations, 1936 33 p.

J. Furs and Fur Trade

See 5262-5264.

11905. Lomer, H. Der rauchwaarenhandel: geschichte, betriebs-
weise und waarenkunde. Leipzig, Der Verfasser, 1864. 109 p.

11906. Buddeus, K. Leipzigs rauchwaarenhandel und industrie. Leipzig, Schmidt, 1891. 74 p.

11907. Pabst, Fritz. Der rauchwaarenhandel, Berlin, Schade, 1902. 116 p.

11908. Brass, Emil. Aus dem reiche der pelze. Berlin, Neuen verlage der Neuen pelzwaaren-zeiting, 1911. 709 p.

11909. Klein, Joseph. Der sibirische pelzhandel und seine bedeutung für die eroberung Sibiriens. Bonn, Foppen, 1906. 206 p.

11910. Краткий очерк о пушной промышленности в Сибири. (A brief sketch of the fur industry in Siberia.) Moscow, Izd. Gromovoi, 1896.

11911. Kogan, M. I.Советская Азия как пушнопромысловый район. (Soviet Asia as a fur-trading region.) Moscow, 1931. 68 p.

11912. Материалы к познанию охотничьего дела. (Materials for the study of hunting methods.) St. Petersburg, Departament zemledeliia, 1913-1916. 9 v.

11913. Труды экспедиций по изучению соболя и исследованию соболиного промысла. (Publications of the expeditions for the study of the sable and the sable trade.) St. Petersburg, 1920. 458 p.

11914. Пушное дело. (The fur trade.) Moscow, Narodnyi komissariat vneshnei torgovli, 1925-1930.

11915. Tretiakov, P. N. "Первобытная охота в Северной Азии." (Primitive hunting in Northern Asia.) Iz istorii rodovogo obshchestva na territorii SSSR. Izvestiia Gosudarstvennoi akademii istorii material'noi kul'tury, vypusk 106 (Moscow, 1935), 220-262.

11916. Schleusing, G. Ad. Neuentdecktes Sibyria oder Sieweria worinnen die zobeln gefangen werden. Stettin, 1690.

11917. IAnitskii, N. "Торговля пушным товаром в XVII в." (Fur trade in the XVII century.) In Kievskie universitetskie izvestiia, 52 (1912):9:1-33   See also Sbornik Istoriko-etnograficheskogo fakul'teta pri Kievskom universitete, Kiev, 1913:61-93.

11918. Bakhrushin, S. V. "Ясак в Сибири в XVII веке." (IAsak in Siberia in the XVII cent.) Sibirskie ogni, Novosibirsk, 3:95-129, May-June 1927.

424   Russia

11919. Bakhrushin, S. "Покрута на соболиннх промыслах XVII века."(Contracts in fur trade in the XVII c.) Trud v Rossii, 1 (1925).

11920. Cherkasov, A.   Записки охотника Восточной Сибири. (Memoirs of an East Siberian hunter.) St. Petersburg, 1884.

11921. Dattan, A. Über tiger, bären und wildschweine des Ussuri gebietes. Der Zool. Gart. 1890.

11922. Jochelson, V. I. Очерк зверопромышленности и торгов- ли мехами в Колымском округе. (Sketch of the hunting and pelt trades in the Kolyma district.) St. Petersburg, 1898.

11923. Schwen, A. I. К вопросу о хищническом истреблении соболя в Сибири. (The problem of predatory extermination of the sable in Siberia.) Irkutsk, 1911.

11924. Timofeev-Tereshkin, M. N. Очерки пушного дела в Якутии. (Sketches of the fur industry in Iakutia.) Irkutsk, 1927. 51 p.

11925. Natol'skii, A. B. Пушное дело в Якутии. (The fur in- dustry in Iakutia.) Yakutsk, 1928. 110 p.

11926. Doppelmair, G. Соболиный промысел на северовосточном побережии Байкала. (Sable trade on the northeastern shore of the Baikal.) Leningrad, 1926.

11927. Промысловне богатства Камчатки, Сахалина и Командор- ских о-вов. (Natural resources of Kamchatka, Sakhalin, and the Commodore islands.) M.Z. i G.I. Dep. Zem., St. Peters- burg, 1895.

11928. Suvorov, E. K. Командорские острова и пушной про- мысел на них. (The Commodore islands and their fur trade.) St. Petersburg, 1912.

11929. Naumov, S. P. Тюлени СССР. (Seals of the USSR.) Mos- cow, 1933. 105 p.

11930. Favorskii, V. P. Соболь Восточной Сибири. (The sable of Eastern Siberia.) Moscow-Irkutsk, OGIZ, 1935. 56, 8 p.

11931. Genrozov, V. V. Пушной промысел. (Fur trade.) Moscow, Gosizdat, 1926.

11932. Fisher, Raymond L. The Russian fur trade. Unpublished Ph.D thesis. Berkeley, University of California, 1932. 409 p.

K. Fisheries

See 899-929.

11933. Takahashi, Kokki. 露領極東ノ魚類毛皮資源. Ro-ryo Kyokuto... (The resources of fish, hides, and furs of the Russian Far East.) Dairen, S.M.R.R., 1929. 2 v.

11934. 蘇聯遠東漁業之發達報告 Su-Lien Yüan tung yü-yeh chih fa-ta pao-kao. (A report on the development of the Soviet Union's Far Eastern fisheries.) Nanking, Ministry of agriculture and mining, Agriculture and mining gazette, 16, September 1929.

11935. Bashkirov, K. A. Потери дальневосточной рыбной промышленности. (Losses of the Far Eastern fishing industry.) Khabarovsk, Dal'giz, 1933. 38 p.

11936. Kriukov, N. A. Некоторые данные о положении рыболовства в Приамурском крае. (Some data on conditions of the fish industry in the Maritime region.) Zapiski Priamurskogo otdela I.R.G.O., St. Petersburg, 1 (1894):1.

11937. Brazhnikov, V. K. Рыбные промыслы Дальнего Востока. (Fisheries of the Far East.) St. Petersburg, Department of agriculture, 1900-1904. 2 v.

11938. Razin, A. I. Морские промысловые моллюски Южного Приморья. (The sea mollusk trade of the southern Maritime province.) Moscow-Khabarovsk, 1934. 110 p.

11939. Driagin, P. A. Рыбные ресурсы Якутии. (Fishing resources of Iakutia.) Leningrad, 1933. 94 p.

11940. Poliakov, I. Остяки и рыбопромышленность в долине р. Оби. (The Ostiaks and the Ob valley fisheries.) St. Petersburg, 1878.

L. Industry

See 846-863.

(1) Periodicals

11941. За индустриализацию. (For industrialization.) Moscow, Vysshii sovet narodnogo khoziaistva, 1921- Supplement: По фабрикам и заводам. (In factories and mills.) Dec.1924-Sept.1925, 1-36.

(2) Statistical Publications

See 11657-11658.

11942. Всероссийская промышленная и профессиональная перепись 1918-го года. Список фабрик, заводов и других промышленных предприятий ... губерний по данным... (All-Russian census of industry and occupations. List of factories, plants and other industrial establishments of ... province according to the data of data of All-Russian census of industry and occupations in 1918.) Moscow, 1918-1920. 8 v.

11943. Промышленность Восточносибирской области за 1912-1935 годы. (Industry of the East Siberian province during 1912-1935.) Irkutsk, 1937. 166.

11944. Материалы по статистике Дальнего Востока. Серия III. Данные о промышленных заведениях. (Statistical material on the Far East. III series. Industrial enterprises.) Chita, Upravlenie Upolnomochennogo tsentral'nogo statisticheskogo upravleniia na Dal'nem Vostoke, 1924. 119 p.

11945. Контрольные цифры пятилетнего плана сибирской промышленности на 1927/28-1932/32 гг. (Statistical data concerning the five year plan of Siberian industry, 1927/28-1931/32.) Novosibirsk, Sibkraisovnarkhoz, 1928.

(3) General Accounts

11946. За индустриализацию Советского Востока. (For the industrialization of the Soviet East.) Izd. Sovetskaia Aziia, 1932-1934. 4 v.

11947. Kanche, A. A. (ed.). За индустриализацию Советского Востока.(For the industrialization of the Soviet East.) Moscow, 1934. 288 p.

11948. Индустриализация Сибири. (The industrialization of Siberia.) Novonikolaevsk, Sibkrai Sovnarkhoz, 1925. 152 p.

11949. Tamarin, A. (ed.). К вопросу индустриализации Сибири. (The problem of industrialization of Siberia.) Novonikolaevsk, 1925. 91, 12 p.

11950. Промышленность за 10 лет. (Industry for 10 years.) Moscow, Vysshii sovet narodnogo khoziaistva, 1927.

11951. Zubashev, E. L. "Сибирская промышленность в 1924-1927 гг. (Siberian industry, 1924-1927.) Vol'naia Sibir', 4 (1928):114-137.

11952. Kornev, V. "Задачи сибирской промышленности." (The problems of Siberian industry.) Zhizn' Sibiri, 7, 1927.

11953. Sato, Takeo. 露領極東 / 資源 ト 産業、 Ro-ryo Kyokuto no shigen to sangyo. (Natural resources and industries of the Russian Far East.) Dairen, S.M.R.R., 1928.

11954. Miliutin, V. P. История экономического развития СССР. (History of the economic development of the USSR.) Moscow, 1928. 491 p. (2) Burns, Emile. Russia's productive system. New York, Dutton, 1930. 288 p.

11955. Wada, Kameji. 露國 / 産業 計劃 ト 極東 Rokoku no sangyo keikaku to Kyokuto. (Russia's industrial plans and the Far East.) Gaiko jiho, 64:4:149-164, November 15, 1932.

11956. Rozhkov, V. Деятельность артиллерии капитана В. Н. Татищева на уральских заводах в царствование Петра Великого. (The activities of Captain Tatishchev in the Ural mills during the reign of Peter the Great.) Gornyi zhurnal, 7-8 (1884).

11957. Комиссия по исследованию кустарной промышленности в России, 1872-1888. Труды.(Commission for the study of peasant arts and crafts in Russia, 1872-1888. Transactions.) St. Petersburg, 1879-1890. 17 v.

11958. Bereznikov, M. Обозрение фабрично-заводской промышленности Приморской области в 1896 г.(An industrial survey of the Maritime province, 1896.) Zapiski Priamurskogo otd. I.R.G.O., Khabarovsk, 4 (1898):2.

11959. Bulakh, V. Химические возможности КССР. (Chemical possibilities of the Kirghiz Soviet Republic.) Orenburg, 1924. 54 p.

11960. Belorusets, L. "К вопросу о сельско-хозяйственном машиностроении Сибирского края." (The problem of the farm-machine industry in the Siberian region.) Planovoe khoziaistvo, September 1925: 258-262.

(4) Special Accounts

11961. Проблемы Урало-Кузбасского комбината. (Problems concerning the Ural-Kuzbas combine.) Akademiia nauk, SSSR., 1932-1933. 2 v.

11962. Chernyshev, A. A. Электро-энергетические проблемы Урало-Кузбасского комбината. (Problems of the electrical energy of the Ural-Kuzbas combine.) Leningrad, Akademiia nauk, 1933. 19 p.

11963. Krivitskii, G. I. Сборник материалов по Урало-Кузнецкой проблеме. (A collection of sources pertaining to the Ural-Kuznetsk problem.) A guide to the literature for 1922-1930. N. p. 1932.

11964. Урало-Кузнецкой комбинат. (The Ural-Kuznetsk combine.) Izd. Sovetskaia Aziia, 1933. 382 p.

11965. Zubashev, E. L. "Урало-Кузнецкая проблема." (The Ural-Kuznetsk problem.) Vol'naia Sibir', 3 (1928):100-118.

11966. Nikitin, M. A. Жемчужина Кузбасса. (The pearl of the Kuzbas.) Moscow, 1935. 107, 28 p.

11967. Strizhkov, P. N. Кузбас. (Kuzbas.) Moscow, Federatsiia, 1932. 148.

11968. Gubkin, I. M. Горючие ископаемые Кузбаса. (Fuel resources of the Kuzbas.) Izd. Akademii nauk SSSR., 1932. 32 p.

11969. Huppert, Hugo. Men of Siberia. Sketchbook from the Kuzbas. Moscow, Cooperative publishing society of foreign workers in the USSR, 1934. 326 p.

11970. Gaister, A. I. Урало-Кузнецкий комбинат. (The Ural-Kuznetsk combine.) Moscow, 1933. 323 p.

11971. Урало-Кузнецкий комбинат. (The Ural-Kuznetsk combine.) Moscow, Sotsekgiz, 1931. 206 p.

11972. Evenchik, Boris, I. Урал в плане Урало-Кузнецкого комбината. (The Urals in the plan of the Ural-Kuznetsk combine.) Moscow, Sovetskaia Aziia, 1932. 104 p.

11973. Материалы пятилетнего плана Башкирской части УКК на 1933-1937 гг. (Sources pertaining to the five-year plan of the Bashkir part of the Ural-Kuznetsk combine for 1933-1937.) Ufa, Khoziaistvo Bashkirii, 1932. 213 p.

11974. Kolosovskii, N. Будущее Урало-Кузнецкого комбината. (The future of the Ural-Kuznetsk combine.) Moscow, Sotsekgiz, 1932. 136 p.

11975. Barsukov, P. F. Социалистическая индустриализация Урала и задачи научного исследования. (Socialist industrialization of the Urals and the problems of scientific research.) Sverdlovsk-Moscow, Uralogiz, 1932. 104 p.

11976. Shchegliaev, F. M. and others. Ангаро-Енисейстрой. (Angara-Yeniseistroi.) Obshchestvo izucheniia Sovetskoi Azii, Moscow, Sovetskaia Aziia, 1933. 80 p.

11977. Ангаро-Енисейская проблема. (The Angara-Yenisei problem.) Moscow, Sovetskaia Aziia, 1932. 414 p.

11978. Tretiakov, S. M. Страна А.-Е. (Ангаро-Енисейская проблема). (The country of A.-E. [The Angara-Yenisei problem].) Moscow, 1932. 149 p.

11979. Popov, F. V., Menshenin, S. A. and Borshchevskii, A. M. (ed.). Социалистическая реконструкция г. Новосибирска. (Socialist reconstruction of the city of Novosibirsk.) Moscow, 1936. 165 p.

11980. Kirillov, S. "Печора как основная сырьевая база индустриализации Нового Севера." (Pechora as the fundamental base of raw materials for the industrialization of the New North.) Sovetskoe kraevedenie, 4:28-37, June 1933.

11981. Lomov, G. I. (ed.). Генеральный план электрификации СССР. (General electrification plan of the USSR.) Moscow, 1933. 407 p.

11982. See 11944.

11983. Saratovskii, I. K. "Перспективный план электрификации Западной Сибири." (The prospective plan of electrification of Western Siberia.) Planovoe khoziaistvo, October 1925:294-298.

11984. Suzuki, Shozo. 勞農露國' 產業ㆍ電化計畫 Rono-Rokoku no sangyo to denka keikaku. (Soviet Russia's industries and electrification plans.) Dairen, S.M.R.R., 1927.

11985. Stepanov, P. "К вопросу о пересмотре плана электрификации Уральской области." (Revision of the plan for the electrification of the Ural province.) Planovoe khoziaistvo, November 1925: 215-246.

11986. Sosnovskii, G. P. "Древнейшие шерстяные ткани Сибири." (Most ancient woolen textiles of Siberia.) Problemy istorii dokapitalisticheskogo obshchestva, 2:92-9£, February 1934.

M. Minerals and Mining

See 10490-10520.

(1) Bibliography

11987. Материалы по библиографии железных руд Урала. (Materials for the bibliography of the iron ores of the Urals.) Moscow, Glavnoe geologo-razvedochnoe upravlenie, Ural'skoe otdelenie, 1929-

11988. Литература о минералах Южного Урала. (Literature concerning the minerals of the South Ural region.) Leningrad, Academy of sciences, Minerological institute, 1933.

(2) Periodicals

See 10490-10495.

11989. Вестник меъеллопромышленности. (Messenger of the metal industry.) Moscow, Glavnoe upravlenie metallicheskoi promyshlennosti, 1921-

11990. Годовой обзор минеральных рессурсов СССР. (Annual report on the mineral resources of the USSR.) Moscow, Geologicheskii komitet, 1925/26-

11991. Осведомительный бюллетень по полезным ископаемым. (Bulletin of information on mineral resources.) Moscow, Glavnoe geologo-razvedochnoe upravlenie, 1928-

(3) Statistics

11992. Сборник статистических сведений по горной части (1862-1865). (Collection of statistical information on mining in Russia, 1862-1865.) St. Petersburg, Gornyi departament, 1864-1867.

11993. Горнозаводская производительность России. (Metallu gical production in Russia.) St. Petersburg, Gornyi depart ment, 1873-1885.

11994. Сборник статистических сведений о горнозаводской промышленности России. (Statistical information on metallu gical industry in Russia.) St. Petersburg, Gornyi departament, 1882-1911.

11995. Сборник статистических сведений по горной и горнозаводской промышленности СССР. (Collection of statistical
data on the mining and metallurgical industry of the USSR.)
Geologicheskii komitet, I, 1911-1924/25; II, 1925/26.

(4)History

11996. Sigov, S. P. Очерки по истории горнозаводской промышленности Урала. (Outlines of history of the metallurgical industry of the Urals.) Sverdlovsk, 1936. 292 p.

11997. Kashintsev, D. "Горнозаводская промышленность Урала и
крестьянская война 1773-1774 годов." (Metallurgical industry of the Urals and the peasant war of 1773-1774.) Istorik marksist, 1 (1936):53:133-185.

11998. R. G. "История горнозаводского труда на Урале до
1917 г." (History of labor in the metallurgical industry in
the Urals until 1917.) In: Istoriia proletariata SSSR, 3-4
(1930):255-284. Bibliography.

11999. Fedorovich, I. I. "Основа металлургической промышленности Западной Сибири." (The foundation of the metallurgical
industry in Western Siberia.) Planovoe khoziaistvo, October
1925: 285-294.

12000. Molchanov, I. A. Поиски месторождений полезных ис-
копаемых в Красноярском крае. (Prospecting for mineral
ores in the Krasnoiarsk region.) Tomsk, Zapadno-Sibirskoe
geologicheskoe upravlenie, 1938. v, 119 p.

(5) General Accounts

See 10496-10520.

12001. Kuzbasov, G. A. Горные богатства Сибирского края.
(Mineral wealth of Siberia.) 1929.

12002. Reutovskii, V. Полезные ископаемые Сибири. (Useful
minerals of Siberia.) St. Petersburg, Department of mining,
1905.

12003. Oyama, Takeo. 露領極東／鑛業利權
Ro-ryo Kyokuto no kogyo riken. (Russian mining rights in
the Far East.) Dairen, S.M.R.R., 1929. 259 p.

12004. Материалы по геологии и полезным ископаемым Восточной Сибири. (Materials on the geology and mineral resources
of Eastern Siberia.) Glavnoe geologo-razvedochnoe upravlenie Vostochno-Sibirskoe raionnoe otdelenie, 1930-

12005. Перспективы развития металлургии черных металлов.
(Prospects of the development of the metallurgy of black
metals.) Material for the five year plan, 1928-1933. Moscow,
Vysshii sovet narodnogo khoziaistva, 1929. 3 v.

12006. Gubkin, I. M. (ed.). Минеральные рессурсы СССР.
(Mineral resources of the USSR.) Moscow, 1937-

12007. Fersman, A. E. The scientific study of Soviet mineral
resources. Moscow, 1935. 149 p.

12008. Maksimov, S. E. Богатства недр СССР. (Mineral
wealth of the USSR.) Leningrad, 1935. 100, 4 p.

12009. Геология и полезные ископаемые Севера СССР. (Geology and mineral resources of the North of the USSR.) Collected articles. Leningrad, 1936. 356 p.

12010. Barmin, A. Горные богатства Урала. (Mineral wealth
of the Urals.) Sverdlovsk, 1934. 109 p.

12011. L. P. "Минеральные рессурсы Дальнего Востока." (Mineral resources of the Far East.) Ekonomicheskaia zhizn' Dal'-
nego Vostoka, Khabarovsk, 4:195-202, April 1926.

12012. Kuznetsov,   "Забайкальские минеральные источники и
их германские конкуренты." (The Transbaikal mineral sources
and their German rivals.) Irkutskaia zhizn', 67, 1915.

12013. Anikeev, N. P. Геология и минералогия Ангаро-Илимских
железнорудных месторождений.   (Geology and mineralogy
o f the Angara-Ilimsk iron ore deposits.) Irkutsk, 1936.
168 p.

12014. 蘇聯五年計劃中之五金問題 Su-Lien
wu-nien-chi-hua chung chih wu-chin wên-t'i. (The problem of
metals in the Soviet Union's five-year plan.) Wai-chiao-pu
kung-pao, 5:1, January 1932.

12015. Горные концессии. (Mining concessions.) Khabarovsk,
Dal'nevostochnaia kontsessionnaia kommissiia, 1925.

12016. Suzuki, Shozo. 露領極東・鑛産 Ro-ryo Kyo-
kuto no kosan. (Mineral production of the Russian Far East.)
Dairen, S.M.R.R., 1927. 2v.

(6) Gold

(a) Bibliography

12017. Golovachev, D. Библиографический указатель статей, корреспонденций и заметок в Сибирской печати по вопросу о золотопромышленности Сибири.(A bibliographical guide to articles, correspondence, and notes in the Siberian press concerning gold mining in Siberia. St. Petersburg, 1890. 60 p.

(b) General Accounts

12018. Serebrovskii, A. P. Золотая промышленность.(The gold industry.) Moscow-Leningrad, Academy of sciences, 1935. 3 v.

12019. Padalka, G. L. Золото и платина. (Gold and platinum.) Moscow, Sovetskaia Aziia, 1932. 62 p.

12020. Drozdov, P. "Из истории золотопромышленности в Восточной Сибири в 60-70 годах XIX века." (From the history of the gold-mining industry in Eastern Siberia in the sixties and seventies of the XIX century.) Istoriia proletariata SSSR, 2 (1935):22:3-32.

12021. Tul'chinskii, K. "Золотопромышленность Сибири." (Gold mining in Siberia.) Sibirskie ogni, Novosibirsk, 1-2:164-173, January-April 1926.

12022. Chang, Yin-tang. 西 比 利 亞 之 金 業. Hsi-pi-li-ya chih chin-yeh. (Gold mines in Siberia.) Northeast mining association journal, 2:1, February 1930.

12023. Pospelov, P. (ed.). Ленские прииски. (The Lena gold mines.) Collected documents. Moscow, 1937. 565 p.

12024. Riazanov, V. Отчет по статистико-экономическому и техническому исследованию золотопромышленности Амурско-Приморского района. (A report on the statistical, economic, and technical study of the gold-mining industry in the Amur-Maritime region.) St. Petersburg, 1905. 2 v.

12025. Petrov, A. A. "Перспективы золотопромышленности ДВК на десятилетие 1926-1936 года." (The gold-mining outlook in the Far Eastern region for the decade 1926-1936.) Ekonomicheskaia zhizn' Dal'nego Vostoka, Khabarovsk, 1-2:287-309, January-February 1927.

12026. Makerov, IA. A.Золоторудные месторождения Забайкалья.
(Gold deposits in the Transbaikal region.) In: Mineral'nye
istochniki Dal'nevostochnogo kraia, Vladivostok, 1927:233-
255.

12027. Ponomarev, I. A. Золотопромышленность Дальнего Востока и Алданское золото--русский Клондайк.   (Gold mining
in the Far East and Aldan gold -- the Russian Klondike.)
Moscow, 1925. 30 p.

12028. Алданское золото. (The Aldan gold.) Yakutsk, 1926.
64 p.

12029. See 12001.

                        (7) Coal

12030. Korovin, M. K. (ed.). Угленосные районы Сибири.(Coal
regions of Siberia.) Novosibirsk, 1933. 144 p.

12031. Bazhanov, V. M. Положение и перспективы каменно-
угольной промышленности в Сибири.   (The condition and perspectives of the coal industry in Siberia.) Moscow, 1925.
64 p.

12032. Пути развития сибирской каменно-угольной промышленности. (Tendencies in the development of the Siberian coal-
mining industry.) Novosibirsk, 1930. 173 p.

12033. Stroilov, M. S. (ed.). Вторая угольная база СССР,
Кузбас. (The second coal base of the USSR -- Kuzbas.)
Novosibirsk, 1935-1936. 2 v.

12034. Grigoriev, V. S. (ed.). Каменные угли Кузбаса.(Types
of Kuzbas coal.) Collected articles pertaining to the quality and nature of the coal. Novosibirsk, 1935. 439 p.

12035. IAvorskii, V. I. and Bulov, P. I. Кузнецкий угольный
бассейн.(The Kuznetsk coal basin.) Leningrad, 1927.

12036. Иркутский угленосный бассейн. (The Irkutsk coal basin.) Collected articles. Moscow-Irkutsk, 1934. 116 p.

12037. Tetiaev, M. M.Южная окраина Иркутского угленосного
бассейна. (The southern fringe of the Irkutsk coal basin.)
Leningrad-Moscow, 1934. 74 p.

12038. Fersman, A. E. (ed.). Челябинские угли. (The Cheliabinsk coal.) Moscow, Academy of sciences, 1935. 143 p.

(8) Oil and Gas

12039. Нефтяное хозяйство. (The oil industry.) Moscow,
Gosudarstvennoe vsesoiuznoe ob"edinenie neftianoi i gazovoi
promyshlennosti, 1920-

12040. Fedorov, S. F. Нефтяные месторождения Советского
Союза. (Oil deposits of the Soviet Union.) Moscow, 1935. 523p.

12041. Нефтяная промышленность СССР в цифрах. (The oil industry of the USSR in figures.) Moscow, 1935. 180 p.

12042. Omura, Ichizo. 露西亜　石油事業 Roshia
no sekiyu jigyo. (The petroleum industry of Russia.) Sekai
chishiki, November 1932.

12043. Riabukhin, G. E. Поиски нефти в Сибири. (Oil prospecting in Siberia.) Moscow-Irkutsk, 1934. 96 p.

12044. Sulin, V. A. Нефть Урала и Сибири. (Ural and Siberian oil.) Moscow, 1934. 67 p.

12045. Ganshin, S. M. and Zhorov, I. D. (ed.). Нефть в Башкирии. (Oil in Bashkiria.) Ufa, 1935. 95 p.

12046. Golubiatnikov, V. D. and Reineke, V. I. (ed.). Природные газы СССР. (Natural gases of the USSR.) Leningrad,
1935. 601 p.

12047. Mautner, Wilhelm. Der kampf um und gegen das russische erdöl. Leipzig, Manz, 1929. 260 p.

(9) Miscellaneous

12048. Lempitskii, M. О соляных промыслах Западной Сибири.
(Salt mining in Western Siberia.) Gornyi zhurnal, 1 (1884).

12049. Ivanov, A. A. Верхне-Камское месторождение калийных
солей.　　(Upper Kama beds of potassium salts.) Leningrad-Moscow, 1932. 154 p.

12050. Kazantsev, V. P. Бариты Урала. (Barytes of the
Urals.) Moscow, 1935. 101 p.

12051. Stepanov, B. L. Роль Восточно-Сибирского края в оло-
вянной проблеме СССР.(The part of the East Siberian region
in the lead problem of the USSR.) Moscow-Irkutsk, 1933. 74p.

12052. Misharev, D. T. Слюда в Восточной Сибири.(Mica in
Eastern Siberia.) Moscow-Irkutsk, 1932. 48 p.

12053. Luchitskii, V. I. Петрографические провинции СССР.
(Petrographic provinces of the USSR.) Moscow, 1936. 704 p.

N. Trade and Commerce

See 864-898; 3857-3882; 4048-4061; 4232-4252.

(1) Periodical Publications

12054. Консульские донесения по торговле и промышленности.
(Consular reports on commerce and industry.) St. Petersburg,
Departament torgovli i manufaktur, 1895-1896. 6 v.

12055. Сборник консульских донесений.   (Collection of consular reports.) St. Petersburg, Ministerstvo inostrannykh
del, 1898-1910. 13 v. (Bi-monthly).

12056. Советская торговля. (Soviet trade.) Moscow, Narodnyi
komissariat snabzheniia, 1922-   Supplements: Внешние
рынки. (Title also in English: The foreign trade.) 1925,
nos. 1-3; 1926, nos. 4-6.

12057. Итоги внешней торговли СССР.   (Returns of foreign
trade of the USSR.) Moscow, Narodnyi komissariat vneshnei
torgovli, 1923/24-

12058. Статистика внешней торговли СССР. (Statistics of foreign trade of the USSR.) Ed. by A. A. Voloshinskii. Pub. by
the Commissariat of foreign trade, Chief of customs administration (Vneshtorgizdat.) 1, February 1924-   (Monthly).

12059. Внешняя торговля союза ССР.(Foreign commerce of the
USSR.) Statistical survey. Moscow, Glavnoe tamozhennoe upravlenie, 1924-

12060. Наша внешняя торговля.   (Our foreign trade.) Moscow, Narodnyi komissariat vneshnei torgovli, 1931-

12061. Торговля России с Востоком. (Russian trade with the
Orient.) Moscow, 1923-1930. (Monthly. Discontinued.)

(2) Statistics

See 12054-12061.

12062. Nebol'sin, G. Статистические записки о внешней торговле России. (Statistical memoranda concerning foreign trade of Russia.) St. Petersburg, 1835. 2 parts.

12063. Материалы по статистике хлебной торговли.   (Statistical material on the trade in grain.) St. Petersburg, Departament torgovli i manufaktur, 1899. 5 v.

12064. Сборник узаконений и циркуляров по таможенной части. (Collection of enactments and circulars on customs.) St. Petersburg, Departament tamozhennykh sborov, 1901-1916.

12065. Энциклопедия советского импорта в 12 томах. (Encyclopedia of Soviet imports.) Moscow, Narodnyi komissariat vneshnei torgovli, 1929. 12 v.

12066. Торговля СССР за ... год по данным сплошного учета ЦСУ. (Commerce of the USSR for the year ... according to the data of the general survey made by the Central statistical board.) Moscow, TSentral'noe statisticheskoe upravlenie, 1924-1927. 3 issues.

12067. Внешняя торговля СССР за период 1918-27-8. (Foreign trade of the USSR for the period 1918-27-8.) Statistical survey. Moscow, Snabkoopriz, 1931.

12068. Внешняя торговля СССР за первую пятилетку (1928-1933) (Foreign trade of the USSR during the first five-year plan, 1928-1933.) Moscow, Vneshtorgizdat, 1933.

12069. Вопросы торговли. (Problems of commerce.) Moscow, Narodnyi komissariat snabzheniia, 1927-1930. 4 v.

12070. 日露年鑑 Nichi-Ro nenkan. (Russo-Japanese yearbook.) Tokyo, Russo-Japanese trade agency, 1931. 795 p.

(3) History

See 11014-11401.

12071. Chulkov, M. Историческое описание Российской коммерции при всех портах и границах от древних времен до ныне настоящего. (Historical description of Russian commerce at all ports and and boundaries from ancient times to the present.) St. Petersburg-Moscow, 1781-1788. 21 v.   (2) История краткая российской торговли.   (A short history of Russian commerce.) Moscow, 1788. 314 p.

12072. Mel'gunov, P. P. Очерки по истории русской торговли IX-XVIII вв. (Sketches on the history of Russian trade, IX-XVIII cent.) Moscow, 1905. 279 p.

12073. Kulisher, I. M. История русской торговли до XIX века включительно. (History of Russian commerce through the XIX century.) Petrograd, 1923. 317 p.

12074. Pokrovskii, V. I. Сборник сведений по истории и статистике внешней торговли России. (Collection of historical and statistical data on Russian foreign commerce.) St. Petersburg, Departament tamozhennykh sborov, 1902.

12075. Обзор внешней торговли России по европейской и азиатской границам. (Survey of the foreign commerce of Russia across the European and Asiatic frontiers.) St. Petersburg, Departament tamozhennykh sborov, 1802-1915.

12076. Vvedenskii, A. A. Торговый дом XVI-XVIII веков. (A trading establishment of the XVI-XVII cent.) Leningrad, 1924. 182 p.   (2) Rasmussen, J. L. De Arabum, Persamque commercio cum Russia et Scandinavia medio aevo. Hauniae, 1825. 60 p.

12077. "О распространении торга с областями Хивинскою, Бухарскою и Индейскими, 1787."(On the expansion of trade with the Khiva, Bokhara, and Indian provinces, 1787.) In: Chteniia v Imperatorskom obshchestve istorii i drevnostei rossiiskikh pri Moskovskom universitete, 2:57-64, April-June 1863.

12078. Sobolev, Mikhail N. История русско-германского торгового договора. (History of the Russo-German commercial treaty.) Petrograd, Ministerstvo finansov, 1915. 202 p.

(4) Laws

12079. Законы о торговле. (Laws on commerce.) Moscow, 1922-1923. 2 v.

(5) General Accounts of Foreign Trade

12080. Budish, Jacob M. and Shipman, S. S. Soviet foreign trade: menace or promise? New York, Liveright, 1931. 276 p.

12081. Knickerbocker, Hubert R. Soviet trade and world depression. London, Lane, 1931. 288 p.

12082. Foreign trade policy of the Soviet government. Foreign policy reports (New York), 6 (1930):20.

12083. Ching-ju. 蘇 俄 國 際 貿 易 之 分 析 觀 察
Su-O kuo-chi mao-i chih fên-hsi kuan-cha. (An analytic observation on Soviet Russia's international trade.) Kung-
shang pan-yüeh-k'an, 3:20, October 1931.

12084. Czechowiez, Paul. "Die exportpolitik und das problem
der export fähigkeit der U.d.S.S.R." Weltwirtschaftliches
archiv, 35:475-513, April 1932.

12085. Kawatani, Commercial commissioner. ソ 聯 邦 ノ 外
國 貿 易 情況 So-Renpo no gaikoku boeki jokyo. (The conditions of foreign trade of the Soviet Union.) Sekai chishiki,
September 1932.

12086. Brutskus, Boris. Die getreideausfuhr Russlands. Weltwirtschaftliches archiv, October 1933.

12087. Yanson, J. D. Foreign trade in the USSR. London,
Gollancz, 1934. 176 p.

12088. Zhirmunskii, M. M. Экспорт СССР. (Export of the
USSR.) Moscow, 1936. 204 p.

12089. Ginsburg, I. S. Внешняя торговля СССР. (Foreign trade
of the USSR.) Moscow, Sotsekgiz, 1937. 160 p.

(6) Domestic Trade

12090. Balkashin, N. Торговое движение между Западною Сибирью, Среднею Азиею и Китайскими владениями. (Movement.
of goods between Western Siberia, Central Asia, and the
Chinese possessions.) Zapiski Zapadno-Sibirskogo otd. I.R.
G.O., Omsk, 1881.

12091. Hage, K. and Tegner, G. Об условиях торгового сношения Европы с Западной Сибирью. (The conditions of trade relations between Europe and Western Siberia.) Zapiski Zap.-
Sib. otd. I.R.G.O., Omsk, 4, 1882.

12092. Subbotin, A. P. Материалы для экономического изучения
России. Торговые сообщения восточной России и Сибири.(Sources for the economic study of Russia. Trade communications
between eastern Russia and Siberia.) St. Petersburg, 1882.

12093. Shvetsov, S. P. Чуйский торговый путь. (The Chuisk
trade route.) Barnaul, 1898.

12094. Tamai, K. Karawanenreise in Sibirien, mit anhang:
weltreise eines Japaners über Sibirien vor hundert jahren.
Berlin, 1898. 163 p.

12095. Schmidt, P. IU. О промыслах острова Сахалина.
(Economic activities of the island of Sakhalin.) St. Petersburg, 1905. 458 p.

12096. Sibiriakov, A. M. О путях сообщения Сибири и морских
сношениях ее с другими странами.   (Communications of
Siberia and her sea routes to other countries.) St. Petersburg, 1907.

12097. Vostrotin, S. V. Северный морской путь и Челябинский
тарифный перелом. (The Northern sea route and the Cheliabinsk tariff station.) St. Petersburg, 1908. 79 p.

12098. Bogolepov, M. Торговля Сибири. (Trade of Siberia.)
In: Sibir', ee sovremennoe sostoianie i ee nuzhdy. [Ed. by
I.S. Mel'nik.] St. Petersburg, 1908.

12099. Sibiriakov, A. Zur frage der äusseren verbindungen
Sibiriens mit Europa. Zürich, 1910.

12100. Bogdanovskii, A. E. Ленская дорога и ее экономическое значение. (The Lena route and its economic significance.) St. Petersburg, 1911.

12101. Внутренняя торговля СССР за 10 лет. (Domestic commerce of the USSR for 10 years.) Moscow, Narodnyi komissariat snabzheniia, 1917-1927.

12102. Smirnov, A. Куяндинская ярмарка.(The Kuiandinsk fair)
Semipalatinsk, 1924. 68 p.

12103. Sosnin, I. V. О торговле и кооперации на Лене.(Trade
and cooperatives of the Lena.) Irkutsk, 1925. 78 p.

12104. Сибпромбюро ВСНХ. Сибторг. Промбанк. Итоги и перспективы.   (The Siberian trading bureau of the Supreme
council of people's economy.) Returns and prospectives.)
Novonikolaevsk, 1925. 80 p.

12105. Popov, V. L. "Сибирь и Монголия как рынок кожевенного
сырья." (Siberia and Mongolia as a market for rawhide
goods.) Severnaia Aziia, Moscow, 1 (1926):37-39.

12106. Материалы по статистике внутренней торговли СССР,
1923-1925. (Statistical material on domestic trade in the
USSR in 1923-1925.) In: Trudy sektsii obsledovaniia dere-
venskoi torgovli, Moscow, Narodnyi komissariat vneshnei i
vnutrennei torgovli, 1928 -

12107. Artamonov, D. S. Транспорт и торговля по восточной границе СССР. (Transportation and trade along the eastern frontier of the USSR.) N.p., 1928.

(7) Trade in Asia

(a) General

12108. Торговля России с Востоком. (Russia's trade with the East.) News organ of the Rossiiskaia torgovaia palata, 1923-1927. Continued as: Торговля СССР с Востоком. 1928- (Published by the Vsesoiuzno-Vostochnaia torgovaia palata.)

12109. Conolly, Violet. Soviet economic policy in the East. Oxford university press, 1933. 168 p.

12110. Conolly, Violet, Soviet trade from the Pacific to the Levant. With an economic study of the Soviet Far Eastern region. London, Oxford university press, 1935. 238 p.

12111. Shavrov, N. О путях для торговли России с Азией. (On the trade-routes between Russia and Asia.) St. Petersburg, 1873. 86 p.

12112. Merkulov, S. D. Возможные судьбы русской торговли на Дальнем Востоке. ((Possible fates of the Russian trade in the Far East.) St. Petersburg, 1903.

12113. Mitinskii, A. Материалы о положении и нуждах торговли и промышленности на Дальнем Востоке. (Sources pertaining to the conditions and problems of trade and industry in the Far East.) In: Trudy Amurskoi ekspeditsii, St. Petersburg, 8 (1911).

12114. Обзор внешней торговли по Европейской и Азиатской границе за 1911 г. (A survey of foreign trade along the European and Asiatic boundaries for 1911.) St. Petersburg, 1913. 2 parts.

12115. Scholz, F. A. Северный морской путь и его значение во внешнем товарообмене. (The Northern sea route and its significance in foreign trade.) Omsk, 1921.

12116. Отчет Российско-Восточной торговой палаты за 1923 год и план деятельности на 1924 год. (An account of the Russo-Oriental chamber of commerce for the year 1923 and the activities planned for 1924.) Moscow, Rossiisko-Vostochnaia torgovaia palata, 1924. 16 p.

12117. Российско-Восточная торговая палата. Год работы.
(1923-1924). (Russo-Oriental chamber of commerce. Annual
report, 1923-1924.) Stenographic account of the General
meeting of the members. Moscow, 1924. 32 p.

12118. Внешняя торговля и экспортные возможности Дальневосточного края. (Foreign trade and export possibilities of
the Far Eastern region.) Moscow, 1926. 120 p.

12119. S. "Наши торговые сношения с Японией." (Our commercial
relations with Japan.) Torgovopromyshlennyi iug, 15, 1912.

12120. ソ 聯邦 , 對 東方 諸國 貿易 So-Renpo no
tai-Toho shokoku boeki. (Foreign trade of the Soviet Union
with the Oriental countries.) Dairen, S.M.R.R., Harbin office, 1928.

12121. "The Great northern route." Quarterly review (USSR
chamber of commerce.) Moscow, 2:35-40, April-June, 1931.
1 map.

12122. 一九二九,一九三〇年度蘇聯對東方各國貿易狀況
I-chiu-erh-chiu i-chiu-san-ling nien-tu Su-Lien tui tung-
fang ko-kuo mao-i chuang-kuang. (The status of the Soviet
Union's trade with the Far Eastern nations in 1929 and 1930.)
Wai-chiao-pu kung-pao, 4:5, September 1931.

12123. 蘇聯 騰賣政策 Su-Lien têng-ping chêng-tsê. (The
dumping policy of the Soviet Union.) Shih-yeh kung-pao, 42,
October 1931. (Prepared by the Chinese consulate at Khabarovsk.)

12124. Barnes, Kathleen. "The Soviet economic stake in the
Orient." Far Eastern survey, 5:3:19-25, January 29, 1936.

(b) Trade with China

12125. Rzhanov, I. Китайский чай. (Chinese tea.) Moscow,
1856.

12126. Skachkov, K. A. О торговле русских в Чугучаке.
(About the Russian trade in Chuguchak.) Extract from the
Vestnik promyshlennosti, 1860. Moscow, 1860. 29 p.

12127. Ostroukhov, P. A. Движение цен на чай на внутреннем
рынке России в XIX ст.(The movement of prices on tea in the
domestic market of Russia in the XIX century [prior to the
reforms of Russo-Chinese trade in Kiakhta in 1861].) Praha,
1937. 46 p.

12128. Skachkov, K. A. Наши торговые дела в Китае. (Our trade in China.) St. Petersburg, 1863. 44 p.

12129. Marthe, Dr. F. "Die wege des landhandels zwischen Russland und China." Zeitschrift der gesellschaft für erdkunde zu Berlin, 2 (1867):10:305-324.

12130. I. N. О русской торговле с Китаем. (On Russian trade with China.) St. Petersburg, 1867. 20 p.

12131. Правила о сухопутной торговли ...   (Rules for land trade...) Hankow, October 15, 1869. 15 p.

12132. Noskov, I. О мерах к поддержанию русской торговли внутри Китая. (Concerning measures to aid Russian trade with China.) N.p., 1875. 5 p.

12133. Записка К. А. Скачкова о нуждах в деле русской торговли в Китае. (K.A. Skachkov's memorandum concerning the problems of Russian trade in China.) Moscow, 1875. 34 p.

12134. Subbotin, A. P. Чай и чайная торговля в России и других государствах. (Tea and tea trade in Russia and in other states.) St. Petersburg, 1892. 657 p.

12135. Digamma. Торговля с Китаем. (Trade with China.) Tomsk, 1899.

12136. "La commerce russo-chinois par route de Kiakhta." Bulletin commercial Asie française, 489-490, October 1904.

12137. Материалы по чайной торговле в связи с проэктом введения в России чайной монополии. (Sources on tea trade concerning the plan of tea monopoly in Russia.) Petrograd, 1915.

12138. Yu, Chien-hsing. 華茶對俄貿易觀 Hua-cha tui-O mao-i kuan. (The Chinese tea trade in Russia.) Chien-yeh yüeh-pao, 11:9, September 1931.

12139. Wu, Chueh-nung. 華茶俄銷問題 Hua-cha O-hsiao wên-t'i. (The problem of Chinese tea trade in Russia.) Kuo-chi-mao-i tao-pao, 2:10, October 1931.

(c) Trade in Central Asia

12140. IAnzhul, I. I. Исторический очерк русской торговли с Средней Азией. (Historical outline of Russian trade with Central Asia.) Mosk. univ. izvestiia, 1869:5.

12141. Bakulin, F. A. Очерк торговли с Персиею. (An outline of the Russo-Persian trade.) St. Petersburg, 1875.

(d) Border Trade and Free Ports

12142. Berezovskii, A. A. Таможенное обложение и порто-франко в Приамурском крае. (Customs duties and free trade in the Amur province.) Vladivostok, 1907.

12143. Kurteev, K. Порто-франко и Амурская область. (Free trade and the Amur province.) Khabarovsk, 1907.

12144. Порто-франко на Дальнем Востоке и российский космополитизм. (Free trade in the Far East and Russian cosmopolitism.) Moscow, 1908.

12145. Borisov, V. V. "Шанхай, как рынок для Приморья." (Shanghai as a market for the Maritime province.) Ekonomicheskaia zhizn' Dal'nego Vostoka, 8 (1924):4:57-67.

O. Railroads and Communications

See 4048-4052; 5380-5581.

(1) Periodical Publications

12146. Почтово-телеграфная статистика. (Postal and telegraph statistics.) St. Petersburg, Glavnoe upravlenie pocht i telegrafov, 1877/78-1914.

12147. Ежемесячный бюллетень транспортной статистики. (Monthly bulletin of transportation statistics.) Moscow, Narodnyi komissariat putei soobshcheniia, TSentral'noe planovo-tekhniko-ekonomicheskoe upravlenie, Sektor statistiki, 1923-

12148. Материалы по статистике путей сообщения. (Statistical material on transportation.) Moscow, Narodnyi komissariat putei soobshcheniia, TSentral'noe planovo-tekhniko-ekonomicheskoe upravlenie, Sektor statistiki, 1920-   (irregular).

12149. Железнодорожный транспорт в ... году. (Railway transportation in the year ...) Moscow, Narodnyi komissariat putei soobshcheniia, TSentral'noe planovo-tekhniko-ekonomicheskoe upravlenie, Sektor statistiki, 1924/25-
(annual).

12150. Речной транспорт ... (Предварительные сведения).
(Inland waterways transportation ... Preliminary data.)
Moscow, Narodnyi komissariat putei soobshcheniia. TSentral'-
noe planovo-tekhniko-ekonomicheskoe upravlenie, 1925-   (irregular).1

12151. Реконструкция транспорта. (Reconstruction of transportation.) Moscow, Narodnyi komissariat putei soobshcheniia, 1931-

(2) History

12152. Исторический очерк развития учреждений и работ Ведомства путей сообщения по статистике путей сообщения в
1798-1898. (Historical outline of the development of the
administration and labors of the Department of roads and
communications statistics, 1798-1898.) St. Petersburg,
Ministerstva putei soobshcheniia, 1898.

12153. Краткий исторический очерк развития и деятельности
Ведомства путей сообщения за сто лет его существования,
1798-1898. (Brief historical outline of the growth and activities of the Department of roads and communications during the hundred years of its existence, 1798-1898.)   St.
Petersburg, Ministerstvo putei soobshcheniia, 1898.

12154. Комиссия для исследования железнодорожного дела в
России, 1876 г. Труды. (Commission for the study of Russian
railways, 1876. Transactions.)   St. Petersburg, 1879. 4 v.

12155. Исторический очерк развития железных дорог в России
с их основания по 1897 г. (Historical sketch of development
of railroads in Russia from their foundation to 1897.) St.
Petersburg, Ministerstvo putei soobshcheniia, 1898. 2 v.

12156. Kislinskii, N. A. Наша железнодорожная политика по
документам архива Комитета министров. (Our [Russian] railway policy based on the documents from the archive of the
Committee of ministers.) St. Petersburg, 1902.

(3) General Accounts

12157. Материалы по исследованию экономическому внутренних
водных путей. (Material for the economic study of inland
waterways.) Moscow, TSentral'noe upravlenie vnutrennikh
vodnykh putei, 1928-

12158. Cleinow, Georg. Roter imperialismus. Einde studie
über die verkehrsprobleme der Sowietunion. Mit 25 karten-
skizzen und 76 abbildungen. Berlin, 1931.

12159. Nikitine, B. Les transports en Asie russe. Paris,
Société d'étude et informations, January 1935.

12160. IAkobi, A. M. Железные дороги СССР в цифрах.   (Railways of the USSR in figures.) Moscow, 1935. 186 p.

12161. Cherskii, I. D. Геологическое исследование Сибирского почтового тракта от оз. Байкала до восточного склона
хребта Уральского, а также путей, ведущих к падунскому по-
рогу на р. Ангаре и в г. Минусинск.(A geological study of
the Siberian post road...) St. Petersburg, 1888.

12162. Sibiriakov, A. О путях сообщения Сибири и морских
сношениях ее с другими странами. (On road communications of
Siberia and its sea communications with other countries.)
St. Petersburg, 1907. 199 p.

12163. Sobolev, M. Пути сообщения Сибири.   (Communications
of Siberia.) St. Petersburg, 1908.

12164. Belousov, M. P. Железнодорожные выходы из Сибири.
(Railway outlets from Siberia.) Moscow, 1929. 84 p.

12165. Takahashi, Kokki. アヂア ロシア / 交通 Ajia Roshia
no kotsu. (The communications of Russian Asia.) Dairen, S.
M.R.R., 1927.

12166. Hopper, Bruce C. "Soviet transport plans: winning
the East." Foreign affairs, 8:4:652-658, July 1930.

12167. Platonov, E. M. "Реорганизация железнодорожного
транспорта СССР." (Reorganization of the railway transportation of the USSR.) Vestnik Man'chzhurii, 5 (1931):82-86.

12168. 蘇聯政府合併西比利亞及遠東四鐵道管
理權之原因 Su-Lien chêng-fu ho-ping Hsi-pi-li-ya chi Yüan-
tung szu-t'ieh-lu kuan-li-chuan chih yüan-yin. (Causes of
the Soviet Union's act on uniting the administration of the
Trans-Siberian R.R. and the other four Far Eastern railroads.) Wai-chiao-pu kung-pao, 5:2, July 1932.

(4) Railroad Rates

12169. Материалы по генеральному пересмотру тарифной системы железнодорожного транспорта в 1929 г. в СССР. (Materials

for the general revision of the railway rates system in the
USSR in 1929.) Moscow, Narodnyi komissariat putei soobshcheniia, 1929. 2 v.

12170. Zagorskii, K. IA. Наша железнодорожная тарифная
политика.(Our [Russian] railway rate policy.) St. Petersburg, 1910.

12171. Belovezhskii, V. I. Система железнодорожных тарифов
на сети Российских железных дорог.(The system of railway
rates on the Russian railways.) 2nd ed. St. Petersburg,
1910.

12172. Ashik, V. Финансовые результаты эксплоатации русской
железнодорожной сети за последнее трехлетие (1907-1909).
(Financial results of the exploitation of the Russian railways for the last three year, 1907-1909.) St. Petersburg,
1911.

12173. Свод грузовых тарифов речного транспорта ᴜССР. Амурское управление. (A code of freight rates of the USSR river transportation. Amur administration.) Moscow, 1933.

12174. Европейско-Азиатское, через Сибирь, товаробагажное
сообщение. (European-Asiatic freight communications across
Siberia.) Moscow, 1933.

12175. See 12159.

(5) The Transsiberian Railroad

See 4048-4052.

(a) Guides

12176. Dmitriev-Mamonov, A. I. Путеводитель во Великой Сибирской железной дороге 1901-1902. (A guide to the Great
Siberian railway, 1901-1902.) St. Petersburg, 1902. 396 p.

12177. Saianskii, L. Великий Сибирский путь. (The Great Siberian railway.) A guide-book. Moscow, 1930. 59 p.

12178. Guide du Grand chemin de fer transsibérien. Édité
par le Ministère des voies de communication, sous la rédac-
tion de A. I. Dmitrief-Mamonov et de l'Ingénieur A. F.
Zdsiarsky, traduit du russe par P. Tacchella. St. Petersburg, Société d'impression artistique, 1900. viii, 572 p.

(b) General Accounts

12179. Miliutin, I. Сибирская железная дорога с точки зрения государственно-экономической.   (The Siberian railway from a political and economic point of view.) St. Petersburg, 1884. 36 p.

12180. Материалы к истории вопроса о Сибирской железной дороге. (Sources pertaining to the history of the Siberian railway.) St. Petersburg, 1891. 284 p.

12181. Геологические исследования и разведочные работы по линии Сибирской железной дороги.   (Geological studies and surveys of the territory adjacent to the Siberian railway.) St. Petersburg, 1896-

12182. Voloshanov, N. V. "Сибирская железная дорога." (The Siberian railway.) Izvestiia Imperatorskogo russkogo geograficheskogo obshchestva, 27 (1891):1:11-39.

12183. Boulangier, Edgar. Notes de voyage en Sibérie; le chemin de fer trans-sibérien et la Chine. Paris, Société d'éditions scientifiques, 1891. xii, 397 p.

12184. Crawford, John Martin. Siberia and the Great Siberian railway. St. Petersburg, 1893. xii, 265 p.

12185. Сибирь и Великая Сибирская железная дорога. (Siberia and the Great Siberian railway.) 2nd ed. St. Petersburg, 1896.

12186. Jefferson, Robert L. Roughing it in Siberia; with some account of the Trans-Siberian railway, and the gold mining industry of Asiatic Russia. London, Sampson Low, 1897. 252 p.

12187. Simpson, James Young. Side-lights on Siberia. Some account of the Great Siberian railroad, the prisons, and the exile system. Edinburgh-London, Blackwood & Sons, 1898. xvi, 383 p.

12188. "The Russian empire and the Trans-Siberian railway." Monthly summary of commerce and finance, Washington, 6: 2501-2599, April 1899. 1 map.

12189. Colquhoun, Archibald R. "The Trans-Siberian-Manchurian railway." Royal united service institution journal, 44:1408-1430, December 1900.

12190. Exposition universelle de 1900 à Paris. Comité du
Chemin de fer transsibérien. Aperçu des explorations géo-
logiques et minières le long du transsibérien. St. Petersburg, Le Comité géologique de Russie, 1900. xiii, 200 p.

12191. Krahmer, Gustav. Sibirien und die grosse sibirische
eisenbahn. Leipzig, Zuckschwert & co., 1897. 2te aufl.,
Leipzig, 1900, iv, 286 p. Russian translation: Сибирь и
значение Великого Сибирского пути. St. Petersburg, 1900.
108 p.

12192. Sabler, S. V. and Sosnovskii, I. V. Сибирская железная дорога в ее прошлом и настоящем. (The Siberian railway,
past and present.) A historical outline...1893-1903. St.
Petersburg, 1903.

12193. Shoemaker, Michael Myers. The Great Siberian railway
from St. Petersburg to Pekin. New York - London, Putnam's
sons, 1903. viii, 243 p.

12194. Koulomzine, A. N. de. Le Transsibérien. Paris, 1904.

12195. Zabel, Eugen. Auf der sibirischen bahn nach China.
Berlin, Allg. verein für deutsche litteratur, 1904. 294 p.

12196. "Military aspects of the Trans-Siberian railway."
Scientific American, 90:308-309, April 16, 1904.

12197. "The Siberian railway in war." World today, 6:607-
615, May 1904.

(6) The Amur Railroad

12198. Subbotich, D. I. Амурская дорога и наша политика на
Дальнем Востоке. (The Amur railway and our policy in the
Far East.) Revel, 1906. 53 p.

12199. Viskovatov, Vl. Амурская железная дорога. (The Amur
railway.) St. Petersburg, 1908.

12200. Sakhanskii, V.A. Очерк Амурской области в связи с
грузооборотом проектируемой Средне-Амурской железной дороги.
(A sketch of the Amur province in connection with the
freightage of the projected Central Amur railway.) St. Petersburg, 1909.

12201. Дальний Восток. (The Far East.) Ed. by Bolkhovitinov.
V.II: Communications... Transbaikal, Amur, and Maritime
provinces and Manchuria, St. Petersburg, 1911.

12202. Molodykh, I. F.Транспортная проблема Восточной Сибири.
(The transportation problem of Eastern Siberia.) Moscow,
1930. 41 p.

(7) The Turk-Sib Railroad

See 7138-7144.

12203. Khalatov, Artemii B. О Туркестано-Сибирской(Семиреченской) железной дороге.(The Turkestan-Siberian railway.)
Leningrad, 1927. 44 p.

12204. Greeg, Nikolai. На Турксибе.(On the Turkestan-Siberian railway.) Leningrad, 1929. 237 p.

12205. Ostrovskii, Z. G. Турксиб. (Turksib [The Turkestan-
Siberian railway].) Collected articles. Moscow, 1930. 256 p.

12206. Ryskulov, T. R. Турксиб.(The Turksib [railway].)
Moscow, 1930. 76 p.

12207. Turksib. On the opening of the Turkestan-Siberian
railway. May 1, 1930.[In English]. Moscow, 1930. 64 p.

12208. D. T. "Турксиб и экономическое развитие районов к
нему тяготеющих." (The Turkestan-Siberian railway and the
economic development.of the adjacent regions.) Voprosy
torgovli, Moscow, 3-4 (1930):113-121.

12209. Chao, Ching-yüan.土西鐵道之完成暨其影響
T'u-Hsi-t'ieh-lu chih wan chêng yü chi ying-hsiang. (The
completion of the Turkestan-Siberian railway and its effects)
Current events, 3:2: August 1930.

12210. Lunin, B. Турксиб. (The Turksib [railway].) Moscow,
1931. 47 p.

(8) Other Railroads

12211. Задачи России в Средней Азии в связи с вопросом о
проведении Средне-Азиатской железной дороги. (The problems
of Russia in Asia in connection to the construction of the
Central-Asiatic railway.) St. Petersburg, 1900.

12212. Dmitriev-Mamonov, A. I. Путеводитель по Туркестану и
Средне-Азиатской железной дороге. (Guide to the Turkestan
and the Central Asiatic railroads.) St. Petersburg, 1903.
454 p.

12213. Maliarevskii, G. IA. О проведении железной дороги до г. Тобольска, как средства к оживлению севера Западной Сибири. (The construction of a railway to Tobolsk as a means to developing the north of Western Siberia.) Tobolsk, 1905.

12214. Lepeshinskii, V. "К проблеме транспорта Западной Сибири." (The transportation problem of Western Siberia.) Planovoe khoziaistvo, October 1925:298-309.

12215. "Н. Н. Романов и американская концессия на железную дорогу Сибирь-Аляска в 1905 г." (N. N. Romanov and the American concession on the Siberia-Alaska railway in 1905.) Krasnyi arkhiv, 43 (1931):173-176.

12216. Egerman, P. and Alskii, S. Новые железные дороги в Западной Сибири. (New railways in Western Siberia.) Novosibirsk, 1932.

P. Economic Zoning

12217. Boldyrev, V. and Gurinovich, P. Районирование Сибири. (The zoning of Siberia.) A brief cultural-economic sketch. Novonikolaevsk, 1926. 46 p.

12218. Cherkunov, A. N. "К вопросу о районировании Средней Сибири (Лено-Байкальская область). (The zoning problem of Central Siberia, the Lena-Baikal region.) Severnaia Aziia, Moscow, 1 (1926):5-29.

12219. Kolosovskii, N. N. "Хозяйство Восточной Сибири и Дальнего Востока в связи с районированием." (Economy of Eastern Siberia and the Far East in its relation to the zoning problem.) Planovoe khoziaistvo, September 1925:239-258.

12220. Charnetskii, L. "Вопросы районирования Приморской губернии." (The zoning problem in the Maritime province.) Sovetskoe primorie, Vladivostok, 1-2:164-178, January-February 1926.

12221. Zalesskii, P. M. Районы Западно-Сибирского края. (The zones of the West-Siberian region.) Novosibirsk, 1931. 256 p. (2) Society for the study of Soviet Asia. Госплан СССР. Труды первой Всесоюзной конференции по размещению производительных сил СССР. (Transactions of the first All-Union conference on the distribution of the productive power of the Soviet union.) Moscow, 1, 1931-

Q. The Five-Year Plans

(1) Periodicals

12222. Плановое хозяйство. (Planned economy.) Moscow, 1924-

12223. Государственная плановая комиссия. Труды. (State planning commission. Transactions.) Moscow, 1924-

12224. Коньюнктура народного хозяйства СССР и мирового хозяйства. (Conjuncture of the economy of the Soviet Union and the world economy.) Moscow, 1924/25-1925/26. Publ. by the Kon'iunkturnyi institut.

12225. Коньюнктурный институт. Бюллетень. (Bulletin of the Conjuncture institute.) Moscow, 1922-1929.

12226. Проблемы мирового хозяйства. (Problems of world economy.) Moscow, Institut ekonomicheskikh issledovanii, 1931- (Bi-monthly).

12227. Центральное планово-технико-экономическое управление. Научно-исследовательский сектор. Издания. (Central department of planning, economics and technology. Section of scientific research. Publications.) Moscow, 1923- (Irregular).

12228. Мировое хозяйство. Сборник материалов за ... (World economy. Collection of data for the period ...) Moscow, TSentral'noe statisticheskoe upravlenie, 1913-1927.

(2) The First Five-Year Plan

12229. Пятилетний план социалистического строительства. (The five-year plan of socialist construction.) Moscow, Gosudarstvennaia planovaia komissiia, 1929-1930. 3 v.

12230. Пятилетний план народно-хозяйственного строительства СССР. (The five-year plan of national economic construction of the USSR.) 3rd ed. Moscow, Plankhozgiz, 1932. 5 v.

12231. Контрольные цифры пятилетнего плана народного хозяйства и социально-культурного строительства Р.С.Ф.С.Р. (Control figures for the five-year plan for the economic, cultural, and social construction of the RSFSR.) Moscow, Gosudarstvennaia planovaia komissiia, 1928-1933. 2 v.

12232. Пятилетний план промышленности ВСНХ РСФСР. (Five-year plan for industry managed by the Supreme economic council of the RSFSR.) Moscow, Vysshii sovet narodnogo khoziaistva, 1929.

12233. Khronin, V. Первая наметка пятилетнего плана развития Сибирского края.(First draft of the five-year plan for the development of Siberia.) Zhizn' Sibiri, 5 (1928).

12234.Проблемы капитального строительства Восточной Сибири. (The problems of capital construction of Eastern Siberia.) Irkutsk, Irkutskaia planovaia komissiia, 1926.

12235. Nanking, Ministry of foreign affairs. 蘇聯遠東州 五年建設計劃之概要 Su-Lien Yüan-tung-chou wu-nien chien-shê-chi-hua chih kai-yao. (The Soviet Union's five-year construction plan for the Far East: a general outline.) Foreign affairs gazette, 3:8:175, December 1930.

12236. Farbman, M. Piatiletka: the five-year plan. New York, New Republic, 1931. 220 p.

12237. Mu-kung. 蘇聯遠東五年計劃 Su-Lien Yüan-tung wu-nien chi-hua. (The Soviet Union's five-year plan for the Far East.) Russia study monthly, 2:1:1, January 1931.

12238. Fu, Shih. 五年計劃實施前俄領亞州之產業 概況 Wu-nien-chi-hua shih-szu chien o-ling-ya-chou chih chan-yeh kai-kuang. (The general conditions of industries in Russian Asia before the completion of the five-year plan.) Chung-tung ching-chi yüeh-k'an, 7:9, September 1931.

12239. Hu, Yü-chih. 蘇俄五年計劃之研究 Su-O wu-nien-chi-hua chih yen-chiu. (A study of Soviet Russia's five-year plan.) Hsin-shê-hui, 1:7, October, 1931.

12240. Strumilin, S. G. Проблемы планирования в СССР. (The problems of planned economy in the USSR.) Leningrad, Akademiia nauk, 1932. 541 p.

12241. Su, Ju-chiang. 蘇俄五年計劃之內容成績及 其批評 Su-O wu-nien-chi-hua chih nei-jung chêng-chi chi ch'i pi-ping. (The contents and the results of the five-year plan of Soviet Russia and its criticism.) Wu-ta wên-hsüeh-yüan chi-k'an, 1:2, 1932.

12242. Ching-ju. 蘇俄五年計劃之輪廓 Su-O wu-nien-chi-hua chih lun-kuo. (An outline of Soviet Russia's five-year plan.) Kung-shang pan-yüeh-k'an, 4:46-47, March-April 1932.

12243. Wang, Yin-chuan. 蘇聯五年計劃奮闘成功史
Su-Lien wu-nien-chi-hua fên-to ch'êng-kung-shih. (A history
of the struggles and success of Soviet Russia's five-
year plan.) Ta-kung daily, 1932.

12244. Panfilov, V. N. "К истории развития планирования в
CCCP." (History of the development of planned economy in
the USSR.) Kommunisticheskoe prosveshchenie, 1 (1933):37-66.

12245. Summary of the fulfillment of the first five-year
plan for the development of the national economy of the
USSR. Report of the State planning commission of the Council of people's commissars of the Union of Soviet Socialist
Republics. Moscow, USSR State planning commission, 1933.
xi, 296 p.

12246. Stalin, I. V. The results of the first five-year
plan. Report delivered at the joint plenum of the Central
committee and the Central control commission of the Communist party of the Soviet Union. January 7, 1933. Moscow-
Leningrad, Co-operative publishing society of foreign workers in the USSR, International press in Moscow, 1933. 61 p.

12247. Ananiev, A. A. Итоги первой пятилетки Западной Сибири.
(Summaries of the first five-year plan of Western Siberia.)
Novosibirsk, 1934. 80 p.

(3) Between the Two Five-Year Plans

12248. T'ang, Tê-hêng. 俄國糧食不足之根本原因及
其前途之推測 O-kuo liang-shih pu-tsu chih kên-
pên yüan-yin chi ch'i ch'ien-t'u chih t'ui-ts'ê. (Fundamental causes of the shortage of food in Russia and the future outlook.) Eastern miscellany, 27:10:23-31, May 1930.

12249. Ching-kuan. 蘇聯關于民食供給的新政策
Su-Lien kuan-yü min-shih kung-chi ti hsin-chêng-tsê. (New
policy in people's food supply in the Soviet Union.) Shên-
pao yüeh-k'an, 1:2, August 1932.

12250. Davis, Jerome (ed.). The New Russia. Between the
first and second five-year plans. New York, John Day co.,
1933. 265 p.

(4) The Second Five-Year Plan

12251. Wang, Yü-t'ung. 蘇俄公布新五年計劃
Su-O kung-pu hsin-wu-nien-chi-hua. (Soviet Russia promulgated her new five-year plan.) Shang-yeh yüeh-pao, 12:2, 1932.

12252. Tang-hsia. 蘇 俄 第 二 五 年 計 劃 決 案 Su-O ti-erh wu-nien-chi-hua chueh-an. (Soviet Russia passed her second five-year plan.) Kuo-wên chou-pao, 9:20, May 1932.

12253. Tao-fêng. 蘇 俄 第 二 次 五 年 計 劃 Su-O ti-erh-tzu wu-nien-chi-hua. (The second five-year plan of Soviet Russia.) Shêng-huo, 7:23, June 1932.

12254. Li, Pai-chiang. 最 近 蘇 俄 經 濟 之 進 展 Tsui-chin Su-O ching-chi chih chin-chan. (Recent economic progress in Soviet Russia.) Chien-yeh yüeh-pao, 12:6, June 1932.

12255. Wên, Hu-shêng. 蘇 聯 第 二 五 年 計 劃 的 目 標 Su-Lien ti-erh wu-nien-chi-hua ti mu-piao. (The aims of Soviet Russia's second five-year plan.) Hsin-chuang-tsao, 1: 6, July 1932.

12256. Chên, Ping-ho. 蘇 聯 的 五 年 計 劃 與 新 五 年 計 劃 Su-Lien ti wu-nien-chi-hua yü hsin-wu-nien-chi-hua. (The Soviet Union's five-year plan plan and her new five-year plan.) Shên-pao yüeh-k'an, 1:1, July 1932.

12257. Molotov, V. M. Tasks of the first year of the second five-year plan. Report delivered at the joint plenum of the Central committee and the Central control commission of the Communist party of the Soviet Union, January 8, 1933. Mos-cow-Leningrad, 1933. 59 p.

12258. Второй пятилетний план развития народного хозяйства СССР. (The second five-year plan of the development of na-tional economy of the USSR, 1933-1937.) Moscow, Gosplan SSSR, 1934. 2 v.

12259. Butkevich, A. Обьско-Иртышская область во второй пятилетке. (The Ob-Irtysh region in the second five-year plan.) Tiumen, 1934. 52 p.

12260. Maimin, I. B. (ed.). Вопросы Ангаро-Енисейской проб-лемы. (Questions concerning the Angara-Eniseisk problem.) Moscow-Irkutsk, 1934. 73 p.

R. Labor

12261. Материалы по истории рабочего движения в России. (Materials for the history of the labor movement in Russia.) Moscow, TSentral'nyi arkhiv, 1925-

12262. Semevskii, V. I. Рабочие на сибирских золотых промыслах. (Laborers of the Siberian gold mines.) St. Petersburg, 1898.

12263. Материалы по бюджетному обследованию рабочих и служащих в 1923. (Materials for the budget investigation of workers and employees.) Novonikolaevsk, Sibirskoe ob"-edinennoe biuro statistiki truda, 1923. 56 p.

12264. Материалы по бюджетному обследованию рабочих и служащих в Сибири в 1923 n (Materials for the budget investigation of workers and employees.) Novonikolaevsk, Sibirskoe ob"-edinennoe biuro statistiki truda, 1924. 64 p. 2nd issue.

12265. Общий очерк работы Сибирских инспекций в 1922 году. (A general sketch of the work of the Siberian inspection in 1922.) Novonikolaevsk, Upravlenie upolnomochennogo po Sibiri narodnogo komissariata raboche-krestianskoi inspektsii SSSR, 1923. 41 p.

12266. Двадцать пять лет деятельности Транспортно-потребительского общества служащих и рабочих Уссурийской железной дороги. (Twenty-five years of activity of the Cooperative society of the Ussuriisk railway employees and workers.) Khabarovsk, Ussuriiskii kooperator transportnik, 1923. 16 p.

12267. Отчет 3-му Губернскому съезду профсоюзов. (Report presented to the 3rd Guberniia congress of trade unions.) [September 1, 1922 - May 14, 1924 . Novonikolaevsk, 1924, Novonikolaevskii gubernskii sovet professional'nykh soiuzov. 100, 15, 56 p.

12268. Бюллетень объединенного бюро статистики труда при Сиббюро ВЦСПС Сибстатуправлении и Сибтруде. (Bulletin of the Siberian bureau of labor statistics.) Novonikolaevsk, no. 4, 1924,October. 36 p.

12269. Социальное страхование на Урале в январе-марте 1924. (Social insurance in the Urals in January-March 1924.) Ekaterinburg, 1924. 14 p.

12270. Uchiyama, Peteru. 露領極東ニ於ケル職業組合 / 組織 Ro-ryo Kyokuto ni okeru shokugyo kumiai no soshiki. (The organization of the trade unions in the Russian Far East.) Dairen, S.M.R.R., 1927.

12271. Banin, D. M. "Рабочие и рабочее движение на Урале." (Laborers and the labor movement in the Urals.) The 1870's. Istoriia proletariata SSSR, Moscow, 1930. 2:72-98.

S. Finances

(1) Gevernment Periodicals and Publications

12272. Комиссия для пересмотра системы податей и сборов.
Труды. (Commission for the revision of the taxation system,
1859-1882. Transactions.) St. Petersburg, 1861-1878. 24 v.

12273. Отчет государственного контроля по исполнению
государственной росписи и финансовых смет. (Report of the
State control on receipts and expenditures in respect to
the state budget and financial estimates.) St. Petersburg,
1866-1914. Объяснительная записка... (Explanatory memorandum.) Отчет... (Report.) Приложения... (Appendices.)

12274. Всеподданнейший доклад министра финансов. О необходи-
мости установить и затем непреложно придерживаться опре-
деленной программы торгово-промышленной политики Империи.
(Report of the Minister of finance to His Majesty. On the
necessity of formulating and thereafter steadfastly adhering
to a definite program of a commercial and industrial policy
of the Empire.) St. Petersburg, 1899.

12275. Государственная роспись доходов и расходов. (State
budget.) St. Petersburg, 1862-1917. Приложение. (Supplement)

12276. Департамент окладных сборов. Поступление казенных
окладных сборов с сельских сословий по месяцам. (Collection
of government direct taxes from peasants, by months ...)
За 14 лет с 1880 по 1893 г. (For 14 years from 1880 to 1893.)
1897. За 21 летний период с 1880 по 1900 г. (For the 21
year period, 1880-1900.) 1903.

12277. Статистический ежегодник. (Statistical year-book.)
Moscow, Narodnyi komissariat finansov, 1923/24-1926/27 (?)

12278. Статистика государственных налогов и пошлин. (Statistics of state taxes and duties.) Moscow, Narodnyi komissariat finansov, 1923/24-   (Annual).

12279. Роспись общегосударственных доходов и расходов РСФСР.
(State budget of the RSFSR for the period when it represen-
ted the whole Soviet Russia.) 1918-1923.

12280. Единый государственный бюджет Союза ССР. (Single
state budget of the USSR.) Moscow, 1924/25-

12281. Исполнение единого государственного бюджета СССР.
(The completion of a single state budget of the USSR.) A
short survey. Moscow, 1924/25-

12282. Единый финансовый план на ... (Single [federal] financial plan for ...) Moscow, 1929-30-

12283. Местный бюджет СССР в ... исполнение бюджетов. (Local budget of the USSR for the year ... Finance accounts) Moscow, 1923/24-

12284. Финансы и экономика. (Finance and economics.) Moscow, 1922. Succeeded by Социалистическое хозяйство. (Social economy.) Moscow, 1923-

12285. Систематическое собрание постановлений, циркуляров и инструкций Наркомфина СССР. (Systematically arranged collection of resolutions, circulars, and instructions of the Commissariat for finance of the USSR.) Moscow, Narodnyi komissariat finansov, 1928-

12286. Отчет Дальневосточного акционерного банка.(Report of the Far Eastern joint-stock bank.) 1923-1924. Khabarovsk, 1925. xiv,22, 41 p.

(2) General Accounts

12287. Kliuchevskii, V. O. Русский рубль XVI-XVIII в. (The Russian ruble XVI-XVIII c.) In: Chteniia Imperatorskogo obschestva istorii i drevnostei pri Moskovskom universitete, Issledovaniia, 1, 1884.

12288. IAsnopol'skii, N. P. О географическом распределении государственных доходов и расходов России. (The geographic distribution of state revenues and expenditures of Russia.) Kiev, 1890-1897. 2 parts.

12289. Migulin, P. P. Русский государственный кредит. (The state credit of Russia.) Kharkov, 1899-1907. 3v. in 7 issues.

12290. Kaufman, I. I. Серебряный рубль в России. (The silver ruble in Russia.) St. Petersburg, 1910.

12291. Vanag, N. I. Финансовый капитал в России накануне мировой войны. (Financial capital in Russia on the eve of the world war.) 2nd ed. Moscow, 192?.

12292. Ronin, S. Иностранный капитал и русские банки. (Foreign capital and Russian banks.) Moscow, 192 .

12293. La dette publique de la Russie. Paris, Payot, 1922. 220 p.

12294. Pogrebetskii, A. Денежное обращение и денежные знаки Дальнего Востока за период войны и революции (1914-1924). (Circulation of currency and paper money in the Far East during the war and revolution, 1914-1924.) Harbin-Chita-Vladivostok, 1924. 419 p.

12295. Kursel', K. P. and Lukasiuk, A. A. Денежное обращение на русском Дальнем Востоке с 1918 по 1924 год. (Circulation of currency in the Russian Far East from 1918 to 1924.) Chita, 1924. 64 p.

12296. Ioffe, A. "Наша концессионная политика на Д.В." (Our [Soviet] concessions policy in the Far East.) Severnaia Aziia, 5-6 (1926):9-23.

12297. See 11918.

12298. Sokol'nikov, Gregory et al. Soviet policy in public finance 1917-1928. Stanford university press, 1931. 470 p.

12299. Pao, Chih. 蘇 俄 之 銀 行 Su-O chih yin-hang. (Banks in Soviet Russia) Ch'ien-yeh yüeh-pao, 11:12, Dec. 1931.

12300. Hubbard, L. E. Soviet money and finance. New York-London, Macmillan, 1936. 339 p.

T. Colonization

See 1047-1060; 2730-2746; 5618-5665;6846-6847.

(1) Bibliography

12301. IAmzin, I. L. Список изданий переселенческого управления. (List of publications of the immigration department.) Petrograd, 1914.

12302. Справочники для ходоков и переселенцев. (Reference-books for the advance-scouts and colonists.) Moscow, Narodnyi komissariat zemledeliia, Otdel pereseleniia, 1928-

(2) History

12303. Цифровый материал для изучения переселений в Сибирь. (Figures for the study of the colonization of Siberia.) St. Petersburg, Ministerstvo vnutrennikh del, 1899-1901. 6 v.

12304. Сборник статистических сведений об экономическом положении переселенцев в Сибири. (A collection of statistical data on the economic conditions of the immigrants in Siberia.) St. Petersburg, 1912. 4 v.

12305. Государственный научно-исследовательский институт
землеустройства и переселения. Бюллетень. (State institute
for scientific study of problems of colonization and of agrarian relations. Bulletin.) Moscow, 1923-

12306. Государственный научно-исследовательский институт
землеустройства и переселения. Труды. (State institute
for scientific study of problems of colonization and of agrarian relations. Transactions.) Moscow, 1924-

12307. Материалы для истории русских заселений по берегам
Восточного океана. (Sources pertaining to the history of
the Russian settlements along the Pacific shores.) Supplement to the Morskoi sbornik, 1-3 (1861):4.

12308. Serpovskii, N. Переселения в России в древнее и новое
время. (Emigration in Russia in ancient and modern times.)
Kharkov, 1885.

12309. Bagalei, D. Материалы для истории колонизации.
(Sources pertaining to the history of colonization.) Kharkov, 1886-1890.

12310. IAdrintsev, Nikolai M. Сибирь, как колония в географическом, этнографическом и историческом отношении. La Sibérie
comme colonie considéré sous le rapport géographique, etno-
graphique et historique. 2nd enlarged and revised edition.
St. Petersburg, 1892.

12311. Stankevich, A. Материалы для изучения быта переселенцев, водворенных в Тобольской губ. (Sources for the study
of the customs of immigrants who were settled in Tobolsk
gubernia.) Late 1870's to 1893. Moscow, 1895, 1897.

12312. Kaufman, A. Сибирское переселение на исходе XIX в.
(Siberian migration at the end of the XIX century.) Histor-
ical-statistical sketch. Russkoe ekonomicheskoe obozrenie,
2 (1901).

12313. Kiriakov, V. V. Очерки по истории переселенческого
движения в Сибирь. (Historical sketches of the colonizing
of Siberia.) Moscow, 1902. 370 p.

12314. Kaufman, A. A. Переселение и колонизация. (Immigration and colonization.) St. Petersburg, 1905.

12315. Kaufman, A. A. По новым местам. (In new places.)
St. Petersburg, 1905.

12316. Turchaninov, N. Итоги переселенческого движения за время с 1896 по 1909 гг. включительно.(Results of the immigration movement during the period 1896-1909.) St. Petersburg, 1910.

12317. Сборник цифровых материалов для изучения крестьянских переселений в Сибирь. (A collection of sources for the study of peasant immigration to Siberia.) 1900-1906. Moscow, 1907-1909.

12318. Vvedenskii, I. Переселение на Дальний Восток за последние годы. (Recent immigration to the Far East.) Voprosy kolonizatsii, St. Petersburg, 4 (1909).

12319. Stolypin, P. A. Die kolonisation Sibiriens. Berlin, 1912.

12320. IAmzin, I. Переселенческое движение в России с момента освобождения крестьян. (The immigration movement in Russia from the period of the emancipation of the peasants.) Kiev, 1912.

12321. Kobozev, P. "Колонизация Дальнего Востока." (Colonization of the Far East.) In: Trudy Gosudarstvennoi kollegii Nauchno-issled. instituta, 1 (1924):213-269. (2) Bakhrushin, S. V. Исторический очерк заселения Сибири до половины XIX века.   (Historical sketch of the settlement of Siberia to mid-nineteenth century.) In: Ocherki po istorii kolonizatsii Severa i Sibiri, Petrograd, 2, 1922.

12322. Belorusets, L. "Колонизация Сибирского края в 1924-1925 г. и перспективы." (The colonization of Siberia in 1924-1925 and its prospects.) Planovoe khoziaistvo, December, 1925:230-237.

12323. Derber, P. "Демография и колонизация советского Дальнего Востока." (Demography and colonization of the Soviet Far East.) Novyi Vostok, 7 (1925):103-114.

12324. Vorobiev, N. I. Материалы по быту русского старожильческого населения Восточной Сибири.   (Materials pertaining to the Russian pioneers of Eastern Siberia.) Naselenie Prichunskogo kraia, Kazan, 1926. v. 33:2-3.

12325. IAmzin, I. L. and Voshchinin, V. P. Учение о колонизации и переселениях. (A study of colonization and immigration.) Moscow-Leningrad, Gosizdat, 1926. 328 p.

12326. IArmosh, A. M. Колонизация Дальневосточного края.
(Colonization of the Far East.) Vladivostok, 1926. 28 p.

12327. Zhemchuzhnikov, N. N. Движение на Восток.   (The
Eastward movement.) Moscow, 1927. viii,9, 142 p.   (2)
Ogorodnikov, V. I. Туземное и русское земледелие на Амуре
в XVII в. (Native and Russian agriculture on the Amur in
the XVII c.) In: Trudy Dal'nevostochnogo universiteta,
Series 3, Vladivostok, 1927.

12328. Losovoi, I. G. "Вопросы переселения и колонизации
Сибири." (The problem of immigration and colonization in
Siberia.) Vol'naia Sibir' (Prague), 3 (1928).   (2) Bakhru-
shin, S. V. Очерки по истории колонизации Сибири в XVI и
XVII вв. (Sketches in history of the colonization of Sibe-
ria in the XVI and XVII centuries.) Moscow, 1928.

12329. Liubavskii, M. K. Образование основной государственной территории великорусской народности. Заселение и объ-
единение центра.(Formation of the main state territory of
the Great Russian nation. Colonization and unification of
the center.) Leningrad, Academy of sciences of the USSR.,
1929.

12330. Rixy, Jan Ing. Kolonisace Ruska ve svém dějinném vý-
voji a významu až po přitomnou dobu (1929). Praha, Nákladem
Masarykovy akademie práce s podporou Ministerstva školství
a národní osvěty, 1929. 137 p.

12331. Sineokov, Vladimir. La colonisation russe en Asie.
Dissertation présentée à l'Université de Lausanne. Paris,
M. Girard, 1929. 227 p.

12332. Mende, Gerhard von. Studien zur kolonisation in der
Sowjetunion. Ost-Europa institut in Breslau. Quellen und
studien, Neue folge, Heft 2, Breslau, Priebatsch, 1933.
(2) Beliaev, N. T. О начале Руси. (Concerning the beginning
of Russia.) In: Trudy kruzhka k poznaniiu Rossii, 2 (1937).
(3) Glinka, G. B. Колонизация русской Азии.   (The colonization of Russian Asia.) In: Trudy kruzhka k poznaniiu Rossii, 2 (1937).

(3) Policy

12333. IAdrintsev, N. M. Колонизационное значение русской
ссылки. (Russian exile system as a colonizing factor.) Zhurnal "Delo", 12 (1872). St. Petersburg.

12334. Отчет высочайше командированного на Дальний Восток по переселенческому делу товарища главноуправляющего землеустройством и земледелием сенатора Иваницкого. (Report of the associate head of the department of land settlement and agriculture, Senator Ivanitskii, appo¹nted by His Majesty to supervise colonization in the Far East.) St. Petersburg, 1909.

12335. Chirkin, G. О задачах колонизационной политики в Сибири. (Problems of the colonization policy in Siberia.) Voprosy kolonizatsii, St. Petersburg, 8 (1911).

12336. "Русская государственная власть и сибирские инородцы XVI-XVIII вв."(The Russian administration and the Siberian natives in the XVI-XVIII cent.) In: Sbornik professorov i prepodavatelei gosudarstvennogo irkutskogo universiteta, Irkutsk, 1 (1921):69-113. (By V. I. Ogorodnikov).

12337. Lavrov, V. (ed.). К вопросу колонизации Сибири. (On the problem of Siberian colonization.) Novosibirsk, Sibirskii kraevoi ispolnitel'nyi komitet sovetov, 1926. 138 p.

12338. Gapanovich, I. I. "Колониальная система на Севере." (Colonial system in the North.) Vol'naia Sibir', 9 (1930): 84-115.

12339. Meerson, O. "Колониальная политика самодержавия." (The colonial policy of [Russian] autocracy.) Revoliutsionnyi Vostok, Moscow, 8 (1930):132-154.

12340. Hsiao-shêng. 蘇俄對於俄領遠東之移民事業. Su-O tui-yü O-ling-yüan-tung chih i-min shih-yeh. (Soviet Russia's policy in the Russian Far East.) Chinese Eastern economics monthly, 7:1, January 1931.

12341. Дальневосточный край. (The Far Eastern region.) A handbook for Far Eastern settlers. Dal'giz, 1932.

(4) Problems

12342. Medvedev, N. Переселенцы в Сибири. (Immigrants in Siberia.) St. Petersburg, 1891. 68 p.

12343. Semenov, P. P. Значение Сибири в колонизационном движении европейских народов. (The significance of Siberia in the colonization movement of the European people.) Izvestiia I.R.G.O., St. Petersburg, 28 (1892):4.

12344. Колонизация Сибири в связи с общим переселенческим
вопросом. (The colonization of Siberia in relation to the
general immigration problem.) St. Petersburg, 1900. 374 p.

12345. Kaufman, A. A. Сибирское переселение на исходе XIX
века. (Siberian immigration at the end of the XIX century.)
St. Petersburg, 1901.

12346. Auhagen, Otto. Besiedlung Sibiriens. Berlin, 1902.

12347. К. В.   Плотность населения северных стран и ее отношение к эмиграции (к вопросу о колонизации Сибири.)
(Density of population in the northern countries and its
relation to the colonization of Siberia.) Moscow, 1906.

12348. Переселение в Сибирь. (Immigration to Siberia.) St.
Petersburg, 1906.

12349. Charushin, A. Вопросы колонизации на Дальнем Востоке.
(Colonization problems in the Far East.) Vestnik finansov,
promyshlennosti i torgovli, 8, 1906.

12350. Strukovskii, I. A. Книжка для крестьян о том, как по
настоящему нужно переселяться в Сибирь. (Instructions to
peasants on how to immigrate to Siberia.) Minsk, 1907.

12351. Averin, N. Переселенческий вопрос и общественные
организации. (The immigration problem and social organizations.) St. Petersburg, 1907.

12352. Bakhrushin, S. V. "Сибирские слободчики в XVII в."
(Siberian freemen, XVII cent.) Trudy Gosudarstvennogo nauchno-issledovatel'skogo kolonizatsionnogo instituta, 2, 1926.

12353. Вопросы колонизации. (Colonization problems.) St.
Petersburg, 1907-1908. 2 issues.

12354. Kuznetsov, V. K. Экономические результаты переселения
в Сибирь и Степной край. (Economic results of the immigration to Siberia and the Stepnoi regions.) In: Voprosy kolonizatsii (St. Petersburg), 2, 1908.

12355. Radchenko, N. A. Земский опыт помощи переселенцам. (The
Zemstvo experiment of aiding the emigrants.) Chernigov, 1908.

12356. Chirkin, G. "Основные задачи колонизации в Сибири."
(The fundamental problems of Siberian colonization.) Tor-
govo-promyshlennaia gazeta, 265, 1908.

12357. Kaufman, A. A. Наш Дальний Восток и его колонизация.
(Our Far East and its colonization.) Russkaia mysl', 12, 1909.

12358. Kokhanovskii, A. Переселенческое дело в Китае и наши
дальне-восточные окраины. (Immigration in China and our
[Russian] Far Eastern border lands.) Izvestiia Vostochnogo
instituta, Vladivostok, 29:2, 1909.

12359. Voshchinin, V. P. Переселенческий вопрос в Государственной Думе III созыва.   (The colonization question in
the Duma, 3rd session.) St. Petersburg, 1912.

12360. Lenskii, Nik. Самовольные переселенцы и переселенческое законодательство.   (Illegal immigrants and legislation pertaining to immigration.) Voprosy kolonizatsii,
St. Petersburg, 14, 1913.

12361. Muganskii, V. Вопросы колонизации ь четвертой Государственной Думе. (The colonization problems in the 4th
Duma.) Voprosy kolonizatsii, St. Petersburg, 13, 1913.

12362. Oganovskii, N. P. Очерки по переселенческому вопросу.
(Sketches dealing with the immigration problem.) Vestnik
Evropy, 11, 1913.

12363. Kapherr, E. von. Die Ansiedler in Sibirien. Leipzig,
1923.

12364. See 12337.

(5) Colonization and Agriculture

12365. Kacharovskii, K. Крестьянское хозяйство и переселение. (Agriculture and immigration.) Russkaia mysl', 3
and 6, 1894.

12366. Shlikevich, S. P. Колонизационное значение земледелия в Приамурье.   (The significance of agriculture for
the colonization of the Amur   region.) In: Trudy komand.
po Vysochaishemu povel. Amursk. ekspeditsii, St. Petersburg,
5, 1911.

12367. Uchiyama, Peteru. 露領極東／農業、ト植民
問題 Ro-ryo Kyokuto no nogyo to shokumin mondai. (Agriculture and the problem of colonization in the Russian Far
East.) Dairen, S.M.R.R., 1926.

(6) Land Settlement

12368. Umanets, F. M. Колонизация свободных земель России. (The colonization of free land in Russia.) St. Petersburg, 1884.

12369. Kaufman, A. A. Сложные формы общинного землевладения
в Сибири по новейшим местным исследованиям 1887 и 1892
г. г.   (Complex forms of communal land-tenure in Siberia.)
Izvestiia Vostochno-Sibirskogo otdeleniia I.R.G.O., Irkutsk,
26 (1896):4,5.

12370. Сборник узаконений и распоряжений о водворении переселенцев и образовании переселенческих участков.
(A collection of laws and regulation pertaining to the settlement of immigrants and formation of immigration allotments.) St. Petersburg, 1907.

12371. Главное управление землеустройства и земледелия.
Обзор деятельности.   (Main office for agrarian reforms [land
settlement] and agriculture. Survey of activities.) St. Petersburg, 1906/07-1915.

12372. Переселение и заготовка земель для переселенцев.
(Immigration and preparation of land for immigrants.) St.
Petersburg, 1907.

12373. Sinel'nikov, N. Хуторские отрубы, образованные в
1907 г. в Томском уезде, на землях Алтайского округа.
(Farmstead lots in the district of Tomsk, settled in 1907
upon the lands of the Altai circuit.) Voprosy kolonizatsii,
3 (n.d.)

12374. Chirkin, G. К вопросу о происхождении земельной общины в Сибири.   (On the question of the origin of communal land-tenure in Siberia.) Voprosy kolonizatsii, 1, 1907.

12375. Andronnikov, I. A. Колонизация Сибири в связи с
землеустройством местного населения.   (Colonization
of Siberia and land allotments of the native population.)
Voprosy kolonizatsii, St. Petersburg, 2, 1908.

12376. Chirkin, G. К вопросу об урегулировании земельных
отношений переселенцев.   (The problem of land regulation
among the immigrants.) Voprosy kolonizatsii, St. Petersburg,
3, 1908.

12377. Chirkin, G. Землеустройство киргизов в связи с
колонизацией степи.   (Land settlement of the Kirghiz in relation to the colonization of the steppe.) Voprosy kolonizatsii, St. Petersburg, 2, 1908.

12378. Andrievskii, A. Значение вопроса о киргизских
зимовках в деле образования переселенческих участков в
Лепинском уезде, Семиреченской области.   (The signifi-

cance of the problem of Kirghiz winter settlements in con-
nection with the immigrant land allotments in the Lepinsk
uezd, Semirechensk province.) Voprosy kolonizatsii, St. Petersburg, 5, 1908.

12379. Отчет по зачислению долей ходокам и водворению
переселенцев в Азиатской России в 1908 году.   (Report
concerning the registering of the land shares by deputies
of the migrating peasants and of the settlement of immigrants in Asiatic Russia in 1908.) St. Petersburg, 1909.

12380. Sokolov, P. Земельный фонд сибирской тайги и значение его для колонизации.   (Land resources of the Siberian
taiga and its significance for colonization.) St. Petersburg, 1908.

12381. Soldatov, V. V. Изменение форм общинного землевладения в Сибири.   (Changing forms of communal land tenure in
Siberia.) Voprosy kolonizatsii, 7, 1910.

12382. Переселение и землеустройство за 5 лет, 1906 - 1909
годы, и отчет по переселению и землеустройству за 1910
год.   (Immigration and land settlement for 5 years, 1906-
1909, and a report concerning immigration and land settlement for the year 1910.) St. Petersburg, 1911. 10 v.

12383. Vvedenskii, I. Частное землевладение в Западной
Сибири. (Private land tenure in Western Siberia.) Voprosy
kolonizatsii, St. Petersburg, 11, 1912.

12384. Vvedenskii, I. Оценка земли в Сибири.   (The val-
uation of land in Siberia.) Voprosy kolonizatsii, St. Petersburg, 14, 1914.

12385. Описание земель предназначаемых для переселения.
(Description of the lands alloted for colonization.) Book
3, Siberia... Moscow, Narodnyi komissariat zemledeliia,
1925. 21 p.

(7) Colonization by Regions

12386. Busse, F. F. Переселвние крестьян морем в Южно-
Уссурийский край в 1883-1893 г. (The immigration by sea of
peasants to the South-Ussuriisk region during 1883-1893.)
St. Petersburg, 1896.

12387. Kirillov, V. N. Движение населения в Верхне-Уссу-
рийском участке Приморской области. 1890-1904 гг. (Population movement in the Upper Ussuriisk district of the

Maritime province. 1890-1904.) Sibirskie vrachebnye vedomosti, 1904:21,22.

12388. Очерк переселенческого дела в Алтайском округе,
1884-1898 гг.(A sketch of the immigration problem in the
Altai region, 1884-1898.) Barnaul, 1900.

12389. Merkulov, S. D. Порто-франко и колонизация Приамурского края русским населением.   (Free-trade and the
colonization of the Amur region by Russian people.) St.
Petersburg, 1908.   (2) The same. Вопросы колонизации Приамурского края.   (Problems concerning the colonization
of the Cisamur region.) St. Petersburg, 1911.

12390. Sokolov, P. I. Население, культура, колонизация
района Туркестан-Сибирской железной дороги.   (The population, culture, and colonization of the territory along
the Turkestan-Siberian railway.) St. Petersburg, 1908.

12391. Описание Приморского переселенческого района.
(Description of the Maritime colonization district.) St.
Petersburg, 1911.

12392. Описание Забайкальского переселенческого района.
(Description of the Transbaikal colonization district.) St.
Petersburg, 1911.

12393. IAkut. К вопросу о переселении в Якутскую область.
(The problem of immigration to the Iakutsk province.) Moscow, 1911.

12394. Украинцы-переселенцы Семипалатинской губернии.
(Ukrainian immigrants of the Semipalatinsk guberniia.) Leningrad, Akademiia nauk, 1930. 253 p.

U. Siberian Exile System

12395. Katorga i ssylka. (Exile and penal servitude). A periodical. Moscow, 1, 1921-

12396. Maksimov, S. V. Сибирь и каторга. (Siberia and penal
servitude.) St. Petersburg, 1871. 3 v.

12397. Foinitskii, I. IA. "Управление ссылки." (Exile administration.) In: Sbornik gosudarstvennykh znanii, 8 (1880).

12398. IAdrintsev, N. M. Ссылка и ссыльные в Сибири.
(The exile system and the exiled in Siberia.) In the miscellany Zhivopisnaia Rossiia; St. Petersburg, 12 (1895):1.

12399. Kennan, George. Siberia and the exile system. New York, 1891. 2 v.

12400. Ссылка в Сибирь. (Exile to Siberia.) St. Petersburg, 1900.

12401. Iden-Zeller, Anita und O. Der weg der tränen. Leipzig, 1924.

12402. Krotov, M. A. Якутская ссылка. (Yakutsk as a place of exile.) 1870's and 1880's. Moscow, 1925. 243 p.

12403. Nikolaev, V. I. "Сибирская периодическая печать и политическая ссылка." (The Siberian periodical press and political exile.) Katorga i ssylka, 1928: 4 (41), 6 (63).

12404. Konstantinov, M."Мартовские дни у Ледовитого океана. Из записок политическ. сс.-каторжан." (The March days on the Pacific. Memoirs of political exiles.) Katorga i ssylka, 2:15:14-48.

XXI. NON-RUSSIANS IN RUSSIAN ASIA

See 10688-10721.

A. Bibliography

12405. Slobodskii, M. "Литература по этнографии Сибири в этнолого-географических повременных изданиях 1901-1917 гг." (Ethnographic literature on Siberia in contemporary ethnogeographic publications, 1901-1917.) Sibirskaia zhivaia starina, Irkutsk, 3-4 (1925):217-240. Also separately, Irkutsk, 1925. 24p.

12406. Zelenin, D. K. Библиографический указатель русской этнографической литературы о внешнем быте народов. (Bibliographical index of Russian ethnographic literature concerning life and manners of various peoples.) Zapiski I.R.G.O., St. Petersburg, 40 (1913):1.

12407. Справочник Народного комиссариата по делам национальностей. (A guide of the People's commissariat for nationalities.) Moscow, 1921. 32 p.

B. Russian Policy

12408. Firsov, N. A. Положение инородцев северо-восточной России в Московском государстве. (Condition of natives in the north-eastern section of the Muscovite state.) Kazan, 1866.

12409. Обзор деятельности Всероссийского национального союза. (Survey of the activities of the All-Russian national union.) St. Petersburg, 1912-

12410. Liubinskii, A. I. Русский национализм как средство борьбы с революционно-инородческим движением. (Russian nationalism as a means of fighting the native-revolutionary movement.) Kiev, 1907. 16 p.

12411. Sergievskii, N. Русское окраинное общество. (Russian border-land society.) St. Petersburg, Balashev, 1908.

12412. Fedorov, P. Вымирание сибирских инородцев. (The gradual extinction of the Siberian natives.) Sibirskaia vrachebnaia gazeta, 29, 1908.

12413. Tyzhnov, I. Эксплоатация сибирских инородцев в XIX в. (The exploitation of Siberian natives in the XIX century.) Vestnik Evropy, 8 (1910).

12414. Sidorov, A. A. Инородческие вопросы и идея федерализма в России. (Native problems and the idea of federalism in Russia.) Moscow, 1912. 68 p.

12415. Stroganov, Viktor. Русский национализм, его сущность и задачи. (Russian nationalism, its essence and problems.) St. Petersburg, 1912. 151 p.

12416. Stalin, K. Национальный вопрос и марксизм. (The national problem and Marxism.) St. Petersburg, 1914. 80 p.

12417. Отечество. (The fatherland.) The nationality problem. Petrograd, 1916. 480, 8 p. [v.I.]

12418. Lazerson, M. Национальность и государственный строй. (Nationality and form of government.) Petrograd, 1918. 187p.

12419. Ogorodnikov, V. I. Из истории инородческих волнений в Сибири. (History of native rebellions in Siberia.) In: Sbornik trudov professorov i prepodavatelei Gosudarstvennogo irkutskogo universiteta, Irkutsk, 1:1, 1924. Also separately, Chita, 1922.

12420. Pletnev, B. D. Национальная проблема в России и методы ее разрешения. (The national problem in Russia and methods for its solution.) Iaroslavl, 1922. 21 p.

12421. Lopatin, I. A. "Национальный вопрос на русском Дальнем Востоке." (The problem of nationality in the Russian Far East.) Problems in ethnography in the Russian Far East. Novyi Dal'nii Vostok, Vladivostok, 4-5 (1923):57-66.

12422. Dimanshtein, S. Прошлое и настоящее. (The past and present.) Life of the peoples of the USSR. Moscow, 1924. 110 p.

12423. Trainin, I. СССР и национальная проблема. (The USSR and the problem of nationalities.) Moscow, 1924. 242 p.

12424. Popov, N. Национальная политика советской власти. (The national policy of the Soviet government.) Moscow, 1924. 127 p.

12425. Шесть лет национальной политики советской власти и Наркомнац. (Six years of Soviet national policy and the People's Commissariat for nationalities.) 1917-1922. Moscow, 1924. 228 p.

12426. Ravich-Cherkasskii, M. Ленин и национальный вопрос. (Lenin and the nationalities problem.) Kharkov, 1924. 96 p.

12427. Bakhrushin, S. V. Сибирские туземцы под русской властью до революции 17 г. (Siberian natives under Russian rule, prior to the revolution of 1917.) Sovetskii Sever, 1926.

12428. Национальный и колониальный вопрос и РКП (б). (National and colonial problems and the Communist party.) Part I. Moscow, 1925. 411 p.

12429. Ota, Sanko. 極東露領ニ於ル黄色人種問題 Ro-ryo Kyokuto ni okeru oshoku jinshu mondai. (The problem of the yellow race in the Russian Far East.) Dairen, S.M. R.R., 1929.

C. The Non-Russian Peoples

12430. "Материалы для истории Сибири." (Sources pertaining to the history of Siberia.) Chteniia v Imperatorskom obshchestve istorii i drevnosei rossiiskikh pri Moskovskom universitete, 4:1-128, October-December 1866. (2) Ogorodnikov, V. I. Русская государственная власть и сибирские

472   Russia

инородцы в XVI-XVIII вв. (Russian government and the Siberian natives in XVI-XVIII cent.) In his: Ocherk istorii Sibiri do nachala XIX v., 2:3. Irkutsk, 1920. Also in: Sbornik trudov i prepodavatelei Gosudarstvennogo irkutskogo universiteta, Irkutsk, 1:1 (1921).   (3) Shashkov, S. S. "Сибирские инородцы в XIX ст." (Siberian natives in the XIX
cent.) Delo, 1867:8,9,10.

12431. Mikhailov, V. Третья Государственная Дума и желтая
опасность. (The third Duma and the yellow peril.) St. Petersburg, 1912. 63 p.

12432. Czaplicka, M. A. My Siberian Year. London, 1915.

12433. Pilsudski, B. Les Polonais en Sibérie. Le Puy, 1918.

12434. Janik, M. L'histoire des Polonais en Sibérie. Cra-
covie, 1928. (2) Grochowski, K. Les Polonais en Extrême-
Orient. Harbin, 1928.

12435. Sokolov, B. "Содружество народов советского Дальнего Востока." (Friendship among the peoples of the Soviet
Far East.) Tikhii Okean, 1:11:49-65, January-March 1937.

D. Legal Rights of Non-Russians

12436. Свод степных законов кочевых инородцев Восточной
Сибири. (The code of laws of the steppe of the nomadic natives of Eastern Siberia.) 1841. (2) Samokvasov, D. IA.
Сборник обычного права сибирских инородцев. (A collection of common law of the Siberian natives.) Warsaw, 1876.

12437. Leontovich, F. I. К истории права русских инородцев.
Калмыцкое право. (Legal history of Russian aborigines.
Kalmuk law.) In: Zapiski Imperatorskogo novorossiiskogo uni-
versiteta, Odessa, 29 (1880).

XXII. SOCIAL LIFE

A. General

12438. Shashkov, S. S. "Очерки русских нравов и обычаев в
старинной Сибири. (Sketches of Russian customs in ancient
Siberia.) Otechestvennye zapiski, 1867:20-22. (2) The same.
"Рабство в Сибири." (Slavery in Siberia.) Delo, 1869:1,3.

12439. Shchapov, A. P. Сибирское общество до Сперанского.
(Siberian society before Speranskii.) Izvestiia Sibirskogo
otd. I.R.G.O., 4 (1873):4,5; 5 (1873):1.

12440. Bakhrushin, S. V. Мангазейская мирская община в
XVII с. (The Mangazeian commune in the XVII cent.) Severnaia Aziia, 1929.   (2) The same. A. Ф. Палицын, русский
интеллигент XVII в. (A. F. Palitsyn, a Russian intellectu-
al of the XVII cent.) Sovetskii Sever, 1926.

B. The Russian Orthodox Church and Its Problems

See 967-1012.

(1) General Accounts

12441. Распределение населения Империи по главным вероиспо-
веданиям.   (Classification of the population of the Empire
by principal religions.) Census. Population 1897. St. Petersburg, 1901.   (2) Хронологический обзор церковно-исторических
событий Сибири и т. д.   (A chronological survey of Siberian church history events.) Tobol'skie eparkhial'nye vedomosti, 1882-1884.

12442. Dolotov, Aleksei S. Церковь и сектанство в Сибири.
(Church and sectarianism in Siberia.) Novosibirsk, 1928.
128 p. (2) Arsenii, bishop. Летопись церковных событий.
(A chronicle of church events.) St. Petersburg, 1900.

12443. Meletii, archimandrite. Древние церковные грамоты
Восточного Сибирского края (1653-1726 гг.) и сведения о
Даурской миссии. (Ancient church charters of the East Siberian region [1653-1726] and data concerning the Daurian
mission.) Kazan, 1876.

12444. Razumovskii, A. Владивостокская епархия за первые
пять лет ее существования (1899-1903). (The Vladivostok diocese during the first five years of its existence, 1899-
1903.) Simferopol, 1906.

(2) Church Schools

12445. Abramov, Nikolai A. "Материалы для истории христиан-
ского просвещения Сибири, со времени покорения ее в 1581
году до начала XIX столетия." (Sources pertaining to the
history of Christian education in Siberia from the time of
its conquest in 1581 until the beginning of the XIX cent.)
Zhurnal Ministerstva narodnogo prosveshcheniia, 81 (1854).

12446. Zverinskii, V. О православных монастырях в Российской Империи.   (Orthodox monasteries of the Russian empire.)
St. Petersburg, 1890.

474   Russia

12447. Сибирские церкви и школы фонда имени Александра III.
(Siberian churches and schools established by the fund in
honor of Alexander III.) St. Petersburg, 1901.

12448. Сибирские церкви и школы. (Siberian churches and
schools, 1894-1904.) St. Petersburg, Kom. Sib. Zh. D., 1904.
119 p.

12449. Miropol'skii, S. Очерк истории церковно-приходской
школы от первого ее возникновения на Руси до настоящего
времени. (An outline of the history of the parochial schools
of Russia from their origin to the present time.) St. Petersburg, 1910. x, 222 p. 2nd ed.

12450. Aleksei, ordained monk. Иркутский миссионерский съезд.
(The Irkutsk missionary congress.) Tomsk, 1910.

(3) Missions

12451. Труды православных миссий Иркутской епархии.   (Publications of the Orthodox missions of the Irkutsk diocese.)
Irkutsk, Irkutsk committee of the Orthodox missionary society, 1878-1883. 4 v.

12452. Труды православных миссий Восточной Сибири.   (Publications of the Orthodox missions of Eastern Siberia.) Irkutsk, 1883-1886. 4 v.

12453. Отчеты годовые православного миссионерского общества.
(Annual accounts of the Orthodox missionary society.)
n. p.

12454. Изложение хода миссионерского дела по просвещению
христианством казанских инородцев.(С 1552 по 1867 год.) (A
narrative concerning the progress of missionary work in the
field of Christian education of natives of the Kazan region,
1552-1867.) Chteniia v Imperatorskom obshchestve istorii i
drevnostei rossiiskikh pri Moskovskom universitete, 1:1-261,
January-March 1880.

12455. Veniamin, archbishop. Жизненные вопросы православной
миссии в Сибири. (The essential problems of the Orthodox
mission in Siberia.) St. Petersburg, 1885.

12456. Miletii, bishop. Пустынник Варлаам, основатель скита
за Байкалом. (Varlaam, hermit-founder of the hermitage beyond the Baikal.) Riazan, 1901.

12457. Vagin, V. I. "Английские миссионеры в Сибири." (English missionaries in Siberia.) Izvestiia Sibirskogo otdela Imperatorskogo russkogo geograficheskogo obshchestva, 4-5 (1870):69-77.

12458. Makarii, bishop. Миссионерство на Алтае и Киргизской степи в 1885 году. (Missionary work in the Altai region and the Kirghiz steppes in 1885.) Tomsk, 1886.

12459. San-Antus. "К вопросу о социально-экономических предпосылках обращения Коми в христианство. (Social and economic premises in the converting of the Komi people to Christianity.) Komi-Mu-Komi krai, Ust'sysol'sk, 3 (61):50-53, February 1929; 4 (62):53-58, March 1929.

12460. Bazanov, A. G. Миссионеры и миссионерские школы на Архангельском севере. (Missionaries and missionary schools in the Archangel North.) Historical sketches. Archangel, 1936. 73 p.

B. The Sectarians

12461. Распределение старообрядцев и сектантов по толкам и сектам. (Classification of the old believers according to creeds and sects.) Census. Population 1897. St. Petersburg, 1901.

12462. Muratov, M. V. К изучению старообрядчества и сектантства в Сибири. (Contribution to the study of sectarianism and the sect of old believers in Siberia.) Irkutsk, 1923. 17 p.

12463. Muratov, M. V. Духоборцы в Восточной Сибири в половине XIX в. (Dukhobors in Eastern Siberia in the middle of the XIX century.) Irkutsk, 1923. 55 p.

12464. Shchepkin, Ivan V. Уральские сектанты прежде и теперь. (The Ural sectarians, past and present.) Sverdlovsk-Moscow, 1930. 48 p.

C. Non-Christian Relgions

12465. Vashkevich, V. Ламаиты в Восточной Сибири. (The Lamaits in Eastern Siberia.) St. Petersburg, 1885. 145 p.

12466. Sosnovskii, I. Ламаизм. (Lamaism.) St. Petersburg, 1898.

12467. Ukhtomskii, Esper. Из области ламаизма. (On Lamaism.)
St. Petersburg, 1904. 128 p.

12468. Popov, A.A. Материалы для библиографии русской литературы по изучению шаманства северо-азиатских народов.
(Sources for a bibliography of Russian literature on the
study of Shamanism of the North Asiatic peoples.) Izd. Instituta narodov Severa TsIK SSSR, 1932. 116, xii p.

12469. Shashkov, S. S. Шаманство в Сибири. (Shamanism in
Siberia.) Zapiski Imperatorskogo russkogo geograficheskogo
obshchestva, 2 (1864):1-105. Also in Sibirskii vestnik,
59-61, 1865.

12470. Banzarov, D. Черная вера или шаманство у монголов.
(The Black faith, or Shamanism, among the Mongols.) St. Petersburg, 1891.

12471. Mikhailovskii, V. M. Шаманство. (Shamanism.) Moscow,
1892.

12472. Anuchin, V. I. Очерк шаманство у енисейских остяков.
(A sketch of shamanism among the Yenisei Ostiaks.) St. Petersburg, 1914. 89 p.

12473. Shirokogorov, S. Опыт исследования основ шаманства у
тунгусов. (An essay in investigating the foundations of
Shamanism among the Tungus.) Vladivostok, Uchenye zapiski
Ist.rfil. fakul'teta Vladivostokskogo universiteta, 1919.

12474. Khangalov, M. "Материалы для изучения шаманства в
Сибири. Шаманство у бурят." (Materials pertaining to the
study of Shamanism in Siberia. Shamanism among the Buriats.)
Izvestiia Vostochno-Sibirskogo russkogo geograficheskogo
obshchestva, 14 (1883):1-2:1-60.

12475. Anokhin, A. V. Материалы по шаманству у алтайцев, собранные во время путешествий по Алтаю 1910-1912 гг. (Sources
pertaining to Shamanism among the Altai natives, collected
during travels through the Altai in 1910-1912.) Leningrad,
Sbornik Muzeia antropologii i etnografii pri Rossiiskoi
akademii nauk, 4 (1924):2. 4,vii, 248 p.

12476. Gondatti, N. L. Следы языческих верований маньзов.
(Traces of paganism among the Manzes.) In: Trudy Etnograficheskogo otd. Obshchestva liubitelei estestvoznaniia, Moscow, 8 (1888).

12477. Shimkevich, P. Материалы для изучения шаманства у гольдов. (Sources for the study of Shamanism among the Golds.) Zapiski Priamurskogo otd. I.R.G.O., Khabarovsk, 2 (1896):1.

12478. Mikhailovskii, V. М. Шаманство. Шаманство у инород-цев Сибири и Европейской России. (Shamanism. Shamanism among the natives of Siberia and European Russia.) Izvestiia Imperatorskogo obshchestva liubitelei estestvoznaniia, antropologii i etnografii, v. 75.

12479. See 12465.

12480. Troshchanskii, V. F. Эволюция "черной веры" (шаман-ства) у якутов. (Evolution of the "Black faith" [Shamanism] among the Yakuts.) Kazan, 1902.

12481. Markov, IU. "Буряты и шаманство."(The Buriats and Shamanism.) Mirskii vestnik, 8 (1871):39-53.

12482. Shirokogorov, S. M. "General theory of Shamanism among the Tungus." Journal of the North-China branch of the Royal Asiatic society, 54 (1922):246-249.

12483. Kosokov, I. К вопросу о шаманстве в Северной Азии. (The problem of Shamanism in Northern Asia.) Moscow, 1930. 78 p.

12484. Zelenin, D. K. "Идеология сибирского шаманства." (Ideology of Siberian Shamanism.) Izvestiia Akademii nauk. Otdelenie obshchestvennykh nauk, series 7. 8 (1935):709-743.

12485. Ionov, V. К вопросу об изучении дохристианских веро-ваний якутов. (The problem of study of the pre-Christian Yakut religious beliefs.) Sbornik Muzeia antropologii i etnografii pri Rossiiskoi akademii nauk, Petrograd, 5 (1918): 1:155-164.

12486. Kulakovskii, A. E. Материалы для изучения верований якутов. (Sources pertaining to the study of the Yakut re-ligious beliefs.) Zapiski IAkutskogo kraevogo geografiche-skogo obshchestva, Yakutsk, 1, 1923. 108 p.

12487. Inostrantsev, K. "Несколько слов о верованиях древних турок." (A few words about the religious beliefs of the ancient Turks.) Sbornik Muzeia antropologii i etnografii pri Rossiiskoi akademii nauk, 5 (1918):1:152-154.

12488. Antsyferov, L. V. Гашишизм в Средней Азии. (Hashishism in Central Asia.) Tashkent, 1934. 45 p.

E. Education and Cultural Conditions

(1) Bibliography

12489. Mezhov, V.Материалы для истории просвещения в России. (Sources pertaining to the history of education in Russia.) St. Petersburg, 1872.

12490. Ulianov, G. K. Обзор литературы по вопросам культуры и просвещения народов СССР. (A survey of the literature on culture and education of the peoples of the USSR.) Moscow, 1930. 246 p.

(2) Periodicals

12491. Статистический сборник по народному просвещению. (Statistical miscellany of public instruction.) Moscow, Narodnyi komissariat prosveshcheniia, 1923/24-   See 10364.

12492. Народное просвещение в СССР. (Public instruction in the USSR.) Moscow, TSentral'noe statisticheskoe upravlenie, 1925/26-   (annual).

(3) Sources

12493. Сборник постановлений по Министерству народного просвещения. (A collection of regulations of the Ministry of public instruction.) St. Petersburg, 1, 1864-

12494. Сборник материалов для истории просвещения в России. (Collection of material on the history of education in Russia.) St. Petersburg, Ministerstvo narodnogo prosveshcheniia, 1893-1902. 4 v.

12495. Rozhdestvenskii, S. V. Материалы для истории учебных реформ в России в XVIII-XIX вв.   (Sources pertaining to the history of educational reforms in Russia in the XVIII-XIX centuries.) St. Petersburg, 1910. xv, 396 p.

12496. Статистические сведения по начальному образованию в Рос. Имп.(Statistical data on primary education in the Russian empire.) St. Petersburg, Ministerstvo narodnogo prosveshcheniia, 1899-1908. 7 v.

(4) General Accounts

12497. Fal'bork, G. and Charnolusskii, V. (ed.). Начальное народное образование в России. (Primary education in Russia.) St. Petersburg, Vol'no-ekonomicheskoe obshchestvo, 1900-1905. 4 v.

12498. Nazarevskii, I. T. Исторический очерк законодательства по начальному народному образованию в России. (Historical outline of the legislation on primary public education in Russia.) Zhurnal Ministerstva narodnogo prosveshcheniia, February-March, 1905.

12499. IUrtovskii, N. S. Очерки по истории просвещения в Сибири. (Sketches regarding the history of education in Siberia.) Novonikolaevsk, 1923. 246, iv p.

12500. Likhovitskii, A. Просвещение в Сибири в первой половине XVIII века. (Education in Siberia in the first half of the XVIII century.) A historical outline. Zhurnal Ministerstva narodnogo prosveshcheniia, 7, 1905.

12501. Kniaz'kov, S. A. and Serbov, N. I. Очерк истории народного образования в России до эпохи реформ Александра II. (An outline of the history of public education in Russia prior to the epoch of reforms of Alexander II.) Moscow, 1910. 240 p.

12502. Shchapov, A. P. "Письмо А. П. Шапова Александру II в 1861 г. (A letter of A. P. Shchapov to Alexander II in 1861.) Krasnyi arkhiv, 19 (1926):150-165.

12503. Народное образование в Западно-Сибирском учебном округе с 1897 г. по 1906 г. (Public instruction in the West-Siberian educational circuit, 1897-1906.) Zhurnal Ministerstva narodnogo prosveshcheniia, 9-11, 1909.

12504. Charnolusskii, V. Земство и народное образование. (Zemstvo and the public instruction.) St. Petersburg, 1911. 2 parts.

12505. Первый общеземский съезд по народному образованию 1911 года. (The first All-zemstvo conference on public education, 1911. Reports.) Moscow, 1911-1912. 2 v.

12506. Charnolusskii, V. Вопросы народного образования на общем земском съезде. (Problems of public education at the general zemstvo conference.) St. Petersburg, Znanie, 1912.

12507. Просвещение в Сибкрае.(Education in the Siberian region.) Novosibirsk, Sibirskii krai, Planovaia komissiia, Statisticheskii sektor, 1930. xxxviii, 105 p.

480   Russia

12508. Ivanitskii, N. S. Нужды народного образования в Приамурском крае. (Needs of public education in the Amur region.) In: Materialy po izucheniiu Priamurskogo kraia, Khabarovsk, 19 (1914). 99 p.

12509. Efanov, Z. D. На фронте просвещения. (On the educational front.) Tashkent, 1924. 41 p.

12510. Furaev, G. Очерк по истории профессионального объединения работников просвещения Омской губернии (1895-1924 гг.) (Historical sketch of the professional organization of educational workers of the Omsk guberniia, 1895-1924.) Omsk, 1924. 43 p.

12511. Состояние просвещения в Сибирском крае. (The state of education in the Siberian region.) Statistical materials. Novosibirsk, Sibirskii krai, Statisticheskii otdel, 1928. xxvi, 114 p.

12512. Материалы для истории академических учреждений за 1889-1914 гг. (Sources pertaining to the history of academic institutions, 1889-1914.) Petrograd, 1917. iii, 631 p.

12513. Manassein, V. S. Возникновение и развитие идеи и учреждения Сибирского университета в связи с историей просвещения в Сибири в первой четверти XIX ст. (The origin and development of the idea for the establishment of a Siberian university in the first quarter of the XIX century.) Irkutsk, 1924. 30 p.

12514. Azadovskii, Mark. "Wissentschaftliche tätigkeit in Sibirien". Slavische rundschau, 1:3:177-182, March 1929.

12515. TSiunchik, I. Просвещение на Камчатке в связи с главнейшими историческими эпохами. (Education in Kamchatka in relation to the main historical epochs.) Vladivostok, 1914. 51 p.

12516. В помощь учителю. (An aid to the teacher.) Collected articles. Novosibirsk, 1935. 96 p.

12517. Chu, Tang (tr.). 新興 俄國 敎育 Hsin-hsing O-kuo chiao-yü. (Education in new Russia.) Shanghai, Chung-hua shu-chü, 1932.

12518. Hsu, Chung-ching. 蘇 俄 之 敎育 Su-O chih chiao-yü. (Education in Soviet Russia.) Shanghai, Commercial press, 1931.

12519. Chêng, I-hua. 新 俄 成 人 的 公 民 教 育 Hsin-0
chêng-jên ti kung-min chiao-yü. (The citizenship education
for adults in new Russia.) Chiao-yü tsa-chih, 23:8, August
1931.

(5) Education of Non-Russians

12520. Инородческое обозрение. (The native review.) Supplement to the magazine "Pravoslavnyi sobesednik." Kazan,
1913 (?) -

12521. Сборник документов и статей по вопросу об образовании инородцев. (A collection of documents and articles pertaining to the problem of the education of natives.) St.
Petersburg, 1869. 522 p.

12522. Zalesskii, V. F. К истории просвещения инородцев
Казанского края в XVIII столетии. (On the history of education of the natives of the Kazan region in the XVIII century.) Kazan, 1911. 19 p.

12523. Труды особого совещания по вопросам образования восточных инородцев. (Transactions of the special conference
concerning the problems of education of the Oriental natives,) Ed. by A. S. Budilovich. St. Petersburg, Minister-
stve narodnogo prosveshcheniia, 1905.

12524. Mashkevich, D. F. О христианском просвещении и русском образовании инородцев Восточной России. (On Christian
enlightenment and Russian education of the natives of Eastern Russia.) Odessa, 1914. 72 p.

12525. Malinovskii, N. "Законодательство об инородческих
школах." (Legislation concerning native schools.) Inorod-
cheskaia shkola (St. Petersburg), 1916:119-157.

12526. Инородческая школа. (The native school.) Miscellany
ed. by G.G. Tumim and V. S. Zenchenko. 1916. 254 p.

12527. Koz'min, N. "Туземная интеллигенция Сибири."(Native
intelligentsia of Siberia.) Sibirskai zhivaia starina, 1
(1923):72-90.

12528. Mainov, I. I. Зачатки народного образования в Якутской области. (Beginnings of public education in the
Yakutsk province.) Irkutsk, 1897. Also in: Sibirskii sbornik, 3, 1897.

12529. I. K."Якуты и просвещение."(The Yakuts and education.) Obraz, 12, 1897.

12530. Chicherina, S. V. Как началось дело просвещения восточных инородцев. (Beginning of education among the orient al aborigines.) Zhurnal Ministerstva narodnogo prosveshcheniia, 9-10, 1907.

12531. Mironov, P. M. Очерк о русско-киргизских школах Уральской области.(Brief description of the Russian-Kirghiz schools of the Ural province.) Zhurnal Ministerstva narodnogo prosveshcheniia, 8 (1910):177-179.

(6) Miscellaneous

12532. Razumov, N. and Sosnovskii, I. Население, значение рода у инородцев и ламаизм. (The population and tribal significance among the aborigines, and Lamaism.) Materialy Komiteta dlia issledovaniia zemlevladeniia i zemlepol'zovaniia Zabaikal'skoi oblasti, St. Petersburg, 6 (1898).

12533. Dmitriev-Mamonov, A. I. Начало печати в Сибири. (The beginning of the press in Siberia.) Omsk, 1891. 82 p. 3rd ed., St. Petersburg, 1900. 72 p.

12534. Выставка культуры народов Востока.(Cultural exhibit of the peoples of the East.) Kazan, 1920. 138 p.

12535. Boldyrev-Kazarin, D. A. Народное искусство в Сибири. (Folk art in Siberia.) Irkutsk, 1924. 18 p.

12536. Faibushevich, D. Большевистская печать на Дальнем Востоке. (The bolshevik press in the Far East.) Moscow-Khabarovsk, 1931. 96 p.

XXIII. RUSSIA AND THE SOVIET UNION IN THE FAR EAST

A. Bibliography

12537. Asatkin, A. N. and Samoilov, V. A. (ed.). Библиография Дальневосточного края, 1890-1931. (Bibliography of the Far Eastern region, 1890-1931.) Moscow, 1935. 40, 415 p.

12538. Grachev, V. A. "Обзор источников по истории Приамурья и Охотско-Камчатского края." (A survey of the sources on the history of the Amur and the Okhotsk-Kamchatka region.) Trudy Gosudarstvennogo dal'nevostochnogo universiteta, Vladivostok, Series 3, 5(1927):1-50.

12539. Georgievskii, A. P. Программа для собирания сведений о старине, быте, творчестве и языке Дальневосточной области. (A program for the gathering of material concerning the history, customs, art and language of the Far Eastern region.) Vladivostok, 1925. 8 p.

B. Maps

12540. Карта Приморской области.   (A map of the Maritime province.) Scale: 40 versts/inch. St. Petersburg, Il'in, n.d.

12541. Карта Амурской области.   (Map of the Amur province.) Scale: 20 versts/inch. St. Petersburg, 1912.

C. Encyclopaedias

12542. Volinskii, V. (ed.). Энциклопедия Дальневосточного края СССР. (An encyclopedia of the Far Eastern region of the USSR.)   [A projected publication.]

12543. Kirillov, N. V. Географическо-статистическии словарь Амурской и Приморской областей.(A geographical-statistical dictionary of the Amur and Maritime provinces.) Blagoveshchensk, 1884.

D. Anthropology--Non-Russians

See 260-272; 10722-10784; 12405-12438.

12544. Shrenk, Leopold I. von. Об инородцах Амурского края. (About the natives of the Amur region.) St. Petersburg, Akademiia nauk, 1883-1903. 3 v.

12545. Przheval'skii, N. M. Об инородческом населении в южной части Приамурской области.   (The native population of the southern portion of the Amur province.) St. Petersburg, 1869.

12546. Soliarskii, V. V. Современное правовое и культурное экономическое положение инородцев Приамурского края.   (Contemporary legal and cultural economic position of the Non-Russian groups of the Amur region.) Khabarovsk, 1916. 173 p.

12547. Resin, A. A. Очерк инородцев русского побережья Тихого океана.(Brief description of the natives of the Russian Pacific coast.) St. Petersburg, 1888.

12548. Shternberg, L. IA. Гиляки, орочи, гольды, негидальцы, айны. (Giliaks, Orochi, Golds, Negidals, Ainus.) Articles and materials. Khabarovsk, 1933. xxxviii, 740 p.

12549. Zeland, Dr. О гиляках. (The Giliaks.) Moscow, 1887.

12550. Shternberg, L. IA. Материалы по изучению гиляцкого языка и фольклора. (Sources· for the study of the Giliak language and folklore.) St. Petersburg, 1908.

12551. Manizer, G. Антропологические данные о Гиляках. (Anthropological data on the Giliaks.) Petrograd, 1916.

12552. Lopatin, I. A. Гольды.(The Golds.) An ethnographic sketch. Zapiski Priamurskogo otdela Obshchestva vostoko-vedeniia, Khabarovsk, 1916. 100 p.

12553. Lopatin, I. A. Гольды амурские, уссурийские и сунгар-ские. (The Amur, Ussuri, and Sungari Golds.) Vladivostok, 1922. 230 p.

12554. Ling, Ch'uan-shêng. 松花江下游的赫哲族、 Sung-hua-chiang hsia-yü ti Ho-chê-tsu. (The Golds on the lower Sungari river.) Nanking, Academia Sinica, 1934.

12555. Anuchin, D. N. Материалы для антропологии Восточной Азии. 1. Племя айнов. (Sources for anthropology of Eastern Asia. 1. The Ainu tribe.) In: Izvestiia obshchestva liubi-telei estestvoznaniia, 20 (1876): 79-203.

12556. Panov, V. A. Желтый вопрос в Приамурье. (The yellow problem in the Amur region.) St. Petersburg, 1910. 66 p.

12557. Pesotskii, V. D. Корейский вопрос в Приамурье. (The Korean problem in the Amur region.) Supplement to: Trudy Amurskoi ekspeditsii, Khabarovsk, 11, 1913. xii, 188 p.

12558. Trave, V. V. Китайцы, корейцы и японцы в Приамурье. (Chinese, Koreans, and Japanese in the Amur region.) Trudy Amurskoi ekspeditsii, St. Petersburg, 11, 1912. iii, 489 p.

12559. Anosov, S. D. Корейцы в Уссурийском крае. (Koreans in the Ussuri region.) Vladivostok, 1928. 86 p.

12560. Vagin, V. "Корейцы на Амуре." (Koreans in the Amur region.) In: Sbornik istoriko-statiskicheskikh svedenii o Sibiri, Irkutsk, 1:2 (1875):1-29.

12561. Nedachin, S. V. "Корейцы-колонисты." (Koreans as colonists.) Vostochnyi sbornik, Izd. Obshchestva russkikh orientalistov, 1:182-204.

12562. Pak, Dinshun. Корейская эмиграция в Россию.(Korean immigration to Russia.) Zhizn' natsional'nostei, 11, 1920.

12563. Serebriannikov, I. I. Албазинцы. (The Albazinians.) Peking, 1922. 15 p.

12564. Hsi-pi-li-ya Hua-chiao jên-shu tsui-chin tung-chi. 西比利亞華僑人數最近統計 (Recent statistics on Chinese emigrants in Siberia.) Wai-chiao-pu kung-pao, 4:5, September 1931.

12565. 赤塔華僑現狀 Ch'ih-t'a Hua-chiao hsien-chuang. (The present condition of Chinese emigrants in Chita.) Nanking, Ministry of foreign affairs, Foreign affairs gazette, 3:5:87, September 1930.

12566. Arseniev, V. K. Китайцы в Уссурийском крае. (Chinese in the Ussuri region.) Zapiski Priamurskogo otdeleniia Geograficheskogo obshchestva, Khabarovsk, 1914.

12567. Yarmolinsky, Avram. The Jews and other minor nationalities under the Soviets. New York, Vanguard press, 1928. 193 p.

12568. Voitinskii, Vl. and Gornshtein, A. Евреи в Иркутске. (Jews in Irkutsk.) Irkutsk, Evreiskii molitvennyi dom, 1915. xvi, 392 p.

12569. Jochelson, Vladimir I. Этнологические проблемы на северных берегах Тихого океана. (Ethnological problems on the northern shores of the Pacific.) Izvestiia Russkogo geograficheskogo obshchestva, St. Petersburg, 18 (1908). 30 p. (2) Jochelson-Brodskaia, D. L. К антропологии женщин племен крайнего северовостока Сибири. (Contribution to the anthropology of the women in the Northeastern Siberian tribes.) Moscow, 1908.

12570. Ivanovskii, I. I. Библиографический указатель книг и статей о Чукчах. (Bibliographical index to books and articles concerning the Chukchi.) Moscow, 1891.

12571. Berkh, V. N. "Разные известия и сказания о Чукотской земле." (Facts and accounts relating to the land of the Chukchi.) Severnyi arkhiv, St. Petersburg, 18 (1825):164-201.

12572. Maidel, G. von. Ответы Чукотской экспедиции на вопросы Академика Бера. (The replies of the Chukchi expedition to the questions of Academician Ber.) In: Izvestiia
Sibirskogo otdela Imperatorskogo russkogo geograficheskogo
obshchestva, 2:1 (1871):60-70.

12573. Grigoriev, V. Чукчи и земля их с открытия этого края
до настоящего времени. (The Chukchi and their land from
the discovery of that region to the present time.) St. Petersburg, 1876.

12574. Bogoraz, V. Краткий отчет по исследованию Чукоч
Колымского округа. (A brief report on the study of·the
Chukchi of the Kolyma district.) Irkutsk, 1899. (2) The
same. Очерк материального быта оленних чукчей, составленный
на основании коллекций Н. Л. Гондатти. (Sketch of the
material life of the Reindeer Chikchi based on the Gondatti
collection.) St. Petersburg, 1901. (3) The same. Материалы
по изучению чукотского языка. (A study of the Chukchi language and folk-lore, collected in the Kolyma district.) St.
Petersburg, 1900. (4) The same. Чукчи. (Chukchi.) English edition, New York - Leiden, 1904-1909. Leningrad,
1934. xxx, 191 p.

12575. Bogdanovich, S. I. Очерки Чукотского плуострова.
(Sketches of the Chukchi peninsula.) St. Petersburg, 1901.

12576. Vasiliev, A. P. Забайкальские казаки.(Transbaikal
cossacks.) Chita, 1917.

12577. Bakhrushin, S. V. Казаки на Амуре. (The cossacks on
the Amur.) Leningrad, 1925. 97 p.

12578. Казаки. (The cossacks.) Anthropological sketches.
Leningrad, Akademiia nauk, 1927. 257 p.

12579. Lopatin, I. A. Орочи -- сородичи Маньчжур. (The Orochi -- kinsmen of the Manchus.) Harbin, 1925. 30 p.

E. General Accounts

12580. Parshin, Vasilii. Поездка в Забайкальский край.(A
journey to the Transbaikal region.) Moscow, 1844. 2 v.

12581. Radde, G. Berichte über reisen im süden von Ostsibir-
ien. St. Petersburg, 1861.

12582. Lezhnin, P. Дальний Восток. Богатства Приамурья и Забайкалья. (The Far East. The wealth of the Amur and Trans-

baikal regions.) Chita, 1922. 91, 354 p. 1 map.

12583. Приморье, природа и хозяйство.(The Maritime region, its nature and economy.) Collected articles. Vladivostok, 1923. iv, 173, 364 p.

12584. Gluzdovskii, V. E. Дальневосточная область.(The Far Eastern region.) Vladivostok, 1925. 240 p. 2nd ed., 1927. 268 p.

12585. Arkhipov, N. B. Дальневосточный край.(The Far Eastern region.) In: Seriia Ekonomicheskaia geografiia SSSR po raionam, Moscow-Leningrad,192 . 159 p.

12586. Georgievskii, A. P. Русские на Дальнем Востоке. (Russians in the Far East.) In: Trudy Dal'nevostochnogo universiteta, Vladivostok, series 3, 3 (1926); 6 (1927); 7 (1928).

12587. Krylov, L. V. "Дальневосточный край, как часть Советского Союза." (The Far Eastern region as a part of the Soviet Union.) Ekonomicheskaia zhizn' Dal'nego Vostoka, Khabarovsk, 3:12-20, March 1926.

12588. See 12584.

12589. Ostrovskikh, P. E. Восточносибирский край. (The East Siberian region.) Moscow, 1932. 40 p.

12590. Diagilev, V. F. Экскурсии в природу Восточносибирского края. (Studies on nature in the East Siberian region.) Irkutsk, 1936. Part 2. 152 p.

12591. Razumov, N. I. Забайкалье.(The Transbaikal region.) Materials compiled by the Kulomzin commission. St. Petersburg, 1899. 349 p.

12592. Sliunin, N. Охотско-Камчатский край. (The Okhotsk-Kamchatka region.) St. Petersburg, 1900. 2 v.

12593. Zepelin, C. von. Das russische küstengebiet in Ostasien (Primorskaja oblastj). Berlin, Siegfried Mittler, 1902. 60 p.

12594. Krahmer, Gustav. Das nordöstliche küstengebiet. (Der Ochotskische, Gischinginskische, Petropawlowskische und Anadyr - bezirk.) Leipzig, Zuckschwerdt, 1902. vii, 295 p.

12595. Журнал совещания по вопросам, касающимся колонизации
Дальневосточных областей. (Proceedings of the conference
concerning the problems of the Far Eastern provinces.) St.
Petersburg, 1908.

12596. See 12606.

12597. Mel'nikov, V. Дальний Восток. Амурская область и о.
Сахалин.   (The Far East. The Amur region and the island
of Sakhalin.) Moscow, 1909. 43 p.

12598. Peace handbook. V. 9. The Russian empire. No. 55.
Eastern Siberia. London, Historical section of the Foreign
office of Great Britain, 1920.

12599. Kobayashi, Kuro. 嚢領沿海地方又北樺太
Ro-ryo enkai chiho oyobi kita Karafuto. (Russian maritime
regions and Northern Sakhalin.) Dairen, S.M.R.R., 1922.

12600. Сборник материалов по политическому и экономическому
состоянию Дальнего Востока.   (Collected materials on the
political and economic condition of the Far East.) Chita,
Dal'nevostochnaia organizatsiia Rossiiskoi kommunisticheskoi partii, 1923. 204 p.

12601. Советское Забайкалье.   Отчет...II Губернскому
съезду советов. (The Soviet Transbaikal region. An account
... to the II Guberniia congress of Soviets.) Chita, Zabái-
kal'skii gubernskii ispolnitel'nyi komitet, 1925. xix, 11,
227 p.

12602. Ichikawa, Tagui. 嚢領沿海地方ノ自然ト經濟
Ro-ryo enkai chiho no shizen to keizai. (The natural sur-
roundings and economic conditions of the Russian maritime
regions.) Dairen, S.M.R.R., 1927. 2 v.

12603. Дальний Восток к концу первой пятилетки. (The Far
East at the end of the first five year-plan.) Khabarovsk,
1930. 51 p.

12604. Gasilovskii, A. N. Дальневосточный край.   (The Far
Eastern region.) Moscow, 1932. 40 p.

12605. Gutstein, Fedor. По побережью Дальнего Востока.
(Along the Far Eastern coast.) Moscow, 1932. 62 p.

12606. Ira, O. G. (ed.). Дальневосточный край в цифрах.
(The Far Eastern region in figures.) Moscow, 1932. 261 p.

12607. Дальневосточный край. (The Far Eastern region.) Khabarovsk, 1934. 52 p.

12608. Arseniev, V. K. В дебрях Приморья. (In the wilderness of the Maritime province.) A geographical sketch. Moscow, 1936. 213 p.

12609. Wang, Hua-yen. 蘇聯遠東設施完況 Su-Lien Yüantung shê-hsi shih-k'uang. (Soviet Russia's construction in Eastern Siberia.) Eastern miscellany, 34:4, February 16, 1937.

F. The Amur Region

(1) General Accounts

12610. Andree, Richard. Das Amur-gebiet und seine bedeutung. Reisen in theilen der Mongolei, den angrenzenden gegenden Ostsibiriens, am Amur und seinen nebenflüssen. Leipzig, Spamer, 1867. xii, 268 p.

12611. Grum-Grzhimailo, G. E. Описание Амурской области. (A description of the Amur region.) St. Petersburg, 1894. 640 p.

12612. Smirnov, E. T. Приамурский край на Амурско-Приморской выставке 1899 года в г. Хабаровске. (The Amur province at the Amur-Maritime exposition of 1899 at Khabarovsk.) Khabarovsk, 1899.

12613. Gruzdev, F. Амур. Природа и люди Амурского края. (The Amur. Nature and people of the Amur region.) St. Petersburg, 1900. 176 p. 1 map.

12614. Приамурье. Факты, цифры, наблюдения. (The Amur region. Facts, figures, and observations.) Moscow, 1909. Supplement to the report of the All-zemstvo organization for 1908.

12615. Karpov, A. Река Амур с его притоками, как пути сообщения. (The Amur river with its tributaries as means of communications.) St. Petersburg, 1909. 134 p.

12616. Труды командированной Амурской экспедиции по высочайшему повелению. (Works of the Amur expedition, dispatched by His Majesty's orders.) St. Petersburg, Amurskaia ekspeditsiia, 1911.

12617. Unterberger, P. F. Приамурский край 1906-1907 гг.
(The Amur region, 1906-1907.) In: Zapiski Russkogo geograficheskogo obshchestva, Otdel statistiki, St. Petersburg,
13 (1912). 428, 21 p.   See also 12654.

12618. Bolotov, A. A. Амур и его бассейн. (The Amur and its
basin.) Harbin, 1925. 36 p.

12619. Valiakhin, S. Николаевский на Амуре порт. (The port
of Nikolaevsk on the Amur.) Its significance, 1923 to Octo-
ber1, 1925. Nikolaevsk, 1926. 169 p.

12620. Wei-chih, Chêng-jung. 黑 龍 江 沿 邊 調 查 記
Hei-lung-chiang yen-pien tiao-ch'a chi. (An account of a
survey of the Amur river basin.) Kuo-wên weekly, 7:35-39,
September 1930.

12621. Hsiao-shêng. 黑 龍 江 俄 領 沿 岸 之 概 光 Hei-lung-
chiang O-ling yen-an chih kai-k'uang. (General condition of
the Russian Amur region.) Chinese Eastern economics monthly,
7:12, December 1931.

12622. Po-chin. 黑 龍 江 沿 岸 之 交 通 狀 況 Hei-lun-
chiang yen-an chih chiao-t'ung chuang-k'uang. (Transportation conditions along the Amur river.) Chinese Eastern
economics monthly, 6:11, 12, November, December 1930; 7:1,
January 1931.

12623. Po-chin. 黑 龍 江 沿 岸 之 一 瞥 Hei-lung-
chiang yen-an chih i-pieh. (A glimpse of the Amur river region.) Chinese Eastern economics monthly, 7:4-5, May 1931;
7:6, June 1931.

12624. Arseniev, V. K. По Уссурийскому краю. (Through the
Ussuri region.) 3rd revised edition. Moscow, 1936. 379 p.

12625. Комсомольск на Амуре. (Komsomolsk on the Amur.)
Moscow, 1936. 128 p.

                (2) Biro-Bidzhan Territory

12626. Druianov, M. B. Еврейская автономная область Биро-
биджан. (The Jewish autonomous province of Birobidzhan.)
Moscow, 1934. 48 p.

12627. Труды Биробиджанской геологической экспедиции, 1933-
1934 гг. (Works of the Birobidzhan geological expedition,
1933-1934.) Collected articles. Leningrad-Moscow, 1937.
197 p.

12628. Vaneev, E. I. Биро-Биджан. Историческая справка.
(Biro-Bidzhan. A historical reference sketch.) Khabarovsk,
1931. 84 p.

12629. Raitsin, E. По Биробиджану. (Through Birobidzhan.)
Sketches. Kharkov, 1933. 88 p.

12630. Goldshtein, M. Биробиджанцы на Амуре. (Birobidzhan-
ians on the Amur.) Moscow, 1934. 132 p.

12631. Trotskii, B. I. Биробиджан в 1935 и 1936 г. (Birobidzhan in 1935 and 1936.) Moscow, 1936. 60 p.

G. Vladivostok

See 12663.

12632. Berezovskii, A. A. К вопросу об экономическом и
торгово-промышленном развитии порта и города Владивостока.
(The problem of economic and industrial development of the
port and city of Vladivostok.) Vladivostok, 1907.

12633. Владивостокский морской торговый порт. (The commercial sea port of Vladivostok.) Vladivostok, 1925. 199 p.

12634. Nikonov, S. "Владивосток и Дайрен. Значение их, как
портов." (Vladivostok and Dairen. Their importance as sea
ports.) Sovetskoe primorie, Vladivostok, 3-4:3-14, March-
April 1926.

12635. Kurteev, K. "Японские банки в Владивостоке."
(Japanese banks in Vladivostok.) Ekonomicheskaia zhizn'
Dal'nego Vostoka, 12 (1923):2-135.

H. History

12636. Müller, G. F. История о странах, при реке Амуре
лежащих, когда оные состояли под Российским владением. (History of the countries lying on the Amur river, when they
were in the possession of the Russian realm.) Ezhemesiach-
nye sochineniia k pol'ze i uveseleniiu sluzhashchie, July-
October 1757.

12637. "Выписки из бумаг Якутского архива, об открытии и
завоевании реки Амура."(Extracts from the papers of the
Yakut archive, concerning the discovery and the conquest of
the Amur river.) Moskovskii telegraf, 2, 3 (1832):266-274,
420-433.

12638. Zenzinov, G. "Исторические воспоминания о реке Амуре."
(Historical recollections about the Amur river.) Six historical documents confirming Russia's possession of the
Amur at the end of the XVII century. Moskvitianin, 7 (1843):
106-118.

12639. Sabir, C. de. Le fleuve Amoûr, histoire, géographie,
ethnographie. Paris, G. Kugelmann, 1861. viii, 160 p.

12640. Ravenstein, E. G. The Russians on the Amur; its discovery, conquest and colonization. With a description of
the country, its inhabitants, productions, and commercial
capabilities; and personal accounts of Russian travellers.
London, Trubner, 1861. xx, 467 p.

12641. Veniukov, M. История реки Амура, составленная из
обнародованных источников, с планами р. Амура. (History of
the Amur river, according to the revealed sources, with
plans of the Amur river.) St. Petersburg, 1859. 148 p.

12642. Veniukov, M. "Исторические изыскания о населении
русских на Амуре." (Historical investigations about the
Russian settlements along the Amur.) Biblioteka dlia chteniia, 3 (1859):22-33.

12643. Veniukov, M. P. Воспоминания о заселении Амура в
1857-1858 гг. (Memoirs, concerning the peopling of the
Amur in 1857-1858.) Russkaia starina, 1879.

12644. Maak, R. Путешествие на Амур, совершенное по распо-
ряжению Сибирского отдела Императорского русского географического общества, в 1855 году. (A journey to the Amur made
by the order of the Siberian branch of the Imperial Russian
geographical society in 1855.) St. Petersburg, 1859. viii,
332, 211, viii, xix p.

12645. Maak, R. Путешествие по долине реки Уссури. (A jour-
néy through the valley of the Ussuri river.) St. Petersburg,
1861.

12646. Collins, P. M. Voyage down the Amoor, with a land
journey through Siberia, and notes on Manchuria, Kamchatka,
and Japan. New York, 1860. 390 p. 4 plates.

12647. Maksimov, S. V. На устье Амура и на море. (At the
mouth of the Amur river and in the sea.) In: Morskoi sbornik, 11 (1861).

12648. Maksimov, A. На востоке: поездка на Амур в 1860-
1861 гг. (In the east: a journey to the Amur, 1860-1861.)
St. Petersburg, 1864.

12649. Andrievich, V. Краткий очерк Забайкалья от древнейших
времен до 1762 года. (A brief account of the Transbaikal
region from ancient times to 1762.) St. Petersburg, 1887.

12650. Tronin, V. История первых времен Амура, 1644-1689.
(Early history of the Amur, 1644-1689.) Blagoveshchensk,
1908.

12651. Gonsovich, E.V. История Амурского края.   (History
of the Amur region.) Blagoveshchensk, 1914. 197 p.

12652. Grachev, V. A. Присоединение Приамурского края к
России. (Annexation of the Amur region to Russia.) Nikol'sk-
Ussuriiskii, 1920. 21 p.

12653. Matveev, Z. N. "История Дальневосточного края."
(History of the Far Eastern region.) Zapiski Vladivostokskogo Otdela Gosudarstvennogo russkogo geograficheskogo
obshchestva, Vladivostok, 3 (20) (1929):2:341-377.

12654. Unterberger, P. Приморская область, 1856-1896 г.
(The Maritime province, 1856-1896.) St. Petersburg, 1900.
324, xx p. See also 12617.

12655. Zolotarev, A. "Из истории народов Амура." (History
of the peoples of the Amur.) Istoricheskii zhurnal, 7:27-
41, July 1937.

12656. TSypkin, S. Дальневосточные большевики на путях к
Октябрю. (Far Eastern bolsheviks or the road to the October revolution.) Khabarovsk, 1934. 170 p.

12657. Vshivkov, P. E. Боевые дни на Амуре.   (Fighting days
in the Amur region.) Moscow-Khabarovsk, 1934. 265 p.

12658. Bezrodnykh, I. Амур в огне. (Amur in flames.)
Sketches of the civil war. Khabarovsk, 1935. 133 p.

I. Economic Conditions

See 11657-12404.

(1) Statistics

12659. Листок Приморского областного статистического коми-

тета за годы 1900, 1901, 1903, 1904, 1908.   (Publications of the Maritime provincial statistical committee for
the years 1900, 1901, 1903, 1904, 1908.) Vladivostok.

12660. Patkanov, S. K. Главнейшие данные по статистике населения Дальневосточной Сибири. (Chief statistical data concerning the population of Far Eastern Siberia.) St. Petersburg, 1911.

12661. Материалы по статистике Забайкальской губернии.
(Statistics of the Zabaikal guberniia.) Chita, Zabaikal'-
skoe gubernskoe statisticheskoe biuro, 1924. 140, 108 p.

12662. Материалы Амурского губернского статистического
бюро. (Publications of the Amur guberniia statistical bureau.) Blagoveshchensk, Amurskoe gubernskoe statisticheskoe
biuro, 1, 1924-

12663. Материалы по статистике Дальнего Востока. (Materials pertaining to the statistics of the Far East.) Khabarovsk, Dal'nevostochnoe oblastnoe statisticheskoe upravlenie, 1, 1924-

12664. Приморская область в цифрах. (The Maritime province
in figures.) Vladivostok, Planning commission of the Maritime province, 1933. 191 p.

12665. Dobrovol'skii, I. D. "Экспорт - импорт - транзит через
Владивостокский порт." (Export - import - transit through
the Vladivostok port.) In: Vneshniaia torgovlia i eksport-
nye vozmozhnosti Dal'nevostochnogo kraia, Moscow, 1926:
81-86.

12666. See 12633.

                     (2) General Accounts

12667. Arshinov, N. V. Экономическая география по районам.
(Economic geography according to regions.) The Far Eastern
region. Gosizdat, 1929.

12668. Экономико-статистический справочник по Восточносибир-
скому краю. (Economic-statistical guide to the East Siberian region.) Irkutsk, Vostochnosibirskii krai, Upravlenie
narodno-khoziaistvennogo ucheta, 1932. 92, 428 p.

12669. Raikhman, E. and Vedensky, B. The economic development of the Soviet Far East. Moscow, Institute of Pacific
relations, USSR council, 1936. 50 p.

12670. Mirotvortsev, K. N. Очерки физической географии
Восточносибирского края. (Outlines of physical geography
of the East Siberian region.) Moscow-Irkutsk, 1933. 161 p.

12671. Природа Восточносибирского края.Фенология. (Nature of
the East Siberian region. Phenology.) Collected articles.
Irkutsk, 1936. 64 p.

12672. Mirotvortsev, K. N. Климат Восточносибирского края.
(Climate of the East Siberian region.) Moscow-Irkutsk,
1934-1935. 206 p.

12673. Bogatkov, G. M. Почвы Восточносибирского края.
(Soils of the East Siberian region.) Moscow-Irkutsk, 1935.
92 p.

12674. Nikolaev, I. V. Почвы Восточносибирского края.
(Soils of the East Siberian region.) Irkutsk, 1934. 164 p.

12675. Shchukin, N. S. "Очерк Забайкальской области."
(A sketch of the Transbaikal province.) Zhurnal Ministerstva vnutrennikh del, 37 (1852):1:11-47.

12676. Отчет Дальэкосо Экономическому совещанию РСФСР. С
приложением брошюры "Камчатка в 1923 году." (A report of
the Far Eastern economic conference to the Economic conference of the RSFSR with an additional pamphlet, "Kamchatka in 1923".) Chita, 1924. 510 p.

12677. Отчет Приморского губернского экономического совещания в С.Т.О. (Report of the Maritime gubernia economic
conference.) For the period January 1 - October 1, 1923.
Vladivostok, 1924. iii, 145 p.

12678. Конъюнктурный обзор народного хозяйства Забайкал-
ской губернии за 1923-1924 год. (A survey of the Zabaikal gubernia national economy, 1923-1924.) Chita, Zabaikal'skaia gubernskaia planovaia komissiia, 1925. 47 p.

12679. Народное хозяйство Дальневосточной области. 1923-
1924 г.(National economy of the Far Eastern province, 1923-
1924.) Khabarovsk, Dal'nevostochnyi revoliutsionnyi komitet,
1925.

12680. Производительные силы Дальнего Востока. Вып. 7.
Транспорт и строительство. (Productive forces of the Far
East. 7. Transport and construction.) Moscow, Konferentsiia
po izucheniiu proizvoditel'nykh sil Dal'nego Vostoka, 1928.
187 p.

12681. Конъюнктурный обзор народного хозяйства Дальневосточного края за 1927-1928 г. (A survey of the national economy of the Far Eastern region for 1927-1928.) Khabarovsk,
1929. lv, 109 p. Also in: Ekonomicheskaia zhizn' Dal'nego
Vostoka, 11-12:71-179, November-December 1928.

12682. Ivanov, A. N."Экспорт леса в Японию из Д.-В. края."
(The export of timber from the Far Eastern region to Japan.)
Ekonomicheskaia zhizn' Dal'nego Vostoka, Khabarovsk, 8-9:
78-94, August-September 1926.

12683. Berezin, E. "Очерк русских портов в Татарском проли-
ве и Японском море." (A description of the Russian ports in
the Tatar strait and in the Sea of Japan.) Morskoi sbornik,
1 (1861):161-170.

12684. Sliunin, N. Промысловые богатства Камчатки, Сахалина
и Командорских островов. (The economic resources of Kamchatka, Sakhalin, and the Commander islands.) St. Petersburg,
1895.

12685. Krasnov, A. По островам далекого Востока. (Among
the islands of the distant East.) travel sketches. St. Petersburg, 1895. 443 p.

(3) Regionalization

12686. Районирование Забайкальской губернии. (The zoning of
the Zabaikal gubernia.) Chita, Zabaikal'skii gubernskii
ispolnitel'nyi komitet, 1925. 58 p.

12687. Материалы по районированию Дальнего Востока.
(Materials pertaining to the zoning of the Far East.) Khabarovsk, Dal'nevostochnaia planovaia komissiia, 1925.

12688. Lagutin, A. N. Районированный Дальневосточный край.
(The zoning of the Far Eastern region.) Vladivostok, 1926.
46 p.

12689. Районы Дальневосточного края. (The zones of the Far
Eastern region.) Excluding Kamchatka and Sakhalin. Khabarovsk, 1931. 224, xcvi p.

(4) Geology and Natural Resources

See 10490-10510.

12690. Batsevich, L. Материалы для изучения Амурского края
в геологическом и горнопромышленном отношении. (Sources

for the study of the Amur region in relation to its geological and mining aspects.) St. Petersburg, 1894. 161 p.

12691. Геологические исследования и разведочные работы по
линии Сибирской железной дороги.   (Geological investigations and explorations along the path of the Siberian railroad.) St. Petersburg, 1896-1899. 20 issues and maps.

12692. Отчет по статистико-экономическому и техническому исследованию золотопромышленности Амурско-Приморского района.
(Report on statistical-economic and technical investigations
of the gold mining industry in the Amur and Maritime regions.) St. Petersburg, 1902-1905. 2 v.

12693. Rippas, P. Ближайшие меры к облегчению развития Приамурского и Удского края.   (Immediate measures to encourage
the development of the Amur and Uda regions.) St. Petersburg, 1907.

12694. Rippas, P. Ближайшие меры к облегчению развития
золотопромышленности горного промысла и колонизации Приамурского и Удского края.   (Immediate measures to encourage the development of gold mining in general and of
colonization in the Amur and Uda regions.) St. Petersburg,
1909.

12695. Anert, E. E. Краткий геологический очерк Приамурья.
(A brief geological sketch of the Amur region.) St. Petersburg, 1913. 199 p.

12696. Материалы по геологии и полезным ископаемым Дальнего
Востока(Publications on the geology and mineralogy of the
Far East.) Vladivostok, Geologicheskii komitet Dal'nego
Vostoka, 1, 1924-

12697. Состояние золотопромышленности Дальнего Востока в
1923-24 опер. году и план работ Горного отдела Дальпромбюро
на 1924-25 опер. год. (Gold mining conditions in the Far
East for 1923-1924 and the plans for 1924-1925 of the Mining department of the Far Eastern economics bureau.) Khabarovsk, 1925. 83 p.

12698. О Томмотских приисках. (The Tommotsk gold mines.)
Blagoveshchensk, Amurskaia gubernskaia planovaia komissiia,
1925. 53 p.

12699. Khlaponin, A. I. Геологические исследования в
Верхне-Амурском районе. (Geological explorations in the
Upper-Amur region.) Collected articles. Moscow, 1932. 102 p.

498   Russia

12700. Rudnev, V. N. Геологические исследования 1930 г. в
юговосточном Забайкалье. (Geological investigations of
1930 in the south eastern Transbaikal region.) Moscow,
1931. 18 p.

(5) Agriculture and Peasantry

See 11778-11938.

12701. Korzhinskii, S. I. Почвы югозападной Сибири. Почвы
Амурской области. (The soils of southwestern Siberia.) Catalogue of the Section on soil science and climatology, at
the All-Russian agricultural expostion of 1895. (On soils
of the Amur region).

12702. Razumov, N. I. Забайкалье.(The Transbaikal region.)
St. Petersburg, 1899. 377 p.

12703. Материалы по обследованию крестьянских хозяйств При-
морск. об.(Sources for the study of rural economy in the
Maritime province.) Saratov, 1911-1912. 4 v.

12704. Материалы, относящиеся до земельного и экономического
положения Амурского и Уссурийского кавачьих войск.
(Sources pertaining to the land and economic situation of
the Amur and Ussuriisk cossack provinces.) St. Petersburg,
Kantseliariia Komiteta ministrov, 1902. 3 issues.

12705. Kriukov, N. A. Восточное Забайкалье в сельскохозяйственном отношении. (The eastern Transbaikal region in relation to agriculture.) St. Petersburg, 1895.

12706. Kriukov, N. A. Западное Забайкалье в сельскохозяйственном отношении. (The western Transbaikal region in relation to agriculture.) St. Petersburg, 1896.

12707. Shchukin, N. S. "Очерк земледельческой промышленности
в Восточной Сибири." (A sketch of agriculture in
Eastern Siberia.) Zhurnal Ministerstva vnutrennikh del, 42
(1853):6:360-417. Also in Trudy Imperatorskogo vol'nogo
ekonomicheskogo obshchestva, 14 (1866):3:220-243.

12708. Golovachev, P. "Приамурье, как русская земледельческая
колония."(The Amur region as a Russian agricultural colony.)
Narodnoe khoziaistvo, 1900.

12709. Bonch-Osmolovskii, A. Хлебный рынок Дальнего Востока.
(The grain market of the Far East.) Khlebhyi rynok, 1,
1925.

12710. Suzuki, Shozo. 露 國 沿 黑 龍 江, 農 業. Ro-koku
en-Kokuryoko no nogyo. (Agriculture along the Russian Amur.)
Dairen, S.M.R.R., 1930.

12711. Vinogradov, S. Амурское земледелие и покупка хлебного
зерна для войск. (Agriculture on the Amur and the purchase
of grain for the Army.) Khabarovsk, 1907.

12712. Shchukin, N. S. "О скотоводстве в Восточной Сибири."
(Concerning cattle breeding in Eastern Siberia.) Zhurnal
Ministerstva narodnogo prosveshcheniia, 27 (1849):9:337-384.

12713. Sosnovskii, G. P. "Древнейшие следы скотоводства в
Прибайкалье." (Most ancient traces of cattle breeding in
the Baikal region.) In: Istoriia dokapitalisticheskikh
formatsii (Moscow, 1933), 210-222.

12714. Tikhonov, N. N. (ed.). Плодово-ягодные культуры
Дальневосточного края. (Fruit and berry culture of the Far
Wastern region.) Moscow-Khabarovsk, 1935. 308 p.

12715. Плодоводство. Дальневосточного края. (Horticulture
of the Far Eastern region.) Moscow, 1937. 124 p.

12716. Berg, L. S. Рыбы бассейна Амура. (The fish of the
Amur basin.) In: Zapiski Imperatoskoi akademii nauk, St.
Petersburg, 24 (1909):9.

12717. Материалы по исследованию землевладения и землепользования в Забайкальсой области. (Materials concerning the
study of land-ownership and land-utilization in the Transbaikal province.) St. Petersburg, 1898.

12718. Kriukov, N. A. Опыт описания землепользования у
крестьян-переселенцев Амурской и Приморской обл. (An essay
on description of land-utilization among the peasant-immig-
rants of the Amur and the Maritime provinces.) Moscow,
1896.

12719. Kaufman, A. A. Земельные отношения и общинные порядки
в Забайкалье по местному исследованию 1897 г. (System of
land-ownership and local management in the Transbaikal region, according to local investigation of 1897.) Irkutsk,
1900.

12720. Kovalev, V. T. О частновладельческих хозяйствах Амурской области. (Private farms in the Amur province.) Khabarovsk, 1902.

12721. Классификация угодий принятая в Амурской партии. (The classification of land property on the Amur.) 2nd ed. Blagoveshchensk, 1908.

12722. Обзор земледельческой колонизации Амурской области. (A survey of the agrarian colonization of the Amur province.) Blagoveshchensk, 1913. 325, 57 p.

12723. Сельское хозяйство Дальневосточной области по данным сельскохозяйственной переписи 1923 г. Губернские итоги. (Rural economy in the Far Eastern province according to the agricultural census of 1923.) Khabarovsk, Dal'nevostochnoe oblastnoe statisticheskoe upravlenie, 1924. 33 p.

12724. Количество хозяйств по Забайкальской губернии и налог падающий на отдельные категории. (The number of farms in the Zabaikal gubernia and the taxes levied on each category.) Chita, Zabaikal'skaia gubernskaia organizatsiia Rossiiskoi kommunisticheskoi partii, 1923.

12725. Материалы по статистике Дальнего Востока. Итоги сельскохозяйственной переписи 1923 года на Дальнем Востоке. Вся Дальневосточная область. Предварительные итоги. (Statistical materials of the Far East. Returns of the census of agriculture in 1923 in the Far East. The entire Far Eastern province. Preliminary returns.) Moscow, 1924.

12726. Brianskii, A. M. Сельское хозяйство Дальневосточной области в годы революции (1917-1923 гг.). (Rural economy of the Far Eastern province during the revolutionary years, 1917-1923.) Khabarovsk, 1925. 35 p.

12727. Предварительные итоги сельскохозяйственной переписи 1923 года в Забайкальской губ. (Preliminary results of the agricultural census of 1923 in the Zabaikal gubernia.) Supplementary issue. Chita, Zabaikal'skoe gubernskoe statisticheskoe biuro, 1924. 15 p.

12728. Оперативный план работ по сельскому и лесному хозяйству на 1924-1925 год. (Operative plan for the agriculture nad forestry in 1924-1925.) Khabarovsk, Dal'nevostochnaia oblast', Upravlenie Upolnomochennogo narodnogo komissariata zemledeliia, 1924. 337 p.

12729. Сельскохозяйственный бюллетень Дальнего Востока. (Agricultural bulletin of the Far East.) Khabarovsk, Dal'nevostochnoe oblastnoe statisticheskoe upravlenie, 1924-

12730. Сельскохозяйственная перепись 1923 г. на Дальнем Востоке. (Agricultural census of 1923 in the Far East.) Village returns. Khabarovsk, Dal'nevostochnoe oblastnoe statisticheskoe upravlenie, 1925. 332 p.

12731. Очерки по землеведению и экономике Восточной Сибири. (Sketches on the agriculture and economics of Eastern Siberia.) In: Izvestiia Vostochnosibirskogo otdela Russkogo geograficheskogo obshchestva, Irkutsk, 1926. 188 p.

12732. Sato, Michio. 黑 領 黑. 龍 江 氣 候 土 壤 Ko-ryo Kokuryuko no kiko, dojo, shokubutsu kenkyu-shi. (Study on the climate, soil, and plants of the Russian Amur district.) Dairen, S.M.R.R., 1927. 2 v.

12733. Ch'ên, Han-shêng and Wang, Yin-shêng. 黑. 龍 江 流 域 的 農 民 與 地 主 Hei-lung-chiang liu-yü ti nung-min yü ti-chu. (Peasants and landlords in the Amur basin.) Peiping, National central research institute, Social science department, Monographs no. 1, 1931.

12734. Соя на Амуре. (The Soy bean in the Amur region.) Narodnyi komissar zemledeliia. Amurskaia oblastnaia sel'-skokhoziaistvennaia opytnaia stantsiia i agbiuro maslozhirsindikata, 1930. 80 p.

12735. Borodin, Ivan V. Вызревание риса на Амуре. (Ripening of rice on the Amur.) Vladivostok, 1933. 40 p.

12736. Drovkin, A. K. Сад в Восточной Сибири. (Gardening in Eastern Siberia.) Moscow-Irkutsk, 1933. 72 p.

12737. Razumov, N. Скотоводство. (Cattle raising.) Materialy komissii dlia issledovaniia zemlevladeniia i zemlepol'zovaniia v Zabaikal'skoi oblasti, St. Petersburg, 13 (1898).

12738. Животноводство Восточносибирского края. (Cattle raising in the East Siberian region.) Irkutsk, 1936. 104 p.

12739. Приморский кооператор. (The Maritime cooperator.) Vladivostok. (Bi-weekly organ of the cooperative organizations of the Maritime region.)

12740. Dneprovskii, S. Кооперация на Дальнем Востоке. (Cooperatives in the Far East in 1922.) Chita, 1923. 52 p.

12741. Крестьянская общественная взаимопомощь. (Peasant social mutual aid.) Chita, Zabaikal'skii gubernskii komitet
krestianskikh obshchestv vzaimopomoshchi, 1924. 81, 15 p.

12742. Кооперация Дальневосточного края. (Cooperatives in
the Far Eastern region.) Khabarovsk, Dal'novostochnyi kraevoi mazhkooperativnyi sovet, 1926. 115 p.

(6) Industry

See 11939-11987.

12743. Kriukov, N. A. Промышленность и торговля Приамурского края. (Trade and industry in the Amur region.) Nizhnii-
Novgorod, 1896. 4 parts.

12744. Отчет Дальневосточного промышленного бюро В.С.Н.Х.
январь-октябрь 1923 г. (Report of the Far Eastern industial
bureau of the Supreme soviet of people's economy.) Chita,
Dal'nevostochnoe promyshlennoe biuro Vysshego soveta narodnogo khoziaistva, 1923. 178 p.

12745. Государственная промышленность Дальнего Востока за
1923-25 гг. (State industry in the Far East for 1923-1925.)
Khabarovsk, 1925. 331 p.

(7) Railroads

See 12146-12216.

12746. Отчет по эксплоатации...за 1923-1924 год. (An account of the operation of the Transbaikal railway for 1923-
1924.) Irkutsk, Zabaikal'skaia zheleznaia doroga, 1925.
504 p.

12747. Отчет по эксплоатации Забайкальской железной дороги
за 1924-1925 год. (An account of the operation of the Transbaikal railway for 1924-1925.) Irkutsk, Zabaikal'skaia
zheleznaia doroga, 1926. 435 p.

(8) Finances

See 12272-12300.

12748. Первый Дальневосточный съезд финработников. 9-14 июля, 1923. (The first Far Eastern conference of finance workers.) Chita, 1923. 242 p.

12749. Госбюджет по Дальневосточной области на 1924-1925 г.
(State budget for the Far Eastern province for 1924-1925.)
Khabarovsk, Dal'nevostochnyi revoliutsionnyi komitet, 1924.
xviii, 82, 63 p.

12750. Финансово-оперативный план Дальцентрсоюза на 1924-
1925 год. (The financial plan of the Far Eastern union of
consumer cooperatives.) Khabarovsk, Dal'nevostochnyi tsentral'nyi soiuz potrebitel'skikh obshchestv, 1925. 68 p.

12751. Местный бюджет Приморской губернии на 1924-1925 год.
(Local budget of the Maritime guberniia, 1924-1925.) Vladivostok, Primorskii gubernskii ispolnitel'nyi komitet, 1925.
11, 115 p.

12752. Концессионные объекты Дальнего Востока. (Concessions in
the Far East.) Khabarovsk, 1925. 2 parts.

12753. Concessions in the Far East. Part 2. Mining concessions. Habarovsk, 1925. 192 p.

12754. Проблемы капитального строительства Восточной Сибири.
(The problem of extensive construction in Eastern Siberia.)
Irkutsk, Irkutskaia planovaia komissiia RSFSR, 1926.

12755. See 12287.

(9) Labor

See 12261-12271.

12756. Материалы по изучению рабочего вопроса в Приамурье.
(Sources for the study of the labor question in the Amur
region.) St. Petersburg, Kantseliariia komiteta po zasele-
niiu Dal'nego Vostoka, 1911-1912. 2 v.

12757. Vil'chinskii, F. L. Рабочие силы промышленных предприятий Приморской области.(Labor in industrial enterprises
of the Maritime province.) Vladivostok, Primorskii oblastnoi statisticheskii komitet, 1904.

12758. Panov, A. "Борьба за рабочий рынок в Приамурье."
(The struggle for the labor market in the Amur region.) Voprosy kolonizatsii, 11 (1912):241-282.

12759. Профсоюзы Дальнего Востока в 1923. (Trade unions in
the Far East in 1923.) Chita-Vladivostok, Dal'nevostochnoe
biuro Vserossiiskogo tsentral'nogo soveta professional'nykh
soiuzov, 1924. 136 p.

12760. Предварительные итоги бюджетного обследования рабочих и служащих Дальнего Востока в марте 1924 года. (Preliminary results of a study of the budgets of the laboring and professional classes of the Far East, March 1924.) Issue I. Budget of a chinese worker in the Amur region. Khabarovsk, Dal'nevostochnoe oblastnoe biuro statisticheskogo truda, 1924. 109 p.

12761. Вторая Дальневосточная конференция профсоюзов. (Second Far Eastern conference of trade unions.) Summaries, results, resolutions, March 31 - April 5, 1924. Chita, Dal'nevostochnoe biuro Vserossiiskogo tsentral'nogo soveta professional'nykh soiuzov, 1924. xx, 46 p.

12762. Дальневосточное совещание профорганизаций. Резолюции. (Conference of the Far Eastern trade unions. Resolutions.) September 21-24, 1924. Khabarovsk, Dal'nevostochnoe biuro Vserossiiskogo tsentral'nogo soveta professional'nykh soiuzov, 1924. 53 p.

12763. Материалы работ первой губернской конференции профсоюзов 11-14 сентября 1924 г. (Records of the first Gubernia conference of trade unions.) Blagoveshchensk, Amurskii gubernskii sovet professional'nykh soiuzov, 1924. 82 p.

12764. Положение труда на Дальнем Востоке. (Labor conditions in the Far East.) Chita, Dal'nevostochnoe biuro Vserossiiskogo tsentral'nogo soveta professional'nykh soiuzov, 1924. 66 p.

12765. Постановления 1-го совещания представителей рабочих кооперативов Дальнего Востока(Resolutions of the first conference of delegates of the Far Eastern labor cooperatives) September 25-27 September, 1924.) Khabarovsk, Dal'nevostochnoe 1-oe soveshchanie predstavitelei rabochikh kooperativov, 1924. 52 p.

12766. Протоколы и резолюции 1-го пленума Забайкальского губпрофсоюзсовета 3-го созыва. (Protocols and resolutions of the first plenum of trade unions of the Zabaikal gubernia.) Chita, 1925. 80 p. Publ. by Zabaikal'skii gubernskii sovet professional'nykh soiuzov.

12767. Материалы к IV-му Приморскому губернскому съезду профсоюзов. (Materials pertaining to the IV congress of trade unions of the Primorsk gubernia.) 1925. 72 p.

(10) Education

See 12489-12536; 12445-12450; 12520-12531.

12768. Труды Государственного дальневосточного университета. (Publications of the Far Eastern state university.) Vladivostok, Dal'nevostochnyi gosudarstvennyi universitet, 1, 1924-

12769. Sokolovskii, I. Русская школа в Восточной Сибири и Приамурском крае. (The Russian school in Eastern Siberia and the Amur region.) Kharkov, 1914. 305 p.

12770. Datskova, A. V. Очерки начального образования в Амурской области. (Outlines of primary education in the Amur province.) Blagoveshchensk, 1910.

12771. Vorotnikov, A. M. Краткий исторический очерк народного образования в амурском казачьем войске. (A brief historical outline of popular education in the Amur cossack community.) Blagoveshchensk, 1913.

12772. Kudriavtsev, P. Церковно-приходские школы Дальнего Востока. (Parish schools of the Far East.) Khabarovsk, 1914.

12773. Ivanitskii, N. S. Нужды народного образования в Приамурском крае. (Problems concerning popular education in the Amur region.) Materials pertaining to the study of the Amur region.) Khabarovsk, 1915.

12774. Народное просвещение в Дальневосточном крае. (Popular education in the Far Eastern region.) Khabarovsk, Dal'nevostochnyi krai, Statisticheskii otdel, 1929. xxi, 453 p.

12775. Markov, K. L. (comp.). Программно-методические материалы для национальных школ Восточного Сибирского края.(Sources pertaining to the programs and methods applied in the national schools in the East Siberian region.) Moscow-Irkutsk, 1932. 56 p.

12776. Начальные и средние школы Дальневосточного края. (Primary and secondary schools of the Far Eastern region.) Khabarovsk, 1935. 275 p.

(11) Communist Party

See 11495-11583.

12777. Lekhov, P. V. "К истории Приамурской Р. К. П." (The history of.the Amur communist party.) Dal'istpart, Chita-Vladivostok, 1 (1923):142-152.

12778. Сборник обязательных постановлений Забайкальского губернского исполнительного комитета советов рабочих, крестьянских и красноармейских депутатов на 1924-1925 г. (A collection of obligatory resolutions passed by the Zabaikal gubernia executive committee.) Chita, 1924. 135 p.

12779. Протоколы и постановления 5 Дальневосточной конференции Р.К.П. 5-8 марта 1923 г. (Protocols and resolutions of the 5th Far Eastern conference of the Communist party, March 5-8, 1923.) Chita, Dal'nevostochnaia organizatsiia Rossiiskoi kommunisticheskoi partii, 1923. 79 p.

12780. Политико-просветительная работа в деревне.(Political education in the village.) Chita, Dal'nevostochnyi politiko-prosvetitel'nyi komitet, 1923. 76 p.

12781. Перед новым годом. Протоколы заседаний и постановление расширенного пленума Приморского губернского исполнительного комитета 18-20 октября 1924 г.(Before the new year. Protocols of the sessions and resolutions passed by the augmented plenum of the Primorsk gubernija executive committee.) Vladivostok, 1924. 126 p.

12782. Два года советской власти в Приморье.(Two years of Soviet rule in the Maritime region.) Vladivostok, 1925. xxxviii, 348 p.

12783. Отчет Дальревкома и Дальэкосо за 1923-1924 г. (Report of the Eastern revolutionary committee and the Provincial economic conference.) Khabarovsk, 1925. 571 p.

12784. Сборник обязательных постановлений. На 1925-1926 г. (A collection of obligatory resolutions for 1925-1926.) Blagoveshchensk, Amurskii gubernskii ispolnitel'nyi komitet, 1925. 92 p.

12785. Два года советской власти в Амурской губернии. (Two years of Soviet rule in the Amur gubernia.) Blagoveshchensk, Amurskii gubernskii ispolnitel'nyi komitet, 1925. 292 p.

12786. Второй Приморский губернский съезд советов, 17-21 фев. 1925 г. (Second Primorsk gubernia congress of soviets.) Vladivostok, 1925. 256 p.

J. Kamchatka

(1) Maps

12787. Карта Камчатки Богдановича. (Map of Kamchatka.) St. Petersburg, Gornyi uchenyi komitet, n.d.

12788. Kell', N. Карта вулканов Камчатки. (Map of the volcanoes of Kamchatka.) Leningrad, 1928.

12789. Восточный берег полуострова Камчатки от м. Столбового до м. Лопатки. (The eastern coast of Kamchatka.) Compiled in 1906, revised in 1911. Scale: 12 miles/inch. St. Petersburg, Glavnoe Gidrograficheskoe upravlenie Morskogo ministerstva, 1911.

(2) History

12790. The history of Kamtschatka and the Kurilski islands ... translated from the Russian by James Grieve. Glocester, 1764. (2) Histoire du Kamtschatka, des îles Kurilski et des contrées voisines publiée à St. Pêtersbourg en langue russe, et trad. par M. E... Lyon, Duplain, 1767. 2 v.

12791. Sgibnev, A. Исторический очерк главнейших событий в Камчатке с 1650 по 1856 г. (Historical outline of the principal events having occurred in Kamchatka in the years 1650-1856.) St. Petersburg, 1869.

12792. Vasenko, P. "Из истории русского господства на Камчатке." (Episodes from the history of Russian domination in Kamchatka.) Russkoe proshloe, 3 (1923):154-156.

12793. Alkor, IA. P. and Drezen, L. K. (ed.). Колониальная политика царизма на Камчатке и Чукотке в XVIII веке. (Colonial policy of tsarism in Kamchatka and Chukotka in the XVIII century.) Collection of archival material. Leningrad, 1935. 211 p. See 11148.

12794. Okun', S. B. Очерки по истории колониальной политики царизма в Камчатском крае. (Outlines of history of the colonial policy of tsarism in the Kamchatka region.) Leningrad, 1935. 149 p.

12795. Ogloblin, N. "Две 'сказки' Вл. Атласова об открытии
Камчатки." (Two 'tales' of V. Atlasov about the discovery
of Kamchatka.) Chteniia v Obshchestve istorii i drevnostei
rossiiskikh (Moscow), 3 (1891):3:1-18.

(3) General Accounts

12796. Steller, G. Beschreibung von dem lande Kamtschatka.
Frankfurt & Leipzig, 1774.

12797. Krasheninnikov, S. Описание земли Камчатки. (A description of Kamchatka.) St. Petersburg, 1818. 2 v.   3rd
ed. [1st ed. St. Petersburg, 1755; 2nd ed. 1786.]

12798. Камчатка, ее естественные богатства и промыслы.(Kamchatka, its natural resources and enterprises.) Pravitel'-
stvennyi vestnik, 17, 1884; 83, 1884.

12799. Margaritov, V. P. Камчатка и ее обитатели. (Kamchatka
and its inhabitants.) Zapiski Priamurskogo otdela Imperatorskogo russkogo geograficheskogo obshchestva, Khabarovsk, 1,
1899.

12800. Sliunin, N. V. Охотско-камчатский край. (The Okhotsk-
Kamchatka region.) St. Petersburg, 1900.

12801. Bogdanovich, K. Очерки Чукотского полуострова.
(Sketches of the Chukotsk peninsula.) St. Petersburg, 1901.
233 p.

12802. Gorovskii, B. Забытые русские земли.(Forgotten Russian lands.) The Chukotka peninsula and Kamchatka. Travel
sketches. St. Petersburg, 1914. 122 p.

12803. Sato, Michio. 勘察加調査書 Kamuchakka chosa-sho.
(Research study on Kamchatka.) Dairen, S.M.R.R., 1927.

12804. Советская Камчатка. (Soviet Kamchatka.) Petropavlovsk-
Kamchatksii, 1930. 28 p.

12805. Polianovskii, Maks L. Среди трех морей. (Between
three seas.) Moscow, 1931. 222 p.

12806. О Камчатке. (On Kamchatka.) Moscow, Kamchatksoe ak-
tsionernoe obshchestvo, 1931. 80 p.

12807. Sergeev, Mikh. "Советская Камчатка." (Soviet Kamchatka.) Sovetskoe stroitel'stvo, Moscow, 8 (60) (1931):81-
96.

12808. Chonaga, Yoshimasa. 九 ム 千 キ ゝ カ 大 觀 Kamuchakka taikan. (A bird's eye view of Kamchatka.) Tokyo, Banrikaku, 1931. 213 p.

12809. Kantorovich, Vladimir IA. По советской Камчатке. (Through Soviet Kamchatka.) Travel sketches. Moscow, 1931. 158 p.

12810. Egorov, D. Земля камчатская. (The Kamchatka land.) Khabarovsk, Ogiz-Dal'giz, 1932. 41 p.

12811. Shabanov, I. На западном берегу Камчатки. (On the western shore of Kamchatka.) Khabarovsk, 1933. 57 p.

12812. Sergeev, M. A. Камчатский край. (The Kamchatka region.). Moscow, Sovetskaia Aziia, 1934. 90 p.

12813. Vasiliev, N. V. (ed.). На Камчатке. (In Kamchatka.) Collection of articles and sketches. Moscow, Academy of sciences, 1936. 213 p.

12814. TSiunchik, I. Просвещение на Камчатке в связи с главнейшими историческими эпохами. (Education in Kamchatka in relation to the most important historical epochs.) Vladivostok, 1914. 51 p.

12815. Zavaritskii, A. N. Северная группа вулканов Камчатки. (The northern group of the Kamchatka volcanoes.) Moscow, Academy of sciences, 1935. 55 p.

(4) Economic Conditions

12816. Bol'shakov, M. Камчатская область. (The Kamchatka province.) Economic sketch. Moscow, 1934. 144 p.

12817. Sergeev, M. A. Народное хозяйство Камчатского края. (National economy of the Kamchatka region.) Leningrad, Academy of sciences, 1936. 815 p.

12818. Shmulovich, I. S. "Камчатка. Экономическо-географический очерк." (Kamchatka. An economic geographic sketch.) Sotsialisticheskaia rekonstruktsiia i nauka, 3 (1936):71-83.

12819. Bol'shakov, M. A."Население Камчатки и его хозяйство." (The population of Kamchatka and its economy.) Sovetskii sever, 11-12 (1931):51-98.

12820. Komarov, V. L. Два года на Камчатке. (Two years in Kamchatka.) Zemlevedenie, 1-2, 1911.

12821. Komarov, V. L. Путешествие по Камчатке в 1908-1909 п (A journey through Kamchatka, 1908-1909.) Kamchatskaia ekspeditsiia Riabushinskogo, Botanicheskii otdel, Moscow, 1, 1912.

12822. Komarov, V. Флора полуострова Камчатки. (Flora of the Kamchatka peninsula.) Leningrad, Akademiia nauk, 1929. 369 p.

12823. Shmidt, P. Камчатская экспедиция Ф. П. Рябушинского. (F. P. Riabushinskii's expedition to Kamchatka.) Zoological department. Moscow, 1916.

K. Sakhalin

(1) Ethnology

See 260-272; 10722-10784;12405-12438.

12824. Funke, м. Die insel Sachalin. Eine ethno-geographische studie. Angewandte geographie. 2 serie, heft 12. Halle a. S., Gebauer-Schwetschke, 1906. viii, 33 p.

12825. Pilsudskii, В. Отчет по командировке к Аинам и Орокам острова Сахалина в 1903-1905 гг. (Report of an expedition to the Ainus and Oroks of Sakhalin, 1903-1905.) St. Petersburg, 1906.

12826. Uralov,   Типы и нравы Сахалина.(Types and customs of Sakhalin.) St. Petersburg, 1906. 26 p.

12827. Alpatov, Lev. Сахалин. (Sakhalin.) An ethnographer's travel sketches. Moscow, 1930. 163 p.

(2) History

12828. Doroshevich, V. M. Сахалин. (Sakhalin.) Moscow, 1907. 2 v.

12829. Isbert, H. Geschichte, natur und bedeutung der insel Sachalin. Dissertation, Bonn, Broch, 1907. 63 p.

12830. Funke, Max. "Geschichlicher abriss Sachalins." Ost-Asien, Berlin, 10 (1907-1908):69-70.

12831. Kowarz, Agnellus. "Aus Sachalins vergangenen tagen."
St. Hedwigskalender. 5 (1929):99-110.

12832. Matveev, Z. N. "К истории Сахалина." (Concerning
the history of Sakhalin.) Vestnik Dal'nevostochnogo filiala
Akademii nauk SSSR, 15 (1935):92-98.

12833. Osnos, IU. "Японская оккупация Северного Сахалина,
1920-1925 гг." (Japanese occupation of Northern Sakhalin.)
Bor'ba klassov, 10:64-75, October 1935.

12834. Aboltin, N. B. "Как был возращен СССР Северный Сахалин." (How Northern Sakhalin was returned to the USSR.)
Severnaia Aziia, 7 (16) (1927):44-54.

12835. Aristov, F. F. "Значение Сахалина в стратегическом
отношении."(The strategic significance of Sakhalin.) Novyi
Vostok, 2 (1922):396-399.

12836. Zepelin, C. v. Die Insel Sachalin. Der kriegsschau-
platz in Ostasien. Berlin, 1905. 18 p.

12837. Funke, M. "Die russische kronkolonie Sachalin."
Deutsche rundschau für geographie und statistik, 29 (1907):
481-487.

12838. "Saghalien." The Japan magazine, 11 (1920-21):533-
549.

(3) General Accounts

12839. Oono, Toun. 樺太地誌 Karafuto chishi. (Topogra-
phy of Sakhalin.) Tokyo, Kokin shoin, 1936. 209 p.

12840. Kantorovich, V. IA. Сахалинские очерки. (Sakhalin
sketches.) 2nd ed., enlarged. Moscow, 1934. 238 p.

12841. Novombergskii, N. Остров Сахалин. (Sakhalin.) St.
Petersburg, 1903. 251 p.

12842. Hawes, Charles Henry. In the uttermost East; being
an account of investigations among the natives and Russian
convicts of the island of Sakhalin; with notes of travel in
Korea, Siberia and Manchuria. London, Harper; New York,
Scribner, 1903. xxx, 478 p.

12843. Labbé, Paul. Un bagne russe l'île de Sakhaline.
Paris, Hachette, 1904. 277 p. 51 gravures.

512   Russia

12844. Sakhalin. Handbooks prepared under the direction of
the Historical section of the Foreign office np. 56. London,
H. M. Stationery office, 1920.

12845. Gluzdovskii, V. E. Советский Сахалин. (Soviet Sakhalin.) Vladivostok, 1926. 50 p.

12846. Ellinskii, B. Сахалин. Черная жемчужина Дальнего Востока. (Sakhalin. The black pearl of the Far East.) Moscow,
1928. 158 p.

12847. Sletov, P. V. На Сахалине. (On Sakhalin.) Sketches.
[Moscow], 1933. 148 p.

12848. Kantorovich, V. IA. Soviet Sakhalin. Moscow-Leningrad, Cooperative publishing society of foreign workers in
the USSR, International press, 1933. 96 p.

12849. Lebedev, E. V. Советский Сахалин. (Soviet Sakhalin.)
Obshchestvo izucheniia sovetskoi Azii, Dal'nevostochnaia
sektsiia. Izd. Sovetskaia Aziia, 1933. 47 p.

12850. Kuznetsov, A. Сахалин. (Sakhalin.) Khabarovsk, Dal-
giz, 1933. 68 p.

12851. Veniukov, M. I. "On the island of Sakhalin." Transl.
from the Russian... by Captain Spalding, 104th regiment.
Journal, Royal geographical society, 42 (1872):373-388.

12852. Basnin, V. N. "Восточная Сибирь." (Eastern Siberia.)
Lieut.-captain Podushkin's memorandum concerning his expedition to Sakhalin. In: Chteniia v Imperatorskom obshchestve
istorii i drevnostei rossiiskikh pri Moskovskom universitete, 2:1-3-188, April-June, 1875.

12853. Miroliubov, I. P. Восемь лет на Сахалине. (Eight
years on Sakhalin.) St. Petersburg, 1901. 287 p.

(4) Economic Conditions

12854. Anert, E. E. Геологические исследования на восточном
побережье русского Сахалина. (Geological studies of the
eastern shore of the Russian Sakhalin.) Report of the 1907
expedition. Trudy Geologicheskoi komissii, new series, 45
(1909). 219 p.

12855. Tikhonovich, N. N. and Polevoi, P. I. Геоморфологический очерк Русского Сахалина. (Geomorphological sketch of
Russian Sakhalin. Trudy Geologicheskogo komiteta, 120 (1915).

12856. Krassnik, A. A. Soils and agriculture on the Sakhalin island. Bulletin Bureau of soils (Leningrad), 1927, 5-59. (In Russian with a conclusion in English.)

12857. Panov, A. A. Сахалин, как колония. (Sakhalin as a colony.) Moscow, 1905.

12858. Sokolov, D. and Tikhonovich, N. Сахалин. (Sakhalin.) Nature, population, natural resources. Moscow, 1925. 126 p.

12859. "Северный Сахалин и его хозяйство." (Northern Sakhalin and its economy.) Ekonomicheskai zhizn' Dal'nego Vostoka, Khabarovsk, 12:148-166, December 1926. By A.Velikopol'skii.

12860. Aboltin, N. V. "Северный Сахалин, его экономическое значение и перспективы." (Northern Sakhalin, its economic significance and possibilities.) Planovoe khoziaistvo, Moscow, 5:270-276, March 1927.

12861. "Экономическое положение Южного Сахалина."(The economic condition of Southern Sakhalin.) Ekonomicheskoe obozrenie, 3 (1927):22-24.

12862. Behaghel, G. The oil fields of Saghalin and the concessions of the China oil company, ltd. Tientsin, 1911. 28p.

12863. Martell, Paul. "Die petroleumfelder auf der insel Sachalin." Asien,Berlin, 12 (1912-13):89-91, 102-103.

12864. Abazov, N. "Сахалинская нефть." (Sakhalin oil.) History of production. Novyi Vostok, Moscow, 12 (1926):121-126.

12865. "Деятельность концессионного предприятия Акционерного о-ва сахалинской нефти." (Activities of the concessional enterprise, The Sakhalin oil co.) Ekonomicheskoe obozrenie, 1 (1928):6-12.

12866. Kirillov, N. V. Морские промыслы Южного Сахалина. (The fishing industry of Southern Sakhalin.) In: Zapiski obshchestva izucheniia Amurskogo kraia, Vladivostok, 7 (1900): no. 7.

(5) Sakhalin as a Penal Colony

See 12437-12440.

12867. Doroshevich, V. M. Как я попал на Сахалин. (How I came to go to Sakhalin.) Moscow, 1903. 163 p.

12868. Kleye, C. F. "Die sträflinge auf Sachalin."Der Ferne Osten, 3 (1905-06):96-113.

12869. Zenbitskii, P. "Половая жизнь в Сахалине." (Sex life in Sakhalin.) Zhivaia starina, 19 (1910):1-2.

(6) Japanese Sakhalin

12870. B., P. Южный Сахалин под властью японцев. (Southern Sakhalin under Japanese rule.) Priroda i liudi Dal'nego Vostoka, 4-5, 1906.

12871. "Russie-Japon. Éxchange de notes en vue d'approuver l'Acte de démarcation entre les possessions russes et japonaises de l'île de Sakhaline, dressé par les commissaires des deux parties à Vladivostok, le 28 mars - 10 avril 1908." Archives diplomatiques, 114 (1910):31-33.

12872. Müller, Max. "Die japanische kolonie Karafuto (Sachalin)." Petermanns geographische mitteilungen, 62 (1916): 1:175-178, 215-220.

12873. Müller, Max. Einiges über kolonisation, ackerbau und viehzucht auf Japanisch-Sachalin und Niederländisch-Indien. Vortrag. Schriften der Ökonomischen gesellshcaft im Königreich Sachsen. Leipzig, Reichenbach, 1918. 17 p.

12874. Правовое положение русских в занятых японцами местностях Сахалинской области. (Legal status of Russians living in the Sakhalin territory occupied by the Japanese.) Vladivostok, 1921. 58 p.

12875. Русский Сахалин, как новая Япония. (Russian Sakhalin as a new Japan.) Collected articles. Vladivostok, 1921.

12876. A., N. Японцы на Сахалине и в низовьях Амура. (Japanese in Sakhalin and the lower region of the Amur.) Zhizn' natsional'nostei, 16, 1921.

12877. Nakamura, Y. The historical relations between Japan and Saghalien. The original of the following article appeared in the Gaiko jiho (Diplomatic review) in March 1923, and was translated by Mr Yeinosuke Nakamura. Tokyo, Foreign office, 1923. 143 p.

12878. "Японский южный Сахалин." (Japanese Southern Sakhalin.) Economic sketch. Sovetskii sever, 1930:3:155-158.

12879. Sasaki, Ryuichi. 樺太拓殖計畫／全貌Karafuto
takushoku keikaku no zenbyo. (General outlook on the colonization plans in Sakhalin.) Tokyo, Chuo johosha, 1935.
195 p.

L. Commander Islands

12880. Grebnitskii, N. A. Commander islands. Transl. by
L. Woehlke. St. Petersburg, 1902.

12881. Stahl, A. Командорские острова и восточный берег Камчатки. (The Commander islands and the eastern coast of Kamchatka.) In: Zapiski po gidrografii, St. Petersburg, 19,
1898.

12882. Suvorov, E. K. Командорские острова и пушной промысел на них. (The Commander islands and their fur-trade.)
St. Petersburg, 1912.

XXIV. AUTONOMOUS BURIAT-MONGOLIAN SSR

See 6447-6872.

A. Bibliography

12883. "Пособия и источники для изучения истории бурят."
(Aids and sources for the study of Buriat history.) Vestnik
Azii, Harbin, 48 (1922):169-173.

12884. Khoroshikh, P. "Указатель историко-этнографической
литературы о бурятской народности." (A guide to historical
ethnographic literature on the Buriat people.) Sibirskaia
zhivaia starina, Irkutsk, 1 (1923):154-178.

12885. Girchenko, V. P., Vil'min, K. M., and Bazhin, A. P.
(comp.). Указатель литературы по Прибайкалью. (A guide to
the literature on the Baikal region.) Verkhneudinsk, 1923.
38 p.

B. Buriat Society Publications

12886. Жизнь Бурятии. (Life of Buriatiia.) Verkhneudinsk,
1, July 1924-   (monthly).

12887. Сборник трудов исследовательского общества   "Saga
Keskile". (Collection of publications of the research society "Saga Keskile".) Yakutsk, August 1925. 112 p. (2) Буря-
тиеведение. (Buriat studies.) Verkhneudinsk, Buriat-Mongol
learned society, 1, 1925-

12888. Бурятоведческий сборник. (The Buriat miscellany.)
Irkutsk, Buriato-mongol'skaia sektsiia Vostochnosibirskogo
otdela Russkogo geograficheskogo obshchestva, 1926. 2 parts.

C. Maps

12889. Карта Бурят-Монгольской АСС Республики, Забайкальской губернии и частей Иркутской губернии и Монголии.
(A map of the Buriat-Mongol republic, Zabaikal gubernia
and parts of the Irkutsk gubernia and Mongolia.) Irkutsk,
1924.

D. Lake Baikal

12890. Taliev, D. N. Байкал. (The Baikal.) A bio-geographic
sketch. Moscow-Irkutsk, 1933. 62 p.

12891. Diagilev, V. F. "Байкал. Географический очерк."
(The Baikal. A geographic sketch.) Sovetskoe kraevedenie,
3:46-61, March 1936.

12892. Dorogostaiskii, V. Ch. Озера Прибайкалья, их природа
и экономическое значение. (The Baikal lakes, their nature
and economic significance.) Irkutsk, 1924. 7 p.

12893. Лоция и физико-географический очерк озёра Байкал.
(Navigation chart and physical-geographical notes of Lake
Baikal.) St. Petersburg, Gidrograficheskoe upravlenie, 1908.

12894. Kozhov, M. M. Моллюски озера Байкала. (Shell-fish
of Lake Baikal.) Moscow, Academy of sciences, 1936. 352 p.

E. Anthropology

See 10722-10784; 12405-12438;12465-12488.

12895. Petrov, G. I. (comp.). Материалы Бурят-Монгольской
антропологической экспедиции 1931 г. (Materials of the
Buriat-Mongolian anthropological expedition of 1931.) [Le-
ningrad], Academy of sciences, 1933. 102 p.

12896. Kovalevskii, G. "О забайкальских бурятах." (Concerning the Transbaikal Buriats.) Kazanskii vestnik, 8 (1829):
26:230-245; 9-10:27:15-54; 11-12:151-214; 2 (1830):28:146-
157; 3-4:283-301.

12897. Astyrev, N. "Монголы-буряты Иркутской губернии."
(The Mongol-Buriats of the Irkutsk gubernia.) Severnyi
vestnik, 1890, 12.

12898. Khangalov, M. N. Юридические обычаи у бурят. (Legal customs among the Buriats.) Moscow, 1894.

12899. Shendrikovskii. Материалы к антропологии бурят. (Materials concerning the anthropology of the Buriats.) St. Petersburg, 1894.

12900. Porotov. К антропологии бурят. (Concerning the anthropology of the Buriats. St. Petersburg, 1895.

12901. Podgorbunskii, I. A. Буряты. (The Buriats.) Irkutskie eparkhial'nye vedomosti, 13-17, 1902.

12902. Turunov, A. N. Прошлое бурято-монгольской народности. (The past of the Buriat-Mongolian nation.) Irkutsk, 1922.

12903. Khangalov, M. N. and Satopliaev, I. Бурятские сказки и поверья. (Tales and beliefs of the Buriats.) Irkutsk, 1889.

12904. Khangalov, M. N. Новые материалы о шаманстве у бурят. (New materials concerning Shamanism among the Buriats.) Irkutsk, 1890.

12905. Krol', M. "О забайкальских бурятах." (The Transbaikal Buriats.) Zapiski Chit. O. R. G. O-va, 1 (1896):1026.

12906. Khangalov, M. N. Свадебные обряды унгинских бурят. (Marriage customs among the Buriats of Unginsk.) Moscow, 1898.

12907. Veselovskaia, N. B. Буряты. (The Buriats.) Moscow, 1901.

12908. Termin, A. I. Среди бурят Иркутской губернии и Забайкальской области. (Among the Buriats of the Irkutsk guberniia and Zabaikal province.) St. Petersburg, 1912.

12909. See 12888.

12910. Zhamtsarano, TS. Zh. Произведения народной словесности бурят. (The lore of the Buriat people.) Bulletin de l' Institut caucasien d'histoire et d'archéologie à Tiflis. 1, 1918. ii, xxiv, 503-648.

12911. Petri, B. "Школа шаманства у северных бурят." (The Shaman school of the northern Buriats.) Sbornik trudov Gosudarstvennogo irkutskogo universiteta, 5 (1923):403-423.

12912. Veselovskaia, B. Буряты. (The Buriats.) Moscow, Kurnin, 1923. See 12907.

12913. Petri, B. E. Брачные нормы у северных бурят. (Matrimonial norms of the northern Buriats.) Irkutsk, 1924. 32 p.

12914. Khoroshikh, P. "Итоги и задачи изучения памятников изобразительного искусства бурят"(Results and problems in the study of the remains of Buriat fine art.) Zhizn' Buriatii, 6 (1924):83-89.

12915. Kliukin, I. A. "Этическая поэзия монголо-бурят." (Ethical poetry of the Mongol-Buriats.) Vostochnaia studiia, 79 (1925):159-171.

12916. Kojeuroff, George P. "Some contributions to the anthropology of the Buriats." British Royal Asiatic society, North China branch, 58 (1927).

F. History

(1) Sources

12917. Bogdanov, M. N. Из истории бурят. (From the history of the Buriats.) Zapiski Sibirskogo otdela Russkogo geograficheskogo obshchestva, Omsk, 38 (1916).

12918. К истории Бурято-Монголии. (Contributions to the history of Buriat-Mongolia.) Materials. Moscow-Leningrad, 1935. 180 p.

12919. Poppe, N. N. Летописи хоринских бурят. (Chronicles of the Khorinsk Buriats.) A reproduction of the Buriat-Mongolian text. Introduction and annotations in Russian. Moscow-Leningrad, Academy of sciences, 1, 1935-

12920. Poppe, N. N. Бурят-монгольский фольклорный и диалектологический сборник. (Collection of the Buriat-Mongol folklore.) Trudy Instituta vostokovedeniia, 21 Obraztsy narodnoi slovesnosti mongolov, v. 5. Moscow-Leningrad, Akademiia nauk SSSR, 1936. 167 p.

12921. See 12928.

12922. Vostrikov, A. I. Летопись баргузинских бурят. (The chronicle of the Barguzinsk Buriats.) Texts and research. Moscow-Leningrad, Academy of science, 1935. 75 p.

12923. Poppe, N. N. Летописи селенгинских бурят. (Chronicles of the Selenginsk Buriats.) Reproduction of the Buriat-Mongolian text with introductory annotations in Russian. Moscow, 1936. 4, 55 p.

12924. "К истории Бурятии в XVII в. Архивные материалы 1629-1705 гг." (Concerning the history of Buriatia in the XVII century. Archival materials, 1629-1705.) Krasnyi arkhiv, 3 (1936):76:156-191.

12925. Сборник материалов по истории Бурятии XVIII-го и первой половины XIX века. (A collection of materials pertaining to the history of Buriatia of the XVIII and first half of the XIX century.) Verkhneudinsk, 1926-

12926. "Хроника Тугултур Тобоева 1863 г." (A chronicle of Tugultur Toboev, 1863.) Materialy dlia istorii buriat-mongolov, Trudy Instituta vostokovedeniia, Akademiia nauk SSSR, 9 (Moscow, 1935), 1-47.

12927. "Хроника Вандана Юмсунова 1875 г." (A chronicle of Vandan IUmsunov, 1875.) Materialy dlia istorii buriat-mongolov, Trudy Instituta vostokovedeniia, Akademiia nauk SSSR, 9 (Moscow, 1935), 49-172.

(2) Accounts

12928. Okladnikov, A. P. Очерки по истории западных бурят-монголов XVII-XVIII вв. (Outlines of history of the western Buriat-Mongols, XVII-XVIII c.) Leningrad, 1937. 424 p.

12929. Gudoshnikov, M. A. and Ubuguné, A. I. (ed.). От царской колонии до советской республики. (From tsarist colony to a Soviet republic.) Moscow-Irkutsk, 1933. 94 p. (2) A later edition, Verkhneudinsk, 1934. 106 p.

12930. Bogdanov, M. N. Очерки истории бурят-монгольского народа. (An outline of the history of the Buriat-Mongolian people.) Verkhneudinsk, 1926. 229 p.

12931. Turunov, A. N. Прошлое бурят-монгольской народности. (History of the Buriat-Mongolian people.) Irkutsk, 1922. 48 p.

12932. Petri, B. E. Далекое прошлое бурятского края. (The distant past of the Buriat region.) Irkutsk, 1922. 43 p.

12933. Koz'min, N. N. К вопросу о времени расселения бурят около Байкала. (The question of the time of settlement of the Buriats along the Baikal.) Trudy Buriato-mongol'skogo uchenogo komiteta, Irkutsk, 1925. 22 p.

12934. Girchenko, Vl. "Хоринские 'происшествия' 1848-1849
годов и православная миссия." (The Khorinsk "events" of
1848-1849 and the Orthodox mission.) Zhizn' Buriatii,
Verkhneudinsk, 1:119-124, January-February 1929.

12935. Ilin, M. "Историческое прошлое Бурятии в Троцкистском
зеркале.   (The historical past of Buriatia in a Trotskist
mirror.) Sovetskaia Buriatia, 2 (1933):61-78.

G. General Accounts

12936. Samoilovich, P. D. Бурят-Монгольская АССР. (Buriat-
Mongolian ASSR.) Moscow, 1934. 117 p.

12937. Koz'min, N. N. Бурят-Монгольская АССР.(Buriat-Mongolian autonomous socialist soviet republic.) Geographical
and economic sketch. Irkutsk-Verkhneudinsk, 1928. 70 p.

12938. Бурят-Монгольская АССР за десять лет.(The Buriat-
Mongolian ASSR after ten years.) Moscow-Irkutsk, 1933.
136 p.

12939. Социалистическое строительство Бурятии за 10 лет.
(Socialist construction of Buriatia in ten eyars.) Verkhneudinsk, 1933. 53 p.

12940. Erbanov, M. N. Строительство Красной Бурятии.(The development of Red Buriatia.) Verkhneudinsk, 1925. 38 p.

12941. Бурят-монгольская автономная область Дальнего Востока.
(The Buriat-Mongolian autonomous province of the Far East.)
Chita, Buriato-mongol'skii revoliutsionnyi komitet, 1923.
120 p.

12942. Бурят-монгольская автономная социалистическая советская республика. Очерки и отчеты 1923-24. (The Buriat-Mongolian autonomous socialist soviet republic.) Verkhneudinsk,
Gosudarstvennaia planovaia komissiia, 1925. 379 p.

12943. Бурят-монгольская автономная советская социалистическая республика. Очерки и отчеты 1925-26. (The Buriat-Mongolian autonomous socialist soviet republic.) Verkhneudinsk,
Gosudarstvennaia planovaia komissiia, 1927. xix, 224 p.

12944. Barshchevskii, D. "Бурят-монгольская автономная ССР."
(The Buriat-Mongolian autonomous socialist soviet republic.)
Sovetskoe stroitel'stvo, Moscow, 55 (1931):2:62-76.

12945. Kireev, B. Бурято-монгольская АССР на пороге второго пятилетия. (The Buriat-Mongolian ASSR on the eve of the second five-year plan.) Moscow, 1933. 32 p.

12946. Ostrovskii, P. IA. Бурято-монгольская АССР. (The Buriat-Mongolian ASSR.) Moscow, 1932. 22 p.

12947. Erbanov, M. N. Бурят-монголы у великого Сталина. (Buriat-Mongols visiting the great Stalin.) Ulan-Ude, 1936. 77 p.

12948. Khangalov, M. N. Несколько данных для характеристики быта северных бурят. (Some data concerning the mode of life of the northern Buriats.) Moscow, 1898.

12949. Dolotov, Aleksei S. Старообрядчество в Бурятии. (The "old-believers" in Buriatia.) Verkhneudinsk, 1931. 52p.

12950. Shashkov, S. S. Предания бурят. (Folk-tales of the Buriats.) Irkutsk, 1889.

12951. Сказания бурят, записанные разными собирателями. (Buriat tales recorded by various collectors.) Irkutsk, 1890.

12952. Poppe, N. N. Бурят-монгольское языкознание. (Buriat-Mongolian philology.) Leningrad, 1933. 119 p.

12953. Поэты Бурят-Монголии. (Poets of Buriat-Mongolia.) Verses. Moscow, 1935. 93 p.

12954. Podgorbunskii, I. D. Русско-монголо-бурятский словарь. (A Russian-Mongolian-Buriat dictionary.) Irkutsk, 1908. v, 340 p. (2) Baradin, B. B. Русско-бурятский словарь. (Russian-Buriat dictionary.) Ulan-Ude, 1935. 195 p.

H. The Communist Party

See 11495-11583.

12955. Gudoshnikov, M., Kuznetsov, I., and Shulunov, F. (ed.) Бурят-Монголия в борьбе за советы. (Buriat-Mongolia in the struggle for soviets.) Collection of memoirs and documents. Irkutsk, 1933. 216 p.

12956. Shulunov, F. "Бурятские национал-демократы и гражданская война в Бурято-Монголии, 1919-1920 гг." (Buriat national-democrats and the civil war in Buriat-Mongolia, 1919-1920.) Bor'ba klassov, 5:49-59, May 1936.

12957. Первый съезд советов Бурят-монгольской социалистической советской респ. (First conference of soviets of the
Buriat-Mongolian socialist soviet republic.) Materials.
Verkhneudinsk, Buriato-mongol'skii oblastnoi s"ezd sovetov,
1923. 39 p.

12958. Резолюции второй Бурят-монгольской областной конференции Российской Коммунистической партии.(Resolutions of the 2nd
Buriat-Mongolian provincial conference of the Russian, communist party.) March 10-15, 1925. Verkhneudinsk, Rossiiskaia
kommunisticheskaia partiia, Buriat-mongol'skaia organizatsiia, 1925. 13 p.

I. Economic and Social Conditions

12959. Бурятия в цифрах. (Buriatia in figures.) Statistical
economic almanach of Buriatia 1927-1930. Verkhneudinsk,
Buriat-Mongol'skaia ASSR, Gosudarstvennaia planovaia komissiia, 1931. 508 p.

12960. Pomus, M. "Советская Бурят-Монголия. Экон.-геогр.
очерк." (Soviet Buriat-Mongolia. Economic geographical
sketch.) Sovetskoe kraevedenie, 3:23-32, March 1936.

12961. Koz'min, N. N. Бурят-монгольская республика-область.
(The Buriat-Mongolian republic-province.) Irkutsk, 1924.
13 p.

12962. Zabelin, K. A. "Очерки по экономике Северобайкаль-
ского района." (Economic sketches of the North Baikal region.) Zhizn' Buriatii, 4:35-57, July 1930.

12963. Кооперация в Бурят-монгольской республике. (Cooperatives in the Buriat-Mongolian republic.) Verkhneudinsk,
Buriat-mongol'skii soiuz kooperativov, 1925. 26 p.

12964. Zhinkin, V. M. Курорты и минеральные источники Бурятии. (Resorts and mineral springs in Buriatia.) Verkhneudinsk, 1925. 51 p.

12965. Единый сельскохозяйственный налог в условиях Бурят-
монгольской республики. (The single tax on agriculture in
the Buriat-Mongolian republic.) Verkhneudinsk, Narodnyi
komissariat finansov Buriat-mongol'skoi SSR, 1924. 88 p.

12966. Kulakov, P. E. Ольхон. Хозяйство и быт бурят Еланцин-
ского и Кутукьского ведомств Верхоленского уезда Иркутской
губернии. (Ol'khon. Occupations and customs of Buriats of

the Elantsinsk and Kutul'sk settlements in the Upper Ol'-
khon district of the Irkutsk guberniia.) Zapiski Imperatorskogo russkogo geograficheskogo obshchestva po otd. statistiki, St. Petersburg, 8 (1898):1.

12967. Chiang-po. 布里雅特蒙古共和國之經济概況
Pu-li-ya-t'ê Mêng-ku kung-ho-kuo chih ching-chi kai-k'uang.
(The economic status of the Buriat-Mongolian republic.)
Chinese Eastern economics monthly, 6:9, September 1930.

12968. Girchenko, Vl. "Социальное расслоение среди бурят-
монголов в XVI-XIX веках." (Social stratification among the
Buriat-Mongolian people during the XVI-XIX centuries.)
Zhizn' Buriatii, Verkhneudinsk, 2 (1929):100-108; 3-4:60-65.

12969. Munkoev, N. I. Десять лет профсоюзов Бурят-Монголии.
(Ten years of Buriat-Mongolian labor unions.) Verkhneudinsk,
1933. 72 p.

12970. Kudriavtsev, V. D. Преподавание русского языка в
Бурятской начальной школе. (The teaching of Russian in
the Buriat primary schools.) Ulan-Ude, 1935. 145 p.

12971. Trebukhovskii, P. F. Бурято-монгольская школа. (The
Buriat-Mongolian school.) Irkutsk, 1931. 46 p.

12972. Программы начальной бурятской школы. (Programs of primary Buriat schools.) Verkhneudinsk, 1933.

12973. Bimbaev, V. Русско-монгольский переводчик халхасского
наречья. (A Russian-Mongolian translator of the Khalkhas
dialect.) Troitskozavsk, 1910. 117, 14, iv p. (2) Boldonov,
N. Русско-бурятский букварь. (A Russian-Buriat ABC book.)
St. Petersburg, 1866.

J. Kiakhta

12974. Stakheev, D. Кяхта. (Kiakhta.) In: Zhivopisnaia Rossiia, St. Petersburg, 12 (1895):1.

K. Nerchinsk

12975. Kotov, A. "Нерчинская Даурия. Экон.-геогр. очерк."
(The Nerchinsk Dauria. An economic geographical sketch.)
Geografiia v shkole, 4:19-27, June-July 1935.

12976. Braginskii, M. A. Нерчинская каторга. (Nerchinsk
penal servitude.) Moscow, 1933. 266 p.

12977. Zhukov, N. N. "Из недр архива. Материалы к истории
Нерчинской каторги. (From the depths of the archive. Materials pertaining to the history of the Nerchinsk penal servitude.) Nerchinskaia katorga, Moscow, 1933, 7-81.

L. Tungusia

12978. Patkanov, S. Опыт географии и статистики тунгусских
племен Сибирипо данным переписи 1897 г. и др. источникам.
(An essay on the geography and statistics of the Tungus
tribes of Siberia according to the census of 1897 and other
sources.) Zapiski Geographicheskogo obshchestva po otd. etnografii, St. Petersburg, 31 (1906).

12979. Mainov, I. I. Некоторые данные о тунгусах Якутского
края. (Some data on the Tungus of the Yakutsk region.) Irkutsk, 1898.

12980. Rychkov, K. M. "The Yenisei Tungus." Zemlevedenie,
3-4, 1917, 1921-1922. Moscow.

12981. Titov, E. I. "Notes on the ethnography of the Tungus,
the Barguzin district of Transbaikalia." Herald of Asia,
Harbin, 52, 1924.

12982. Shirokogorov, S. M. "Northern Tungus migrations. The
Goldi and their ethnical affinities." Journal of the North
China branch of the Royal Asiatic society, 57, 1926. Shang-
hai.

12983. Тунгусский сборник. (A Tungus miscellany.) Leningrad,
Akademiia nauk, 1, 1931-

12984. Rástsvetaev, M. K. Тунгусы Мямяльского рода. (Tungus
of the Miamial tribe.) A social-economic sketch. Leningrad,
Academy of sciences, 1933. 178 p.

12985. Kurilovich, A. P. and Naumov. Советская Тунгусия.
(Soviet Tungusia.) Moscow, 1934. 178 p.

12985a. Postyshev, P. P. Первый партизанский тунгусский от-
ряд. (The first Tungus guerrilla detachment.) Reminiscences
of the civil war in the Far East. Tiraspol, 1935. 39 p.
2nd ed. Moscow, 1935. 70 p.

XXV. AUTONOMOUS YAKUT SSR

A. Bibliography

12986. Gribanovskii, N. N. Библиография Якутии. (A bibliography of Yakutia.) Leningrad, Akademiia nauk SSSR i Yakutskii gosizdat, 1932-1935. 2 v.

12987. Khoroshikh, P. P. Якуты. (The Yakuts.) A guide to historico-ethnological literature of the Yakut people. Irkutsk, 1924. 48 p.

12988. Priklonskii, V. L. Материалы для библиографий Якутской области. (Sources for the bibliography of the Yakutsk province.) Irkutsk, 1893.

B. Maps

12989. Gerasimov, A. S. Описание карты 1924 г. Якутской автономной республики. (A description of the map of the Yakutsk autonomous republic.) Leningrad, Partiia po issledovaniiu rek Lenskogo i Baikal'skogo basseinov Upravleniia vodnymi putiami Sibiri, 1924. 46 p.

12990. Kozhevnikov, M. IA. Описание карты Якутской АССР 1932 г., составленной Советом по изучению производительных сил Академии наук СССР. (Description of the map of the Yakutsk autonomous socialist soviet republic, prepared by the Council for the study of productive forces at the Academy of sciences.) Leningrad, 1933. 66 p.

C. Academy Publications

12991. Материалы по изучению Якутской АСС Республики. (Materials pertaining to the study of the Yakut ASS republic.) Leningrad, Akademiia nauk SSSR, 1925-1932 13 v.

12992. Якутская АССР. (The Yakut autonomous socialistic soviet republic.) Miscellany, ed. by A. A. Grigoriev. Trudy Soveta po izucheniiu proizvoditel'nykh sil. K desiatiletiiu IaASSR. Leningrad, Akademiia nauk SSSR, 1932.

12993. Комиссия по исследованию Якутской АССР в 1925 году. (The Commission for the study of the Yakut ASSR in 1925.) Leningrad, Akademiia nauk SSSR, 1926.

12994. Vittenburg, P. V. Якутская экспедиция Академии наук. (The Yakut expedition of the Academy of sciences.) Leningrad, Academy of sciences, 1925. 154 p.

12995. Краткие отчеты о работах отрядов Якутской экспедиции
Академии наук СССР, 1925-1926 г. (Brief accounts of the
sections of the Yakut expedition of the USSR Academy of
science, 1925-1926.) Leningrad, Akademiia nauk SSSR, 1929.
432 p.

12996. See 12887.

12997. Очерки по изучению Якутского края. (Essays on the
study of the Yakutsk region.) Irkutsk, Geograficheskoe obshchestvo, Vostochnosibirskii otdel, IAkutskaia sektsiia,
1928.

D. Anthropology

See 10722-10784.

12998. Priklonskii, V. L. Материалы по этнографии якутов
Якутской области. (Sources pertaining to the ethnography of
the Yakuts of the Yakutsk province, 1887.)

12999. Gekker, N. A. К характеристике физического типа
якутов.(Materials for the description of the physical chara
racteristics of the Yakuts.) Irkutsk, 1896. (2) Ovchin-
nikov, M. Из материалов по этнографии якутов.
(Selection from the materials for the ethnography of the
Yakuts.) Moscow, 1897.

13000. Vrutsevich, M. S. Обитатели, культура и жизнь в Якутской области. (Inhabitants, culture, and life in the Yakut
province.) St. Petersburg, 1891.

13001. Seroshevskii, V. L. Якуты. Опыт этнограф. исследования.   (The Yakuts. An attempt at ethnographic investigation.) St. Petersburg, Geograficheskoe obshchestvo,
1896. 719 p. (2) Kon, A. IA. Физиологические и биологические
данные о якутах.   (Physiological and biological data concerning the Yakuts.) Minusinsk, 1899.

13002. Jochelson, V. I. Материалы по изучению юкагирского
языка и фольклора, собранные в Колымском округе. (Materials
for the study of the Yukagir language and folk-lore, collected in the Kolyma district.) St. Petersburg, 1900. (2)
The same. Бродячие роды тундры между реками Индигирской и
Колымой. (Wandering tribes of the trundra between the Indigirka and Kolyma rivers.) St. Petersburg, 1900.

13003. Troshchanskii, V. F. Якуты в их домашней обстановке.
(The Yakuts in their homes.) 1908. (2) The same. Наброски

о Якутах. (Sketches on the Yakuts.) Kazan, 1911.

13004. Ionov, V. M. Дух-хозяин леса у якутов. (The spirit-master of the forest among the Yakuts.) Petrograd, 1916. 89 p.

13005. Popov, G. A. "Народность севера Якутии в XVIII веке." (Peoples of the north of Yakutia in the XVIII century.) Sbornik turdov Issledovatel'skogo obshchestva "Saga Keskile", Yakutsk, 3 (1926):3-4.

13006. Togmitov, B. D. Современный ламаизм в Бурятии и задачи дальнейшей борьбы с ним. (Modern Lamaism in Buriatia and the problems of further struggle with it.) Verkhneudinsk, 1932. 48 p.

13007. Kostrov, N. A. Юридические обычаи якутов. (Common law of the Yakuts.) St. Petersburg, 1878.

13008. Kochnev, D. A. "Очерки юридического быта якутов." (The legal customs of the Yakuts.) Izvestiia Obshchestva arkheologii, Kazan, 1899. xv, 5-6.

13009. Pavlinov, D., Vitashevskii, N., and others. Материалы по обычному праву и по общественному быту якутов. (Sources pertaining to common law and social customs of the Yakuts.) Trudy po izucheniiu IAkutskoi ASSR, Izd. Akademii nauk SSSR, 4, 1929. 461 p. (2) Pavlinov, D. Брачное право у якутов. (Marriage law of the Yakuts.) Yakutsk, 1871.

13010. Якутский фольклор. (Yakut folklore.) Ed. by M. A. Sergeev. Leningrad, 1936. 319 p.

13011. Khudiakov, I. A. Верхоянский сборник. Якутские сказки, песни и пословицы. (Verkhoiansk anthology. Yakut tales, songs, and proverbs.) Irkutsk, 1891.

13012. Potapov, S. G. Национальное искусство Якутии. (The national art of Yakutia.) Yakutsk, 1932. 30 p.

E. History

13013. Ksenofontov, G. V. Урянгхай-Сахалар. Очерки по древней истории якутов. (Urianghai-Sakhalar. Outlines of ancient history of the Yakuts.) Irkutsk, Ogiz, 1937. xi, 572 p.

13014. Strod, I. IA. Якутия в прошлом и настоящем. (Yakutia past and present.) Yakutsk, 1933. 40 p.

13015. Popov, G. A. Очерки по истории Якутии. (Essays on the history of Yakutia.) Yakutsk, 1924. 119 p.   (2) Ogorodnikov, Vl. I. Из истории покорения Сибири. Покорение Юкагирской земли.   (From the history of the Siberian conquest. Conquest of the Yukagir territory.) Chita, 1922. Also in: Trudy Gosudarstvennogo instituta narodnogo obrazovaniia v Chite, 1.

13016. Bakhrushin, S. V. Исторические судьбы Якутии. (Historical destinies of Yakutia.) Leningrad, Akademiia nauk SSSR, 1927. 48 p.

13017. Nikolaev, V. Якутский край и его исследователи. (The Yakut region and its explorers.) 1913. 88 p.

13018. Khoroshikh, P. Исследователи Якутии.   (The explorers of Yakutia.) Irkutsk, 1925. 20 p.

13019. Якутская трагедия 22 марта (3 апреля) 1889 года.(The Yakutsk tragedy of March 22 [April 3] 1889.) Recollections and materials. Moscow, 1924-1925. 224 p.

13020. Braginskii, M. A. (ed.). Сто лет якутской ссылки. (A hundred years of Yakutsk exile.) Moscow, 1934. 392 p.

13021. "К истории 'Союза якутов'. Материалы о революционном движении в Якутии в 1906 г." (Concerning the history of the "Union of Yakuts".Materials pertaining to the revolutionary movement in Yakutia in 1906.) Krasnyi Arkhiv, 3 (1936):76:67-82.

F. General Accounts

13022. Kolesov, G. G. Советская Якутия. (Soviet Yakutia.) Moscow, 1937.   (2) Vittenburg, P. (ed.). Якутия. (Yakutia.) Collected articles. Leningrad, 1927. 746 p.

13023. Kosven, M. Якутская республика. (The Yakut republic.) Moscow, 1925. 155 p. 1 map.

13024. Khaldeev, V. Якутская АССР.   (The Yakut ASSR.) Moscow, 1927. 97 p.

13025. Десять лет Якутской АССР. (Ten years of the Yakut ASSR.) Yakutsk, IAkutskoe gosudarstvennoe izdatel'stvo, 1932. 91 p.

13026. Goldin, L. B. (ed.). Якутская республика за десять лет. (Ten years of the Yakut republic.) Collected articles. Moscow, 1933. 138 p.

13027. Pinegin, N. V. В стране песцов. (In the land of arctic foxes.) Leningrad, Izdatel'stvo pisatelei, 1932. 245 p.

13028. Самолет над Якутией. (The aeroplane over Yakutia.) Moscow, 1933. 60 p.

13029. Buzanov, D. I. (ed.). Воздушная служба в Якутии. (Air service in Yakutia.) Collected articles. Moscow, 1934. 224 p.

13030. Anvel't, IA. IA. Самолеты над Якутией. (Aeroplanes over Yakutia.) Moscow, 1934. 56 p.

13031. Meidel, Gerhart. Путешествие по северовосточной части Якутской области в 1868-1870 годах. (Travels in the northeastern part of the Yakut province, 1868-1870.) St. Petersburg, 1896. 2 v.

13032. Chekanovskii, A. L. Дневник экспедиции по рекам Нижней Тунгуске, Оленеку и Лене в 1873-1875 гг. (Diary of the expedition along the rivers Lower Tunguska, Olenek, and Lena, 1873-1875.) St. Petersburg, 1879.

13033. Priklonskii, V. L. Три года в Якутской области. (Three years in the Yakutsk province.) St. Petersburg, 1890-1891.

13034. Melikov, D. I. Отчет старшего советника Якутского областного правления Д. И. Меликова по командировке его в Колымский округ в 1893 г. (Report of the senior counsellor of the Yakutsk territorial administration, D. I. Melikov, on his inspection of the Kolyma district in 1893.) St. Petersburg, 1894.

13035. Strod, I. В якутской тайге, 1922-1923. (In the Yakut taiga, 1922-1923.) Moscow, 1934. 232 p.

13036. Maak, R. Вилюйский округ Якутской области. (The Viliusk district of the Yakut province.) St. Petersburg, 1883-1887. 3 v.

13037. Parkhomenko, S. G. Отчет о поездке в Вилюйский округ. (An account of the journey to Viliuisk.) Materialy Komissii po izucheniiu IAkutskoi ASSR, Izd. Akademii nauk SSSR, 1928. 64 p.

13038. Obruchev, S. V. В неведомых горах Якутии. (In the unknown mountains of Yakutia.) Moscow, 1928. 247 p.

13039. Obruchev, S. V. Колымская землица. Два года скитаний. (The land of Kolyma. Two years of wandering.) The expedition of 1929-1930. Moscow, Sovetskaia Aziia, 1933. 174 p.

13040. Polevoi, P. Анадырский край. (The Anadyr region.) Petrograd, 1915.

G. The Communist Party

See 11495-11583.

13041. Постановления третьей сессии Якутского центрального исполнительного комитета II созыва. (Decrees passed by the third session of the Yakut central executive committee.) Yakutsk, 1924. 23 p.

13042. Бюллетень четвертого Всеялутского съезда советов. (Bulletin of the fourth All-Yakut congress of soviets.) Yakutsk, 1-5, February 2-25, 1926.

13043. Potapov, S. "Социалистическое строительство в Якутской республике." (Socialist development in the Yakut republic.) Sovetskoe stroitel'stvo, Moscow, July 1931, 7 (60):119-129.

H. Economic Conditions

(1) Statistics

13044. Sokolov, M. P. Якутия по переписи 1917 года. (Yakutia according to the census of 1917.) Irkutsk, 1925. 2 issues.

13045. See 12959.

(2) Geology and Geography

13046. Геология Якутской АССР и Чукотского национального округа. (Geology of the Yakut ASSR and Chukotsk national circuit.) Collected articles. Leningrad, 1936. 187 p.

13047. Геофизические проблемы Якутии. (Geophysical problems of Yakutia.) Miscellany, ed. by P. V. Vittenburg. Materialy Komissii po izucheniiu IAkutskoi SSR, Izd. Akademii nauk, Leningrad, 1928. 258 p.

13048. Elenevskii, P. A. "Природа Алданского края." (The nature of the Aldan region.) Prirodnye resursy IUzhnoi IAkutii (Moscow, 1933), 10-79.

13049. Tugarinov, A. IA. Общий обзор фауны Якутии. (A general survey of the fauna of Yakutia.) Leningrad, Akademiia nauk SSSR, 1927.

13050. Petrov, V. A. Флора Якутии.(The flora of Yakutia.) Leningrad, Akademiia nauk SSSR, 1930. 221 p.

13051. Vize, V. IU. Климат Якутии. (The climate of Yakutia.) Leningrad, Akademiia nauk SSSR, 1927. 33 p.

(3) General Accounts

13052. Kolesov, G. G. Сельское хозяйство Якутии. (Rural economy of Yakutia.) Summaries. Problems. Perspectives. Yakutsk, 1932. vii, 199 p.

13053. Volens, N. V. Очерк хозяйственного строя Якутии. (A study of the economic organization of Yakutia.) Leningrad, Akademiia nauk SSSR, 1927. 28 p.

13054. Krotov, Viktor A. Земледелие в бассейне Колымы. (Agriculture in the Kolyma basin.) Moscow, 1932. 220 p.

13055. Kolesov, G. G. Колхозы Якутии по переписи 1930 г. (Collectivized farms of Yakutia according to the 1932 census.) Yakutsk, 1931. xxv, 125 p.

13056. Народно-хозяйственный план Якутской АССР на 1932 год. (The national economic plan of the Yakut ASSR for 1932.) Yakutsk, Gosudarstvennaia planovaia komissiia, 1932. xx, 182 p.

13057. Генеральный план реконструкции народного хозяйства Якутской автономной ССР на ближайшие 10-15 лет. (A general plan for the reconstruction of national economy of the Yakut ASSR for the coming 10-15 years.) Yakutsk, Gosudarstvennaia planovaia komissiia, 1927. 235 p.

13058. О пятилетнем плане развития народного хозяйства Якутской АССР. (The five-year plan for the economic development of the Yakut ASSR.) Yakutsk, Gosudarstvennaia planovaia komissiia, 1929. xviii, 75 p.

13059. Материалы по изучению сельского хозяйства Якутского округа по данным Агрономического отряда Якутской экспедиции Академии наук СССР 1926 г. (Materials for the study of rural economy in the Yakutsk circuit.) Leningrad, 1930. 388 p.

13060. К экономическим вопросам Якутии. (Economic problems of Yakutia.) Yakutsk, 1924. 34 p.

13061. Khaldeev, V. D. Крестьянское хозяйство Якутии в войне и революции. (Rural economy in Yakutia during the war and revolution.) Leningrad, 1924. 74 p.

13062. Итоги земельной переписи в Якутии. (Results of the land census in Yakutia.) Moscow, Statisticheskoe upravlenie Iakutskoi SSR, 1924. 25 p.

13063. Налоги и сборы в ЯАССР. (Taxation and collection in the IaASSR.) A collection of instructions, orders, regulations... Yakutsk, Narodnyi komissariat finansov IaSSR, 1924. 140 p.

13064. Levental, L. G. "Подати, повинности и земля у якутов (от 1766 г.)." (Taxation, duties, and land among the Yakuts.) Trudy Komissii po izucheniiu IAkutskoi avtonomnoi sovetskoi sotsialisticheskoi respubliki, Leningrad, 1929: 4:221-448.

13065. Окружной и волостной бюджет ЯАССР. (Regional and county budgets in the Yakut ASSR.) Yakutsk, Narkomfin IaSSR, 1924. 107 p.

13066. Potapov, S. "Реконструкция народного хозяйства Якутии." (Reconstruction of the national economy of Yakutia.) Sovetskaia Aziia, 7-8:202-210, July-August 1931.

13067. Shchukin, Nikolai S. О хлебопашестве в Якутской области. (Farming in the Yakut province.) Zhurnal Ministerstva vnutrennikh del, 4, 1846. (2) Krasovskii, M. A. Русские в Якутской области в XVII в. (Russians in the Yakut province in the XVII century.) In: Izvestiia Obshchestva istorii, arkheologii i etnografii pri Kazanskom universitete, Kazan, 12 (1894):2.

13068. Mainov, I. I. Русские крестьяне и оседлые инородцы Якутской области. (Russian peasants and the settled natives of the Yakut province.) St. Petersburg, 1913. 292 p. [Zapiski Russkogo geograficheskogo obshchestva, v. 12.]

13069. Nedrigailov, S. N. (ed.). Лесные ресурсы Якутии.
(The forest resources of Yakutia.) Collected articles. Leningrad, 1932. 179 p.

13070. Elenevskii, P. A., Kremnev, A. I., and others. Природные ресурсы Южной Якутии в связи с социалистической реконструкции сельского хозяйства. (Natural resources of Southern Yakutia in relation to the socialist reconstruction of
rural economy.) Moscow, 1933. 148 p.

13071. Krotov, M. A. Работа ЯАССР на экспорт в 1932 году и
задачи 1933 года. (Activity of the IaASSR in relation to
export in 1932 and the problems of 1933.)· Yakutsk, 1933.
17 p.

I. Along the Lena

13072. Borisov, P. Современное состояние рыбного промысла
в низовьях реки Лены и пути его развития. (The present condition of the fishing industry in the lower part of the
Lena river and means for its development.) Materialy Komissii po izucheniiu IAkutskoi SSR, Leningrad, Akademiia nauk
SSSR, 1928. 32 p.

13073. Bogdanovskii, A. Ленская дорога и ее экономическое
значение. (The Lena route and its economic significance.)
St. Petersburg, 1911. 296 p.

13074. Lenin, V. I. О ленских событиях. (Concerning the
Lena events.) Moscow, 1937. 64 p.

13075. Vladimirova, V. F. (comp.). Событие на Лене в документах. (The Lena events in documents.) Moscow, 1932. 86 p.

13076. Takopulo, T. Ленский расстрел. (The Lena executions.)
Moscow, 1932.

13077. Ленско-Колымская экспедиция 1909 г. под начальством
К. А. Воллосовича. (The Lena-Kolymsk expedition of 1909 under the leadership of K. A. Vollosovich.) Leningrad, Akademiia nauk, 1930. 395 p.

J. Dictionaries

13078. Popov, I. N. Якутско-русский словарь. (Yakut-Russian
dictionary.) Yakutsk, 1931. 1v, 288 p.

534 Russia

13079. Pekarskii, E. K. Словарь якутского языка. (Yakut dictionary.) Yakutsk, 1899.

XXVI. THE SIBERIAN REGION (SIBIRSKII KRAI)

A. The Siberian Region

13080. Boldyrev, V. and Skurskii, F. Сибирский край в цифрах. (The Siberian region in figures.) Sibkraiizdat, 1925.

B. Along the Yenisei

(1) Maps

13081. Карта Енисейской губернии. (Map of the Yenisei gubernia.) Scale: 50 versts/inch. St. Petersburg, Il'in, n.d.

(2) General Accounts

13082. Ископаемые растения Иркутского угленосного бассейна. (Fossil plants of the Irkutsk coal basin.) Izvestiia Sibirskogo otdeleniia Geologicheskogo komiteta, Tomsk, 4 (1924): 2. 39 p.

13083. Klements, D. Архив Енисейского музея. (Archives of the Yeniseisk museum.) Tomsk, 1886.

13084. Chudnovskii, S. Енисейская губерния к 300-летнему юбилею Сибири. (The Yenisei gubernia contribution to the 300 anniversary of Siberia.) Tomsk, 1885. 195 p.

13085. Smirnov, V. A. Исторический очерк Енисейского края. (A historical sketch on the Yenisei region.) Krasnodar, 1926.

13086. Zavadskii-Krasnoploskii, A. K. Очерк Енисейской губернии. (A sketch of the Yenisei gubernia.) Krasnoiarsk, 1885.

13087. Lebedev, N. K. Енисейский район. (The Yenisei region.) Moscow, 1929. 68 p.

13088. Latkin, N. V. Енисейская губерния, ее прошлое и настоящее. (The Enisei gubernia: its past and present.) St. Petersburg, 1892. 466 p.

13089. Latkin, N. V. Красноярский округ Енисейской губернии. (The Krasnoiarsk circuit of the Yenisei gubernia.) St. Petersburg, 1890.

13090. Obruchev, S. V. Тунгусский бассейн. Южная и западная части. (The Tungus basin. Southern and western parts.) Leningrad, 1933. 353 p.

13091. Protopopov, K. I. "Енисейская политическая ссылка от декабристов до 1917 года." (The Yenisei political exile system from the Decembrists to 1917.) Eniseiskaia ssylka, Moscow, 1934. 5-16.

13092. Kalmykova, K. V. "Политическая ссылка бывшей Енисейской губернии в цифрах. (Political exile system of the former Yenisei gubernia in figures.) Eniseiskaia ssylka, Moscow, 1934. 144-157.

13093. Kon, F. IA. "В Минусинске. Воспоминания о Енисейской ссылке 90-х годов." (In Minusinsk. Reminiscences concerning the Yenisei system of the 90's.) Eniseiskaia ssylka, Moscow, 1934. 54-68.

13094. Shapovalov, A. S. "Минусинский округ. Место ссылки т. Ленина. Воспоминания о енисейской ссылке 90-х годов." (The Minusinsk circuit. The place of exile of comrade Lenin. Reminiscences of the Yenisei exile system of the 90's.) Eniseiskaia ssylka, Moscow, 1934. 33-53.

13095. Kriukov, N. A. Западное Забайкалье в сельскохозяйственном отношении. (Agriculture in the Western Transbaikal region.) St. Petersburg, 1896.

13096. Материалы по исследованию землепользования и хозяйственного быта сельского населения Иркутской и Енисейской губерний. (Materials concerning the study of land utilization and economic conditions of the rural population of the Irkutsk and Yenisei gubernia.) Irkutsk, 1889-1893. 4 v.

13097. Edel'shtein, IA. S. Геоморфологический очерк Минусинского края. (A geomorphological sketch of the Minusinsk rerion.) Moscow, Akademiia nauk, 1936. 82 p.

13098. Kuznetsov, A. A. and Kulikov, P. E. Минусинские и Ачинские инородцы. (The Minusinsk and Achinsk aborigines.) Krasnoiarsk, 1898.

13099. Matseevskii and Poiarkov. Краткие этнографические заметки о туземцах бывшего Кульджинского района.(Brief ethnographic notes on the natives of the former Kulja district.) Omsk, 1883.

13100. Grigoriev, V. IU. К вопросу о поземельном устройстве инородцев Минусинского края.   (The problem of land settlement among the aborigines of the Minusinsk region.) St. Petersburg, 1906. 133 p.

13101. Lappo, D. Общественное управление минусинских инородцев в 1909 г.   (Public administration among the Minusinsk aboriginies in 1909.)

13102. Argunov, Pavel. Очерки сельского хозяйства Минусинского края и объяснительный каталог сел.-хоз. отдела музея. (Essays on the Minusinsk province and an explanatory catalogue of the agricultural museum.) Kazan, 1892.

13103. Stasevich, A. N. Почвенные исследования в Минусинском уезде, Енисейской губ. (Soil investigations in the Minusinsk uezd, Yenisei gubernia.) St. Petersburg, 1911.

13104. Vatin, V. A. Город Минусинск. (The city of Minusinsk. A historical essay.) Minusinsk, 1916-1922.

13105. Krapotkin, A. A. Саянский хребет и Минусинский округ. (The Saian ridge and the Minusinsk circuit.) In: Zhivopisnaia Rossiia, St. Petersburg, 12 (1895):1.

13106. Prazdnikov, A. A. and Sborovskii, N. A. Нарымский край. (The Narym region.) Tomsk, 1910.

13107. Kiselev, S. V. Разложение рода и феодализм на Енисее. (Disintegration of the clan and feudalism on the Yenisei.) Leningrad, 1933. 34 p.

13108. Shukhov, Innokentii N. Охотничий промысел Приенисейского края. (Hunting in the Yenisei region.) Krasnoiarsk, 1933. 24 p.

13109. Енисейский губернский совет народного хозяйства. (The Yenisei gubernia soviet of people's economy.) Krasnoiarsk, 1923. 423 p.

C. Irkutsk

13110. Lukashuk, A. I. Прибайкалье. (The Baikal region.) Leningrad, 1933. 21 p.

13111. Girchenko, V. P., Vil'min, K..M., Bazhin, A. P.
Указатель литературы по Прибайкалью. (Guide to the literature of the Baikal region.) Verkhneudinsk, 1923.

13112. Материалы к изучению лесов Дальнего Востока.(Materials for the study of Far Eastern forests.) Chita, 1923. 2
parts.

13113. Иркутская архивная ученая комиссия. (The Irkutsk archival scientific commission.) Trudy, 1913-1916. 3 v. Irkutsk.

13114. Иркутск. материалы для истории города XVII и XVIII
столетий. (Irkutsk. Materials pertaining to the history of
the city of the XVII-XVIII centuries.) Moscow, 1883.   (2)
Pezhemskii, P. I. "Летопись г. Иркутска (1652-1807)." (Chronicle of the town of Irkutsk, 1652-1807.) Irkutskie gubernskie vedomosti, 1858-1861.

13115. Serebrennikov, I. I. Покорение и первоначальное заселение Иркутской губернии.   (Conquest and original settlement of the Irkutsk gubernia.) Irkutsk, 1915.

13116. N. A. N. Сибирские города. Материалы для их истории.
XVII и XVIII ст. Нерчинск, Селенгинск, Иркутск. (Siberian
cities. Materials on their history, XVII and XVIII centuries. Nerchinsk, Selenginsk, Irkutsk.) Moscow, 1886.

13117. Sokolov, M. P. Историческое прошлое Иркутской губернии. (Historical past of the Irkutsk gubernia.) Irkutsk,
1925. 14 p.

13118. Sukachev, V. P. Иркутск. (Irkutsk.) Moscow, 1891.

13119. Bustrem, V. V. (ed.). Иркутская ссылка.   (Exile to
Irkutsk.) Miscellany of the Irkutsk society. Moscow, [1934].
317 p.

13120. Rozenoer, S. M. Растопленный полюс.   (The melted
pole.) Yakutsk exile, 1900-1917. Moscow, 1935. 44 p.

13121. Обзор революционного движения в округе Иркутской
судебной палаты за 1897-1907 гг.   (A survey of the revolutionary movement, 1897-1917, made by the Irkutsk judiciary
circuit.) St. Petersburg, 1908. 203, ix p.

13122. Gudoshnikov, M. A. Декабрьские бои 1917 г. в Иркутске.
(December battles of 1917 in Irkutsk.) Moscow-Irkutsk,
1932. 64 p.

13123. Kudriavtsev, F. На баррикадах Иркутска 1917-1919.
(On the barricades of Irkutsk, 1917-1919.) Sketches. Moscow-Irkutsk, 1935. 64 p.

13124. Отчет о деятельности Иркутского губернского исполнительного комитета ... 4-го созыва.   (An account of the
activities of the Irkutsk gubernia   executive committee.)
Irkutsk, 1925. 398 p.

13125. Резолюции и постановления V Губернского съезда советов. (Resolutions and decrees passed by the V gubernia
congress of soviets.) Irkutsk, 1925. 15 p.

13126. Материалы Иркутского губернского статистического
бюро. (Publications of the Irkutsk gubernia   statistical
bureau.) Irkutsk, 1, 1921-

13127. Sokolov, M. P. Иркутская губерния в цифрах.   (The
Irkutsk gubernia in figures.) In: Materialy Irkutskogo
gubernskogo statisticheskogo biuro, Irkutsk, 26 (1924).
85 p.   See 13126.

13128. Cherkunov, A. N. Сельское хозяйство, хлебный баланс,
подсобные и кустарные промыслы Иркутской губернии. (Rural
economy, grain balance, handicraft and allied trades of the
Irkutsk gubernia.) Irkutsk, Materialy Irkutskogo gubernskogo statisticheskogo biuro, 24 (1925). 40 p. See 13126.

13129. IUnitskii, L. D. Единый сельско-хозяйственный налог в
Иркутской губернии на 1924-1925 гг. (The single agricultural tax in the Irkutsk gubernia   for 1924-1925.) Irkutsk,
1924. 71 p.

13130. Kokoulina, L. A. Бюджеты крестьянских хозяйств Иркутской губернии. (Budgets of the peasant households of the
Irkutsk gubernia.) In: Materialy Irkutskogo gubernskogo
statisticheskogo biuro, Irkutsk, 27 (1924). 83 p. See 13126.

13131. Kats, IA. Основные показатели положения наемного труда в Иркутской губернии в 1923 г. (Basic index of hired labor in the Irkutsk gubernia in 1923.) Irkutsk, 1924. 38 p.

13132. Pisarev, V. Пшеница в Иркутской губернии.   (Wheat in
the Irkutsk guberniia.) Irkutsk, 1922. 70 p.

13133. Nanking, Ministry of industry and commerce. 伊爾庫次
克之實業情形   I-êrh-k'u-tzu-k'o chih shih-
yeh ching-hsing. (Industrial conditions in Irkutsk.) Industry and commerce gazette, 15, August 1929.

13134. Chernykh, A. B. Торговля Иркутской губернии в
освещении второго торгового учета.   (Trade of the Irkutsk
gubernia in the light of the second trade census.) In:
Materialy Irkutskogo gubernskogo statisticheskogo biuro,
Irkutsk, 22 (1924). 59 p.

13135. 伊爾庫次克華僑近况 I-êrh-k'u-t'zu-k'o
Hua-chiáo chin-k'uang. (The recent status of the Chinese in
Irkutsk.) Central people abroad affairs monthly, 2:59, Oc-
tober 1929.

13136. Известия Биолого-географического научно-исследователь-
ского института при Государственном иркутском университете.
(Publications of the Bio-geographic scientific institute of
the Irkutsk state university.) Irkutsk, Gosudarstvennyi
universitet, 1, 1924-

13137. Сборник трудов Государственного иркутск.   (Publications of the Irkutsk state university.) No. 8. Social-his-
torical sciences and education. Irkutsk, 1924.

13138. Сборник трудов Иркутского государственного университета.   (Publications of the Irkutsk state university.)
No. 9. Problems of a new school. Irkutsk, 1925. 181 p.

13139. Материалы к проекту сооружения районной гидро-элек-
трической станции на реке Иркуте.   (Information pertaining
to the project for the erection of a regional hydro-elect-
ric station on the river Irkut.) Irkutsk, Irkutskii gubernskii sovet narodnogo khoziaistva, 1924. 143, [56] p.

D. Omsk

13140. Карта Тобольской губернии.   (Map of the Tobolsk
gubernia.)   By A. A. Dunin-Gorkavich, 1902. Scale: 40 versts
/inch. St. Petersburg, 1911.

13141. Районы Омской области. Справочник.   (Regions of the
Omsk province. Guide.) Omsk, 1936. 238 p.

13142. Хозяйство и культурное строительство Омской губернии.
(Economic and cultural development in the Omsk gubernia.)
Omsk, Gubernskii ispolnitel'nyi komitet, 1925. 367 p.

13143. Конъюнктурный обзор народного хозяйства Омской губернии за апрель 1925 г.   (Economic survey of the Omsk gubernia for April 1925.) Omsk, Gubernskaia planovaia komissiia, 1925. 22 p.

13144. Отчет Омского губернского исполнительного комитета
пятому Губернскому съезду советов.   (Report of
the Omsk guberniia executive committee to the fifth conference of the Gubernia soviets.) Orel, Omskii gubernskii
ispolnitel'nyi komitet, 1923. 149 p.

13145. Перспективный план развития сельского хозяйства Омской губернии.   (Prospective plan for the development of
agriculture in the Omsk gubernia.) Omsk, Gubernskoe zemel'-
noe upravlenie, 1924. 426 p.

13146. Лесной факультет Сибирской сельскохозяйственной
академии.   (The Forestry department of the Siberian agricultural academy.) Omsk, 1925. 52 p.

13147. Местный бюджет Омской губернии на 1923-24 г. (Local
budget of the Omsk gubernia for ...) Omsk, Gubernskii
ispolnitel'nyi komitet, 1923-1924.

13148. Из прошлого и настоящего (Омской области).
(From the past and present [of the Omsk region].) Collection of materials. Omgiz, 1938. 48 p.

E. Tomsk

13149. Карта Томской губернии.   (Map of the Tomsk gubernia.)   Scale: 50 versts/inch. St. Petersburg, Il'in, n.d.

13150. Adrianov, A. V. Город Томск в прошлом и настоящем.
(The City of Tomsk, past and present.) Tomsk, 1890.

13151. Экономические очерки Томской губернии.   (Economic
sketches of the Tomsk gubernia.) Tomsk, Gubernskii ispolnitel'nyi komitet, 1925. 264,40,4.p.

13152. Экономический и статистический обзор Томской губ.
(An economic and statistical survey of the Tomsk gubernia.)
Tomsk, Gubernskii isponitel'nyi komitet, 1924. 280 p.

13153. Конъюнктурный обзор народного хозяйства Томской
губернии. (An economic survey of the Tomsk gubernia.)
Publ. by the Tomskaia gubernskaia planovaia komissiia.

13154. Nagnibeda, V. IA. Сельское хозяйство Томской губ.
(Rural economy of the Tomsk gubernia.)   Tomsk, 1924. 135 p.

13155. Kaufman, A. A. Экономический быт государственных крестьян восточной части Томского округа и сев.-зап части
Мариинского округа. (Economic condition of the state peas-

ants of the eastern part of the Tomsk region and northwestern part of the Mariinsk region.) St. Petersburg, 1892.

13156. Народное хозяйство Томской губернии. (People's economy of the Tomsk gubernia.) Tomsk, Gubernskóe ekonomicheskoe soveshchanie, 1923.

13157. Потребительская кооперация Томской губернии за три года новой экономической политики.   (Consumers' cooperative of the Tomsk gubernia during three years of the new economic policy.) June 1, 1921-July 1, 1924. Tomsk, Gubernskii soiuz potrebitel'nykh obshchestv, 1924. 68 p.

13158. Результаты кампании по реорганизации методов преподавания в 1923-1924 учебном году. (Results of a campaign for educational reforms, 1923-1924.) Tomsk, Tomskii tekhnologicheskii institut, 1924. 24 p.

13159. Руководящие материалы по работе в учреждениях народного образования.   (Information concerning the work of the department for public instruction.) Tomsk, Gubernskii otdel narodnogo obrazovaniia, 1924. 43 p.

13160. Томский губернский исполнительный комитет. Местный бюджет Томской губернии.   (The Tomsk gubernia executive committee. The local budget of the Tomsk gubernia.) Tomsk, 1923.

13161. Отчет 4-го Губернского съезда советов рабочих, крестьянских и красноармейских депутатов Томской губернии 1-5 декабря 1923 года. (An account of the 4th Congress of soviets..of the Tomsk gubernia.) Tomsk, Tomskii gubernskii s"ezd sovetov, 1924. 85 p.

13162. Четыре года работы Томского рабфака.   (Four years' work of the Tomsk workers' preparatory college.) Tomsk, Tomskii rabochii fakul'tet, 1924. 67 p.

13163. Известия Томского технологического института. (Publications of the Tomsk politechnic institute.) Tomsk, 1, 1903-

13164. Известия Томского государственного университета. (Publications of the Tomsk state university.) Tomsk, 1, 1889-

F. Turukhansk

13165. Mordvinov, A. Инородцы, обитающие в Туруханском крае.
(Natives of the Turukhansk region.) St. Petersburg, Imperatorskoe russkoe geograficheskoe obshchestvo, 1860.

13166. Tretiakov, P. I. Туруханский край, его природа и жи-
тели. (The Turukhansk region, its nature and inhabitants.)
St. Petersburg, 1871.

13167. Dobrova-IAdrintseva, L. N. Туземцы Туруханского края.
(Natives of the Turukhansk region.) Novonikolaevsk, 1925.
81 p.

13168. Tarasenkov, G. N. Туруханский край. (The Turukhansk
region.) Krasnoiarsk, 1930. 517.

13169. Shumiatskii, IA. B. "Туруханское дело. О вооруженном
побеге ссыльных анархистов в 1908 году." (The Turukhansk
case. Concerning the armed escape of exiled anarchists in
1908.) Eniseiskaia ssylka, (Moscow, 1934), 69-77.

G. Uriankhai (Tannu Tuva)

13170. Kabo. Очерки по истории Тувы. (History of Tuva.)
Uzgiz, 1933. (2) Kodevich, V. Урянхайский край и его обитатели. (The Uriankhai region and its inhabitants.) In: Izvestiia Imperatorskogo russkogo geograficheskogo obshchestva, St. Petersburg, 48 (1912):1-5. See 6548-6872.

13171. Shoizhelov, S. A. Тувинская народная республика. (The
Tuva national republic.) Materials and documents. 1929. (2)
L'vov, A. Современный Урянхай. (Contemporary Uriankhai.)
Novyi Vostok, 6 (1924):161-172.

13172. Mintslov, S. R. Секретное поручение. (A secret commission.) Riga, 1928. 276 p.

13173. Berlin, L and Grumm-Grzhimailo, G. Западная Монголия
и Урянхайский край. (Western Mongolia and the Uriankhai region.) 3 v. 1930.

H. Khakassk

13174. Хакасская автономная область -- индустриальный район
Западной Сибири. (The Khakass autonomous province -- the
industrial region of Western Siberia.) Minusinsk, Planovaia
komissiia Khakasskoi avtonomnoi oblasti, 1931. 105 p.

I. Oirot Autonomous District (Altai)

(1) Geology and Natural Resources

13175. Kalesnik, S. V. (ed.). Алтай. (The Altai region.)
A geological study. Leningrad, 1936. 192 p.

13176. Samoilovich, A. N., Obruchev, V. A., and others.
Большой Алтай. (The Great Altai.) Collection of materials.
Leningrad, Academy of sciences, 1934-1936. 3 v.

13177. Blumberg, O. K. Белый уголь Алтая. (White coal of
the Altai.) Leningrad, Akademiia nauk SSSR, 1930. 193 p.

13178. Suslov, S. P. Материалы по геоморфологии Ойротии.
(Materials pertaining to the geomorphology of Oirotia
[Northwestern Altai].) Moscow, Academy of sciences, 1936.
76 p.

13179. Roerich, Nikolai K., Altai-Himalaya. New York,
Stokes, 1929. 407 p.

13180. Bogdanov, D. P. Материалы для геологии Алтая.
(Sources pertaining to the geology of the Altai region.)
Moscow, 1911.

13181. IAkovlev, A. К вопросу о ледниковом периоде на Алтае.
(The glacial period in the Altai region.) Trudy Sankt-Peter-
burgskogo obshchestva estestvoznaniia, Otdel geologii i
mineralogii, 40 (1909):1.

13182. Krylov, P. N. Флора Алтая. (Flora of the Altai region.) Tomsk, 1898-1914. 7 v.

13183. IAdrintsev, N. M. "Сибирская Швейцария." (The Siberian Switzerland.) Russkoe bogatstvo, 8 (1880):47-66.

13184. Vereshchagin, V. Алтай, как район образовательных экс-
курсий. (The Altai as a region for educational excursions.)
Novonikolaevsk, 1925. 23 p.

13185. Cherepanov, D. Золотой Алтай.   (The golden Altai.)
An essay. Alma-Ata, 1933. 42 p.

13186. Shemelev, V. I. По Алтаю.   (Through the Altai region.) Novosibirsk, 1933. 46 p.

13187. Serebriakov, G. У Алтайских гор. (At the Altai
mountains.) Leningrad-Moscow, 1933. 147 p.

13188. Ovalov, L. Июль в Ойротии. (July in Oirotia.) Travel
sketches. Moscow, 1933. 136 p.

13189. Путешествие по Алтаю. (Travel through the Altai.)
Moscow, 1935. 64 p.

13190. Koptelov, A. L. В горах Алтая. (In the mountains of
Altai.) Moscow, 1937. 137 p.

(2) History

13191. Potapov, L. P. Очерк истории Ойротии. Алтайцы в
период русской колонизации. (An essay on the history of
Oirotia. The Altai natives during the period of Russian
colonization.) Novosibirsk, 1933. 204 p.

13192. Brainin,S. Очерки по истории Алаш-Орды. (Studies on
the history of the Alash-Horde.) Alma-Ata, 1935. 149 p.

13193. Краткий исторический очерк Алтайского округа (1747-
1897). (A brief historical sketch of the Altai region,
1747-1897.) St. Petersburg, 1897. 137 p.

13194. Potapov, L. P. "Исторический путь Ойротии." (Historical development of Oirotia.) Sovetskaia etnografiia, 5-6
(1932):55-87.

13195. Bakai, N. "Легендарный Ойрат-хан." (The legendary
Oirat-khan.) Sibirskie ogni, Novosibirsk, 4:117-124, July-
August 1926.

13196. Castrén, M. A. Ethnologische vorlesungen über die
altaischer völker. St. Petersburg, 1857.

13197. IAdrintsev, N. M. Об алтайцах и татарах Черни.
(The Altaians and Tatars of Chern.) St. Petersburg, 1881.

13198. Nikolas', V. I. "Февральская революция на Алтае."
(The February revolution in the Altai.) Severnaia Aziia,
1 (13):29-35.

13199. Vegman, V. (ed.). Повстанческое движение на Алтае.
(The revolutionary movement in the Altai region.) Collected
articles. Novosibirsk, 1935. 122 p.

13200. Zakharov, Rodion. Алтайские партизаны.   (The Altai
guerrillas.) Novosibirsk, 1934. 110 p.

13201. Kuiat, F. Десять лет Советской Ойротии. (Ten years
of Soviet Oirotia.) Novosibirsk, 1932. 56 p.

13202. Письмо ойротского народа великому Сталину. (A letter from the Oirot people to the Great Stalin.) Novosibirsk,
1937. 47, 4 p.

(3) General Accounts

13203. Ostrovskikh, P. E. Ойратская автономная область.
(The Oirot autonomous province.) Moscow, 1932. 23 p.

13204. Gordienko, P. Ойротия. (Oirotia.) Novosibirsk, 1931.
144 p.

13205. Shvetsov, S. P. Горный Алтай и его население. (The
mountainous Altai region and its population.) Barnaul,
1896. 3 v.

13206. Очерки Алтайского края. (Sketches of the Altai region.) Collected articles. Barnaul, 1920, 192, xvii p.

13207. Алтайский ежегодник за 1922-1923 хоз. год.(The Altai
year-book for 1922-1923.) Barnaul, 1924. xv, 425 p.

13208. Shvetsov, S. P. Примитивное земледелие на Алтае.
(Primitive agriculture in the Altai region.) Zapiski Zapadnosibirskogo otdela Imperatorskogo russkogo geograficheskogo-
go obshchestva, 27 (1900).

13209. IArkho, A. I. "Казаки русского Алтая." (Cossacks of
the Russian Altai.) Severnaia Aziia, Moscow, 31-32 (1930):
1-2:76-99.

13210. Stonov, D. M. Повести об Алтае.   (Tales about the
Altai.) Moscow, 1930. 297 p.

(4) Economic Conditions

13211. Алтайский крестьянин. (The Altai peasant.) Barnaul,
September 1912 - December 1918. (Monthly).

13212. Golubev, P. Алтай. (The Altai.) A historico-statis-
tical miscellany on the problems of economic and civil development of the Altai mountainous district. Tomsk, 1890.

13213. Koposov, N. A. Почвы северовосточной части Ойротии.
(Soils of the northwestern part of Oirotia [Northeastern
Altai].) Moscow, 1936. 72 p.

13214. Golubev, P. A. (ed.). Алтай. (The Altai.) Tomsk,
1890.

13215. Государственная и кооперативная торговля в Алтайской
губернии в 1923 году. (State and cooperative trade in the
Altai gubernia in 1923.) Barnaul, Altaiskii gubernskii ispolnitel'nyi komitet, 1924. 44 p.

13216. Borzenko, A. Кедровый и зверовый промыслы в Бийском
имении Алтайского округа. (Fur and cedar tree industry in
the Biisk domain, Altai region.) Barnaul, 1910. 34 p.

13217. Tokarev, S. A. Докапиталистические пережитки в
Ойротии. (Survivals of the pre-capitalist era in Oirotia.)
Moscow, 1936. 153 p.

13218. Potapov, L. P. Поездка в колхозы Чемальского аймака
Ойротской автономной области. (A journey to the collective
farms of the Chemal county of the Oirot autonomous province.) Trudy instituta po izucheniiu narodov SSSR, Izd.
Akademii nauk SSSR, 1932. 48 p.

13219. Breshchinskii, M. A. Исследование путей в Алтайском
крае. (A study of the roads in the Altai region.) Zapiski
Zapadnosibirskogo otdela Imperatoskogo russkogo geograficheskogo obshchestva, Omsk, 1881, 3.

13220. Dmitriev-Mamonov, A. I. Алтайская железная дорога.
(The Altai railway.) St. Petersburg, 1904.

(5) Communist Party

See 11495-11583.

13221. Отчет ... 7-му очередному Губернскому съезду советов
за 1923-1924 хозяйственный год. (Report of the seventh Altai
gubernia executive committee to the Gubernia congress of
soviets.) Barnaul, Altaiskii gubernskii ispolnitel'nyi komitet, 1925. 281 p.

13222. Сборник обязательных постановлений и правил к ним
Алтайского губернского исполнительного комитета.(A collection of obligatory statutes and regulations of the Altai
gubernia executive committee.) Barnaul, 1924. 102 p.

13223. Резолюции VII Алтайского губернского съезда советов.
(Resolutions of the VII Altai gubernia congress of soviets.)
Barnaul, 1925. 40 p.

13224. Резолюции и постановления.   (Resolutions and decrees.)
Barnaul, Altaiskii V Gubernskii s"ezd professional'nykh soiuzov, 1925. 71 p.

13225. Koptelov, A. L. Молодой Алтай.   (The young Altai.)
Novosibirsk, 1935. 179 p.

XXVII. WESTERN SIBERIA

(Chiefly the Ural Autonomous District)

A. Western Siberia (General)

13226. Карманный путеводитель по Западной Сибири.   (Pocket
guide to Western Siberia.) Novosibirsk, 1936. 246 p.

13227. Krylov, P. N. Флора Западной Сибири. (The flora of
Western Siberia.) Tomsk 1933. 368, xiv p.

13228. Morkovkin, N. A. Кунгурский район Уральской области.
(The Kungur district of the Ural province.) Kungur, 1932.
169 p.

13229. Polikashin, A. I. Советская Печора.   (The Soviet
Pechora.) Travel sketches. Archangel, 1934. 142 p.

13230. Tashkin, S. F. Инородцы Приволжско-Приуральского
края и Сибири по материалам Екатерининской законодательной
комиссии. (Native tribes of the Volga-Ural region and of Siberia, the data collected by the Legislative commission of
Catherine II.) Kazan, 1922. 190 p.

13231. Nikol'skii, N. Сборник о народностях Поволжья.
(A collection of sources pertaining to the history of the
peoples of the Volga region.) Kazan, 1919. 479 p.

13232. Материалы для истории калмыков. (Sources pertaining
to the history of the Kalmuks.) Kazan, Obshchestvo arkheologii, 1910. 69 p.

13233. IAkinf. Историческое обозрение ойратов и калмыков с
XV столетия до настоящего времени. (A historical survey
of the Oirots and Kalmuks from the XV century to the present.) St. Petersburg, 1834. 253 p.

13234. Chonov, E. Калмыки в русской армии XVII в., XVIII в. и 1812 г. (Kalmuks in the Russian army in the XVII century, XVIII century, and in 1812.) Piatigorsk, 1912. 72 p.

13235. Калмыки. (The Kalmuks.) Research in sanitary conditions and vitality. Moscow, Institut sotsial'noi gigieny, Ekspeditsiia po izucheniiu voprosa o vymiranii i vyrozhdenii kalmytskogo naroda (1925-1926), 1928. 345 p.

13236. Novoletov, M. Калмыки. (The Kalmuks.) St. Petersburg, 1884. 77 p. (2) Badmaev, I. Сборник калмыцких сказок. (A collection of Kaluk stories.) Astrakhan, 1899. (3) Zaikovskii, Bogdan V. Среди калмыков. (Among the Kalmuks.) Moscow, 1930. 101 p.

13237. IAkobii, A. I. Остяки северной части Тобольской губернии. (The Ostiaks of the northern part of the Tobolsk gubernia.) Ezhegodnik gubernskogo muzeia, 4 (1895).

13238. Novitskii, G. Краткое описание о народе остяцком, сочиненное в 1815 г. (A brief description of the Ostiak people, written in 1815.) St. Petersburg, 1884.

13239. Gorokhov, N. Религиозные языческие воззрения остяков. (The pagan of the Ostiaks.) Tomsk, 1890. (2) Patkanov, S. Стародавная жизнь остяков и их богатыри по былинам и сказаниям. (Ancient life of the Ostiaks, and their heroes according to their poems and legends.) St. Petersburg, 1891.

13240. Nosilov, K. У вогулов. (With the Voguls.) St. Petersburg, 1904. (2) Pavlovskii, V. Вогулы. (The Voguls.) Kazan, 1907.

13241. Smirnov, I. Вотяки. (The Votiaks.) Kazan, 1890.

13242. Martynov, M. N. "Удмурты (вотяки) в эпоху раннего феодализма." (The Udmurts [Votiaks] in the epoch of early feudalism.) Istoricheskii sbornik, 1 (1934):49-87.

13243. Smirnov, I. Черемисы. (The Cheremis.) Kazan, 1889.

13244. Smirnov, I. Пермяки. (The Permiaks.) Kazan, 1891.

13245. Mainov, V. N. Очерк юридического быта мордвы. (A sketch of the common law of the Mordvins.) St. Petersburg, 1885.

13246. Smirnov, I. Мордва. (The Mordvins.) Kazan, 1902.

13247. Rudnev, A. О происхождении финнов. (On the origin
of the Finns.) St. Petersburg, 1910. Also in: Finliandiia,
7, 1910.

13248. Islavin, V. Самоеды в домашнем и общественном быту.
(The Samoeds, their home and social life.) St. Petersburg,
1847.

13249. Kostrov, N. A. Обзор этнографических сведений о само-
едских племенах в Сибири. (A survey of ethnographic information on the Samoeds of Siberia.) St. Petersburg, 1879.

13250. Borisov, A. A. У самоедов. От Пинеги до Карского моря.
(Among the Samoeds. From the Pinega to the Kara Sea.) Travel sketches of an artist. St. Petersburg, Devrien, 1907.
104 p.

13251. L'vov, Vl. Самоеды. (The Samoeds.) Moscow, 1910.
32 p.

13252. Donner, Kai. Bei den Samojeden in Sibirien. Stuttgart, 1926.

13253. Народное хозяйство Западного сибирского края. (National economy of the West Siberian region.) A statistical
annual. Novosibirsk, 1936. 424 p.

13254. Semenov, V. F. "Очерк пятидесятилетней деятельности
Зап.-Сиб. отд. Русского государственного географического
общества. (An outline of fifty years of activities of the
West Siberian division of the Russian state geographic society.) Zapiski Zap.-Sib. otd. Russkogo geograficheskogo
obshchestva, Omsk, 39 (1927).

13255. Baryshnikov, M. K. Луга Оби и Иртыша тобольского севера. (Meadows of the Ob and Irtysh of the Tobolsk north.)
Moscow, 1933. 95 p.

13256. Kuznetsov, I. D. Крестьянское движение среди чуваш,
мари и удмуртов во время революции 1905-1907 гг. (Peasant
movement among the Chuvashes, Maris, and Udmurts during the
revolution of 1905-1907.) Cheboksary, 1935. 46 p.

13257. Материалы для изучения экономического быта государственных крестьян и инородцев Зап. Сибири. (Sources for the
study of the economic conditions of the state peasants and
aborigines of Western Siberia.) St. Petersburg, 1890.

13258. Материалы по обследованию переселенческих хозяйств в степном крае, Тобольской, Томской, Енисейской и Иркутской губ. (Sources pertaining to the immigrant homesteads in the prairie regions of the Tobolsk, Tomsk, Eniseisk, and Irkutsk gubernias.) St. Petersburg, 1906.

13259. Makarov, N. Крестьянское кооперативное движение в Западной Сибири. (Peasant cooperative movement in Western Siberia.) Moscow, 1910.

13260. Dronin, G. "Борьба за хлеб в Западной Сибири." (The struggle for bread in Western Siberia.) Bor'ba klassov, 1-2: 120-129, January-February 1935.

13261. Puzin, A. A. Высшая школа и техникумы Западной Сибири. (The university and technical schools in Western Siberia.) Novosibirsk, 1934. 128 p.

B. The Ural District

(1) Publications

13262. Известия Уральского государственного университета. (Publications of the Ural state university.) Sverdlovsk, 1920-1925.

(2) Geology and Natural Resources

13263. Природа Урала. Сборник татей. Климат, почвы, недра, флора и фауна. (Nature and the Urals. Collected articles. Climate, soil, minerals, flora and fauna.) Sverdlovsk, 193(. 252 p.

13264. Didkovskii, B. V., Garan, M. I. Ushakov, N. A. and Serzhant, A. A. (ed.). За недра Урала. (For the development of the Urals.) Collected articles. Sverdlovsk, 1934. 250 p.

13265. Barmin, A. Сокровища каменного пояса. Большой Урал. (Treasures of the stone belt. The Great Urals.) Sverdlovsk, 1935. 144 p.

13266. Soshkina, E. Геологические исследования в районе Подчеремского северного Урала.   (Geological exploration in the Podcheremsk region of the northern Urals.) Leningrad, 1933. 12 p.

13267. Berezov, N. F. Урал -- база качественной металлургии Союза. (Urals -- the base of quality metallurgy of the USSR.) Sverdlovsk, 1933. 84 p.

13268. Gulin, V. Медные богатства Урала и пути их использования. (Copper resources of the Urals and means of their development.) Moscow, 1924. 43 p.

13269. Pal'chinskii, P. "Урал и. его минеральная база для промышленности областного и государственного значения." (The Urals as a mineral base for industry of local and state significance.) Poverkhnost' i nedra, Leningrad, 1 (29):7-12, January 1927.

13270. Andronnikov, V. N. and Rusanov, A. D. (ed.). Водные ресурсы Урала. (Water resources of the Urals.) Moscow, Sovetskaia Aziia, 1933. 212 p. 59 maps.

13271. Проблема Урало-Кузбасского водного пути. (The problem of the Ural-Kuzbas water route.) Mosoow, Sovetskaia Aziia, 1932. 44 p.

(3) History

13272. Butsinskii, P. N. К истории Сибири. Сургут, Нарым и Кетск до 1645 г. (Concerning the history of Siberia. Surgut, Narym, and Ketsk to 1645.) Kharkov, 1893. 28 p. (2) The same. Мангазея и Мангазейский уезд, 1601-1645 гг. (Mangazeia and the Mangazeisk uezd, 1601-1645.) Kharkov, 1893. 66 p. See 11108.

13273. Bers, Aleksandr A. Прошлое Урала. (The Urals in the past.) Moscow, 1930. 132 p. (2) Savich, A. A. Прошлое Урала. (The Urals in the past.) Perm, 1925. 133 p.

13274. Oksenov, A. V. Сношения Новгорода Великого с Югорской землёй. (Relations of the Great Novgorod with the IUgra land:). St. Petersburg, 1885. (2) The same. Политические сношения Московского государства к Югорской земле. 1455-99. (Political relations pf the Muscovite state with the IUgra land, 1455-1499.) Zhurnal Ministerstva narodnogo prosveshcheniia, 4:273, February 1891.

13275. Былое Урала. (The Urals in the past.) Orenburg, 1924. xi, 248 p.

13276. Andriiashev, A. M. Материалы по исторической географии Новгородской земли. (Materials on the historical geography of the Novgorod lands.) Moscow, 1914. 550 p.

13277. Древности Камы по раскопкам А. А. Спицына в 1898 г. (Antiquities of the Kama according to A. A. Spitsyn's excavations of 1898.) Leningrad, Historical academy of material culture, 1933. 27 p.

13278. Kapterev, L. M. История Урала. (History of the Ural region.) Russian colonization of the Ural region. Sverdlovsk, 1927. 15 p.

13279. Danilevskii, K. V. Урало-Каспийский край. (The Ural-Caspian region.) Ural'sk, 1927. 232 p.

13280. Двадцать лет революции 1905 года. (Twenty years since the revolution of 1905.) Sverdlovsk, Ural'skii oblastnoi politiko-prosvetitel'nyi komitet, 1925. 91 p.

13281. Город Свердловск. (The city of Sverdlovsk.) A historical economic sketch. Sverdlovsk, Ural'skii oblastnoi ispolnitel'nyi komitet, 1924. 113 p.

13282. Rychkova, G. Красная гвардия на Урале. (The Red guard in the Ural region.) Sverdlovsk, 1933. 170 p.

(4) General Accounts

13283. Уральская советская энциклопедия. (Soviet encyclopedia of the Urals.) Sverdlovsk-Moscow, 1, 1933-

13284. Урал. (The Urals.) A physical and economic geography. Sverdlovsk, Uralkniga, 1926.

13285. Округ и район в Уральской области. (The district and the circuit in the Ural region.) Moscow, 1925. 207 p.

13286. Konstantinov, Oleg A. Уральская область. (The Ural province.) Moscow, 1929. 207 p.

13287. Startsev, V. Южный Урал и Зауралье. (The southern Urals and the Transural region.) Geographic sketch. Cheliabinsk, 1926. 114 p.

13288. Hofmann, A. and Kowalski, M. Das nördliche Ural und das küstengebirge Pai-choi. St. Petersburg, 1853-1856. 2 v.

13289. Oparin, F. P. Река Чусовая. Путеводитель. (The river Chusovaia. A guide.) Sverdlovsk, 1936. xv, 146 p.

13290. Urban, I. I. Очерк реки Верхнего Урала. (Description of the upper part of the Ural river.) Leningrad, 1933.

(5) Economic Conditions

(a) Statistical Publications

13291. Труды Уральского областного статистического бюро.
(Publications of the Ural provincial statistical bureau.)
Sverdlovsk, 1, 1925-   (2)Уральское хозяйство в цифрах.
(Statistics on Ural economy.) Sverdlovsk, Ural'skaia ob-
last', Planovaia komissiia, Statisticheskii sektor, 1, 1925-

13292. Сборник статистических сведений по округам Уральской
области, образовавшимся на территории Екатеринбургской губ.
(A collection of statistical information on the regions of
the Ural province formed on the territory of the Ekaterinburg gubernia.) Ekaterinburg, Gubernskii ispolnitel'nyi
komitet, 1923. 51 p.

(b) General Accounts

13293. Nemchinov, V. S. Народное хозяйство Урала.(National
economy of the Urals.) Ekaterinburg, 1923. 104 p.

13294. Обзор хозяйства Урала за ...   (A survey of Ural economy for ...) Sverdlovsk, 1925-   Publ. by the Ural'skoe
pblastnoe statisticheskoe biuro.

13295. Stepanov, P. "Швеция и Урал."   (Sweden and the
Urals.) Planovoe khoziaistvo, Moscow, 2:267-285, February
1926.

13296. Социалистическое строительство Урала за 15 лет.
(Socialist construction in the Ural region during the [last]
15 years.) Sverdlovsk, 1932. 57 p.

13297. Районирование Урала. (The zoning of the Urals.)
Sverdlovsk, Ural'skii oblastnoi ispolnitel'nyi komitet,
1925. 136 p.

13298. Материалы по районированию Урала.   (Materials on
the zoning of the Urals.) Ekaterinburg, Ural'skoe oblastnoe
ekonomicheskoe soveshchanie, 1924-

13299. Уральский округ и его районы. (The Ural circuit and
its zones.) Ural'sk, Ural'skii okrug, Planovaia komissiia,
1929.

13300. Klimenko, K. Плановое овладение хозяйством на Урале.
(Introduction of planned economy in the Urals.) Planovoe
khoziaistvo, March 1926, 207-217.

554   Russia

                      (c) Agriculture

See 11778-11882.

13301. Уральский кооператор. (Cooperator of the Urals.)
Sverdlovsk, 1, 1924-   (bi-weekly).

13302. Vorobiev, A. Сельское хозяйство Урала. (Rural economy of the Urals.) Sverdlovsk, 1926. 120 p.

13303. Ishmaev, N. "Проблема сельскохозяйственного сырья на
Урале." (The problem of agricultural raw materials in the
Urals.) Planovoe khoziaistvo, December 1926, 207-219.

13304. Lartsev, N. I. Огородничество на Урале. (Gardening in
the Urals.) Ekaterinburg, 1924. 116 p.

13305. План кредитования на восстановление сельского хозяйства Уральской области на 1924-1925 операционный год. (The
credit plan for the restoration of agriculture in the Ural
province   for   the   fiscal year 1924-1925.) Sverdlovsk, Bank
ural'skii oblastnoi   sel'skokhoziaistvennyi, 1924. 107 p.

13306. План кредитования на восстановление сельского хозяйства Ирбитского округа на 1924-1925 операционный год. (The
credit plan for the restoration of rural economy in the Irbitsk circuit, 1924-1925.) Irbitsk, Bank ural'skii oblastnoi sel'skokhoziaistvennyi, 1925. 38 p.

13307. Краткий отчет о работе сельхозбанка за 1923-1924 г.
и за октябрь-январь 1924-1925 года и план кредитования на
1924-1925 год. (A brief account of the work of the Ural
provincial agricultural bank.) Sverdlovsk, Bank ural'skii
oblastnoi sel'skokhoziaitsvennyi, 1925. 28 p.

13308. Труды первого Областного съезда крестьянских начальников Уральской области в 1904 г. (Publications of the
first Provincial congress of peasant captains on the Ural
province.) Ural'sk, 1905.

13309. Prokoshev, V. N. Пшеница в северном Предуралье.
(Wheat in the northern part of the Cisural region.) Soli-
kamsk, 1936. 136 p.

(d) Industry

See 11939-11987.

13310. De Hennin, Wilhelm. Описание уральских и сибирских заводов, 1735. (A description of the Ural and Siberian mills, 1735.) Moscow, 1937. 656 p.

13311. Доклады и резолюции Уральского областного промышленного съезда 20-25 октября 1923 года. (Reports and resolutions of the Ural provincial industrial conference, October 20-25, 1923.) Ekaterinburg, 1923. 113 p.

13312. Обзор работы уральской промышленности за первое полугодие 1923-1924 опер. года. (A survey of industry in the Urals for the first half year of 1923-1924.) Ekaterinburg, Ural'skii oblastnoi sovet narodnogo khoziaistva, 1924. 417 p.

13313. Обзор хозяйства Урала за 2-ой квартал 1923-1924 г. (A survey of industry in the Urals for the second quarter of 1923-1924.) Ekaterinburg, Ural'skoe oblastnoe statisticheskogo biuro, 1924. 146 p.

13314. Обзор работы уральской крупной промышленности за 1-ый квартал 1924-1925 опер. год. (A survey of the principal industry of the Urals for the 1st quarter of 1924-1925.) Sverdlovsk, Ural'skii oblastnoi sovet narodnogo khoziaistva, 1925. 142 p.

13315. Металлургическая промышленность Урала. (The metallurgical industry of the Urals.) Ekaterinburg, Ural'skii oblastnoi sovet narodnogo khoziaistva, 1924. 116 p.

13316. Kruchinskii, M. A. "Сельскохозяйственное машиностроение на Урале." (Farm-machine industry in the Urals.) Planovoe khoziaistvo, July 1925, 245-250.

13317. Lovin, K. P. Челябинский тракторный завод. (The Cheliabinsk tractor plant.) [Cheliabinsk], 1933. 19 p.

(e) Labor

See 12261-12271.

13318. Тезисы докладов и материалы к 2-му Уральскому областному совещанию инспекторов труда и председателей страховых касс 6-го января 1925 г. (Reports and materials for the 2nd Ural provincial conference of labor inspectors and

556 Russia

chairmen of insurance organizations.) Sverdlovsk, Ural'skii
oblastnoi otdel truda, 1924. 87 p.

13319. Труд на Урале в 1924 году. (Labor in the Urals in
1924.) Sverdlovsk, Ural'skoe oblastnoe biuro statistiki
truda, 1925. 300 p.

13320. Труд на Урале в 1926-1927 г. (Labor in the Urals in
1926-1927.) Sverdlovsk, Biuro statistiki truda, 1928, 211 p.

13321. Труд и профсоюзы на Урале 1924 г. (Labor and trade
unions in the Urals, 1924.) Sverdlovsk, Ural'skoe oblastnoe
biuro statistiki truda, 1925.

13322. Обзор положения труда и профессиональных организаций
на Урале. (A review of the labor conditions and trade organizations in the Urals.) Ekaterinburg, Ural'skoe oblastnoe biuro Vserossiiskogo tsentral'nogo soveta professional'-
nykh soiuzov, 1924. 70 p.

13323. Baranov, A. and Sibiriachka, Z. Женщина Урала в
борьбе и за работой. (Woman in the Urals in the social
struggle and at work.) Sverdlovsk, 1928. 120 p.

13324. Итоги и ближайшие задачи Соцстрахования на Урале.
(Results and problems of Social insurance in the Urals.)
Sverdlovsk, 1925. 15 p.

(f) Trade

See 12054-12145.

13325. Статистика торговли. (Trade statistics.) Trudy Ural'-
skogo oblastnogo statisticheskogo biuro, series 4, Sverdlovsk, 1, 1924-

13326. Bobylev, D. M. Экспортное хозяйство Урала, как экономическая проблема. (Exports of the Urals as an economic
problem.) Ekaterinburg, 1924. 112 p.

(g) Finances

See 12272-12300.

13327. Второе Приуральское районное финансовое совещание
13-17 июня 1924 г. (The 2nd Ural regional financial conference, 13-17 June, 1924.) Svedlovsk, 1924. 7p.

13328. Местный бюджет районированной Уральской области на январь-сентябрь 1924 года. (Local budget of the Ural province, for January-September, 1924.) Ekaterinburg, Ural'skii oblastnoi finansovyi otdel, 1924. 433 p.

13329. Кассы взаимопомощи на Урале.   (Mutual aid banks in the Urals.) Ekaterinburg, Ural'skii oblastnoi sovet professional'nykh soiuzov, 1924. 45 p.

(h) Cossacks

13330. Levshin, A. Историческое и статистическое обозрение уральских казаков.   (A historical and statistical survey of the Ural cossacks.) Severnyi arkhiv, 12-15, 1823.

13331. Riabinin, A. Яицкое казачество.(Cossack settlements along the river Iaik [now called the Ural river].) Russkii vestnik, 7, 1863.

13332. Riabinin, A. Уральское казачье войско. (The Ural cossacks.) Materials for the geography and statistics of the Russian empire. 1866.

13333. Shustov, A. Описание южной части земли Уральского казачьего войска. (A description of the southern territory of the Ural cossacks.) Ural'skie voiskovye vedomosti, 13-15, 1871.

13334. Borodin, N. Уральское казачье войско.   (The Ural cossacks.) Ural'sk, 1885.

13335. Golubykh, M. "Уральская казачья деревня."   (The Ural cossack village.) Khoziaistvo Urala, Sverdlovsk, 15-16: 92-106, August-Sptember 1926.

(i) The National Question

13336. IUren', Ivan M. Национальный вопрос на Урале. (The national question in the Urals.) Sverdlovsk, 1930. 80 p.

(j) Tobolsk

13337. Dunin-Gorkavich, A. A. Географический очерк Тобольского севера. (A geographic sketch of the northern Tobolsk region.) Izvestiia Imperatorskogo russkogo geograficheskogo obshchestva, St. Petersburg, 40 (1904).

13338. Dmitriev-Mamonov and Golodnikov, K. Памятная книжка Тобольской губернии. (Directory of the Tobolsk gubernia.)

Tobolsk, 1884. (2) Тобольск. Материалы для истории города
XVII и XVIII ст. (Tobolsk. Materials for the history of
the town during the XVII and XVIII centuries.) Moscow, 1885.

13339. Andronnikov, I. A. Тобольская губерния, как район
колонизации. (The Tobolsk gubernia as a district for colonization.) Voprosy kolonizatsii, St. Petersburg, 9, 1911.

13340. Kaufman, A. A. Экономический быт государственных
крестьян Ишимского округа Тобольской губернии. (Economic
conditions of the state peasants of the Ishimsk district of
the Tobolsk gubernia.) St. Petersburg, 1889.

13341. Medvedev, P. V. Теплые посолы в Тобольском районе.
(Warm salting in the Tobolsk region.) Tobolsk, 1935. 48 p.

13342. Bazanov, A. G. Очерки по истории миссионерских школ
на крайнем севере. (Outlines of history of the missionary
schools in the extreme north.) The Tobolsk northern region.
Leningrad, 1936. 132 p.

(k) Cheliabinsk

13343. Волостной справочник по округам: Златоустовскому,
Курганскому, Троицкому и Челябинскому.(Volost-directory of the
former Cheliabinsk gubernia.) Cheliabinsk, Okruzhnoe statisticheskoe biuro, 1924. 17 p.

13344. Статистический сборник Челябинской губернии ·за
1922-1923 гг. (Statistical miscellany of the Cheliabinsk
gubernia, 1922-1923.) Cheliabinsk, Gubernskoe statisticheskoe biuro, 1923. 396 p.

13345. Сельское хозяйство Челябинского округа и его районов. (Rural economy of the Cheliabinsk district and its
administrative subdivisions.) Cheliabinsk, 1924. 39 p.

13346. Обзор хозяйства Челябинского округа. (Economic
survey of the Cheliabinsk district.) Second and third quart-
ers of 1923-1924. (January-June 1924). Cheliabinsk, Okruzhnoi ispolnitel'nyi komitet, 1924. 237 p.

13347. Резолюции принятые по докладам на 2-м Съезде уполно-
моченных Челябинского окружного сельпромсоюза. (Resolutions adopted by the Cheliabinsk conference of the deputies
of the Agricultural union.) December 2-4, 1924. Cheliabinsk,
1925. 12 p.

13348. Smirnov, M., Orlov, V., Lisin, A., Korol'kov, A.
(ed.). Индустриальный Челябинск. (Industiral Cheliabinsk.)
Cheliabinsk, 1934. 133 p.

13349. Промышленность Челябинской губернии в 1921-1922 гг.
(Industry of the Cheliabinsk gubernia, 1921-1922.) Cheliabinsk, Gubernskoe statisticheskoe biuro, 1923. 66 p.

13350. Торговля, кредит и кооперация Челябинского округа в
начале 1924 года.   (Trade, credit, and cooperation in the
Cheliabinsk district at the beginning of 1924.) Cheliabinsk, Okruzhnoi ispolnitel'nyi komitet, 1924. 67 p.

13351. Краткий обзор деятельности ... за 1923-1924 г.(Brief
survey of activities, 1923-1924.) Cheliabinsk, Okruzhnaia
kassa sotsial'nogo strakhovaniia, 1924. 27 p.

                    (1) Communist Party

See 11495-11583.

13352. Moiseev, S. К истории Уральской областной конференции
РСДРП(б). (History of the Ural provincial conference of the
RSDW [bolshevisk] party.) Sverdlovsk, 1929. 128 p.

13353. Отчет о деятельности Уральского губернского исполни-
тельного комитета, его отделов и общественных организаций и
централизованных государственных учреждений на территории
Уральской губернии. (An account of the activities of the
Ural gubernia executive committee...) October 1, 1923 -
October 1, 1924. Ural'sk, 1925. 243 p.

13354. Отчет ... о работе с 14 декабря 1923 г. по 1 января
1925 г. к V Съезду советов Уральской области.   (Report
of the Provincial executive committee to the V Congress of
the soviets of the Ural province.) December 14, 1923 - January 1, 1925. Sverdlovsk, Ural'skii oblastnoi ispolnitel'-
nyi komitet, 1925. 243 p.

13355. II сессия Уральского областного исполнительного комитета Совета рабочих, крестьянских и красноармейских депутатов 13-18 марта 1924 г.   (Second session of the Ural
provincial executive committee.) Ekaterinburg, 1924. 148 p.

13356. Отчет о работах Уральского уездного съезда советов
8-го созыва протекавшего с 10-13 ноября 1924 г.   (Report
of the Ural uezd congress of soviets, November 10-13, 1924.)
Ural'sk, 1924. 20 p.

13357. Уральский областной съезд советов. Бюллетень. (Conference of the Ural regional soviets. Bulletin.) Ekaterinburg, 1, 1923-

13358. Moiseev, S. Задачи партийной чистки на Урале. (Problems concerning the party purge in the Urals.) Sverdlovsk, 1933. 56 p.

XXVIII. RUSSIAN CENTRAL ASIA

See 6873-7236.

A. Bibliography

See 13724-13725.

13359. Vitkind, N. IA. Библиография по Средней Азии. (A bibliography of Central Asia.) Trudy Kommunisticheskogo universiteta trudiashchikhsia vostoka imeni I. V. Stalina, Moscow, 1929. 165 p.

13360. Burov, N. A. and Garritskii, A. A. Краткий библиографический указатель литературы по Туркестану. (A brief bibliographical guide to the literature on Turkestan.) Tashkent, 1924. 110 p.

13361. Galkin. Этнографические и исторические материалы по Средней Азии и Оренбургскому краю. (Ethnographical and historical sources concerning Central Asia and the Orenburg region.) St. Petersburg, 1868.

13362. IA. Zh. "Архивное дело в Туркменской ССР." (Work in the archives in the Turkmen SSR.) Arkhivnoe delo, 16 (1928):3:78-80.

13363. Krachkovskii, I. IU. "О подготовке свода арабских источников для истории Восточной Европы, Кавказа и Средней Азии. (The preparation of a digest of Arabic sources for the history of Eastern Europe, the Caucasus, and Central Asia.) Zapiski Inztituta vostokovedeniia Akademii nauk SSSR, 1 (1932):55-63.

13364. Gurevich, A. M. "О некоторых актуальных вопросах истории Средней Азии." (Concerning some actual problems of history of Central Asia.) Literaturnyi Uzbekstan, 1 (1936): 186-193.

13365. Ravenau, L. "Travaux des Russes dans l'Asie septen-
trionale." Annales de géographie, 7:350-359.

13366. Каталог No. 3 книжного магазина.(Catalogue No. 3
[of books published by the Turkestan state publication].)
Tashkent, Gosudarstvennoe izdatel'stvo Turkestanskoi SSR,
1924. 30 p.

13367. Отчет Туркестанской государственной библиотеки.(Report
of the Turkestan state library for 1923.) Tashkent, 1924.
24 p.

B. Periodicals and Newspapers

13368. Туркестанские ведомости. (The Turkestan news.) Tashkent, 1870-   (Weekly; from 1893 semi-weekly).

13369. Туркестанская газета. (The Turkestan newspaper.)
1885-1887. From 1887: Туркестанская туземная газета.
(The Turkestan native newspaper.) 1887-   [Published
by the Turkestan Governor-general office. In Russian and
Sart.]

13370. Среднеазиатский вестник.   (The Central-Asiatic messenger.) March-Decmeber 1896. (Monthly).

13371. Русский Туркестан. (Russian Turkestan.) 1898-

13372. Туркестанская правда. (The Turkestan truth.)   Tashkent, 1918-

13373. Труды Туркестанского научного общества(Publications
of the Turkestan scientific society.) Tashkent, 1, 1924-

C. Guide-books

13374. Mysovskii, Ivan E. Тянь-Шань. Путеводитель. Казакстан. Киргизия. (Tian-Shan. A guide. Kazakstan. Kirgizia.)
Moscow, 1931. 144 p.

13375. Mysovskii, Ivan. E. По Средней Азии. От Ташкента до
Красновоска. Путеводитель.(Through Central Asia. From Tashkent to Krasnovodsk. A guide.) Moscow, 1933. 125 p.

13376. Ivanov, P. P. "Среднеазиатская хозяйственная термино-
логия." (Central Asiatic economic terminology.) Izvestiia
Akademii nauk, Otdelenie obshchestvennykh nauk, Series 7,
8 (1934):745-758.

D. Directories

See 13726-13727.

13377. Вся Средняя Азия.(The entire Central Asia.) Directory. Tashkent, 1926. xlvi, 743 p.

13378. Средняя Азия в учреждениях. 1917-1927. (Central Asia in the institutions, 1917-1927.) Leningrad, Akademiia nauk, 1927.

E. Travels and Explorations

13379. Собрание путешествий к татарам и другим восточным народам в XIII, XIV и XV столетиях. (A collection of travels to the Tatars and other Oriental peoples in the XIII, XIV, and XV centuries.) St. Petersburg, 1825. 2 v.

13380. D'iakonov, M. A. Путешествие в Среднюю Азию от древнейших времен до наших дней. (Travels in Central Asia from ancient times to our own days.) Leningrad, 1932. 83 p.

13381. Veniukov, M. "Aperçu historique des découvertes géographiques faites dans la Russie d'Asie depuis les temps les plus reculés jusqu'à nos jours." Revue de géographie, 5 (1879):58-64, 199-205, 359-365; 6 (1880):40-44, 197-202.

13382. Deniker, J. "Les explorations russes en Asie Centrale (1871-1895)." Annales de géographie, 6.

13383. Huntington, Ellsworth. "Problems in exploration, Central Asia." Geographical journal, 35 (1910):395-418.

13384. Arkhangel'skii, N. P. Среднеазиатские вопросы географической терминологии и транскрипции. (Questions concerning geographic terminology and transcription of Central Asia.) Tashkent, 1935. 53 p.

13385. Khrisanf, Metropolitan. "О странах Средней Азии, посещенных им в 1790 годах." (On the countries of Central Asia visited by him in 1790.) In: Chteniia v Imperatorskom obshchestve istorii i drevnostei rossiiskikh pri Moskovskom universiteta, 1:1-28, January-March 1861.

13386. Russov. Путешествие из Оренбурга в Хиву самарского купца Рукавкина в 1753 г. с приобщением разных известий о Хиве с отдаленных времен до-ныне.(A journey from Orenburg to Khiva in 1753 of the Samara merchant Rukavkin, with additional information concerning Khiva from ancient times to

the present.) Zhurnal Ministerstva vnutrennikh del, 34
(1839):10.

13387. Khanykov, IA. V. Поездка Поспелова и Бурнашева в
Ташкент в 1800 году.   (The journey of Pospelov and Burna-
shev to Tashkent in 1800.) Vestnik Imperatoskogo russkogo
geograficheskogo obshchestva, 1 (1851):1.

13388. Nazarov, Filip. Записки о некоторых народах и землях
средней части Азии.   (Memoranda about some peoples and
lands of the central part of Asia.) St. Petersburg, 1821.

13389. Semenov, P. P. Первая поездка на Тянь-Шань, или Небе-
сный хребет, до верховья системы р. Яксарта или Сыр-дарьи
действительного члена П. П. Семенова в 1857. (The first expedition [1857] to Tian-Shan or the Celestial ridge up to
the river Iaksart or Syr-Daria.) Vestnik Imperatorskogo
russkogo geograficheskogo obshchestva, 23 (1858):2.

13390. Severtsov, N. A. Путешствия по Туркестанскому краю и
исследование горной страны Тань - Шаня. (Journeys through
Turkestan and the study of the mountainous country of Tian-
Shan.) St. Petersburg, 1873.

13391. Przheval'skii, N. M. От Кульджи за Тянь-Шань и на Лоб-
Hop, 1876 и 1877. St. Petersburg, 1879. English translation
by E. D. Morgan: Kulja to Lob-nor. London, 1879.

13392. Uspenskii, V. M. Страна Кукэнор или Цин-хай. (The
country of Kokonor or Tsing-hai.) In: Imperatorskoe russkoe
geograficheskoe obshchestvo po otd. etnografii, Zapiski,
St. Petersburg, 6 (1880).

13393. Przheval'skii, N. M. Третье путешествие в Центральной
Азии. (A third journey in Central Asia.) St. Petersburg,
1883.

13394. Przheval'skii, N. M. Четвертое путешествие в Центральной Азии. (A fouth journey in Central Asia.) St. Petersburg,
1888.

13395. Palladii, Archmandrite. Письмо (по поводу некоторых
этнографических и географических показаний Пржевальского.)
(A letter concerning some ethnographic and geographic statements of Przheval'skii.) In: Izvestiia Imperatorskogo russkogo geograficheskogo obshchestva, St. Petersburg, 9 (1891).

13396. Obruchev, V. A. Центральная Азия, Северный Китай и
Наньшань. (Central Asia, Northern China, and Nan-Shan.) St.
Petersburg, 1900.

13397. Almasy. Reise nach West-Turkestan und in den zentralen Tien-schan. Mitteil d. Géogr. gesell. Wien, 44 (1901).

13398. Roborovskii, V. I. Труды экспедиции И. Р. Г. О. по
Центральной Азии 1893-1895 гг. (Publications of the expedition of the Russian geographic society, in Central Asia,
1893-1895.) St. Petersburg, 1905.   See also edition 1899.

13399. See 7148.

13400. IAvorskii, Iv. L. Отчет о географической и антропологической поездке в Туркестан летом 1894. (A report on the
expedition to Turkestan, summer 1894.) In: Zapiski Imperatorskogo novorossiiskogo universiteta, 67.

13401. IAvorskii, Iv. L. Краткий отчет о научной командировке в Среднюю Азию, исполненную летом 1894.(A brief report on
the scientific expedition to Central Asia, summer 1894.)
Odessa, 1895.

13402. Zaleman, Karl G. Отчет о поездке в Среднюю Азию.(An
account of an expedition to Central Asia.) In: Izvestiia
Imperatorskoi akademii nauk, 1898.

13403. Explorations in Turkestan. Expedition of 1903 under
the direction of R. Pumpelly. Washington, 1905.

13404. Liubchenko, A. E. Экспедиция в Каракумскую степь ор-
ганизованная в 1908 г. (The expedition to the Karakum steppe
organized in 1908.) Moscow, 1910.

13405. "Английская экспедиция А. Штейна в Центральной Азии
1914-1916 гг." (The English expedition of A[urel] Stein to
Central Asia, 1914-1916.) Izvestiia Turkestanskogo otdela
Russkogo geograficheskogo obshchestva, 13:1, 17:148-153.

13406. Bartol'd, V. "Отчет о командировке в Туркестан авг.-
дек. 1920 года."(Report on the mission to Turkestan, August-
December 1920.) Izvestiia Rossiiskoi akademii nauk, Series
6, 15 (1921):188-219.

13407. Anuchin, D. "Экспедиция П. К. Козлова в Центральную
Азию." (The expedition of P. K. Kozlov to Central Asia.)
Novyi Vostok, 3 (1923):399-404.

13408. Bartol'd, V. "Археологические работы в Самарканде
летом 1924 г." (Archeological explorations in Samarkand,
summer 1924.) Izvestiia Rossiiskoi akademii ist. mat. kul't.
4:119-132.

13409. Willfort, F. Turkestanisches tagebuch. Sechs jahre
in Russisch-Zentralasien. Wien-Leipzig, Braumüller, 1930.
viii, 327 p.

13410. Andrews, Roy Chapman. On the trail of ancient man;
a narrative of the field work of the Central Asiatic expeditions. New York, Putnam, 1926. xxiv, 375 p.

13411. Filchner, W. "My Central Asian expedition of 1925-
1928." Journal of the Royal Central Asian society, 16:3:
298-307, July 1929.

13412. Druzhinin, Nikolai M. В страну туркмен и узбеков.
(Into the land of Turkmens and Uzbeks.) Leningrad, 1927.
115 p.

13413. Памирская экспедиция 1928 г. (The Pamir expedition
of 1928.) Leningrad, Akademiia nauk, 1930-1931. 8 issues.

13414. Иссыкульская экспедиция, 1928. (The Issykulsk expeditions, 1928.) Leningrad, Akademiia nauk, 1930. 136 p.

13415. Roerich, Nikolai. Сердце Азии. (The heart of Asia.)
Southburg, Conn., Alatas, 1929. 160 p.

13416. Kaftor, S. 30 тысяч километров по Центральной Азии.
(30,000 kilometers in Central Asia.) Moscow, 1930. 96 p.

13417. Penck, Albrecht. "Central Asia." Geographical journal, 76 (1930):477-487.

13418. Maslov, Pavel. Конец Урянхая. (The end of Uriankhai.) Journey notes. Moscow, 1933. 141 p.

13419. Poppe, N. N. "Значение путешествий П. К. Козлова
для археологического изучения Центральной Азии." (The significance of P. K. Kozlov's travels for archeological study
of Central Asia.) Izvestiia Gosudarstvennogo geograficheskogo obshchestva, 68 (1936):5:748-753.

13420. Pavlenko, P. A. Путешествие в Туркменистан. (A journey to Turkmenistan.) Moscow, Federatsiia, 1928. 214 p.

13421. McCallum, D. "The discovery and development of the new land route to the East." Journal of the Royal Central Asian society, 12:1:44-67, January 1925.

13422. Teichman, Sir Eric. Journey to Turkestan. London, Hodder & Stoughton, 1937. 221 p.

13423. Zav'ialov, V. V. Исторический обзор путешествий в Бухаре. (A historical survey of travels in Bokhara.) Orenburgskie gubernskie vedomosti, 20, 1854.

13424. Kostenko, L. F. Путешествие в Бухару.русской миссии в 1870 году. (Travel in the Bokhara of the Russian mission in 1870.) St. Petersburg, 1871.

13425. Alenitsyn, V. Несколько замечаний о путешествии Дженкинсона в Хиву в 1559 году. (A few notes concerning Jenkinson's travels to Khiva in 1559.) St. Petersburg, 1879.

13426. Ukhtomskii, Esper E. От Калмыцкой степи до Бухары. (From the Kalmuk steppes to Bokhara.) St. Petersburg, 1891.

F. Anthropology and National Zoning

See 260-272; 1379-1395; 10722-10784.

13427. Zarubin, I. I. Список народностей Туркестанского края. (A list of the peoples of Turkestan.) In: Izvestiia Rossiiskoi akademii nauk, Leningrad, 1925. 23 p.

13428. Rashid al Din, Fazl Allah. Vollständige übersicht d. ältesten Türkisch., Tartar., u. Monghol., völkerstämme bearbeitet v. F. von Erdmann. Kazan, 1841.

13429. See 6955.

13430. Galkin, M. N. Этнографические материалы по Средней Азии и Оренбургскому краю. (Ethnographic material concerning Central Asia and the Orenburg province.) St. Petersburg, 1867.

13431. Radlov, V. V. Этнографический обзор тюркских племен Южной Сибири и Дзунгарии. (An ethnographic survey of the Turkic tribes of South Siberia and Dzungaria.) 1887.

13432. Katanov, N. F. Этнографический обзор турецко-татарских племен. (Ethnographical survey of the Turco-Tatar tribes.) Kazan, 1894.

13433. Talko-Gryntsevich, IU. D. "Древние обитатели Центральной Азии." (Ancient inhabitants of Central Asia.) Trudy Troitskosavsko-Kiakhtinskogo otd. Priamurskogo otd. Imperatorskogo russkogo geograficheskogo obshchestva, 2 (1899):1-2:61-76.

13434. Vorobiev, N. I. Казанские татары. (The Kazan Tatars.) Kazan, 1925. Also in: Materialy po izucheniiu Tatarstana, 2 (1925):133-166.

13435. Fedorov, E. Очерки национально-освободительного движения в Средней Азии. (An outline of the national-liberal movement in Central Asia.) Tashkent, 1925. 80 p.

13436. Академия наук СССР республикам Средней Азии, 1924-1934. 1934. (Contributions of the Academy of sciences of the USSR to the republics of Central Asia [on the occasion of the tenth anniversary of national zoning].) Collected articles. Moscow-Leningrad, 1934-1935. 2 v.

13437. Abolin, P. I. Основы естественно-исторического районирования советской Средней Азии. (Basis for the natural historical zoning of Soviet Central Asia.) Trudy Sredneaziatskogo universiteta, Tashkent, 1929. Series 12.

13438. Vareikis, I. and Zelenskii, I. Национально-государственное размежевание Средней Азии. (National state zoning of Central Asia.) Tashkent, 1924. 86 p.

13439. Cleinow, Georg. "Die grundlagen der nationalitatenpolitik in Russisch-Zentralasien." Ost-Europa, 4:559-573, June 1929.

13440. Khodorov, I. "Национальное размежевание Средней Азии." (National zoning of Central Asia.) Novyi Vostok, 8-9 (1925): 65-81.

13441. Alkin, I. "Национально-государственное размежевание Средней Азии и VII Съезд советов СССР. (The national state delimitation of Central Asia and the seventh Congress of soviets of the USSR.) Revoliutsionnyi Vostok, 6 (1934):28: 114-136.

13442. Khodzhaev, Faizulla. "Вопросы национально-территориального размежения советской Средней Азии." (The problem of national territorial zoning of Soviet Central Asia.) Kommunisticheskii internatsional, 8 (1924):218-236.

13443. О национальном размежевании Средней Азии.   (Concerning the national zoning of Central Asia.) Moscow-Tashkent, 1934. 34 p.

13444. Vasilevskii. "Фазы басмаческого движения в Средней Азии."   (Phases of the Basmach movement in Central Asia.) Novyi Vostok, Moscow, 29 (1930):126-141.

13445. Nemchenko, M. Национальное размежевание Средней Азии. (National zoning of Central Asia.) Moscow, 1925. 28 p. Also in Mezhdunarodnaia zhizn', 4-5 (1924):67-92.

G. History

(1) General

13446. Parker, E. H. A thousand years of the Tartars. 2nd ed. New York, 1924. xii, 288 p.

13447. Bartol'd, V. Туркестан в эпоху монгольского нашествия. (Turkestan during the epoch of the Mongolian invasion.) St. Petersburg, Fakul'tet vostochnykh iazykov, 1896-1900. 2 v. English translation by H. A. R. Gibbs: Turkestan down to the Mongol invasion. Oxford university press, 1918.

13448. Bartol'd, V. История Туркестана.   (The history of Turkestan.) Tashkent, 1922. 50 p.

13449. IAkubovskii, A. IU. Самарканд при Тимуре и Тимуридах. (Samarkand under Timur and the Timurides.) Leningrad, 1933. 68 p. (2) Grousset, R. L'empire des steppes. Paris, 1939. 639 p.

13450. Hartmann, M. Der islamische Orient, berichte und forschungen. Berlin, 1900-1910. 3 v.

13451. Bretschneider, Emil. Mediaeval researches from Eastern Asiatic sources. London, 1910. 2 v.

13452. Bartol'd, V. V. Улугбек и его время.   (Ulugbek and his time.) In: Zapiski Rossiiskoi akademii nauk po Istoriko-filologicheskomu otd., Petrograd, 17 (1918):5. ii, 160, 24p.

13453. Vasiliev, A. История и древние памятники восточной части Средней Азии. (History and ancient remains of the eastern part of Central Asia.) St. Petersburg, 1857.

13454. Terentiev, M. A. История завоевания Средней Азии. (History of the conquest of Central Asia.) St. Petersburg, 1906. 3 v. See 13809.

13455. Courant, Maurice. L'Asie Centrale aux XVIIe et XVIIIe siècles. Empire Kalmouk ou Empire Mantchou? Lyons, 1912. 151 p.

13456. Материалы по истории Татарской АССР. (Sources pertaining to the history of the Tatar ASSR.) Leningrad, Istoriko-arkheograficheskii institut, 1932. 240 p. (2) McGovern, W.M. The early empires of Central Asia. Univ. of N. C. press, 1939.

(2) Russia in Central Asia

See 7138-7144.

13457. Акты исторические об отношении России к государствам Средней Азии. (Historical documents pertaining to Russia's relation with the states of Central Asia.) In: Sbornik Kniazia Khilkova, St. Petersburg, 1879: 269-273; 303-579.

13458. Valikhanov, Veniukov, and others. The Russians in Central Asia... Translated from the Russian by John and Robert Mitchell. London, Stanford, 1865. xvi, 552 p.

13459. Kostenko, L. F. Средняя Азия и водворение в ней русской гражданственности. (Central Asia and the establishment of Russian civil administration.) St. Petersburg, 1871.

13460. Hellwald, Friedrich von. Die Russen in Centralasien. Eine geographisch-historische studie. Vienna, 1869. 121 p. English tr.: The Russian in Central Asia. A critical examination down to the present time of the geography and history of Central Asia. Tr. by Lieut.-Col. Theodore Wirgman. London, King & co., 1874. 332 p.

13461. Lansdell, H. Russian Central Asia. London, 1885. 2 v.

13462. Krahmer, Gustav. Russland in Mittel-Asien. Leipzig, Zuckschwert, 1898. iv, 181 p.

13463. See 13518.

13464. Bartol'd, V. Историко-географический обзор Ирана. (A historico-geographical survey of Iran.) St. Petersburg, 1903.

13465. Krahmer, Gustav. Das Transkaspische gebiet. Berlin, 1905. viii, 232 p.

13466. Krahmer, Gustav. Die beziehungen Russlands zu Persien. Leipzig, Zuckschwert, 1903. iv, 126 p.

13467. Иран.   (Iran.) A miscellany. Leningrad, Akademiia nauk, 1927-1930. 3 v.

13468. Ulianitskii, V. A. Сношения России с Средней Азиею и Индиею в XVI-XVII в.в. (The relations of Russia with Central Asia and India in the XVI-XVII centuries.) Moscow, 1889.

13469. Veselovskii, N. Иван Данилович Хохлов. Русский посланник в Персию и Бухару в XVII ст.   (Ivan Danilovich Khokhlov. Russian envoy to Persia and Bokhara in the XVII century.) St. Petersburg, 1891.

13470. Veselovskii, N. I. Очерк историко-географических сведений о хивинском ханстве от древнейших времен до настоящего. (An outline of historical and geographical information concerning the Khiva khanate from ancient times to the present time.) St. Petersburg, 1877.

13471. Sobolev, L. Новейшая история Бухарского и Кокандского ханств.   (Recent history of the Bokharan and Kokand khanates.) Turkestanskie vedomosti, 26-28, 1876.

13472. Logofet.   Бухарское ханство под русским протекторатом. (The Bokharan khanate under Russian protectorate.) St. Petersburg, 1911.

13473. Veselovskii, N. Киргизский рассказ о русских завоеваниях в Туркестанском крае.   (The Kirgiz story concerning the Russian conquest in the Turkestan region.) St. Petersburg, 1894.

13474. Abaza, K. Завоевание Туркестана. (The conquest of Turkestan.) St. Petersburg, 1902. 310 p.

13475. Zhukovskii, S. V. Сношение России с Бухарой и Хивой за последнее 300-летие. (The relations between Russia and Bokhara and Khiva for the last three hundred years.) Trudy obshchestva russkikh orientalistov, Petrograd, 2, 1915. xii, 214 p.   (2) The same. "К истории сношений России с Бухарой и Хивой конца XVIII века."   (History of the relations between Russia and Bokhara and Khiva at the end of the XVIII century.) Vostochnyi sbornik izd. obshch. russk. orient., 2 (1916):273-340.

13476. Pokrovskii, S. P. Международное отношение России и Бухары в дореволюционное время и при советской власти до национального размежевания среднеазиатских республик. (Russo-Bokharan relations before the revolution and during the Soviet period prior to the national zoning of the Central Asiatic republics.) Biulleten' Sredneaziatskogo gosudarstvennogo universiteta, Tashkent, 16 (1927).

13477. Popov, A. N. Сношения России с Хивою и Бухарою при Петре Великом. (Russia's relations with Khiva and Bokhara during the reign of Peter the Great.) Zapiski Imperatorskogo geograficheskogo obshchestva, 9 (1853).

13478. Lebedev. Посольство в Хиву в 1716, 1717 и 1718 гг. (The embassy to Khiva in 1716, 1717, and 1718.) Zhurnal Ministerstva narodnogo prosveshcheniia, 51 (1846).

13479. Zalesov, N. Очерк дипломатических сношений России с Бухарой с 1836-1843 гг. (An outline of the diplomatic relations between Russia and Bokhara, 1836-1843.) Voennyi sbornik, 27 (1862):9:3-46.

13480. Golosov, D. Поход в Хиву в 1839 г. отряда русских войск под начальством ген.-адъютанта Перовского. (The 1839 expedition to Khiva of the detachment of Russian troops under the command of Adjutant-General Perovskii.) Voennyi sbornik, 29-30 (1863):1-3:3-72, 309-358, 3-75.

13481. Veselovskii, N. I. Прием в России и отпуск среднеазиятских послов в XVII и XVIII столетиях. (The reception and dismissal of Central-Asiatic ambassadors in the XVII and XVIII centuries.) St. Petersburg, Zhurnal Ministerstva narodnogo prosveshcheniia, 7, 1884.

13482. Kusheva, E. N. "Среднеазиатский вопрос и русская буржуазия в 40-е годы XIX века." (The Central-Asiatic problem and Russian bourgeoisie in the forties of the XIX century.) Istoricheskii sbornik, 3 (1934):133-162.

13483. Maksheev, A. I. Показание сибирских казаков Милюшина и Батарышкина, бывших в плену у кокандцев с 1849 по 1952 г. (Testimony of the cossacks Miliushin and Bataryshkin, formerly imprisoned by the Kokands from 1849 to 1852.) Vestnik Imperatorskogo russkogo geograficheskogo obshchestva, 17 (1856).

13484. Zalesov, N. Посольство в Хиву и Бухару полковника Игнатьева. (The embassy of Colonel Ignatiev to Khiva and Bokhara. Russkii vestnik, 91,92.

13485. Shepelev, A. Материалы для истории хивинского похода
1873 года. (Sources pertaining to the history of the Khiva
expedition in 1873.) A sketch of military and diplomatic relations of Russia with Central Asia. Tashkent, 1879.

13486. Lobysevich, F. Взятие Хивы и Хивинская экспедиция
1873 г. (The capture of Khiva and the Khivan expedition of
1873.) Vestnik Evropy, 8, 9, 10: 1873.

13487. See 7138.

13488. Бухара. (Bokhara.) Collected articles and memoirs.
Moscow, 1924. 35 p.

13489. Galuzo, P. G. "Туркестан и царская Россия."   (Turkestan and tsarist Russia.) Revoliutsionnyi Vostok, Moscow,
1929:6:95-119.

13490. Grigoriev, V. V. Русская политика в отношении к Средней
Азии. (Russian policy in regard to Central Asia.) St. Petersburg, 1874.

13491 Minkin, G. "Колониальная политика царизма в Калмыкии
в второй половине XIX и начале XX века." (The colonial
policy of tsarism in Kalmukia during the second half of the
nineteenth century and beginning of the twentieth.) Istorik
marksist, 6 (1933):34:51-67.

13492. Ledenev, N. История Семиреченского казачьего войска.
(History of the Semirechensk cossack army.) Vernyi, 1908.

13493. Kiiashko, A. Секретная часть "Военного обзора За-
каспийской области." (The secret part of the "military survey of the Transcaspian province.) Askhabad, 1896. 115 p.

13494. See 13459.

            (3) The Revolution and Recent History

See 11189-11345.

13495. Gor'kii, M., Ivanov, V., and others (ed.). Война в
песках. (War in the sands.) Materials pertaining to the civil war. Leningrad, 1935. 547 p.

13496. Safarov, G. Колониальная революция.   (Colonial revolution.) Moscow, Gosizdat, 1921. (2) Революция и культура
в Средней Азии. (Revolution and culture in Central Asia.)
Tashkent, 1934. 126 p.

13497. IUzhakov, IU. D. Итоги двадцати-семи-летнего управления нашего Туркестанским краем. (Twenty-seven years of Russian administration in Turkestan.) St. Petersburg, 1891.

13498. Mel'kumov, A. Материалы революционного движения в Туркмении, 1904-19. (Sources of the revolutionary movement in Turkmenia, 1904-1919.) Tashkent, 1924. vi, 194 p.

13499. Muravievskii, S. D. Очерки по истории революционного движения в Средней Азии. (An outline of the history of tne revolutionary movement in Central Asia.) Tashkent, 1926. 37 p.

13500. Baratov, A. "Октябрь и гражданская война в Средней Азии." (The October revolution and civil war in Central Asia.) Istoriia proletariata SSSR, 1 (1934):17:144-155.

13501. Sykes, Percy. "Persia and the Great war." Journal of the Royal Central Asian society, 9:4:175-188, October 1922.

13502. Blacker, L. V. S. "Wars and travels in Turkestan." (1918-1920). Journal of the Royal Central Asian society, 9:1:4-20, January 1922.

13503. Shestakov, A. V. "20-летие восстания в Средней Азии (1916-1936 гг.)" (Twentieth anniversary of the uprising in Central Asia.) Revoliutsiia i natsional'nosti, 9:79:38-44, September 1936.

13504. Ryskulov, T. "Восстание в Средней Азии в 1916 году." (The uprising in Central Asia in 1916.) Bor'ba klassov, 6: 1-15, June 1936.

13505. "Восстание 1916 г. в Средней Азии." (The uprising of 1916 in Central Asia.) Krasnyi arkhiv, 34 (1929):39-94.

13506. "Бухара в 1917 г." (Bokhara in 1917.) Krasnyi arkhiv, 20 (1927):78-122.

13507. "К истории восстания киргиз в 1916 г." (On the history of the Kirghiz uprizing of 1916.) Krasnyi arkhiv, 16 (1926):53-75.

13508. Knollys, D. E. "Military operations in Transcaspia 1918-1919." Journal of the Royal Central Asian society, 13: 2:89-110, April 1926.

13509. Malleson, Wilfred. "The British military mission to Turkestan." Journal of the Royal Central Asian society, 9: 2:96-110, April 1922.

13510. Lobanov-Rostovsky, A. "The Soviet Muslim republics in Central Asia." Journal of the Royal institute of international affairs, 7:4:241-255, July 1928.

13511. Chirol, Valentine. "Storm waves in the Mohammedan world." Journal of the Royal Central Asian society, 9:4: 193, 244, October 1922.

13512. Cleinow, Georg. "Russland im Zentralasien." Europäische gespräche, 7:2:60-80, February 1929.

13513. Abdul Qadir Khan. "Central Asia under the Soviets." Journal of the Royal Central Asian society, 17:3:285-291, July 1930.

13514. Chokayev, Mustafa. "Turkestan and the Soviet Regime." Journal of the Royal Central Asian society, 18:3:403-420, July 1931.

H. General Accounts

13515. Kostenko, L. F. Туркестанский край. (The Turkestan region.) A military statistical survey of the Turkestan military circuit. St. Petersburg, 1880. 3 v.

13516. Gaister, A. I. (ed.). Средняя Азия. (Central Asia.) Moscow, 1933. 205 p.

13517. Alkin, I. Средняя Азия. (Central Asia.) Moscow, 1931. 389 p.

13518. Servet, C. La Turkestan soviétique. Paris, 1931. 131 p.

13519. Huntington, Ellsworth. The pulse of Asia. Boston, Houghton Mifflin, 1919.

13520. Biddulph, C. E. "Russian Central Asia." Royal Asiatic society of Great Britain and Ireland, 1891.

13521. Hughes, Langston. A negro looks at Soviet Central Asia. Moscow-Leningrad, Cooperative publishing society of foreign workers in the USSR, 1934. 52 p.

13522. Levin, I. "Среднеазиатские советские республики и
их международное значение." (The Central Asiatic soviet republics and their international significance.) Revoliutsiia
i natsional'nosti, 12:58:36-47, December 1934.

13523. Veniukov, M. I. Туркестанские вопросы. (Turkestan
problems.) Russkaia mysl', 9, 1899.

13524. Bekchurin, Mir Salikh. Туркестанская область. (The
Turkestan province.) Kazan, 1872.

13525. Frideriks, N. "Туркестан и его реформы." (Turkestan and its reforms.) Vestnik Evropy, 6, 1869.

13526. Khoroshkhin, A. P. Сборник статей, касающихся до
Туркестанкого края. (Collected articles pertaining to the
Turkestan region.) St. Petersburg, 1876.

13527. Akarskii, B. Кара-Калпакская автономная ССР. (The
Kara-Kalpak ASSR.) Moscow, 1932. 20 p.

I. Anglo-Russian Rivalry

See 7138-7144; 7189-7223; 13867-13884.

13528. Grulew, M. Das ringen Russlands und Englands in Mittel-Asien. Berlin, Zuckschwert, 1910.

13529. Noyce, Frank. England, India, and Afghanistan. London, 1902. 174 p.

13530. Curzon, George N. Russia in Central Asia in 1889 and
the Anglo-Russian question. London, Longmans, Green, and co.,
and New York, 1889. xxiii, 477 p.

13531. Dobson, George. Russian railway advance into Central
Asia. Notes of a journey from St. Petersburg to Samarkand.
London, Allen & co., and at Calcutta, 1890. xxii 439 p.

13532. Tarasenko-Otreshkov, N. Индия и ее отношение к России.
(India and her attitude toward Russia.) St. Petersburg,
1858. 142 p.

13533. Martens, F. F. Россия и Англия в Средней Азии.
(Russia and England in Central Asia.) St. Petersburg, 1880.

13534. Romanovskii, D. I. Заметки по среднеазиатскому вопросу. (Notes on the Central·Asiatic problem.) St. Petersburg, 1868. 291 p.

13535. Curzon, George N. "The fluctuating frontier of Russia in Asia." Nineteenth century, 25 (1889):267-283.

13536. Curzon, George N. "British and Russian commercial competition in Central Asia.) Asiatic quarterly review, 8: 438-457, July-October 1889.

13537. Subbotin, A. P. Россия и Англия на среднеазиатских рынках. (Russia and England on the Central Asiatic markets.) St. Petersburg, 1883.

13538. See 13876.

13539. Kastel'skaia, Z."К истории англо-русского соперничества в Средней Азии, с первой половины XIX века по 1907 год. (Anglo-Russian rivalry in Central Asia from the first half of the XIX century to 1907.) Na zarubezhnom Vostoke, 2 (1934):7:49-60.

13540. "Английская политика в Индии и русско-индийские отношения в 1897-1905 гг." (English policy in India and Russo-Indian relations in 1897-1905.) Krasnyi arkhiv, 19 (1926):53-63.

13541. "Англо-русское соперничество в Персии в 1890-1906 гг." (Anglo-Persian rivalry, 1890-1906.) Krasnyi arkhiv, 1 (1933):56:65-79.

13542. Mazzoleni, G. B. L'Antagonismo anglo-russo in Asia nell'ultimo ventennio, 1907-1927. Pavia, 1927.

13543. Etherton, P. T. "Central Asia. Its rise as a political and economic factor." Journal of the Royal Central Asian society, 10:2:88-103, April 1923.

13544. Moore, Arthur. "Britain and Islamic Asia." Journal of the Royal Central Asian society, 10:1:3-24, January 1923.

13545. Bosshard, W. "Politics and trade in Central Asia." Journal of the Royal Central Asian society, 16:4:433-454, October 1929.

13546. Ross, E. Denison. "The new Middle East." Journal of the Royal Central Asian society, 16:3:308-318, July 1929.

13547. Andersson, J. G. "The highway of Europe and Asia." Journal of the Royal Central Asian society, 16:2:191-195, April, 1929.

13548. Blue Book. Central Asia. A "Copy of Mr. Davies' report..." Ordered... to be printed, 17 February, 1864.

J. Economic Conditions

See 7013-7047; 7224-7228; 11657-12404.

(1) Statistics

13549. Материалы Всероссийских переписей 1920 года. Перепись в Туркестанской республике. (Materials on the All-Russian census of 1920. Census of the Turkestan republic.) Moscow, 1922-1924. 6 v.

13550. Туркестан. Статистический ежегодник. (Turkestan. A statistical year-book.) Tashkent, TSentral'noe statisticheskoe upravlenie, 1917-1923.

13551. Статистический ежегодник, 1917-1923 гг. (Statistical annual, 1917-1923.) Tashkent, 1924. 581 p.

13552. Классовой и профессиональный состав городского населения ТССР в 1923 г. (Urban population of the Turkestan SSR on the basis of class and profession.) Tashkent, TSentral'noe statisticheskoe upravlenie TSSR, 1924. 142 p.

13553. Некоторые статистические итоги. (Some statistical totals.) Semipalatinsk, Gubernskoe statisticheskoe biuro, 1923. 53 p.

(2) General

13554. Страны Востока. (Countries of the East.) Economic guide. V. II: Central Asia. Moscow, 1936. 400 p.

13555. Arkhipov, N. B. Среднеазиатские республики. (The Central Asiatic republics.) 3rd edition. Moscow-Leningrad, 1930. 160 p.

13556. Balashov, N. Экономическая география Средней Азии. (An economic geography of Central Asia.) Tashkent, 1924. 73 p.

13557. Minkin, G. Z. "О феодализме в Калмыкии." (On feudalism in Kalmukia.) Izvestiia Saratovskogo nizhnevolzhskogo instituta kraevedeniia, 5 (1932):31-48.

13558.Balashev, N. I. Несколько страниц из экономической
географии Туркестана. (A few pages from the economic geography of Turkestan.) Tashkent, 1923. 59 p.

13559. Народное хозяйство Средней Азии. (National economy
of Central Asia.) Tashkent, Sredneaziatskii ekonomicheskii
sovet, 1, 1924-

13560. See 13376.

13561. Отчет 2-го съезда экономических совещаний Туркестанской республики. (Account of the second Congress of the
economic conferences of the Turkestan republic.) November
26-30, 1922. Tashkent, 1923. 110 p.

13562. Kondrashev, S. K. "Об ускорении хозяйственного строительства в Средней Азии." (Acceleration of the economic
development in Central Asia.) November 1925, 246-261.

13563. Gessen, S. IA. "К вопросу о хозяйственном строительстве Средней Азии." (Economic development of Central Asia.)
Sovetskoe stroitel'stvo, Moscow, 6:58-78, January 1927.

(3) Natural Resources

13564. Petrosiants, A. IA. and Shmidt, M. A. Материалы по
геологии Средней Азии. (Materials concerning the geology
of Central Asia.)Tashkent, 1935.

13565. Gorbunov, N. P. (ed.). Минеральные богатства Средней
Азии. (The mineral wealth of Central Asia.) Collected articles. Leningrad, 1935. 606 p.

13566. Природные богатства Семипалатинской губернии КССР.
(Natural resources of the Semipalatinsk gubernia.) Semipalatinsk, 1924. 156 p.

13567. Nikiforova, A. F. Каменноугольные отложения Средней
Азии.   (Coal deposits of Central Asia.) Leningrad,
1933. 76 p.

13568. Limarev, I. Угольная промышленность Средней Азии во
втором пятилетии. (The coal industry of Central Asia during
the second five-year plan.) Tashkent, 1935. 52 p.

13569. Brodskii, A. L. Охрана природы в Туркестане. (Preservation of natural resources in Turkestan.) Tashkent,
1923. 20 p.

13570. Табличная характеристика к статистико-экономическому очерку бассейна реки Мургаб. (A statistical and economic sketch of the basin of the river Murgab.) Tashkent, 1923. 55 p.

(4) Agriculture

See 1178-11882.

13571. Климатическое районирование Туркестана. (Climatic zoning of Turkestan.) Tashkent, 1924. 39 p.

13572. Olovianishnikov. Почвы Средней Азии. (Soils of Central Asia.) Stalinbad-Samarkand, 1934. 12, 2 p.

13573. Davydov, M. M. Водное хозяйство Туркестанских областей КССР. (Irrigation of the Turkestan provinces.) Orenburg, 1925. 40 p.

13574. Khodorov, I. "К вопросу об исторической эволюции землевладения в Туркестане." (The problem of historical evolution of landownership in Turkestan.) Istorik marksist, Moscow, 10 (1928):121-153.

13575. Труды Семинария экономики и организации сельского хозяйства. (Publications of the Department of economics and agriculture.) Tashkent, Sredneaziatskii gosudarstvennyi universitet, 1924. 330 p.

13576. Вопросы сельского хозяйства и ирригации Туркестана. (The problems of agricultural economy and irrigation in Turkestan.) Tashkent, 1924. 200 p.

13577. Табличная характеристика к статистико-экономическому обследованию ирригационных систем рек Чирик и Келес. (A statistical and economic table of the examined irrigation systems of the rivers Chirik and Keles.) Tashkent, 1923. 119 p.

13578. Управление водных хозяйств. Институт ирригационных исследований. (Administration of irrigation. Institution of irrigation research.) Material on the irrigation and water supply of Turkmenistan. Tashkent, 1927-

13579. Annenkov, N. M. Средняя Азия и ее пригодность для водворения в ней русской колонизации. (Central Asia as a place for Russian colonization.) Izvestiia Imperatorskogo russkogo geograficheskogo obshchestva, 25 (1889).

13580. Труды первого областного съезда крестьянских начальников Семипалатинской областей. (Publications of the first provincial congress of peasant captains of the Semipalatinsk province.) Semipalatinsk, 1905.

13581. Fitrat.   "Три документа по аграрному вопросу в Средней Азии." (Three documents concerning the agrarian problem in Central Asia.) Tr. from the Persian by F. B. Rostopchin. Zapiski Instituta vostokodeveniia Akademii nauk SSSR, 2 (1933):2:69-87.

13582. Korovin, E. P. Растительность Средней Азии и Южного Казакстана. (Vegetation of Central Asia and Southern Kazakstan.) Moscow-Tashkent,   480 p.

13583. IUferev, V. I. Хлопководство в Туркестане. (The cotton industry in Turkestan.) Leningrad, 1925. 160 p.

13584. Gorodetskii, V. D. Пособие по дендрологии для Средней Азии. (A textbook of dendrology for Central Asia.) Moscow, 1934. 323 p.

13585. Prashutinskii, A. Виноградное хозяйство Самаркандской области.   (Cultivation of grapes in the Samarkand province.) Tashkent, 1925. 20 p.

13586. Polozov, V. Рисовое хозяйство Ташкентского уезда. (Cultivation of rice in the Tashkent uezd.) Tashkent, 1924. 18 p.

13587. Маслобойная промышленность Средней Азии. (Butter produce in Central Asia.) Tashkent, 1933. 82 p.

13588. Конские породы Средней Азии. (Horse breeds of Central Asia.) Collected articles. Moscow, 1937. 255 p.

13589. Sevastianov, I. Саранча в Туркестане и борьба с ней. (The locust in Turkestan and the struggle with it.) Tashkent, 1923. 49 p.

13590. Vinogradov, Boris, S. Грызуны Средней Азии. (Rodents of Central Asia.) Moscow, 1936. 228 p.

13591. Семипалатинский кооператор. (The Semipalatinsk co-operator.) Semipalatinsk.   (Bi-weekly.)

(5) Industry and Labor

See 11939-11987; 12261-12271.

13592. Материалы по промышленной статистике Туркестанской
ССР. (Industiral statistics on Turkestan.) Tashkent, TSentral'noe statisticheskoe upravlenie TSSR, 1, 1924-

13593. Промышленная перепись в Туркестанской республике.
(The industrial census in the Turkestan republic.) Tashkent, TSentral'noe statisticheskoe upravlenie TSSR, 1924-

13594. Материалы по статистике труда Туркреспублики. (Labor
statistics of the Turkestan republic.) Tashkent, TSentral'-
noe statisticheskoe upravlenie TSSR, 1, 1924-

13595. Отчет о деятельности Сыр-Дарьинского областного
совета профессиональных союзов.   (An account of the activities of the Syr-Daria provincial soviet of trade unions.)
January 1, 1923--March 1, 1924. Tashkent, 1924. 219 p.

13596. Gavrilov, Michel. "Les corps des metiers en Asie
Centrale et leurs statutes." Revue des études islamiques, 2
(1928):209-230.

13597. Itkin, A. Социально-экономические предпосылки кол-
лективизации хлопководства в Средней Азии. (Socio-economic
precedents of the collectivization of the cotton industry
of Central Asia.) Tashkent, 1932. 298 p.

13598. Permanov, A. Потребительская кооперация Средней
Азии к начали хозяйственного года. (The consumers' cooperative in Central Asia.) Tashkent, 1924. 5 p.

13599. Обзор деятельности Главного управления социального
этрахования Н. К. Т. Туркреспублики и его местных страховых
органов.   (A survey of the work of the main administration
for social insurance in the Turkestan republic.) October
1922 - October 1923. Tashkent, 1924. 32 p.

(6) Trade

See 12054-12145.

13600. Popov, N. (tr.). "Примечание о невыгодной торговле с
Бухарией писанные в 1730 Пьером Куки."   (Notes on the
unfavorable trade with Bokhara.) In: Chteniia v Imperatorskom obshchestve istorii i drevnostei rossiiskikh pri Moskovskom universitete, 1:120-136, January-March 1861.

13601. Kingsmill, T. W. "Intercourse of China with Eastern
Turkestan, etc., in 2nd century B.C." Royal Asiatic society
of Great Britain and Ireland, 1882.

13602. Stefanov, N. "Внешняя торговля СССР в Средней Азии."
(Foreign trade of the USSR in Central Asia.) Planovoe khoziaistvo, Moscow, 10:199-215, October 1926.

(7) Railroads and Highways

See 12146-12216.

13603. Transkaspien und seine eisenbahn. - Nach acten des
erbauers generallieutenant M. Annenkow bearbeitet von Dr.
O. Heyfelder, staatsrath in St. Petersburg, ehemals chef-
arzt der Skobelew-Achal-Teke-expedition. Hannover, 1888.
x, 159 p.

13604. Aliev.   "Туркестан--Сибирская железная дорога и
Киргизстан." (Turkestan -- the Siberian railway and Kirgiz-
stan.) Ekonomicheskaia zhizn', l. 3 (1927):49.

13605. Краткий обзор коммерческой деятельности Ташкентской
железной дороги за 1922 и 1923 гг. и экономического состояния районов, тяготеющих к дороге.(A brief sketch of the commercial activities of the Tashkent railway for 1922-1923
and the economic conditions of the regions dependent upon
it.) Orenburg, 1924. 103 p.

(8) Finances

See 12272-12300.

13606. Роспись государственных доходов и расходов Туркестанской социалистической советской республики на октябрь-сент-
ябрь 1923-1924 г.   (State budget. Income and expenditures
of the Turkestan SSR for the year 1923-1924 [October 1923-
September 1924].) Tashkent, Sovet narodnykh kommissarov
TSSR, 1923. xxiii, 81 p.

13607. Делопроизводство и отчетность советских общественных и частных учреждений и промышленных предприятий Туркреспублики.   (The management and accountability of Soviet
public and private institutions and commercial enterprises
in Turkestan.) Tashkent, Sovet narodnykh kommissarov TSSR,
1924.

13608. Khodorov, I. "Денежный и товарный рынок Средней Азии."
(Currency and commodity markets of Central Asia.) Planovoe
khoziaistvo, April 1926, 207-217.

(9) Economic Planning and Zoning

See 12217-12221.

13609. Хозяйственный план Туркреспублики на 1923-1924 год.
(The economic plan of the Turkestan republic for 1923-1924.)
Tashkent, Turkestanskaia planovaia komissiia, 1923.

13610. Перспективы хозяйства Туркреспублики 1924-1929 гг.
(Economic perspectives of the Turkestan republic, 1924-
1929.) Tashkent, Turkestanskaia planovaia komissiia, 1924.
1034 p.

13611. Aleksandrov, I. G. Материалы по гидрометрии рек бассейна Сыр-Дарьи с 1900 по 1916 г. (Sources on hydrometry
of the rivers of the Syr-Daria basin, 1900-1916.) Moscow,
1924. 249 p.

13612. Kondrashev, S. K. "Плановой завоз товаров в Среднюю
Азию." (Planned import into Central Asia.) Planovoe khoziaistvo, June 1925, 209-216.

13613. Kondrashev, S. K. "Среднеазиатское размежевание."
(The zoning of Central Asia.) Planovoe khoziaistvo, April
1925, 255-264.

13614. Материалы изысканий по устройству водохранилищ в бассейне р. Сыр-Дарьи. (Research in the construction of water
reservoirs in the basin of the Syr-Daria.) Moscow, 1923.
319 p.

13615. Электрификация Средней Азии. (The electrification
of Central Asia.) Trudy 1/go Sredneaziatskogo energetiche-
skogo s"ezda. Materialy k gosplanu elektrifikatsii UzSSR,
TadzhSSR, TSSR, KSSR i KKAO. Moscow, VSNKh SSSR, 1932.

13616. Материалы по районированию Туркестана.   (Materials
on the zoning of Turkestan.) Tashkent, 1, 1924-

13617. Dinaev, G. "Плановое хозяйство вСредней Азии."
(Planned economy in Central Asia.) Planovoe khoziaistvo,
March 1926, 217-229.

13618. Aleksandrov, I. G. Проект орошения юговосточной
Ферганы. (Project for the irrigation of southeastern Fer-
gana.) Moscow, 1924. 234 p.

K. Social and Cultural Conditions

See 12439-21536.

13619. Borozdin, I. "Из области татарской культуры."
(On Tatar culture.) Novyi Vostok, Moscow, 25 (1929):185-200.

13620. Bashkirov, A. S. Памятники булгаро-татарской культуры
на Волге. (Monuments of Bulgaro-Tatar culture on the Volga.)
Kazan, 1928. 118 p.

13621. Суд над безграмотным. (The trial of an illiterate.)
A sketch for the stage. Tashkent, Turkestanskaia chrezvy-
chainaia komissiia po likvidatsii bezgramotnosti, 1923. 9 p.

13622. Стенографический отчет Расширенного совещания дея-
телей культуры и просвещения, созванного 11 ноября 1923 г.
Советом народных комиссаров по вопросу народного просвещения. (An account of the Conference of educational workers.)
Tashkent, 1924. 47 p.

13623. Garritskii, A. "Библиотеки в Средней Азии до русского
завоевания." (Libraries in Central Asia before the Russian
conquest.) Novyi Vostok, 10-11 (1925):381-382.

13624. Radlov, V. Proben der volkslitteratur der nördlichen
türkischen stämme. St. Petersburg, 1885.

13625. Radlov, V. Proben der volkslitteratur der türkischen
stämme Süd Sibiriens. St. Petersburg, 1866.

13626. Hsü, Tun-ku (tr.). (Hazama Riote, author). 西 域
佛 敎 之 研 究 Hsi-yü Fo-chiao chih yen chiu. (Studies
on the history of Buddhism in ancient Central Asia.) Yen-
ching journal, 4:653-701, December,1928.

13627. Denike, Boris P. Искусство Средней Азии. (Art of
Central Asia.) Moscow, 1927. 55, 23 p.

13628. Искусство Средней Азии. (Art of Central Asia.) Collected articles. Moscow, 1930. 113 p.

13629. IAvorskii, I. L. Средняя Азия. (Central Asia.) Cultural success and problems of Russia in Central Asia. Odessa,
1893.

13630. Ganiev, Medjid Sultan. Русско-татарский словарь составленный в порядке русского алфавита по Толковому словарю В. Даля. (A Russian-Tatar dictionary.) Baku, 1909. 416 p.

L. Communist Party

See 11495-11583.

13631. TSvibak, M. "Классовая борьба в Туркестане." (Class struggle in Turkestan.) Istorik marksist, Moscow, 1929:11: 130-151.

13632. Bozhko, F. Октябрьская революция в Средней Азии.(The October revolution in Central Asia.) Tashkent, 1934. 43 p.

13663. Туркмения. Съезд советов. Стенографический отчет. (Congress of soviets. Stenographic report.) 1925-

13634. Постановление Центрального исполнительного комитета Туркестанской автономной советской социалистической республики. (A decree passed by the Central Executive committee of the Turkestan ASSR.) Moscow, 1924.

13635. Ksenofontov, F. Узбекистан и Туркменистан. К вопросу об их вхождении в СССР. (Uzbekistan and Turkmenistan. The problem of the entrance of Uzbekstan and Turkmenistan into the Soviet Union.) Moscow, 1925. 40 p.

13636. Nepomniashchii, P. M. Алфавитно-предметный указатель к постановлениям и распоряжениям ЦККПТ, ЦИК'а и СНК Туркреспублики. (An alphabetic and subject index of the decrees and orders made by the Central executive committee and the Council of the people's economy of the Turkestan republic.) Tashkent, 1923. 114 p.

13637. Сборник важнейших декретов, постановлений и распоряжений Правительства ТССР. За 1917-1922 гг.(A collection of the most important decrees, decisions, and orders of the Turkestan soviet government, 1917-1922.) Tashkent, 1923. ii, 213, vi p.

13638. Сборник важнейших декретов и постановлений Правительства ТССР. За 1923 г. Сентябрь-октябрь. (A collection of the most important decrees and decisions of the Turkestan soviet government. September-October 1923.) Tashkent, 1924. 46, ii p.

586   Russia

13639. Сборник дектеров и постановлений правительства ТССР.
За 1923 г. Ноябрь-декабрь. (A collection of decress and
decisions made by the Turkestan Soviet government.) November-December, 1923. Tashkent, 1924. 65 p.

13640. Сборник важнейших декретов, постановлений и распоряжений Правительства СССР и РСФСР. За 1924 г. Январь-июнь.
(A collection of the most important desrees, resolutions,
and orders passed by the government of the USSR and RSFSR
for the period January-June 1924.) Tashkent, 1924. 155 p.

13641. Бюллетень 3-й Чрезвычайной сессии Турцика. (Bulletin of the 3rd extraordinary session of the Turkestan
central executive committee.) Tashkent, 1924.

13642. VIII Всетуркестанский съезд Коммунистической
партии Туркестана. (The 8th All-Turkestan congress of the
Communist party.) Tashkent, 1924. 11 nos.

13643. III Партийная конференция Туркестанского фронта.
(3rd Communist party conference of Turkestan.) Tashkent,
1924. 35 p.

13644. Работа среди женщин в Туркестане. (Work among women
in Turkestan.) Tashkent, Kommunisticheskaia partiia Turkestana, 1924. 14 p.

13645. Отчет Центрального комитета Коммунистической партии
Туркестана. За период с VII по VIII съезд 1923-1924 гг.
(An account of the Central committee of the Communist party
of Turkestan for the Period between the 7 and 8 sessions
1923-1924.) Tashkent, 1924. 40 p.

13646. К VIII Всетуркестанскому партсъезду. (Тезисы).
(Reports for the 8th Congress of the Turkestan communist
party.) Tashkent, 1924. 15 p.

13647. Сборник положений, программ и инструкций по агитпро-
работе на зимний период 1924-1925гг. (A collection of decrees, programs, and instructions pertaining to agitational
work for 1924-1925.) Tashkent, Politicheskoe upravlenie
Turkestanskogo fronta, 1924. 122 p.

M. By Republics

(1) Autonomous Tatar SSR

See 13359-13647.

(a) History

See 13447-13514.

13648. Ermolaev, V. M. Демографический очерк Татарской республики. (A demographic sketch of the Tatar republic.) In: Materialy po izucheniiu Tatarstana, Kazan, 2 (1925):113-131.

13649. Korbut, M. K. "К вопросу об изучении истории пролетариата Татарстана." (The problem of the study of the history of the Tatarstan proletariat.) Istoriia proletariata SSSR, 3-4 (1930):138-157.

13650. Firsov, N. A. "Научное общество татароведения в Казани." (The Kazan scientific society for the study of the Tatars.) Novyi Vostok, 10-11 (1925):377-378.

13651. Vekslin, Noson-Ber Zalmanovich. Изучение Татарстана за 10 лет. (The study of the Tatar republic for the past 10 years. 1920-1930.) Kazan, 1930. 97 p.

13652. Татарстан в годы первой революции. (Tatarstan during the years of the first revolution.) Kazan, 1931. 181 p.

13653. Firsov, Nikolai A. Инородческое население прежнего Казанского царства в новой России до 1762 года и колонизация Закамских земель в это время. (The native population of the former Kazan kingdom up to 1762 in new Russia and the colonization of the Kama lands during the same period.) Kazan, 1869.

13654. Evseviev, M. E. Мордва Татреспублики. (The Mordvins of the Tatar republic.) In: Materialy po izucheniiu Tatarstana, Kazan, 2 (1925):179-196.

(b) General Accounts

See 13515-13527.

13655. Конституция Татарской социалистической советской республики. (The constitution of the Tatar socialist soviet republic.) Kazan, 1926. 21, 26 p.

13656. Отчет Областного правления Союза работников просвещения Автономной Татарской ССР за время с 1-го июля 1923 г. по 1-е сентября 1924 г. (An account of the Provincial administration of the Autonomous Tatar SSR Union of educational workers, June 1, 1923 - September 1, 1924.) Kazan, 1924. 74 p.

13657. Стенографический отчет 2-го Съезда работников юстиции
Татарской социалистической советской республики. (A steno-
graphic account of the 2nd Congress of legal workers of the
Tatar SSR.) Kazan, 1924. 164 p.

13658. Резолюции и постановления 6-го Областного съезда
Союза Медсантруд Татреспублики. (Resolutions and decrees
passed by the 6th Congress of Medical workers of the Tatar
republic.) Kazan, 1924. 74 p.

13659. Каталог выставки картин Тат. АХРР при Ак. Ц Татнар-
компроса. (Catalogue of paintings exhibited.) Kazan,
Tatarskaia assotsiatsiia khudozhnikov revoliutsionnoi Rossii, 1923. 8 p.

                 (c) Economic Conditions

See 13549-13618.

13660. Краткая экономическая характеристика районов Татарии.
(A short economic sketch of the Tatar districts.) Kazan,
Tatarskaia ASSR, Gosudarstvennaia planovaia komissiia, Sta-
tisticheskii sektor, 1930. 92 p.

13661. Серия популярных справочников. Выпуск 1-ый. Статистический справочник по сельскому хозяйству Та АССР.
(A series of popular guides. 1st issue. A statistical guide
to agriculture in the Tatar SSR.) Kazan, Statisticheskoe
upravlenie Tatarskoi SSR, 1, 1924.

13662. Ermolaev, V. M. Сельское хозяйство Татарской республики. (Rural economy of the Tatar republic.) In: Materialy po izucheniiu Tatarstana, Kazan, (1925):2:197-274.

13663. Sabirov, R. Деревня Татреспублики после голода.
(The village of the Tatar republic after the famine.) Kazan,
1923. 59 p.

13664. Отчет профсоюзов Татреспублики за время с 15 сентаб-
ря 1922 г. по 1 ноября 1923 г.   (An account of the
Concil of trade unions of the Tatar republic for the period
September 15, 1922-November 1, 1923. Tashkent, 1923. xxiii,
81 p.

13665. Отчет Совета профсоюзов Татреспублики за время с
декабря 1923 г. по ноябрь 1924 г. (An account of the Council
of trade unions of the Tatar republic for December 1923 -
November 1924.) Kazan, 1924. 120, 106 p.

13666. Хозяйственный план Хорезмской народной республики на 1923-1924 г. (The economic plan of the Khorezm peoples' republic, 1923-1924.) Tashkent, Sredneaziatskii ekonomicheskii sovet, 1924. 32 p.

(d) Communist Party

See 13631-13647.

13667. Отчет ЦИК и СНК Татарской ССР. За время с III по IV Съезд. (An account of the Central executive committee and the Soviet of people's commissars of the Tatar SSR for the period between the 3rd and 4th conferences.) Kazan, 1923. 304 p.

13668. Отчет о деятельности ЦИК и СНК Татарской ССР, 1922-23. (An account of the work of the Central executive committee and the Soviet of people's commissars of the Tatar SSR for 1922-1923.) Kazan, 1923. 40 p.

13669. Отчет Цик и СНК Татарской ССР к V Съезду советов. (An account of the Central executive committee and the Council of people's commissars to the 5th Congress of soviets.) Kazan, 1925. 200 p.

13670. Отчет о деятельсности ЦИК и СНК за 1923-1924 г. (A report of the activities of the Central executive committee and the Soviet of people's commissars for 1923-24.) Kazan, Tatarskaia SSR, TsIK, 1924. 88 p.

13671. Бюллетень IV Съезда советов Татарской ССР 17-24 декабря 1923 года. (Bulletin of the 4th Conference of soviets of the Tatar SSR, December 17-24, 1923.) Kazan, 1923.

13672. Положение о Центральном исполнительном комитете Автономной Татарской ССР. (Statute concerning the Central executive committee of the Autonomous Tatar SSR.) Kazan, 1924. 30, 57 p.

13673. V Съезд советов Татарской ССР. (The 5th Congress of soviets of the Tatar soviet republic.) Stenographic account. January 5-9, 1925. Kazan, 1925. iv, 198 p.

13674. План работы парторганизации Тат ССР в области национального вопроса. (A plan for party organizations of the Tatar SSR in the field of national policy.) Kazan, Tatarskaia oblastnaia organizatsiia Rossiiskoi kommunisticheskoi partii, 1924. 26 p.

13675. Отчет Областной контрольной комиссии РКП Автономной Татарской ССР. (An account of the Control commission of the Russian communist party of the Autonomous Tatar SSR.) Kazan, 1924. 35 p.

(2) Autonomous Bashkir SSR

See 13359-13647.

(a) Maps

13676. Схематическая карта Башреспублики. (A map of the Bashkir republic.) Ufa, 1924.

(b) Anthropology

See 10722-10784; 13427-13446.

13677. Rudenko, S. Башкиры. (The Bashkirs.) Petrograd, 1916.

13678. Nikol'skii, D. Башкиры. (The Bashkirs.) St. Petersburg, 1899. 377 p.

13679. Krasheninnikov, N. Угасающая Башкирия. (The waning Bashkiria.) Moscow, 1907.

(c) History

See 13447-13514.

(i) Sources

13680. Башкирский краеведческий сборник. (The Bashkir miscellany.) Materialy Obshchestva po izucheniiu Bashkirii, Ufa, 1926-   v. I, 69 p.

13681. Tukhvatullin, Fatikh. Материалы к истории башкир. (Sources for the history of the Bashkirs.) Ufa, 1928. 124 p.

13682. See 13448.

(ii) Accounts

13683. Tipeev, Shamson. Очерки по истории Башкирии. (Historical sketches of Bashkiria.) Ufa, 1930. 222 p.

13684. Ishcherikov, P. F. Очерки из истории колонизации
Башкирии. (Sketches from the history of the colonization
of Bashkiria.) Ufa, 1933.

13685. Материалы по истории Башкирской АССР. Часть I.
Башкирские восстания в XVII и первой половине XVIII вв.
(Materials pertaining to the history of the Bashkir ASSR.
Part I. Bashkir uprisings in the XVII and first half of the
XVIII centuries.) Moscow, Akademiia nauk, 1936. 631 p.

13686. Karmin, M. S. "Очерки из истории классовой борьбы в
Башкирии в XVIII-XIX веках."(Outlines of the history of
class struggle in Bashkiria in the XVIII-XIX centuries.)
Sotsial'noe khoziaistvo Bashkirii, 3-4 (1934):9-49.

13687. Samoilov, Feodor N. Малая Башкирия в 1918-1920 гг.
(Bashkiria in 1918-1920.) From the history of the experiment of Soviet national policy. Moscow, 1933. 95 p.

13688. Murtazin, M. L. Башкирия и башкирские войска в
гражданскую войну. (Bashkiria and the Bashkir troops in
the civil war.) Moscow, 1927.

13689. Tipeev, Shamson. К истории национального движения
в советской Башкирии. (The national movement in Soviet
Bashkiria.) 1917-1929. Ufa, 1929. 150 p.

13690. Башкирское национальное движение, 1917-1920 гг.
(The Bashkir national movement.) Ufa, 1926. 27 p.

13691. Кулацкие восстания в Башкирии в 1918 г. (Kulak uprisings in Bashkiria., 1918.) Memoirs. Ufa, 1935. 206 p.

(d) General Accounts

See 13515-13527.

13692. Gasilovskii, A. N. Башкирская АССР. (The Bashkir
ASSR.) Moscow, 1932. 17 p.

13693. Stepanov, P. N. Уральская область с приложением
очерка: Башкирская АССР. (The Ural province. With a supplementary essay on the Bashkir ASSR.) Moscow, 1928. 116 p.

13694. Mironova, O. География Башкирии. (The geography of
Bashkiria.) Ufa, 1926. 72 p.

13695. Kirianov, S. Советская Башкирия. (Soviet Bashkiria.)
Ufa, 1931. 157 p.

13696. Десять лет советской Башкирии. 1919-1929. (Ten
years of Soviet Bashkiria.) Ufa, Bashkirskaia ASSR, Sovet
narodnykh komissarov, 1929. 426 p.

13697. Atnagulov, S. Башкирия. (Bashkiria.) Moscow, 1925.
123 p.

13698. Пять лет Народного комиссариата юстиции Автономной
Башкирской ССР. (Five years of the People's commissariat of
justice of the Autonomous Bashkir SSR.) Ufa, 1924. 24 p.

13699. Культурное строительство Башкирии за пятнадцать лет.
(Cultural construction of Bashkiria for fifteen years.)
Ufa, 1934. 110 p.

13700. Lisovskii, A. A. Башкирская АССР. (The Bashkir
ASSR.) Moscow, 1932. 28 p.

13701. Пятнадцать лет советской Башкирии. (Fifteen years
of Soviet Bashkiria.) Collected articles. Ufa, 1934. 283 p.

13702. Пятнадцать лет Башкирской республики.(Fifteen years
of the Bashkir republic.) Collected articles. Ufa, 1934.
246 p.

13703. Krasheninnikov, N. A. Под солнцем Башкирии. (Under
the Bashkir sun.) 4th ed., revised. Moscow, 1936. 346 p.

(e) Economic Conditions

See 13549-13618.

13704. Башкирское центральное статистическое управление.
(The Bashkir central statistical administration.) Ufa, 1923.
145 p.

13705. Экономическая география Башкирской ССР. (Economic
geography of the Bashkir SSR.) Minsk, 1936. 306 p.

13706. Районы Башкирской АССР. (Zones of the Bashkir ASSR.)
Statistical guide. Ufa, 1931. 325 p.

13707. Налоговая работа Народного комиссариата финансов
БАССР в 1922-1923 бюджетном году. (Taxation in the Bashkir
ASSR, 1922-1923.) Ufa, Narodnyi komissariat finansov, 1923.
64 p.

13708. Налоговая работа Народного комиссариата финансов
БАССР в 1923-1924 бюджетном году. (Tax procedure of the
People's commissariat of finance of the Bashkir republic.)
Ufa, 1924. 91 p.

13709. Основные сведения по неналоговым доходам Башреспублики в 1923-1924 операционном году. (Information concerning revenues other than those derived from taxes.)
Ufa, 1924. 44 p.

13710. Мероприатия по восстановлению сельского хозяйства
Башреспублики за 1922-1923 год. (Measures for the restoration of agriculture in the Bashkir republic.) Ufa, Narodnyi komissariat zemledeliia Bashkirskoi ASSR, 1923. 103 p.

13711. Животноводство в Башкирии. (Cattle breeding in Bashkiria.) Ufa, 1934. 169 p.

13712. Ivanov, V. I. Новые бобовые культуры в Башкирии.
(New bean cultures in Bashkiria.) Ufa, 1935. 94 p.

13713. Kavtsevich, M. Энергетические ресурсы Башкирской ССР
и проблема их использования. (Power resources of the Bashkir SSR and the problem of their utilization.) Minsk, 1935.
24 p.

13714. IAgudin, Gimat Z. Индустриализация Башкирии. (Industrialization of Bashkiria.) Ufa, 1934. 72 p.

13715. Ozhiganov, D. G. Полезные ископаемые Башкирии.
(Minerals of Bashkiria.) Ufa, 1934. 111 p.

13716. Отчет о деятельности Правления Башпрома за 1923-1924
операционный год. (An account of the activities of the
Administration of the Bashkir trading enterprises for 1923-
1924.) Ufa, 1925. 107 p.

13717. Справочник по профессиональному образованию. (Guide
to trade schools.) Ufa, 1924. 29 p.

(f) Communist Party

See 13631-13647.

13718. Gnedkov, L. G. (comp.). Башкирская организация ВКП(б).
(Bashkir organization of the Communist party.) Ufa, 1933.
viii, 184 p.

13719. Протокол заседаний IV Всебашкирского съезда советов рабочих, крестьянских и красноармейских депутатов. (Protocol of the sessions of the IV All-Bashkir conference of soviets) Ufa, 1924. 136 p.

13720. Отчет о деятельности ЦИК и СНК БАССР IV созыва V Всебашкирскому съезду советов. (An account of the activities of the Central executive committee and the council of people's commissars of the Bashkir ASSR to the 5th All-Bashkir congress of soviets.) Ufa, 1925. 46 p.

13721. VIII Башкирская областная конференция РКП (б). (The 8th Bashkir provincial conference of the Communist party.) Ufa, 1924. 3 nos.

13722. IX Башкирская областная конференция РКП (б).   (The 9th Bashkir provincial conference of the Communist party.) January 30 - February 4, 1925. Ufa, 1925. 103 p.

13723. Годовой отчет Башкирского областного комитета РКП(б). (Annual report of the Bashkir provincial committee of the Communist party.) 1923-1924.   Ufa, 1924. 194 p.

(3) Autonomous Kazak SSR

See 13359-31647.

(a) Bibliography

See 13359-13367.

13724. Voznesenskii, E. and Piotrovskii, A. Материалы для библиографии по антропологии и этнографии Казакстана и среднеазиатских республик.   (Sources for bibliography on the anthropology and ethnography of Kazakstan and the Central Asiatic republics.) Leningrad, Akademiia nauk SSSR, 1927. 247 p.

13725. Gorban, N. V. Архивные богатства Казакстана. (Archival wealth of Kazakstan.) A guide to the archival depositories of the Kazakstan central archives.   Alma-Ata, 1933. 16 p.

(b) Directories

See 13376-13377.

13726. Bol'shakov, L. (Grazhdanskii). Справочная книга по Казакстану.   (A Kazakstan directory.) Orenburg, 1925. 364 p

13727. Bondarchuk, Z. P., Bulin, N. P., and others. Весь Казакстан. (All Kazakstan.) A guide. Alma-Ata, 1932. 482 p.

13728. Briakin, M. I. Справочник по курортам Казакстана. (Guide to the resorts of Kazakstan.) Alma-Ata, 1935. 66,3 p.

13729. Gorbunov, V. Путеводитель по Казакстану. (A guide through Kazakstan.) Moscow - Alma-Ata, 1932. 156 p.

13730. Begaliev, G. B. Казахско-русский словарь. (Kazakstan-Russian dictionary.) Alma-Ata, 1936. 266 p.

(c) Statistics

See 13549-13553.

13731. Южный Казахстан в цифрах. (South Kazakstan in figures.) Statistical guide. Chimkent, 1936. 314 p.

(d) History

See 13447-31514.

13732. Asfendiarov, S. D. (ed.). Прошлое Казахстана в источниках и материалах. (Past of Kazakstan. Sources and materials.) Alma-Ata - Moscow, 1935. 293 p.

13733. Asfendiarov, S. D. История Казахстана с древнейших времен. (History of Kazakstan from the earliest times.) Alma-Ata, 1935. 259 p.

13734. Asfendiarov, S. D. Очерки истории казахов. (Outlines of the history of the people of Kazakstan.) Alma-Ata, 1935. 91 p.

13735. Togzhanov. "О казакском феодализме." (Concerning Kazakstan feudalism.) Revoliutsionnyi Vostok, 6 (1936): 21:120-138.

13736. Chuloshnikov, A. P. "К истории феодальных отношений в Казахстане в конце XVII в." (Contributions to the history of feudal relations in Kazakstan at the end of the XVII century.) Izvestiia Akademii nauk SSSR, Otdelenie obshchestvennykh nauk, 3 (1936):497-524.

13737. Lebedev, V. "Из истории завоевания Казахстана царской Россией (1730-1732 годы)." (From the history of the conquest of Kazakstan by tsarist Russia, 1730-1732.) Bor'ba klassov, 10:60-65, October 1936.

13738. Shakhmatov, V. "Очерки по истории уйгуро-дунганского
национально-освободительного движения в XIX веке." (Outlines
of the history of the Uigur-Dungan national liberation movement in the XIX century.) Trudy Kazakhstanskogo nauchno-
issledovatel'skogo instituta natsional'noi kul'tury, 1 (1935):
51-118.

13739. Mel'nikov, G. N. Октябрь в Казакстане.   (October in
Kazakstan.) Alma-Ata, 1930. 233 p.

13740. "Летопись важнейших событий Октябрьской революции и
гражданской войны в Казакстане." (A chronicle of the most
important events of the October revolution and the civil war
in Kazakstan.) Bol'shevik Kazakstana, 52-53:133-144, January-February 1936; 54:67-72, March 1936.

13741. Asfendiarov, S. D.   Национально-освободительное восстание 1916 года в Казакстане." (National liberation uprising of 1916 in Kazakstan.) Alma-Ata, 1936. 150 p.

13742. Казакстан к IX съезду советов. (Kazakstan at the IX
convention of soviets.) 1931-1934. Alma-Ata, 1935. xvi, 258p.

13743. Nurpeisov, S. N., Isaev, U. D., and Gusev, N. I.(ed.)
15 лет Казакской АССР. (15 years of the Kazakstan ASSR.) 1920-
1935. Alma-Ata, 1935. 268 p.

13744. Burkidbaev, A. "От царской колонии к советскому
аграрно-индустриальному Казакстану." (From a tsarist colony to a soviet agrarian-industrial Kazakstan.) IUnyi kommunist, 1 (1931):52-65.

13745. Zhurgenev, T. Культурная революция в Казакстане. (The
cultural revolution in Kazakstan.) Alma-Ata, 1935. 44 p.

(e) General Accounts

See 13515-13527.

13746. Cherdantsev, G. N. Казакстан.   (Kazakstan.) Moscow,
1930. 203 p.

13747. Skosyrev, P., Popov, V., and others. Люди нового
Казакстана. (People of new Kazakstan.) Sketches. Alma-Ata,
Moscow, 1933. 100 p.

13748. Maimin, I. B. Казакстан в 1932 году. (Kazakstan in
1932.) Alma-Ata, Moscow, Ogiz, 1932. 74 p.

13749. Gorban, N. V. Алма-Ата--столица социалистического Казакстана. (Alma-Ata , the capital of socialist Kazakstan.) Alma-Ata - Moscow, 1933. 36 p.

(f) Economic Conditions

See 13549-13618.

13750. Goloshchekin, F. I. Казакстан на путях социалистического переустройства.(Kazakstan on the road to socialist rebuilding.) Moscow - Alma-Ata, 1931. 248 p.

13751. Voshchinin, V. P. Казакстан. (Kazakstan.) An economic geography. Moscow-Leningrad, 192 . 91 p.

13752. Pototskii, A. P. "Народное хозяйство Казакстана и основные тенденции его развития." (National economy of Kazakstan and its main tendencies of development.) Narodnoe khoziaistvo Kazakstana, Kzyl Orda, 1927: 5:3-35.

13753. Isaev, U. Контрольные цифры народного хозяйства Казакстана на 1933 год. (Control figures concerning the national economy of Kazakstan for 1933.) Alma-Ata - Moscow, 1933. 58 p.

13754. Grinev, V. I. Геологические исследования вдоль Туркестано-Сибирской железной дороги от ст. Алма-Ата до ст. Биже в 1928 году. (Geological explorations along the Turkestan-Siberian railway from the station Alma-Ata to the station Bizhe in 1928.) Leningrad--Moscow, 1933. 80 p.

13755. Shcherba, A. G. Почвы Казакстана и их сельскохозяйственное использование. (The soils of Kazakstan and their agricultural utilization.) Alma-Ata, 1935. 118 p.

13756. Matusevich, S. P. Почвенный покров Казакстана. (Soil surface of Kazakstan.) Alma-Ata, 1934. 93 p.

13757. Pavlov, N. V. Флора центрального Казакстана. (Flora of Central Kazakstan.) Moscow, 1935. 550 p.

13758. Grossman, I. M. Казакская АССР. (The Kazak ASSR.) The fur resources. Moscow, Sovetskaia Aziia, 1932. 57 p.

13759. Казакстан. (Kazakstan.) Economic problems of the second five-year plan. Leningrad, Akademiia nauk, Konferentsiia po izucheniiu proizvoditel'nykh sil Kazakstana, 1932. 484 p.

13760. Shnitnikov, V. N. Животный мир Казахстана. (The animal kingdom of Kazakstan.) Alma-Ata, 1935. 242 p.

13761. Kiiatkin, P. F. Козоводство в Казахстане. (Goat breeding in Kazakstan.) Alma-Ata, 1934. 50 p.

13762. Selivonov, P. K. Кролиководство в Казахстане. (Rabbit breeding in Kazakstan.) Alma-Ata, 1933. 128 p.

13763. Favorskii, V. V. Энергетика Казахстана. (Water power resources of Kazakstan.) Alma-Ata, 1935. 66 p.

13764. Safronov, V. I. Топливо в Казахстане. (Fuel in Kazakstan.) Kzyl-Orda, 1935. 112 p.

13765. Sarkisian, D. A. Золотая промышленность Казахстана. (Gold industry of Kazakstan.) Moscow, 1935. 36 p.

13766. Труды и итоги работ Семипалатинского губернского съезда советов РКК депутатов IV созыва. (Work and activities of the 4th session of the Semipalatinsk conference of soviets.) September 13-18, 1923. Semipalatinsk, Kazak ASSR, Semipalatinskii gubernskii s"ezd sovetov, 1923. 131 p.

13767. Работа Семипалатинского губернского комитета РКП. (An account of the activities of the Semipalatinsk gubernia committee of the Russian communist party.) Semipalatinsk, 1924. 167 p.

13768. Бюллетени ... V созыва. (Bulletins of the Semipalatinsk gubernia congress of soviets, 5th session.) March 10-14, 1925. Semipalatinsk, Gubernskii s"ezd sovetov, 1925. 106 p.

(4) Turkmen SSR

See 13359-13647.

13769. Shteinberg, E. L. Очерки истории Туркмении. (Outlines of the history of Turkmenia.) Moscow, 1934. 168 p.

13770. Туркмения. (Turkmenia.) Colected articles. Leningrad, 1929. 2 v.

13771. Akarskii, V. N. Туркменская ССР. (The Turkmen SSR.) Moscow, 1932. 18 p.

13772. Kozlov, T. S. Зачатки большевизма в революционном движении Туркмении, 1904-1916 гг. (Beginnings of bolshevism in the revolutionary movement of Turkmenia, 1904-1916.) Ashkhabad, 1928. 18 p.

13773. Askochenskii, A. N. Водное хозяйство Туркмении. (Administration of water resources of Turkmenia.) Moscow, 1934. 110 p.

13774. Tikhonov, N. Кочевники. (Nomads.) Sketches of Turkmenia. Stalinbad-Samarkand, 1933. 140 p.

13775. Проблемы Туркмении. Труды I Конференции по изучению производительных сил Туркмении.(Problems of Turkmenia. Transactions of the first Conference for the study of the productive forces of Turkmenia.) Moscow, Academy of sciences, 1934. 2 v.

13776. See 13362.

13777. Lavrov, A. P., Malykin, P. IA., and Khanmagometov, T. Курорты Туркмении. (Resorts of Turkmenia.) Ashkhabad-Baku, 1935. 128 p.

13778. Туркмения в 1933 г. Бюджет Туркменской ССР в связи с нар.-хоз. планом. . (The Turkmen republic in 1933. Budget of the Turkmen SSR in relation to the national economic plan.) Moscow, 1933. 69 p.

13779. Государственный бюджет Туркменской советской социалистической республики на 1927-1928 год. (State budget of the Turkmen SSR for 1927-1928.) Moscow, Turkmenskaia SSR, Narodnyi komissariat finansov,1928. 172 p.

13780. Zhuravleva, E. V. Искусство советской Туркмении. (The art of Soviet Turkmenia.) Moscow, 1934. 133 p.

13781. Поэты советского Туркменистана. (Poets of Soviet Turkmenia.) Moscow, 1934. 79 p.

13782. Stalin, I. V. Речь на Совещании передовых колхозников ... Туркменистана. (Speech made at the meeting of leading collective farmers.) Revoliutsiia i natsional'nosti, 93:21, November 1937.

13783. See 13412.

(5) Uzbek SSR

See 13359-13647.

13784. Узбек. Правда Востока. (Uzbek. Truth of the East.)
1, 1924-

13785. Всесоюзная перепись 1926 г.(The All-Union census of
1926.) V. 49, The Uzbek SSR. Moscow, 1930.

13786. Frolov, S. I. Узбекистан.   (Uzbekistan.) Samarkand, 1930. 276 p.

13787. Lutskii, V. Узбекистан и Египет. Итоги двух систем.
(Uzbekistan and Egypt. A summary of two systems.) Moscow,
1934. 60 p.

13788. Kastel'skaia,Z. D. Восстание 1916 года в Узбекистане.
(The uprising of 1916 in Uzbekistan.) Tashkent, 1937. 65 p.

13789. Узбек. Съезд советов. Стенографический отчет. (Uzbek.
Congress of soviets. Stenographic report.) 1, 1925-

13790. Узбек. Высший совет народного хозяйства. Сборник
узаконений и распоряжений по промышленному строительству
ВСНХ, Узбекской ССР и его местных органов. (Supreme economic council. Collection of laws and ordinances on industrial
reconstruction issued by the Supreme economic council of
the Uzbek SSR and by its organs.) 1928-

13791. Государственный бюджет Узбекской ССР.   (State budget of the Uzbek SSR.) With an explanatory memorandum.
1926/27-

13792. Два года работы правительства Узбекской ССР. (Two
years' activities of the government of the Uzbek SSR.)
TSentral'nyi izpolnitel'nyi komitet, 1926/27-1927/28.

13793. Ermilov, V. and Madzhidi, P. (ed.). Литература Узбекистана. (Literature of Uzbekistan.) Collected articles.
Moscow, 1935. 387 p.

13794. Madzhidi, R. Литература советского Узбекистана.
(Literature of Soviet Uzbekistan.) Tashkent, 1934. 105 p.

13795. Chepelev, V. N. Искусство советского Узбекистана.
(Art of Soviet Uzbekistan.) Leningrad, 1935. 2 v.

13796. Отчет о деятельности Ташкентского новогородского Совета РК и КД XII Созыва и его отделов.   (An account of the work of the Tashkent novgorodskii soviet and its divisions.) October 1922 - October 1923. Tashkent,1923. 151 p.

(6) Kirghiz SSR

See 13359-13846.

(a) Bibliography

See 13359-13367.

13797. Проспект-каталог.   (A catalog of publications of the Kirghiz state publication office.) Orenburg, 1923. No.3.

(b) Anthropology

See 13427-13446.

13798. Ibragimov, I. I. Этнографические очерки киргизского народа.   (Ethnographic sketches of the Kirghiz people.) In: Russkii Turkestan, Moscow, 2 (1872).

13799. Zeland, N. L. Киргизы. (The Kirghiz.) Zapiski Sibirskogo otdela Imperatorskogo russkogo geograficheskogo obshchestva, 7 (1885):2.

13800. Kharuzin, A. К вопросу о происхождении киргизского народа. (The origin of the Kirghiz people.) Moscow, 1895.

13801. Kharuzin, A. N. Киргизы Букеевской орды. (The Kirghiz of the Bukeev Horde.) Moscow, 1889.

13802. Chormanov, M. Заметка о киргизах Павлодарского уезда. (Note on the Kirghiz of the Pavlodarsk uezd.) Zapiski Zapadnosibirskogo otdela Imperatorskogo russkogo geograficheskogo obshchestva, Omsk, 1906.

13803. Vul'fson, E. Киргизы. (The Kirghiz.) Moscow, 1910. 79 p.

13804. Bukeikhanov, A. Киргизы. (The Kirghiz.) 1910.

13805. See 13473.

(c) History

See 13447-13514.

13806. Tynyshpaev, M. Материалы к истории киргиз-казакского народа. (Sources pertaining to the history of the Kirghiz-Kazak people.) Tashkent, 1925. 75 p.

13807. Rumiantsev, P. P. Киргизский народ в прошлом и настоящем. (The Kirghiz people, past and present.) St. Petersburg, Pereselencheskoe upravlenie, 1910.

13808. Romanovskii, G. Краткий очерк исследований восточной части киргизской степи Западной Сибири с 1816 по 1893 г. (A brief study of the eastern part of the Kirghiz steppes of Western Siberia from 1816 to 1893.) St. Petersburg, 1903.

13809. Katanaev, G. Киргизские степи, Средняя Азия и Северный Китай в XVII и XVIII ст. по показаниям, разведкам, доезжим записям, отчетам и исследованиям зап.-сиб. казаков и. прочих служилых сибирских людей. (The Kirghiz steppes, Central Asia, and Northern China...) Zapiski Zapadnosibirskogo otdela Imperatoskogo russkogo geograficheskogo obshchestva, 14 (1893):1.

13810. Chuloshnikov, A. Очерки по истории казак-киргизского народа в связи с общими историческими судьбами других тюркских племен. (Historical sketches of the Kazak-Kirghiz people in its relation to the development of other Turkic tribes.) Orenburg, 1924. 294 p.

13811. Zorin, A. N. Революционное движение в Киргизии. (Revolutionary movement of Kirghizia.) Frunze, 1931. 59 p.

13812. Труды Общества изучения Киргизского края. (Publications of the Society for the study of the Kirghiz region.) Orenburg, 1922-1923. 2 v.

13813. See 13448.

13814. Kraft, I. Принятие киргизами русского подданства. (Russian naturalization of the Kirghiz.) Izvestiia Orenburgskogo otdela Imperatorskogo russkogo geograficheskogo obshchestva, 12 (1897).

13815. "Заселение Киргизских степей." (The settling of the Kirghiz steppes.) Vostochnoe obozrenie, 19, 1882.

13816. Grodekov, N. I. Киргизы и кара-киргизы Сырдарьинской области. (The Kirghiz and Kara-Kirghiz of the Syr-Daria province.) Tashkent, 1889.

13817. Zagriazhskii, G. Юридические обычаи киргиз. (Legal customs among the Kirghiz.) Materialy dlia statistiki Turkestanskogo kraia, 4 (1876).

13818. Katanaev, G. E. Киргизский вопрос в Сибирском казачьем войске. (The Kirghiz problem in the Siberian cossack army.) Omsk, 1904.

13819. Советская литература Киргизии. (Soviet literature of Kirghizia.) Frunze, 1935. 15, 150 p.

(d) General Accounts

See 13515-13527.

13820. Belotskii, M. Киргизская республика. (The Kirghiz republic.) A popular sketch. Moscow, 1936. 134 p.

13821. Akarskii, B. I. Киргизская АССР. (The Kirghiz ASSR.) Moscow, 1932. 24 p.

13822. Smirnov, Nikolai A. Киргизские очерки. (Kirghiz sketches.) Moscow, 1930. 101 p.

13823. Конституция Киргизской социалистической советской республики. (The constitution of the Kirghiz SSR.) Orenburg, S"ezd sovetov Kirgizskoi SSR, 1924. 21 p.

13824. Zorin, A. "Десять лет советской Киргизии." (Ten years of Soviet Kirghizia.) Revoliutsionnyi Vostok, 6 (1934):28:158-172.

13825. Kivman, M. S. Чуйский район Киргизской АССР. (The Chuisk region of the Kirghiz ASSR.) Frunze, 1931. 51 p.

13826. Shmidt, IUlii A. Очерк Киргизской степи к югу от Арало-Иртышского водораздела в Акмолинской области. (A description of the Kirghiz steppe.) Zapiski Zapadnosibirskogo otdela Imperatorskogo russkogo geograficheskogo obshchestva, Omsk, 17 (1894):2.

(e) Economic Conditions

See 13549-13618.

13827. Isakeev, B. D. 10 лет Киргизской АССР и ее ближайшие народнохозяйственные задачи. (10 years of the Kirghiz ASSR and its impending economic problems.) In: Problemy Kirgizskoi ASSR, Moscow - Leningrad, 1936, 9-28.

13828. Ryskulov, T. R. Киргизстан. (Kirghizstan.) An economic geographic sketch. Moscow, 1935. 188 p.

13829. Karpinskii, A. P., Aleksandrov, I. G., Keller, B. A.,
and others (ed.). Киргизстан.(Kirghizia.) Publications of
the first Conference for the study of the productive forces
of the Kirghiz ASSR.) Leningrad, Akademiia nauk, 1934.
521 p.

13830. Хозяйственное развитие Киргизской ССР.   (The economic development of the Kirghiz SSR.) Orenburg, Kirgizskoe
ekonomicheskoe soveshchanie, 1924. 410 p.

13831. Материалы по районированию Киргизской республики.
(Materials pertaining to the zoning of the Kirghiz republic.) Orenburg, Obshchegosudarstvennaia planovaia komissiia,
1924.

13832. Операционный план на 1923-1924 год. (Operative
plan for the year 1923-1924.) Orenburg, Narodnyi komissariat po prodovol'stviiu Kirgizskoi SSR, 1923. 134 p.

13833. Vel'man, V. I. Народное хозяйство КССР и наши
очередные задачи. (The economy of the Kirghiz SSR and its
allied problems.) Orenburg, 1924. 44 p

13834. Dzosokhov, V. "Киргизстан." (Kirghizstan.) Sovetskoe stroitel'stvo, Moscow, 54:104-123, January 1931.

13835. Glinka, K. D. Почвы Киргизской республики.
(Soils of the Kirghiz republic.) Orenburg, 1923. 85 p.

13836. Shkapskii, O. A. Киргизы-крестьяне. (The Kirghiz
peasants.) Izvestiia Imperatorskogo russkogo geograficheskogo obshchestva, St. Petersburg, 41 (1905):4.

13837. Отчет о деятельности за 1923-1924 г. и план на
1924-1925 операционный год, со сметой расходов. (An account
of the activities of 1923-1924 and the plan for the operative year 1924-1925, of the Kirghiz agricultural society.)
Orenburg, 1924. 156, 108 p.

13838. Сельское хозяйство Киргизской советской социалистической республики.1923.(Agricultural economy in the Kirghiz
SSR in 1923.) Orenburg, Kirgizskoe TSentral'noe statisticheskoe upravlenie, 1924. 143, 45 p.

13839. Постановления II Всекиргизского съезда земельных
работников. (Decrees passed by the 2nd All-Kirghiz confer-

ence of land workers.) June 20-27, 1923. Orenburg, 1923.
35 p.

13840. Резолюции и постановления III Всекиргизского съезда
земельных работников. (Resolutions and decrees of the 3rd
All-Kirghiz congress of agricultural laborers.) Orenburg,
1924. 41 p.

13841. По вопросу о поземельном устройстве туземного киргиз-
ского населения в Семиреченской области.
(Concerning the Kirghiz agrarian system in the province of
Semirechensk.) Vernyi, 1908.

13842. TSabel, L. Схема землеустройства киргиз Тургайской
и Уральской областей. (A scheme for land settlement among
the Kirghiz of the Turgaisk and Uralsk provinces.) Voprosy
kolonizatsii, St. Petersburg, 3 (1908).

13843.)Рыбное хозяйство Киргизской АССР. (Fishing industry
of the Kirghiz ASSR.) Collected articles. Moscow, 1936.
295 p.

13844. Slavinskii, M. M. (ed.). Сборник статей о строительстве Памирского и Великого киргизского трактов. (A miscellany pertaining to the construction of the Pamir and Great
Kirghiz highways.) Frunze, 1935. 110 p.

13845. Работа профсоюзов Киргизии.   (Activities of the
Kirghiz trade unions.) November 1922-April 1924. Orenburg,
1924, 142 p.

13846. Резолюции и постановления Киргизского областного
совещания профсоюзов. (Resolutions and decrees passed by
the Kirghiz provincial conference of trade unions.) October 22-25, 1924. Orenburg, 1925. 54 p.

13847. Сборник материалов по социальному страхованию в КССР.
(Social insurance in the Kirghiz SSR.) Orenburg, 1924.
196 p.

13848. Valeev, A. V. Очерк о деятельности и состоянии инва-
лидной кооперации в Киргизской республике.(A sketch of the
activities and condition of the cooperatives of the in-
valids in the Kirghiz republic.) Orenburg, 1924.

13849. Труды III Всекиргизского съезда здравотделов.
(Transaction of the 3rd All-Kirghiz conference of health
departments.) June 3-8, 1923. Orenburg, 1923. 230 p.

(f) Communist Party

See 13631-13647.

13850. Стенографический отчет IV Всекиргизского съезда советов. (Stenographic account of the 4th All-Kirghiz conference of soviets.) January 5-10, 1924. Orenburg, 1924.

13851. III Сессия Киргизского центрального исполнительного комитета IV созыва. (3rd session of the Kirghiz central executive committee.) September 29-30, 1924. 46, 11 p.

13852. Постановления II сессии Киргизского центрального исполнительного комитета IV созыва. (Resolutions passed by the 2nd session of the Kirghiz central executive committee.) Orenburg, 1924.

13853. Отчет о деятельности Киргизского ЦИК и Народных комиссариатов КССР. (An account of the activities of the Kirghiz central executive committee and the People's commissariats o f the Kirghiz SSR.) Orenburg, 1923. 456 p.

13854. Отчетный доклад Революционного комитета Кара-Киргизской автономной области РСФСР. (An account of the Revolutionary committee of the Kara-Kirghiz autonomous province.) November 1924 - March 1925. Pishpek, 1925. 142 p.

(7) Tadjik SSR

See 13359-13647.

13855. Таджикистан. Физико-географический очерк. (Tadjikistan. Physical geographic sketch.) Collected articles. Leningrad, 1936. 399 p.

13856. Таджикская экспедиция. Труды. (Tadjik expedition. Publications.) Leningrad, 1935.

13857. Проблемы Таджикистана. Труды первой Конференции по изучению производительных сил Таджикистанской ССР.(Problems of Tadjikistan.) Transactions of the first Conference for the study of the productive forces of the Tadjikistan SSR. Leningrad, Akademiia nauk, 19 . 251 p.

13858. Khodorov, I. E. "Таджикистан в народном хозяйстве СССР." (Tadjikistan and its rôle in the national economy of the USSR.) Planovoe khoziaistvo, Moscow, 1930:1:205-209.

13859. Государственный бюджет Таджикской ССР на ... бюджетный год с объяснительной запиской. (State budget of the Tadjik SSR for the fiscal year ... with an explanatory note.) 1929/1930-

13860. Lapin, B. "Заметки о Таджикистане." (Notes on Tadjikistan.) Nashi dostizheniia, 1:2-12, January 1933.

13861. Adov, I. O. Таджикистан ко второй пятилетке. (Tadjikistan on the way to the second five year plan.) Moscow-Tashkent, 1933. 131 p.

13862. Alkin, Il'ia. "Таджикская социалистическая советская республика." (The Tadjik Socialist soviet republic.) Revoliutsionnyi Vostok, 3 (1935):31:129-149.

13863. Goncharov, N. F. Очерк растительности Центрального Таджикистана. (A sketch of the vegetation of Tadjikistan.) Moscow, Academy of sciences, 1936. 236 p.

13864. Vinogradov, B. S. Звери Таджикистана, их жизнь и значение для человека.(Animals of Tadjikistan, their mode of living and significance to man.) Moscow-Leningrad, Academy of sciences, 1935. 276 p.

13865. Соляные месторождения Югозападного Таджикистана. (Salt deposits of Southwest Tadjikistan.) Materials pertaining to geology. Moscow, 1935. 504 p.

13866. Ali-Zade, S. P. Полный русско-таджикский словарь. (Complete Russo-Tadjik dictionary.) Stalinbad, 1933. 325 p.

XXIX. ANGLO-RUSSIAN RIVALRY IN AFGHANISTAN

See 6873-7236.

13867. Ahmad, Jamal-ud-Idin and Aziz, Mohammud Abdul. Afghanistan. A brief survey. New York, Longmans, 1937.

13868. Schwager, Joseph. Die entwicklung Afghanistans als staat und seine zwischenstaatlichen beziehungen. Leipzig, Noske, 1932. 100 p. (2) Gervais, Lyons. Afghanistan, the buffer state. New York, 1910.

13869. Sirdar Ikbal Ali Shah. The tragedy of Amanullah. London, 1933. 274 p.

13870. Filchner, Wilhelm. Sturm über Asien. Berlin, 1924.

13871. IUzhakov, S. Афганистан и сопредельные страны.
(Afghanistan and the adjacent countries.) St. Petersburg,
1885. 195 p. (2) Zinoviev, I. Россия, Англия и Персия.
(Russia, England, and Persia.) St. Petersburg, 1912. 176 p.
(3) Афганское разграничение. (Delimitation of Afghanistan.)
Russo-British negotiations, 1872-1885. St. Petersburg, 1886.

13872. Skerskii, K. V. "Русско-афганские торговые взаимо-
отношения." (Russo-Afghan trade relations.) Novyi Vostok,
Moscow, 10:199-211, October 1926.

13873. Viollis, Andrée. Tourmente sur l'Afghanistan. Paris,
Valois, 1930.

13874. Morrish, C. Afghanistan in the melting pot. Lahore,
Civil and military press, 1930.

13875. Le Conte, Rene. "L'organization politique de l'Afghanistan." Revue du droit publique, 46:2:330-340, April-
June 1929.

13876. Habberton, William. Anglo-Russian relations concerning Afghanistan, 1837-1907. Illinois studies in the social
sciences, v. 21, no. 4. Urbana, University of Illinois
press, 1937. 102 p.

13877. Comyn, Platt Thomas. "Afghanistan and the Soviet."
Nineteenth century, 105:625:297-305, March 1929.

13878. Beveridge, A. S. "The Khaibar pass as the invader's
road for India." Journal of the Royal Central Asian society, 13:3:250-288; 13:4:368-374, July, October 1926.

13879. Potocki, Joseph. "Afghanistan looks abroad." Foreign
affairs, New York, 7:1:110-117, October 1928.

13880. Ravich, N. "Приподнятая завеса. Борьба в Афганистане
в период империалистической войны." (The lifted curtain.
The struggle in Afghanistan during the period of the Imperialist war.) Zvezda, 10:139-156, October 1933.

13881. Thomson, William. "The problem of Afghanistan."
Journal of the Royal Central Asian society, 13:3:187-204,
July 1926.

13882. Abdul Qadir Khan. "Afghanistan since the revolution."
Journal of the Royal Central Asian society, 17:3:331-334,
July 1930.

13883. Macmunn, George. "The defense of India and the Simon report." Army quarterly, 21:1:99-106, October, 1930.

13884. Anderson, J. G. "The highway of Europe and Asia." Journal of the Royal Central Asian society, 16:2:191-196, April 1929.   (2) Аравия, Турция, Персия, Афганистан, Индия, Западный Китай. (Arabia, Turkey, Persia, Afghanistan, India, West China.) A political and economic guide. Tashkent, 1928.

SUBJECT INDEX

Numbers refer to separate items in the Bibliography, not to pages. Only the first item under a subject is given in each case

AFGHANISTAN: 13867; Anglo-Russian rivalry, 13867
AGRICULTURE: Asia, Far East, Pacific, 833; China, 2147; Manchuria, 5195; Manchukuo, 6376; Japan, 9094; Korea, 10206; Russia-Siberia, 11778, 12365; Soviet Far East, 12701; Western Siberia, 13301; Russian Central Asia, 13571
AMUR: Railroad, 12198; Region, 12610
ANGLO-JAPANESE ALLIANCE: 4283, 4310
ANGLO-JAPANESE RELATIONS: 4253, 4283, 4310
ANGLO-RUSSIAN RIVALRY: Central Asia, 13528; Afghanistan, 13867
ANTHROPOLOGY: Asia, Far East, Pacific, 260; China, 1379; Manchuria, 4856; Mongolia, 6561; Northwestern China, 6954; Japan, 7474; Korea, 9859; Siberia, 10722; Russia in the Far East; 12544; Buriat-Mongolian SSR, 12895; Yakutsk SSR, 12998; Russian Central Asia, 13427; Tatar SSR, 13677; Kirghiz SSR, 13798
ARCHAEOLOGY: Asia, Far East, Pacific, 256; China, 1367; Manchuria, 4852; Northwestern China, 6942; Japan, 7464; Korea, 9860; Siberia, 10688
ARCHIVAL GUIDES: Russian 10361, 11060

ARCTIC: 10885
ART: Asia, Far East, Pacific, 1017; China, 2855; Japan, 9810; Korea, 10253
ASIA: 1; Japanese expansion, 8855; Russian studies, 10652; Russia in Asia, 10785
ASIATIC MONROE DOCTRINE (JAPANESE): 8692
ATLASES: See Maps and Atlases
AUSTRALIA: 4341
AVIATION: China, 2538; Manchuria, 5380, 5451; Japan, military, 8533, 8661; Japan, commercial, 9470; Russia, 12157
BAIKAL, LAKE: 12890
BANKS AND BANKING: See Finance
BARGA: 6542
BASHKIR SSR: 13676
BEANS: Soya, 5232
BIBLIOGRAPHY: Asia, Far East, Pacific, 1, 148, 781, 984; China, 1061, 1195, 1235, 1526, 1795, 2147, 2730, 2824, 3198, 3906, 4362; Manchuria, 4706, 4783, 5452; Northwestern China, 6873; Japan, 7237, 7502, 8886, 9650; Korea, 9843; Russia, 10291, 10521, 10885, 11179, 11528, 11649, 11778, 11988, 12017, 12301, 12405, 12489, 12537, 12883, 12986, 13359, 13724, 13797
BIOGRAPHIES: China, 1162, 1164, 2546; Japan, 7338

Subject Index ≀

7343, 7759; Russia,10465, 10468
BIRO-BYDZHAN: Territory, 12626
BOYCOTTS: China, 2716
BUDDHISM: Asia, Far East, Pacific, 984; China, 2932; Manchuria, 5666; Mongolia, 6860; Tibet, 7229; Japan, 9731; Korea, 10258; Russia, 12465, 12959
BURIAT-MONGOLIAN SSR: 12883
CANADIAN RELATIONS: 4359
CENTRAL ASIA: General, 1,43, 148, 182, 256, 273, 343, 450, 781, 937, 1047; Chinese Central Asia, 1061, 1145, 1162, 1164, 1176, 1195, 1235, 1346, 1367, 1526, 1922, 2004, 2029, 2747, 2824, 2987, 3022, 3198, 3696, 4253; Northwestern China, 6873; Japan, 8690, 8736, 8855; Russia, 10291, 10364, 10465, 10468, 10478,10485, 10490, 10521,10584,10652, 10688, 10722,10785,11014, 11402, 11437,11465,11495, 11584, 11657,12405,12439, 13080, 13226; Russian Central Asia, 13359, 13457, 13867
CHAHAR: 6504
CHELIABINSK: 13343
CHINA: See Table of Contents, volume I; see also Sino-
CHINESE REPUBLIC: 1717
CHRISTIANITY: Asia,Far East, Pacific, 997; Japan,9756; Korea, 10265; Russia, 12451
CHRONOLOGICAL AIDS: Asia,Far East, Pacific (History), 273; China (History), 1532; Japan (History), 7518
CHRONOLOGIES: See Chronological Aids

CHURCH: See Christianity, Missions, Religions
CITIES: Russia, Revolution, (1905), 11231; (1917) 11332
CLIMATE: Asia, Far East, Pacific, 165; China, 1201, 1343; Manchuria, 4783; Mongolia, 6548; Northwest China, 6879; Japan, 7407, 7438; Russia, 10496,10560, 10885, 11799, 12691
COAL: Asia, Far East, Pacific, 804; China, 1224; Manchuria, 4803; Japan, 7416; Russia, 10496,12001, 12030; Soviet Far East, 12691; Sakhalin, 12854; Buriat-Mongolian SSR, 12959; Yakutsk SSR,13046; Siberian Region, 13203; Western Siberia, 13263, 13291; Central Asia,13564
COLONIZATION: Asia,Far East, Pacific, 1047; China, 2730, 2987; Manchuria, 5618; Northern Manchuria, 5785; Manchukuo, 6430; Mongolia, 6846; Japan, 8805; Siberia, 12301
COMMANDER ISLANDS: 12880
COMMERCE AND TRADE: Asia, Far East, Pacific, 864; China, 2362; Manchuria, 5582; Manchukuo, 6393; Mongolia, 6480; Northwestern China, 7013; Tibet, 7224; Japan, 9222; Korea, 10231; Russia in Asia, 12054; Soviet Far East, 12655; Buriat-Mongolian SSR, 12959, 12974, 12975; Siberian Region, 13325; Russia in Central Asia, 13600
COMMUNICATIONS: China, 2478; Manchuria, 5380, 6405; Japan, 9430; Siberia, 12146; Russian Central

Asia, 13603
COMMUNIST PARTY (COMMUNISM):
China, 1795, 3696, 4132,
4679; Manchuria, 5014;
Manchukuo, 6183;Mongolia,
6700, 6763; Northwestern
China, 7138; Japan, 8156,
8430; Russia, 11242,11495;
Soviet Far East, 12777;
Buriat-Mongolian SSR,
12955; Yakutsk SSR,13041;
Siberian Region, 13221;
Western Siberia, 13352;
Central Asia, 13631;Tatar
SSR, 13667; Bashkir SSR,
13718; Kirghiz SSR, 13850
CONFUCIANISM: China, 2911;
Japan, 9754
COSSACKS: 13330
COOPERATIVES, AGRICULTURAL:
Asia, Far East, Pacific,
833; China, 2261, 2270;
Manchuria, 5195; Manchu-
kuo, 6376; Japan, 9094;
Russia, 11839; Soviet Far
East, 12701; Western Sib-
eria, 13301; Russian Cen-
tral Asia, 13571
COOPERATIVE MOVEMENT: 2261;
See also Cooperatives,Ag-
ricultural, and Labor
COTTON: Asia, Far East, Pac-
ific, 804, 833; China,
2241, 2300, 3395; Russia,
11778; Russian Central
Asia, 13571, 13704, 13750,
13769, 13784, 13827
CULTURE AND CIVILIZATION:
Asia, Far East, Pacific,
937; China, 2824; Manchu-
ria, 5666; Mongolia,6487;
Soviet Outer-Mongolia,
6848; Japan, 9581; Korea,
10253; Siberia, 12439,
12497; Soviet Far East,
12768; Buriat-Mongolian
SSR, 12886, 12959; Yak-
utsk SSR, 12991; Russian
Central Asia, 13619

CURRENCY: See Financial Pro-
blems
CZECHO-SLOVAKS IN SIBERIA:
11346, 11358
DAIREN: 5681
DEMOCRACY: In Japan, 8341
DICTIONARIES: China, 1162,
1164; Japan, 7338, 7343,
7522; Russia, 10465,
10468; Yakutsk SSR,13078;
Russian Central Asia,
13726
DIRECTORIES AND GUIDES:Asia,
Far East, Pacific, 144;
China, 1182; Manchuria,
4745, 4747; Manchukuo,
6051; Japan, 7358, 8928,
8932; Russia, 10478,10485,
11703; Russia in Central
Asia, 13374, 13376; Kazak
SSR, 13726; See also Archival Guides
EARTHQUAKE OF 1923: 7461
ECONOMIC FACTORS: Asia, Far
East, Pacific, 781; China
(geography), 1339; China,
2029; Sino-Japanese,3652;
Sino-Russian, 3857; Trans-
siberian Railroad, 4054;
Russo-Japanese, 4232;Phil-
ippines, 4600; Dutch-Chi-
nese-Japanese, 4675; Man-
churia, 5117; China (com-
munications), 5515; South
Manchuria Railroad, 5574;
Manchukuo, 6317; Mongolia,
6480; Soviet Outer-Mon-
golia, 6808; Northwestern
China, 7013; Tibet, 7224;
Japan (war economics),
8681, (expansion) 8881,
8886; Korea, 10185;Russia
(economic periodicals),
10425, (general accounts),
10997, 11657; Soviet Far
East, 12655; Kamchatka,
12818; Sakhalin, 12854;
Buriat-Mongolian SSR,
12959; Yakutsk SSR, 13044;

Siberian Region, 13211;
Western Siberia, 13289;
Russian Central Asia,
13549, 13609; Tatar SSR,
13660; Bashkir SSR,13704;
Kazak SSR, 13750; Kirghiz
SSR, 13827
EDUCATION: Asia, Far East,
Pacific, 1013; China,2783;
Japan, 9650; Korea, 10280;
Russian Asia, 12445; of
non-Russians, 12489; Sov-
iet Far East, 12768
ENCYCLOPEDIAS: China, 1162;
Japan, 7338; Russian Em-
pire, 10465; Soviet Far
East, 12542
ENGLAND: Asia,Far East, Pa-
cific (treaty and docu-
mentary collections),514;
British-Chinese-Japanese
Relations, 4253; Tibetan-
Chinese-British Relations,
7209; Anglo-Russian Ri-
valry, 13528
ETHNOLOGY: 12824; See Anthro-
pology
EURASIA: 11045; see also
Pan-Mongolian and Pan-
Asiatic Movements
EXCHANGE (MONETARY): See
Finance
EXILE SYSTEM: Russia in Asia,
12395; Soviet Far East,
12867
EXPLORATIONS: See Travels
and Explorations
EXTRATERRITORIALITY: China
(international relations),
3169
FAMINES: China, 2289
FAR EAST, THE: See Table of
Contents; also 11286,
11766
FASCISM: China, 4679; Japan,
8123, 8430
FEUDALISM: Japan, 8255
FINANCIAL PROBLEMS AND CUR-
RENCY: Asia, Far East,

Pacific, 930; China,2540;
Manchuria, 5344; Manchu-
kuo, 6414; Japan, 9291;
Korea, 10231; Russia in
Asia, 12272; Russia in
the Far East, 12748; Wes-
tern Siberia, 13327; Rus-
sian Central Asia, 13606
FISHERIES: Asia, Far East,
Pacific, 899; Japan, 8990;
Russia, 11931, 12890
FIVE-YEAR PLANS: Russia,
12222
FLORA AND FAUNA: Manchuria,
5228; Russian Asia,11804
FLOUR: China, 2239; Manchuria, 5243; Russia, 11763,
11813, 13211, 13301
FOOD-SUPPLY: China, 2285,
2289, 2684; Manchuria,
5265; Japan, 9545; Korea,
10206; Russia, 11839,
11877, 11931; see also
Agriculture, Famines,Pop-
ulation Problems
FORESTRY: China, 2249; Manchuria, 5269; Japan, 9169;
Russia in Asia, 11883
FRANCE: Asia, Far East, Pacific (treaty and document-
ary collections), 531;
French-Chinese Relations,
3696; French-Chinese-Jap-
anese Relations, 4621;
Franco-Japanese Relations,
4638; Franco-Russian Re-
lations, 11346, 11358,
11402, 11437
FRONTIER PROBLEMS: China,
2987
FRUIT: China, 2248
FUR TRADE: See Furs
FURS: Manchuria, 5262;Russia
in Asia, 11905
GAS: See Oil
GAZETTEERS: China, 1318;Man-
churia, 4870, 5750, 5759,
5764, 5788; Northwestern
China, 6897

GEOGRAPHY: Asia, Far East,
Pacific, 148; China,1235;
Manchuria, 4824; Mongolia,
6548; Northwestern China,
6879; Tibet, 7149; Japan,
7384, 7436, (economic geography) 9010; Korea,9853;
Russian Asia, 10521,(economic geography) 11711;
Yakutsk SSR, 13046
GEOLOGY: Asia, Far East, Pacific, 804; China, 1195;
Manchuria, 4783;Mongolia,
6548; Japan, 7384; Korea,
9853; Russia in Asia,
10490, 10537; Russian Far
East, 12691; Yakutsk SSR,
13046; Siberian Region,
13175; Western Siberia,
13263; Russian Central
Asia, 13564
GERMANY: Asia, Far East, Pacific, 536; German-Chinese-
Japanese Relations, 4679,
8156
GOLD: China, 1209, 1233;Man-
churia, 4815; Mongolia,
6548; Siberia, 10490,
12017
GOVERNMENT AND POLITICS:
China, 1922, 1938;Manchu-
ria, 5097, 5540; Japan,
7607, 8225, 8327; Korea,
10054; Russia, 11282,
11584
GUIDES: China (periodical
literature) 1094, (geo-
graphy and cartography)
1268, (commerce and trade)
2364; Manchuria, 4745;
Russia (archival guides)
10361, (guides and hand-
books) 10485, (Transsiberian railroad guides)
12176; Russia in Central
Asia, 13374
HANDBOOKS: China (Periodical
publications), 11703
HARBIN: 5786

HARBORS: Asia, Far East, Pacific, 864; China, 2362;
Manchuria, 5600, 5681,
5699; Japan, 8533, 9222,
9235, 9447; Korea,10231;
Russia, 11465, 12054,
12090, 12108, 12655
HAWAIIAN ISLANDS: 4585
HEILUNGKIANG: 5788
HISTORY: Asia, Far East, Pacific, 273; China, 1322,
1526, 1933, 2057, 2367,
2437, 2486, 2549, 2824,
2897, 2824, 2897, 3042,
3203; Sino-Russian Rela-
tions, 3736; Franco-Chi-
nese Relations, 4621;
Dutch-Chinese-Japanese
Relations, 4664; Manchu-
ria, 4870, 5136; Chinese
Eastern Railroad, 5456;
South Manchuria Railroad,
5542; Manchukuo, 6058,
6322; Eastern Inner Mon-
golia, 6449; Outer Mon-
golia, 6625; Northwestern
China, 6960; Japan, 7366,
7502, 8053, 8289, 8473,
8990, 9094, 9177, 9222,
9291, 9430, 9476, 9587,
9655; Korea, 9912, 10185;
Russia, 10410, 10557,
10694,10889, 11014,11495,
11704,11997, 12071,12152,
12303,12636, 12790,12828,
12919,13013, 13191,13272,
13447,13648, 13680,13732,
13806
HOLLAND: Dutch-Chinese-Japanese Relations, 4658
HOPEI: 3458; see North China
IMMIGRATION: China, 2684,
2730, 2987; Manchuria,
5618, 5785; Mongolia,
6846; Northwest China,
7013; Tibet, 7224;Japan,
9545, 9571, 10148; see
also Colonization, Fron-
tier Problems, Popula-

Subject Index

tion Problems
INDUSTRY: Asia,Far East, Pa-
cific, 846; China, 2298;
Manchuria, 5289; Manchu-
kuo, 6389; Japan, 9177;
Korea, 10220; Russia in
Asia, 11939; Russian Far
East, 12743; Siberian Re-
gion, 13310; Russia in
Central Asia, 13592
INTERNATIONAL LAW: Asia, Far
East, Pacific, 538, 647;
China, 3110, 3113, 3169,
3188, 3982; Manchuria,
4992, 5027, 5097, 5106;
Manchukuo, 5805, 5907,
6088, 6128, 6174, 6183;
Mongolia, 6685, 6700;
Tibet, 7209; Japan, 8053,
8123, 8156, 8496; Korea,
9912, 10001, 10036,10156;
Russia, 11440
INTERNATIONAL RELATIONS:
Asia, Far East, Pacific,
450; China, 2459, 3022;
Manchuria, 4992, 5479;
Manchukuo, 6088; Mongol-
Chinese, 6685; Japan,
8044; Korea, 9912; Rus-
sian Empire, 11402; Sov-
iet Russia, 11437
INTERNATIONAL SETTLEMENT:
Shanghai, 3346
INTERVENTION: Siberia, 4133,
11346, 11358
IRKUTSK: 13110
IRON: 4812; see Minerals and
Mining
JAPAN: See Table of Contents,
volume I
JAPANESE: Expansion, 8690,
8736; Colonies, 8805; Pa-
cific, 8842; Asia, 8855
JAPAN SOCIETIES: 7329
JEHOL: 6519
JOURNALISM: see Newspapers
KAMCHATKA: 12787
KANSU: 7065
KAZAK SSR: 13724

KHAKASSK: 13174
KIAKHTA: 12974
KIAO-CHOW: 3446
KIRGHIZ: 13797
KIRIN: 5750
KOKONOR: 7125
KOREA: see Table of Contents,
volume I
KOREAN-CHINESE RELATIONS;
10156
KOREAN-JAPANESE RELATIONS:
10001, 10036,10101,10148
KOREAN-MANCHURIAN PROBLEM:
5652
KOREAN NATIONAL MOVEMENT:
10054
KUOMINTANG: 1775
KWANTUNG: 5667
LABOR: Asia, Far East, Paci-
fic, 846; China, 2662;
Manchuria, 5611; Japan,
9523; Russia in Asia,
12261; Russia in the Far
East, 12756; Western Si-
beria, 13318; Russia in
Central Asia, 13592
LAND SYSTEM: China, 2187;
Manchuria, 5265; Japan,
9094, 9545, 9571; Russia
in Asia, 11867; Russian
Colonization, 12368; see
also Agriculture
LAWS: China, 1980;Manchuria,
5106, 5540; Manchukuo,
6315; Japan, 8225, 8289,
8471; Korea, 10168; Rus-
sia, 11060, 11071, 11584,
12079, 12436; see also
Government
LEAGUE OF NATIONS: 647, 658;
Manchuria, 5907
LEGISLATION: see Laws
LENA REGION: 13072
LIAONING: 5704
LIBRARIES: China, 1088; Ja-
pan, 7269, 7303
LIBRARY METHODS: Japan, 7303
LIMITATION OF ARMS AND DIS-
ARMAMENT: Asia, Far East,

Pacific, 760; China,2004;
Japan, 8533;Russia,11465
LITERATURE: Asia, Far East,
Pacific, 1015; China,2876
Mongolia, 6867; Japan,
9797; Russia, 12489
LOANS: China, 2540, (foreign,
2650; Manchuria, 5344; Japan, 9358, 9427; Russia,
12272; Soviet Far East,
12748; see also Financial
Problems
MANCHU DYNASTY: 1685, 1933,
2057, 2147, 2748, 2825,
3042, 6449, 6960, 7189
MANCHUKUO: 5805; see Table
of Contents, volume I
MANCHURIA: 4706; see Table
of Contents, volume I
MANDATES IN THE PACIFIC:658
MAPS AND ATLASES: Asia, Far
East, Pacific, 149; Asia
(Historical) 278; China,
1240; Manchuria, 4731,
(economic) 5134, (commun-
ications) 5380; Mongolia,
6447; Outer-Mongolia,
6548; Northwestern China,
6875; Japan, 7387; Russia
in Asia, 10525, (geologi-
cal) 10537, (general)
10539, (special) 10547;
Arctic, 10886; Far East,
12540; Kamchatka, 12787;
Buriat-Mongolian SSR,
12889; Yakutsk SSR, 12989;
Siberian Region, 13081;
Bashkir SSR, 13676
MEDICINE: China, 2893
MENGKUKUO: Eastern Inner Mongolia, 6447; see Table of
Contents, volume I
MILITARY AFFAIRS: Asia, Far
East, Pacific, 663; China,
2004, (Undeclared War,
1937) 3519; Russo-Japanese
War, 3906; Manchukuo,5836,
5892; Japan, 8533, 8589;
Russian Asia, 11465

MILLETT: China, 2147, 2239;
Manchuria, 5246
MINERALS AND MINING; China,
1209; Manchuria, 4783;
Manchukuo, 6410; Japan,
7416; Russia in Asia,
11988
MISSIONS: Asia, Far East,
cific, 131, 967; China,
2897; Japan, 9706, 9756;
Russia in Asia, 12451
MOHAMMEDANISM: Asia, Far
East, Pacific, 1011;
China, 2939
MONGOLIA: Eastern Inner Mon-
golia (Mengkukuo), 6447;
Outer Mongolia, 6548; see
Table of Contents, volume
I
MONROE DOCTRINE: American,
4575; Japanese, 8692
MUKDEN: 5759
MUSIC: Asia, Far East, Paci-
fic, 937, 1045; China,
2887; Japan, 9842;Russia,
12489
NATIONALISM: Asia, Far East,
Pacific, 283; China, 1717,
1775; Japan, 7992, 8690;
Korea, 10054; Russia
11027,12408, 12430, 13336,
13427; see also Anthro-
pology, Ethnology
NATURAL RESOURCES: see Geol-
ogy
NAVAL AFFAIRS: Asia, Far
East, Pacific, 663, 722;
China, 2004; Russo-Japan-
ese War, 4013; Japan,
8533, 8627; Russia in
Asia, 11465
NERCHINSK: 12975
NEWSPAPERS: Asia, Far East,
Pacific (bibliography of),
34, (periodical publica-
tions) 142; China, 1182;
Manchuria, 4721; Japan,
7366, 7372; Russia in
Asia, 10403; Russian Cen-

tral Asia, 13368
NON-RUSSIANS IN RUSSIAN ASIA:
12405; Education of,12520;
Anthropology, 12544; see
also Nationalism
OIL: Asia, Far East, Pacific,
804; Manchuria, 4817; Si-
beria, 12039
OIRAT: Autonomous District,
13175
OMSK: Siberian Region, 13140
OPEN DOOR: Policy, 450, 538,
647, 864, 2362, 3188
ORIENTALS: in the U.S., 4558
OUTER MONGOLIA, SOVIET:6763;
see Table of Contents,
volume I
PACIFIC OCEAN: Asia, Far
East, Pacific, 1; Scien-
tific Studies and Pilot
Directions, 224; Interna-
tional Relations, 564;
Mandates in the, 658;
Trade, 864; Fisheries,
899; Japanese Expansion
in, 8842; Russia on the,
10851
PAN-ASIATIC MOVEMENTS: 8690,
8716
PAN-MONGOLIAN MOVEMENTS:
8690, 8713
PEASANTRY: Asia, Far East,
Pacific, 833; China,2256;
Manchuria, 5195, 5265,
6376; Mongolia, 6848; Ja-
pan, 9100, 9491, 9523,
9545; Russia in Asia,
11846, 11867; Russian Far
East, 12701; Western Si-
beria, 13301; See Agriculture, Social Conditions
PEIPING: City, 3477
PERIODICALS: Asia, Far East,
Pacific, 43; Pacific Oc-
ean (scientific and pilot
directions), 224; China,
1100, (geology and natur-
al resources) 1196, (geo-
graphy and cartography)

1236, (history) 1528,(government and politics)
1922, (military and naval
affairs) 2004, (economic
factors) 2029, (agricul-
ture) 2149, (industry)
2298, (commerce and trade)
2362, (inland trade)2414,
(financial) 2540, (labor)
2662, (colonization and
immigration), 2731,(social
conditions) 2747, (learn-
ed societies) 2795, (in-
ternational relations)
3022; Japanese Interven-
tion in Siberia, 4132;
Manchuria, 4716, 4721,
5541; Manchukuo, 6046;
Northwestern China, 6874;
Japan, 7299, 7305, (geol-
ogy, geography) 7384,7436;
(archaeology, anthropolo-
gy) 7464, 7474, (history)
7509, (international re-
lations) 8044, (politics)
8225, (legislation) 8471,
(economic conditions)
8889, (social conditions)
9473, (culture, religion,
philosophy) 9581, 9651,
9768; Korea, 9849; Russia
(bibliographical) 10295,
(articles) 10333, (gener-
al) 10364, (historical)
10419, (local, Siberian)
10438, (geology) 10490,
(geography) 10523, (arch-
aeology) 10688, (Arctic)
10887, (revolutions)11185,
(international relations)
11402, 11437, (military
and naval) 11465, (government) 11584, 11650, (ec-
onomic conditions) 11657,
11696, 11783, 11939,11990,
12054,12146, 12222,12272,
12395, (religion) 12491;
Russia in Central Asia,
13368

PHILIPPINES: American Far
Eastern Relations, 4590
PHILOSOPHY: Asia, Far East,
Pacific, 952; China,2970;
Japan, 9581, 9768; see
also Government
POLITICS: see Government
POPULATION PROBLEMS: Asia,
Far East, Pacific, 824;
China, 2684; Japan, 9545;
Russia in Asia, 11659;
see also Agriculture,Col-
onization, Frontier Pro-
blems
PORT ARTHUR: 4062, 5699
PORTSMOUTH: Peace of, 450,
538, 3883, 4076, 4083
PORTUGUESE-CHINESE RELATIONS:
4705
PRINTING: China, 2890
PUBLIC HEALTH: China, 2819
RADIO: China, 2537
RAILROADS: China, 2478;Trans-
siberian railroad, 4048;
Manchuria, 5380; Chinese
Eastern Railroad, 5452;
South Manchuria Railroad,
5541; Manchukuo, 6405;
Japan, 9430, 9432; Korea,
10241; Russia in Asia,
12146; Russia in the Far
East, 12746; Russia in
Central Asia, 13603
RELIGIONS: Asia, Far East,
Pacific, 967; China,2897;
Mongolia, 6860; Tibet,
7229; Japan, 9581, 9765;
Korea, 10258; Russia in
Asia, 12439, 12461, 12465
REVOLUTIONARY MOVEMENTS:
Asia, Far East, Pacific,
1047; China, 1717, 1775,
1795, 1915; Manchuria,
6030; Mongolia, 6454,
6638, 6763, 6808; Japan,
8430; Korea, 10054; Sib-
eria, 11179; Russian Rev-
olutionary Movement to
1905, 11189; Third Inter-

nationale, 11495, 11528,
11549, 13495
RICE: Asia, Far East, Pacific, 833; China, 2217;
Manchuria, 5247; Japan,
9147; see also Agricul-
ture
RIVERS: Russia in Asia,10580
ROADS: China, 2532; Manchuria, 5380; Russia in Cen-
tral Asia, 13603; see al-
so Geography, Communica-
tions, Railroads
RURAL RECONSTRUCTION: Asia,
Far East, Pacific, 833;
China, 2270; Manchukuo,
6376; Japan, 9094; Korea,
10206; Russia, 11813
RUSSIA: see Table of Con-
tents
RUSSO-JAPANESE ALLIANCE:4108
RUSSO-JAPANESE WAR: 3906
SAKHALIN: Russian, 4053,
12824; Japanese, 12870
SCIENCE: Asia, Far East, Pacific, 182, 224, 899,937,
1013; China, 2893; Japan,
9650, 9703; Korea, 10253,
10280; Russia, 12489
SHAMANISM: Asia, Far East,
Pacific, 1013; Russia,
12465
SHANGHAI: 3340
SHANSI: 7063
SHANTUNG: 3430
SHENSI: 7056
SHINTOISM: Japan, 9725
SHIPPING: Asia, Far East,Pa-
cific, 224, 864; China,
2414, 2430; Japan, 9222,
9447; Korea, 10231; Rus-
sia, 12054, 12108; see al-
so Commerce, Harbors
SIBERIA: see Table of Contents
SIK'ANG: 7069
SILK: Asia, Far East, Pacific, 833, 846, 864;China,
2228; Japan, 9152; see

also Agriculture,Commerce
SINGAPORE: 4351
SINKIANG: 7096
SINO-JAPANESE: Relations,
  3198, 3245,(war,1894)3215,
  (incident, 1932) 3353,
  (North China) 3395, (undeclared war, 1937-) 3519,
  (economic relations) 3652
SINOLOGY: 1145
SINO-RUSSIAN: Relations,3696,
  3736, 3790, (general accounts) 3802, (economic
  relations) 3857
SOCIAL CONDITIONS: Asia, Far
  East, Pacific, 343, 782,
  937; China, 2747, 2824,
  2825; Manchuria, 5666;
  Mongolia, 6848; Northwestern China, 7013; Japan,
  9473; Korea, 10253;Russia
  in Asia, 12439; Buriat-
  Mongolian SSR, 12959;Rus-
  sia in Central Asia,13619
SOCIALISM: Asia, Far East,
  Pacific, 1047; China,
  1766, 1795; Japan, 8430,
  9523; Russia, 11495,11615,
  11754
SOILS: 11811; see also Agriculture
STATISTICS: China (economic
  factors) 2046; Manchuria,
  5117, (communications)
  5381, (Colonization) 5618
  Manchukuo, 6317; Japan,
  8938; Russia, 11657, (agriculture) 11779, (industry) 11940, (mining)
  11993, (trade and com-
  merce) 12062; Russia in
  the Far East, 12655; Yakutsk SSR, 13044; Western
  Siberia, 13289; Russia in
  Central Asia, 13549; Kazak SSR, 13731
STOCKS AND STOCK EXCHANGES:
  see Finance
STRATEGY: Asia, Far East,Pa-

cific, 674, 682; China,
  2020, 3990; Japan, 8670
SUIYUAN: 6489
SUN YAT-SEN: 1766
SZECHWAN: 7048
TADJIK SSR: 13855
TANNU TUVA: 13170
TARIFFS: Asia, Far East, Pa-
  cific, 864; China, 2437,
  2459, 2462, (likin) 2473,
  (commercial treaties)
  2462; Japan, 9280
TAOISM: China, 2923
TATAR SSR: 13648
TAXATION: Asia, Far East,Pa-
  cific, 906; China, 2540,
  2600; Manchuria, 5376;
  Manchukuo, 6414; Japan,
  9409; Russia, 11704,11718,
  12222, 13327, 13606
TEA: 2221, 9168
THEATRE: Asia, Far East, Pa-
  cific, 1045; China, 2886;
  Japan, 9841
THIRD INTERNATIONAL: 11528
TIBET: 7145; see Table of
  Contents, volume I
TIENTSIN: 3477
TOBOLSK: 13337
TOMSK: 13149
TRADE: see Commerce and
  Trade
TRANSSIBERIAN RAILROAD: Rus-
  so-Japanese War, 4048;
  12176
TRAVELS AND EXPLORATIONS:
  Asia, Far East, Pacific,
  182; China, 1346; Manchu-
  ria, 4753; Mongolia,6568;
  Northwestern China, 6898;
  Tibet, 7145; Russia in
  Asia, 10584, 10920; Rus-
  sia in Central Asia,13378
TREATIES: for all Powers,
  450; China, 2462,
  (sources) 3022; Mongolia,
  6685; Northwestern China,
  6960; Japan (sources)
  8048; Korea, 9912; Russia

11060, 11403
TSINGTAO: 3454
TUNGUSIA: 12978
TURKMEN SSR: 13769
TURK-SIB RAILROAD: 12203
RUSSIAN ORTHODOX CHURCH:
12439; see Religions
TURUKHANSK: 13165
UNITED STATES: Asia, Far
East, Pacific (treaty and
documentary collections)
527; American-Chinese-
Japanese Relations, 4362
URAL DISTRICT: Siberia,13262
URIANKHAI (TANNU TUVA):13170
UZBEK SSR: 13784
VLADIVOSTOK: 12632, 12054,
12090, 12108, 12139
WAR: Asia, Far East, Pacific
(problems) 663; China
(Taiping Rebellion) 1672,
(Sino-Japanese, 1894-95)
3215, ("Incident" of 1932)
3353, (Undeclared War,
1937) 3519, (Russo-Japan-
ese, 1904-05) 3906, 3988;
Manchuria, 5836, 5892;
Japan (in the World War)
7727, (finance) 9427; Re-
volution in Siberia,11179;
Central Asia, 13495
WAR ECONOMICS: Japan, 8681

WASHINGTON CONFERENCE:
Sources, 722; General Ac-
counts, 729; Limitation
of Arms and Disarmament,
760
WATER POWER: Russia in Asia,
11756
WATER TRANSPORTATION: China,
5578
WESTERN SIBERIA: 13226
WHEAT: China, 2239; see also
Agriculture
WOMEN: China, 2747; Japan,
9511; Korea, 10253; Rus-
sia, 11506, 11627, 12489
WOOL: Asia, Far East, Paci-
fic, 822; China, 2247;
Mongolia, 6480, 6808;
Northwestern China, 7013;
Tibet, 7224
YAKUTSK SSR: 12986; see
Table of Contents, volume
II
YEARBOOKS: Asia, Far East,
Pacific (periodicals)144;
China, 1177, (economic
factors) 2546; Manchuria,
4747; Manchukuo, 6051;
Japan, 7358, (economic
conditions) 8928; Russia
in Asia, 10478
YENISEI: 13081

D. Archaeology and Anthropology

See 256-272.

9860. 朝鮮總督府古蹟調査報告 Chosen Sotokufu ko-seki chosa hokoku (Annual report of the Archaeological survey in Korea.) Published by the Goverment-general of Chosen, 1916-1922. 7 v.

9861. Tsuboi, Heigoro. 朝鮮, 人種 Chosen no jinshu. (Korean racial origins.) Chiri to rekishi, 141-146, November 1, 1910. (Special edition: Annexation of Korea.)

9862. Hulbert, Homer B. "Korean and Ainu." Korea review, 6 (1906):223-228.

9863. Kubo, T. Beitrage zur physischen anthropologie der Koreaner. Mitteilungen der Medizinischen fakultät der Kaiserlichen universität, 12. Tokyo, 1913. 676 p.

9864. Korf, Baron N. A. "О численности населения в Корее." (On the number of inhabitants in Korea.) Izvestiia Imperatorskogo russkogo geograficheskogo obshchestva, 40:330-354.

9865. Shinoda, Jisaku. 朝鮮民族, 北進 Chosen minzoku no hokushin. (Northward advance of the Korean race.) Gaiko jiho, 81:5:98-113, March 1937.

E. General Accounts

See 343-449.

9866 . Oppert, Ernst. A forbidden land. London, 1880. 349 p. (2) Lowell, Percival. Chosön, the land of the morning calm. Boston, 1888. 412 p. (3) Carles, W. R. Life in Korea. London-New York, 1888. 317 p.

9867. Podzhio, M. Очерки Кореи. (Sketches of Korea.) St. Petersburg, 1892. 391 p. (2)Chaillé-Long, Colonel Charles. La Corée ou Tchösen (La terre du calme matinal. Paris, 1894. (3) Landor, Arnold H. S. Corea; or, Cho-sen, the land of morning calm. London, 1895.

9868. Bishop, Isabella L. (Bird). Korea and her neighbours. London, 1898. 2 v. (2) Gale, James S. Korean sketches. New York, 1898. 256 p. (3) The same. The vanguard. New York, 1904. 320 p.

9869. Genthe, Siegfried. Korea: reiseschilderungen... Berlin, 1905. 343 p.

9851. 青丘學叢 Seikyu gakuso. (Quarterly review of the Korean historical society.) Keijo, 1929-1938. Discontinued. (2) 震檀學報 Chindan hakpo. (Quarterly journal of Korean studies.) Seoul, 1934-

9852. 대 평 양 주 보 T'aep'yŏngyang chubo. (Korean Pacific weekly.) Honolulu, 1, 1914-   (irregular in early years.)   (2) Minjok hyŏngmyŏng. 민 족 혁 명 (National revolution.) Nanking, 1936-   (Monthly). 　(3) 신 한 민 보 Sinhan minbo. (The New Korea.) San Francisco, 1906-1937; Los Angeles, 1938-   . [The first few volumes under: 공 립 신 보 Kongnip sinbo. (United Korea.).]   (4) 국 민 보 Kungminbo. (Korean national herald.) Honolulu, 1, October 1907-   (Weekly).

C. Geology, Natural Resources, and Geography

See 1235-1345.

9853. Karte der russisch-asiatischen grenzendistrikte. Sektion 16: Korea. Neue ausgabe, July 1913. 1:1,680,000.

9854. Inouye, K. (comp.). General geological map of Korea. Tokyo, Imperial survey, 1911. 1:1 500 000.   (2) Kawasaki, S. Geology and mineral resources of Korea. Tokyo, 1916.

9855. O, Taehwan. 大韓地理 대 한 지 리 Taehan Chiri. (Geography of Korea.) Seoul, Pangmunsa, 1904. 2 v.

9856. Fukuchi, N. 朝鮮鑛產物 Chosen kosanbutsu. (The minerals of Chosen.) Beiträge zur mineralogie von Japan, Tokyo, 1915, 207-305.   (2) Shihara, Genzo. 新朝鮮風土記 Shin-Chosen fudo-ki. (The natural features of new Korea.) Tokyo, Banrikaku, 1930.

9857. Robbins, H. R. "The mineral resources of Korea." Transaction of the American institute for mining and engineering, 1908, 587-800. (2) Fermor, L. Leigh. "On the geology and coal resources of the Korean state, Central provinces." Memoirs, Geological survey of India, 41 (1914):2:I-III, 148-245.   (3) Mills, E. W. "Gold mining in Korea." Transactions of the Korea branch of the Royal Asiatic society, 7 (1916):1:3-39.

9858. Niu-shan. 朝鮮鑛業的現狀 Ch'ao-hsien k'uang-yeh ti hsien-chuang. (Korean mining at present.) New Orient monthly, 1:10:87, October 1930.

9859. Chong, Unmo. 대 한 십삼도유람하 Taehan sipsamdo yuramha. (Geography of the 13 provinces of Korea.) Seoul, 1909. 2 v.